T0347396

Annual Survey of Eastern Europe and the Former Soviet Union 1998

EWI

The EastWest Institute (EWI) is an independent, international, not-for-profit institution established in 1981 and was formerly known as The Institute for EastWest Studies. It works to defuse tensions and conflicts that threaten geopolitical stability and to promote democracy, free enterprise, and prosperity in Central and Eastern Europe, Russia, and other states of Eurasia.

The EWI has centers in New York, Moscow, Prague, Kyiv, Brussels, and Košice and maintains a large global network of relationships with leaders in the business, governmental, non-governmental and intellectual communities. This network is dedicated to providing assistance to regional leaderships dealing with critical issues at both the local and global levels.

The EWI seeks to cooperate with individuals and institutions sharing our values and mission. For more information please contact us at:

EastWest Institute
700 Broadway, Second Floor
New York, NY 10003
Tel: (212) 824 4100
Fax: (212) 824 4149

We also invite you to visit our Website in English or Russian at http://www.iews.org/.

John Edwin Mroz
Founder and President

ANNUAL SURVEY 1998
of Eastern Europe and the Former Soviet Union

Holding the Course

Edited with an Introduction by

Peter Rutland

EASTWEST INSTITUTE
New York Prague Moscow Kyiv Brussels Košice

Routledge
Taylor & Francis Group
LONDON AND NEW YORK

First published 2000 by M.E. Sharpe

Published 2015 by Routledge
2 Park Square, Milton Park, Abingdon, Oxon OX14 4RN
711 Third Avenue, New York, NY 10017, USA

Routledge is an imprint of the Taylor & Francis Group, an informa business

Library of Congress Cataloging-in-Publication Data

EastWest Institute
Annual Survey of Eastern Europe and the former
Soviet Union : 1998—Holding the course / by The EastWest Institute
p.   cm.
Includes bibliographical references (p.) and index.
ISBN 0-7656-0360-8 (alk. paper)
1. Europe, Eastern—Politics and government—1989– .
2. Former Soviet republics—Politics and government.
3. Europe, Eastern—Economic conditions—1989– .
4. Former Soviet republics—Economic conditions.
5. Post-communism—Europe, Eastern.
6. Post-communism—Former Soviet republics.
I. Title
CIP

ISBN 13: 9780765603609 (hbk)

In memoriam

This book is dedicated to the memory
of Professor Yutaka Akito, 1950–1998.

Professor Akito, from Tsukuba University
in Japan, was killed on 20 July 1998 while
serving as a political affairs officer with
the United Nations peace observer mission
in Tajikistan.

Contents

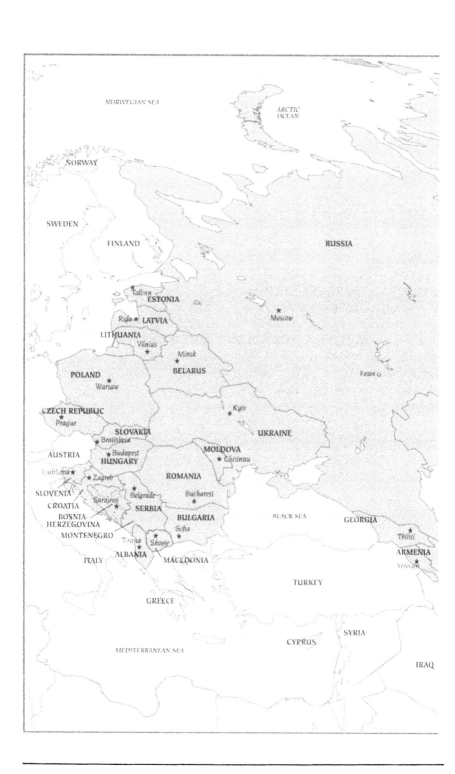

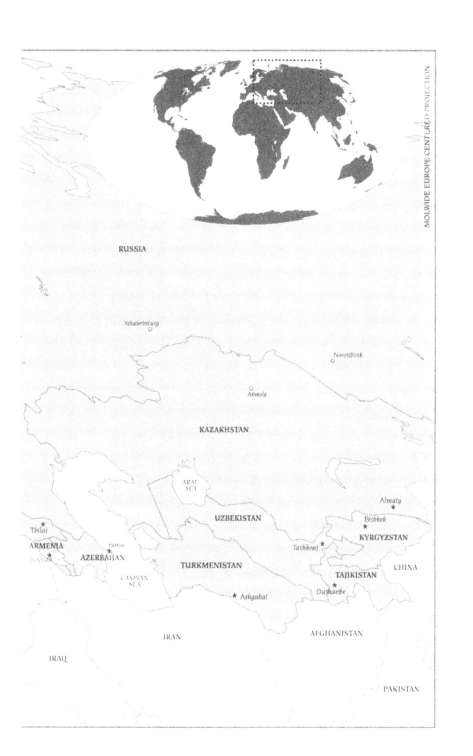

Annual Survey of
Eastern Europe and the
Former Soviet Union
1998

INTRODUCTION

I

WAITING FOR THE NEXT STEP

by PETER RUTLAND

For most of the post-socialist countries of Eurasia, 1998 was something of a wasted year. There were few transition successes to report, and quite a bit of back-sliding. It looked increasingly as if most of the major structural reforms that were going to take place had already occurred. Those countries unfortunate enough to have missed the chance at radical change during the early, chaotic years of socialist collapse seem doomed to endless failed efforts at tackling the chronic problems of political corruption, economic inefficiency, and/or ethnic disharmony. With each thwarted effort at change it becomes more difficult to regain the reform momentum, and politicians and citizens alike resign themselves to a treadmill of abortive reform; a sort of political "Groundhog Day."

The news was brightest, as usual, in Central Europe. Slovakia shattered its image as the bad boy of the region. September saw parliamentary elections in which the opposition parties united their forces and kicked out the entrenched government of Prime Minister Vladimir Meciar, which had dominated politics since 1990. Meciar resorted to some last-minute skullduggery to try to stay in power, including a bid to gain control of the main private TV station. In the end, democratic procedures prevailed. Slovakia's neighbors breathed a sigh of relief—and Slovakia can in turn expect to be advanced to the fast track for entry to the European Union (EU) and NATO.

While Meciar was toppled in Bratislava, the neighboring Czechs also saw the end of a political era. The bristly libertarian Vaclav Klaus refused to follow up corruption allegations, causing the defection of leading members of his Civic Democratic Party in late 1997. However, Klaus managed to fight back against his critics and retain control of the Civic Democratic Party. Elections to the parliament in June proved rather indecisive, in that the soft-left Social Democrats failed to win a clear majority. Their leader Milos Zeman cut a cynical deal with Klaus to keep the smaller centrist parties out of power.

Poland was free of elections in 1998, although its political class managed to create a furor over a plan to rationalize the number of provincial administrations.

Poland at least deserves credit for tacking the question of local government reform—something which has stayed off the agenda of just about all the other new democracies. The Polish economy saw a slowdown in 1998, although annual growth still came in at close to 5 percent, while inflation was in single digits and foreign investment boomed.

The Slovak and Czech experiences proved that democracy can fulfill its core function of bringing about a change in national leadership. But they also illustrated the three factors that seem to dominate political life in the transitional democracies—the strong role played by individual leaders' personalities; battles for control over the media; and the vagaries of coalition politics. These factors often combine to make political life unpredictable and frustrating for voters. The multiplicity of parties in East Europe reflects the variety of ethnic and regional interests within each country and the personal followings of individual politicians, plus the general immaturity of the political system. In order for stable party systems to emerge, these mini-parties have to show themselves willing to cooperate, although many established Western democracies share this fractured-coalition quality, which is hard to understand for observers coming out of the Anglo-American political tradition. Several countries are still experimenting with electoral reform (raising the threshold of votes required for parties to enter parliament, for example) in a bid to produce a more effective party system.

The foreign policies of Central and Eastern Europe were dominated by the carrot of eastward expansion of NATO and the EU. In December 1997 five post-communist states were selected for the "fast track" of negotiations for accession to the European Union (Czech Republic, Estonia, Hungary, Poland, and Slovenia). The painstaking process of adjusting their economic and legislative policies to European norms got under way. As the enormity of the task sank in, the optimistic timetable of leaders in Poland and elsewhere who talked of full entry by 2002 started to look more and more unrealistic. Absent a consensus within the EU to radically overhaul its agricultural support system and cumbersome decision-making processes, it is hard to see any of the Eastern aspirants gaining entry before 2005. At the same time, the mere process of preparing for entry is having a profound impact on how the aspirant countries' economies are being managed. Trade has been radically liberalized, and prices (of food products for example) have quickly moved to near-European levels. Indeed, it is no exaggeration to say that most of the costs and benefits of EU entry are likely to occur *before* actual entry to the union.

Regional economies were hit by the double-whammy of the Asian crisis of late 1997 and its echo, the Russian meltdown of August 1998. This caused external balances of most countries to deteriorate as export demand dried up and foreign investors took their cash and ran for safer harbors.

Despite these problems the Baltics continued to steer their course for Europe. Latvia persisted in liberalizing its economy, while the Estonian government, under pressure from farmers unable to compete with subsidized EU imports, became enmeshed in a debate over tariffs. By the year's end the EU was actually rating Latvia as a more liberal economy than Estonia, casting doubt on the wisdom of singling out Estonia as the sole Baltic country on the fast-track for EU entry. (A decision usually explained as a political sop to Sweden.) On the downside, Latvia experienced an indecisive election in October that produced a minority coalition government, and saw a deterioration in relations with Russia over the treatment of its Russian minority.

Among the second-tier of Euro-aspirants, Romania was gripped by recession and political stalemate. The new reformist government elected in 1996 failed to break the mould of Romania's patrimonial political system. Feuding within the governing coalition led to the resignation of Prime Minister Victor Ciorbea in April 1998. Old, unresolved problems continued to dog the new leadership, such as the controversy over a draft law opening the files of the feared Securitate secret police, and another over demands for a Hungarian-language university. In a break with previous tradition, Bulgaria managed to pull off a crisis-free year. Thanks to the introduction of a currency board tying the lev to the German mark, inflation fell from 600 percent in 1997 to 10 percent in 1998.

THE LOOMING SHADOW OF KOSOVO

Politics in the former Yugoslavia continued to dance on the edge of the abyss. The international community maintained its gravity-defying effort to turn Bosnia-Herzegovina into a functioning entity, although elections in its three component parts failed to produce victories for moderates who favored building a multiethnic Bosnia. Precious few victims of ethnic cleansing returned to their homes. In Montenegro the accession to power of President Milo Djukanovic, a foe of Yugoslav President Slobodan Milosevic, posed a serious challenge to the Belgrade ruler's grip on power. But Milosevic clamped down on internal opposition, while launching a bloody campaign of repression in Kosovo, using as a pretext the attacks launched by the Kosovo Liberation Army (UCK). Already in 1998 perhaps a quarter of a million Kosovars fled their homes. International efforts to broker a deal between Milosevic and the moderate Albanian leader Ibrahim Rugova fell through, and in October NATO issued a threat of military action. This persuaded Milosevic to agree to the insertion of a UN sponsored "verification mission," although the cease-fire between Yugoslav forces and the UCK soon broke down.

Meanwhile, over the mountains in Albania the political stand-off between government and opposition continued. The Democratic Party of ousted president Sali Berisha boycotted meetings of the parliament, while in August the prosecutor arrested six former high-ranking officials of the Democratic government and accused them of violent repression of anti-government protests in 1997. The tension culminated in a bout of street-fighting in Tirana in September, which the government was able to swiftly suppress. In the wake of the violence Prime Minister Fatos Nano resigned and was replaced by 30-year-old Pandeli Majko, who became the youngest head of government in Europe. Unlike his fellow premiers, Majko faced the daunting task of disarming the population, who had emptied the state's armories during the 1997 unrest. In a November referendum boycotted by the Democrats, a new constitution was approved, but Berisha—a firm backer of independence for Kosovo—was aiming to use the violence in Kosovo to lever his way back into power.

Across the other border, in Macedonia, parliamentary elections in November saw a turnover of power, with the ouster of the ruling Social Democrats. The elections strengthened the hand of nationalist-oriented parties among the ethnic Macedonian and Albanian communities, but the Democratic Party of Albanians did agree to join the new coalition government, a hopeful sign that mounting inter-ethnic tension could perhaps be held in check.

Up in Croatia, August saw the emergence of a coalition of opposition parties, prepared for the first time to coordinate their efforts to dislodge President Franjo Tudjman. Their chances were increased by the outbreak of faction-fighting within the ruling Croatian Democratic Union. Perhaps in the near future another strongman of the transition to democracy will be ready to fall. In the meantime, Tudjman shrugged off Western pressures to liberalize his stance toward ethnic minorities, and there was zero chance of the displaced Serbs being allowed to return to Krajina.

RUSSIA'S AUGUST EPIPHANY

Political developments in Russia stumbled forward from tragedy into farce. The political stability which had been symbolized by President Boris Yeltsin's 1996 electoral victory and the six-year tenure of Viktor Chernomyrdin as prime minister was shattered by Chernomyrdin's abrupt dismissal in March and by the even more dramatic ejection of his replacement, the youthful Sergei Kirienko, in August. Despite a $22 billion rescue package assembled by the IMF in June, investors were scared by the mounting pyramid of unpaid treasury bills and stampeded out of the Russian market in early August. On 17 August the ruble collapsed, losing 75 percent of its value, while the government suspended payments on all foreign debts. The August crisis was a crushing blow to those who believed that market reform was still in some sense on track in Russia, and could drag the country out of its eight-year recession.

The political stability of preceding years had in any case been illusory, since it disguised bitter fighting between Kremlin clans and astonishing incompetence when it came to policy implementation. Still, it had been a comforting illusion. Some interpreted the arrival of Yevgenii Primakov as premier as a sign that the "old structures" of the Soviet era were returning to the saddle. Others concluded that the breakdown of governability at the national level was irretrievable, and salvation would only come through a strengthening of the regional governors.

The August financial crisis also dashed hopes of economic revival in many of the countries of the Commonwealth of Independent States (CIS), for most of whom Russia was still the largest single trading partner. Countries with energy exports that could be sold elsewhere (Azerbaijan, Kazakhstan, Turkmenistan) were hit by the fall in world commodity prices. This meant that Western oil companies yet again postponed a definitive decision on when and where to build the main export pipeline for Caspian oil. The Russian crisis brought a new wave of financial instability to the CIS—the flight of foreign capital; a large risk premium on lending to the region; the collapse of Russian banks that had been active from trade credit to privatization; and the likelihood of domino devaluations. These trends threatened to undermine not only growth prospects but also the stable exchange rates and low inflation (below 30 percent) which were among the few positive achievements that the countries had to show after seven years of half-hearted reform.

Like Russia, most of the CIS countries (with the notable exception of Belarus) had formally privatized a large proportion of their economy, but none of them had made much progress toward real industrial restructuring, tackling corruption, or building a solid tax base. First prize in tax collection must go to Ukrainian Prime Minister Valerii Pustovoitenko, who interned 1,500 executives in a summer resort camp until their companies made a cash contribution toward their tax arrears. In October, Kyrgyzstan was rewarded for its efforts at economic liberalization by being granted entry to the World Trade Organization—the first CIS state to be so honored. The practical benefits of this step were not immediately apparent, however.

POLITICS AS USUAL

While the CIS economies seemed to be heading backwards, the region's political regimes were at best marking time. Parliamentary elections were held in Ukraine and Moldova in March, and in both cases the Communists emerged as the largest single party. In Moldova they fell short of winning a majority, and could not prevent the formation of a centrist coalition government. Executive–legislative relations in Russia and Ukraine followed their familiar pattern—a truculent parliament in noisy opposition to a Western-leaning president and government, but lacking the cohesion and commitment to come up with an alternative program for governing the country. All sides talked about the need to do something about corruption—but all sides feared giving a green light to prosecutors to arrest the guilty, for fear that this power would be misused by their political opponents. In December former Prime Minister Pavlo Lazarenko was charged in Switzerland with money laundering, the second Ukrainian ex-premier since 1991 to be indicted for corruption.

Economic woes only served to redouble the determination of CIS presidents to consolidate their grip on power. They learned their lesson from the defeat of incumbent presidents Leonid Kravchuk in Ukraine and Stanislau Shuskevich in Belarus in 1994—and the near-defeat of Boris Yeltsin in 1996. Kyrgyz President Askar Akayev showed the way in his December 1995 re-election, manipulating registration rules to keep strong opponents out of the race—but leaving some small fish in the pond, in order to create a plausible veneer of electoral competition. This was precisely the model followed by Azerbaijan's President Heydar Aliev in preparing the ground for his triumphal re-election in October 1998, and by Kazakh President Nursultan Nazarbaev in the run-up to his re-election bid in January 1999.

Nazarbaev also followed his Kyrgyz counterpart in getting permission to run again despite the constitutional provision limiting the president to two terms in office—on the grounds that his first term, originating before independence, did not count. (The Kazakhstani parliament changed the constitution to suit Nazarbaev: in Akayev's case, it was done through a ruling by the constitutional court.) Other tools in the super-president's arsenal include periodic referenda; rapid turnover of government officials; and a strong dose of media control. The latter is based on the carrot of state financing and, increasingly, the stick of inventive law suits to shut up opposition journalists—for treason, for inciting ethnic hatred, or even through civil libel suits (how wonderful is the rule of law!).

Central Asian publics seem resigned to the view that there is no viable alternative to their present leaders. This is precisely the sort of opinion which those leaders deliberately cultivate, and which helps to sustain them in power. Nazarbaev could probably have won even without electoral manipulation—but that is beside the point. What is important is to have a landslide victory (80 percent, in his case). Exactly the same point was made by observers with regard to the re-election of Aliev, with 78 percent support.

Breaking the pattern of permanent presidents, Armenian President Levon Ter-Petrossian was forced to resign in February. But this was driven by factors external to the political system—his willingness to cut a deal over Nagorno-Karabakh. His removal was the product of back-room politics—the desertion of his own security establishment—and did not reflect a democratic opening of the political system.

JAW-JAW AND WAR-WAR

On the surface, inter-state relations in Central Asia started 1998 on a positive note. The June 1997 Tajik peace accord was holding up, and members of the United Tajik Opposition were amnestied and brought into a government of national unity. President Nazarbaev cemented good relations with his neighbors, signing a treaty of "eternal friendship" with Uzbekistan and marrying his youngest daughter to the oldest son of Kyrgyz President Akayev, a Shakespearean touch.

However, neither side in Tajikistan had disarmed its fighters, and violence flared on several occasions. The low point of the year was the killing of three United Nations peace observers, including Japanese political science professor Yutaka Akito, in July. In August Afghanistan's Taliban movement overran the last major bastion of resistance, the northern city of Mazar-i-Sharif, and brought their forces right up to the Tajik and Uzbek border. Uzbekistan grew increasingly nervous of Islamic influence, given the entry of UTO leaders into the Tajik government, and was implicated in the launching of an abortive anti-Islamicist insurrection in November in the Leninabad region of northern Tajikistan.

While the Tajik conflict seemed to be creeping toward resolution, there was scant progress to report from other conflict zones in the CIS. Russia refused to withdraw its troops from the breakaway enclave of Transdniester in Moldova, and stepped up its military cooperation with the new hard-line government of Armenia. The replacement of Ter-Petrossian as president of Armenia by Robert Kocharian, the former head of Nagorno-Karabakh, made early resolution of that conflict even less likely. In Georgia, the separatist republic of Abkhazia saw a fresh outbreak of fighting in May. Attacks by Georgian militias seeking the return of refugees to the Gali district triggered an assault by Abkhaz forces, as a result of which some 30,000 returned refugees were once more driven from their homes.

Many observers pinned high hopes on the strengthening of horizontal ties among the southern tier states, exemplified by the GUAM group (Georgia, Ukraine, Azerbaijan, and Moldova) and the involvement of those countries in NATO Partnership for Peace exercises. The fact that countries were increasingly spurning the Commonwealth of Independent States is a development which few would regret. The CIS is an organization that had long ago outlived its original purpose—whatever that was. The most bizarre diplomatic behavior of the year, as usual, was displayed by Belarusian President Alyaksandr Lukashenka, who decided in April to expel all foreign diplomats from their current residencies, so that he could incorporate their properties into his presidential estate. Fortunately, such antics merely served to make the prospect of an actual union between Russia and Belarus seem even more far-fetched.

IN CONCLUSION

Once one moves beyond the northwestern edge of the region, therefore, there is scant cause for celebration. The political systems are democratic, but not very; the economies reformed, but not very. Francis Fukuyama's 1989 vision of the "end of history" is partly fulfilled, in the sense that there are no serious, explicit rivals to the prevailing doctrines of liberal democracy and market economics. But despite much excited debate, the eastward expansion of NATO and the European Union only really engaged the countries of Central Europe. Beyond that zone, the international community proved woefully inadequate at coming up with ideas for solving the ethnic conflicts inherited from the break-up of the multinational socialist states of Yugoslavia and the Soviet Union; or for restarting economies that obstinately refuse to recover.

REGIONAL ISSUES

II

CENTRAL AND EAST EUROPEAN ECONOMIES: SLOW GROWTH, SLOWER REFORM

by BEN SLAY

In the 1993–1997 period two key economic trends were apparent in the economies of Central and Eastern Europe (CEE—understood as the Visegrad countries, the Balkans, and the Baltic states). The first trend was economic growth, as countries began to recover from the "transition recession" that followed the collapse of Soviet system at the turn of the decade. By 1997, this growth had become increasingly broad-based, reflecting not only stronger consumer spending (thanks in part to falling unemployment rates) but also rising investment by domestic and foreign firms that increasingly saw the region as a platform for exports to the European Union (EU).

The second trend was a fairly strong link between the strength and longevity of this recovery and the ambition of the reform initiatives pursued in individual economies. Macroeconomic performance—broadly understood as export growth, foreign direct investment, and enterprise restructuring, as well as GDP growth and inflation—tended to be best in countries like Poland and the Czech Republic that had done the most with systemic reform. By contrast, the economies that prior to 1998 had not experienced strong recoveries seemed to share a small set of common characteristics. These included the poor management of macroeconomic policy that resulted in the loss of external and internal balance, and the failure to pursue ambitious privatization and structural reform agendas, particularly in the financial sector.

Both of these trends underwent important changes in 1998, as economic growth in 1998 slowed broadly across the region, and the slowdown hit both reform leaders like Poland and laggards like Yugoslavia. Only six economies—Albania, Bosnia-Herzegovina, Bulgaria, Hungary, Macedonia, and Slovenia—reported strong or accelerating growth in 1998. External tensions also sharpened across the region in 1998: current account deficits expanded or remained large; and a number of currencies underwent controlled (e.g., the Croatian kuna, the Slovak koruna) or uncontrolled (e.g., the Yugoslav dinar) depreciation. The growth that was recorded in some CEE countries in 1998 may therefore have been unsustainable. In addition, economic performance in the Czech Republic and Romania—two of the region's largest and most important countries—was much worse than many observers expected, as both countries were gripped by recession and political stalemate.

The 1998 growth slowdown was exacerbated by a deteriorating regional and global context that exhibited four sobering trends. First, 1998 was not a good year for emerging markets in general. As a result of the "Asian flu" that precipitated the East Asian meltdown in late 1997, the banner year for stock exchanges in Budapest, Warsaw, and elsewhere was not repeated in 1998. Hungary, which possessed one of the region's most sophisticated and modern financial systems, saw the Budapest Stock Exchange's market index plummet by 57 percent between April and October. Market indices in Riga, Tallinn, and Vilnius over the course of 1998 fell by 75, 66, and 40 percent, respectively. Smaller capital inflows in 1998 meant difficulties in financing current account deficits, which in turn slowed growth in imports, output, and incomes.

Second, matters were further aggravated by Russia's financial crisis associated with the botched ruble devaluation in mid-August. CEE exports to countries in the Commonwealth of Independent States (CIS) fell sharply in the second half of 1998, as otherwise healthy economies like Hungary found themselves viewed by global investors as susceptible to the "Russian contagion," even though most of their ties to the Russian economy had been cut in the early 1990s. Fears about the "Russian contagion" were linked to a third factor: a growing lack (if not crisis) of confidence in the international monetary system. If the IMF and G-7 were unable to protect Russia—a country regarded by many as "too big and too nuclear to fail"—from financial meltdown, should lending of last resort be expected for Macedonia? If (as economists increasingly argued) standard IMF programs do not work for countries whose external imbalances result from pathological financial systems rather than too much domestic demand, had the "Washington consensus" policy framework lost its effectiveness? These unanswered questions cast long shadows across Central and East Europe, which is full of small open economies implementing IMF-backed (and financed) stabilization programs.

Fourth, 1998 was not a particularly good year for economies on the EU periphery. Not only did Brussels choose not to broaden the list of countries invited to begin accession negotiations beyond the region's five "fast-track" economies (Poland, Hungary, Czech Republic, Slovenia, and Estonia) tapped in 1997: it also failed to make much headway in resolving its own internal disputes over governance and subsidies. Moreover, economic growth in the EU slowed in the second half of 1998, and since the EU is the largest purchaser of CEE exports, this slowed growth in the region as well. Baltic exporters in particular therefore found themselves caught between EU stagnation and Russia's collapse in 1998.

NO GROUNDS FOR PANIC

The CEE economies have not yet emerged from their challenging and difficult transition, and complacency about the final outcome of this transition is far from warranted. Still, the region's 1998 growth slowdown should not be taken as a sign of doom, and it should certainly not be seen as analogous to the economic problems besetting Russia and many countries in the CIS. Barring cataclysmic international economic developments, the East European growth slowdown is not likely to become a full-blown regional recession in 1999, and the region should stage a strong recovery once growth in the EU accelerates.

Moreover, closer inspection shows that many of the worrisome global trends described above did not have a strong impact on the region in 1998. Although Central and East Europe is full of current account deficits and quasi-fixed exchange rate regimes, only Yugoslavia experienced a sharp, Russian-like uncontrolled currency depreciation in 1998. Controlled devaluations/depreciations in 1998 promoted external adjustment in Slovakia and Croatia, as had been the case in Macedonia in 1997. While the Romanian leu depreciated by some 29 percent in nominal terms in 1998, this corresponded to a real effective appreciation of some 9 percent for the year. Meanwhile, currency boards in Bulgaria, Bosnia-Herzegovina, Estonia, and Lithuania provided the monetary stability critical to the resumption or continuation of growth. Claims (made with surprising frequency after Russia's botched devaluation) that fixed exchange rates and/or devaluations are disasters in the making were not consistent with the East European experience in 1998.

In contrast to the many criticisms leveled against the activities of international financial institutions in Russia, the IMF, World Bank, and European Bank for Reconstruction and Development in 1998 were generally perceived as part of the solution rather than part of the problem. In addition to helping some countries (e.g., Albania, Bulgaria) restore macroeconomic stability and growth, IMF-backed stabilization programs also promoted structural reforms in the financial and enterprise sectors in these countries and elsewhere (e.g., Macedonia, Romania). These were precisely the kinds of structural reforms that the Fund had been criticized for not supporting more vigorously in Russia. Most of the CEE countries receiving IMF assistance stayed within the framework of their programs; only Romania presented the sorts of non-compliance dilemmas the Fund routinely faces in Russia, Ukraine, and some other CIS countries. Moreover, the IMF was barely on the policy screen in Budapest, Ljubljana, Prague, and Warsaw. The Czech Republic and Poland have not had to avail themselves of IMF assistance since the early 1990s and 1995, respectively, while Hungary paid off its final IMF obligation in early 1998.

Finally, it is important to note that the 1998 growth slowdown was accompanied by some very favorable macroeconomic developments in the region. These included sharp declines in inflation rates, and further progress in the geographic reorientation of trade, away from Russia and the CIS and toward the EU. These developments, which also contrasted sharply with economic trends in much of the CIS in 1998, seemed set to continue in 1999. Indeed, with the exception of Yugoslavia and Romania, the entire region could be experiencing single-digit annual inflation rates by the end of 1999.

These developments showed that economic trends in CEE in 1998 should not be understood solely, or even largely, in terms of slowing growth precipitated by ominous trends in Russia or the international economy. Instead, the 1998 growth slowdown resulted from the interplay of different factors in different countries, reflecting different phases in economic transition, business cycles, and geographic reorientation of trade. This interplay can be seen by considering the following country groupings.

The first group includes Albania, Bosnia-Herzegovina, and Macedonia. These are small, open, and poor transition economies that starting from a very low base posted rapid or accelerating GDP growth in 1998. This favorable growth reflects four somewhat unique factors: (1) recovery and emergence from the chaos of war; (2) progress in state building in the southern Balkans; (3) geographic proximity to EU markets (Greece, Italy); and (4) generous international assistance, much of which reflected geopolitical (rather than economic) considerations. The Albanian economy, whose 1993–1995 GDP growth rates were among the world's highest, collapsed into anarchy in early 1997. A solid recovery seems to have resulted in 1998, however, as preliminary estimates put 1998 GDP growth at around 8.0 percent. Macedonia seemed to have finally emerged from the chaos of the Yugoslav break-up and the Greek economic embargo: GDP growth accelerated from 1.5 percent in 1997 to around 5.0 percent in 1998. In Bosnia-Herzegovina, peace and reconstruction generously financed by external assistance made possible another year of 30 percent GDP growth in 1998, with more of the same likely in 1999. Since all three countries had large current-account deficits that were financed primarily by the IMF and external donors, questions can be raised about the sustainability of this growth. Still, 1998 economic performance in these three countries was not significantly affected by the four global factors mentioned above.

The second group consists of Poland, Estonia, Latvia, Croatia, and Slovakia—countries in which GDP growth fell sharply in the latter part of 1998 as policy makers faced up to the need to reduce current-account deficits. This was particularly the case in the first three economies, as they were among the region's most vulnerable to the Russian contagion. In Estonia, for example, GDP growth slowed from 11.4 percent in 1997 to 9.3 percent in the first quarter, 5.2 percent in the second quarter, 1.8 percent in the third quarter, and 0.2 percent in the fourth quarter. The current-account deficit nonetheless stayed high (at 9.5 percent of GDP through the first three quarters), although it was nonetheless down on 1997's 12.0 percent. This pattern was also apparent in Poland, where GDP growth dropped from 6.9 percent in 1997, to 6.5 percent in the first quarter of 1998, to 2.5 percent in the fourth quarter. But despite this growth slowdown, the current-account deficit rose to 4.5 percent of GDP (from 3.2 percent in 1997). Likewise, Latvia saw GDP growth drop 7.4 percent in the first quarter of 1998 to 1.9 percent in the third quarter, while the current-account deficit rose from 6.3 percent of GDP in 1997 to 9.2 percent at the end of the third quarter of 1998.

While Croatia and Slovakia also enjoyed rapid growth during 1996–1997, this growth was fueled by booming domestic demand while exports languished. Large current-account deficits therefore resulted, which were financed by short-term borrowing rather than foreign direct investment. (This contrasted with the growth in Poland, Hungary, Estonia, and Slovenia, where rapid export growth boosted GDP, and current-account deficits were financed primarily via foreign direct investment.) External adjustments in 1998 were therefore inevitable in both countries, irrespective of global trends. Croatia's external adjustment began in 1998: GDP growth fell to about 4.0 percent (down from 6.5 percent in 1997), as the current-account deficit dropped to 8.8 percent of GDP (from 11.9 percent in 1997). Further reductions in both are expected in 1999. Slovakia's current-account deficit rose from 6.9 percent of GDP in 1997 to 9.0 percent in 1998, even as GDP growth fell to about 5.0 percent in 1998 (down from a scorching 7.0 percent in 1996 and 6.5 percent in 1997). Both GDP growth and the current-account deficit are likely to fall further in 1999. Moreover, both the Slovak koruna and the Croatian kuna experienced significant, albeit controlled, depreciations in 1998.

The third group consists of Hungary, Lithuania, and Slovenia—countries where the deterioration in external balance was not sufficient to slow GDP growth. Slovenia was virtually alone in the region in managing to keep its current account in balance in 1998 while still pushing GDP growth up to 4.3 percent for the year (up from 3.8 percent in 1997). But while GDP growth in Hungary accelerated from 4.6 percent in 1997 to 5.2 percent in 1998, the EU slowdown combined with surging domestic demand to produce a dramatic expansion in the current-account deficit, from 2.2 percent of GDP in 1997 to 4.2 percent in 1998. In Lithuania, GDP growth during the first three quarters of 1998 was largely unchanged on 1997's 6.1 percent rate, and the 7.0 percent industrial output growth recorded for the year was well above 1997's 0.7 percent growth. However, Lithuania's 1998 current-account deficit rose to 13 percent of GDP during the first three quarters, up from 10.3 percent in 1997. In contrast to Slovenia, GDP growth in Hungary and Lithuania was likely to slow in 1999, as these economies experience the external adjustment that befell the Group 2 countries in the second half of 1998.

The fourth group consists of Bulgaria, the Czech Republic, and Romania. To be sure, these economies were quite different: the Czech Republic is much richer (in per-capita GDP) than the other two, and despite its problems remained on the fast track to join the EU. The Czech Republic had also attracted much more FDI than Bulgaria and Romania, and had a much better record on growth and inflation. Differences were apparent among the two Balkan economies as well: inflation, which averaged 60 percent in Romania in 1998, dropped dramatically in Bulgaria (to 22 percent), and by the end of the year had basically stopped altogether. Still, all three economies were in the midst of painful external adjustments, and were also paying for their previous unwillingness to pursue bolder structural reform initiatives, especially in the financial sector. Macroeconomic performance in 1998 was disappointing in all three countries: GDP in the Czech Republic and Romania declined by some 2.5 percent and 4.8 percent, respectively, while Bulgaria managed only the weakest of recoveries from its economic collapse of 1996–1997 (when GDP declined by 18.0 percent).

Yugoslavia, the Balkan Belarus, was once again the odd man out. The rapid GDP growth officially reported for 1994–1997 seems to have flagged in 1998, under the weight of the fiscal costs associated with the attempted military solution to the Kosovo question and the resulting tightening of international financial sanctions. GDP growth in 1998 probably slowed to 4.0 percent, due to increased difficulties in financing the imports needed to grease the wheels of Yugoslavia's largely unreformed economy. The Yugoslav financial system was shaky and the National Bank alternated between large credit emissions to support insolvent industries and monetary tightening to forestall a collapse in the exchange rate.

CENTRAL EUROPE

Poland

Tighter monetary and fiscal policies combined with falling export demand to produce a substantial slowdown in the Polish economy starting in the second quarter of 1998. Following a 6.5 percent rise in January–March 1998, GDP growth slowed to 5.3 percent in the second quarter, 5.2 percent in the third quarter, and 2.5 percent in the fourth quarter. The resulting 4.8 percent 1998 GDP growth was Poland's slowest since 1993. Despite this slowdown, Poland's current-account deficit rose from 3.2 percent of GDP in 1997 to 4.5 percent in 1998. Poland's economic boom, which had been such a constant feature of the Central European economy since the mid-1990s, was facing its first serious test.

A number of good things happened to the Polish economy in 1998. Inflation rates fell sharply, and ran at single-digit levels in the last quarter of 1998. These lower inflation rates allowed the National Bank of Poland to sharply cut interest rates in the fourth quarter, which should help boost investment demand and lower the government's debt-servicing costs. Poland netted another $6.2 billion in foreign direct investment in 1998, which was sufficient to cover 90 percent of the current-account deficit. The year 1998 also saw the introduction or preparation of ambitious reforms of the pension and health care systems, as well as of the steel industry and local government. Still, GDP growth was unlikely to return to pre-1998 levels until the EU economies strengthen.

Hungary

The Hungarian economy in 1998 shed its perennial "sick man of Central Europe" status. GDP growth rose to 5.2 percent for the year, as industrial output was up 12.9 percent, fixed investment increased 10.2 percent, retail sales grew 8.7 percent, and exports rose by more than 20 percent. Consumer price inflation, which remained stubbornly high in 1997, dropped sharply to about 14.3 percent in 1998, and was running in single-digit levels in January 1999. Unemployment rates also fell dramatically in 1998, from 11.0 percent at the start of the year to around 9.0 percent by December.

Unfortunately, the specter of the "twin deficits" on the current account and the consolidated government budget had returned by the end 1998. These deficits, which rose to 8–9 percent of GDP (each) in 1994, forced the government to introduce the March 1995 stabilization program. After recording dramatic reductions in both deficits during 1996–1997, the consolidated budget deficit rose to 6.8 percent of GDP in 1998, thanks to a New Year's Eve bank bailout that absorbed some 2.0 percent of GDP all by itself. This fiscal boost, combined with accelerating consumption and investment spending, pushed the current-account deficit up to 4.8 percent of GDP (up from 2.1 percent in 1997), and by early 1999 was threatening to undo much of Hungary's progress since March 1995. Slowing the growth of fiscal red ink, domestic demand, and the current-account deficit were the major challenges facing policy makers at year's end.

Czech Republic

The Czech economy went from bad to worse in 1998, as the external adjustment that began with the May 1997 currency crisis gave way to recession. GDP fell by an estimated 2.5 percent in 1998, and the downturn is likely to extend at least through mid-1999. Retail sales were down 7.0 percent in 1998, and after growing strongly over the first eight months of 1998, industrial output fell in the last four months of the year, so that industrial growth for the year was an anemic 1.9 percent. Although the slowdown in domestic demand pulled down import growth, export growth was also lackluster, so that the trade balance still recorded a sizable ($2.5 billion) deficit in 1998 (albeit below 1997's $4.5 billion). The unemployment rate rose from 5.6 percent in January 1998 to 8.1 percent in January 1999, and was likely to be in double digits by the end of the year.

On the other hand, inflation dropped sharply over the course of 1998: annual growth in consumer price inflation fell from 13.1 percent in January 1998 to 3.5 percent in January 1999. A 44 percent increase in foreign direct investment during the first three quarters of 1998 helped stabilize the koruna and the Czech Republic's external accounts. Still, prospects for arresting the downward slide in incomes and output depended in part on the ability of Prime Minister Milos Zeman's minority government to get an economic program through parliament. They also depended on progress in the structuring of the cumbersome financial-industrial conglomerates that were created in the mid-1990s, as well as on more rapid economic growth in the EU.

Slovakia

The National Bank of Slovakia finally let the Slovak koruna float on 1 October 1998, right after the September parliamentary elections. The koruna immediately fell 12–13 percent. This devaluation marked the end of the era of rapid GDP growth stimulated by government-sponsored investment and consumption: policies that kept Slovakia's external accounts in the red. Slovakia's current-account deficits on average absorbed 9.0 percent of GDP during 1996–1998, and the external borrowing required to finance these deficits pushed Slovakia's foreign debt up from $4.2 billion at the end of 1993 to $12.2 billion as of August 1998. The burden of servicing these debts was one of the reasons that Slovakia's GDP growth in 1998 slowed to about 5.0 percent (from an annual average of 6.5 percent during 1995–1997), and is likely to drop below 3.0 percent in 1999. Debt servicing costs will also force Slovakia to curb its current-account deficits, which rose to 9.0 percent in 1998.

In many respects, Slovakia's economic situation was worse than these numbers suggest. Although Slovakia's voters rejected the government of former Prime Minister Vladimir Meciar in the September parliamentary elections, the new government of Prime Minister Mikulas Dzurinda inherited the difficult economic problems left by his predecessor. The new government also faced the need to repair the damage to Slovakia's prospects for EU accession done by the corruption and authoritarian politics of the Meciar era. An ambitious privatization program, as well as initiatives to bring Slovakia's regulatory and legal frameworks into closer compliance with EU norms would be a good start. But feuding among the parties that supported Dzurinda's government, as well as popular dissatisfaction with the low living standards associated with Meciar's economic policy mismanagement, left the government with little room to maneuver.

Slovenia

Slovenia was virtually the only economy in Eastern Europe in 1998 with rising GDP growth, falling inflation, and a balanced current account. GDP grew by about 4.5 percent (up from 3.8 percent in 1997), while consumer price inflation fell to about 8.0 percent (from 9 percent in 1997). Solid export growth (of about 7.0 percent) played an important role in these numbers; and since Slovenian exports consisted primarily of manufactured goods, export growth boosted industrial output, which rose by about 5.0 percent in 1998. Rising exports also helped finance import growth, especially of the intermediate goods needed for the recovery of Slovenian industry. Industry also benefited from a sharp reduction in inflation and real interest rates: the cost of short-term enterprise credits fell by 53.7 percent during January–October. Lower credit costs in turn sparked growth in investment spending, particularly in manufacturing, where investment spending rose at double-digit levels throughout most of the year.

THE BALTIC ECONOMIES

Estonia

Like many other economies in the region, Estonia saw GDP growth decelerate sharply over the course of 1998. After posting a 9.3 percent increase in the first quarter, GDP growth slowed to 5.2 percent in the second quarter, 1.8 percent in the third quarter, and 0.2 percent in the fourth quarter. GDP growth for the year was projected at 4.1 percent, a sharp drop from 1997's 11.4 percent growth rate. The growth slowdown was accompanied by some good news on inflation and the current account, however. Consumer price inflation dropped to an average rate of 10.6 percent for the year, thanks to sharp declines in inflation during the last quarter of 1998. And while the current-account deficit in 1998 stayed high (at 9.5 percent of GDP through the first three quarters), it was nonetheless down on 1997's 12.0 percent.

These developments were in part attributable to business-cycle trends in Estonia. Under Estonia's currency board, large current-account deficits tend to reduce foreign exchange reserves, which slows subsequent growth in the domestic money supply and spending. External factors were also at work, as exports to both the CIS and EU countries slowed. While its extensive trade with Germany and Scandinavia provided Estonia with some protection against the "Russian contagion" (trade with Russia through the first 11 months of 1998 made up only 13 percent of total exports and 11 percent of total imports, respectively), falling exports to CIS countries also played a role in the growth slowdown. This was particularly the case for Estonian agricultural and food processing exports. Still, balance-of-payments losses on exports to Russia were partially offset by 30 percent growth in cargo transit of Russian goods through Estonian ports during 1998.

Estonia in 1999 would face the challenge of restoring economic growth without causing unsustainable increases in the current-account deficit. Since the currency board ruled out a devaluation to boost exports and cut imports, GDP growth would have to be financed by capital inflows, preferably in the form of direct investment. Much therefore would depend on the success of Estonia's 1999 privatization program, which featured the sale of the Eesti Energia utility, oil shale producer Eesti Polevkivi, two state rail companies, and alcohol producer Liviko.

Latvia

"Russian contagion" effects may have been greater on Latvia than on the other two Baltic economies in 1998. Latvian exports to Russia during the first 11 months of 1998 dropped by about 50 percent over the same period in 1997, and Riga's role as an "off-shore" center for Russian finance meant additional strains on the Latvian financial system. As a result, GDP growth in Latvia slowed from 7.4 percent in the first quarter to 5.4 percent in the second quarter to 1.9 percent in the third quarter, and probably averaged around 3.5 percent for the year (down from 6.5 percent in 1997). Growth in industrial production also slowed dramatically, from 6.1 percent in 1997 to 2.0 percent in 1998. Industrial production in

December 1998 was some 13 percent below December 1997 levels. But despite this growth slowdown, Latvia's current-account deficit grew sharply in 1998, rising from 6.3 percent of GDP in 1997 to 9.2 percent at the end of the third quarter of 1998. On the other hand, consumer price inflation in Latvia was only 4.7 percent for 1998–the lowest in Eastern Europe. Also, much of the decline in trade with Russia occurred prior to the ruble's August crash, as Moscow at mid-year introduced economic sanctions over Riga's alleged mistreatment of Latvia's Russian minority. Since the Russian trade shock began earlier for Latvia than for Estonia and Lithuania, it may also end sooner. Unlike Estonia and Lithuania, its relatively flexible exchange-rate regime allows Latvia to devalue the lats in order to boost exports; and 1998's very low inflation rate suggests that a devaluation would have a minimal effect on Latvian prices. Moreover, Latvia in 1998 became the first Baltic state to gain admission to the World Trade Organization, and the EU's November progress report gave Latvia high marks for progress in legal and structural reform. If the government can continue to push ahead in these areas, and if the economy recovers from the worst of the Russian contagion, Latvia could conceivably be invited to begin EU accession negotiations in the near future.

Lithuania

In many respects, Lithuania's economic performance in 1998 was the best in the Baltics. In contrast to Estonia and Latvia, Lithuania's growth slowdown in 1998 was quite moderate. GDP during the first three quarters increased by 5.7 percent, largely unchanged on 1997's 6.1 percent growth rate. Industrial output in 1998 also grew by some 7.0 percent. This was well above 1997's 0.7 percent industrial growth, as well as Estonia's 1.5 percent industrial growth and Latvia's 2.0 percent growth in 1998. And preliminary reports indicate that consumer price inflation in Lithuania averaged only 5.1 percent in 1998, second only to Latvia's 4.7 percent annual rate.

On the other hand, Lithuania's current-account deficit expanded in 1998, rising to 13 percent of GDP over the first three quarters from 10.3 percent in 1997. Lithuania's economic performance in 1998 was therefore similar to Hungary's, in that impressive growth and inflation numbers may have been purchased at the cost of unsustainable deterioration in external balance. As such, Lithuania could be in for a rough external adjustment in 1999. Moreover, Lithuania's currency board ruled out devaluing the litas in order to boost export growth and slow imports. As in Estonia, Lithuania faced the challenge of attracting capital inflows in order to maintain sustainable GDP growth. Some 13 large state enterprises were slated for initial public offers in 1999, and much may hinge on the outcome of these sales.

THE BALKANS

Albania

The Albanian economy grew by some 8 percent in 1998, and as such seems to have essentially recovered from the turmoil of early 1997, which caused GDP to drop 7.0 percent in that year. Agriculture, construction, and transport seemed to be the leading growth sectors. Sharp reductions in inflation were also recorded in 1998: year-on-year inflation rates fell from 42 percent in 1997 to 10 percent by the end of 1998. Although the 1998 fiscal deficit absorbed close to 12 percent of GDP, this was smaller than 1997's nearly 16 percent deficit. On the other hand, export growth did not keep pace with surging imports in 1998, and the trade deficit probably rose to above 20 percent of GDP.

Bulgaria

Having achieved price and exchange-rate stability thanks to its currency board, 1998 was to be the year in which Bulgaria enjoyed a sustained, rapid recovery. But while Bulgarian GDP grew by 4.5 percent in 1998, this expansion was due primarily to a rebound from the drastic downturn suffered in the first half of 1997. Falling exports to Russia and the CIS, which began earlier in 1998, accelerated after the August collapse of the ruble. While the region did not dominate Bulgarian trade as it did in the days of the Soviet bloc, the drastic contraction of CIS exports nonetheless had a serious impact. Exports to the developed West were disappointing as well, especially outside the EU. Export competitiveness and import competition for domestic producers became more problematic as the lev—which was pegged to the Deutsche mark under a currency board—appreciated significantly in real terms in 1998.

Privatization and restructuring in Bulgaria went forward in 1998, but in fits and starts. The government of Ivan Kostov pledged to accelerate this process, to make it more transparent, and to improve the environment for foreign and domestic investors. With the currency board in place and IMF credits only sufficient to keep Bulgaria current on foreign debt service, the financing of the 1999 state budget would depend critically on the government's ability to follow through on its privatization pledges. The government also promised to liquidate loss-making enterprises, eliminating their burden on the economy and freeing up resources for productive activities. While this restructuring, together with continuing difficulties in key export markets, may constrain growth in 1999, in the medium term it should help generate the long-awaited, sustained, and robust recovery of aggregate output.

Croatia

Croatia's burgeoning current-account deficit and the possibility of a currency crisis were key worries for policy makers in Zagreb during 1997–1998. In 1997, strong domestic demand pushed the current-account deficit to $2.43 billion, or 12.6 percent of GDP. Croatia could not sustain this situation in the medium term, and many analysts predicted that the kuna would have to depreciate sharply. In response, fiscal and monetary policy was tightened in the second half of 1997, and these restrictions remained in place throughout 1998. As a result, increases in domestic demand—the catalyst for booming imports—slowed to more sustainable levels. While growth in aggregate demand slowed, the industrial sector recovered in the second half of 1998 due to growth of exports, while tourism also staged a second-half comeback. These developments allowed Croatia to weather the emerging market crises of 1998 and avoid a sharp depreciation.

Gross industrial output was up 6.7 percent for the first three quarters of 1998, year-on-year. While dollar exports were up 9.5 percent through October, dollar imports declined by 1.9 percent during this time. The retail price index January through October was up 5.7 percent on an annual basis, but this was due largely to the one-off effect of the introduction of the VAT in January. Unemployment remained dangerously high, but real wages and retail trade turnover continued to grow, albeit at a slower pace than in 1997. Through the first three quarters of 1998, Croatia's budget was in surplus by 1,194 million kunas.

The political situation in Croatia may have a negative effect on the economy in the near future. President Franjo Tudjman's apparent support for the hard-liners in the ruling party may reduce foreign assistance, investment, and even trade agreements. In the medium term, this would jeopardize Croatia's external balance, and in turn macroeconomic stability. Already, foreign investment stagnated during the first half of 1998. If not for the sale of Pilva, the pharmaceutical giant, foreign direct investment would be about the same as 1997's disappointing level. Foreign portfolio investment was essentially non-existent in 1998, while "other" investment has fallen almost $200 million below the previous year's level. Excluding the Pliva sale, total foreign investment was running 25 percent less than in 1997.

Romania

Prospects for restructuring in Romania were revived yet again when Radu Vasile became prime minister in April, but little action resulted thereafter, and inflows of foreign investment and progress on privatization remained slow. In early December, Vasile called on Romanians for six months of "social peace" to allow the government to develop a new reform program—and vowed to resign if significant progress had not been made by then. Most of the trade unions refused to honor the request for a moratorium on strikes and protests. Nonetheless, in December, the government gave the go-ahead to immediately shut down the 49 largest cash sinkholes among the remaining state-owned enterprises. The EU and other international financial institutions had made radical restructuring a precondition for additional assistance and support—and with several credit downgrades in the second half of 1998, Romania desperately needed to restore its credibility with Western investors.

Restructuring and privatization become more vital each day to rescue Romania's sagging economy. First-half GDP declined 5.2 percent year-on-year, primarily due to the 19.1 percent decline in industrial output. Industry lagged because its products were not competitive on international markets—in the first eight months of 1998 relative to the same period last year, exports declined 2.8 percent, while imports rose 5.1 percent. By the end of the third quarter, the trade deficit had risen to $2,431 million, 26 percent higher than the same period in 1997, with a concomitant rise in the current-account deficit. Inflation continued to fall, and fiscal targets are relatively on track. However, a successful turnaround in Romania's economy will require immediate restructuring of the real economy, on top of the continuation of existing fiscal and monetary policies.

Yugoslavia

Yugoslavia remained under international financial sanctions and an investment ban due to the crackdown in Kosovo. Prospects for lifting these sanctions in 1999 seemed increasingly remote. The sanctions also made financing the trade and current-account deficits more difficult, although Yugoslavia managed to avoid a sharp external correction. Yugoslavia's fragile recovery appeared under threat, as GDP growth has slowed sharply in 1998 to about 4.0 percent from over 7.0 percent in 1997. Part of this was due to Yugoslav industry struggling to finance raw material imports. The economy as a whole was largely unreformed, characterized by multiple distortions and a degree of government intervention. The financial system was shaky and National Bank policy alternated between large credit emissions to support insolvent industries and monetary tightening to support the fixed exchange rate. Due to high inflation fueled by credit emissions, the dinar peg was once again under threat. The country's foreign exchange reserves were minimal and provided almost no import coverage.

The political situation remained the key to the future of the country. Nineteen ninety-eight saw a sharp deterioration in Yugoslavia's political outlook, as President Slobodan Milosevic cracked down in Kosovo and launched a clampdown in Serbia. Tensions with Montenegro were escalating, while dissatisfaction with the regime was high. Milosevic was bent on staying in power whatever the cost and continued to sacrifice the economy and the country to this end.

Macedonia

Macedonia witnessed its long anticipated acceleration in growth in 1998, as GDP growth picked up from 1.5 percent to an estimated 5.0 percent. Growth was fueled by the industrial sector and stronger exports. Inflation should come in at under 3.0 percent for 1998, and reforms to strengthen the financial sector and improve corporate governance were continuing. The election of a new reformist government should accelerate this process. Macedonia's external accounts continued to worsen in 1998, though at a slower pace. The current-account deficit remained high, though it was increasingly being financed by direct foreign investment and long-term loans from official creditors. Continued growth depends on restructuring in the industrial sector.

Despite its impressive recovery, Macedonia's economic situation remained fragile, and industrial growth may have been slowing in the second half of 1998. Long-term Macedonian economic development requires regional stability and good relations with its neighbors. Yugoslavia was Macedonia's largest single trading partner and instability there combined with Belgrade's renewed isolation could hurt Macedonian exports. Macedonia was seeking to reorient its trade toward the EU and is improving relations with Greece to that end. The new government hoped to conclude an association agreement and significantly boost foreign investment.

Bosnia-Herzegovina

Bosnia continued its rapid post-war recovery and growth is set for 30 percent in 1998. This growth was becoming more even as the Republika Srpska's (RS) economic situation was also improving. Inter-entity trade increased and other signs suggested that the internal Bosnian economy was integrating. The Convertible Mark was accepted in the Federation, while in the RS the Yugoslav dinar still prevailed. This was a significant factor behind the higher inflation rate in the RS. Continued progress was made over budgets and pension reform. Privatization, which was slated for introduction in the Federation in 1998, was delayed until 1999 due to a number of technical problems. Despite these signs of progress, the country was still deeply divided and governance structures were weak. Elections in September produced mixed results as a hard-line nationalist won in the RS. A meeting of international donors stressed that Bosnia must end its dependence on foreign aid and more aggressively pursue reforms to make its economic recovery self-sustaining. Donors also expressed dissatisfaction over the slow pace of refugee returns and other efforts to integrate the country. The situation in the county was clearly dependent on the continued presence of foreign troops and the active role played by international administrators.

RUSSIA CASTS A LONG SHADOW OVER CIS ECONOMIES

by BEN SLAY

Economic developments in the Commonwealth of Independent States (CIS) prior to 1998 seemed to be following a trajectory that was broadly similar to the patterns of recovery and growth apparent in most of Central and Eastern Europe (CEE). As was the case in the CEE countries, the CIS economies in the early 1990s experienced a period of high inflation (often hyperinflation), large declines in GDP, and sharp drops in intra-regional trade. Virtually all of these economies then saw inflation rates fall sharply, and most saw their transition recessions stop, by the mid-1990s. In East Europe, recovery began in Poland in 1992; in the CIS, it began with Armenia in 1994. By 1997, virtually all of these economies—including Russia—had reported at least one year of economic growth. Likewise, inflation had generally fallen well below the 30 percent annual rate often seen as compatible with GDP growth. Prior to 1998, only Moldova, Ukraine, and Turkmenistan had been unable to turn the growth corner.

There were, of course, some important differences between the recoveries in the CIS and CEE economies. The inflation rates were generally higher, and the transition recessions longer, in the CIS countries. The odd combination of large wage and pension arrears, perpetual shortages of household electricity and heat, and strong GDP growth apparent in many CIS economies also differed from the CEE experience, where growing GDP was more likely to mean significant improvements in living standards. Also, whereas the CEE economies that succeeded in stabilizing their exchange rates and bringing inflation down could count on rapid export growth to EU countries to offset the decline in intra-regional trade, this option was not available for most CIS economies for a host of reasons, not least of which was sheer physical distance. Moreover, the recipe for recovery in Central and Eastern Europe was broadly consistent with the advice governments were receiving from international financial institutions (the "Washington consensus"), emphasizing stabilization, liberalization, and international economic integration. The CIS experience was much more heterogeneous in this respect. While some of the economies with strong post-1994 growth robustly embraced the Washington consensus (e.g., Georgia, Kyrgyzstan, Armenia), others did not. Belarus reported large increases in GDP during 1996–1998 after recreating quasi-Soviet central planning; while Uzbekistan combined continued strong administrative controls over economic activity with the region's smallest post-1991 cumulative decline in GDP.

Prior to 1998, these differences between the CIS and CEE economies could be seen as relatively minor. Developments in 1998, especially following the Russian financial collapse in August, made this argument much less tenable. Instead, due to the ruble's sharp depreciation and Russia's second burst of high inflation of the 1990s, many of the CIS economies began what is likely to be their second bout of inflation, recession, and exchange-rate instability. Some of these economies may escape being ravaged by the Russian flu, of course: Azerbaijan and Armenia both reported higher GDP growth and lower inflation in 1998, for example. But for most CIS economies, the links to Russia were still very strong. The sharp declines in Russian import purchases devastated exports for many CIS countries in 1998, and those countries with energy exports that could be sold elsewhere (Azerbaijan, Kazakhstan, and Turkmenistan) were hit by sharp declines in world energy prices, as well as by on-going problems with pipeline access. The sharp declines in Russian imports also reduced transit incomes for Belarus and Ukraine, while the ruble's slide reduced the value of the remittances sent home by Georgians and Armenians working in Russia. The shock of Russia's sovereign default damaged the external creditworthiness of the other CIS countries (Ukraine, Moldova, and Kazakhstan) that had issued Eurobonds to tap international capital markets. And the banks in other CIS countries with strong ties to Russian financial institutions and markets often came to regret these links after August 1998.

These "second recessions" that began in a number of CIS economies in 1998 were highly worrisome. Officially reported GDP remained far below the levels reported at the beginning of the transition; and while comparisons between GDP in 1991 and 1998 are highly problematic, there can be no doubt that most citizens of CIS countries at the end of 1998 were living much worse than they were in 1988. Perhaps more importantly, the new recessions curtailed private-sector activities and in many cases delayed the private- and public-sector institutional restructuring that is crucial for the region's long-term growth prospects. Some countries—like Belarus, Uzbekistan, and Georgia—will have to make sure that 1998's sharp rises in inflation will not lead to a return to the triple- (or quadruple) digit inflation rates of the early 1990s. And since the other CIS countries' exports to Russia are unlikely to return to 1997 levels before 2002 at the earliest, growth cannot be based on waiting for the "coming Russian boom." Instead, due to current-account pressures and unfavorable conditions on international financial markets, CIS economies that wish to avoid more pressures on prices and currencies may have to make further reductions in domestic demand in general, and fiscal deficits in particular. Given the important elections slated for 1999 in a number of CIS countries, including Ukraine and Armenia, it is difficult to be optimistic about the region's growth prospects during 1999–2000.

THE WESTERN CIS ECONOMIES

Ukraine

The Ukrainian economy seemed poised to recover from its long transition recession in the second half of 1998: GDP during January–August actually posted a

0.2 percent increase relative to the same period in 1997. GDP then fell sharply in the wake of the Russian financial collapse, so that the output decline for the year was set at 1.7 percent. Although the hryvnya depreciated by some 72 percent (in an average annual sense) during 1998, a relatively tight fiscal policy and the more extensive use of price controls kept inflation from spiraling out of control: retail prices at the end of the year were only rising at a 20 percent annual rate.

Despite a sharp decline in exports (which dropped from $15.4 billion in 1997 to $12.5 billion in 1998), Kyiv managed to push the current-account deficit down to $1.1 billion (from $1.3 billion in 1997). Official reserves nonetheless fell sharply, from $2.3 billion at the end of 1997 to only $680 million by the end of 1998. By mid-March 1999, these had dropped to a mere $410 million, and Kyiv was living on IMF life support. However, even though the consolidated fiscal deficit had fallen to only 2.1 percent of GDP by the end of 1998, and even though domestic demand fell by some 2.0 percent that year, Kyiv was unable to keep its relationship with the IMF on solid footing. As a result, Ukraine began 1999 with its Extended Fund Facility from the IMF on hold, and close to $1.6 billion in debt payments falling due later in the year.

President Leonid Kuchma and Prime Minister Valerii Pustovoitenko were therefore in the unenviable position of having to impose continued macroeconomic austerity that is simultaneously deeply unpopular politically and perceived as inadequate by foreign investors, in terms of boosting Ukraine's external creditworthiness. The presidential elections slated for 1999 are likely to bring domestic political considerations to the fore, and these in turn could well prevent the austerity measures necessary to avoid a Russian-type meltdown. Ukraine is therefore likely to flirt with sovereign default for much of 1999—and, depending on the outcome of the presidential elections, afterwards as well.

Belarus

In all probability, 1998 marked the end of President Alyaksandr Lukashenka's "Belarusian economic miracle," although the official statistics continued to portray it as another banner year for Minsk: GDP grew by 8.3 percent, while industrial output rose by 11 percent. On the other hand, despite extensive price controls, consumer price inflation rose from 63 percent at the end of 1997 to 182 percent by December 1998. Likewise, the official exchange rate collapsed, falling from $1 = 31,000 Belarusian rubles at the end of 1997 to $1 = 107,000 rubles by December 1998. Money-losing enterprises were kept afloat by soft credits issued through the banking system, while burgeoning wage arrears were increasingly monetized. The rapid devaluation of the Belarusian ruble which resulted prompted attempts to artificially prop up the value of the currency through restrictions on trading, to little avail. Much of this output growth clearly ended up in inventory rather than adding value, and reports of shortages and labor unrest proliferated over the course of the year.

Belarus's "economic miracle," such as it was, was based on close integration with Russia. Minsk's ties to Moscow allowed Belarusian firms to export to Russia on exceptionally favorable terms, while Belarusian enterprises and households benefited from soft Russian credits that subsidized imports of cheap Russian energy. Official data show that Belarus's foreign trade did not fall off substantially in 1998, presumably due to barter deals among enterprises and Moscow's continuing willingness to finance the Lukashenka regime. However, the collapse in the exchange rate suggests that an increasing share of Belarusian GDP had to be devoted to maintaining trade with Russia. The failure to rein in domestic demand in light of these developments then resulted in the high inflation of 1998. Preventing prices and the exchange rate from surging further out of control will require the introduction of austerity policies that Minsk will have a hard time accepting. The combination of an increasingly unruly economy and rising political tensions within Belarus could well make 1999 a "memorable" year.

Moldova

The ruble devaluation and sovereign default in Russia interacted with pre-existing tensions in the Moldovan economy—in the form of large current-account deficits, acute energy shortages, and negligible levels of foreign investment—to precipitate a potentially devastating economic and political crisis in the second half of 1998. Moldovan GDP declined by 8.6 percent in 1998—the largest drop recorded in the CIS—due to a large decline in exports to Russia, which in turn reflected 11 percent reductions in industrial and agricultural output. Domestic confidence in the leu collapsed: the exchange rate fell from $1 = 4.7 at the end of 1997 to $1 = 8.7 as of December 1998. The leu's collapse in turn ignited inflationary expectations: December-on-December consumer price inflation jumped from 11.1 percent in 1997 to 18.2 percent in 1998 and was likely to accelerate further in 1999. The rapid depreciation of the leu also caused Moldova to accumulate arrears on its debt-servicing obligations during the first quarter of 1999; this could force Russia to halt all natural gas shipments to Moldova in 1999.

Due to Chisinau's inability to draft and implement an economic program supported by the IMF and World Bank, Moldova had to face these problems without significant multilateral assistance in 1998. Although the IMF promised to resume lending in January 1999, financial support from the IMF and World Bank has remained on hold following the resignation of Prime Minister Ion Ciubuc in February. Although a new government was approved in March, it faces the unpleasant task of imposing painful reforms on a formidable parliamentary opposition and in very difficult macroeconomic circumstances. It is difficult therefore to be optimistic about Moldova's economic prospects during 1999–2000.

CENTRAL ASIA

Kazakhstan

GDP fell by 2.5 percent in 1998, as Kazakhstan suffered from a triple whammy of the Russian crisis, falling energy prices, and a bad harvest: crop output fell by nearly 40 percent last year. The unfavorable external environment caused exports to drop by some 17 percent (to $5.5 billion) last year, while the current-account deficit ballooned to $1.7 billion, or 7.1 percent of GDP. While large inflows (about $1.2 billion) of foreign direct investment helped finance this deficit, this represented a departure from previous years, when the current-account shortfall was entirely financed by incoming investment. On the plus side, inflation in Kazakhstan had essentially stopped by the end of 1998: consumer prices in December were only 1.8 percent above their December 1997 levels. This helped the government and central bank to keep the currency relatively stable during 1998, as the tenge only depreciated by some 4 percent between December 1997 and December 1998. Nonetheless, due to Kazakhstan's deteriorating external circumstances, official reserves shrank from $1.7 billion at the end of 1997 to only $917 million at the end of the third quarter of 1998, and did not recover much thereafter. A currency crisis seemed likely in 1999 if the current-account imbalance was not reduced.

The Kazakhstani government in response to these pressures sought to tighten fiscal policy in 1999: the central government deficit was to be cut from 1998's target level of 5.5 percent of GDP to 3.1 percent of GDP in 1999. In Astana's battle for fiscal and external balance, much will depend on the success of the government's program to raise nearly $600 million in privatization revenues. Still, a second consecutive year of falling GDP was likely in 1999; and if the tenge collapses as well, inflation could return with a vengeance. A revival in world oil prices could ease the pressure.

Uzbekistan

Uzbekistan's 4.4 percent GDP growth in 1998 was the fifth highest recorded in the CIS (after Belarus, Azerbaijan, Armenia, and Tajikistan), and put Uzbekistan's cumulative GDP decline for the 1990–1998 period at only 9.0 percent—the lowest of all the Soviet successor states, including the Baltics. Annual inflation rates remained roughly constant during 1998: the 27.3 percent consumer price inflation rate recorded in December was essentially unchanged on December 1997's 27.5 percent rate. Although both imports and exports declined sharply in 1998, the 33 percent drop in exports turned 1997's $136 million trade deficit into a $129 million trade surplus. Much of the export decline occurred before the ruble devaluation, and was due to low world prices for Uzbekistan's exports, most notably cotton.

Tashkent likes to attribute its success to its purposeful isolation from international capital markets and extremely gradualist transition strategy. According to the regime of President Islam Karimov, the Russian financial crisis further vindicated Uzbekistan's economic policies. However, despite its splendid international economic isolation, Uzbekistan was not immune to the fallout from the financial crises in Russia and Asia. This was most apparent in the exchange rate: the som fell 25 percent in the fourth quarter of 1998 (to $1 = 113 som); and the black market rate, which typically hovered at about twice the official one, fell to almost 400 som to the dollar in early 1999. As was the case in Belarus, the administrative nature of Uzbekistan's economic system exacted some important costs. The introduction of currency controls in 1996—which resulted in the cut-off of IMF assistance—led to draconian reductions in imports: these fell from $4.7 billion in 1996 to $3.0 billion in 1998. In addition to removing many consumer goods from the shelves, these controls have kept many Uzbekistani factories from obtaining the equipment needed to modernize and restructure. Still, given the developments in Russia, the Karimov regime was not likely to abandon the "Uzbek economic model" in 1999.

Kyrgyzstan

Like many other CIS countries, economic growth in Kyrgyzstan slowed sharply in 1998: GDP growth dropped to 1.8 percent from 9.9 percent in 1997. Russia's financial crisis triggered a run on the som in November, so that consumer price inflation in December had risen to an annualized rate of 18.4 percent. Perhaps the most worrisome developments in 1998 were in Kyrgyzstan's external accounts: the trade deficit widened from $15 million in 1997 to $195 million; while the current-account deficit rose from $139 million to $225 million (13.8 percent of GDP). Only some $90 million of the current-account deficit was financed by foreign direct investment. As a result, the accumulation of Kyrgyzstan's foreign debt continued unabated.

These unfavorable developments in 1998 were due in part to Russia's financial crisis: the som's collapse was precipitated by the losses sustained by Kyrgyzstan's banks when the Russian treasury bill market collapsed, as well as by the withdrawal of Russian banks from Kyrgyzstani financial markets. Still, Kyrgyzstan's main problems remained within the domestic economy itself: the industrial sector remained largely unrestructured and depressed, while the agricultural sector's growth potential was not being realized. However, reforms at the micro level continued to advance in 1998, especially in terms of strengthening corporate governance, legal reform, land privatization, and private sector development. The authorities in early 1999 were tightening monetary and fiscal policies in order to maintain macroeconomic stability, and both the IMF and World Bank have agreed to up their assistance to Kyrgyzstan in 1999.

Tajikistan

Tajikistan's economic recovery from the four-year civil war strengthened in 1998: the reported 5.3 percent GDP growth was the highest of Tajikistan's transition, and the fourth highest growth rate recorded among CIS countries (after Belarus, Azerbaijan, and Armenia) in 1998. Industrial production posted 8.1 percent growth, while agricultural output was up 6.5 percent. Inflation essentially stopped by the end of 1998: consumer prices in December were only 2.7 percent above their December 1998 level. But despite these encouraging developments, the exchange rate fell from $1 = 747 Tajik rubles as of December 1997 to $1 = 995 rubles by December 1998 (a 33 percent decline in nominal terms), as the current-account deficit swelled to $180 million (nearly 20 percent of GDP). Although IMF and World Bank assistance funded most of this deficit—Tajikistan remains the poorest CIS country, with per capita annual income (at purchasing power parity rates) of only $149 in 1998—such assistance cannot be expected indefinitely.

Turkmenistan

The 4.7 percent GDP growth recorded in Turkmenistan in 1998 was an impressive figure considering the continuing fall in gas production, the poor cotton harvest in 1998, and sharp declines in exports and imports (by 32 and 34 percent, respectively). The tightening of foreign exchange controls introduced after the ruble devaluation in August helped prevent a sharp nominal depreciation of the manat, which in turn reduced price pressures: consumer price inflation averaged only 19.3 percent last year, down from 86.1 percent in 1997. Still, Turkmenistan's longer-term economic prospects depend on gaining access to paying customers for its gas exports. Although Ashgabat was able to secure a new gas deal with Ukraine in early 1999 (shipments had been cut off completely in 1997 due to a payments dispute) the resolution of Turkmenistan's central dilemma—reducing its reliance on Russia's gas pipeline network system—came no closer to fruition in 1998.

THE CAUCASUS

Armenia

Armenia was one of the CIS's best economic performers in 1998. GDP grew by 7.2 percent, while inflation essentially disappeared: consumer prices at the end of December were actually 1.2 percent below December 1997 levels. The dram remained stable: 1998's average exchange rate of $1 = 504 drams was not much below 1997's $1 = 490 average rate. And, in sharp contrast to most other CIS countries, Armenia's foreign trade did not undergo dramatic shrinkage in 1998: exports and imports remained essentially unchanged at $223 million and $895 million, respectively. Although the resulting trade deficit absorbed some 36 percent of GDP, this was below the 41 percent share of 1997's deficit.

Armenia's solid macroeconomic performance, which occurred despite a 10 percent decline in exports to other CIS countries (due mostly to the Russian financial crisis), primarily reflected three factors. First, Armenia continued to benefit from substantial cash inflows from the diaspora and multilateral lenders.

These inflows stimulated domestic demand and boosted GDP growth while simultaneously allowing Armenia to finance very large trade and current account deficits (the latter constituted some 36 percent of GDP in 1998). Second, 1998 was an exceptionally good year for Armenian agriculture: gross agricultural output was up 13 percent, which helped offset a 2.5 percent decline in industrial production. Finally, the government under President Robert Kocharian and Prime Minister Armen Darbinian restored reform momentum and implemented sound fiscal and monetary policies. In contrast to Georgia, which saw economic growth drop sharply, inflation accelerate, and the domestic currency undergo sharp depreciation due to an escalating budget crisis in late 1998, Armenia recorded impressive growth in revenues from both taxes and privatization in 1998. In the longer run, however, the Armenian economy remains heavily dependent on multilateral transfers from abroad. Also, the Kocharian regime was unwilling to take the steps necessary to reduce tensions with Azerbaijan that will probably be required to end the Azerbaijani-Turkish blockade. Armenia's long-term growth prospects are unlikely to improve without at least some progress towards resolving these problems.

Azerbaijan

Azerbaijan posted 10.0 percent GDP growth in 1998 as $1.3 billion in foreign direct investment in the oil sector boosted rapid growth in services and construction. This rapid growth, which occurred despite sharp declines in world energy prices, was accompanied by deflationary pressures and a strong manat. In contrast to Russia and many other CIS economies, consumer prices in Azerbaijan at the end of December were actually 2.8 percent below December 1997 levels; and the average exchange rate for the year remained essentially unchanged, at $1 = 3,869 manats. These developments occurred despite a 24 percent decline in exports (to $593 million) and a sharp (56 percent) rise in imports (to $1.2 billion).

By contrast, industry and agriculture grew more slowly than GDP: gross industrial output increased by just 2.2 percent in 1998, while agricultural production increased 4.0 percent. Likewise, the current account deficit in 1998 rose to $1.5 billion (about 36 percent of GDP). While virtually all of this was financed by foreign direct investment in the oil sector, the fall in international oil prices and poor drilling results at a few fields caused some international consortia to leave the area, while others delayed exploratory drillings. Azerbaijan showed signs of catching a whiff of the Dutch disease, as the economy's reliance on the oil sector may be driving down investment in other sectors. Still, while enthusiasm for Caspian production may have waned slightly, international energy companies and markets continued to believe that Azerbaijan possesses significant amounts of proven offshore crude oil reserves. Azerbaijan's economy should continue to grow rapidly as long as this is the case.

Georgia

Like Kyrgyzstan, Georgia saw its macroeconomic performance deteriorate dramatically in the wake of Russia's financial collapse. The lari, which had traded at $1 = 1.35 prior to the ruble's devaluation, had slipped to $1 = 1.8 by early December. On 7 December the National Bank of Georgia (NBG) announced that it could no longer support the lari, and in the ensuing float the lari by March 1999 had slipped to $1 = 2.15. GDP, which had grown at 8.9 percent during the first half of 1998, fell by some 3.1 percent during the second half of the year, due to the effects of a bad harvest and the collapse of Georgia's exports to (and remittances from) Russia. The 2.9 percent GDP growth recorded for the year was Georgia's lowest since 1995, and was well below the 11.3 percent growth recorded in 1997. Exports in 1998 fell by some 23 percent, while industrial and agricultural output were down 2.7 and 8.0 percent, respectively. The current-account deficit also swelled to $691 million (13.9 percent of GDP), up from $499 million (10.1 percent of GDP) in 1997.

While many of Georgia's macroeconomic problems could be ascribed to developments in Russia and the bad harvest, these difficulties were compounded by serious underlying problems within the Georgian economy. A deepening budget crisis, spawned by persistent, massive shortfalls in tax revenues, continued to severely restrain public sector spending on capital investment and led to mounting public salary and pension arrears. Expenditures were cut in line with revenue shortfalls, which in turn weakened spending that had already been cut by falling export receipts. The inability to collect taxes also hurt Georgia's prospects for continued assistance from international multilateral institutions, which have played a key role in covering Georgia's large current-account deficits and servicing its external debt. The IMF in early 1999 froze a $37 million dollar tranche from Georgia's $240 million Enhanced Structural Adjustment Facility (ESAF) due, in large part, to the anemic performance of the government in collecting tax revenue in 1998. Although the IMF approved Georgia's austere budget for 1999, it planned to withhold disbursement of the frozen tranche until the government records several months of improved tax receipts.

NATO'S OSTPOLITIK: CONSOLIDATION, BUT KOSOVO LOOMS

by ANDREW COTTEY

After the major decisions of 1997, 1998 was a year of consolidation for NATO's Ostpolitik. In 1997, after five years of debate, NATO took its first decisive steps towards eastward enlargement by inviting the Czech Republic, Hungary, and Poland to join the alliance as full members. At the same time, other measures were agreed to "sweeten the pill" for Russia and disappointed Central and Eastern European candidates: the NATO-Russia Founding Act and a NATO-Russia Permanent Joint Council (PJC); the NATO-Ukraine Charter on Distinctive Partnership; an "enhanced" Partnership for Peace (PfP); a new Euro-Atlantic Partnership Council (EAPC) bringing together NATO with almost all other European states; and an official "open door" to further enlargement. Nineteen ninety-eight saw the ratification of the Visegrad three's integration into NATO by the legislatures in the alliance's existing members and the consolidation of the other new institutional arrangements established in 1997. The escalating crisis in Kosovo, however, posed a growing challenge to NATO's credibility and dragged the Alliance ever deeper into the Balkans.

RATIFYING ENLARGEMENT

The accession of the Czech Republic, Hungary, and Poland to NATO—more specifically to the North Atlantic Treaty, which defines NATO's collective defense guarantee and provides the basis for the Alliance—required the formal assent of legislatures in the 16 existing NATO members. Although such assent was always likely once NATO's governments had agreed to invite the three countries to join, it was not entirely a foregone conclusion. Canada was the first country to ratify the accession of the three Visegrad states to NATO in February 1998. The most important debate was in the US Senate. If the Senate refused to ratify NATO enlargement, the process would likely collapse and the US commitment to NATO itself might be called into serious doubt. On the other hand, US ratification would virtually ensure ratification by the other NATO legislatures. The Senate formally debated ratification of NATO enlargement in April. Critics from the left argued that enlargement was unnecessary and risked fundamentally undermining relations with Russia and existing arms control arrangements. Critics from the right argued that enlargement risked weakening NATO and turning it from a powerful defense alliance into an amorphous collective security organization, while conceding too much to Russia via the Founding Act and the PJC.

With NATO already committed to enlargement, the Clinton administration pressing the issue, and bipartisan centrist support, opponents were not strong enough to prevent ratification. On 30 April 1998 the Senate voted 80–19 in favor of the Czech Republic, Hungary, and Poland's accession to NATO. Proposals for a three year "strategic pause" before further enlargement and a suggestion to link NATO enlargement to prior expansion of the European Union (EU) were defeated. President Bill Clinton expressed delight at the "overwhelming majority" in favor of enlargement and praised the vote as one "in the tradition of Harry Truman, George Marshall, and Arthur Vandenberg and the other giants who kept America in the world after World War II and were present at NATO's creation." Led by Senator Jesse Helms, the Republican Majority Chairman of the Senate Foreign Relations Committee, the Senate attached to its ratification of enlargement a resolution reaffirming collective defense as NATO's core mission, demanding that enlargement not lead to a major increase in the economic costs to the United States of NATO, and seeking to limit Russia's influence over the Alliance.

With US assent secured, ratification proceeded without significant problems in the other NATO legislatures. Despite French differences with the United States over NATO enlargement, the French Senate and National Assembly approved the invitation to the Visegrad three in May and June. Similarly, despite earlier fears that Greece or Turkey (or perhaps even both countries) might veto NATO enlargement because of their bilateral disputes and differences over Turkey's desire to join the European Union (EU), their parliaments ratified the move in May and October. Ratification was completed by all 16 NATO legislatures by the end of 1998, opening the way for the Czech Republic, Hungary, and Poland to join the Alliance in March 1999 in time for its fiftieth anniversary summit the following month.

WHERE NEXT?

With the Visegrad three's membership of NATO assured, attention shifted to the other Central and Eastern European states. At the July 1997 Madrid summit where the Czech Republic, Hungary, and Poland were invited to join the Alliance, NATO had stated that it would "continue to welcome new members," expected "to extend further invitations," and specifically acknowledged the membership ambitions of Romania, Slovenia, and the Baltic states. It quickly became clear, however, that no new membership invitations would be issued at NATO's 50th anniversary summit in April 1999. The "first wave" of enlargement had proved controversial within NATO, the Alliance wanted time to integrate the Visegrad three, NATO members remained wary of antagonizing Russia, and there was no consensus on which countries (if any) might be invited to join the Alliance next.

During 1998, efforts focused on intensifying ties with the Central and Eastern European states remaining outside NATO, while those states seeking NATO membership sought to enhance their credentials as potential members. In July 1997, the United States had committed itself to a "strategic partnership" with Romania, based on closer political ties and increased US support for reforms in that country. In February 1998, the United States committed itself to a similar "strategic partnership" with Bulgaria—an implicit recognition of progress made in political and economic reforms by Bulgaria's reformist center-right government since it came to power in April 1997. In January 1998, the United States also signed a special "Charter of Partnership" with Estonia, Latvia, and Lithuania, which stated its "real, profound and enduring interest in the independence, sovereignty, and territorial integrity" of the Baltic states and established frameworks for closer political, economic, and military ties with them. While these new arrangements deepened US ties with Romania, Bulgaria, and the Baltic states and emphasized US support for their full integration into NATO and the EU, they did not extend a US security guarantee to these countries, nor did they guarantee NATO membership. NATO continued its regular "Individual Dialogues" with the Central and Eastern European countries which had formally expressed their interest in joining the Alliance (Albania, Bulgaria, Estonia, Latvia, Lithuania, Macedonia, Slovakia, Slovenia, and Romania), advising these countries on foreign and defense policy reforms and how to integrate more closely with the Alliance.

The Partnership for Peace (PfP) continued to provide the primary framework for much of NATO's Ostpolitik, with growing cooperation both between NATO and individual partners and multilaterally. Partner countries participated for the first time in all aspects of a major NATO crisis management exercise in February. From September, partner countries began to work within NATO's political and military command structure, via PfP Staff Elements (PSEs) at NATO's headquarters in Brussels and in NATO's military commands. Various multilateral PfP military exercises took place during 1998, including a major peacekeeping exercise in Denmark in May which brought together forces from six NATO members and 11 partner nations.

The Euro-Atlantic Partnership Council (EAPC) grew in importance as a framework for cooperation between NATO and its eastern partners. The EAPC now involves twice yearly meetings of foreign ministers and defense ministers (alongside official NATO meetings), monthly meetings of ambassadors, and regular meetings of officials at NATO's headquarters in Brussels. Throughout 1998, the EAPC provided a framework for consultations between NATO and its partners on Kosovo. At the beginning of the year, a 1998–2000 EAPC Action Plan was adopted, laying out the areas for cooperation between NATO and its partners (at the EAPC level, between NATO and individual partners and between ad hoc groups of states). This covered areas such as general foreign and security policy discussions; arms control, disarmament, and non-proliferation; international terrorism; peacekeeping; defense economics; and civil emergency planning. Regional cooperation emerged as one of the most important issues on the EAPC agenda, with NATO holding special EAPC seminars on regional cooperation in the Baltic and the Caucasus and supporting the establishment of a multinational peacekeeping force by Southeast European states. The second major issue on the EAPC's agenda was the development of a "political-military framework" to provide guidelines for NATO-led PfP military operations, which it was hoped could be agreed in time for the Alliance's April 1999 summit. A Euro-Atlantic Disaster Response Coordination Center was also established in May 1998 and subsequently helped to coordinate emergency aid for relief operations in Albania and Ukraine.

Although PfP and EAPC activities continued to grow in scope, Central and Eastern European states were disappointed at the lack of progress on enlargement beyond the Visegrad three and continued to press for early membership. Debate on this issue also began to emerge in the West. US Senator William Roth, the president of NATO's parliamentary wing, the North Atlantic Assembly, supported Slovenia's candidacy, suggesting that it had made sufficient progress in democratization, economic reform, and integration with the Alliance to warrant a membership invitation. In a November *National Interest* article, influential former US National Security Adviser Zbigniew Brzezinski argued that Slovenia and Lithuania should be invited to join NATO, as the two most stable candidates with good relations with their neighbors. There clearly remained much to play for when it came to further enlargement of NATO. The long-term question of the eventual limits of NATO's borders had barely begun to be addressed.

RUSSIA, UKRAINE, AND THE FORMER SOVIET UNION

During 1998, the NATO–Russia relationship continued to be characterized by both cooperation and tension. The NATO–Russia Permanent Joint Council met at the level of foreign ministers, defense ministers, and chiefs of staff, with monthly meetings at ambassadorial level. NATO and Russian political and military experts discussed a wide range of issues, including peacekeeping, disarmament and arms control, proliferation, defense policy, nuclear weapons, and defense industry conversion. Russian ground forces participated for first time in the NATO PfP exercise in Denmark in May and in a NATO-led exercise in Albania in August. NATO and Russia also agreed to establish military liaison missions at various levels of their military structures and a NATO Documentation Centre for European Security Issues was opened in Moscow. Discussions in the PJC focused on Bosnia and especially Kosovo. While the two sides agreed on the need for a political solution based on autonomy for Kosovo, Russia opposed possible NATO air strikes and threatened to veto a UN Security Council resolution authorizing such action. Russia was also strongly critical of the US-U.K. air strikes against Iraq towards the end of the year. Russian leaders continued to describe the borders of the former Soviet Union as a "red line" that NATO must not cross, warning that Russia would have to reconsider its entire relationship with the Alliance if the Baltic states were invited to become members. Domestically, the Russian government continued to face pressure from the State Duma and the military to take a harder line against NATO.

Parallel to its ties with Russia, NATO continued its efforts to build a "Distinctive Partnership" with Ukraine. The NATO–Ukraine Commission (NUC) met at foreign minister, defense minister, chief of staff, ambassador, and expert level. In February a Joint Working Group on Defense Reform was established to facilitate NATO's support for Ukrainian military reform. A Ukrainian military liaison mission to NATO was opened and agreement was reached on the establishment of a similar NATO mission in Kyiv. In contrast to its relations with Russia, NATO's relations with Ukraine were relatively unburdened by disputes over enlargement and Kosovo. Ukraine welcomed the coming accession of the Czech Republic, Hungary, and Poland to the alliance, worked with NATO in Bosnia and Kosovo, and announced a special "State Program of Cooperation with NATO to the Year 2001," while retaining its position that it was not seeking membership of the Alliance. Nevertheless, NATO officials privately acknowledged that deeper cooperation with Ukraine would depend on the country making more serious efforts to reforms its still large, Soviet-era armed forces.

NATO also sought to expand its ties with Moldova, the Caucasus, and Central Asia, but this proved controversial in the region. In September and October, NATO Secretary-General Javier Solana visited Moldova, Georgia, Armenia, and Azerbaijan, to explore the intensification of the Alliance's relations with these states. Although Moldova was formally a neutral state, the Moldovan government had sought stronger ties with NATO and the Alliance's political support in securing the withdrawal of Russian troops from the Transdniestr region. In March left-wing politicians in Moldova accused the government of "flirting with NATO." During 1998, the issue of the possible deployment of NATO forces in the Caucasus became a controversial issue within the region. In January Georgian politicians suggested that a NATO force might intervene to impose peace in the country's Abkhazia region. Azerbaijani officials suggested that NATO could deploy forces to protect future oil export pipelines, act as a peacekeeper along the "line of contact" between Armenian and Azerbaijani forces, and should help to prevent the "militarization of Armenia." The on-going debate about pipeline routes for Caspian oil and gas, Armenia's close military ties with Russia, and Azerbaijan's efforts to build ties with the US, Turkey, and NATO raised the possibility of NATO being drawn into the complex competition for influence in the region. Senior NATO officials also visited the Central Asian states and in September NATO supported the annual CentrasBat peacekeeping exercises. NATO has not yet even considered the deployment of forces into the Caucasus and would be wary of antagonizing Russia or being drawn into open-ended commitments. Nevertheless, the debate on these issues indicated the sensitive ground onto which the Alliance was stepping in the southern tier of the former Soviet Union.

INTO KOSOVO?

NATO's greatest challenges in 1998 were in the Balkans, above all in Kosovo. The year began with NATO formally announcing in February that the alliance's Stabilization Force (SFOR) would remain deployed in Bosnia-Herzegovina beyond the end of its then mandate of June 1998. SFOR continued to support the implementation of the 1995 Dayton peace agreement: deterring a return to arms in Bosnia-Herzegovina, supporting the work of the High Representative and the Organization for Security and Cooperation in Europe (OSCE) in the civilian sphere, and helping with economic reconstruction. NATO leaders used SFOR to intervene more proactively than they had done in the past in Bosnia's politics, supporting the moderate Bosnian Serb government of Prime Minister Milorad Dodik, arresting a number of people indicted for war crimes, and establishing a Multinational Specialized Unit within SFOR to support the International Police Task Force (IPTF) and local police in maintaining law and order. NATO also established a Security Cooperation Program with Bosnia-Herzegovina, designed to promote confidence and cooperation amongst the country's various armed forces and to encourage democratic and central state control of the military. The September 1998 elections indicated the limits of what NATO—and the West in general—had achieved in Bosnia-Herzegovina: nationalist Nikola Poplasen won the Republika Srpska presidential elections and nationalists did well in all three communities, while Western-backed moderates received only limited support. At the end of the year, NATO defense ministers agreed that SFOR should be maintained at essentially the same size and with its mission unchanged. Despite talk of the need to establish a "sustainable peace" and avoid a "culture of dependency," the time when NATO would be able to withdraw its forces without precipitating renewed conflict seemed far away.

With the outbreak of violence in Kosovo in spring 1998 NATO faced a more severe crisis. Just as the Bosnian conflict had in the early 1990s, it was feared Kosovo might stretch NATO's unity and credibility to the breaking point. The conflict in Kosovo, further, might easily spill over into neighboring Albania and Macedonia, threaten the NATO-enforced peace in Bosnia-Herzegovina and perhaps drag in NATO members Greece and Turkey. NATO was torn between the desire to act decisively, avoid a bloody conflict, and prevent a return to Bosnia-style divisions within the Alliance on the one hand and uncertainty as to how to act and fear of being drawn into escalating conflict on the other. NATO's member states quickly rallied around a position supporting extensive autonomy (but not outright independence) for Kosovo and demanding that both the Yugoslav authorities and the Kosovo Liberation Army (UCK) cease military operations and pursue a political solution.

As Serb attacks against Albanian villages escalated in the summer, NATO's calls for a political solution became increasingly hollow and the alliance was driven to consider military intervention to halt the fighting. In June air exercises were held over Albania and Macedonia, their purpose being, in Secretary-General Solana's words, to "demonstrate NATO's capability to project power rapidly into the region." NATO began to plan for air strikes against Yugoslav forces. NATO's members, however, were unwilling to deploy ground forces before a peace settlement was agreed, were divided over the effectiveness of air strikes alone, and were wary of becoming the "airforce of the Kosovo Liberation Army." September and October saw a period of brinkmanship between the alliance and Yugoslav President Slobodan Milosevic, with NATO stepping up the threat of air strikes and Milosevic continuing military operations but stopping short of provoking airstrikes. In mid-October, with Serb attacks continuing, NATO issued activation orders for air strikes, indicating that military action might be only days away. Against this background, US envoy Richard Holbrooke brokered a ceasefire, a withdrawal of Yugoslav forces, and the deployment of an unarmed OSCE verification mission. With the agreement of the Yugoslav authorities, NATO began to undertake aerial verification of the ceasefire. NATO also agreed to establish an Extraction Force, to be deployed in Macedonia, to remove the OSCE verifiers from Kosovo if war broke out again. The ceasefire in Kosovo remained fragile. There was no long-term political solution in sight and neither the Kosovar Albanians nor the Yugoslav government was satisfied with the status quo. As the year ended, the dilemmas of military intervention in Kosovo were clear.

The Kosovo conflict resulted in a major upgrading of NATO's relations with Albania and Macedonia, as the alliance sought to prevent the crisis from spilling over into these two countries. NATO Secretary-General Solana and NATO political and military experts visited both countries at various points in 1998. NATO established assistance programs to help both countries secure their borders. PfP exercises were held in Albania in August and in Macedonia in September. A NATO/PfP cell was established in the Albanian capital Tirana to facilitate cooperation with the Alliance and NATO's Standing Force Mediterranean visited the port of Durres. From December, the NATO Extraction Force began to be deployed in Macedonia. Implicitly, the Extraction Force might not only help to rescue the OSCE verifiers if necessary but could also provide a logistical base for any eventual NATO deployment of ground forces into Kosovo and the basis for a NATO-led successor to the United Nations UNPREDEP peacekeeping force already in Macedonia.

HEADING FOR 50

The ratification of the Czech Republic, Hungary, and Poland's coming membership by NATO's legislatures, the consolidation of ties with Russia and Ukraine, and the continuing development of PfP and the EAPC represented significant successes for the alliance in 1998. With NATO approaching its 50th anniversary summit in Washington in April 1999, the alliance had grounds for congratulating itself on a successful first decade of post–Cold War Ostpolitik. In particular, the successful management of the first wave of enlargement into Central and Eastern Europe seemed to be disproving the dire warnings of many critics. The post-communist world, however, seemed likely to continue to pose major challenges for NATO. The alliance had yet to seriously address the issues involved in further enlargement into Central and Eastern Europe. Whether, when, and how to extend NATO membership to countries such as Romania and the Baltic states may pose great dilemmas. NATO's relations with Russia remained troubled and could yet drift into confrontation. The peace in Bosnia-Herzegovina remained fragile and NATO was not able to create the circumstances that would allow it to withdraw from that troubled country. Continuing instability in Kosovo pointed towards more not less NATO involvement in the province and in neighboring Albania and Macedonia. As 1998 ended, there could be little doubt that Central and Eastern Europe would continue to preoccupy NATO.

EUROPEAN UNION FACES EAST

by MILADA ANNA VACHUDOVA

In 1998 the European Union invited five associated states from East Central Europe—Poland, Hungary, Estonia, the Czech Republic, and Slovenia—to begin negotiations on membership. The five countries welcomed the invitation as a confirmation of the success of their political and economic transformation from communism to market democracy. It was widely understood, however, that for two main reasons the first applicants would not enter the EU until 2004, at the earliest. First, none of the applicants were close to fulfilling the EU's entry requirements. Moreover, EU governments lacked the political will to push through a rapid enlargement due to political opposition to enlargement at home and the difficulties of reforming the institutions and reworking the budgets in Brussels.

ACCESSION PARTNERSHIPS AND REGULAR REPORTS

In July 1997, the Commission had published its "Opinions" on the fitness of each of the ten eastern candidates for accession. To research the Opinions, Commission officials scrutinized the political and economic reforms of each applicant. The Commission thus came to a better understanding of what reforms each candidate had yet to implement to qualify for EU membership. By way of the Opinion and of contact with Commission officials in 1998, applicant governments received more detailed instructions—in myriad policy areas—on how to proceed toward EU membership.

On the basis of the Opinions of 1997, the EU member states agreed to begin negotiations in 1998 with only five of the candidates: Poland, Hungary, the Czech Republic, Estonia, and Slovenia. The Commission created a separate Task Force on Accession Negotiations with a negotiating team for each of the five countries. However, a favorable assessment of any of the five latecomers—Slovakia, Bulgaria, Romania, Lithuania, and Latvia—in a Regular Report could prompt EU member states to decide to open negotiations with that state as well. Indeed, it was felt likely that at the Helsinki European Council Summit in December 1999, Slovakia, Latvia, and Lithuania would be invited to begin negotiations on accession. Bulgaria and Romania may be invited as well, in a show of support for the reform programs of their governments.

Following on the Opinions of July 1997, the Commission created a sharper tool for influencing the policy choices of the governments of the applicant states. The "Accession Partnerships" published in March 1998 set out what the Commission believed should be the priorities of each applicant's reform program. PHARE assistance became conditional on addressing these priorities, which are based on the membership requirements laid down by the EU's European Council at its Copenhagen meeting in 1993. These comprised political criteria (democracy and rule of law); economic criteria (market economy); and ability to meet the obligations of membership. The Accession Partnerships therefore address broader issues beyond the 31 chapters of the acquis communautaire (the body of common EU law), such as the protection of ethnic minorities.

The Accession Partnerships proved successful at times in inspiring reform in areas where political inertia had blocked it, such as the judiciary and the state administration. While domestic civil society still has little access to the policy process in East Central Europe, EU norms tend to be the standard against which public policy is being made. In such cases, the Accession Partnerships can act as a surrogate for civil society by promoting reforms that are in the interest of the public and the state, but not in the interest of entrenched institutions or government bureaucracies.

The progress of each applicant was measured in the first of a series of "Regular Reports," published in November 1998. Of the frontrunners, Hungary and Estonia received the best report cards, while Slovenia and the Czech Republic were warned of serious deficiencies and dangerous complacency. Of the second group, Bulgaria was praised for its ambitious economic reform program, although the Commission warned that much work remained ahead. In contrast, very little progress was registered in Romania. The ousting of Vladimir Meciar in the September 1998 elections in Slovakia was warmly welcomed. Slovakia had been the only country held back from the negotiations due to political as opposed to economic shortcomings. Although Slovakia's new government promised to uphold democratic standards, the November 1998 Vienna summit of the EU came too soon for Slovakia to be moved up to the negotiating group.

The EU emphasized inclusiveness in its approach to the ten applicant states. For all ten, Opinions and Accession Partnerships were written, followed up by Regular Reports. After the exit of nationalist governments in Romania and Bulgaria, a significant challenge for the accession process and for regional stability became how to keep governments and publics committed to reform when the confluence of geography, economic backwardness, incompetence, and years of counterproductive government meant that EU accession was still a long way off. Almost two years after the election of more European and reform-oriented governments in Bulgaria and Romania, Bulgaria was doing much better in building political consensus and pushing through difficult economic reforms than Romania, where incompetence and political infighting blocks progress.

THE NEGOTIATIONS

The "screening" process, during which the Commission is examining the legislation and practice of the five negotiating applicants in light of the 31 chapters of the "acquis communautaire," officially launched negotiations in April 1998. Where a candidate falls short during screening, its negotiators are forced to promise adoption of the acquis by a certain date. The negotiators, however, cannot themselves deliver on their promises. Once the actual negotiations begin, other candidates may move ahead while EU negotiators wait for a government to fulfill the promises of its negotiators.

The Accession Partnerships and the Regular Reports create a framework that endeavors to be a meritocracy: the priorities for reform are clear, and states which address these priorities will move closer to membership. The negotiation process, however, will take on its own momentum that is likely to be increasingly influenced by diverse political considerations. Moreover, the vast quantity of requirements to be met make it difficult to hold the candidate to perfection in all areas. The decision about which shortcomings are acceptable, for example meeting environmental standards, and which are not, for example applying the rules of the internal market, will be a political one.

THE CHALLENGE OF STABILIZING SOUTHEASTERN EUROPE

The European Union has been forced to rethink its approach to Southeastern Europe in response to the economic and political turmoil caused by the Kosovo crisis in 1998. The EU has recognized that the long-term goal must be the democratization of Southeastern Europe and its inclusion in the process of European integration. But while this goal underpins the EU's Common Strategy toward the Western Balkans and the EU-sponsored Stability Pact for Southeastern Europe, neither is likely to succeed if EU governments do not change the way that they think about enlargement. Over the last decade, they have not treated association and accession to the EU as a powerful tool for promoting democratization and economic reform in the applicant countries of post-communist Europe. Instead, they have dwelled on domestic opposition to enlargement within EU member countries and on the institutional and budgetary difficulties of absorbing new members.

But the prospect of joining the EU is promoting reform in Central and Eastern Europe as governments work to fulfill the requirements of accession. The incentives of membership have put Hungary and Slovakia, for example, on the road to liberal democracy and greater prosperity by helping reformers to get elected and by encouraging elected governments to pursue reform. This can work in the Balkans as well, but only if elites and citizens come to believe that their states are also credible future members of the EU.

The EU's potential to exercise substantial leverage in the region was recognized in the Commission's proposal to conclude bilateral Stabilization and Association Agreements with those Southeast European states who are not yet associated to the EU. But of the five relevant states—Macedonia, Albania, Croatia, Bosnia-Herzegovina, and the Federal Republic of Yugoslavia—only Macedonia is likely to meet the conditions for negotiating an agreement in 1999.

As Slobodan Milosevic's Serbia, Franjo Tudjman's Croatia or even Meciar's Slovakia amply demonstrated, Western carrots and sticks do not induce pro-European behavior on the part of governments controlled by extremists. It is therefore an onerous prerequisite to regional stability that moderate politicians win power in all Southeast European states.

When relatively moderate politicians do win power, they should be given substantial incentives to orient their states towards the EU. And when, in the name of joining the EU, they implement reform despite difficult domestic conditions (or support NATO air strikes despite strong domestic opposition), they should be rewarded for their efforts, even if their countries are still a long way away from membership.

If they are not rewarded in a way that can be understood by their electorates, moderate politicians may be discredited for having followed the "dictates" of the West but having little to show in return. They may become less Western oriented themselves, or they may be succeeded in government by more extreme parties. The former risks taking place in Bulgaria, and the latter in Romania, unless the EU moves to start negotiations on membership with these two countries along with better-prepared candidates such as Slovakia.

Over the next decade, the most substantial rewards short of membership that EU governments will be able to offer Southeast European governments for a domestic job well-done are visa-free travel for citizens and unrestricted market access for goods. But these will be politically much more sensitive than the large-scale financial transfers being pondered in the wake of the Kosovo crisis.

The most sensitive issue will be visa-free travel. At the moment, of the citizens of the EU's ten states associated, only Bulgarians and Romanians are required to obtain visas before entering the zone of EU countries which have implemented the Schengen accords on border-free travel between them. This is also the case for citizens of Macedonia, Bosnia-Herzegovina, Albania, Croatia, and Yugoslavia. European leaders seem unaware of or indifferent to the negative consequences of restrictive visa policies for the long-term project of democratizing the Balkans.

Elites from business, academic, civic, and policy circles on whom the West must rely to Europeanize their countries are often discouraged from traveling to professional meetings in Western Europe. It can take three months to obtain a visa and many find the process humiliating. Elites as well as ordinary citizens are frustrated, resentful, and feel like third-class Europeans. This decreases the willingness of politicians and other public figures to portray themselves as pro-European, undermines the popularity of those who do, and feeds a sense of futility about ever being allowed into the European club. Balkan frustration will only mount as first wave candidates to the EU such as Hungary and Slovenia are required to implement Schengen visa policies in order to make good on their bids for membership.

The visa requirements stem from the fear and the reality of illegal immigration from the Balkans into the EU. Still, expedited visa procedures for professional meetings and family visits should be considered. Moreover, the removal of well-behaved countries from the EU's common visa list should be on the agenda as part of a strategy to strengthen the hand of pro-Western elites in the Balkans while integrating the region into Europe instead of excluding it.

A second critical issue will be market access. For the economic revival of Southeastern Europe over the next decade, the ability to export to the EU market will be more important than financial assistance. The East-Central European states that signed association agreements with the EU in 1991 found the EU a mean negotiating partner when it came to trade. The sectors in which they were most competitive—textiles, steel, and agriculture—were those that member states were most eager to protect. The EU severely restricted market access in these sectors by writing anti-dumping provisions and long transition periods (now over for textiles and steel) into the agreements. As a result, in the early 1990s the EU enjoyed a large trade surplus with its impoverished Eastern partners.

This time around, in the wake of the economic devastation of the wars of Yugoslav succession, EU governments seemed to be trying to resist their protectionist impulses. The new Stabilization and Association Agreements should offer producers from qualifying Balkan states access to EU markets, restricted only by fairly applied health and safety standards and local content rules. This should prove to be no great sacrifice: economists generally agree that the losses to West European producers would have been minimal had the EU thrown its markets wide open to East-Central European goods in 1991. While some Balkan countries may now have precious little to export, the prospect of being able to export freely to the EU market may prove to be the single most effective way to attract essential foreign investment to the region. But West European politicians fear that the specter of cheap goods arriving in their countries from the southeast will hurt their chances for re-election.

THE EUROPEAN UNION OPENS THE DOOR

by RORY WATSON

To its critics in the early days, the European Community was a small club of rich Western nations. It was a label that stuck for years, as the six founding members met for cozy chats in small rooms. Subsequent enlargements have taken away ammunition from the detractors, but it is today's commitment to expand membership into Central and Eastern Europe that will finally rid the European Union of the cynical tag.

At the genesis of the union in 1957, it was explicitly stated in its constitution, the Treaty of Rome, that "any European state may apply to become a member of the Community" (as it was then called). That invitation has been taken up on many occasions in the intervening years. The first to join, in 1973, were the United Kingdom, Denmark, and Ireland. Greece followed in 1981, Spain and Portugal five years later, and in 1995 Austria, Sweden, and Finland became part of what had already become the European Union.

But during those 40 years, not all eligible candidates opted for union membership. Norwegians twice rejected the option of joining after their government had painstakingly negotiated entry terms. Greenland, despite being an integral part of Denmark, voted in 1982 to leave the EC and finally did so four years later—the only example of an actual departure from the alliance. Even the small Mediterranean island of Malta is getting cold feet at the thought of entering the EU arena. After the recent change of government, the country has formally placed its membership application on the back burner.

Whether any applicants in the current group will have second thoughts about finally joining the union as the lengthy negotiations approach their end is not a question anyone is prepared to voice. From the EU's point of view, the prevailing current, after some hesitation in the early 1990s, is gradually to expand and to bring under one roof countries that meet the entry criteria and can take on the responsibilities of membership.

In that sense, the latest accession negotiations are a logical part of the historic continuum and were specifically foreseen by EU leaders at their summit in Copenhagen in June 1993, when they agreed that "the associated countries in Central and Eastern Europe that so desire shall become members of the Union."

It may sound sentimental, but there was a distinct family feeling of togetherness when the leaders of the existing and applicant EU members sat down to lunch at their Luxembourg summit shortly before last Christmas. It was not just the champagne talking when French President Jacques Chirac and the European Commission President Jacques Santer described the gathering as "a moving occasion."

UNSENTIMENTAL JOURNEY

But no one is going to allow emotion to cloud hard-headed realism, despite unrealistic calls in recent years for Polish or Hungarian accession by 2000. One of the proponents of such an optimistic timetable was Chirac, partly to underline France's close links with Poland and partly to establish his country's commitment to enlargement. Everything, however, indicates that the process will be lengthy and at times acrimonious.

In purely economic terms, the gap that must be bridged is huge. The per capita gross domestic product in some applicant countries is only about a third of that in the EU. The figure is nearer 60 percent for Slovenia and the Czech Republic, but it falls to below 30 percent for Estonia, Bulgaria, Lithuania, Romania, and Latvia.

No serious politician is prepared to risk his reputation by predicting when the negotiations will be concluded for the first set of new members. The usual diplomatic response is that while Austria, Sweden, and Finland managed to wrap up their own negotiations in 13 months, it took Spain and Portugal seven years. And, unlike the current batch of countries, they had all been long-standing members of the Organization for Economic Cooperation and Development, a forum of the world's developed nations.

The European Commission's budgetary calculations—particularly regarding regional and social spending—for the opening years of the next century envisage at least some new members as of 2002. But to many in Brussels, this reflects a combination of political and budgetary caution. Given the range of issues on the table and the fact that each membership agreement must be ratified by all the countries involved before taking effect, realists see 2003 or 2004 as more likely dates. And, they note, just because negotiations have been opened simultaneously with several countries does not mean they will be concluded at the same time.

The union's hard-headedness has already been demonstrated by its decision to divide the applicants into two groups. Negotiations with the first, which consists of Poland, Hungary, Slovenia, Estonia, the Czech Republic, and Cyprus, were slated to start in the spring of 1998. As a European Commission recommendation stated in July 1997, the five ex-communist countries "could be in a position to satisfy all the conditions of membership in the medium term if they maintain and strongly sustain their efforts of preparation."

Before the EC made its final choice, some commissioners—notably the commission president, Jacques Santer—suggested restricting the first group to Poland, Hungary, and the Czech Republic. The rationale was essentially political. It would have established a clear link between NATO's eastward enlargement and would have lessened the pressure for internal institutional reform, particularly regarding the number of European commissioners to be appointed and member governments' voting weight. But the EU's Nordic members—particularly Finland—were keen on including all three Baltic states in the initial group, while Italy and Austria were pushing for Slovenia. External Affairs Commissioner Hans van den Broek, the commission member responsible for the accession negotiations, argued that there were no objective grounds for excluding any applicant that met the criteria set for the first wave of negotiations. His opinion ended up winning the day, and Slovenia and Estonia were ultimately added to the list.

SECOND-DIVISION GRUMBLING

In EU jargon, the first wave of expansion is described as "five plus one." The one is Cyprus, which in fact staked a claim to negotiate EU membership before any of the ex-communist countries. The deal was sealed at the June 1995 European summit in Corfu, when the Greek hosts successfully persuaded their EU partners that accession talks with Cyprus would open no later than six months after the end of the negotiations on the Amsterdam Treaty.

Members of the second group—Latvia, Lithuania, Bulgaria, Romania, and Slovakia—will be subject to an annual screening exercise. The European Commission monitors how these countries are adapting their political and legal systems to EU standards. The findings will be given to union governments at the end of the year, along with recommendations on which countries, if any, have progressed enough in economic and legislative reforms to be invited to start negotiating their union membership.

The union insists that the decision to begin the enlargement process with a handful of applicants was taken on objective grounds, after a year-long examination. The head of the Enlargement Task Force, Klaus van der Pas, denies assertions that the separate tracks were created because the union did not have sufficient resources to handle all ten at once.

But the distinction rankled some of those in the second group. For example, it is already common practice for Latvian diplomats, annoyed that Estonia is the sole Baltic state in the first group of six, to suggest to Brussels that Latvia should be the seventh applicant to open negotiations.

So far, the EU has managed to achieve a sense of unity and inclusiveness among the Central and Eastern European countries. At the Luxembourg summit in December 1997, EU leaders successfully downplayed the differences by agreeing that the enlargement process with all ten Central and Eastern European applicants and Cyprus would begin in March, and that the actual negotiations with the first wave would open a few weeks later. All applicants welcomed the formula, not least because some of them feared that a blunter distinction between those deemed ready to open negotiations and the rest could have undermined public support for domestic reforms.

MAPS FOR UNCHARTED WATERS

Both current and future members know that they are entering uncharted waters; the union will be irrevocably changed when the first ex-communist country joins. For that reason, the EU is working to create a framework to enable the expansion to be a success. For the ex-communist aspirants to EU membership, it means that whenever possible, EU standards and legislation are applied from the first day of membership (if not before), and lengthy exemption periods are kept to a minimum. For the union, it means adapting its existing policies—particularly costly agricultural, regional, and social ones—so the arrival of these new members will not break the bank or cause politically unpalatable sacrifices for existing members.

The EU's favored strategy is to provide aspiring members with "road maps" containing legislative, administrative, and political signposts on the route to accession and timetables by which they should be reached. The most important one concerns the single market, which provides for the free movement of people, goods, capital, and services among EU member countries. The single market, with its 1,100 separate items of legislation, in principle tolerates no exceptions. This is bound to be tested, because acceding countries are sure to seek waivers.

Toward the end of last year, the European Commission began to draw up single-market road maps with the applicants. The subjects covered range from minute details on standardized parts for cars, tractors, and motorcycles to implementing environmental clean-ups and rules for major financial services such as banks and the insurance industry. Failure to meet the targets set out in individual accession agreements could jeopardize the applicants' access to EU funding.

One of the key conditions set by the union is respect for human rights and the rule of law. The recently negotiated Amsterdam Treaty, due to come into force next year, includes a confirmation that the EU "is founded on the principles of liberty, democracy, respect for human rights, and fundamental rule of law, principles which are common to the member states." Another novelty is the assertion that "a serious and persistent breach" of the commitments would lead to sanctions against the offending state. Those are not spelled out but could involve suspension of EU aid and temporary removal from the union's main decision-making body, the Council of Ministers.

The importance the EU attaches to the rule of law and to the effective implementation of over 80,000 pages of existing EU legislation, was underlined by commissioner van den Broek. "Constitutional text and supplementing legislation are important but no panacea," he warned the aspiring members at a June conference. "The implementation and enforcement of constitutional and legal principles is just as important as the adoption of the texts themselves. The right laws and institutions must be coupled with a political and legal culture conducive to the rule of law and human rights."

THE GOVERNING CLASSES

Two specifics set this enlargement apart from earlier ones. For the first time, the EU is not confident that a new batch of applicants has the capacity to implement EU legislation in the civil service, courts, and various channels of government. In addition, this is the first time new members will have to take on a corpus of legislation and practices in whose genesis they had no hand. Their predecessors had a smaller volume of legislation to contend with, and they did not have to try to catch up on a 40-year head start.

As a result, over the next ten to 15 years, the union will be heavily involved in what it terms "institution-building" in the ten ex-communist applicant countries. The objective is to ensure that each new member has the administrative capacity to enforce EU legislation effectively from the start. For this purpose, the EU will annually disburse some 500 million euros ($550 million) for training key personnel in the applicant countries. At the outset, efforts will be concentrated in the central policy areas of finance, agriculture, justice, and the environment, although other sectors, such as nuclear safety, may be added later.

Brussels recognizes that the challenge cannot be met by simply parachuting in international consultants on short-term contracts. Instead, experienced officials from member states will spend at least two years helping their counterparts in the applicant countries. EU member states are negotiating reforms to their regional, agricultural, and social programs, which should come into effect from 2000. For much of the next 12 months, the union will be heavily preoccupied with internal issues, and the applicants will not know until 1999 the final details of the legislation they will be expected to apply in those areas.

Overall, imminent expansion policy debates will be dominated by money. Aware of the general reluctance to transfer more national finances to the EU budget, the commission and most member states believe that with adequate reforms and steady economic growth, the cost of enlargement can be carried within the existing budgetary structure. The EU levies an annual contribution of no more than 1.27 percent of GDP on its members, which gives it a current yearly budget of some $90 billion. The levy is now slightly lower than the maximum. It is anticipated that expansion will necessitate coming closer to that ceiling—a move that is unlikely to be greeted with unanimous enthusiasm.

Current EU members have to resolve a number of institutional issues prior to the accession of the new members. They must agree on a reduction in the number of European Commissioners, for instance, boost flexibility in EU decision-making procedures, and even on the number of official languages. Also, major beneficiaries of intra-EU fund transfers, notably Spain and Portugal, are likely to take a tough line in the enlargement negotiations for fear that their subsidies will be diverted to Central and Eastern Europe.

But supporters present this expansion as an opportunity and a historic stage in Europe's development. They point to the commercial opportunities that stem from an increase in the single market from 370 million citizens to 500 million. Above all, they say, how can one put a price on peace?

NOTE

Reprinted with kind permission from *Transitions* magazine, April 1998.

VESTIGES OF VISEGRAD

by JEREMY DRUKER

After some five years of stagnation, politicians across Central Europe have revived the theme of regional cooperation, offering up grand pronouncements that suggest past disagreements have healed and new frontiers for cooperation have opened up. The term "Visegrad"—referring to the early 1990s meetings designed to spur greater cooperation between Czechoslovakia, Poland, and Hungary—has even received a new lease on life. In May, for example, some of the region's eminent intellectuals took part in a discussion entitled "Visegrad After Madrid" at the Hungarian Cultural Center in Prague. A packed hall listened to the likes of Poland's Adam Michnik and Hungary's Gyorgy Konrad gush over the possibility of a collegial, harmonious team of nations entering Europe under a purported slogan of "all for one, and one for all."

GRAND IDEAS

Ideas of a close-knit Central European grouping that would counter the influence of Germany and Russia had come to a head at the end of the 1980s and in the early 1990s. Sparked partly by Milan Kundera's 1983 article "The Tragedy of Central Europe," intellectuals across the Soviet bloc had begun to offer their own visions for regional cooperation as a cure for the Stalinist system of isolation, provincialism, and forced cooperation that had survived long after the dictator's death. In the past, elites throughout the bloc rarely understood the problems faced by their neighbors; meeting only in Moscow on special occasions—and under the Kremlin's watchful eye—they almost never had a chance to sit together and hammer out local disputes, even in the spirit of so-called socialist brotherhood. The compelled and inefficient cooperation of the Soviet-engineered Council for Mutual Economic Assistance and the Warsaw Pact were hardly outlets for true cooperation.

After the dissolution of the Soviet bloc, proposals for a vibrant regional grouping gained popular appeal. Across Central Europe, many people warmed to the idea that expansive economic, political, and cultural cooperation—on both the national and local level—could help revitalize the entire region and further integration into the West. Because the Central European countries were facing similar problems after breaking free from the Soviet Union, some even hoped that detailed information about the successes and failures in one country's transition could help guide the policies of its neighbors and that officials who supervised a successful economic transition could be called upon to advise a country at a lower stage of development. The time seemed ripe: many of the dissident supporters of greater cooperation, such as Vaclav Havel, suddenly found themselves catapulted to power, with the ability to follow through on their grand schemes.

Yet very little of that actually happened, for a whole range of reasons: the European Union's failure to encourage such projects; the division of Czechoslovakia into two smaller nations searching for their own identities; Slovakia's worsening democratic reputation and its tensions with Hungary over minority issues; and the understandable but shortsighted goal of destroying all remnants of previous bloc arrangements. Perhaps most importantly, in the mad rush to enter NATO and the EU, some leaders worried that regional integration might slow their progress toward becoming part of the West. The fear was that Western leaders might come to view those countries as a bloc rather than judging them on their individual merits. Some projects—such as the Central European Initiative and the Visegrad Three—did develop, but these were hardly what their originators had had in mind.

A HUMBLER PRAGUE

By 1998, however, diplomats were saying a new mood was in the air—especially in the Czech Republic. "I found for the first time after some years the awareness of the importance of such cooperation," said Bronislaw Geremek, the longtime chairman of the Polish parliament's Foreign Affairs Committee before his appointment as foreign minister. "The idea of Visegrad cooperation is considered now by the [Czech] political spectrum and by public opinion as a good project for the future."

Other Central European diplomats, who preferred not to be named in this article, say much of the shift in attitude has to do with the 1997 crash of the Czech economic miracle and the fall of Prime Minister Vaclav Klaus, a hardened opponent of Visegrad cooperation, at the end of that year. Amid the worsening economic situation, Klaus was no longer able to claim that strengthening ties with other Central European countries would stall the Czech juggernaut. "To a certain level, they were forced to change their position," says one diplomat. A more friendly approach set in even before Klaus's departure, the diplomat says, but it accelerated under the caretaker government of Josef Tosovsky and Foreign Minister Jaroslav Sedivy, the latter an old dissident friend of Geremek's. Leaders in the new Social Democratic government in Prague also vowed to jump-start Visegrad cooperative efforts in economic, environmental, political, and social fields but also wanted to draw in Austria and Slovenia.

The more humble stance adopted by Czech politicians also coincided with NATO's decision to invite Hungary, the Czech Republic, and Poland to join the alliance—announced in Madrid in July 1997—and the EU's near-simultaneous decision to open up accession negotiations with the three countries. Very rapidly, competition was out and cooperation was in. "It's now very clear that Madrid served as a major boost," said Gabor Iklody, head of the NATO and the Western European Union department at the Hungarian Foreign Ministry. "We have realized we can achieve more this way than by hiding things behind one another's backs."

In 1997, the three foreign ministers jointly lobbied the US Senate to ratify their countries' entrance into NATO, the climax of an intense three-way campaign organized by their Washington embassies. In March of 1998, the three countries' prime ministers promised to closely coordinate their negotiations for membership in NATO and the EU.

Regular consultations now take place, at both high and lower levels, as those involved in the entrance talks brief one another on their concerns, said Edita Hrda, who is in charge of Central European affairs at the Czech Foreign Ministry. "In this, the cooperation works very well. It is some kind of return to the idea of Visegrad, even if we don't think it makes sense to call it that anymore." She says the close ties of the various Polish, Czech, and Hungarian officials involved in EU affairs have even irritated their counterparts in Estonia and Slovenia, who feel excluded because their countries are also slated for first round admission. "But it's not really that we are leaving them out. It's just that these ongoing consultations are important for our regional cooperation, because our problems are similar in so many cases."

Such cooperation may in itself be productive, as various Central European diplomats say, but they also understand that it looks very good to those making the calls in Brussels. "No one told us to [cooperate], but we realized long ago—even before Madrid—that if we can, it will be very well received both in NATO and the EU," said Iklody.

Geremek said the EU stresses that ascension depends strictly on the talks between the European Commission and the candidate countries. "But at the same time," he says, "for the European Union, it's extremely important—it's not always presented in an open and clear way—to see the maturity of the candidate countries toward international cooperation."

FAIR-WEATHER RIVALS

Ties among the three countries' officials probably haven't been better in years, but the much lauded new era of cooperation isn't exactly what it's billed to be. Consultations are a good step forward, critics say, but where are the practical projects that could have an immediate impact? An initiative to purchase fighter planes together—and save money by buying in bulk—fell through, partly because the three nations had various strategic partners they didn't want to offend by shopping elsewhere. The calls for regional flood-prevention programs—made after the tragic deluges of the summer of 1997—have not progressed. Only the Central European Free Trade Agreement (CEFTA) has brought concrete results by liberalizing trade, but its scope remains narrow.

Lubos Palata, who covers Central Europe and Germany for the popular Czech daily *Mlada fronta dnes*, has written about the potential strength of a combined, regional lobbying force representing 60 million people in Brussels—especially when the time comes to ask for exemptions or subsidies. But, said Palata, despite all the talk of partnership, the countries' foreign ministers quickly pushed their own agendas at the formal opening of EU enlargement in April.

Particularly striking were comments by Laszlo Kovacs, Hungary's foreign minister at the time, who made clear that Hungary feared its application might be hindered by the lack of progress elsewhere. "The large number of applicants results in a kind of competition, even a kind of rivalry," he said.

A few days later, Hungarian Finance Minister Peter Medgyessy advised, "It would be prudent for the EU to conclude negotiations with the most prepared countries, and if there are only one or two, so be it."

"This [approach] was totally the same [as the old Czech attitude] because Hungary is in the same situation as the Czechs were four years ago," said Palata. "It's crazy, but that's the way Central European cooperation works. We are friends only when we're all in a bad situation. In good times, people want to single themselves out."

Some analysts and diplomats chalked up the Hungarian politicians' comments to last spring's pre-election fever, but others suspect the comments signal that although one race has ended (NATO admission), another has begun (to be the first into the EU). With no guarantees that all three countries will be admitted simultaneously, some say it's unrealistic to expect the three countries to team up and fight the EU over matters that do not directly concern them. "No one wants to get left behind, and in the end it will be national interests that take precedence," said Renata Dwan, deputy director of the European Security Program in the Budapest office of the EastWest Institute. In the last few years, many fruitful bilateral initiatives have emerged—both between Visegrad countries and with other neighbors like Austria—and talk of a revived Visegrad may simply be passe, said Dwan. "Some argue that it came to its natural end. It helped define the states as a group and set them up for European integration."

A PEOPLE'S VISEGRAD

Josef Vesely, a veteran Czech journalist and commentator on EU affairs, thinks that no matter how sincere the current hopes for greater political cooperation may be, they are nonetheless unfeasible. "In my view, it's only talking, nothing more," he said. The window of opportunity that had opened in the early 1990s has shut now that EU and NATO membership is on the horizon. The whole diplomatic mindset has changed, said Vesely, mentioning a conversation he had with Kovacs in Strasbourg before the Hungarian elections. Vesely said he asked the then–foreign minister about the chances for a coordinated, trilateral policy toward Slovakia, but Kovacs immediately responded by saying that impending NATO membership would supersede anything like that.

"That's a big difference," said Vesely. "He focused on a common approach much larger than Visegrad cooperation, which must be seen in the framework of NATO and the EU. That is why this remake of the Visegrad situation is impossible." As preparation for the EU accelerates in the coming years, Austria will also play an extremely important role, he added. "What would Visegrad be without Austria in the next three, four, or five years?"

While the grand visions of Havel and others in the early 1990s may no longer be feasible, grassroots cooperative efforts will be vital in keeping a lid on nationalistic strife in Central Europe. Vesely, for one, advocates arranging exchanges of journalists; creating networks of people who run small and medium-sized businesses; and sponsoring language training. The goal, he said, is to break down provincialism and head off the new tensions that will naturally develop once EU membership arrives and borders disappear. "It's like in a multi-family house: if you take a wall out between neighbors, they all suddenly find themselves in a big room together. That's why you need to establish contacts before," he said. There are regional models to build on: the Transcarpathian Euroregion and the Alpe-Adria Work Community. The latter—formed in 1978 by then-Yugoslav republics of Slovenia and Croatia, several provinces in Austria, and three Italian provinces—has an extensive agenda, including collaborative efforts on tourism, ecology, and traffic; cultural exchanges; and economic cooperation. Five western and southwestern Hungarian counties joined in the late 1980s.

"I was in favor of Visegrad, arguing against Klaus in many articles," says Vesely. "Now I'm not for cooperation between governments, political parties, and presidents. It's really necessary to create a new Visegrad on the level of common people, the man on the street."

NOTE

Reprinted with kind permission from *Transitions* magazine, September 1998.

XENOPHOBIA IN CENTRAL AND EASTERN EUROPE

by CLAIRE WALLACE

Xenophobia is often reported as being on the rise in Central and Eastern Europe. However, in fact there are few studies which can show this in any systematic or comparative way, and we have no information about what happened before 1989 because xenophobia was officially discouraged by the former regimes.[1] Nevertheless, all the factors which have been associated with xenophobia in Western Europe, both past and present, are to be found in post-communist Europe in a very stark form.

For example, there has been a steep economic decline in nearly all Central and Eastern European countries, where more than half of the people are now worse off than in the past and two thirds are unable to live from their earned incomes. Economic conditions are often seen as one of the causes of xenophobia in Western Europe as poor economic performance means more competition in the labor market and more people wanting to share the welfare cake. Although in some East-Central European countries there has been an economic recovery, others are continuing decline. Second, the opening of borders has resulted in an influx of immigrants, something for which these countries were unprepared and unfamiliar. This factor has been identified as a cause of xenophobia elsewhere in Europe. These immigrants come both from neighboring countries and from far afield—China, Pakistan and elsewhere. Some remain in the Central and Eastern European countries and some are trying to get further west. The opening of borders has also resulted in the opening to international crime with the smuggling of people, drugs and weapons in addition to other forms of criminality. Third, the people of these countries have been rapidly subject to globalization. The introduction of Hollywood, Hip Hop, and Hamburgers as well unemployment could be seen as a threat to indigenous cultures and traditions which were fostered and preserved under the former regimes. Furthermore, the growing influence of international organizations can likewise be seen to be a threat for small nations struggling to become independent. Alternatively, international organizations such as the European Union or NATO are seen by many as the best guarantee of that independence. Fourth, as these countries are finding a route into a new world order, one response is for states to become increasingly nationalistic in order to define a new identity. In some countries there have even been civil wars as the unity imposed by communism fragmented. Xenophobia has been helped along by the emergence of right wing and nationalistic movements or political parties which a newly open media has allowed to flourish but which is unrestricted by the kind of civil society organizations such as human rights groups and antiracist movements because these are underdeveloped. If we look at these factors altogether, then the conditions appear to be ripe for the emergence of xenophobia. In order to see if this is the case, we conducted a survey of xenophobia in 11 post-communist countries. The countries covered were: Poland, Hungary, Czech Republic, Slovakia, Slovenia, Bulgaria, Romania, Yugoslavia, Croatia, Belarus, and Ukraine. These countries include the more prosperous Central European countries which are candidates for the European Union, the more unstable southern European countries as well as two countries from the former Soviet Union. The survey was based upon face-to-face interviews with 12,310 post-communist citizens, at least 1,000 in each country, and was carried out in spring 1998. This was a representative sample survey from which generalizations can be made and which is large enough to permit analysis of particular sub-groups. The survey formed part of the New Democracies Barometer and is referred to as NDB V because this was the fifth round of this survey.[2]

Previous surveys of xenophobia have tended to identify particular population groups as being likely to be xenophobic. These are especially young males with lower education. These young males have been the focus of attention in Eastern Germany and German sociologists have argued that marginalized groups which have been hit by economic decline and what they like to call "modernization" are the ones most likely to be xenophobic—that is the unemployed, lower educated people. The most xenophobic people are found in the former communist regions of Eastern Germany. Another reason often provided for the rise in xenophobia in Germany is the very large number of immigrants there, immigrants who may compete with the low educated young males in the labor market. Germany has indeed received the largest numbers of migrants out of any country in Europe, but we should note that the Eastern regions, where most xenophobia is to be found, is also the region with the least number of immigrants. Yet, similar patterns of xenophobia have also been discovered in other European countries with young males being xenophobic.

In order to see if this was also the case in Central and Eastern Europe, we constructed a "xenophobia index" which combined attitudes to foreigners with social distance from generic groups such as Jews, Gypsies, Russians, Germans, Austrians, and Arabs/Chinese. These groups were chosen because they are familiar ones for the citizens of Eastern and Central Europe. Jews and Gypsies were historically persecuted minorities in the region, whilst Germans, Austrians, and Russians were representative of ruling empires against which many of these Central and Eastern European countries have struggled. Arabs and Chinese are new ethnic groups, unfamiliar in the region but with very different civilizations and cultures, sometimes identified as being a different "race." Thus we combined fear of foreigners—the literal meaning of xenophobia—with attitudes towards particular generic groups, sometimes termed racism. This meant that together we had a total of 29 items altogether on the scale.

In Table 1 we see the breakdown of xenophobia by country. We can see that

Table 1: Xenophobia By Country

Country	Least xenophobic (%)	Quite xenophobic (%)	More xenophobic (%)	Most xenophobic (%)
Hungary	13	22	20	45
Poland	25	17	18	41
Czech Republic	11	20	31	38
Croatia	18	19	29	34
Belarus	22	24	28	27
Romania	24	29	24	24
Ukraine	23	28	26	23
Slovakia	12	32	36	20

Source: NDB V, 1998. Some countries are missing—Bulgaria, FRY, Slovenia—because the questions were asked in a slightly different way in those countries so we could not construct the same scale.

the Central European countries—Hungary, Poland, and the Czech Republic—are the most likely to have xenophobic people. The former Soviet countries are not very likely to be xenophobic, by contrast. Some explanations for this are offered later. Austria was included in a separate analysis to see if the same patterns could be found in a country which had not had the experience of post-communist transition.

In the following analysis we begin by looking at objective indicators of xenophobia including social structure, economic performance, and levels of immigration. We then go on to look at subjective, attitudinal indicators of xenophobia including political attitudes of the respondent, national pride, national security, personal security, and concepts of citizenship.

OBJECTIVE INDICATORS OF XENOPHOBIA

Xenophobia and Social Structure

Following the literature, we expected to find young males to be the most xenophobic. However, this was not the case. Gender did not make any difference to xenophobic attitudes (we have to remember that the margin of error in such a survey is about 3 percent so we can discount any variation below that level as insignificant). Rather than young people being the most xenophobic, we found quite the opposite—the older people were the most xenophobic: 32 percent of those over 60 were in the most xenophobic category, compared with only 22 percent of those aged 20–29 and 27 percent of those aged 18–19. It is possible therefore that teenagers are indeed more xenophobic than other groups of young people, but not as xenophobic as the elderly. Xenophobia was strongest amongst the over 60s in particular, indicating that this was maybe a generational phenom-

Table 2: Xenophobia by Age and Education

	Least xenophobic (%)	Somewhat xenophobic (%)	Very xenophobic (%)	Most xenophobic (%)
Gender				
Males	26	26	24	25
Females	25	24	24	27
Age				
18–19	28	24	21	27
20–29	29	26	23	22
30–39	27	27	26	22
40–49	25	25	25	25
50–59	24	25	25	26
60+	22	23	23	32
Education				
Elementary	25	23	22	29
Vocational	23	25	24	28
Secondary	25	26	26	23
University	31	27	24	18

Source: NDB V 1998.

enon. This is shown in Table 2. However, xenophobia was indeed associated with having a lower education. It decreases with the rise in education.

Next we looked at whether economic marginalization leads to xenophobia. We considered the personal income of the respondent and we found that there is indeed a tendency for those in the bottom income quartile to be slightly more xenophobic (27 percent in the most xenophobic compared with 24 percent least xenophobic group), but in the upper income quartile there was no consistent tendency and the Eta association was very weak.[3] Using another measure of social marginalization, we found a slightly stronger tendency for people to be more xenophobic if they felt that their situation had deteriorated compared to what it had been in the past. Unemployment also did not really affect attitudes to xenophobia although those who were unemployed were slightly more likely to be xenophobic. Thus, of the employed, 25 percent were in the most xenophobic group—exactly the quartile—whilst for the unemployed with benefits it was 29 percent and for the unemployed without benefits it was 26 percent. Of the pensioners, however, 35 percent were in the most xenophobic category, reflecting the fact that they are the older group. In general then, we could not really say that social marginalization had much of an effect on attitudes to xenophobia in Central and Eastern Europe.

Therefore, from our analysis by social groups, the only variables which were at all strongly associated with xenophobia were those of age—xenophobia rises with age—and education—xenophobia decreases with education.

Xenophobia and Economic Performance

One possible source of xenophobia is the general performance of the economy. It could be that foreigners and generic groups of various kinds can be seen as a threat if the economy is generally in bad shape and if unemployment is rising. This has less therefore to do with individual characteristics than with the state of the economy as a whole and people's sense of collective well-being. For this reason it is necessary to look at macro-economic indicators and here we have chosen GDP per capita and unemployment as indicators. In terms of economic performance and unemployment, our countries under consideration fall into three distinct groups: the Central European countries (Czech Republic, Poland, Hungary, Slovakia, and Slovenia); the Southern European countries (Romania, Bulgaria, Croatia, and Yugoslavia); and the former Soviet Union countries of Belarus and Ukraine—the Eastern European countries.

If we now look at these countries and compare their economic performance with attitudes to xenophobia, we do not find that those with the poorest performance are the most xenophobic. In Table 1 we showed the indicators of xenophobia per country.[4] We can see that the most xenophobic are actually the most prosperous countries, whilst Romania and Ukraine, some of the least prosperous countries, are also least likely to have the most xenophobic population. Ukraine also has some of the lowest official unemployment. We cannot say therefore that xenophobia is caused by poor economic performance in any direct way, although high unemployment in general may be a factor.

Xenophobia and Immigration

Another factor which has been thought to cause a rise in xenophobia has been the influx of immigrants. In the case of all of these countries, there has been a rise in the number of migrants, but the main countries which have been the destination for migrants are the Central European "buffer zone" countries, which lie on the edge of the European Union: Poland, Hungary, Czech Republic, and Slovakia. These countries are the recipients of many transit migrants who are trying to get into Western Europe, but under various bilateral agreements can be sent back to the last country they came from—in many cases the buffer zone countries. As Western European countries closed their doors to asylum seekers and refugees after 1992, so many of these have also gone instead to the buffer zone countries, although they may not officially register as refugees. In addition, these countries have themselves become the destination for many different kinds of migrants, usually of short duration, including small scale traders from the East, professionals from the West involved in new businesses or multi-national enterprises, labor migrants from the East, and business people from China and from other parts of

Eastern Europe. Although the numbers are still small relative to the numbers of migrants in Germany or Austria, they are very great compared to the past and therefore cause concern in those countries, especially since they are associated in the popular imagination with a rise in crime. For the Central European countries which have an image of themselves as being ethnically "pure" this kind of multi-cultural influx comes as something of a shock. In fact data on migration is incomplete and so we do not have very accurate or comparable information for the post-communist countries. Nevertheless, from data collected by various international organizations we can get some idea of the general trends and it is clear that Hungary, Poland, and the Czech Republic have been the targets of a new round of migration. The countries of the former Yugoslavia have probably had the highest number of migrants, but most of these are refugees from the other republics and this is a rather exceptional situation.

If we look at these data together, we see that indeed it is the case that the countries with the highest numbers of migrants are also the most xenophobic. However, we should be cautious about assuming that the numbers of migrants per se is sufficient to explain the rise in xenophobia: we also need to look at how this is dealt with by politicians and the press. The numbers of migrants can be presented as either a problem or an asset. This is a debate at present in Poland, where migration restrictions being negotiated as part of the accession to the European Union mean that Poland will have to impose visas upon visitors from the neighboring East. Yet these visitors, who come to buy goods, are a great economic asset to Poland, representing a significant part of Poland's external trade.

SUBJECTIVE INDICATORS

In the next section we look at a range of attitudes which are associated with xenophobia. We know from previous analysis that attitudes to migrants and minorities is much more strongly associated with other attitudes than it is with social characteristics.[5] In other words, in Eastern and Central Europe people form attitudinal clusters in this respect but these clusters are only weakly associated with social and economic characteristics.

Xenophobia and National Pride

The first group of attitudes we have considered therefore, is national pride. There is a general assumption that xenophobia is on the rise because nationalism is on the rise. Our indicator of nationalism was a series of questions asking people how proud they were of their country on the one hand and their nationality on the other. Xenophobia is extremely strongly associated with pride in nationality in particular but also strongly associated with pride in one's country. Thus of the most xenophobic group, 58 percent were very proud of their nationality compared with 37 percent in the least xenophobic group. The more proud a person is of their nationality or country, the more likely they are to be xenophobic.

Xenophobia and Political Attitudes

Xenophobia was strongly associated with various political attitudes. For example those who were most xenophobic were less likely to trust parliament, civil servants, or government. They were also more likely to be pro-communist, supporting a return to communist rule and were most likely to be critical of the current regime: 39 percent of those who wanted a return to communist rule were in the most xenophobic group, compared with 18 percent in the least xenophobic group. We also asked about alternatives to democracy, and here the most xenophobic were more likely to think that the Army should govern. There was a very strong positive association between xenophobia and preferring a strong leader to elections. Thus, 41 percent of those who felt very strongly that a strong leader would be better were in the core xenophobic group, whilst only 16 percent were in the least xenophobic group. We could say therefore, that xenophobes were generally anti-democratic.

Xenophobia and National Security

One indicator of the increasing globalization of Central and Eastern Europe is the increasing influence of western international organizations such as the European Union, NATO, and various economic institutions. We could assume that xenophobia could be one reaction against the influence of these supra-national bodies. Indeed we found this to be the case. The most xenophobic were also those the most against their country joining the European Union and also strongly disapproving of NATO membership.[6] Thus, 45 percent of those who disapproved very strongly of EU membership were core xenophobes compared with just 15 percent who were the least xenophobic, and 37 percent of those who thought that joining the EU would be "very bad" were the most xenophobic as against 12 percent who were the least xenophobic. We could say therefore that opposition to these international institutions was associated with xenophobia, especially in the case of NATO.

It is perhaps related to this issue that xenophobia was strongly associated with people having a strong sense of threat or insecurity. The most xenophobic were also the most likely to see everything as threatening. Most strong was the sense of threat from Russia, followed by the sense of threat from neighboring countries and then Germany and the United States in that order. Xenophobes felt threatened not only by international institutions but also by international powers.

Xenophobia and Personal Security

Xenophobic respondents were also likely to have a personal sense of insecurity. The questions about personal insecurity were asked only in Poland, Hungary, and the Czech Republic. Here we found that xenophobia was associated with having poor emotional and mental health, with a lack of feeling of control over one's life, with having given up trying to make changes to one's life, and with feeling unfairly treated. Finally xenophobes were likely to feel that it was unsafe for them to walk the streets at night.

Thus, xenophobia was associated with various more psychological measures of threat and insecurity.

Xenophobia and Concepts of Citizenship

In the survey we compared attitudes to two different concepts of citizenship. On the one hand there was *republican* model of citizenship, meaning the idea that everybody who is born on the territory should have the right to be a citizen or *jus soli*. On the other hand, there is the *ethnic* model of citizenship, that citizenship should be by ethnic descent, regardless of where one is born or *jus sanguinis*. Part of the debate about xenophobia in Germany hinges around the fact that many people are defined as "foreigners" in Germany even if they are born there because the German constitution is based mainly on the ethnic model of citizenship. Foreigners are therefore by definition marginalized as non-citizens of the country, not entitled to so many rights as full citizens. However, there is some debate about this in European politics because the republican model of citizenship, found for example in France, can also be associated with a strong assimilationist tendency which can be also racist—with a refusal to acknowledge different lifestyles and cultures.

In Central and Eastern Europe we found that whilst most people in general supported the republican model of citizenship (71 percent), 28 percent overall favored the ethnic model of citizenship and these were also most likely to be the most xenophobic people. There was a very strong positive association between xenophobia and the ethnic model of citizenship and a negative association between xenophobia and the republican model of citizenship. Thus, 44 percent of people who agreed very strongly citizenship should be by ethnic descent were core xenophobes, compared with only 13 percent who were the least xenophobic. We could say therefore in Central and Eastern Europe it was certainly the case that the idea of an ethnic model of citizenship was supported by those who were xenophobic.

However, this was also associated in Central and Eastern Europe with a tendency for xenophobes to want to assimilate minorities rather than allow them separate identity and culture, although there was a lot of variation between countries, with more than 70 percent of people in Slovenia and Romania supporting assimilation but less than 30 percent in Hungary and Ukraine, so the support or otherwise for the assimilation or separate development of minorities probably depends upon the historical circumstances in each country and is difficult to generalize.

CONCLUSIONS

Our survey of xenophobia in 11 East-Central European countries shows some clear patterns of association. Some of these confirm the tendencies found in studies in other Western European countries and some tendencies are disconfirmed. In general it is believed that there has been a rise in xenophobia in East-Central Europe since the collapse of communism. However, our data from previous analysis of the NDB survey, admittedly with fewer and less detailed questions about xenophobia than were asked in the current round of the survey, seems to show that the general tendency is in the opposite direction. There has been a tendency for people to see migrants and minorities as less of a threat in 1996 and 1998 than they did in 1992 and this reflects a growing sense of security with the international situation in most of these countries. There may be variations, however, within particular countries.

We divided our analysis into objective indicators of xenophobia on the one hand and subjective indicators on the other. For the objective indicators, we found that xenophobia was not something which was generally associated with young males as is the case in Germany and other countries. On the contrary, it was associated with older people, especially those over 60, and gender did not feature significantly at all. There did seem to be a tendency, however, for teenagers to be more xenophobic than other groups of young people. However, it was the case that the less educated were the most xenophobic and this confirms the findings of other European studies. Going to university significantly decreases the chances of being xenophobic. Nor were the xenophobic people necessarily the ones who were most economically marginalized by restructuring of the economy. Xenophobia was weakly associated with unemployment, but not in any consistent way with poverty or wealth. However, people who are xenophobic are more likely to think that things got worse since the collapse of communism—this is an attitude held mainly by older people.

Xenophobia was not related at an aggregate level to economic performance either. Those countries which were the most xenophobic were also in relative terms the most prosperous and successful transition countries, although they do suffer high unemployment. One factor which could be important however, is the experience of immigration. The most xenophobic countries—Poland, Hungary, and the Czech Republic—are the ones subject to the most immigration in recent years. However, we know from other studies in Western Europe, that it is less the numbers of migrants which are important than how these are dealt with politically. Politically, the numbers of migrants, though in absolute terms still small compared with Germany or Austria, are seen as problematic in countries which never had any immigration in the past and where there was until recently no policies for dealing with migration or integrating people of different cultures and origins.

Of the subjective indicators of xenophobia, we could say that national pride is very strongly associated with xenophobia as are certain political attitudes—support for communism, skepticism of the current regime, and a tendency to support alternatives to democracy. Xenophobes were therefore anti-democratic. Xenophobia was also very strongly associated with a sense of international insecurity—seeing other countries as a threat to their own country—and with personal insecurity. International organizations, such as the EU and NATO, were particularly rejected by the most xenophobic, especially the latter. Finally, xenophobia is very strongly associated with an ethnic model of citizenship rather than a republican model, a model of citizenship which defines those who are not part of the ethnos as "foreigners."

The subjective indicators were far more strongly associated with xenophobia than the objective indicators, which means that in terms of xenophobia, people fall into attitudinal groups rather than xenophobia being caused in any strong way by economic conditions or associated with social structure.

We also carried out the same survey in Austria. The comparison with Austria is important because it can help us to understand to what extent these features of xenophobia are associated particularly with the problems of post-communist transition and to what extent they are more generally common in Europe. In fact we found that the people of Austria were generally less xenophobic than their post-communist neighbors (especially their immediate neighbors in Central Europe). However, there were the same patterns of association with xenophobia as there were in the post-communist countries. In Austria, indeed, xenophobia was even more strongly concentrated among the elderly, lower educated population than in the post-communist countries. We could say perhaps that this reflects the historical experiences of this generation of people.

NOTES

This paper was originally written for a *Xenophobia* volume edited by E. Menasse-Wiesbauer. For full references, please contact the author.

[1] A regular survey was carried out in Hungary which found a steady increase in xenophobia—Gyorgy Csepeli and Endre Sik, "Changing Content of Political Xenophobia in Hungary—Is the Growth of Xenophobia Inevitable?" Budapest: Hungarian Academy of Sciences, Institute of Political Science, 1995. However, there is also evidence that xenophobia may be declining: Christian Haerpfer and Claire Wallace, *Attitudes to Migrants and Minorities in Central and Eastern Europe*. Vienna, Austria: Institute for Advanced Studies, 1997.

[2] For a full report see Claire Wallace, *Xenophobia in Transition: Austria and Eastern Europe Compared. Final Report to the BMWV*. Vienna: Institute for Advanced Studies, 1999.

[3] In fact we tried a range of variables which measured social marginalization in addition to personal income, but none showed any very consistent tendencies.

[4] Some countries are missing from this index because the questions were not asked in exactly the same way in these countries. However, they are included in the pooled data set.

[5] Haerpfer and Wallace, 1997.

[6] The EU question was asked only in Poland, Czech Republic, Hungary, Slovakia, Slovenia, Croatia, FRY, Belarus, and Romania. The NATO question was asked only in Poland, Hungary, Czech Republic, Slovakia, and Yugoslavia.

Appendix 1

Eta Values of Different Variables

Strength of association between individual variables and the 4 point xenophobia scale

Variable	Eta value
Social Structure	
Gender	0.030
Age	0.084
Education	0.076
Personal income	0.035
Economic situation compared to past	0.066
Employed/unemployed	0.054
Political Attitudes	
Trust in Parliament	0.067
Trust in civil servants	0.062
Trust in government	0.054
Return to communist rule	0.087
Current political system	0.100
Army should govern	0.073
Strong leader better than elections	0.119
Return to a monarchy	0.011
National Identity	
Pride in nationality	0.267
National Security	
Russia a threat	0.167
Germany a threat	0.133
USA a threat	0.103
Neighboring countries a threat	0.158
Personal Security	
Poor health	0.091
Poor emotional and mental health	0.095
Lack of control over life at home	0.072

Things happen beyond my control   0.076
Feeling treated unfairly   0.112
Not feeling safe on the streets   0.131

Citizenship
Support for ethnic citizenship   0.199
Support for republican citizenship   0.134

Globalization
Support for EU membership   0.092
Support for NATO membership   0.214

CENTRAL EUROPE

III

Czech Republic
Slovakia
Hungary
Poland

Czech Republic

Population:	10,331,206
Capital:	Prague (pop. 1,215,000)
Major cities:	Brno (pop. 390,000), Ostrava (pop. 331,000), Plzen (pop. 175,000)
Area:	78,864 sq. km.
Major ethnic groups:	Czech 94%, Slovak 3%, Romani 2.4%
Economy:	GPD growth: 2.5%
....	Inflation rate: 7%
....	Unemployment rate: 8.1%

BETWEEN STAGNATION AND INTEGRATION

by JONATHAN STEIN

After years of priding itself on political stability and an unwavering commitment to market reform, the Czech Republic entered a period of deepening uncertainty in 1998. While its democratic institutions remain vigorous, relations among the main political parties deteriorated sharply, leading to the formation of a weak and inexperienced minority government by the center-left Social Democrats (CSSD) following elections to the parliament's lower house in June. Meanwhile, the economy slipped into recession for the first time since GDP growth resumed in 1993, with the full-year contraction estimated at 2.5 percent. This, along with mounting evidence of widespread economic crime and corruption, brought to the fore longstanding doubts concerning the "Czech way," the reform strategy pursued under two coalition governments led by the neoliberal economist and former prime minister, Vaclav Klaus, from 1992 until his resignation at the end of 1997.

The Czech Republic's main successes in 1998 were achieved in the field of foreign policy. With the CSSD dropping its demand for a referendum on NATO membership, admission (along with Hungary and Poland) was set for April 1999. In December 1997 the Czech Republic had been selected (with Estonia, Hungary, Poland, and Slovenia) as one of five post-communist states on the "fast track" of negotiations for accession to the European Union. Bilateral relations with Slovakia improved dramatically following the defeat of Vladimir Meciar's authoritarian government in late September, with both new governments pledging to complete the division of former Czechoslovak federal property and to develop "above-standard" ties, including the possibility of dual citizenship. Similarly, the Social Democrats' victory in Germany implied an end to official support for restitution claims pressed against post-1989 Czech administrations by the Bavaria-based Sudeten German Landsmannschaft, which had formed a key constituency in Helmut Kohl's Christian Democratic governments.

The CSSD was considerably more predisposed to the EU than Mr. Klaus, who favored admission into the Common Market but opposed key aspects of political unification, particularly the Social Charter. Nevertheless, domestic developments tarnished the Czechs' international reputation as a post-communist success story. The first annual re-evaluation by the European Union's executive body, the European Commission (EC), released in November 1998, highlighted the seriousness of the inherited institutional deficits the new Czech administration must redress to ensure effective implementation and enforcement of public policy and improved conditions for sustainable economic growth. By the end of the year, however, the constraints imposed on the cabinet by its lack of a parliamentary majority and an electoral base vulnerable to the short- and medium-term costs of delayed economic restructuring served to reinforce the prevailing political and economic malaise.

THE PARTIAL ECLIPSE OF VACLAV KLAUS

The political scene was dominated through the first half of 1998 by the fallout from the resignation of Vaclav Klaus's center-right coalition government in November 1997 following a split within his Civic Democratic Party (ODS) and the withdrawal of one of its two junior coalition partners, the Christian Democratic Union-People's Party (KDU-CSL). The government was weakened by its adoption of two austerity packages and the currency devaluation earlier in 1997, and tensions within the ODS and the coalition continued to mount as Klaus's autocratic style and ideological stridency met widening recognition of the need for improved economic and financial regulation. An official report released in September 1997 catalogued 1,420 cases of privatized companies whose assets had been "tunneled out," as a piquant Czech neologism phrased it, by their new owners in 1996 and another 892 cases over the first half of 1997. The coalition's collapse was precipitated by the resignation of two ODS ministers amid withering allegations (supported by other senior party officials) of illegal donations to the party by beneficiaries of direct sales of companies approved by the government.

The ODS's anti-Klaus wing, led by former interior minister Jan Ruml and Finance Minister Ivan Pilip, clearly hoped that forcing the government's resignation would sideline Klaus and give them control of the party. They promised a thorough investigation of the ODS's finances, better relations with the KDU-CSL and the third coalition partner, the Civic Democratic Alliance (ODA), and support for improved economic regulatory and enforcement measures, such as increased legal protection for minority shareholders (the primary victims of "tunneling"), a step that had been rejected by Klaus in July 1996 as a piece of unnecessary state intervention. After several spectacular tunneling cases forced the resignation in May 1997 of his close ally and Pilip's predecessor as finance minister, Ivan Kocarnik, Klaus reluctantly agreed to establish an independent body to ensure adequate capital market supervision.

By the end of 1997, however, Klaus had lost control of the policy agenda. Notwithstanding his avowed adherence to laissez faire, a key feature of his reform strategy had been continued partial state ownership of the three largest banks, which, as he admitted in an interview at the end of 1998, ensured continued lending to loss-making enterprises. The de facto tolerance of soft budget constraints on firms by what critics dubbed "bank socialism" prevented bankruptcies and kept unemployment low. However, despite high reported rates of investment, it also removed pressure for significant microeconomic restructuring and caused a gradual loss of competitiveness, with wage increases consistently outstripping productivity gains and feeding demand-driven growth. Combined with poor oversight and enforcement by the central bank, it also led to a dramatic weakening of the domestic financial sector, with the volume of bad loans, estimated at 29 percent in 1998, reaching roughly three times the level in Hungary and Poland.

While these developments hindered macroeconomic stability, necessitating the austerity packages adopted in 1997, Klaus's credibility was most powerfully undermined by a loss of confidence in the privatization process. Most of the asset tunneling was carried out by poorly regulated investment funds established to concentrate ownership of the nominal shares distributed to the more than 6 million adult citizens who participated in the "voucher" privatization completed in 1994. Just as the voucher program, with which Mr. Klaus was closely identified, had been a potent element of elite consensus in the early 1990s, so the widely publicized reports of tunneling by fund managers now seemed to vindicate CSSD leader Milos Zeman's longstanding portrayal of the scheme as "the theft of the century."

With Klaus politically isolated, President Vaclav Havel, although constitutionally weak and in poor health, openly supported Klaus's opponents and asked the outgoing agriculture minister and KDU-CSL leader, Josef Lux, to form an interim government to guide the country to early elections. The new cabinet, headed by Czech National Bank governor Josef Tosovsky and composed of several other non-party-aligned ministers, was only partly technocratic, with the remainder of the portfolios given exclusively to Klaus's opponents from the previous government. Responding to public fears and reflecting its members' desire to distance themselves from Klaus, Tosovsky's interim government launched an investigation in March of 26 "suspicious" privatization decisions taken by the two previous governments on direct sales of companies.

However, Klaus refused to leave political life quietly, portraying his government's collapse as the result of political intrigue and personal betrayal. Even as the police began investigating well-founded reports of a Swiss bank account estimated to contain nearly $6 million in illegal contributions to the ODS, Klaus received the backing of an overwhelming majority of delegates at a hastily convened extraordinary party congress, defeating Ruml by a vote of 227 to 72. While he conceded that "mistakes" had been made in the past, he left them unspecified and steadfastly denied any knowledge of secret donations to the party—a position he maintained throughout 1998 despite a steady stream of similar revelations and an independent audit that uncovered numerous unregistered contributions. (See accompanying document, "Mea Culpa.")

Klaus's victory inside the ODS, accompanied by his opponents' replacement in all senior leadership positions and a ban on separate internal "platforms," split the party irremediably. In January, those members who had joined Tosovsky's cabinet were ordered to leave either the ODS or the interim government. They quickly established the Freedom Union (US) under Ruml's leadership, gaining the support of 30 of the ODS's 69 parliamentary deputies. While the ODS resolved to be a "constructive" opposition to the interim government, Klaus's loyalists voted in late January with the Communists and the far-right Republicans in the parliament against President Havel's reelection to a second (and final) five-year term. Havel, a powerful international symbol of democracy and stability, won reelection on the second ballot, but the outcome was decided by a single vote, thus heightening the atmosphere of political division and mistrust.

THE JUNE ELECTION: A PYRRHIC VICTORY

The main beneficiary of the coalition's declining popularity and eventual collapse was the center-left CSSD, whose support under Zeman's leadership had risen from just over 6 percent in 1992 to more than 26 percent in the 1996 election. The party further consolidated its electoral base as the economic downturn accelerated during the run-up to the early election on 19 June. Accompanied by devaluation, the 1997 austerity packages had cut public spending by 42 billion crowns ($1.3 billion) and liberalized prices for energy, transport, and housing rents. Tosovsky's government pursued similar policies over the first half of 1998, increasing the value-added tax on fuels from 5 to 22 percent, raising duties on alcohol and tobacco, and announcing increases in household electricity prices by an average of 43 percent, gas prices by 28 percent, and regulated housing rents by a further 27 percent as of 1 July. While clearly necessary to restrain domestic demand and reverse the country's growing external deficit, these measures caused a sharp reduction in real incomes and private consumption in the months prior to the election.

Moreover, the deep fiscal cuts and the emphasis on price increases for basic necessities led to a widening income gap, with those dependent on state support faring worse than those in the labor force, and public sector employees losing ground relative to those in private enterprises. Health and education employees, for example, suffered an 8 percent decline in real earnings, while for pensioners the price increases meant a 17 percent rise in the cost of living.

Thus, while the economic austerity measures' effects were widely felt, the 1.7 percent fall in GDP over the first half of 1998 had a particularly adverse impact on the CSSD's natural electoral constituencies. This was reflected in strong support for the CSSD among state employees and in the poorer industrial regions of northern Bohemia and Moravia (where unemployment was also higher), as well as among pensioners, many of whom appear to have responded to the party's promise of slower price liberalization by dropping their support for the new party Pensioners for Life Security, which had gained as much as 9 percent backing in opinion polls conducted in early 1998. According to exit polls, the CSSD also won support from younger, less educated, and disaffected voters that in the past had gone to the far-right Republican Party, whose anti-Romani and anti-German platform failed for the first time since 1992 to secure the 5 percent electoral threshold required to enter parliament.

While the CSSD clearly appealed to the most economically vulnerable social groups, it failed to make significant inroads into the former coalition's electoral

Parliamentary Election Results (19–20 June 1998)		
	percent	*(seats)*
Czech Social Democratic Party (CSSD)	32.3	(74)
Civic Democratic Party (ODS)	27.7	(63)
Communist Party of Bohemia and Moravia (KSCM)	11.0	(24)
Christian Democratic Union–People's Party (KDU-CSL)	9.0	(20)
Freedom Union (US)	8.6	(19)
Total	100	(200)

support. With the partial exception of the newly established Freedom Union, each of the former coalition parties received roughly the same share of the popular vote as in 1996. While the ODS's support slipped to around 10 percent immediately after Klaus's government fell, the extraordinary congress demonstrated that he retained the loyalty of the party's powerful network of regional and local organizations, which it inherited and developed as the main successor to the revolutionary Civic Forum movement in 1991. Combined with Klaus's charismatic appeal and his campaign's highly polarizing portrayal of a CSSD victory as threatening a return to pre-1989 authoritarian socialism, this enabled the ODS to mobilize 80 percent of those who supported the party in 1996. Similarly, the KDU-CSL's results reflected the party's stable electoral base centered in the agricultural, primarily Catholic region of southern Moravia. Finally, the composition of support for the US, which polled as high as 20 percent in early 1998, in the end closely resembled that of the ODA, which withdrew from the election after its own series of financing scandals and internal splits drove its popular support down to less than one percent. Like the ODA, the US appealed mainly to educated urban voters and, as a party based on national political elites, suffered from low membership and a poor organizational apparatus with which to maintain broader support among initially disillusioned ODS voters.

THE NEW GOVERNMENT: A SOLUTION WITHOUT RESOLUTION

Despite a parliamentary majority of 102 seats for the ODS, KDU-CSL, and US, the ODS's strong performance ensured that the Right would remain too divided to govern. The KDU-CSL and the US, whose main objective had been the removal of Klaus, could not seriously consider joining a government in which he would again be premier. On the other hand, the ODS had little incentive to compromise, as the departure of his opponents had left the party even more closely identified with Klaus himself, making it unlikely that he would forego the prime minister's portfolio. Moreover, having regained its popular support while in opposition to the interim government, the ODS had little to lose by remaining out of power, particularly given the need for further unpopular economic measures by the next government, regardless of its composition.

The KDU-CSL and the US were thus left with the prospect of cooperating with the CSSD, which had resolved at its 1995 congress that it would not govern with the unreformed Communist Party (KSCM) and similarly ruled out a grand coalition with the ODS prior to the election. With its broadly compatible support for a market economy preserving elements of "social solidarity," a coalition with the CSSD was clearly the preferred option for the KDU-CSL, while Zeman offered the party half the cabinet portfolios and proposed Lux as prime minister. However, the KDU-CSL refused to enter a coalition with the CSSD that would depend on tacit support from the KSCM and proposed sharing some posts with the US. Despite his description of Ruml's party as "ODS 2," Zeman was willing to accept this arrangement in order to gain a parliamentary majority.

While this option received clear encouragement from President Havel, the US refused to support a government containing the CSSD either directly or tacitly, evidently assuming that the only remaining alternative would then be a rapprochement on the Right. The US demanded that no party should hold a majority in a re-formed center-right coalition and that it should follow the interim government's program of improved regulation, price liberalization, and privatization of enterprises previously classified as "strategic." When the smaller parties rejected the ODS's insistence on a cabinet majority, the prime minister's post, and the support of the US and KDU-CSL for all government legislation, Klaus and Zeman reached a novel agreement on the formation of a minority CSSD government that left the US and KDU-CSL completely marginalized.

Under the terms of the "opposition agreement," which could be annulled if either party fails to fulfill its provisions, the ODS agreed neither to initiate nor support a parliamentary vote of no confidence over the four-year electoral term. However, it is not obliged to support any particular policy measures. The CSSD, in turn, agreed to regard the ODS as the "official" opposition party with which all parliamentary leadership posts would be divided. Thus, Klaus became chairman of the parliament's lower house and the ODS gained one of three deputy chairman posts, control of the intelligence oversight and budget committees, and the right to name the head of the Supreme Audit Office. The CSSD was further obliged not to invite any other party into a government coalition or conclude a "lasting agreement" with another party in parliamentary voting.

With the ODS and the CSSD controlling the three-fifths majority of both the lower house and the Senate required to amend the constitution, the agreement promised proposals within 12 months to "enhance the significance of the outcome of the competition of political parties" and "define with more precision the powers of the different constitutional bodies." The first of these, clearly directed at the US and the KDU-CSL, implies either a change from party-list proportional representation to a first-past-the-post electoral system or an increase in the electoral threshold, possibly to 10–15 percent. The second category of proposed changes introduces even greater uncertainty, opening the possibility of a revision of presidential powers in anticipation of the post-Havel era or, perhaps more likely, elimination of the 81-member Senate. Both parties have expressed strong doubts about the need for an upper house in a unitary, ethnically homogeneous state that appear to resonate with Czech voters, only 20 percent of whom turned out in November for the second round of elections of one-third of its members.

THE CSSD IN POWER: TOSOVSKY PLUS WHAT?

While Zeman's description during the June election campaign of a "scorched earth" economy was an exaggeration, the CSSD inherited a profoundly difficult set of problems whose resolution was further complicated by the high costs implied for the party's electoral base. While it fulfilled its promise of a 17 percent wage increase for public sector employees—a move that drew praise as a hedge against corruption in the EC's 1998 reassessment—this did not eliminate the gap that had appeared over the previous two years, when public sector wages fell to 81 percent of the average wage in enterprises. Moreover, despite a 31 billion crown deficit planned for the 1999 budget, the government was unable to specify how it would finance its promises of increased spending on housing construction, education, and health care.

In fact, the CSSD came to power with very little room for maneuver on fiscal policy, facing not only a recession, but also two other constraints in addition to mandatory entitlements spending (which makes up about two-thirds of expenditures). First, despite claims of balanced budgets, Klaus's governments built up considerable hidden public debt, with the World Bank estimating the figure at 270 billion crowns ($9 billion), of which 130 billion crowns was attributable to Konsolidacni banka, a state institution that had been subsidizing enterprises and banks by taking over their bad debts. While still manageable, the rapid growth of the debt raised strong concerns about the longer-term sustainability of public finances. Second, joining NATO and the EU entails commitments to increase defense expenditures by 0.1 percent of GDP per year until 2000, and spending on research and development from 0.45 percent to 0.7 percent of GDP by the time of EU accession.

Indeed, during its first months in power, the government had little choice but to continue pursuing many of the Tosovsky cabinet's policies. The interim government successfully privatized the state's share of Investicni a postovni banka in March, and the CSSD pledged to sell the state's stake in the two leading banks Ceska sporitelna and Komercni banka by mid-2000. The government did, however, decide to regain a majority stake in other strategic sectors, namely gas production and distribution, in the hope that this would ensure higher prices when they are finally put on sale, and in order to establish a regulatory framework to prevent monopoly practices following their sell-off. Similarly, with foreign direct investment reaching barely $100 per capita (placing the Czech Republic behind Hungary, Slovenia, Latvia, Estonia, Poland, and Croatia), the CSSD embraced the Tosovsky government's incentive package, announced in April, emphasizing tax holidays, duty-free technology imports, and retraining grants. The government's support for the Securities Commission, which was finally established in early 1998, should also improve the climate for portfolio investment. While the EC's reassessment noted that it is undermanned and dependent on the finance ministry for funding, by the end of the year the Commission had begun enforcing new licensing requirements for traders and brokerages, levied significant fines, and closed several investment funds.

It was less clear how the CSSD would proceed with enforcement of bankruptcy provisions, which were streamlined by the Tosovsky government. An important consideration noted by the EC was the lack of administrative capacity in the judiciary, with the Institute for the Further Training of Judges unreformed since 1989 and facing serious deficiencies in both staffing and basic equipment. Equally important, however, was the CSSD's reluctance to accept a sharper rise in unemployment, which the government forecast to reach 10 percent by the end of 1999. Indeed, with the banks' bad loan portfolios reflecting the scope of insolvency in the enterprise sector, the prospect of a wave of bankruptcies prompted the government to support an enterprise "revitalization" plan produced by Minister of Industry and Trade Miroslav Gregr. However, the plan, which called for 60 billion crowns in state guarantees, appeared to stand little chance of gaining parliamentary approval.

More broadly, the dilemma for the CSSD government was that while it controlled the levers of administrative power, it failed to craft economic policy legislation that could gain majority support and signal a fundamental shift away from Klaus's discredited "Czech way." The ODS voted against the first reading of the 1999 budget in October, while the prospect of a majority coalition emerging was diminished by the US's continued opposition and uncertainty within the KDU-CSL following the resignation in September of Lux, who was diagnosed with leukemia.

Instead, the CSSD's attention focused on following up the investigation of past corruption in the privatization process by the Tosovsky government, which released a report on 1 July concluding merely that the prices at which direct sales of companies were approved by the Klaus government were frequently "anomalously low." However, while the interim government also amended the penal code to increase the sanctions for bribery, the CSSD's "clean hands" campaign, centered in the newly-established Committee for the Protection of Economic Interests (VOEZ), appeared to be entirely backward-looking. As the EC noted, the government made no progress on drafting legislation to reform and professionalize the civil service, despite clear deadlines set out in an indicative timetable approved in March. More disturbing was the possibility that "clean hands" will be open to political manipulation, particularly given the ambiguous relationship between the CSSD and the ODS. Indeed, at the end of the year, senior police officials expressed little confidence in the VOEZ and complained that their investigation of the allegations surrounding the ODS's Swiss bank account had met with a "lack of political will."

GLOSSARY

CSSD	Czech Social Democratic Party
KDU-CSL	Christian Democratic Union–People's Party
KSCM	Communist Party of Bohemia and Moravia
ODA	Civic Democratic Alliance
ODS	Civic Democratic Party
US	Freedom Union

Document: *MEA CULPA*

Former Prime Minister Vaclav Klaus and his Civic Democratic Party (ODS) tried hard to improve their images—shattered after a party financing scandal, including allegations of secret foreign accounts, brought down Klaus's government in November 1997 and led to the defection of many of the party's deputies. To make amends for the financial machinations, ODS decided recently to publicize the results of an audit of the party's accounting.

The audit's findings made clear that ODS had broken accounting laws; cheated on its financial reporting; and played loose with loans, membership fees, and other contributions. Even though the report criticized the lack of control by ODS's leadership, Klaus and other top officials refused to resign, prompting criticism from many journalists.

Below is the full text of ODS's mea culpa advertisement, published on 13 May in several of the country's daily newspapers:

ODS on the Results of the Forensic Audit of [Party] Financing: Open admission of past mistakes is the only path to a speedy cure.

Of its own free will, ODS decided to use the specialized services of the internationally renowned firm Deloitte and Touche and requested that it, through the help of a forensic audit, analyze the problems of ODS financing in past years. The main reason was our effort to ascertain the true state of things and, after learning from personal or systematic mistakes, to draw up measures that would prevent their future repetition and would ensure the regular and problem-free financing of ODS.

We are publicizing the results of the forensic investigation regardless of the fact that elections are approaching, and that some political parties and media might be tempted to abuse its results in the election campaign. We are convinced that citizens will understand and appreciate our attempt to openly admit past mistakes and above all our effort to remedy them as quickly as possible. The forensic inquiry revealed:

— serious defects and mistakes in ODS's accounting, and this because of insufficient internal control mechanisms and methods that would have prevented irregularities;
— cases of irregular documentation, accounting, and manipulation of gifts, loans, and membership dues. These cases were also caused by not following internal regulations or their imperfection or incompleteness;
— that not even the annual accounting audit fulfilled its purpose: it didn't identify mistakes and irregularities and did not call for their remediation;
— and that a serious defect was the imperfect control of the financial staff by the political leadership of ODS.

For all these reasons:

1. We will prepare a complete plan of preventive and remedial measures of a systematic and organizational type;
2. We will judge the personal responsibility of individuals who up to now have a legal working relationship with ODS;
3. We will pay off all possible debts to the state, which could result from this audit;
4. We will provide the police not only the results of this audit, but also maximum cooperation.

For these mistakes, ODS has already paid a not-insignificant political price. To our members, sympathizers, and to the voters, we apologize for all of these past problems and mistakes.

NOTE
Reprinted with kind permission from *Transitions* magazine, June 1998.

Slovakia

Population:	5,324,632 (1993)
Capital:	Bratislava (pop. 448,785)
Major cities:	Kosice (pop. 238,886); Presov (pop. 90,963), Nitra (pop. 86,679)
Area:	49,036 sq. km.
Major ethnic groups:	Slovak 86%; Hungarian 10.7%; Romani 1.6%; Czech, Moravian, and Silesian 1.1%; Ruthenian, Ukrainian 0.6%
Economy:	GDP growth: 5.0%
	Inflation rate: 5.6%
	Unemployment rate: 15.6%

A YEAR OF DRAMATIC CHANGE

by SHARON FISHER

Slovakia's parliamentary elections on 25–26 September overshadowed other events of 1998, marking a major turning point in post-independence politics and bringing an end to the era of Prime Minister Vladimir Meciar. Citizens demonstrated their desire for change by giving four opposition parties a constitutional majority. Still, the new government, headed by Slovak Democratic Coalition (SDK) Chairman Mikulas Dzurinda, faced major hurdles, including resolving economic difficulties, restoring the rule of law, dampening inter-party conflicts, and catching up with Slovakia's neighbors in European integration efforts.

TENSE PRE-ELECTION POLITICS

Given the expiration of President Michal Kovac's five-year term in office on 2 March, the year began with continued controversy over the question of the presidency. Recognizing that the parliament would be unable to agree on a new candidate since the approval of three-fifths of the 150 deputies was needed, the opposition had tried the previous year to push forward a law on direct presidential elections. Such moves were rejected by the ruling coalition, however, and the interior minister removed a question on direct presidential elections from a referendum which was held in May 1997. On 29 January, the first attempt to elect a new president through the parliament was made, but Meciar's party—the Movement for a Democratic Slovakia (HZDS)—and its coalition partners demonstrated their lack of interest in the vote by failing to propose a candidate. At the same time, the ruling parties refused to support the opposition's candidates, who were far short of winning the required 90 votes. Shortly before leaving office, Kovac called a new referendum on direct presidential elections.

When Kovac's term expired, most presidential powers transferred to the prime minister, including the right to grant amnesty and pardons, to declare referenda, to veto legislation, and to approve and dismiss ambassadors. In a session on 3 March that was symbolically held in the presidential palace, the Meciar government canceled the newly-called referendum on direct presidential elections, dismissed 28 ambassadors, and granted amnesty to those individuals who had disrupted the 1997 referendum as well as to those who were accused of involvement of the 1995 kidnapping of Kovac's son. The amnesty decision in particular attracted strong international and domestic criticism. Undeterred, the Meciar government clearly enjoyed holding the extra powers, and the ruling parties showed little interest in subsequent rounds of presidential elections. Only in the fifth round, held on 9 July, did the HZDS put forward a serious candidate and get the backing of its coalition partners; however, the candidate lost by four votes. Additional rounds were canceled because of lack of interest from all parties.

As the elections approached, tension in Slovak society increased. On 20 May, the parliament approved government-sponsored amendments to the election law that were seen as an effort by the ruling parties to shut out the opposition. The most controversial amendments included one that prohibited campaigning through the private electronic media and another that required each party entering the parliament to have at least 5 percent of the vote, even if competing in a coalition. Although all parties running in the elections were allowed equal time to run ads on state-run Slovak TV and Slovak Radio, many saw the former amendment as a limitation of freedom of speech. Meanwhile, the provision on coalitions was seen as a direct attack on the three-party Hungarian Coalition and five-party Slovak Democratic Coalition (SDK), both of which included several parties that were under the 5 percent barrier. The SDK was a particularly tempting target for the HZDS since many opinion polls showed that it had replaced the HZDS as the most popular political grouping in Slovakia. To avoid probable failure, each of the two coalitions took steps to merge into a single party. While Dzurinda become SDK chairman, Bela Bugar became the leader of the new Party of the Hungarian Coalition (SMK).

After failing to destroy its major competitor through amendments to the electoral law, the HZDS tried another approach. Although the SDK was officially registered as a party with the interior ministry and narrowly managed to be accepted by the Central Election Commission, on 10 August the HZDS brought a complaint before the Supreme Court arguing that the SDK was not a party but a coalition. The opposition showed a united front in response to the HZDS move, and there was even discussion of boycotting the elections should the SDK be barred from running. On 14 August the court ruled in the SDK's favor.

Although the opposition remained concerned that the ruling parties would try in some other way to manipulate the elections, two developments in July and August helped to calm such fears. The first was the approval on 14 July of a constitutional amendment transferring certain presidential powers to the parliament chairman in the absence of the president, including the right to appoint and dismiss the government. Before that change was made, many were afraid that a constitutional crisis would occur after the elections and that Meciar would misuse the situation to remain power. The second important development was the Slovak government's much delayed invitation on 18 August to the Organization for Security and Cooperation in Europe allowing international observers to monitor the elections. Even with these provisions, however, many opposition representatives and their supporters were worried that more surprises were on the way, creating a mood of paranoia.

The election campaign, which started on 26 August, was especially tense. The HZDS ran a lavish campaign, with estimates showing that the party far surpassed the 12 million crown ($370,000) spending limit for parties during the pre-election period. Probably the most controversial aspect of the HZDS campaign was the participation of a number of international celebrities who were offered considerable sums of money to attend HZDS rallies and events. Although many refused, figures such as model Claudia Schiffer and French actor Gerard Depardieu appeared at Meciar's side during the campaign. In an effort to further boost support, Meciar called a referendum banning the privatization of strategic energy and gas firms, to be held at the same time as the parliamentary elections.

The use of the media during the election campaign was a particularly controversial issue. Although formally a "public interest" station, Slovak Television (STV) ran a smear campaign against the opposition, focusing mainly on the SDK and the newly-created Party of Civic Understanding (SOP). This was thought to have been especially harmful to the latter, as a new party whose supporters were less committed than those of other parties. The Council for Radio and TV Broadcasting took administrative action against a number of television and radio stations, including STV, requiring that they broadcast statements saying that they had violated the media law. Even so, many believed that the Council did not go far enough against STV.

The biggest media story of the election campaign involved private TV Markiza, Slovakia's most popular television station. On 18 August, Markiza was mysteriously taken over in a move that many suspected had political overtones and that could have significantly influenced the election results. Although director-general Pavol Rusko was temporarily reinstated and no major changes occurred in the news programs, on 15 September Markiza was occupied by the new owners' security guards, and several top TV representatives were fired, including Rusko. Markiza staff reacted by asking its viewers for support, leading to several days of protests by thousands of citizens around Slovakia. Live broadcasts of demonstrations outside Markiza headquarters near Bratislava became a showplace for opposition deputies, some of whom used the chance to promote themselves and their parties, trying to convince people that the Meciar cabinet and secret service were involved. Meciar, concerned about how these events would influence the election results, on 16 September complained about the extra airtime that the opposition gained through the Markiza affair and asked whether the opposition really wanted the elections to take place. The crisis calmed down after the new owner and his security guards left Markiza on 17 September and agreed not to make personnel changes or interfere in the station's news programs until after 11 October. Still, Markiza was charged 3.5 million crowns, near the top level of fines for election law violations.

CITIZENS VOTE FOR CHANGE

Despite the pre-election tension and fear of manipulation, the voting process itself went smoothly, and voter turnout was high at 84 percent. Although the

HZDS managed to win the most votes, with 27 percent and 43 seats, the SDK was close behind with 26.3 percent and 42 seats. Most importantly, the SDK combined with the other opposition parties—the Party of the Democratic Left (SDL) with 14.7 percent and 23 seats, the SMK with 9.1 percent and 15 seats, and the SOP with 8.0 percent and 13 seats—won a constitutional majority of 93 out of 150 parliamentary seats. HZDS attempts to form a new cabinet were welcomed only by the Slovak National Party (SNS), which won 9.1 percent and 14 seats. At the same time, the referendum failed to gain approval since only 44 percent of eligible voters participated, less than the 50 percent required for a referendum to be valid. It was generally believed that the informal ("third") sector played an important role in encouraging the high voter turnout in the elections, since several non-governmental organizations ran campaigns encouraging citizens to participate in the electoral process.

Some feared that the HZDS would try to "buy" SDL or SOP support to create a new cabinet; however, the opposition's success in winning a constitutional majority offered these parties a clear sign that Slovaks wanted a change. The four opposition parties held round-table talks on 27 September and announced that they would set up a cabinet of their own. Three days later, Meciar gave his first post-election public address. In an emotional speech he accepted defeat, claimed he never hurt anyone, and criticized those who did not vote for the HZDS. He also announced that he would not try to form a new cabinet and promised to give up his parliamentary seat. Meciar later kept his promise, giving his seat to former Slovak Information Service (SIS) director Ivan Lexa, ostensibly to provide his ally with parliamentary immunity.

Although some HZDS representatives readily admitted that the party would be unable to form a government, the HZDS proposed Jan Smerek of the east Slovak steel giant, VSZ, to make an attempt. However, the SDL rejected Smerek's best offer, and the four opposition parties signed a coalition agreement on 28 October, one day before the constituent parliament session. On 30 October, newly-elected parliament chairman Jozef Migas of the SDL appointed the new government. In the 20-member cabinet, which included four deputy prime ministers, the breakdown by party was: nine for the SDK, six for the SDL, three for the SMK, and two for the SOP. Of the new cabinet members, 13 had previous ministerial experience, while of the remaining seven, one had served as a state secretary and another three were well-known politicians.

Although differences of opinion within the cabinet were unavoidable given the broad spectrum they represented, all four parties in the new cabinet agreed on the need to bring Slovakia closer to Europe, to renew democracy, and to restore rule of law. Pressing problems involved the economy as well as personnel in key organizations such as the SIS and STV. To contribute to renewing rule of law, Dzurinda made an unprecedented move on 8 December, canceling the amnesties that were granted by Meciar in March and thereby allowing for the continuation of the criminal investigations. The following day, the parliament approved a law allowing for the dismissal of Prosecutor General Michal Valo before the end of his five-year term because of his role in several controversial criminal cases. Another key question facing the Dzurinda cabinet was that of the presidency, and there was considerable controversy among the four coalition parties regarding whether to elect a new president in the parliament or through direct elections. In dividing the top posts among the parties, the SOP was given only two cabinet representatives on the understanding that its chairman, Rudolf Schuster, would be the ruling parties' joint candidate for the presidency. In early November, the ruling coalition decided in favor of direct elections, which would be held in the first part of 1999. Several weeks later, on 24 November, former President Michal Kovac announced that he would also run for president. In early December, Meciar vowed that he would not compete in the presidential elections, and he said he would withdraw from public life.

The first coalition crisis occurred in December, when Justice Minister Jan Carnogursky, a Christian Democrat, refused to vote for the government's program because of its lack of support for certain religious questions. During the parliamentary vote on the program on 2 December, some SDK deputies voted with the opposition to approve legislation calling for a treaty between Slovakia and the Vatican; the creation of equal conditions for religious, private, and state schools; and the establishment of a Catholic university. Pressure also arose within the SDK to return to its previous make-up as a coalition of five parties.

Local elections were initially scheduled for 13–14 November, but the Constitutional Court ruled on 15 October that changes in the election law sponsored by the previous Meciar government were unconstitutional. The new parliament amended the law and delayed the elections until 19–20 December. Former Prime Minister Jozef Moravcik, who had ties to the SDK, was elected Bratislava's new mayor, beating HZDS deputy Jozef Binder, who was closely linked with the controversial Gabcikovo dam project, a bone of contention with Hungary. Of the eight regional capitals, the opposition was victorious in six and the SNS in two, while the HZDS did not win any. Although the HZDS won the most council seats, independent candidates won the most mayoral positions. The election turnout was 54 percent.

ECONOMIC TROUBLES LOOM

In 1998, Slovakia's GDP growth continued to be strong, with an expected annual increase of approximately 5 percent, while annual inflation rose just 5.6 percent in December. Still, numerous imbalances signaled that the country was headed for an economic crisis due to growing foreign trade and state budget deficits as well as rising public debt, which emerged mainly from the Meciar cabinet's huge infrastructure projects, including highway construction and the Mochovce nuclear power plant. The state budget deficit soared to 65.2 billion crowns, or more than 10 percent of GDP, while the trade deficit reached 73 billion crowns. In October, foreign debt totaled $12.2 billion, or over 60 percent of GDP. Despite several years of high economic growth, unemployment remained high, at 13.8 percent in September.

While privatization moved quickly under Meciar's cabinet, many firms were sold at rock-bottom prices to government supporters. In many cases, the necessary restructuring was not carried out, and the management of some firms was accused of "tunneling," or secretly moving valuable corporate assets into privately controlled firms. The banking sector in particular was in need of emergency measures, while the capital markets were virtually stagnant because of low transparency and an inconsistent legislative framework. Prior to the elections, the National Bank of Slovakia (NBS) and the International Monetary Fund warned the Meciar government to take action, while international agencies such as Standard & Poor's and Moody's lowered Slovakia's credit rating. Just after the elections, with the currency under strong pressure, the NBS was forced on 1 October to float the currency and abolish the 7 percent fluctuation band within which the crown was fixed against a mark/dollar basket.

Given the economic difficulties facing the country, the new cabinet took office in an unenviable situation. Although responsibility for the devaluation and other economic problems was placed with the outgoing Meciar government, the Dzurinda cabinet faced a number of tough decisions that were expected to cause internal controversy during the coming years and which could cost the new government considerable public support. Its first economic priorities included drafting a provisional state budget for the first quarter of 1999; resolving the acute problems in health care, education, and agriculture; and preparing the budget for the remainder of 1999. Longer-term goals included the attraction of new foreign investment, which was very low in Slovakia compared with its neighbors. The new government also promised to review the privatization projects approved by its predecessor.

NEW OPTIMISM IN FOREIGN RELATIONS

Prior to the elections, Slovakia's relations with the West as well as with some of its neighbors were rocky. Slovak-Austrian ties were troubled by the Meciar government's decision to start operation of the Mochovce nuclear power plant, while the Gabcikovo-Nagymaros dam complex continued to be a source of controversy in bilateral relations with Hungary. Hungary failed to come to agreement with Slovakia by the 25 March deadline that was set by the International Court of Justice in The Hague, leading the Meciar government in early September to return the case to the court. Slovak-Czech relations were strained in the first half of the year since Meciar refused to negotiate outstanding bilateral issues with the transitional government of Josef Tosovsky, and they remained cool even after the June elections. Relations with Great Britain were troubled given an exodus of Slovak Roma applying for refugee status there. The situation of Roma in Slovakia was particularly difficult in 1998 since summer floods hit two villages and killed some 50 people. Britain imposed a visa requirement for Slovaks on 7 October.

With the appointment of the new Dzurinda government, Slovakia's relations with the West and with its immediate neighbors improved dramatically. The Czech Republic, Poland, and Hungary began actively pushing for Slovakia's European integration, while Dzurinda made a number of foreign trips designed to promote Slovakia abroad. In hope of being included in the first round of EU expansion talks, the new government began to address the organization's recommendations on democratization and minority rights that had been made to the previous Meciar cabinet. Although at its Vienna summit on 11–12 December the European Union decided against reassessing Slovakia's case before the next scheduled review in late 1999, the Slovak government remained optimistic and hoped that after some fundamental changes Slovakia's case would be reconsidered. In terms of bilateral ties, the most dramatic improvement occurred between Slovakia and the Czech Republic.

GLOSSARY

HZDS   Movement for a Democratic Slovakia
SDK   Slovak Democratic Coalition
SDL   Party of the Democratic Left
SMK   Party of the Hungarian Coalition
SNS   Slovak National Party
SOP   Party of Civic Understanding

Hungary _____

Population:	10,277,000 (January 1994)
Capital:	Budapest (pop. 1,996,000)
Major cities:	Debrecen (pop. 218,000), Miskolc (pop. 190,000), Szeged (pop. 179,000)
Area:	93,030 sq. km.
Major ethnic groups:	Hungarian 90%, Romani 4%, German 2.6%, Slovak 1%
Economy:	GDP growth: 5.2%
....	Inflation rate: 14.3%
....	Unemployment rate: 9.0%

THE RIGHT RETURNS TO POWER

by JAMES TOOLE

Following four years of socialist-liberal rule in Hungary, the May general elections produced a surprising win for the revitalized parties of the right. The Young Democrats–Hungarian Civic Party (Fidesz), the onetime party of youth and liberalism, narrowly bested the Hungarian Socialist Party (MSzP) of outgoing prime minister Gyula Horn and went on to form a three-party conservative coalition. The new government, led by 35-year-old Fidesz leader Viktor Orban, inherited a booming economy. It will also have the honor of presiding over Hungary's one-thousandth anniversary in the year 2000, and over the country's formal entry into the NATO military alliance in 1999. But for the government, considerable challenges remain. Its majority in parliament is far smaller than that of its predecessor, and relations among the parties of the new governing coalition are likely to be more unstable. Its aggressive governing style aroused domestic and foreign concerns from its very first days in office. And with the most intensive phase of negotiations over EU entry just beginning, the government has signaled its intention to strike a hard bargain.

VICTORY OF THE RIGHT

As the May election approached, it was not at all clear who would emerge victorious. While most opinion polls predicted that the MSzP would finish first, the potentially poor showing of its coalition partner, the Alliance of Free Democrats (SzDSz), threatened the government's chances of retaining a parliamentary majority. After the first round of elections on 10 May, the MSzP did indeed top the list, but only narrowly ahead of Fidesz. The SzDSz, meanwhile, won only 8 percent of the vote, down from nearly 20 percent in 1994. The closeness of the MSzP and Fidesz results, combined with the dramatic fall of the SzDSz, ensured that the second round would be the decisive one, and set off a frenzy of speculation and negotiation. In the ensuing two weeks, several polling firm projections suggested a Fidesz win. In the second round of elections on 24 May Fidesz pulled ahead, winning 148 parliamentary seats to the MSzP's 134. With the MSzP and SzDSz unable to form a majority, responsibility for forming a new government fell to Fidesz. Yet Fidesz and its electoral ally, the Hungarian Democratic Forum (MDF), together held only 165 seats, 29 shy of a parliamentary majority. Orban rejected the oft-mentioned idea of a grand coalition with the MSzP, favoring instead a clear coalition of the right. On 8 July, after protracted negotiations, Fidesz formed a government that included not only the MDF but also the Independent Smallholders' Party (ISP), a right-wing populist party led by the charismatic and often volatile Jozsef Torgyan.

with a 76–seat majority in the 386-seat National Assembly, the new coalition began with a majority of only 19. Among coalition parties, Fidesz won 148 seats and 30 percent of the party list vote, while the ISP won 48 seats and 13 percent of the vote. The MDF failed to pass the 5 percent threshold for representation in the party list voting, but maintained its presence in parliament by winning 17 seats in single-member constituency races. The Christian Democratic People's Party, a conservative group in parliament since 1990, failed to win any seats following a dramatic 1997 party split. To the dismay of many, the Hungarian Justice and Life Party, the extreme nationalist party led by Istvan Csurka, entered parliament with 14 seats and 5 percent of the party list vote. It was excluded from the coalition.

The closeness of the outcome was shown by the MSzP results. Although the MSzP won fewer seats than Fidesz, it won a greater share of the first-round party list vote (33 percent) than its opponent. Had the Socialists been able to build on their first-round showing, they might have saved the governing coalition. In the end, they lost over a third of their parliamentary seats. But blame for the coalition defeat may lie even more heavily with the SzDSz, which won only 24 seats and seemed unable to articulate any positive identity separate from that of its larger coalition partner. The Free Democrats suffered a humiliating defeat, losing approximately two-thirds of their 1994 vote and seat totals. With their dismal first-round result convincing many that a continued socialist-liberal majority was unlikely, the SzDSz may well have cost the coalition its hold on government.

The election cemented a shift that had been developing for some time among the parties of the right. The 1994 election, a landslide victory for the MSzP, had left the right in shambles, controlling less than a quarter of parliamentary seats. Fidesz, which had joined neither the conservative government in 1990 nor the socialist-liberal government in 1994, moved to fill the gap, evolving steadily away from its roots as a liberal party of Hungarian youth. An increasingly outspoken opponent of the socialist-liberal government, Fidesz presented itself as a center-right party representing middle-class Hungarians of all ages. By securing the leadership of the Hungarian right, Fidesz inherited the mantle of the once-dominant MDF, now reduced to smallest partner in the coalition. As though to underscore the point, Orban readily professed affection and admiration for the late Jozsef Antall, who as MDF leader served as Hungary's first post-communist prime minister.

Though the current economic boom began in early 1997, improvement in living standards seemed to come too late to save the socialist-liberal coalition. Despite its socialist base, the MSzP-SzDSz government was far more economically liberal than its predecessor. While this won it credit abroad for Hungary's economic success, many voters had yet to feel the benefits. The MSzP suffered, and the SzDSz even more so. The SzDSz, never able to shake their association with the wildly unpopular austerity plan introduced by Finance Minister Lajos and the SzDSz even more so. The SzDSz, never able to shake their association with the wildly unpopular austerity plan introduced by Finance Minister Lajos Bokros in 1995, were greatly hurt by their failure to adequately explain the long-term benefits of their commitment to free-market economics. Fidesz and its conservative allies, meanwhile, ran on more statist economic platforms that appealed to apprehensions formed over years of economic decline. They also benefited from a spate of pre-election bombings, some directed at conservative political leaders, that helped to divert attention away from economic growth and toward the public security issues on which the right was viewed as more credible.

A NEW GOVERNING STYLE

In its campaign, Fidesz had promised a break from the past. During its first six months in office, it worked aggressively to project an image of change, provoking no small measure of controversy. Its administrative reforms were lauded by supporters, but viewed by opponents as producing an excessive centralization of coalition authority. Its renewed assertion of nationalist concerns, downplayed by the previous government, reassured Hungarian conservatives but aroused suspicions in Romania and Slovakia, where large ethnic Hungarian minorities reside. Less confidently, the new government backtracked within days of taking office on economic positions that had worried foreign observers during the campaign.

By rejecting a grand coalition with the Socialists, Fidesz ensured that it would be the dominant influence in the new government. Allying with the Smallholders' Party, however, brought its own share of difficulties. The Smallholders' strong nationalism and economic protectionism moved the coalition further away from the political center, while Torgyan's outspoken and confrontational character would likely make for many tense and awkward moments. In his last tenure as a junior partner in government, Torgyan lasted less than two years, defecting in 1992 from the MDF-led government formed in 1990. With only a narrow governing majority, much will depend on Orban's ability to keep Torgyan loyal and content. Of the 16 cabinet-level ministerial appointments, Fidesz ended up with 10, the ISP with four, the MDF with one, and the CDU, a CDPP remnant affiliated with Fidesz, with one. Though denied the post of deputy prime minister, the Smallholders won the right to nominate the government's candidate for president in 2000, a nomination likely to be Torgyan's for the taking.

Two of the government's administrative reforms provoked considerable controversy. The first was a visible expansion of the powers of the prime minister's office. The office was now to be managed by a cabinet-level minister, with office staff projected to increase from the approximately 300 used by the previous government to around 470 in 1999. The second reform was a proposal to decrease the number of parliamentary sessions by two-thirds. Though opponents contended that these actions were designed to weaken the opposition's ability to influence policy making, the government argued that they were overdue improvements in governmental efficiency.

LOCAL ELECTIONS

Though Fidesz continued to score well in opinion polls following the general election, it was unable to capitalize on its popularity at local elections in October. While Fidesz won the most mayoral posts in the country's larger cities and towns, the MSzP won the most mayorships overall and the most votes nationwide for all local posts combined. In the most important race in the country, the SzDSz's Gabor Demszky won a third consecutive term as mayor of Budapest. With the MSzP and SzDSz also winning enough Budapest city council seats to form a governing coalition, the opposition won control of the capital.

Controversy arose soon after the local elections when the national government announced its unilateral withdrawal from two major public works projects in the capital. Construction of a new national theater was canceled on 29 October, after ground had already been broken. Two weeks later, the government withdrew from a much larger project, the planned construction of a fourth underground metro line for the city. The project was to have been funded jointly by the national and Budapest governments and was supported by a loan already secured from the European Investment Bank. The latter cancellation in particular angered many in Budapest. Though the government claimed that it could no longer afford the project, opponents called the cancellation retribution for the capital's support for opposition parties in the local elections. "The prime minister wants to punish Budapest," Demszky told the weekly *HVG*, "and thus has withdrawn support from all proposed projects." The magazine noted that while withdrawing its 35 billion forint ($155 million) contribution to the metro project for lack of money, the government was nonetheless planning to spend 20 billion forints ($90 million) on the country's millennial anniversary celebrations.

CONTINUED ECONOMIC GROWTH

Despite crises in emerging markets worldwide, the Hungarian economy continued its robust growth in 1998. Improving on a 1997 annual growth rate of 4.6 percent, GDP grew in 1998 by 5.2 percent. Inflation continued to fall, from an annual rate of 18 percent in January to 11 percent in October. Unemployment fell from 10.5 percent in October 1997 to 9.2 percent in October 1998. In February the government finished payment of its last debt to the IMF, nearly two and a half years ahead of schedule. And with mass privatization completed in 1997, 80 percent of the economy was estimated to be in private hands.

The country's newfound economic strength, however, still continued to bypass many Hungarians. Years of economic contraction and stagnation had left many worse off than ever before. The November Transition Report from the European Bank for Reconstruction and Development found that GDP in Hungary had reached 95 percent of its 1989 levels, a figure fifth best among 25 postcommunist countries but still down from communist-era levels. Regional economic disparities were still pronounced, with eastern regions of the country faring the worst.

few major criticisms contained in the European Union's November accession progress report on Hungary. The report concluded that Hungary had "not yet adequately addressed the [required] priority relating to reinforcement of institutional and administrative capacity in regional development" and that "human and financial resources are lacking at all levels" of the regional development program.

A major development in economic policy was the launch on 1 January 1998 of the country's new privately-funded pension program. Though participation in the program was only compulsory for new entrants to the job market, voluntary participation was widespread. Overall, changes in economic policy by the new government were expected to be small, despite the campaign promises of the winning parties. Many analysts and international investors, generally pleased with the Horn government's economic record, believed that Fidesz had promised excessive increases in state spending and unrealistic or destabilizing levels of economic growth. They were also concerned by the ISP's unabashed economic interventionism and protectionism. The Budapest Stock Exchange (BUX) fell 8 percent in the week following Fidesz's strong showing in the first round of the election. Fidesz worked hard, however, to reassure investors that economic policy would remain substantially unchanged. Soon after its second-round victory, the party played down its hopes for a 7 percent increase in GDP growth, its opposition to the crawling-peg currency devaluation regime, and its previous critical assessments of the current state of the national economy.

Thanks to the Russian currency crisis, the BUX suffered a more severe drop in the fall. On 21 September the index reached a low of 3,795, down 58 percent from the year's high of 9,016. By year's end, however, investor confidence in the economy pushed the index back to 6,308, up 67 percent from its September low. According to London's *Financial Times*, the market rebounded because "the message struck home that the country had moved into a different category of risk and that its fortunes are much more influenced by economic developments in the EU than in countries to the east."

INTERNATIONAL RELATIONS

Relations with NATO and the European Union continued to prosper. By December, all NATO members had ratified the country's application for membership, clearing the way for accession in 1999. Substantive negotiations with the EU began in November; soon after, Orban relaxed the Hungarian government's long-held insistence on EU accession by 2002, a date that had been widely viewed as unrealistic. In its November accession progress report, the EU was highly complimentary. In addition to regional development, weaknesses noted were a failure to adequately address the concerns of the Roma (Gypsy) minority, a poor showing in the fight against corruption, and a low level of environmental safeguards. Concerning the Roma and other minority groups, the EU specifically regretted the failure of parliament to approve a pending bill designed to add reserved minority seats to the National Assembly.

Though strongly supportive of EU entry, Orban advocated a tough negotiating strategy, and as an opposition leader he had criticized the Horn government for being too eager to please. Among the new government's negotiating demands was a 10-year ban on foreign ownership of Hungarian agricultural land. Fidesz and its allies had failed to bring the issue to a national referendum in two previous attempts—alongside the NATO membership referendum in November 1997 and in March 1998—but now intended to raise it directly in EU negotiations.

In a departure from its liberal past, Fidesz became a steadfast advocate of Hungarian national concerns. Its rise to power, alongside the adamantly nationalist ISP, aroused fears that the new government would mirror the controversial policies of the Antall government of 1990 to 1994 in its relations with neighboring states. Officials failed to dismiss such impressions in the months following the election. In one controversial statement, made on a July visit to the Romanian province of Transylvania, Orban raised eyebrows by describing his new government as one "whose horizon does not stop at the borders of the Hungarian state when it looks around the world."

Though policy toward Romania and Slovakia became more assertive under Orban, Hungarian relations with its two neighbors improved in some respects. By the end of 1998, for the first time since the end of communist rule ethnic Hungarians were serving as ministers in both the Romanian and the Slovak cabinets. In Romania, the Hungarian Democratic Union of Romania continued its membership in the government formed after the electoral victory of reformist parties in 1996. In Slovakia, the September victory of opposition parties over the government of Vladimir Meciar led to the formation of a new ruling coalition that included the Hungarian Coalition Party, which was granted three cabinet ministries. Both the Horn and Orban governments also continued to voice support for future Romanian and Slovak membership in both NATO and the European Union.

Hungarian-Romanian relations were strained, however, by a flare-up in the longstanding controversy over the Hungarian Democratic Union's proposed reestablishment of a Hungarian-language university in the Transylvanian city of Cluj-Napoca. In September, after an unfavorable parliamentary committee ruling led some members of the governing coalition to consider reversing their support for the university proposal, the Hungarian Democratic Union threatened to leave the government. The Orban government involved itself in the affair by emphasizing the importance of the university to bilateral relations and by declaring itself ready to financially support the institution's establishment. Reports that Orban had delivered an ultimatum on the university to Romanian Prime Minister Radu Vasile while on a visit to Bucharest caused anger in much of the Romanian press, but were downplayed by the Hungarians and repudiated by *Adevarul*, the leading Bucharest newspaper. While a compromise resolution proposing the establishment of a Hungarian-German dual-language university eventually persuaded the HDUR to remain in government, the Hungarian government's active participation in the debate provoked considerable opposition in Romania. Relations with Slovakia, long bedeviled by controversy over the Nagymaros-Gabcikovo dam project on the Danube River, remained tense for most of the year. Though bilateral talks mandated by the International Court of Justice (ICJ) continued, the two sides failed to reach agreement by the Court's March deadline. Hungary and Czechoslovakia had agreed to build the dam in a 1977 treaty, but Hungary withdrew from the agreement in 1989 over environmental concerns. A September 1997 ICJ ruling was generally viewed as favoring Slovakia's claim that Hungary should return to work on the project. In February, one month before the Court's deadline, a Horn government delegation reached a preliminary agreement with the Slovaks that proposed the building of a Hungarian dam. The accord outraged many Hungarians, prompting a large street demonstration in the capital and strong opposition from all major parties, including the government's own Free Democrats. On 23 July, the new Fidesz-led government reversed the Horn policy, rejecting any Hungarian dam construction. The move was followed in September by a Slovak petition to the ICJ asking for stricter enforcement against Hungary of the 1997 ruling. By year's end, the issue remained unresolved.

Controversy also continued throughout much of the year on other issues, including the Hungarian-Slovak basic treaty, a Slovak nuclear power plant, and Slovak minority educational and language policy. The new Hungarian governing parties were vocal both before and after the election in their dissatisfaction with the terms of the treaty, negotiated with the Slovaks by the socialist-liberal government. The new government also announced its opposition to the opening of a new Slovak nuclear power plant not far from the Hungarian border. Conflict over language policy arose in the run-up to the September election, when the Slovak government, citing the country's controversial language law, barred the Hungarian Coalition Party from displaying its Hungarian name more prominently than its Slovak name. Hope for improved relations increased dramatically with Meciar's electoral defeat. But with the new government installed so close to the end of the year, it remained unclear just how much the change in government would affect the two countries' long-strained relations.

Document: HORN BLASTED OVER ROMA

The Hungarian government has made a very public effort to show its willingness to improve the life of the country's Romani minority. That said, a group of Hungarian human-rights organizations—including the European Roma Rights Center and Hungarian Helsinki Committee—circulated a letter protesting comments made by Prime Minister Gyula Horn, whom they accused of reinforcing "Gypsy" stereotypes. Horn's office responded by calling the accusation "entirely false and unfair" and saying that "certain nongovernmental organizations consciously misinterpret the statements of a prime minister who took sides with the Gypsy issue in a way that is unique in Europe." Below are excerpts from one of Horn's most controversial speeches, made at the Szolnok meeting of the Lungo Drom Romani organization on 16 January 1998.

I want to stress again: the situation of the Gypsies is a grave challenge for both the Roma and the majority of society. If we do not treat the problem intelligently, with programs, it may endanger the whole society. . . . It must also be said outright that a significant portion of society has an unfavorable experience regarding Gypsies' willingness to work, abuse of public goods, and observance of community norms and rules. Of course—and we have to admit it just as openly—we can encounter many prejudices, but the minority cannot get along opposed to the majority, and the same thing applies vice versa. . . . We have to state some basic principles, and we have to realize them in practice. We do not think it acceptable—I hope that the Gypsies agree—that for Romani families the only form of making ends meet is the allowance received for the children, and this could be helped only if they [the parents] started working. It is harmful for the ethnic minorities as well, if masses of families build their lives, or are forced to build their lives, on an unemployed existence. We have to change this, first of all by creating workplaces, but also by looking for workplaces.

In this field, we can already observe the traces of a change: in 1997, more than 100,000 Roma were given employment opportunities through the work programs for the public good, 25,000 through public work, and about 30,000 Roma through the support of small regional programs and small entrepreneurs. I wish to make it quite unambiguous that positive discrimination is not the same as favoritism. It would be unacceptable if layers of a similar social situation received less support than the Romani needy. One's otherness, one's origins, does not give any right to social partiality. . . .

It is a well-known fact that Romani society has well-organized local communities, and that inner solidarity is very strong among them. This fact has several positive results. Unfortunately, for historical reasons, this solidarity is often extended to offenders of the laws as well. Today, however, such phenomena are unacceptable even for an ethnic minority. It is my conviction that this phenomenon results in grave damage in the moral reputation of minorities. This is why I believe it is very important for the Gypsies to face this problem and to separate themselves from the criminals.

Translated by David Olah

NOTE

Reprinted with kind permission from *Transitions* magazine, March 1998.

Poland

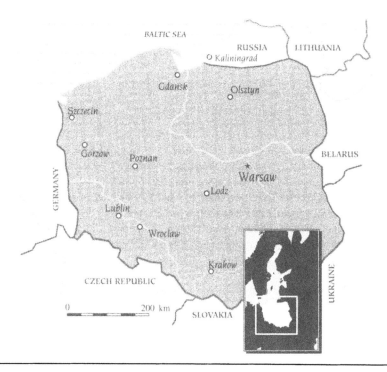

Population: 8,600,000
Capital: .... Warsaw (pop. 1,638,300)
Major cities: .... Lodz (pop. 825,600), Krakow (pop. 745,400),
Wroclaw (pop. 642,700)
Area: .... 312,685 sq. km.
Major ethnic groups: .... Polish 97.6%, German 1.3%, Ukrainian 0.6%,
Belarusian 0.5%
Economy: .... GDP growth: 4.8%
.... Inflation rate: 8.5%
.... Unemployment rate: 10.4%

FORGING AHEAD, BUT STRAINS SHOW

by PETER RUTLAND

1998 was the year in which Poland returned to the path of structural market reform, which had been partly interrupted by the election of a socialist government in 1993. The November 1997 parliamentary election resulted in a coalition government led by Prime Minister Jerzy Buzek and composed of Marian Krzaklewski's Solidarity Electoral Action (AWS), itself an amalgam of two dozen labor unions and center-right parties, with Leszek Balcerowicz's Freedom Union (UW) as a junior partner. The enthusiasm with which the market liberals returned to power was blunted over the course of 1998, as it became apparent that they were politically outnumbered by their AWS coalition partner, whose leaders had their own populist agenda.

The magnet of European Union entry was an important force driving the renewal of reform. The pace of adaptation of laws and administrative structures to European Union norms rapidly accelerated. Although economic growth continued at a brisk pace, the government's determination to press ahead with structural reforms in local government, health, pensions, and education, while cutting the remaining sectors of state-subsidized industry, ran the risk of provoking a social backlash.

ALL POLITICS IS LOCAL

The ruling coalition of AWS and UW which replaced the left-wing government of the Democratic Left Alliance (SLD) and the Polish Peasant Party (PSL) was a curious hybrid of market liberals, union activists, and Catholic nationalists whose strains became increasingly apparent over the course of the year. Although the AWS held 201 seats in the Sejm and the UW only 60, the AWS provided only 16 ministers and the UW six, filling the important ministries of foreign affairs (Bronislaw Geremek), justice (Hanna Suchocka), and defense (Janusz Onyszkiewicz), not forgetting Deputy Prime Minister and Finance Minister Leszek Balcerowicz. Because of the wealth of talent in the UW ranks and their unity behind energetic reform, in contrast to the fractionalism of the AWS, the UW was able to punch above its weight and provide more leadership to the government's program than the party's level of public support would warrant.

The new center-right government also had to learn the art of cohabitation with socialist President Aleksander Kwasniewski, elected in 1995. Their main problem was mustering a two-thirds majority in parliament to overcome presidential vetoes: the governing coalition had only 261 of the Sejm's 460 seats. The new 1997 constitution clarified the respective duties of the two branches of government—and the new cabinet stopped the former practice of inviting the president to send representatives to its meetings. Since passage of the 1997 constitution the Constitutional Tribunal has emerged as an important arbiter, and respect for the rule of law seems to have been strengthened.

The main political event of the year was the controversy over the introduction of a new three-tier system of local government to replace the old two-tier arrangement (that in itself had only been introduced in 1975). This was the biggest reform of domestic administrative and political structures seen in any post-Communist country to date. It provoked fierce political debate, threatening the unity of the ruling coalition and showing the limits of its power. Elections to the new councils, originally scheduled for June, were delayed until October.

In order to rationalize regional government the previous 49 provinces (*wojewodztwo*) were cut to 16. The new middle tier consists of 308 districts (*powiat*) and 65 towns with the status of district. Beneath them are 2,500 municipalities (*gmina*). The idea was that the new, larger provinces would be better able to coordinate regional economic development, while beneath them the new layer of district councils would be more responsive to democratic input from the community. The government originally proposed to create only 12 provinces, but faced fierce protests in May from cities that would lose their status as provincial centers. Opponents demanded a referendum on the issue. President Aleksander Kwasniewski vetoed the bill on 2 July, to widespread public approval, and the government lacked the two-thirds majority to overcome the presidential veto. The government was forced to compromise and upped the number to 16. Protests continued in some towns even after the new borders were signed into law on 27 July.

The AWS expelled the Confederation for an Independent Poland–Patriotic Camp (KPN-OP) led by Adam Slomka, one of its member parties, for opposing the creation of larger provinces. The KPN-OP formed a new four-party right-wing alliance, the Fatherland Patriotic Movement, to compete in the October elections.

The new councils will have enhanced responsibilities for providing government services, and will control roughly half of public spending. In July an ambitious educational reform was adopted, to be introduced in September 1999. Primary education will stay with the municipalities, but primary school will be shortened from 8 to 6 years and new two-year gymnasiums will be set up under the control of the districts. The measure was criticized by the Peasant Party, afraid of losing the patronage it formerly enjoyed in small rural communities.

Local government elections finally took place on 11 October. Turnout was 46 percent, higher than the previous local election (34 percent), but less than some had expected given the protests over the reforms. AWS, campaigning on the slogan "Family-Community-Fatherland," won 16 percent of the vote and 10,613 of the 63,765 seats. They were closely followed by the Democratic Left Alliance (SLD) who won 14 percent (8,840 seats). Third place was taken by the Social Alliance (PS), a coalition of the Polish Peasants' Party (PSL), the Labor Union

(UP), and the National Pensioners Party (7 percent), ahead of the liberal Freedom Union with only 2 percent (1,141 seats). The right-wing Fatherland Patriotic Movement and Catholic Polish Family won only 0.4 percent and 0.2 percent respectively; 38,000 seats went to independents.

The main political lessons of the elections were a resurgence in the fortunes of the socialist SLD and the PSL, a denting of prestige for the ruling UW, and no sign of any deep grassroots for the Catholic right. Because of differing regional concentrations in party support, the SLD ended up in control of eight of the 16 provinces (alone or in coalition), the AWS six, and UW only one—Wroclaw, where they ran in coalition with a popular local mayor. Despite the UW's weakened position in local government, it was still a necessary partner for AWS in order to fend off the threat from the SLD.

AWS was keen to beat back the revived fortunes of the SLD, especially with an eye to the presidential election forthcoming in 2000. AWS made some efforts to gain control over the state television network, Telewizja Polska (TVP), or at least weaken the grip of its head, Robert Kwiatkowski, who ran President Kwasniewski's 1995 election campaign and stayed close to the SLD. AWS pressed for the appointment of a new board to replace the existing five-person panel, which included two persons tied to the SLD, two with the PSL, and one with the UW. AWS threatened to declare TVP bankrupt to try to force changes in the board.

In July the government approved a plan to reform the judicial system in order to cut down on delays (it can take up to four years for civil cases to reach their first hearing), creating some 400 new local courts to deal with minor offenses. Organized crime has made inroads in Poland, as elsewhere in Eastern Europe. The former head of Poland's police force, Marek Papala, was shot dead on 25 June. Russia formally protested a wave of attacks on Russian tourists, but Polish police responded with the remark that the attacks were probably carried out by other Russians. A new criminal procedure code and penal code took effect on 1 September. They were aimed at bringing the criminal justice system into line with the European Convention on Human Rights, and included greater emphasis on defense rights, a reduction of the maximum detention time without charge from 72 to 48 hours, and abolition of the death penalty. A new Commissioner for Civil Rights Protection was introduced, with a staff of 130.

Meanwhile, much anxiety was generated by the travails of Polish soccer. The government's tourism officer suspended the entire leadership of the Polish Soccer Association in May for incompetence and corruption, but was forced to reinstate it after the International Federation of Football Associations threatened to exclude Poland from international soccer events. Dissatisfaction with the association's leadership led to a boycott of matches by some clubs. Perhaps the most noteworthy social trend of the year was that for the first time per capita beer consumption in Poland exceeded that of spirits.

LEGACIES OF THE PAST

Finding a place for the Catholic Church in a democratic, secular Poland continued to be a source of friction. A major step forward was the signing of a formal concordat with the Vatican on 13 February, recognizing the rights of the church but also noting the separation of church and state. The previous leftist government had delayed signing the pact, which had been ready in 1993. Pro-church forces did not have the votes in the Sejm to do much to advance the Church's agenda, although on 17 December the Sejm did vote to ban sex education from schools. The church complained that the government was too slow in returning church property that was seized during communist rule.

Controversy over the site of the former death camp in Auschwitz flared up once again in August. In response to appeals from the Catholic radio station Radio Maryja and sundry anti-Semitic activists, more than a hundred new crosses were planted in a gravel pit adjacent to the camp, in protest against efforts to remove an 8 meter cross that had been erected a year earlier. Jews complained that the crosses were politicizing a place of mourning, while the cross-planters argued that Catholics had also died at Auschwitz. Cardinal Jozef Glemp called protests from the Israeli parliament an attempt to "impose foreign will" and refused to call for the removal of the cross. Government efforts to gain possession of the land, with a view to removing the crosses (or at least reducing the number), were blocked by a Oswiecim (Auschwitz) municipal court decision in October. One positive development was the March handover of the former synagogue in Oswiecim to the Jewish community, the first such property to be transferred as part of a new restitution program.

Despite the presence of vociferous anti-communists on the right wing of the political spectrum, Poland has made little progress in confronting the legacy of the communist years. Back in 1990 Solidarity Prime Minister Tadeusz Mazowiecki adopted the position that Poland should draw "a thick line" to mark off the communist past from the democratic future, which came to be interpreted as doing nothing. Mainly this was because of fears that such an exercise would be too socially divisive: memories of martial law were still raw. Indeed, in 1992 a scandal around a list (later proved false) of alleged secret police collaborators brought down the government of Jan Olszewski. After social democrats took power in 1993, dealing with the past was quietly dropped from the national agenda.

With the return of the right to power in 1997 the issue once again became the focus of attention. In December 1997 parliament passed a law allowing the dismissal of judges and prosecutors who took part in political trials between 1944 and 1989. The Constitutional Tribunal decreed on 24 June 1998 that the law was unconstitutional interference with the judiciary, although it did allow former judges to be stripped of some retirement bonuses. In December Justice Minister Hanna Suchocka announced that prosecutors who handed down unfair verdicts during the period 1944–1956 will have special pension benefits withdrawn.

Poland

On 18 June the Sejm took a symbolic but important vote to condemn communism as a system alien to Polish traditions. (The vote was 250 to 150, with 31 abstentions.) President Kwasniewski opposed the measure, arguing that it was trying to divide Polish society "into good and bad people." The AWS pressed ahead with proposals to expose former collaborators with the secret police, a process known as "lustration" (from the Latin, meaning "to cast light"). Parliament passed a law requiring those seeking elected positions or senior posts in state service to declare whether they had cooperated with the security police. Kwasniewski refused to sign the bill, citing constitutional concerns, until ordered to do so by the Constitutional Tribunal on 22 October. Officials who are later found (by a special lustration prosecutor) to have lied in such declarations will be barred from public office for 10 years. (Even before the new law candidates to the Sejm and Senate already had to declare that they had not willingly cooperated with the secret police.) By year's end 23,000 declarations had been filed, and at least 100 admitted some sort of involvement with the communist secret police.

On 18 December parliament overrode a presidential veto, and passed a law allowing victims of repression to see their former secret police files. The bill also created an Institute of National Remembrance to hold the former state archives. The vote (by 282 to 164) was the first time since taking office that the AWS-UW coalition was able to override a presidential veto. In June the trial began in Gdansk of seven former officials accused of involvement in the shooting of 44 workers in the December 1970 protests. At the end of the year it was announced that Poland will pay $366,000 to Colonel Ryszard Kuklinski, an intelligence officer who passed thousands of documents to the CIA before fleeing Poland in 1984. In absentia he was sentenced to death and his property was confiscated, although these sentences were revoked in 1995.

WELFARE REFORMS

Contrary to the image of austerity associated with the imposition of "shock therapy," in reality social spending had mushroomed in Poland in 1989–90 as eligibility criteria for pensions were relaxed. In 1998 Balcerowicz, former prime minister and since 1997 serving as deputy prime minister, boldly tackled this problem by introducing a new pension system, modeled on reforms introduced in Chile and Argentina. All workers under the age of 30 would henceforth be required to contribute part of their social security taxes to one of two dozen private and self-financing pension funds. Workers over the age of 50 will stay in the existing pay-as-you-go system (funded directly out of the state budget), while those aged 30 to 50 can choose to join the new system or stay in the old one. Time will tell whether Polish capital markets will be robust enough to make the new private pension funds viable. A similar radical reform was introduced to generate more reliable funding for the health care system. Sixteen new health insurance funds are to be created, financed by mandatory worker contributions equaling 7.5 percent of their gross income.

Balcerowicz ran into opposition within his own government with his proposals to overhaul the tax system. He initially proposed a flat rate 22 percent income tax, but had to settle for a two-tier income tax system. The Catholic-nationalist Christian-National Union (ZChN), a member of the AWS, pushed Balcerowicz to introduce more pro-family measures. Initial proposals to grant tax exemptions for children would eventually have cost 1 billion zlotys ($250 million) a year. On 6 November the government agreed on a compromise measure granting relief to families with three children, which will cost $44 million. Other factions in the AWS were pushing hard for tax exemptions for union contributions.

ECONOMY MOVES FORWARD

Poland saw its GDP growth rate slow to 5 percent in 1998; down on previous years, but still a trail-blazer among the transition economies. Under a law passed in August 1997 a new autonomous Council for Monetary Policy came into operation in January 1998, which slowed the pace of nominal depreciation of the zloty and brought inflation down to 9 percent by year's end. Exports continued to grow, but so did imports, leaving a persistent trade deficit of around $9 billion, which was easily covered by incoming investment and by unreported exports (thought to be worth $3 billion a year).

In addition to maintaining previous polices of liberalization and macroeconomic stabilization, the government also tackled some of the remaining sectors of state-subsidized industry. In June they revealed a plan to cut 45,000 jobs in steel mills. In July the government announced a restructuring plan which should halve employment and close 24 of the 50 plus coal mines over three years. Poland's mines lose 3 billion zlotys ($750 million) a year: since 1989 output has fallen from 180 million to 133 million tons, while employment fell from 400,000 to 240,000. The scheme included generous severance pay of 44,000 zlotys ($11,000) per miner to win the acceptance of the politically-powerful mining unions. It will cost some $4 billion, about $1 billion of which will come from the EU and World Bank. It was endorsed by the Sejm in November.

Also in April the government adopted a medium-term strategy for agriculture. Long-term, the sector's fate is intimately connected with the conditions of Poland's entry to the EU. (See the accompanying article by Andrzej Rudka.) According to an EU study released in September, the average yearly income of a family farm in Poland is 2,500 ecus ($2,700) compared with some 17,500 ecus in the EU. The agricultural sector accounts for only 6 percent of Poland's GDP (down from 13 percent in 1989), despite the fact that it involves 27 percent of the population.

Throughout June–August farmers blocked railroad lines and public roads in protest against government policies which were flooding the country with cheaper food imports—including subsidized food from the EU. On 10 July 10,000 farmers marched in Warsaw. The government eventually responded to the protests, imposing higher customs duties on imported grain, but not pork.

In July 1998, the Polish government adopted a plan to sell most of the remaining state assets by the end of 2001, involving 1,800 companies and 35 percent of Polish employees. The plan includes the two largest steel mills (Katowice and Sendzimira), the national airline LOT, and insurance giant PZU. Revenue, which is hoped to reach $30 billion, will be used to pay compensation claims of former private owners and to finance the new pension system. Two state-owned banks were privatized in 1997 and several more will be sold off in 1999. Back in 1995 15 National Investment Funds had been created to manage the privatization of about 500 enterprises (and citizens were given vouchers in the funds). Since June 1998, the funds have been listed on the Warsaw Stock Exchange. On 19 October Poland began selling a 15 percent stake in the national phone company Telekomunikacja Polska (TPSA). Foreign investors were wary, given that a regulatory agency to monitor the industry had not yet been set in place. Poland has lagged three to four years behind other transition economies in liberalizing and privatizing its state telephone monopoly.

Social unrest was relatively muted, with the farm protests causing the most disruption. There were some strikes by miners against the pension reform, and by arms factory workers over wage arrears. The most sustained strike action came from railway workers, who were pressing for a 30 percent salary hike. Half the nation's trains were idle on 18 June as a result of their strike. The most serious social unrest came in the northern city of Slupsk in January, where youths rioted for three days following the killing of a young demonstrator by police.

Perhaps the biggest block to economic development is the appalling road system. Poland has a grand total of 260 kilometers of divided highway. In Europe, only Albania and Romania have worse roads. For most of its length across Polish territory the Berlin-Warsaw-Moscow "highway" has a single lane in each direction, which is shared by speeding Mercedes, sputtering Fiat 650s, huge TIR trailers, and the occasional tractor. For the past six years there have been plans to build 2,600 km of limited access, four-lane highways at an estimated cost of $8 billion. The problem is that these roads are supposed to be funded through private investment, to be recouped from tolls. Such schemes have been disastrous in Mexico and Hungary (drivers find the tolls exorbitant and use local roads). Hence private developers are not rushing to build these roads, and in the meantime the death rate on Polish roads is 10 times the UK level.

GETTING READY FOR EUROPE

At a meeting in Brussels on 30 March the foreign ministers of the 15 European Union member countries signed accession partnership agreements with the 10 countries being considered for membership. The five countries in the fast track for entry are Poland, Hungary, Czech Republic, Slovenia, and Estonia (plus Cyprus). The others are Bulgaria, Romania, Slovakia, Latvia, and Lithuania. The European Commission began screening each applicant's compliance in 31 separate policy areas (involving 80,000 pages of regulations). On 10 November talks formally opened with the five first-line countries in Brussels. Agreement was reached on three non-controversial chapters (education, science, and research): next in line are foreign and security policy; audiovisual policy, industrial policy, and telecommunications. Tough subjects, such as farming and labor mobility, will be left till the end.

However, expansion of EU membership cannot proceed until the EU resolves its own problems of internal governance and reforms its budgetary spending. Decision-making is already a problem with 15 members: if that number goes up to 25, the "democratic deficit" will become impossibly wide. Currently most of the 85 million ecu ($95 billion) budget is spent on the Common Agricultural Policy and on regional subsidies for poorer countries (Ireland, Greece, Portugal). One or both of these programs will have to be radically cut if funds are to be available to help the new member-countries catch up. The new entrants are poorer than any of the existing members: Slovenia's per capita GDP is 68 percent of the EU average, but Poland's is only 40 percent. Closer harmonization of civic and economic rights will not work if such large disparities in living standards persist. The EU leaders' summit in Vienna in December 1998 was dominated by financial wrangling and failed to resolve any of these budgetary and governance issues.

In May Poland presented a National Program for the Adoption of the Acquis Communautaire (EU laws), which laid out a busy legislative agenda for the next two years, covering everything from the sewage sludge directive to national emergency oil stocks. The Polish parliament has already passed much legislation to bring Poland in line with EU practices, but laws are still lacking in some areas such as environmental policy. As the legislative program moves forward, attention is now shifting to the question of administrative implementation. Only 10 percent of 18,000 product standards have been harmonized, for example.

The European Commission issued country reports in November detailing each applicant's progress in preparing itself for entry. Poland received high marks for its democracy and competitive market economy. Trade liberalization was well advanced, though the report noted "some serious reverses" in 1998 (Poland's ban on beef gelatin imports, and its refusal to cut tariffs on steel imports), and "notable difficulties persisting in the field of agricultural products (spirits tariffs, livestock, fruit, and vegetables)." In January the EU suspended Polish milk imports, citing quality concerns. While Poland's legislative program was generally deemed satisfactory, there were doubts about the effectiveness of its administrative machinery, hampered by shortage of funds and personnel.

At a 29 October conference Tadeusz Mazowiecki, head of the Sejm Committee for European Integration, remarked "Without losing our Slavic identity, we need to get rid of our Slavic sluggishness." There is a special European Integration Committee with 270 staff to hasten the process along, but its head, Ryszard

Czarnecki, was fired in July after the EU announced on 25 May it was cutting aid to Poland by 32 million ecu ($35 million) to 178 million ecu ($200 million), because Poland had failed to prepare sufficient projects requesting the funds. The European Commission report concluded that Poland should be able to meet single market criteria "in the medium term," which presumably means Poland cannot expect to enter for at least four or five years. Time is not necessarily on their side, since there is a danger that as awareness of the costs of entry increase, public opinion could become more skeptical. A poll carried put in June showed that some 58 percent of citizens supported entry into the EU—about 20 percent lower than polls in previous years.

FRIENDS TO THE WEST . . .

There were a few hiccups during the year in Poland's normally excellent relations with Germany, mainly connected to uncertainty over the timetable for Polish entry to the EU. German fears about being swamped by cheap Polish labor were matched by Polish fears of being swamped by German investors, buying up cheap Polish land.

German Chancellor Helmut Kohl, French President Jacques Chirac, and Polish President Kwasniewski held a "Weimar Triangle" meeting in Poznan on 21 February, reaffirming the three countries' close collaboration. However on 25 February the German ambassador to the EU Dietrich von Kyaw said that open access for Poles to the German labor market would be "unthinkable" immediately upon entering the EU. In May, the Bundestag passed a resolution calling on Poland to acknowledge the right of German exiles to settle in areas from which they had been expelled in 1945. The Polish Sejm responded with a 3 July statement reaffirming the inviolability of Polish borders and property rights. Germany's Union of Expellees, which claims to represent 12 million former residents of Polish and Czech territories and their descendants, suggested that Poland's EU membership should be conditional on its meeting their claims. In response Poland's former slave laborers in Germany (for whom the German government has already created a $300 million fund) started upping their compensation demands. (Poland has already paid its own compensation to Poles expelled from territories taken by Soviet Union in 1945.)

When Chancellor Kohl was at the helm, Poland was confident that its interests would be respected. On 20 October Kwasniewski presented Kohl with the Order of the White Eagle, and in his acceptance speech Kohl reiterated that "Europe without Poland is not complete." The next week saw the electoral victory of Gerhard Schroeder of the Social Democrats, who did not share Kohl's sense of historical mission, and who was expected to take a harder line over protecting German jobs. While the new government repeated its willingness to see Poland enter the EU it also started to espouse a "new realism" about the timetable for entry. While Polish politicians were still talking about 2002 or 2003 as possible entry dates, Germans were talking about 2006 or thereabouts.

...AND TO THE EAST

Poland has been pursuing an ingenious policy of reaching out to its Eastern neighbors as part and parcel of its efforts to integrate with the West. (See the accompanying article by Timothy Snyder.) 1998 saw some strains in relations with its eastern neighbors, however.

First and foremost these arose because of Poland's steps to tighten control over its eastern border—steps taken at the urging of the EU, keen to stem the flow of illegal immigrants as far away from German borders as possible. (Since 1993, Germany has given Poland $67 million to reinforce border posts on its eastern frontier.) From 1 January 1998 Poland introduced a law requiring visitors without a visa to prove they have the financial resources to pay for their stay. Visitors from Russia and Belarus were required to buy a visa, costing $20—something that was not required of visitors from Ukraine and Lithuania, whose governments had signed re-admission agreements under which they pledge to take back persons illegally crossing the border into Poland. Border crossings fell 80 percent as a result, severely hitting the cross-border trade, much of it unregistered, which generates at least $2 billion (and possibly as much as $7 billion) per year. Later in the year, in response to protests from market traders, Russians and Belarusians were allowed to purchase multiple-entry visas for about $10.

The EU was not happy with the relaxation of the visa rules, nor were they pleased in July when Poland (and Lithuania) broke ranks and decided not to join the EU's visa restrictions against Belarus, introduced in retaliation for the closure of the embassy compound in Minsk.

The August crisis in Russia caused some panicked reactions in Warsaw. Fears of economic catastrophe and civic unrest led to offers of food aid especially for Kaliningrad enclave. President Kwasniewski urged "sensible silence," and the crisis passed. Relations with Moscow remained rather tetchy—for example, there was an angry Russian reaction to the appearance of rebel Chechen President Aslan Maskhadov at an international conference on human rights in Warsaw on 13 October.

Despite the advances made toward market democracy, geography still obliges Poland to look over its shoulder at Russia. But with Russia's share of Poland's trade down to 10 percent, the likely economic consequences of disorder further east should not be exaggerated.

ON COURSE FOR NATO

At the Madrid summit back in July 1997 Poland, Hungary, and the Czech Republic were told they would be invited to join NATO, and formal accession protocols were signed in December 1997. Polish politicians breathed a huge sigh of relief. One of the main goals of the democratic transition had been realized: NATO entry was seen as wiping clean the betrayal of Poland at Yalta in 1945.

The last possible barrier fell in April 1998, when the U.S. Senate voted to confirm NATO expansion. Pending full entry (which was to happen in April

1999), Poland seemed to be doing relatively little to prepare itself. The 1999 budget allocation for the army was only 1.91 percent of GDP, down from 2.3 percent in 1997. Poland will spend 8 billion zlotys ($2.3 billion) by 2003 to upgrade its armed forces to NATO standards, mainly involving language training and modernization of communications and air traffic control systems.

The defense ministers of Poland, Germany, and Denmark met in Szczecin on 5 September and agreed to create a joint NATO military corps, with 60,000 troops in three mechanized divisions, one from each country.

In November the government announced that from 1999 compulsory military service will be cut from 18 to 12 months, and exemptions for higher education will be tightened. (In 1997 of 220,000 young men who were issued draft notices, 130,000 took deferments based on continuing education.) The intent is to shrink the armed forces from 240,000 to 180,000 over five years.

1998 saw the revival of the Visegrad group of Poland, Hungary, and Czech Republic, with a view to coordinating these nations' policies as they move toward NATO and EU entry. The Visegrad group was originally formed in 1991, but ceased meeting after 1995, in large part due to the skeptical attitude of then Czech Premier Vaclav Klaus. On 21 October the prime ministers of Hungary, Poland, and the Czech Republic gathered in Budapest and agreed to resume regular meetings.

Polish Foreign Minister Bronislaw Geremek took over as chair-in-office of the 54-country Organization for Security and Cooperation in Europe in 1998. He tried to play an active role in the Kosovo conflict, in monitoring developments in Belarus, and in restarting negotiations over frozen conflicts in Caucasus, Central Asia, and Moldova. There was not much to show for his efforts at year's end, but at least Poland was trying to solve problems rather than cause them.

GLOSSARY

AWS	Solidarity Electoral Action
PS	Social Alliance
PSL	Polish Peasant Party
SLD	Democratic Left Alliance
UW	Freedom Union

LOOK EAST, FACE WEST

by TIM SNYDER

Since 1989, Poland has played an increasingly important role as a foreign policy leader in Central and Eastern Europe. It has devised its own Ostpolitik, navigating the rocky shores of national memory, ethnic identity, immigration, and trade. The U.S. State Department has recognized Poland's success in its domestic and foreign policy, calling on the country to serve as "an exporter of democracy to its neighbors" (referring primarily to Belarus and Slovakia). At the same time, as Poland approaches full membership in the European Union (EU), it faces new pressures from its Western European partners to close its eastern borders, creating new tensions that threaten to undermine the successes of its eastern policy.

Trade with Poland is critical to all of the country's eastern neighbors. Hundreds of thousands of Russians, Lithuanians, Belarusians, and Ukrainians make their livelihoods on the Polish border or in the enormous bazaars near major cities. The volume of this trade in 1997 was estimated by the Polish Foreign Ministry at between $2.2 billion and $3 billion. But more than money is at stake. In Poland, eastern visitors gain some experience in a society where capitalism works and learn that economic reform can bring prosperity.

As Poland negotiates for accession to the EU, however, it is losing room to maneuver with the countries on its eastern frontiers. Not only trade, but hard-won successes in regional cooperation are at risk.

POLAND'S QUIET OSTPOLITIK

Since 1989, Poland's eastern policy has been based on the simple premises that Poland, Lithuania, Belarus, and Ukraine all deserved independence within their present borders, and that they were all interested in improving relations with Western states and institutions. These ideas may seem simple, but they were the fruits of long reflection and debate within Polish emigrant circles (especially those associated with the journal *Kultura* in Paris) and the Polish opposition. In practice, they put Polish policy a step ahead of those of the United States and of Western European powers. In 1990, Foreign Minister Krzysztof Skubiszewski, who served in every Solidarity cabinet between August 1989 and September 1993, initiated a two-track eastern policy. By engaging the Soviet republics as equal partners well before the collapse of the Soviet Union, Skubiszewski blazed trails for the West to follow.

As then-U.S. President George Bush delivered his "Chicken Kiev" speech in August 1991, urging Ukraine to stay in the Soviet Union, Poland had already paved the way for official relations with the new Ukrainian Republic. When the Soviet Union disintegrated, Western attention turned to potential ethnic and border conflicts among the newly-independent states. In 1992, Poland initiated a policy of what Skubiszewski called "European standards," designed to stabilize the region and thereby smooth the way for Poland's return to Europe. The aim was to persuade the country's eastern neighbors that certain norms of international law were binding in Europe, and that their acceptance would help post-communist states join Western institutions.

In particular, Poland told Lithuania, Belarus, and Ukraine that relations should be based on recognition of existing borders, that national minorities should be granted cultural rights, and that historical disputes should be relegated to the domain of historians.

Armed with draft treaties along these lines, Poland succeeded in propagating these simple European standards and signed comprehensive treaties with those three countries. In the early 1990s, talk of anticipated problems of the Polish minority (there are at least 260,000 Poles in Lithuania, 420,000 in Belarus, and 220,000 in Ukraine) and of Polish revanche in the East silently disappeared from Western intelligence reports and newspapers.

These principles, however, were quickly tested by all three of Poland's eastern neighbors. One of the first acts of independent Lithuania in September 1991 was to dissolve the local governmental authorities of its Polish minority, which the country charged with supporting the coup plotters in Moscow and cooperating with the KGB. The country then refused to hold fresh elections to replace those authorities, which froze Polish-Lithuanian relations. While Poland opposed the ethnic Polish minority's demands for territorial autonomy, it demanded that it enjoy equal civil rights. In late 1992, Lithuania finally held local elections but then made signing a treaty with Poland dependent on a Polish apology for its inter-war occupation of Vilnius. Poland stuck to its European standards approach (in this case, to the idea that international law trumps historical myth), and Lithuania finally compromised in 1994. As Polish efforts to join the European Union and NATO began to bear fruit, Lithuanian leaders realized that they risked falling behind and accepted that good relations with Poland were necessary to join European institutions.

Whereas Lithuania initially wanted nothing to do with Poland, Ukraine at first wanted more help than Poland was willing to provide, hoping for a strategic alliance to balance the power of Russia. Poland was unwilling to ally itself with Ukraine, though it did its part in explaining to the West that Kyiv's reticence to surrender its nuclear weapons to Moscow was not unfounded. By the mid-1990s, Ukraine was balancing its foreign policy, forging close political ties with Western states and Poland, while sustaining healthy economic relations with Russia.

Belarus is a different story. During the early 1990s, while the country sought closer ties with the West, its relations with Poland were cordial, evolving in a friendly fashion. But the election of Alyaksandr Lukashenka as Belarus's president in July 1994 turned Belarusian foreign policy to the East and ended political cooperation with Poland.

The successes of Skubiszewski's eastern policy bolstered a leading goal of the post-communist governments of 1993–1997: a common return to Europe. With most of the difficult problems solved, and Poland well on the way to membership in the EU and NATO, Skubiszewski's successors could explain to their eastern neighbors that better relations with Poland would expedite their own return to the West. In Lithuania and Ukraine, where the elite consensus in favor of European integration was solid, this approach was successful. Poland now enjoys regular consultation at the level of presidents, parliaments, and governments with both Ukraine and Lithuania. In particular, Ukrainian President Leonid Kuchma and Polish President Aleksander Kwasniewski have cultivated close ties: Kwasniewski jokes that he sees more of his Ukrainian counterpart than he does of his wife. Surveys show that 99.5 percent of Ukrainians, despite a history of bloody conflict with Poland, do not regard Poland as a threat. The two countries have even formed a joint peace-keeping battalion meant to serve in future missions of the United Nations or of the Organization for Security and Cooperation in Europe.

Lukashenka, on the other hand, regards European integration as Western imperialism. In his eyes, Poland is the front line of the West's assault on the Slavic heartland. Lukashenka does not want to return to Europe and seeks to limit contacts with Poland to trade. In this, he has not been entirely successful. Belarusian patriots, generally suspicious of Poland in the early 1990s, now seek Poland's help. The country has sustained trade with Belarusian entrepreneurs, and private Polish and American institutions may open a Belarusian-language radio station on Polish territory. Such measures—economically important trade to support an emerging middle class, and objective information to counter the government-dominated media—could play a critical role in helping sustain the beleaguered Belarusian democratic opposition.

Trade matters more than may be apparent. Anyone who takes a train from Belarus to Poland is likely to see Belarusian travelers alight with a plastic bag full of vodka, which they hide from the border guards and then sell at the next station for Polish zloty.

They spend the zloty (or convert them to dollars) and return home. Of the 70,000 registered Belarusian private entrepreneurs, 40,000 got their start in Poland. These traders showed their political clout earlier this year, successfully resisting Lukashenka's attempt to tax them out of existence. Unlike the marches of Belarusian patriots, their strike got results. Lukashenka can afford to mock Belarusian patriots as the lackeys of the West, but he cannot afford to close down access to the consumer goods that petty traders provide.

EAST-WEST SQUEEZE

At the moment when Belarusian traders recognized their political clout, Poland pulled the rug out from under them. Under pressure from the EU, the new center-right, post-Solidarity government tightened Poland's border with Belarus early in 1998. The policy change targeted the Belarusian government, which had refused to sign a readmission agreement with Poland—that would have permitted the return of illegal immigrants to their country of origin (Lithuania and Ukraine have signed similar agreements). But it hit Belarusian and Polish traders, who responded by blockading roads. Polish Foreign Minister Bronislaw Geremek stoically declared that Poland was willing to part with billions of dollars of eastern trade in order to join the EU. The EU signaled that such a gesture was not yet necessary, Poland eased entry requirements, and trade resumed.

Although the Polish Interior Ministry insisted that all of this was simply the implementation of the new immigration law, the flip-flopping indicates that Poland's eastern policy is now hostage to the EU: Ostpolitik is beholden to Westpolitik. On the touchy question of its long eastern border, Poland's slow adoption of the EU's acquis communautaire (body of law) weakens its negotiating position, and Poland is aware that the country cannot risk being perceived by any of its western neighbors as a source of illegal immigrants.

The successes of Poland's eastern policy since 1989 were achieved in Europe's name. Now that Poland must play Europe's game, these achievements are at risk. Poland's Ostpolitik healed old wounds and popularized the idea of Europe. It succeeded by anticipating problems before they arose and by not abusing a position of relative power. Now that Poland's hands are tied, a dose of the same farsightedness would help the EU promote peace and prosperity along what will soon become, after all, its own eastern border.

NOTE

Reprinted with kind permission from *Transitions* magazine, September 1998.

RURAL RECKONING

by ANDRZEJ RUDKA

Poland has become a battleground for fighting out the explosive issue of European Union agriculture policies. On both sides of the negotiating table, vested interests, social and political realities, and disputes over who will receive the substantial EU subsidies for agriculture all complicate the process of bringing Polish produce to the new open market.

As the country enters accession talks, the politics of governments in Warsaw and of the EU itself have postponed the day of reckoning, especially for Poland's small farming sector, at the expense of the modernization of Polish agriculture as a whole. Meanwhile, the EU is slow to reform its agricultural subsidy program and takes advantage of its stronger bargaining position to shortchange its new partners and protect existing EU agricultural structures.

There is no question that Polish agriculture must change. Poland's 2 million farms average under 8 hectares while the average EU farm has about 18 hectares; over a third of the country's farms are just 1 to 3 hectares. Only the larger farms have a good chance of surviving accession to the EU. Small farms will have to be consolidated, and infrastructure and services in the countryside must be developed. Such changes are essential, not only to help increase the efficiency of the Polish agricultural industry but also to dramatically improve the quality of life for Polish farmers.

Agriculture's share of Poland's gross domestic product has been slowly decreasing, although in 1996 at 6.5 percent it was still much higher than the 2.5 percent EU average. About 25 percent of the Polish population works in agriculture, though only 11–12 percent make their living exclusively or mainly from it. The food industry constitutes an increasingly important part of the Polish economy. In 1995, it accounted for 12.9 percent of total industrial employment and 18.5 percent of production, while investment in the sector doubled between 1993 and 1995. Some of the largest Polish companies, 90 out of 500 major Polish enterprises, operate in this still mostly state-owned sector. The privatization program, just shaping up, is attracting foreign investment.

Polish agriculture does offer comparative advantages over the EU's, notably lower labor costs and ecologically healthier products. Both of these characteristics are threatened, however. In 1990, Poland created the Agricultural Market Agency, which follows the EU's Common Agricultural Policy (CAP) by establishing minimum prices to stabilize the markets and protect farmers' income. Yet the policy has not brought stability in prices or farm incomes. The removal of most subsidies to farmers in the early 1990s as part of economic reform and the widening gap between prices and costs contributed to a drop in production in the early years of transition, and in 1993 Poland's traditional agricultural trade surplus turned into a deficit. Any improvement in this situation will require substantial modernization of the agriculture industry. The difficulty of such modernization is complicated by the fact that the agricultural policies of Brussels themselves must be reformed. The CAP has been as much a political as an economic program, and enlargement agreements will have to cope with pressure from such major beneficiaries of the program as France, Germany, and Britain against increasing contributions. The subsidies continue to be a major burden to the overall EU budget, and there are plans for further reductions, by 10 percent to 30 percent, to make EU products more competitive in world markets, which would also narrow the gap between Polish and EU agricultural prices.

RULES OF THE GAME

The Polish association agreement, signed on 16 December 1991, is the foundation for agricultural trade between Poland and the EU. It subjects agricultural products to selective and limited liberalization, but it only applies to some products and for most of them only reduces—not abolishes—trade barriers. But agricultural trade performance after the agreement has been particularly disappointing, despite the improved access for Polish products to the EU market; Poland's growing agricultural trade deficit with the EU has fueled fears that in fact the union is not ready to open its agricultural market to countries like Poland.

Since 1995, Brussels has provided guidelines to help the applicant countries prepare to join the EU internal market. Some 40 percent of EU legislation and regulations concern agriculture. But Poland, like its Central European neighbors, has been dissatisfied with many of the provisions, such as those requiring applicants to meet more stringent environmental standards than current EU members.

In July 1997, the European Commission presented detailed evaluations of applicants and proposed timetables for EU enlargement. In February 1998, the commission adopted draft accession partnership agreements for each first-tier applicant, setting out the requirements for membership, and on what terms the EU will provide aid before accession. It also announced that from the year 2000 the PHARE program would provide 500 million euros ($550 million) a year in agricultural aid to pre-accession applicants, and pre-accession structural funding of 1 billion euros a year. On 18 March, the European Commission revealed its budget proposal for years 2000–2006 and suggested the creation of a steadily growing fund for modernizing agriculture for all new members, assuming they will join the EU in 2002. This is to grow from 600 million euros in 2002 to 2.5 billion euros in 2006. In addition, under the system of guaranteed prices the European Commission is to offer them 1.1 billion euros in 2002, increasing that to 1.4 billion euros in 2006; structural funds will contribute 3.5 billion euros in 2002, to be raised to 11.6 billion euros in 2006. Of course, the new members would also contribute their own dues to the overall EU budget.

These measures suggest that the EU has decided to quickly include Poland and some other applicant countries into the CAP. However, a closer look at the package raises some doubts. And the European Commission has said that a longer adjustment period would be needed for agriculture, during which Poland and other new members would not fully participate in the CAP. Likely rationales suggested for this approach include: agricultural prices in Central and Eastern Europe would still be lower than the EU's at accession, and applying CAP rules and prices would strongly stimulate production there, producing EU surpluses; a sudden rise in Polish farmers' income would create income discrepancies, provoking social stress in the country; agriculture in Central and Eastern Europe needs protection against the strong competition from the West; and a one-time increase in prices to EU levels would cause a rapid increase in raw material prices for food industries in the region, which, combined with a sudden opening to free competition from Western producers, could imperil farmers.

EU EXCUSES?

These arguments can be readily challenged. First, no one can predict that prices paid to Central and East European farmers when they join the Union will necessarily be lower than current EU rates. At the moment, they remain below the average EU level, but prices paid to Polish farmers have been rising steadily over the last few years. In fact, wheat prices in 1996–1997 were higher than the EU's. In any case, denying Polish farmers the same compensation paid to farmers in current EU countries would flout the principles of the common market and fair competition. Expecting an outburst of social conflicts because of growing income differences smacks of alarmism, at least in Poland. Equally, one cannot argue that agriculture in the region is weak and non-competitive, while claiming that a sudden increase of prices would result in huge production increases and exports to the West.

That means that under EU pricing conditions, Polish agriculture would be fully competitive, which is also suggested by the quickly rising flow of foreign investment into the food business. And the view that the poor quality of agricultural products in Central and Eastern Europe inhibits the integration process is rebutted by the modernization already achieved with the help of foreign investment.

It appears that the EU proposal for long adjustment periods for the agricultural sectors in Central and Eastern Europe has little or nothing to do with preparing them for integration. In fact, the EU might fear competition with its own slowly reforming farms. While continuing the CAP in the EU in a slightly reformed but still very expensive form, EU countries appear unwilling to finance the growth of competitive agricultural sectors. At the same time, Poland also faces growing arguments, particularly from the United States, that Central and East European countries should not adjust their agriculture to the EU's inefficient standards because the present CAP system will be transformed to become more competitive in ten years or so.

But that is a long time to wait. Understanding the economic and political importance of agriculture in Poland, the EU will have no choice but to make some concessions during the negotiations. But there is likely to be a price for Poland too. In return for concessions in agriculture, Brussels will press for compromises in other important areas, such as telecommunications and access to Western labor markets. Whatever the terms, it is clear that Poland can count on some EU financial support, especially after accession. But Poland itself has not developed a consistent agricultural policy, and it is not yet clear whether it will use this money efficiently by, for example, assisting young farmers and supporting adjustment to Western competition.

POLITICAL WILL

The autumn 1997 change of government in Poland should have an important, if not necessarily straightforward, impact on the adjustment of Polish agriculture to EU requirements. The former Democratic Left Alliance (SLD), dominated by the Social Democratic Party (SDRP) and the Polish Peasants' Party (PSL) had a comfortable majority in the parliament and could enact practically any laws it wanted. This was especially true after December 1995 when Poland chose a new president, Aleksander Kwasniewski, former leader of SLD and SDRP. But the coalition never established a coherent, long-term program of agricultural reform. The SDRP, although definitely more pro-European than its partner, did not push the issue. Its leaders spoke generally about the need for deep reforms and adjustment to EU requirements but never produced a concrete agenda. It left agricultural policy almost entirely in the hands of its coalition partner, PSL.

The Peasants' Party claims to represent the interests of all Polish farmers and the whole agricultural sector. Yet the dominant faction of the PSL mostly represented less reform-oriented, poorer farmers and was more interested in protecting their short-term interests than championing radical changes. This more traditional approach to agriculture delayed the necessary changes and protected and coddled smaller and inefficient farms. A reform-minded faction within the party lost out, and after unfavorable results in last autumn's parliamentary elections left the party. The PSL's policy provoked conflicts with the European Commission on agriculture, which also limited the chances for quick progress on these issues in the impending pre-accession negotiations.

Jerzy Buzek's winning coalition in 1997, led by the Solidarity Election Action, a conglomerate of right-wing parties and social groups headed by the Solidarity labor union, with the reform-oriented Freedom Union as junior partner, does not have as much of a parliamentary majority as its predecessor. It is also condemned to cohabitation with a leftist president until the end of 2000. As a result, it has to reckon with the threat of a presidential veto if it seeks to introduce radical changes, although the president is much more reform-oriented than many of his colleagues.

Poland will need successful negotiating skills and structural economic reforms; combined with efforts to adjust agriculture to EU requirements before accession, this will give Poland its best shot at favorable terms of membership in the European Union.

NOTE

Reprinted with kind permission from *Transitions* magazine, April 1998.

EASTERN EUROPE

IV

Lithuania
Latvia
Estonia
Belarus
Ukraine

Lithuania

Population:	3,709,100
Capital:	Vilnius (pop. 575,700)
Major cities:	Kaunas (pop. 415,300), Klaipeda (pop. 202,800)
Area:	62,500 sq. km.
Major ethnic groups:	Lithuanian 81.3%, Russian 8.4%, Polish 7%, Belarusian 1.5%, Ukrainian 1%
Economy:	GDP growth: 5.7%
	Inflation rate: 5.1%
	Unemployment rate: 6.7%

THE YEAR OF THE PRESIDENT

by TERRY D. CLARK with ANDREA ADAMS

The biggest political news of the year in Lithuania was the election in January of Valdas Adamkus as president. A Lithuanian-American recently retired after a distinguished career in the U.S. Environmental Protection Agency (EPA), Adamkus won in the second round runoff by fewer than 15,000 votes. Assuming the role of head of state in a French-style political system with a somewhat constitutionally weaker presidency, the newly elected president signaled his intent to play a more activist role in domestic affairs than his predecessor, who had focused on foreign policy matters. Adamkus's efforts were largely successful as he engaged in a number of major initiatives throughout 1998.

1998 was also a year of political scandals as numerous government officials resigned for reasons of corruption or incompetence. Several cases involved questionable ties with organized crime. By year's end the country was headed toward an open declaration of war against organized crime. Adamkus was partially responsible for bringing the issues of crime and corruption to center stage, having committed himself in his inaugural speech to cleaning up the country's political system. However, the implementation of alcohol taxes contributed to much of the growing crime problem by making the illegal import of spirits from neighboring countries a lucrative business.

Economic growth slowed at the end of 1998 leading to renewed charges that the government lacked any real economic plan. Nonetheless, privatization continued apace, and it appeared that the country would weather the fallout from the Russian ruble crisis. Relations with neighbors were generally good, but the primary goal of obtaining membership in NATO and the European Union continued to elude the country. While some progress was made toward NATO entry, the election of a Social-Democratic government in Germany was seen as dimming hopes for Lithuania's early accession.

AN ACTIVIST PRESIDENCY

Assuming office amid doubts that he knew Lithuania's political situation well enough to serve effectively as president, Adamkus moved quickly to dispel such concerns. Employing his enormous public popularity (for most of the year he occupied first place in the country's public opinion polls with an approval rating near 75 percent), he was able to successfully pursue a number of major initiatives. Collectively these initiatives had a significant impact on the further development and interpretation of the Lithuanian Constitution (adopted in an October 1992 referendum), redefining not only the role of the presidency but executive-legislative relations as well. Among the arenas in which Adamkus focused in 1998 were reorganization of the government and government corruption.

Despite a Constitutional Court decision denying him the right to appoint a new prime minister, Adamkus succeeded in requiring that the entire cabinet retake the oath of office. (The Constitutional Court ruled that a newly elected president was required to resubmit a sitting prime minister's name for a renewed vote of confidence from the Seimas. Only in the event the Seimas refused to reaffirm its confidence in the government could the president could then appoint a new prime minister.) Hence Adamkus re-appointed Gediminas Vagnorius as prime minister. Shortly thereafter Adamkus pursued rationalization of the government, calling for a reduction in the number of ministries from 17 to 11. Part of the reorganization plan envisioned replacing the Ministry of European Affairs with a Department of European Affairs subordinate to the prime minister. This eventually engendered the greatest level of opposition from the ruling coalition in the Seimas, comprising the Homeland Union (Conservatives of Lithuania) led by Vytautas Landsbergis, the chair of the Seimas, and the Christian Democrats. While few believed the president would succeed in the ambitious reorganization plan, he ultimately gained legislative approval to reduce the government to 14 ministries.

The strengthening of the presidency was further facilitated by Adamkus's use of the veto. On six occasions during 1998, the Seimas changed legislation in accordance with the president's wishes, or discarded it altogether. On no occasion did it muster the absolute majority necessary to override the president's veto. The year's most notable case involving the presidential veto concerned a law forbidding former KGB employees from occupying positions in the government, courts, Seimas, presidential staff, key communications and transportation enterprises, the energy sector, and banking. Authored by Landsbergis and strongly backed by the Conservatives, Adamkus nonetheless succeeded in getting the Seimas to agree to a delay in the implementation of the legislation until the end of the year. Further, upon expiration of the moratorium he refused to make the necessary appointments to a commission charged with reviewing and making decisions on individual cases until the Constitutional Court had ruled on the constitutionality of the law.

Adamkus's successes owed to a number of factors, not the least of which were the broad public support that he enjoyed and his ability to form a working relationship with all political parties. Perhaps just as importantly, however, he was helped by an intra-party feud that emerged within the Homeland Union (Conservatives) between Prime Minister Vagnorius and Seimas Chair Landsbergis, as well as differences within the ruling coalition between the Conservatives and the Christian Democrats. All parties, including Vagnorius, the Conservatives, and the Christian Democrats sought the support of the president in the ensuing confrontations. As a consequence, the authority of the president further increased in relation to that of all other political institutions.

THE POLITICAL FALLOUT

A number of other political consequences attended the strengthening of the presidency. Among the most important of these was the increasing coordination of the two components of Lithuania's split executive, the presidency and the government headed by the prime minister. As a result, the Lithuanian political system began a marked transition from one dominated by the legislature to one in which the government, when supported by the president, is dominant. The latter is much more consistent with French-style political systems.

In accordance with the Lithuanian constitution, the prime minister is nominated by the president and approved by the Seimas. Further, the prime minister and the government are dependent upon the Seimas for a continued vote of confidence. However, in the event of a vote of no confidence, the president may choose to hold elections to a new Seimas instead of removing the prime minister. Using these powers, a popular president can provide the government with some degree of freedom from the Seimas. Several instances related to the appointment and removal of ministers in 1998 demonstrated that Adamkus and Vagnorius had recognized the potential that the Constitution gave them for doing just this. In one of the more controversial cases the president removed the minister of internal affairs, a Landsbergis protégé, at the prime minister's request while Landsbergis was abroad.

These events contributed to a deepening rift between Vagnorius and Landsbergis, a rift which had first emerged when Landsbergis was reportedly upset by Vagnorius's less than enthusiastic support for his failed presidential campaign. On several occasions during the year the Homeland Union (Conservatives) met to discuss measures to resolve the differences between the two party leaders. Following each meeting, the Conservatives announced that there was broad consensus within the party on all essential matters. However, the most significant outcome of these efforts was a renewed commitment to party discipline. While some observers suggested that this would permit Landsbergis and the Seimas to more tightly control the government, it appears that it was Vagnorius who succeeded in using it to stifle criticism of the government, with two former Landsbergis allies being ejected from the party at year's end.

As Vagnorius worked more closely with the president and skillfully maneuvered with the Party, Landsbergis found himself increasingly marginalized and less able to influence the course of political events as speaker of the Seimas. Further undermining Landsbergis's position was a scandal which erupted in May when *Lietuvos Rytas*, the country's major daily, reported allegations that the Third Section of the Security Department under the ministry of internal affairs had conducted surveillance on both Adamkus and the prime minister, reporting the results to Landsbergis. An investigation by the Seimas, headed by the Conservatives, found no evidence to support the allegations. Nonetheless, the Third Section was disbanded by a presidential decree reorganizing the Security Department and making clear that all elements of the ministry of internal affairs were responsible only to the government. Perhaps even more importantly however, the fate of the minister of internal affairs, himself a Landsbergis ally, was sealed, his resignation having already been demanded by the prime minister for alleged incompetence and mismanagement the week immediately preceding the scandal. This resignation together with the ministers removed by the government reorganization left Landsbergis with no allies in the government.

Nonetheless, Landsbergis succeeded by the end of the year in serving notice that he was determined not to permit any further renegotiation in executive-legislative relations. Late in the year, the president sent a nomination for the post of government ombudsman, Kestutis Lapinskas, to the Seimas only to be rejected by the Conservative majority. Declaring that the Conservatives were attempting to politicize government appointments, Adamkus renominated Lapinskas. Landsbergis countered that the president was creating a political incident that would only hurt the government, which found itself caught in the middle between the president and Seimas. The Lapinskas nomination seemed doomed to defeat, giving Landsbergis perhaps his first political victory over the president.

Public approval of the Conservatives fell as a result of the intra-party dissension and political maneuvering between the executive branch and the Seimas. Having won a plurality (two seats shy of an absolute majority) in the elections to the Seimas in October 1996, the party fell to second place in public opinion surveys behind the Center Union by the end of 1998. Worse still, their Christian Democratic coalition allies, wracked by internal discord, fell to fifth place while the Democratic Labor Party (the former Communist Party and an ardent foe of the Conservatives) regained its position as a credible political force and was the third most popular party in the country. At the same time, President Adamkus remained the most popular politician in the country throughout the year, achieving public approval ratings above 70 percent. The next most popular political figures possessed approval ratings near 50 percent while the two most public figures among the Conservatives, Prime Minister Vagnorius and Seimas Chair Landsbergis, had approval ratings near 40 percent and 25 percent respectively. Landsbergis's negative ratings exceeded his approval rating.

CRIME AND CORRUPTION

The country also saw a large number of high-level government resignations in 1998. Among them were the health minister, the minister of internal affairs, the minister of communications, the director-general of the Security Department, the head of the Special Investigations Division, the chief of the Tax Inspectorate, and the head of Customs. Many of the resignations were part of a campaign initiated by the president to clean up the country's political institutions, a campaign actively supported by the prime minister. Several involved scandals related to the personal use of government property, as in the case of the minister of communications. Others occurred over alleged incompetence, as was the case with the Customs chief.

A number of others involved scandals related to organized crime, which continued to be a serious problem and may have even increased from previous years due to the implementation of new alcohol taxes. In October, it was announced that there were 13 cases of murder, five cases of attempted murder, six cases of blackmail, and two cases of armed robbery under investigation and thought to be connected to organized crime. A European Commission study estimated that 20 organized crime groups were operating in Lithuania. Government officials involved with organized crime were a particular target of the anti-corruption campaign. The chief of the Special Investigations Division, for instance, resigned amidst allegations that he had ties with an alcohol smuggling operation. Customs officials were relieved of their duties in the port of Klaipeda and elements of the police unit fighting organized crime division in the city of Panevezys were arrested after being implicated in criminal activity. A judge was also impeached for overturning a judgment on a smuggling operation on appeal, and a second judge was indicted for taking a bribe.

Feeling the pressure of the campaign, organized crime engaged in a series of retaliatory actions, bombing automobiles and homes of police and judges. The wave of bombings culminated in the January 1999 slaying of a procurator in the city of Panevezys. In response, the prime minister declared war on organized crime and announced the formation of special units to combat organized crime throughout the country. 1999 could be a very difficult year pitting organized crime and law enforcement agencies in a protracted conflict.

THE ECONOMY

While problems of crime and corruption worried many Lithuanians in 1998, the economy was of greater concern. Year end statistics indicated that one-sixth of the population was living at or below the poverty level; according to public opinion surveys one-fourth of the country considered herself/himself "impoverished." Low incomes and the threat of unemployment remained the paramount concern of many. Indeed, there appeared to be reason for concern. Despite continued strong macroeconomic statistics and the first balanced government budget in the post-Soviet period, the country was facing balance of payments problems by the end of the year. Further, economic growth slowed, ending below 6 percent. Adding to the pessimism was the Russian financial crisis. While the prime minister declared that the crisis would have minimal effect on the Lithuanian economy it was still the case that much of Lithuania's trade was with its eastern neighbor. The Russian refusal to deliver oil to the Mazeikiai refinery at previously agreed prices and quantities reinforced this point.

However, not all of the economic news was bad. The country experienced continued strong growth for the third year in a row alongside very low inflation (5.1 percent) for the year. Further, privatization continued. The year began with the privatization of the country's telephone company, 60 percent going to Amber Teleholdings, a Swedish-Finnish consortium. The sale was attended by the announcement that telephone subscribers would be charged by the minute for local calls. The ensuing public furor involving large protests by pensioner groups eventually ended with the government's decision to raise the number of hours of free calls per month allotted to pensioners. The other major privatization in 1998 involved Williams International's investment in the country's oil industry. Williams was permitted by an act of the Seimas to purchase up to a 33 percent stake in both the Mazeikiai oil refinery and the oil terminal being constructed at Butinge. The Seimas decision was vehemently opposed by the Social Democrats and Democratic Labor Party. As a result of monies realized in the continued privatization program, the government was able to fulfill its promise to recompense citizens for their losses in ruble savings accounts in 1992 following the collapse of the Soviet Union and resultant hyperinflation.

RETURN TO EUROPE?

In his inaugural speech, President Adamkus stated that his primary foreign policy goals were accession to NATO and the European Union (EU). In a demonstration of its determination to rejoin Europe, Lithuania changed time zones (moving to the Central European Time Zone); announced that defense expenditures would be raised to 2 percent of GDP by 2001; ratified an agreement on a joint Baltic peacekeeping battalion; changed national stock exchange regulations to meet EU requirements; and abolished the death penalty. Nevertheless, prospects for early entry into either organization appeared somewhat dimmer at year's end, particularly in regard to EU membership.

Given Adamkus's contacts in the U.S. government, many had hoped that his election would accelerate Lithuania's entry into NATO. Several high level discussions during the year helped raise the country's hopes. NATO Secretary General Javier Solana visited Vilnius in July and reaffirmed that all countries wanting membership in the security organization would eventually be granted entry. In October, Adamkus met President Bill Clinton to discuss the country's accession to NATO, saying that there was "unfinished business" in Europe as long as Lithuania remained outside of European security structures. The country also participated in Baltic Challenge naval exercises with 11 member and candidate member states of NATO. However, the election of Social Democrat Gerhard Schroeder as chancellor in Germany resulted in a notable diminution in German support for NATO eastward expansion. The newly elected chancellor called for the full integration of Poland, Hungary, and the Czech Republic into the alliance before any new invitations were made. The Western powers had not resolved the issue as 1998 ended.

Prospects for entry into the European Union (EU) were even less sanguine. The EU criticized the Lithuanian government for not having a realistic economic plan, pointing to the slow rate of privatization and a tendency to bail out failed enterprises at the expense of the state instead of permitting them to go into bankruptcy. The EU was further concerned by unresolved problems of crime and corruption. Not surprisingly given these assessments, the European Commission did not include Lithuania in its November list of six states most prepared for membership. However, even Lithuanians themselves appeared unsure about EU membership given the EU's insistence that the Chornobyl-style nuclear reactor at Ignalina be closed. The demand generated considerable debate. Many worried that closing the country's primary energy source would leave Lithuania overly dependent on others for energy. The Democratic Labor Party suggested that the EU wanted to close the reactor for fear of the competition it would give to EU nuclear energy. Others questioned whether the prize of national sovereignty, only recently achieved at such a high price, was worth sacrificing for the sake of EU membership. Those supporting EU membership suggested that a compromise could be achieved with the EU. President Adamkus and both ruling parties, the Conservatives and the Christian Democrats, indicated their support for keeping the reactor in operation for another 10 to 15 years.

Lithuania's relations with its neighbors continued to be relatively stable. The most problematic relations were those with Belarus, which experienced continued difficulties in paying its energy debt to Lithuania. The behavior of Belarusian President Alyaksandr Lukashenka was also troubling. Hoping to avoid any break in relations that might hurt trade between the two countries, Adamkus took a low-key approach in the diplomatic crisis erupting over Minsk's eviction of foreign ambassadors from their compounds in Drazdy. In contrast to Western states, Adamkus lodged a protest with Minsk but did not recall Lithuania's ambassador. Relations with Poland continued to improve, with Poland supporting Lithuanian entry into NATO. However, the major issues between the two countries remained unresolved: treatment of national minorities and the border crossing from Lithuania to Poland, where vehicular traffic was backed up for extended periods. Relations with Latvia became somewhat charged when Vilnius lodged a formal protest with Riga over the desecration of the Lithuanian flag by Greens protesting the construction of the oil terminal at Butinge near the border of the two countries. Overall, however, relations between the Baltic states remained good. Finally, relations with the United States at the diplomatic level remained relatively good. However, Lithuanians were divided in their reactions to pressure exerted by the U.S. Ambassador in the trial of Aleksandras Lileikis, a 91-year-old Lithuanian and former head of security in Vilnius who was accused of genocide during the German occupation of World War II.

Latvia

Population:	2,485,400
Capital:	Riga (pop. 820,577)
Major cities:	Daugavpils (pop. 117,835), Liepaja (pop. 97,917), Jelgava (pop. 70,943)
Area:	64,610 sq. km.
Major ethnic groups:	Latvian 54.8%, Russian 32.8%, Belarusian 4.0% Ukrainian 3.0%, Polish 2.2%,
....	Lithuanian 1.3%, Jewish 0.5%
Economy:	GDP growth: 3.5%
....	Inflation rate: 4.7%
....	Unemployment rate: 9.2%

TWELVE MONTHS ON A ROLLER COASTER

by ANDREJS PLAKANS

The year 1998—marking Latvia's 80th anniversary as an independent state—demonstrated that the country's ongoing search for improvements in all domains of life could easily be sidetracked. The generally good economic performance of 1997 continued in the first third of 1998; and the signing of the U.S.-Baltic Charter on 16 January by Estonia, Latvia, and Lithuania signaled good relations with "the one remaining superpower." But, starting in March and lasting into the summer months, a series of unforeseen events left Latvians despairing about their international "image" and opened once again the painful question of citizenship for the Russophone population. Then the decision by NATO to move ahead with membership for Poland, Hungary, and the Czech Republic seemed to move the question of Latvia's entry into some distant and unspecified future. The European Union's choice of Estonia but not Latvia or Lithuania for membership discussions had a similar dispiriting effect on Latvian hopes for "the move into Europe."

The October parliamentary (Saeima) elections—the third since the 1991 restoration of independence—produced a coalition government (cabinet) backed by only 46 of 100 parliamentary votes, with the party that had won the most seats remaining in opposition. At the year's end, both demographic and crime indicators continued to be alarming; though some sense of accomplishment came from the country's entry in October into the World Trade Organization. The year 1998, in other words, started high but, on balance, ended low.

TRAVAILS OF SPRING

For the past few years Latvia's capital, Riga, had become used to small and evanescent demonstrations by those on fixed government pensions—mostly the elderly—whose incomes did not match the rise in the cost of living. Most such demonstrations make it to the local news programs, but one of them, on 3 March, became international news. Several hundred picketers, reportedly mostly Russians, formed a crowd at the Riga City Council building on Valdemars Street—a main thoroughfare—and spilled into the street, blocking traffic. Police efforts to clear the street involved upraised nightsticks and pushing. The TV footage of the incident became fodder for claims, especially in Russian-language newspapers, about police attacks on the elderly, violations of Russians' human rights in Latvia, and similar negative portrayals.

Soon thereafter, on 16 March, a World War II commemoration reached a similar level of notoriety. On that date, fixed by the government as "Soldier's Day," about 500 Latvian veterans participated in a march to lay flowers at the Freedom Monument in the center of the city. These veterans—now mostly in their seventies—were former members of the "Latvian Legion," the Latvian military units that were conscripted into the German war effort in 1943 and 1944 and, organizationally, were made a part of the Waffen SS. Local Russians, and also Moscow officials, reacted to the march with outrage, adverting to the "rebirth of fascism" in Latvia and threatening an economic boycott of the country. The participation in the commemoration by the Commander of the Latvian Armed Forces, Juris Dalbins, made matters worse, because it seemed to symbolize official endorsement of the march. Dalbins was fired from his job shortly thereafter.

These events were followed on 6 April by several explosions of the kind Riga had become used to (some 23 in 1998), as the city's criminal element (the "Mafia") settled scores and battled rivals. The explosions on 6 April, however, were different: a plastic explosive was set off at Riga's only synagogue and a land mine exploded in a park next to the Russian Embassy. Latvian officials immediately condemned the bombings and launched investigations. The Russian foreign ministry in Moscow reacted with claims that "explosions thunder in Latvia, monuments are defiled, and fascists raise their heads. This must be put to an end." The governor of Saratov province in Russia announced that "There is no place for genocide and revival of fascism on the threshold of the third millennium." Foreign Minister Valdis Birkavs observed that this and other recent events were part of a planned effort "to destabilize the political situation in Latvia [and] discredit Latvia before the international community."

The speed with which these incidents reached the international media, and the manner in which Latvia's internal affairs were described in the ensuing reportage, made a good case study of how nation-states in the "global village" use (and misuse) the media for purposes other than news reporting. Beyond that, the incidents themselves made plain that at the level of state diplomacy the relations between Latvia and Russia (and Latvians and Russians in Latvia) remained strained. Adding to the tensions, in early April a work group of the Latvian Parliament (Saeima) proposed revising the 1994 citizenship law so as to enable certain categories of non-citizens (mostly Russian-speakers) to obtain citizenship faster. The revisions were meant to boost the very slow naturalization pace: only a small proportion of those eligible to register for naturalization under the existing law had done so. The debates over the revisions revived the argument about, on one side, the survival of Latvian language and culture, and, on the other, denial of "the human rights" of the non-citizen population in Latvia (about 26.5 percent of the total population). Eventually, the Saeima passed the revisions, but their implementation was stopped by the Fatherland and Freedom/LNNK Party, which, drawing on a provision of the Latvian constitution, collected enough signatures to place the question of the proposed revisions on a national referendum. The referendum was set to take place in October, simultaneously with the parliamentary elections.

PARLIAMENTARY ELECTIONS

The run-up to the third (since 1991) regular parliamentary election—scheduled for 2 October—started in January, when the former prime minister Andris Skele announced the formation of a new political party called the People's Party (Tautas Partija). Skele had not withdrawn from politics and his reentry was entirely expected. Over the next half-year the list of parties and party coalitions contending for parliamentary seats continued to swell, also as expected, until their number reached 21. Thus the political arena continued to look fragmented and to carry the message to the voters that Latvian politics would remain a matter of dealmaking, before and after the elections. The list of contenders included some parties that were ancient by current Latvian standards: the right-of-center coalition For Fatherland and Freedom/Latvian National Independence Movement (Tevzemei un Brivibai/Nacionalas Neatkaribas Kustiba), both partners of which were founded in the heady days of the "Singing Revolution" of 1989; the centrist Latvia's Way (Latvijas Cels), founded for the 1993 elections; the leftist National Harmony Party (Tautas Saskanas Partija), also founded for the 1993 elections and by now having a well-established reputation as "friendly" to the "Russian" population in Latvia; and the center-left Saimnieks party, which had won the most seats in the 1995 elections. An entirely new entry was the New Party (Jauna Partija), built around the personality of Raimonds Pauls, the popular composer and former minister of culture.

Campaigning for the election started in early summer, but hit the high-water mark in the months of August and September. The campaign platforms lacked clear distinctions: all favored the "move toward Europe," all promised to improve the economic situation. Some differences appeared on whether joining the EU and NATO was as highly desirable as the leading parties claimed; other, nuanced differences appeared over how to deal with the question of non-citizens. More notable was the emphasis on personalities—the People's Party's Skele, the New Party's Pauls, Harmony Party's Janis Jurkans, TB/LNNK's Guntars Krasts (the current prime minister), Latvia's Way's Anatolijs Gorbunovs (who successfully headed the National Council during the 1990–1991 transition period). The electoral atmosphere was muddied somewhat by the concurrent referendum debate about the citizenship amendments. The political right wanted the amendments defeated; the center and the left supported them. Latvian President Guntis Ulmanis (elected in 1993 and now in his final term) came out in support of the amendments.

The election and referendum results did not signal a major shift in Latvian politics, but rather a continuing centrist stance by the voters. The citizenship amendments received approval by 53 to 44 percent—and within two months the number of non-citizens who had begun the naturalization process had already tripled. Still, the country had a long way to go to diminish the significance of the vexing citizenship question. At the end of 1997 72.3 percent of the resident population were citizens; at the end of 1998, the proportion had barely moved—to

72.7 percent. Resident non-citizens, numbering some 672,000, were mostly ethnic Russians.

The election results were generally in line with what public opinion polls had suggested during the previous two months. The People's Party, which received 24 parliamentary seats, showed the continuing popularity of Andris Skele. Moreover, the voters were reluctant to diminish the relative strength of the parties with experience in governing: Latvia's Way received 21 seats, and TB/LNNK 17 seats. The New Party's eight seats showed the enduring popularity of Raimonds Pauls, though some interpreted this "new" party as a creature of Latvia's Way. Somewhat surprising was the relatively good showing of the parties of the left: Jurkan's Harmony Party received 16 seats, and the Social Democratic Union 14. Neither of these two parties had been in previous governments, and, if able to work together, would constitute a formidable opposition bloc.

No party, of course, received sufficient seats to govern by itself, and therefore, as happened after the 1995 election, the final months of the year consisted of negotiations for the purpose of creating a coalition cabinet. The result was undistinguished: the deal-makers produced a minority government consisting of Latvia's Way, the New Party, and TB/LLNK—46 seats. Selected as PM was Vilis Kristopans of Latvia's Way, the minister of transportation in the outgoing Krasts government. In spite of having won the larger number of parliamentary seats, Andris Skele and his People's Party remained in opposition, as did the two parties of the left. The unwillingness of Latvia's Way, the New Party, and TB/LLNK to bring Skele's party into the coalition was attributed to Skele's prickly and somewhat authoritarian personality, as well as to the obvious fact that his presence in the government and his high scores in public popularity polls would overshadow the efforts of all other party leaders, including those of Kristopans. In early 1999 Kristopans enlarged his Saeima vote count to 60 by appointing a Social Democrat as minister of agriculture, thus securing the promise of the Social Democrats to support most of the new government's legislative initiatives.

DEMOGRAPHIC WORRIES

Behind the economic stability and the smoothly functioning political system lay demographic trends that continued to be a source of worry. The aggregate population of the country declined again in 1998 (from 2.45 million in January to 2.44 million in December), as it has every year since 1991. Emigrants were mostly from the working population (rather than from the young or the retired). The ethnic composition of the country changed slightly in favor of the Latvian population (now 56.5 percent), at the expense of the Slavic-language minorities. The absolute number of Latvians, however, was smaller at the end of 1998 than it had been in 1939.

Two important indicators seemed to shift in 1998, promising, perhaps, further growth in the total population. First, life expectancy appeared to be increasing for both men and women. The increase, however, means an eventual enlargement of the proportion of pensioned and pensionable persons (those living on fixed incomes), with state pensions rising very slowly and private pension plans still in their infancy. Moreover, whether this change meant an overall improvement of Latvian health was unclear. In 1998, only 38 percent of the 8,000 young men who answered the draft for the Latvian army were found to be fit to serve by the army's medical commission—a decline from 44 percent in 1997. And in December a survey by the journal *Healthcare Europe*, using 14 criteria and carried out in 35 countries, listed Latvia along with Estonia, Belarus, Ukraine, and Russia as the unhealthiest countries in Europe.

The second positive sign was a leveling off in the downward slope of the birth curve in Latvia in the middle months of 1998, when more children were born than in the corresponding period of 1997. But this statistic embodied problems. The proportion of children born to unmarried mothers (in and out of consensual unions) continued to be high—about a third of all newborns—placing additional strains on the already under-funded programs to aid unmarried mothers. At the same time, Latvia's economy provided little incentive for families to have many children. The UN Development Commission in Latvia reported that the highest risk of experiencing poverty—officially defined as 24 lats ($14) per person per month—belonged to families having three or more children.

CRIME AND CORRUPTION

If demographic statistics remained ambiguous, those pertaining to criminality provided some comfort, but just barely. The presence of criminal gangs continued: in November, the Council of Europe reported in Latvia two major and about 100 minor criminal gangs. Still, there were some improvements. The police registered 0.5 percent fewer criminal acts in 1998 than in 1997, and the proportion of solved cases rose by 5.2 percent in 1998 over the previous year. The absolute number of crimes against persons (murder, beatings, rape) fell somewhat by comparison with 1997. The huge share still contributed by Riga to these statistics—about a half—fell only slightly from 1997. The absolute number of criminal acts connected to drugs diminished slightly, but those connected to alcohol rose. The most troubling change was in the rise of repeat offenders, as well as the number of criminal acts by those below 18 years of age. The crimes perpetrated by the young made up almost a fifth of all criminal acts (19.4 percent), increasing by 10.6 percent over 1997. The general category of economic crimes—mostly counterfeiting and fraud—continued to be a significant proportion (45.5 percent) of all crime.

Latvia's citizens continued to assume the existence of widespread corruption. In December, a survey of 1,756 respondents (1,100 private families, 438 employees in business enterprise, 218 employees in governmental institutions) by the World Bank reported that some 60 percent believed that corruption over the past four years had grown worse, and only 10 percent believed that the situation had improved. Some 37 percent of the respondents in business enterprises and some 13 percent of private individuals in families said that they had had to make "unofficial" payments (bribes) to various officials. Respondents named as "most corrupt" customs officials, traffic police, Lattelekom (the national phone company), the national government, the parliament, the courts, local governments, various licensing offices, and the privatization agency. The institutions reported to be most honest were the church, the mass media, and educational institutions.

ECONOMIC STABILITY

Throughout 1998 the strong macroeconomic trends visible in 1997 continued. Since the first quarter of 1996, there had been no quarter which has failed to exceed the GDP figures of the corresponding period of the previous year. By year's end, the GDP had grown by about 3.5 percent and annual inflation in consumer prices continued to be comparatively low, at about 4.7 percent. As in 1997, services and consumer-oriented enterprises remained the principal growth sectors, with industrial output growing by a slight 2.0 percent. The year 1998 also ended with the budget of the national government in balance, indeed, with a slight surplus. The Latvian lats remained stable against the U.S. dollar: $0.59 in January and $0.57 in December.

The process of privatization neared completion, with some 98 percent of the enterprises slated for privatization having been sold. Official unemployment levels, however, rose somewhat during the year, from 7.1 percent in January to 9.2 percent in December. Yet these indicators did not change materially certain features of the economy that Latvia shared with other post-communist countries. The mean monthly wage income grew only slightly, from 123 to 140 lats ($71) during the year. Most of the population was still living below the "official poverty" level, and the income differentials between the richest and the poorest remained substantial. In comparison with the economic travails of the Russian Federation, the Latvian economy looked good, but officials had hoped for signs of more robust economic growth.

AN EXASPERATING YEAR

The statistics for any given year do not constitute a trend, and Latvia's hopes are attached to the development of positive trends in all aspects of life. In this respect, the year 1998 proved to be ambiguous. Latvia's expectation that 1998 would contain a significant turn of events constituting an irreversible trajectory "toward Europe" were not realized, but nor were they dashed. Actual membership in NATO and the EU were not in the cards, and at year's end it was not altogether clear at what point in the future these organizations would accept Latvia as a member. Frustrated in these domains, Latvia turned to improving its international image, which, however, suffered—in Latvian eyes—serious damage because of the events of the spring and summer months. In the fall, approval of the naturalization amendments lifted the spirits of those for whom international acceptance was important, but the minority government produced by the fall's parliamentary elections meant that the country would enter 1999 with a somewhat unstable legislature. The economy performed well, and seemed not to be unduly impacted by the economic turmoil in Russia, but problematic demographic indicators suggested that Latvia had not yet escaped some typical characteristics of "post-communist" states. Belief that corruption was widespread remained pronounced. Little about the year 1998 suggested that Latvians should consider the glass half full rather than half empty.

ON THE STREETS WITH LATVIA'S LANGUAGE PATROL
by STEVEN C. JOHNSON

It's a sunny autumn morning, and the cobblestone streets of Riga's old town are alive with commerce. Merchants hawk amber jewelry. Men in smart suits, armed with mobile phones, ply the thoroughfares and alleyways. Nearby, Ilze Berzina casually walks into the Tatiana beauty salon, in the shadow of St. Peter's Cathedral. One of three young hairdressers on duty hovers over an attractive woman seated before a mirror. Berzina greets them all cheerfully in Latvian: "Labdien."

It isn't until she flashes her license that she betrays the reason for the visit. She's come because the municipal language inspection office has received a complaint about salon employees—not enough Latvian spoken. The hairdressers quickly shuffle about the room to accommodate Berzina, neatly dressed in a business suit. Berzina, quick to smile, is easygoing, despite the at-times intimidating nature of her task: enforcing Riga businesses' compliance with the Latvian language law.

"Some inspectors enter undercover, pretending they're clients, but I prefer the up-front approach," Berzina says. "Otherwise, there is potential for arguments and harsh words, and nobody needs that." The salon manager is not in, but Berzina speaks with the employees one by one. The first, a blonde, ethnic-Russian girl in her 20s named Julia, greets Berzina in Latvian. The inspector checks her language certificate, which all non-native speakers must produce upon demand. The certificate says Julia has intermediate command of the language—the second of three proficiency levels and the necessary level for a hairdresser. The law is precise in its requirements: those in high-profile public positions—such as doctors or members of parliament—must command the highest level of Latvian fluency. Shop-owners are also expected to be at that level, although for shop employees, the intermediate level is acceptable. Occupations that involve little public interaction—such as garbage collectors or bus drivers—require only minimal proficiency.

Berzina politely asks some everyday questions to test Julia's knowledge of Latvian. "What is your name? Where did you study?" The girl's responses come quickly at first but begin to slow with each question. When Berzina asks, "How long have you worked at this salon?" Julia answers, in broken Latvian, that her work day is eight hours long. When Berzina asks for nail polish in Latvian, Julia answers with the word for paint. She cannot supply the Latvian words for other tools of the trade—curling irons, hair dryers, scissors. Berzina then shifts into Russian, asking Julia to repeat in Russian the questions Berzina asked in Latvian. She can't do it.

"She doesn't speak according to the second level," Berzina says, and suggests that her language certificate may even be counterfeit, a problem that language inspectors encounter more and more frequently. If it is, it will cost Julia 50 lats ($30), a hefty fine in a country where the average monthly salary in 1997 was about 116 lats. Another hairdresser named Ingrida, half Latvian, half Russian, answers quickly and correctly—she's been working for five years, she trained in a cosmetology school.

A third, Olga, in her mid-20s, falls somewhere in the middle. She knows enough words to communicate and gets most of the technical terms correct. She grabs a pen to jot down one word she doesn't know, a move that impresses Berzina. When questioned about how to address a customer who wants a short haircut, Olga gets the words right but not the syntax: "Nogriezt matus?" (Cut short hair?) Berzina nods knowingly and writes notes to herself. "You know enough to communicate," she tells Olga, "but you need to concentrate on acquiring a richer vocabulary, brushing up your grammar."

Later, Berzina says, "I'm quite certain she could not write in the language at all, but her job doesn't require writing, so it's OK." Olga has forgotten to bring her language certificate to work and Berzina must check the authenticity of Julia's, so she leaves without assessing any fines but promises to return to speak with the manager.

"It's pretty clear this complaint was justified," Berzina says. "Sometimes, they turn out to be false, one person being vindictive toward a particular shop or business, but it looks like there will be fines here." On her way out, Olga calls out in Latvian, "Please, I invite you to sit in my chair. Tell me what you want. I'll do it, everything you want, just as you say. I can do my job."

Berzina has worked as a language inspector for the past four years. An architect by profession, Berzina left the firm she worked for after finding herself giving Latvian lessons to her fellow employees, who fell far short of the legal requirements for proficiency. She went to work directly for the State Language Center, the institution assigned the weighty role of guardian of the Latvian language, one of the oldest in Europe and one many locals say may face extinction if its use is not enforced. The center oversees 18 language inspectors nationwide, nine of whom are stationed in Riga.

Formed in 1992, shortly after Latvia became independent, the center has its hands in everything from printing Latvian language textbooks and learning kits to roving the streets to ensure the language is being used—and used properly. Almost every one of the 1.5 million Latvians born in the country speak the language, but that is not the case for some 1 million Russians who moved here following the Soviet takeover in 1940. "The Russian language still has self-sufficiency here, and we need to establish a place for Latvian," explains Dzintra Hirsa, director of the State Language Center. "We need to give it room to breathe."

The language cops who work for the center react to complaints—last year, the municipal inspectors who patrol Riga received 483 of them—from residents who say they cannot get served in Latvian. Inspectors also perform spot checks at businesses and in shops. Signs can be emblazoned with Latvian words only and are subject to strict grammatical review. Imported goods, from toothpaste to pasta, must have Latvian directions pasted onto the package.

In a Riga pharmacy, it's clear Berzina knows how to zero in on potential violations, which carry a fine of 58 lats. She passes up imported over-the-counter drugs such as Bayer aspirin, many of which already include Latvian instructions added by the manufacturer, and singles out a particular ointment for back aches and lozenges for sore throats. "It's good that we have these American drugs," she says, holding up a small box of imported lozenges, "but it's even better if we know how to use them." This time, the packages are duly labeled, but one pharmacist on duty admits to having been fined in the past.

PLAYING THE NUMBERS

During the Soviet years, Latvia was among the most heavily Russified of the Soviet republics. As a result, Latvians make up just 54 percent of the country's 2.5 million inhabitants, down from three-fourths of the population before World War II. The remainder are primarily Russian-speakers, with ethnic Russians making up a third of the population, according to government figures. In the country's seven largest cities, including Riga, native Latvian speakers are a minority. But for the most part, Latvian and Russian speakers coexist peacefully. They sit next to each other on the trams and carry on conversations in their own languages. They live side by side in Brezhnev-era apartment blocks; they work together; they communicate.

Even before the Soviet Union's collapse, the country moved to establish Latvian as the official state language. In 1989, as part of the country's drive for independence, the Latvian Supreme Soviet passed a law requiring the use of Latvian in public places—establishing the three-tiered levels of proficiency and limiting the use of foreign languages (i.e., Russian) in public and private sectors. The law also banned the use of bilingual (Russian-Latvian) signs, except in a few cases, such as tourist establishments and cultural institutions. In essence, the law established the principle that, when it comes to private businesses like the Tatiana beauty salon, everyone has the right to be served or to ask questions—and expect answers—in Latvian. "People are ready to learn the language, but if there is no requirement, they're not going to do so," says Irena Birkova, head of the Riga Language Center. "We can't rely on their good will."

Since the inspections began in 1992, adding enforcement teeth to the initial language law of 1989, most officials say the situation has improved. As Berzina walks through the Old Town, pointing out the few exemptions to the ban on bilingual advertising—a sign with the English word "Hotel" on it (tourism), a Russian-language theater with Russian billboards (culture)—she recalls when it was common to find as many Russian signs as Latvian ones, few Latvian-speaking employees, and surly managers unwilling to cooperate.

The language requirements continue to be controversial. Parliament has divided over an effort by the nationalist For Fatherland and Freedom Party to strengthen the law—for example, by requiring state employees to ignore any correspondence written in a foreign language. That proposal has been opposed by members of Europe-oriented parties such as Latvia's Way, who argue that such measures will only increase the country's isolation and doom its chances for joining the European Union. It has also inflamed relations with Russia, which habitually accuses Latvia and its Baltic neighbor Estonia of discriminating against ethnic Russian minorities and recently threatened economic sanctions. Russia remains Latvia's biggest single trading partner, a fact that puts Berzina and the country's other language inspectors on the front line of a difficult path between its Russia-dominated past and what it hopes to be its Western future.

Berzina's week has not been spent in vain. On her return visit to the Tatiana beauty salon, she finds the owner, an ethnic Russian, speaks nary a word of Latvian. For a business owner, this offense carries a fine of 116 lats. The hairdressers, however, fare better. Julia's certificate turns out to be genuine after all, and Berzina decides to reprimand rather than fine Julia and Olga. This means they get off without their pockets lightening but must be on guard for a repeat inspection in the coming months.

Berzina's philosophy: sometimes the carrot goes farther than the stick. "We have to provide space for the language to enter life," she says, "but punishment is not always the way to do that."

NOTE

Reprinted with kind permission from *Transitions* magazine, November 1998.

Estonia

Population:	1,466,900
Capital:	Tallinn (pop. 434,763)
Major cities:	Tartu (pop. 104,907), Narva (pop. 77,770), Kohtla-Jarve (pop. 55,415)
Area:	45,000 sq. km.
Major ethnic groups:	Estonian 64.2%, Russian 28.7%, Ukrainian 2.7%, Belarusian 1.5%, Finnish 1%
Economy:	GDP growth: 4.0%
	Inflation rate: 10.0%
	Unemployment rate: 9–10%

STRUGGLING TO REMAIN THE REFORM LEADER
by JOAN LOFGREN

While still the wunderkind of post-Soviet reformers, 1998 showed that Estonia could not afford to take economic or political stability for granted. Estonia moved closer to membership in the European Union (EU), and waited out an ineffective governing coalition in what was yet another year of party realignment. The country weathered the effects of Russia's August financial crisis fairly well, but indirect shocks from the Russian crisis together with the fallout from too rapid expansion provoked severe problems in the banking sector.

MINORITY COALITION REACHES OUT

Prime Minister Mart Siimann's minority coalition government, including his own Coalition Party, the Country People's Party, the Rural Union, and the Pensioners and Families Party (together known as the KMU) had the backing of only 37 out of 101 members of parliament and seemed to unite politically strange bedfellows. The coalition was considered increasingly ineffective and in the spring Siimann sought unsuccessfully to expand the coalition by reaching out to the opposition Reform Party, but the conflict it had with the coalition rural parties over the state's role in agriculture prevented any new agreements from being concluded. The Coalition Party then started talks with the Development Party and the Farmers' Party (ETRE). The Development Party's representative, Andra Veidemann, served as population affairs minister and the Farmers' Party leader, Toomas Herrik Ilves, was serving as foreign minister; both parties occupied an intermediate position between government and opposition.

In April Siimann proposed early elections through staging a no-confidence vote, but other coalition partners wanted the government to continue. Although his government was cursed with what some called "political bankruptcy," a change of government would have to wait until the elections scheduled for March 1999.

Instability in the ruling coalition revealed ongoing problems in Estonia's party system, with its array of small parties and shifting ideological positions. The 1992 elections had seen no less than 38 parties running for seats in the legislature, and 30 ran in the 1995 elections. As of 1998 the parliament included representatives of 13 parties, with no single party dominating. In past elections, small parties put their candidates together, but the list retained the names of all the parties involved.

In November parliament adopted a new electoral law, which states that parties cannot cooperate unless they either merge or agree to issue one joint list of candidates that come under the banner of one political party. The new law also required that a party has a minimum of 1,000 individual members and passes a 5 percent minimum electoral threshold for representation in parliament. This is certain to cause a sharp fall both in the number of parties eligible to compete in the 1999 elections, and the number winning representation in parliament. It was predicted that the biggest victims of the ban were likely, ironically, to be the Coalition and Rural Union parties, both members of the then-ruling coalition. The Coalition Party relied heavily on rural votes that only partnership with farm parties could bring. The Russian parties were also considered possible losers.

By the end of the year, the popularity of the right-wing Pro Patria Union was on the rise, after former prime minister Mart Laar was elected leader. A November poll showed highest support for the Pro Patria Union Party, followed by the Reform Party and Center Party. The ruling alliance, led by the Coalition Party, saw its approval rating drop several percentage points.

Siimann's ruling coalition was also shaken by attacks on leadership. Controversy arose over the decision of Foreign Minister Toomas Henrik Ilves to give up his independent status and join the non-parliamentary Farmers' Party (ETRE) in December 1997. Interior Minister Robert Lepikson publicly protested the move by Ilves, and was fired by Siimann, who replaced him with former banker Olari Taal. Ilves resigned in October, blaming pressure and attacks on him and his ministry.

Elites in the opposition also came under attack. Siim Kallas, Reform Party leader and former president of the Bank of Estonia, was charged in connection with the loss of $10 million from the former North Estonian Bank (NEB) under his leadership at the Bank. The $10 million had been invested by the NEB in a Swiss company, with money borrowed from the Bank of Estonia. Waiving his own immunity as a member of parliament, Kallas was charged with abuse of power, submission of false information, and preparing to embezzle and was later (in 1999) cleared of the charges. The Bank of Estonia assumed no responsibility in connection with the deal.

SOME MEMBERSHIPS MORE ELUSIVE THAN OTHERS

Estonia started formal negotiations for EU membership in March, with actual talks beginning in November as Latvia and Lithuania continued lobbying for the start-up of their own negotiations. The EU Commission recommended that Latvia start entry talks by the end of 1999 and with Lithuania "within a reasonable period," but the proposal was rejected at the December EU summit in Vienna. The EU Commission had evaluated Estonia's readiness for membership in its "Avis" (Opinion) in mid-1997, according to the 1993 Copenhagen Criteria that focus on broad issues such as democracy and protection of human rights. The negotiations according to the "Acquis," the legal framework with which EU members must comply, are stricter and more technical and in 1998 Estonia took a major step forward in this painstaking process.

Accession negotiations concerned seven of the 37 chapters of EU legislation, including areas such as science and research, telecommunications and information technology, education, training, and culture. Estonia promoted a frontrunner image by not asking for a transition period in any of the seven areas under discussion. Also in 1998 Estonia introduced some changes in agricultural policy in the direction of harmonizing with EU practices, such as allowing for direct subsidies per hectare sown and per cow. Estonia's extremely liberal economy has practically permeable, tariff-free borders, which should make the introduction of EU external tariffs relatively easy later on. Politicians predicted Estonia would be ready for accession by 2002, but acknowledged that much depends on the willingness of current EU members to devote resources to enlargement and expand the number of countries eligible for subsidies.

Besides the huge body of legislation requiring harmonization, Estonia continued to demonstrate its solid human rights record to Western institutions. In March Estonia abolished the death penalty, although the parliamentary vote was rather close (39 to 30), reflecting some reluctance among the public but also realism in terms of criteria for EU accession. In December the parliament adopted constitutional amendments designed to ease citizenship requirements for approximately 6,000 Russian-speaking children. Children born in Estonia after February 1992 to stateless parents resident in Estonia five years, who do not have the citizenship of another country, are now to be allowed to apply for Estonian citizenship without passing an Estonian language test. The Organization for Security and Cooperation in Europe and EU were strongly in favor of the amendment (which resembled one adopted by Latvia in October), stating that it would be the last requirement they would make in this area. The final version of the amendments included a clause limiting application to children who are not considered citizens of any other country under that country's laws and not just under Estonia's laws. Technically, if the Russian Duma granted Russian citizenship to former Soviet citizens living outside the Russian Federation, this could disqualify some children, but opinions were divided as to how likely this scenario would be.

A proposed amendment to the constitution adopting tougher language requirements for elected officials, which was narrowly defeated, would have required all people running for public office to speak and read Estonian. Current law required a basic knowledge of Estonian, but the proposed change would have required public officials to demonstrate the highest proficiency in the language. The main target of the law was elected officials on the municipal level whose native language is not Estonian. Since non-citizens were able to vote in local elections, increasing numbers of Russian-speaking representatives were getting elected. Russian MPs opposed the proposed law, arguing it would infringe on the free choice of the electorate. In the event, President Lennart Meri vetoed the bill, arguing that it gave too much power to the executive by authorizing it to check the language proficiency level of already elected MPs and local government council members. This issue illustrated the dilemmas of integration—would the integration of Russian-speakers be better served by more or less demanding language standards for their elected representatives? A government program for integrating aliens was adopted in February, aiming to strengthen the role of the Estonian language in society, especially through the education system.

Estonia naturalized over 9,000 people in the first 11 months of 1998, up from about 6,700 in the same period of 1997. Of the new citizens, about 5,900 were children. Altogether over 105,000 people have been naturalized since 1992. According to the Interfax news agency, only 22,000 out of 320,000 non-citizens of Estonia had been issued permanent residence permits by the end of 1998.

Some politicians argued that Estonia is moving too far too fast, promising reforms to Brussels before they are voted on in Tallinn. "Euroskepticism" seemed to be on the rise, as critics of rapid EU accession pointed to issues such as agriculture and immigration and the need for more information from government agencies concerning the process. They also pointed out obvious financial constraints, at least in the short term, asking why the fast track to the EU, and at what price? A May poll found that only 44 percent of the Estonian population favored EU accession, while 57 percent supported NATO membership.

Membership in the World Trade Organization was hindered in 1998 by harsh evaluations of Estonia's anti-piracy efforts, also damaging its reputation for free competition in the EU. The International Intellectual Property Alliance estimated that 80 percent of recordings and 99 percent of videos produced in Estonia were illegal.

In contrast to EU or WTO membership, joining NATO remained in 1998 an even more elusive goal for Estonia. While it was clear the Baltic states would not be included in the first round of NATO expansion in 1999, Estonia's prospects for eventual membership were not excluded, but were still unclear. Politicians spoke of increasing defense spending from the 1998 rate of 1.1 percent to 2 percent of GDP in order to match the NATO member country average (Latvia spent 0.62 percent and Lithuania 1.5 percent). Lithuania seemed to have better prospects for future membership than Estonia or Latvia, due to a higher defense spending, its border with Poland, and a relatively small ethnic minority population.

The signing of the U.S.-Baltic Partnership Charter in January marked a symbolic step toward linking the country's security with Western interests, although U.S. officials steered clear of supporting full NATO membership for the Baltic states. Establishment of the Baltic-American Partnership Fund was also announced, which was to offer $15 million dollars from U.S. Agency for International Development and the Soros Foundation to support better economic ties.

Meanwhile, joint operations continued to show Estonia's willingness to cooperate at regional level and to bring their forces into line with NATO standards. Projects included: Baltbat, the Baltic peacekeeping battalion (200 from each country); Baltron, the joint Baltic naval squadron, supported by 9 Western countries; Baltnet, the airspace monitoring system; and Baltdefcol, the Tartu-based Baltic Defense College set to open in 1999. A Tallinn-based joint minesweeper squadron was organized to remove more than 40,000 mines that were planted during the World Wars on the Baltic seabed. Estonian, Finnish, and Russian border guards also engaged in joint naval exercises, practicing how to detect and seize a ship carrying illegal immigrants.

Military assistance and sales from Western countries attracted attention, for example when Sweden agreed to increase the sale of arms and ammunition to the Baltic states, incurring criticism from the Swedish peace movement. The United States also decided to extend to Estonia credit of $5.7 million, most of which will be used for regional airspace monitoring. A training program and the transfer of used military equipment were also introduced.

RUSSIAN RELATIONS: IMPERCEPTIBLE PROGRESS?

Relations with Russia were at a relative standstill in 1998, with some moderate improvements but also the usual setbacks. At times it seemed the heat had been taken off Estonia, as Russian diplomatic attention was focused on tensions with Latvia. On other occasions, Moscow's hostile rhetoric was directed at Estonia and Latvia together for their alleged abuse of human rights. For example, Russian Foreign Minister Igor Ivanov in his address to the UN General Assembly in the autumn, said Latvian and Estonian authorities were adopting "brutal repressive measures" against Russians living within their borders. He called on the international community to impose sanctions on countries that abuse human rights.

Estonia's relations with Russia were nonetheless calmer in 1998 relative to Latvia's. An intergovernmental commission continued its work at a mid-diplomatic level and, after several postponements, the first high level meeting between Estonia and Russia since the fall of the Soviet Union took place. Agreements were signed relating to education and culture, but the issue of double tariffs remained unresolved. A draft agreement for abolishing the double tariffs had been prepared, but its adoption was linked to the treatment of Estonia's ethnic Russian minority, e.g. easing naturalization laws for children, improving the treatment of pensioners, and handing over the Nevskii cathedral to the Moscow-affiliated Orthodox Church. Any optimism concerning relations with Russia was thus tempered by the realization that foreign policy elites would continue to use the "diaspora card" if deemed useful.

The utility of the diaspora card was nowhere clearer than in Estonia's foiled attempts to reach a border agreement with Russia. Negotiations have taken place over six years and a draft agreement was concluded in 1996, but no agreement had been signed at year's end.

ECONOMY WEATHERS EASTERN STORMS

The Estonian economy was badly shaken by the volatility of world stock markets in late 1997, with stock values falling in Tallinn. Since bank shares accounted for much of the stock market capitalization, Estonian commercial banks incurred heavy losses and cut back on lending. The Estonian banking sector had been relatively healthy since the crash of 1992 that led to the closure of smaller and weaker banks. Amidst the Asian crisis, the Bank of Estonia set new and tighter reserve requirements for local banks.

In contrast to the economic overheating which had caused some worry in 1997, economic growth "cooled down" in 1998. Real GDP growth in 1998 was around 4 percent, and inflation was about 10 percent. The current account deficit narrowed from the 1997 level of 12 percent to 8.6 percent of GDP (6.3 billion kroons or $452 million). In Latvia and Lithuania the deficit grew, respectively, to over 11 percent and 12 percent. The deficit was accompanied by a healthy increase in trade: exports were up 18.5 percent and imports 12.6 percent from 1997 levels. The kroon continued to be pegged to the German mark at the rate of 8:1. Growth in tourism contributed to the surplus in the balance for services, covering 55 percent of the trade deficit. The real rate of unemployment (considerably higher than the officially recorded rate) for the year is estimated to be 9–10 percent, and it was much higher in areas where ethnic Russians predominate.

Estonia's main trading partner in 1998 was the EU, with 54 percent of exports, mainly in machinery and equipment, and 60 percent of imports (mainly to Finland and Sweden). Early in the year, however, the EU denied Estonia access to market its dairy products, due to hygiene regulations, and dairy producers succeeded in shifting some of the exports to Russian markets. Later in the spring Russia imposed a new customs accounting system, calculating import duties on the amount of goods and not their reported price, which cut into Estonian sales. Shifting exports to the other Baltic states was also difficult: the 1997 Baltic Free Trade Agreement on agricultural products was found wanting due to varying price support policies, and there were disputes over quality in what was labeled the "pork war." By year's end a resolution of the pork dispute was reached, but the ongoing tension between cooperation and competition in Baltic agreements was still evident.

The current account deficit continued to be a worrisome issue, as experts warned that it could threaten the country's ability to repay the large loans being received from the IMF and the European Bank for Reconstruction and Development (EBRD). Others considered the deficit normal for a transitional economy in need of massive re-investment. Potential policy responses included subsidizing export production and introducing protectionist tariffs on imports.

Advocacy of import tariffs increased in the wake of Russia's economic crisis. Russia was one of Estonia's most important trading partners, holding third place in exports (13 percent) and second in imports (11 percent). Half of all Estonian exports to Russia were foodstuffs, accounting for 33 percent of dairy exports and 80 percent of fish sales. In the first half of 1998, Estonia's total export of goods increased by 17 percent, in the last half the increase was only 6 percent, due to the Russian crisis. The Russian share of Estonia's merchandise exports fell from 16 percent in January to 7 percent by October. The Russian crisis was also felt in the Russian-speaking "diaspora," since the Russian government failed to pay the pensions of over 8,000 former Soviet soldiers living in Estonia over several months in the latter part of the year.

Although state officials initially attempted to play down the effects of the crisis, the impact on GDP was clear: growth fell from 9.3 percent in the first quarter of 1998 to 1.8 percent in the third. Many businesses announced layoffs or mandatory vacation leave for thousands of employees. A survey by the Estonian Chamber of Commerce and Industry (ECCI) found 27 percent of the 200 companies surveyed were cutting back on their labor force. The government cut penalties for late payment of taxes but avoided dipping into its stabilization fund, held in a German bank, keeping it for a more severe crisis.

A crisis in agriculture mounted in the latter part of the year. In the summer of 1998 rain and storms damaged the harvest in some areas. In addition, many farmers had put their money into the now collapsed Maapank; creditors feared they might not get back all their money. Farmers found it impossible to compete with foreign importers and subsidized goods and lacked the cash to invest in new equipment; one third of Estonian farmland remained uncultivated. In October 2,000 farmers staged a peaceful protest in front of the parliament building in Tallinn. They demanded compensation for crop losses and more consultation in EU trade. After protracted negotiations, agricultural producers backed down from their 820 million kroon demand and accepted the government's offer of 730 million kroons ($52 million) in support for 1999. In the wake of the farm protests, in November the government proposed introducing import duties starting in January 1999—a step which would violate its trade agreements with the EU and other countries. The measure was defeated in parliament, but in early December farmers once again protested the lack of tariffs by demonstrating near border checkpoints.

UPHEAVAL IN THE BANKING SYSTEM

Major upheaval occurred during 1998 in the banking sector. By the end of the year the nation's 11 banks had shrunk to five (plus one foreign subsidiary). Tallinna Pank and Uhispank agreed to merge under the latter's name in April, making it the second largest bank in Estonia after the merged Hansapank-Hoiupank (Hansapank), which is controlled by Sweden's Swedbank. Hansapank was the only major bank in the country to make a profit in 1998. Hansapank and Uhispank together accounted for 80 percent of the market share.

In June, the Central Bank revoked the operating license of Maapank, the sixth largest bank, marking the first of many bank closures during the year; it was declared bankrupt by the Tallinn City Court in August. The government was criticized for having previously deposited state funds in the bank when it was already clear it had financial problems. Eventually the government offered to compensate 80 percent of private and 100 percent of government deposits, allowing for a total of 270 million kroons to be paid out.

Other banks were threatened with closure during the year. A medium-sized bank (Forekspank) was recapitalized in October by the Bank of Estonia in order to forestall its collapse due in part to large withdrawals of Russian funds. The central bank also took control of the new Optiva bank, the nation's third largest, which reported a loss of 179 million kroons in 1998. The Bank planned to sell its stake to a strategic investor by the end of 1999

On a brighter note, direct foreign investment in Estonia reached in 1998 a record high of 7.94 billion kroons ($550 million), doubling the 1997 level (EEK 3.7 billion). This was equal to 11 percent of GDP, and was the third highest per capita figure in the post-socialist bloc after Hungary and the Czech Republic. Forty-nine percent of the total foreign investment in 1998 was in the banking sector and 20 percent in industry; Finland and Sweden topped the list of foreign investors. Offering low costs and a skilled workforce, Estonia became a base for assembly and semi-manufacturing of modern high-tech goods such as mobile phones, many of which were exported to Russia. In 1998 Telia of Sweden and Sonera of Finland jointly bought 46.5 percent of Eesti Telecom shares.

Overall, the year ended on a sobering note for the economy, with a clear slowdown of sales in industrial and consumer goods and predictions for a low growth rate in 1999.

The growing gap in Estonia between rich and poor became more evident in 1998. The winners are more likely to be aged 25 to 34; people over 50 and women are increasingly losers in Estonian society. Estonia spent a smaller proportion of its GDP on social benefits than any other EU country except Greece. For example, the unemployment benefit in 1998 in Estonia was about 300 EEK, or $23 a month, and only about a quarter of the unemployed were actually receiving benefits in 1998. The United Nations Development Project annual report divided Estonian society into three groups: the top 23 percent enjoyed 50 percent of total income; the middle group 33 percent received 30 percent of total income; and the bottom 44 percent received 20 percent of total income.

In conclusion, 1998 was a sobering year for Estonia, including: painstaking efforts at EU accession; fighting a trade imbalance in the face of Eastern and Western barriers; surviving the fallout from too rapid economic expansion and deepening social inequality. Taking steps to consolidate its party system, strengthen its human rights record, and broaden its citizenry, revealed, however, that Estonia could enjoy some small victories as its neighbors recovered from an even more turbulent year.

Belarus

Population:	10,279,000
Capital:	Minsk (pop. 1,693,000)
Major cities:	Homel (pop. 383,000), Vitsebsk (pop. 297,000), Mahileu (pop. 290,000)
Area:	207,600 sq. km.
Major ethnic groups:	Belarusian 77.9%, Russian 13.2%, Polish 4.1%, Ukrainian 2.9%, other 1.9%
Economy:	GDP growth: 8.3%
	Inflation rate: 180%
	Unemployment rate: 2.8% (1997)

BOTTOMED OUT?

by USTINA MARKUS

Just as every year since the election of Alyaksandr Lukashenka as president of Belarus in 1994, in 1998 the country experienced more international isolation, a strengthening dictatorship, and zero progress in market economic reform. With such a record of authoritarianism and economic stagnation, it is an open question whether the downward spiral can continue much longer, or whether the country has finally bottomed out.

INTERNATIONAL ISOLATION

One of the noteworthy achievements of Lukashenka's regime in 1998 was to outdo its previous records of international gaffes, and make Belarus even more of an international pariah. This was not an easy achievement. Back in 1995, Lukashenka made quite a splash on the international arena when the country's air defense forces shot down a hot-air balloon competing in an international competition, killing its two American pilots. Lukashenka refused to apologize or accept any blame on the country's part. Over the next two years, Belarus made international headlines for a series of negative incidents. Lukashenka's security forces beat parliamentary deputies protesting his policies; the president made a speech admiring the powers Adolf Hitler had held, and saying how he would like that kind of authority; Belarusian UN diplomats got into a fight with New York police when the police tried to apprehend them for drunken driving, and Lukashenka blamed American imperialism for the incident.

While such a record of international faux pas is difficult to beat, President Lukashenka succeeded in doing so. The major international scandal in 1998 was Lukashenka's decision to have all of the foreign diplomats living in the Minsk diplomatic compound at Drazdy locked out of the residences because the complex allegedly needed repairs. While it is difficult to gauge the real reason for the eviction of the 22 ambassadors (including the Russian ambassador) from their residences, it appears to be simply that Lukashenka wanted the compound, or part of it, for himself. The ambassadors received the initial eviction notice in April. The justification for their vacating the premises was that the sewage system and plumbing in the complex needed repairs. The ambassadors balked at the notice, pointing out that under the Vienna Convention, ambassadors' residences are treated like embassies and are considered the property of the ambassadors' countries. They offered to assist in any necessary repairs themselves so they would not have to move, but Lukashenka was adamant that the diplomats leave. The president then demonstrated that the repair issue was a pretext when he changed the reason for the eviction. He declared the complex his own residence, and his foreign minister publicly stated it was inappropriate for the president to live next door to the foreign dignitaries.

In May, the ambassadors received notice that as of 10 June, they would have no further access to the Drazdy compound. In order to underscore the point, on 8 June a team of workers was sent to U.S. Ambassador Daniel Speckhard's residence to weld the gates shut. The welders did not manage to complete the job, since they drove off when the ambassador arrived with a band of journalists. As a result of the bizarre eviction notice, and the determination to enforce it, the United States, five EU countries, Turkey, and Japan recalled their ambassadors and asked that the Belarusian ambassadors to their countries return to Minsk. In addition, in July all European Union (EU) foreign ministers and the United States adopted a resolution to impose travel restrictions on Belarusian officials. Those restrictions applied to President Lukashenka, his cabinet ministers and their deputies, parliamentary speakers and deputy speakers, Constitutional Court justices, military and KGB generals, and several other officials. In all, 131 Belarusian officials were barred from entering any of the 15 EU countries or the United States.

Following the imposition of the travel restrictions, Minsk made an effort to work some damage control when Foreign Minister Ivan Antanovich suggested that the Western ambassadors could return after sewage repairs were completed in Drazdy. In August, this proposal was changed when Lukashenka offered new residencies in lieu of the Drazdy housing. This solution was unacceptable to the evicted ambassadors, who demanded that Lukashenka abide by the Vienna Convention in his diplomatic dealings. Minsk made a play at dividing the united front presented by the Western countries, by offering concessions to some over the matter. Overtures were made to countries that appeared more flexible over the issue to have their ambassadors return. The German charge d'affaires in Belarus, Peter Kolb, rejected any substitute housing and maintained the EU stance that Belarus had to abide by the Vienna Convention in its dealings with foreign officials.

At the end of October Antanovich announced the matter was closed when he invited the evicted ambassadors to return to their embassies except for the American, German, and French ambassadors, whose residences had been absorbed by President Lukashenka's. Those three were to have alternative housing. That did not satisfy the three Western capitals. They reiterated that the problem was not one of where they lived, but a political problem regarding the position of foreign diplomats in Belarus and their rights under the Vienna Convention. Lukashenka had a different interpretation of the dispute. He dismissed the travel restrictions imposed by the EU and United States as blackmail and provocation, finding instead that Belarus was opening the doors for the Western ambassadors to come and work in the country and it was the West that was not cooperating.

The situation remained unresolved at the end of the year. Nonetheless, there were indications in December that some progress was being made towards the issue's resolution when the five evicted EU ambassadors agreed to return and stay in temporary housing while they transferred their belongings out of their Drazdy residences. The United States refused to participate in the exercise.

The Drazdy dispute did not serve to allay other Belarusian disputes with the West. With the exception of Russia, no other European country had accepted the results of the 1996 constitutional referendum that replaced the democratically-elected 13th parliament with a Lukashenka-appointed bicameral legislature. In July, soon after the Drazdy conflict had erupted, the Organization for Security and Cooperation in Europe (OSCE) met in Copenhagen. Representatives from the 13th parliament and delegates from the new Belarusian legislature showed up to represent the country. This forced the OSCE to decide which of the two they would recognize as the legal representatives of Belarus. The vote was overwhelmingly against Lukashenka's parliament. Only Russia and Kazakhstan voted to recognize Lukashenka's lawmakers, while 52 countries voted in favor of the 13th parliament. Rather than stymieing his virulent rhetoric, the Belarusian president took the opportunity to tell his compatriots that the vote was further evidence of the West's evil intentions towards Belarus.

THE RUSSIA–BELARUS CONUNDRUM

While Lukashenka's poor relations with the West were a matter of record, his nebulous relations with Belarus's main ally, Russia, continued to defy easy categorization. Relations between the two were strained at the end of 1997 over a number of issues. These included: the incarceration of the Russian Public Television (ORT) correspondent in Belarus, Pavel Sheremet, by Belarusian authorities over his critical reports on Belarus; Minsk's chronic indebtedness to Russia's Gazprom; and the lack of progress in achieving a union. The new year did not see any real resolution to those issues. In January, Sheremet and his cameraman Dmitry Zavadsky were given suspended sentences of two years and eighteen months respectively. While this kept the journalists out of jail, and made it a less provocative sentence from the Russian perspective, the Russian media were still concerned over the treatment of journalists in Belarus. Sheremet's lawyer commented that "You don't often see journalists tried for doing their job." The United States also joined in condemnation over the treatment of Sheremet when Belarusian authorities barred him from traveling to the United States in November to receive a press freedom award.

The elusive Russian-Belarusian union continued to fail to materialize. The newly-appointed Russian Prime Minister Sergei Kirienko was inclined to follow policies for market reforms, including the cessation of subsidies to countries in the Commonwealth of Independent States (CIS). His September replacement by Yevgenii Primakov was greeted with approval in Minsk, since the new premier was considered to favor the Russian-Belarusian union, which many Belarusians equate with continuing subsidies from their larger neighbor.

The appointment of Primakov as Russian prime minister did not lead to any real progress towards union between the two countries. That appointment had been made as a result of the economic crisis that hit Russia in the summer and led to a devaluation of the ruble. Lukashenka was critical of the way the Russian government had managed the crisis. The Russian devaluation affected the Belarusian ruble, since its value was closely tied to the Russian currency. Lukashenka offered to speak with Russian President Boris Yeltsin and advise him on how to deal with the economy, touting the Belarusian economic model as the road for Russia. Lukashenka also generously offered to send aid to Russia to help it get through its crisis. Former Chairman of the National Bank of Belarus and opposition leader Stanislau Bahdankevich was startled by the offer, noting that Belarus itself was not in good shape economically and could not afford to aid a giant like Russia.

Along with Lukashenka's criticism of Russian economic management, and his insistence that Belarus would continue to manage its economy its own way even inside a union with Russia, his attitude towards the CIS Collective Security Pact ensured there would be little progress in union on that front. During the summer, Tajikistan and other Central Asian republics became increasingly concerned about Taliban aggression from Afghanistan. Rather than standing by Belarus's CIS Security Pact allies, in August Lukashenka reiterated the country's stance that it would not send troops to serve in Asia, saying that whatever the Taliban did there did not concern Belarus.

Another issue that continued to plague Russian-Belarusian relations was Minsk's gas debt to Gazprom. By June, the energy giant reduced its gas supplies to Belarus by 40 percent and threatened to continue supplying Belarus with 40 percent less than contracted for if the country did not start taking specific steps to reduce the debt. Specifically, Gazprom demanded $1 million per day if it was not to reduce the country's supplies further. In October the debt reportedly rose to $220 million, and Lukashenka was working out a loan arrangement with Primakov so that Minsk could borrow from Moscow to meet its energy payments. Owing to a shortage of rubles in Belarus, Belarusian officials made plain that much of the payment would have to be accepted through barter.

One clear sign that Russian-Belarusian relations were nowhere near the close union aspired to by Lukashenka or the Russian State Duma was the lack of real interest from Russian governors in dealing with Belarus. In July, Belarusian media announced there would be a meeting of 40 Russian regional leaders in Minsk. In fact, only five arrived. Ukrainian governors had also been invited to the Slavic jamboree, but not one showed up.

At the end of the year, on 25 December, another set of agreements was signed between Russia and Belarus over the Russian-Belarusian union. Just as previous agreements had been vague documents without definite time-tables, the new accords called for a staged integration of the Russian and Belarusian economies and political systems over the following year. They failed to specify what exactly was meant to be achieved in those areas over that year, making it doubtful that much would actually be achieved. This discrepancy between rhetoric and deed was underlined by statements made by Lukashenka just two weeks before the signing of the accords. At that time the Belarusian president said the two countries could integrate without synchronizing their economies, and continued to press for any synchronization to be along the lines of Belarus's economic policies, not Russia's.

Relations with Ukraine did not help balance out any of the difficulties with Russia. Lukashenka continued to be critical of Ukraine's refusal to join the Russian-Belarusian union. For its part, Kyiv continued to voice its concerns over the political situation in Belarus. Trade between the two declined sharply, falling by 20 percent, from $1.4 billion in 1997 to $1 billion in 1998. Both parties lamented the downward trend and called for measures to improve the situation. Other issues clouded their relations. Kyiv was concerned over Belarus's failure to ratify an agreement on the Ukrainian-Belarusian border, while Minsk wanted Kyiv to pay off earlier debts of some $17 million.

As a result of the problematic relations with East and West, Lukashenka sought to tie the country to other foreign partners. Unfortunately, given Belarus's human rights and economic records, he tended to attract partners with dubious records themselves. One of the new twists in this was Serbia's new interest in the Russian-Belarusian union. At the beginning of the year, Lukashenka visited Belgrade and received a visit from the Serbian deputy Foreign Minister Vojislav Seselj at the end of the year. During that meeting the subject of the Russian-Belarusian union was raised, with the Serbians purporting interest in joining it themselves. Other putative new partners included Iran, Syria, and Vietnam. At mid-year, Lukashenka stated that Belarus intended to join the Non-Aligned Group of countries, but did not attend a UN session to address that issue. It may have been that Lukashenka worried the United States would deny him a visa to UN headquarters in New York due to the Drazdy conflict. The previous year, Russia had denied him permission to fly over Russian airspace because of the Sheremet affair.

The appointment of a former KGB officer as the new foreign minister at the end of the year made it doubtful that Belarusian foreign relations would improve in the near future. On 4 December, Lukashenka appointed Ural Latipau foreign minister. Lapitau had been an advisor on foreign affairs to the president before his appointment. At the time of Lapitau's appointment, Lukashenka also incorporated the Ministry of External Economic Relations and the Ministry of CIS Affairs into the Ministry of Foreign Affairs.

OPPOSITION CONTINUES

Lukashenka's war against multiple enemies, both within and outside of Belarus continued. In January, the Belarusian television program *Rezanans* aired a show alleging a plot involving Western countries and the 13th parliament to perpetrate a coup d'etat against the regime. Such broadcasts had already been aired on several occasions against different foes. In 1994, the culprits were Turkish spies. The following year Belarusian state media accused the Polish Solidarity union of collaborating with the American CIA against Belarus. In 1996, Russian Duma deputy Viktor Ilyukhin announced he had evidence of another CIA, Polish, and Belarusian democratic opposition plot against Lukashenka. In 1997, the new threat to the country was Lithuanian terrorists. The 1998 conspiracy had Western countries funding anti-government forces in Belarus to the tune of $32 million, with the intention of toppling the president. The speaker of the 13th parliament, Syamyon Sharetsky, was to receive $800,000 of the money for his services, while a further $11 million was earmarked for terrorism. The opposition in Belarus dismissed the allegations as nonsense, but voiced concerns over the repeated references to terrorism. A new law on terrorism had been passed allowing for the execution of terrorists, and there had been several alleged terrorist incidents reported the year before. Some opposition members worried that groundwork was being laid for a severe repression under the guise of anti-terrorist measures.

Demonstrations in opposition to Lukashenka and his policies continued to be a feature of Belarusian politics. One of the more colorful was the Valentine's Day rally. About 1,000 protesters marched in Minsk carrying signs saying "I Love NATO," "I Love EU," and various other slogans which contradicted Lukashenka's love list. Protests were also organized on 2 April to mark the anniversary of the signing of the Russian-Belarusian union. That rally ended with clashes between demonstrators and security forces. That month, two young oppositionists who had been arrested for painting anti-Lukashenka graffiti, 19-year old Alyaksei Shydlouski and 16-year-old Vadzim Labkovich, received hefty sentences of eighteen months in a penal colony and an eighteen month suspended sentence, respectively. The OSCE opined that the severity of the sentences was to serve as deterrence to others. On 25 April, the usual Chornobyl anniversary demonstration took place. It also resulted in arrests, including 17 Russians belonging to the Russian Anti-Fascist Youth Movement. Rather than risking a new confrontation with Moscow, Belarusian authorities deported the Russians the following day.

The OSCE attempted to mediate in the ongoing conflict between the Belarusian president and democratic and nationalist opposition. At the end of April, the OSCE sponsored a conference inviting both government officials and the opposition. The conference did not resolve any of the issues between the two, as the crux of the matter was Lukashenka's new constitution, which replaced the 1994 constitution in 1996, and gave the president extremely broad powers and extended his term in office. Immediately after the conference, on 1 May, the opposition staged another demonstration in which some 5,000 participated. It ended in the arrest of 40 protesters. On 5 May, another small demonstration took place, which resulted in the arrest of ten demonstrators. Another protest followed on 14 May. Following a lull, demonstrations were held again in September to mark the 1514 victory of Belarusians against Moscow in the Battle of Orsha. In October, another rally took place commemorating the founding anniversary of the opposition group, the Belarusian Popular Front (BPF). November saw demonstrations commemorating the victims of Stalin's terror in Kurapaty, and a two-day rally organized by the Belarusian Free Trade Union to protest the government's social policies. The final major rally of the year was held on 24 November on the anniversary of the 1996 constitutional referendum which supplanted the first post-Soviet constitution with Lukashenka's own. That demonstration ended with the opposition vowing to hold presidential elections in 1999 as mandated by the 1994 constitution, and not in 2001, as Lukashenka's constitution has it. In all, it was estimated that over 500 people were arrested or beaten by authorities during the demonstrations in 1998.

LUKASHENKA'S SUPPORT

The issue of holding presidential elections in 1999 became the main item on the opposition's agenda. Lukashenka made some moves to secure his position in any upcoming elections, whether in 1999 or 2001. In December, a new law was passed barring anyone found guilty of any offense, even administrative, from running in local elections scheduled for March 1999. That law affected some 300,000 individuals, mostly from the opposition, who had been detained or fined for their participation in unsanctioned rallies. As for the presidential elections, Lukashenka still repeatedly came out as the country's most popular politician in opinion polls, indicating that he would win even in a fair election. One poll conducted in October showed Lukashenka enjoyed the support of 55 percent of the population, while the main opposition leaders—Zyanon Paznyak, Henadz Karpenka, and Stanislau Shushkevich—were each supported by only 3 percent of those surveyed. Nonetheless, a survey conducted by the independent news agency Belapan found that a 62 percent majority in Minsk supported the idea of holding elections in 1999, while only 21 percent preferred the 2001 date. It is difficult to assess how the rest of the country feels, since Minsk has always stood out as the most cosmopolitan city in Belarus and the stronghold of the opposition. During the 1994 presidential elections, Minsk was the only area in the country where Lukashenka had not won a majority.

The Belarusian Patriotic Youth Union, organized the previous year with the help of Lukashenka's son and his friends, continued to support the president. Sometimes referred to as Luksomol due to its similarities with the Soviet-era Komsomol, its members received a variety of benefits including better housing, assured places in the universities, and travel abroad. When the organization was founded in 1997, the opposition declared the privileges were essentially bribes for support, and found the union's members to be of dubious integrity. One of the more questionable actions by one of its members in 1998 was that of Lukashenka's own son Viktor. *Belorusskaya delovaya gazeta* reported the young man shot the head coach of the Belarusian hockey team in the stomach following an argument over who would be on the team for an upcoming international match. Rather than arresting the president's son, security personnel on the scene at the time drew memory blanks over the incident, and the young Lukashenka was still at liberty for his wedding that took place a month after the incident.

AN UNFATHOMABLE ECONOMY

Lukashenka's continued popularity was surprising given the economic situation in the country and his failure to deliver on the Russian-Belarusian union. In the summer, Lukashenka announced that mandatory labor would be imposed during harvesting in August, a system known as the *subbotnik* in the Soviet era. The notion was decried by the opposition as contrary to European labor laws. Wages and pensions continued to be in arrears, international financial institutions such as the World Bank and IMF still refused to release loans, and foreign investment remained painfully low. Lukashenka issued decrees curtailing the activities of independent lawyers and financial companies. There were only some 50 independent lawyers in the country in 1998, but the decree made their continued operations doubtful. As for financial companies, it was reported that there were no independent legal financial companies operating in Belarus anymore in 1998.

The real state of the economy was difficult to assess. Official statistics showed a relatively positive picture, with an increase in trade of 17 percent in the first quarter of the year. The previous year, the country had registered an incredible 18 percent increase in industrial output, but Western economic analysts found that much of that growth had been achieved through a command system which meant goods were being produced according to central directives, but were not necessarily sold. By the end of 1998, the remarkable GDP figures which official Belarusian statistics were reporting were beginning to fall.

Much of Lukashenka's real economic strategy relied on a cozy relationship with Russia. It is difficult to imagine that Russia, in the midst of its own crisis, could help its smaller neighbor, and many Russian politicians and economic leaders made it clear that they opposed subsidizing CIS states. After the Russian ruble devaluation, Lukashenka felt vindicated in following policies opposed to privatization and other market economic reform. Yet the lower inflation rates were artificial, in that they were largely due to government price controls. That real problems existed beneath the surface was clear from the issuance of a presidential decree on rationing various foods and consumer products in September. In addition, despite the price controls, by the third quarter of the year recorded inflation was above 20 percent. Another factor pointing to economic problems was the fact that the exchange rate of the Belarusian ruble plunged from 30,740 to the U.S. dollar at the beginning of the year to 78,000 by November. Trade figures also looked problematic despite the increase registered in the first quarter. The country's trade with Russia consumed an even larger portion of trade than before, amounting to over 60 percent of its total trade. Following the devaluation of the Russian ruble, trade with Russia reportedly declined. In all, Belarus registered a negative trade balance of $214 million in the first half of the year.

BOTTOMING OUT?

The continuing active opposition to President Lukashenka, his increased international isolation, and the economic problems facing Belarus raise the question of how much longer the country can continue along its current path. As early as 1995, some members of the opposition had been predicting that the rambunctious president would eventually self-destruct. This has not happened, and he continues to rule with an iron fist, finding scapegoats for the country's woes, while increasingly placing the economy, media, education, and almost everything else under his centralized control. Both domestic and foreign criticism have had little impact on his policies, and he has become politically well entrenched. Under the circumstances, barring some severe crisis that would mobilize massive support for the opposition, it is unlikely that Lukashenka would lose control. And under Lukashenka's leadership, it is probable there will be more confrontation in Belarus's future, especially with the prospect of a new Russian leader looming over the horizon, and the determination of the Belarusian opposition to push forward with presidential elections.

WIDENING CRACKS IN THE WALL
by ALEXANDER LUKASHUK

A truck carrying seven men gets stuck while navigating its way down a muddy forest road. One by one, each of the passengers disembarks and takes a turn at trying to dig the vehicle out of the mire. In doing so, each man becomes an unwitting accomplice to his own demise, for the truck's place of origin is the garage of the notorious secret police, the NKVD, and its destination is the killing field of the Kurapaty forest on the outskirts of Minsk. The seven passengers are the doomed human cargo of a transport bound for execution.

The personal stories of these seven very different men, their thoughts and insights, the dialogues and conflicts that erupt among them during this fateful journey, are the subject of "Fine Yellow Sand," one of 18 short stories written by Vasil Bykau and recently collected in a single volume titled *The Wall.*

Bykau is by far the most renowned of contemporary Belarusian writers. His works have been translated into more than 50 languages. Until recently, publishing houses in Belarus would print several hundred thousand copies of any new work written by Bykau.

But for the past several years, Belarusian President Alyaksandr Lukashenka has repeatedly denounced Bykau, a man who has come to be regarded not only as a brilliant author but as the moral leader of the democratic opposition. *The Wall* was to have been published three years ago by the state publishing house Mastatskaya Litaratura. Since then the house has deleted Bykau from its list of publishable authors.

After Mastatskaya Litaratura refused to publish *The Wall*, the independent publishing firm Nasha Niva launched its campaign for "the people's book." This campaign generated the finances necessary to publish Bykau's collection by soliciting advance orders directly from the public. *The Wall* finally saw print at the beginning of 1998.

In the short story from which the collection takes its name, a prisoner methodically widens a tiny crack in the wall of his cell, day after day, month after month, year after year. He escapes from the cell only to find himself in the prison yard, which is surrounded by an insurmountable wall.

Such is the situation for many artists in today's Belarus, where the relationship between artists and the government is very similar to the one that existed in Soviet times. In July, Lukashenka agreed to a formal meeting with approximately 30 members of Belarus's Union of Writers. Representatives of the union's board of directors addressed the leader of the nation with various complaints and appeals for assistance; some made impassioned pleas in defense of the Belarusian language.

But the president himself did most of the talking. First, Lukashenka declared that all those present were raised on the same ideals; he modestly conceded, however, that he was perhaps incapable of shedding those ideals as quickly as certain members of the literary world. Then the president tried to convince the assembled men of Belarusian letters that the vast majority of the republic's population did not want to read books written in their own language. At the conclusion of the meeting, Lukashenka promised to award stipends to the ten most talented of the 30 writers present. He seemed to take considerable pleasure in the uncomfortable silence that ensued following this obvious attempt at baiting the writers.

This was not the first time Lukashenka employed such tactics. At the beginning of his term, Lukashenka ordered the president of the Belarusian Academy of Sciences to submit a list of the 100 most talented people in Belarus. As the majority of Belarusian academics worked for the Soviet military-industrial complex, they are far more accustomed to following orders than to enjoying the free thinking usually associated with their status. The chief academician soon dutifully submitted the requested list.

Since then, members of the academy have not uttered a word in defense of the constitution, freedom of the press, or democracy. When prominent researcher Yurii Khadyka was jailed in 1996 and conducted a 25-day prison hunger strike, academic groups the world over, from New York to Japan, registered their outrage and demanded his release. The Belarusian Academy of Sciences, Khadyka's very employer, was mute.

During the Soviet Union's perestroika period, writers' unions were considered an important political force. This was particularly true in Belarus—and for far longer than anywhere else. Unlike analogous organizations in other former Soviet republics and socialist countries, the Union of Writers of Belarus never evolved into a purely professional organization; it always wielded a certain amount of political authority. Once Lukashenka took power, however, this role quickly evaporated, as the president brooked no rivalry. Lukashenka's administration took control of all state publishing houses, deciding which books to publish and how much to pay the authors. Suddenly, Belarusian writers were divested of both the economic and ideological independence they had enjoyed up to the early 1990s. In 1997, the president's administration took control of the union headquarters. The union is now merely a tenant at the House of Writers, where it is forced to seek permission even for something as routine as holding a readers' conference.

July's meeting with the president effectively wiped out any moral authority the union may have retained. The integrity of Belarusian literature remained untarnished, however, as Bykau—the soul of the literary community—did not attend the meeting. Bykau has been called everything from the Belarusian Solzhenitsyn, to the conscience of the nation, to the most profound writer of European existentialism alive today. None of these tributes seem to have any impact on the 74-year-old author and president of the Belarus Pen Center. Bykau's novels were mutilated by Soviet censorship; his texts were disseminated by *samizdat*; his every word and deed were monitored by KGB chairman Yurii Andropov. But even Soviet authorities could not ignore Bykau's talent and popularity. While the state had the KGB spy on Bykau, it also awarded him with the highest national honors. Bykau's name was even reportedly submitted for consideration for the Nobel Prize in Literature.

A monument in western Ukraine commemorating the fallen heroes of 1944 erroneously bears the name of Lieutenant Vasil Bykau. The writer in fact survived after being wounded in battle and saw the war come to an end while stationed in Austria. Bykau's personal war as a writer of truth battling against the hypocrisy of the state was just beginning, however. His short stories, which brought Bykau his greatest fame, also earned him the enmity of Soviet authorities, who had little regard for truth, be it about the war or any other subject. Bykau's stories about the war were not the routine jingoistic tales of vanquishing the enemy or saving the motherland; they were simple but eloquent musings about man in the midst of the hellish, incomprehensible madness of the trenches.

Although Bykau's earliest work is often compared to that of Erich Remarque and Ernest Hemingway, he in fact took realism a step further. Bykau's protagonists live in a world where defeat is inevitable. While Hemingway's old man loses his battle with the sea, he at least gains the respect of others; in individual dignity, at least, there is victory. For Bykau, the only victory possible is the simple victory of death.

Pessimism was anathema in the former Soviet Union, and critics branded Bykau's work pessimistic so often that the author himself was forced to respond. "It is the absolute right of the artist to determine his central theme. Every birth bears the mark of death. Final defeat is encoded genetically even on the cellular level," he said.

In one of his last interviews, academician Andrei Sakharov said he was rereading Bykau's works because they had a profoundly moving effect on him. As a deputy of the Supreme Soviet, Mikhail Gorbachev was often known to express his appreciation and deep respect for the famed Belarusian writer. Bykau's work received the Vatican's award for humanity. At the other end of the spectrum of Bykau's admirers was popular underground novelist Venedikt Yerofyeyev, author of the poem *Moscow-Petushki*, who named Bykau as his favorite living author.

In his writings, Bykau succeeds in identifying one of the core moral truths of the modern world—that at the end of the millennium, man is as impotent in the face of cruelty as he was 2,000 years ago. The slaughter in Rwanda happened only three years ago; the Balkans are still bleeding.

"I'm afraid that we do not properly understand the changes that are taking place at the end of the century," Bykau told *Transitions*. "Not only is the cultural paradigm changing, but perhaps also the paradigm of the entire modern civilization." Albert Camus once said that man only begins to seek the meaning of life when he is threatened by death. Yet Bykau points out that even after a calamity as threatening to man's survival as Chornobyl, many continue to resist looking inward.

It is in the post-Chornobyl period that Bykau's latest, as-yet unpublished novel, *The Wolf's Hole*, takes place. An embittered young soldier deserts the army where he was mercilessly abused and finds refuge in the polluted, radioactive Chornobyl zone, where the mere act of breathing or drinking water may result in death. Not so long ago, such a macabre place seemed to exist only in the realm of science fiction; today the deadly perimeters of Chornobyl's reach are clearly defined on the map of Belarus. And within these boundaries live simple people with simple needs—food, water, shelter. Simple also is the fate these hapless inhabitants of a poisoned land will undoubtedly share.

What, after all, can be simpler than death?

NOTE

Reprinted with kind permission from *Transitions* magazine, October 1998.

Ukraine

Population:	50,090,000
Capital:	Kyiv (pop. 2.5 million)
Major cities:	Kharkiv (pop. 1.5 million), Odesa (pop. 1.1 million), Dnipropetrovsk (pop. 1.1 million)
Area:	603,700 sq. km.
Major ethnic groups:	Ukrainian 72.7%, Russian 22.1%, Jewish 0.9%, Belarusian 0.9%, Moldovan 0.6%, Bulgarian 0.5%, Polish 0.4%
Economy:	GDP growth: –2%
	Inflation rate: 25%
	Unemployment rate: 2.9%

TREADMILL POLITICS
by USTINA MARKUS

Parliamentary elections under a new electoral law were held in Ukraine in 1998. The law allowed for an equal number of both single candidate and party seats in the hopes that this would give parties wider representation the legislature. In fact, the newly elected parliament was dominated by conservatives and closely mirrored the political alignment of the previous two legislatures. The result was that the conflicts between the executive and parliament continued along the same lines as before. This meant the country's economic policies also continued along the same road as before. President Leonid Kuchma and his government were more responsive to international financial institutions such as the IMF and World Bank in formulating economic policy, while the legislature was more responsive to its largely conservative electorate and was at odds with the market reform programs advocated by the IMF.

The usually virulent conflict over economic policies did not become as intense as might be expected, since they were swamped by the shock to the Ukrainian economy which followed the Russian financial crisis in August. By the end of the year there was little political will on the part of the executive to push through any tough programs, since presidential elections were due to be held in 1999. This discouraged the president from taking any overly harsh measures by the autumn as the pre-election campaign had effectively already begun. Ultimately, the domestic situation in Ukraine continued to be dominated by the stagnation in living standards. In addition, corruption remained a high-profile element of political and business life. Since these negative trends have been a constant feature of Ukraine since its independence, Ukraine can be said to have remained *stable* or *stagnant*, depending on the reader's proclivity for optimism or pessimism, throughout 1998.

ELECTIONS AND POLITICAL VIOLENCE

Back in 1997 Ukraine's parliament approved a new election law. The previous legislation governing elections had been regarded as flawed, since it enshrined some Soviet-era assumptions about desired electoral practices. It required a minimum voter turnout of 50 percent for an election to be considered valid, and a candidate had to garner over 50 percent of that vote to win. In reality this meant that few candidates won in the first round of elections, necessitating run-off elections. If these failed owing to low voter turnout, or the invalidation of votes leaving both candidates with fewer than 50 percent of the votes cast, then by-elections had to be held. The result of the electoral law was that repeat elections had to be held in many districts several times over, and some districts failed to elect deputies altogether. The new electoral law was meant to correct those short-comings by lowering the minimum voter turnout requirement to 25 percent, and doing away with the 50 percent of votes cast requirement for a candidate to win. It was also meant to give parties more representation by dividing the 450 seats in the legislature evenly between party tickets and individual candidates. For a party to win representation on the party list it had to win the support of at least 4 percent of the electorate. Previously, the majority of candidates elected had been independent candidates, and parties with considerable support found their candidates losing out because of the multiple candidates being fielded per slot.

Elections were held on 29 March. Despite the new election legislation, the composition of the new parliament did not differ much from the previous one. The largest number of party seats was won by the Communist Party of Ukraine, just as before. In all, the communists won 84 party seats, and 40 more communist deputies were elected from the individual candidates. The centrist national-democratic People's Rukh took a total of 46 seats—33 from the party lists and 13 from individual slots. The United Socialist Democratic Party (USDP) took 29 seats total; the Green Party garnered 19 party seats; the People's Democratic Party (PDP), which supported President Kuchma, won 17 seats; its rival Hromada, which supported former Prime Minister Pavlo Lazarenko, took 22 party seats; the Progressive Socialist Party (PSP) and the Social Democratic Party (SDP) each won 14 seats. The Peasants' Party (SelPU) did not manage to pass the 4 percent barrier, but its candidates won ten places on individual tickets. Independent candidates filled 114 seats. The Central Electoral Commission voided eleven out of the 225 single-mandate races. Among those who found their elections annulled were the former justice minister, Serhii Holovaty, and the leader of the leftist PSP, Natalya Vitrenko. In addition, as legislation banned individuals from holding both government posts and parliamentary seats simultaneously, a slew of newly-elected parliamentarians had to choose which post they would hold. In all, seven ministers, 12 deputy ministers, four heads of state committees, 13 deputy heads of state committees, and eight chiefs of central authorities had to give up their posts.

Once the independent candidates and parliamentary factions had forged their alliances, the new legislature was divided fairly evenly between leftists and centrist-reformists. In June the communists had 121 supporters; the PDP claimed 90; Rukh could count on 47; Hromada was backed by 44; the SDP was supported by 35; the Peasants' Party (which had not cleared the 4 percent barrier) also found it had the support of 35 deputies; the USDP had 27 supporters; the Green Party had 25; and Vitrenko's PSP had 15. Only 41 deputies from the 225 single mandate slots remained uncommitted to any faction. While ideologically the Hromada party would have had more common ground with the centrist-reformists, owing to the PDP's inclusion in that faction Hromada found itself supporting the leftists in opposition to Kuchma on many issues.

The relatively even divide between left and center made the election of a parliamentary speaker problematic. A simple majority of the total number of deputies, or 226 votes, was needed to elect a speaker. While that appeared fairly straightforward, since the legislature was so evenly divided it took 20 rounds of voting before the leftist Oleksandr Tkachenko, a member of the Peasants' Party, was finally elected as parliamentary chairman with 232 votes in his favor. The repeated rounds of voting and bargaining that took place between leftists and centrists prior to Tkachenko's election illustrated that neither faction would be able to dominate the new parliament.

International monitors reported that during the elections the voting itself had run smoothly without irregularities. Nonetheless, a high degree of violence accompanied the ballot. Just before the votes were cast, on 23 March, the head of the Ukrainian Security Service, Volodymyr Radchenko, reported that 34 candidates had been seriously assaulted in the run-up to elections. A month after the elections, Vadim Hetman, the head of Ukraine's currency exchange and one of the country's most influential bankers, was killed outside his apartment in Kyiv. Hetman had previously chaired the parliamentary budget and finance committee. He lost his seat in the March elections, but filed an appeal with the Central Electoral Commission contesting the voting results and asking that the commission review the voting. The murder remained unsolved at the end of the year.

Political violence was also seen in Odesa. There, the incumbent mayor, Eduard Hurvits, defeated the head of the regional administration appointed by Kuchma, Ruslan Bodelan, in the mayoral race. Bodelan had complained to the local court just before the elections that Hurvits was violating campaign laws. The court found Bodelan's charges valid, and ordered that Hurvits's name removed from the ballot. The Odesa City Court overturned the local court's ruling, and reinstated Hurvits on the ballot. This prompted Kyiv to act against the mayor. Prime Minister Valerii Pustovoitenko personally oversaw the operation, which entailed sending a platoon of special security forces to occupy the Odesa City Hall. The same day, special security forces also took over the local ART television station, which had been supportive of Hurvits. Hurvits was not in Odesa when the operations took place, but was quick to denounce the maneuvers. He attacked Bodelan and accused him of connections with Russian organized crime. Bodelan retorted that Hurvits was the one with criminal connections, specifically with the Chechen mafia. Following the operation, Pustovoitenko appointed a temporary acting mayor for the city, Mykola Biloblotsky. Hurvits's strong-arm tactics in Odesa had come under criticism from the media before his replacement. Two publishers critical of Hurvits had been killed since 1997, and a third went missing.

MEDIA AND CORRUPTION

While Ukraine did not score high marks in its economic performance, it managed to score high for its level of corruption. A report put out by an independent anti-corruption watchdog, Transparency International, ranked Ukraine as the 16th most corrupt country out of 85 it had studied. The most notorious perpetrators appeared to be the country's prime ministers. In 1992, Vitalii Fokin was forced to resign from that post following mass protests against his policies and accusations of corruption. Another of Ukraine's premiers, Yukhym Zvyahilsky, was forced out of office and moved to Israel to escape charges of corruption. He was eventually granted immunity and allowed to return without threat of arrest in exchange for cooperating with authorities. The latest ex-prime minister to face corruption accusations was Pavlo Lazarenko. He was forced to resign from the premiership in 1997, owing to his unsavory reputation as one of Ukraine's most corrupt individuals. Following his resignation, he became a parliamentary deputy and one of the most vocal critics of President Kuchma. Lazarenko founded his own party, Hromada, which was vehemently critical of Kuchma, and began laying the groundwork for his own presidential election campaign against Kuchma in 1999.

The result of Lazarenko's declared war on Kuchma was to mobilize Kuchma to move against his former appointee. In March, Chief Prosecutor Mykhailo Potebenko appealed to parliament to lift Lazarenko's immunity as a deputy so he could be charged with holding illegal bank accounts abroad, stealing state property, misappropriating public funds, and abusing his position when he served as prime minister. The appeal came just days before parliamentary elections, so no vote was taken on the request. Despite the legislature's inaction against Lazarenko in the first quarter of the year, other government authorities were putting pressure on the former premier through various means, besides the threat of arrest.

One tactic that came under criticism from the international community was the government's use of media intimidation against Kuchma's opponents. In January, *Pravda Ukrainy* was banned from printing because it was allegedly improperly registered. The paper was closely associated with Kuchma's political rival, Lazarenko. Just before the elections, another paper associated with Lazarenko, *Vseukrainskie viedomosti*, was also forced to close after being fined a hefty $2.5 million in a libel suit. Just days before the election, on 24 March, another Lazarenko mouthpiece, *Kievskie vedomosti*, reported a serious incident. Several bombs exploded in its headquarters and the editor-in-chief, Volodymyr Ilchenko, claimed the attack was instigated by the authorities themselves—a reference to Kuchma. The police opined that the bombing was contrived by the paper itself. Western media watchdogs were critical of the Ukrainian government's handling of the media, finding that Kuchma's administration was indeed heavy-handed towards unfriendly media.

Lazarenko's questionable business dealings and dubious bank accounts caused more problems for the former premier than Kuchma's tactics. On 2 December, he was arrested by Swiss authorities while trying to enter the country on a Panamanian passport. The Swiss froze Lazarenko's bank accounts in Switzerland and held him in jail while an investigative judge traveled to Kyiv to look into charges of money laundering. The freezing of the accounts had been prompted by over 20 requests from the Ukrainian government. Kyiv did not, however, request Lazarenko's extradition. After two weeks in detention, Lazarenko was released from jail after an unnamed associate put up a $3 million bond. He was scheduled to appear before a Swiss court in February 1999, to answer questions regarding the suspicious accounts. In the meantime, he returned to Ukraine where the new parliament began to debate the issue of lifting his immunity so he could be tried on charges of corruption.

Corruption charges against the current prime minister also made the headlines in 1998. At the beginning of the year, Prime Minister Valerii Pustovoitenko was under fire in parliament for allegedly embezzling some $40 million out of $80 million in contracts during the reconstruction of the Palace of Culture. The charges were based on the findings of an investigation by Lazarenko's Hromada faction. Kuchma defended the prime minister and threatened to dissolve the parliament over the issue. The president's cabinet rejected the charges of Pustovoitenko's financial improprieties and refused to dismiss him. In response, the legislature took a vote on including the question of the premier's impeachment in parliamentary debates. That issue was approved by the parliament in February by a vote of 194 to 327. Owing to the upcoming parliamentary election, however, the debate was never held. Once elected, however, the new parliament held a no-confidence vote on Pustovoitenko. In October, Hromada and their newfound allies, the leftists, again failed to remove the prime minister when they could not muster the simple majority of 226 votes necessary for his removal. A key factor preventing his ouster was the intervention of Tkachenko. The conservative speaker had been elected after many deals were brokered between the left and center in parliament. He made good on his purported debt to the centrists for their support of his chairmanship, and appealed to independent deputies to support Pustovoitenko against the vote to remove him. The leftists garnered 203 votes in favor of removal, 23 short of the number needed. As only one no-confidence vote on the prime minister is allowed per parliamentary session, the remainder of the fall/winter session proceeded without further attempts to remove Pustovoitenko.

ECONOMY

There were some positive trends beginning to appear in Ukraine's economy in the first part of 1998. For the first time since independence GDP and manufacturing were up, even if by only one percent. Unfortunately, the effect of the East Asian crisis on Russia eventually made itself felt in Ukraine. This led the hryvnya to fall, depleted Ukraine's hard currency reserves, and led the government to attempt to forcibly rollover its treasury bill issues in September. By the end of the year, instead of registering the slight growth predicted in January, Ukraine's economy shrunk 2 percent. It was the ninth year in a row that a contraction of the economy was recorded. Debt to pensioners topped 3 billion hryvnyas, and the budget shortfall was 8 billion hryvnyas. As a result, both the World Bank and IMF became even more reluctant to release funds to the country.

The national currency, the hryvnya, had been slowly declining in value from the beginning of the year. The currency corridor stood at 1.8–2.25 hryvnyas to the U.S. dollar at the beginning of the year. In August the currency was devalued when the band was changed to 2.5–3.5 hryvnyas to the dollar. By November it stood at 3.42 to the dollar, or a loss of 75 percent of its value to the dollar since the beginning of the year. The accompanying price inflation reached around 25 percent by the end of the year.

The country's currency reserves suffered as a result of trying to prop up the hryvnya. At the beginning of the year they had stood at $2.34 billion. By September, they had fallen to $860 million. In order to shore up the hryvnya, in September the government decreed that Ukrainian banks had to keep at least 75 percent of their currency holdings in the national currency. After protests, the government relented and decreased the minimum to 50 percent.

In August, the IMF had agreed to a $2.2 billion credit line to Ukraine. Although the first tranche of the loan was released in September, that same month when an acceptable budget had still not been passed by parliament, the IMF suspended the release of further credit installments. This prevented the government from being able to buy back its treasury bills. As a result, the government took a controversial step and passed a resolution on 10 September on domestic debt conversion, which restructured treasury bills maturing that month by rolling them over into longer-term Eurobonds. Most of that domestic debt was held by Ukrainian banks. Although the "conversion" was called "voluntary," some economists viewed it as tantamount to default. At that point, the government backed away from its resolution and made it genuinely voluntary. The bills yielded 33 percent annual interest, but with the decline of the hryvnya, there was little enthusiasm for retaining the bills even at that rate, although the government reported a high percentage agreed to the rollover in October.

In November, the IMF agreed to release $78 million to Ukraine. The release of the tranche was due partly to Kyiv's innovative, if not necessarily popular, method of dealing with its maturing treasury bills. Nonetheless, immediately after the release of that tranche the IMF made clear that Kyiv would not see any further credits until a realistic budget was passed. By the end of the year, Ukraine's foreign debt had risen to almost $15 billion. At the same time, the country had attracted only some $2.7 billion in foreign investment since its independence.

The 1999 state budget once again became a major point of contention between president and parliament. In October, the draft budget came under criticism from the IMF as being overly optimistic in its revenue projections. At the same time, it was unacceptable to conservatives who opposed cutting social spending. By November it had still not been passed, and the head of the parliamentary budget committee, Lazarenko's close crony Yuliya Tymoshenko, said her committee would work out their own budget as an alternative proposal to that of the government. Most deputies found her budget unrealistic. At the end of the year, after some 20 attempts to get a budget approved, parliament finally passed a budget by a vote of 226 to 2. The budget assumed a 4:1 hryvnya to dollar exchange rate. It also assumed that the deficit would be held to one percent of GDP deficit, or 1.24 hryvnyas ($354 million). Half of the deficit is to be covered by foreign loans, while the rest is to be funded internally, partly by issuing more bonds. The deficit was the smallest Ukraine had projected since its independence, and was a victory for the economically right-leaning deputies. Although the budget was not completely in line with IMF recommendations, it was aimed at convincing the IMF to release further loan tranches.

There was bad news on Ukraine's agricultural front. The 1998 harvest amounted to 26.5 million metric tons of grain. This was a quarter less than the previous year's harvest, and the second worst since independence. In the Soviet era, the country had been producing around 50 million metric tons. The Ministry of Agriculture laid the blame for the low crop on the weather, but others said it was the direct result of the government's own failure to reform the agricultural sector.

Ukraine's steel industry also suffered setbacks in 1998. The country produced some 25 million tons of raw steel annually and it has been one of its major cash earners. The Southeast Asian crisis had a negative effect on Ukraine's steel exports. That part of the world had accounted for half of Ukraine's steel exports in 1997. With the onset of its economic crisis, the Asian market drastically reduced its imports, and took steps to protect their local producers. Thailand filed an anti-dumping suit in November against Ukraine seeking to limit its steel exports. Just before that, a European steel lobby announced it planned to petition the EU to further limit Ukrainian steel exports to the EU. The previous year, the United States cut Ukraine's quota of steel exports from 500,000 tons in 1997 to just 158,000 in 1998.

Ukraine's debt to Russia's Gazprom remained an issue. Kyiv succeeded in reducing the debt from $1.5 billion at the beginning of the year to either $740 million (Ukraine's figure), or $900 million (Gazprom's figure), by November. Negotiations between Gazprom and Ukraine over the debt went relatively smoothly. By this time, Gazprom had accepted that Ukraine would be unable to pay in cash, and barter was a key element in payment negotiations. In addition, since Gazprom transported its gas to the West via pipelines passing through Ukraine, the transit fees charged by Ukraine also figured into the negotiations. In the first years of independence, Moscow had tried to use the issue of Ukraine's energy debt for political leverage, but by 1998 negotiations had lost much of their previous acrimony, and were handled less by politicians in Moscow than by representatives from Gazprom itself. This changed the character of negotiations and payments to more practical economics, rather than being driven by the desire to extract political concessions. In November, Ukrainian gas officials met with Gazprom representatives in Moscow to figure out payments. Unfortunately for Ukraine, the meeting came on the heels of a U.S. announcement that it would provide Russia with food aid. The Russian officials found the U.S. grain deal was more cost effective for Russia than importing grain from Ukraine, dashing Ukrainian hopes that it would be able to barter grain for gas. Nonetheless, a deal was hammered out owing to the practical considerations that Gazprom needed Ukraine's pipelines for its own gas exports. Details of the deal were not made public.

One of the main problems for Ukraine remained revenue collection. In order to alleviate the problem, Prime Minister Pustovoitenko adopted a colorful tactic in dealing with tax collection from delinquent companies. In July, the prime minister invited 2,000 company executives to the Palace of Culture and informed them they were there to stay until they paid their tax arrears, or signed promissory notes to pay a third of their debts to the state pension fund and 5 percent of their total debts by the end of August. Journalists reported that once the executives ascertained that the premier seriously intended to keep them locked up, they pulled out their cell phones and made the appropriate arrangements. Within a day, payment arrangements totalling $480,000 to the state budget were made. In August, Pustovoitenko resorted to similar tactics. This time he sent some 1,500 executives to a tent camp at Pereyeslav Khmelnytsky outside of Kyiv, and told them they could watch films and attend lectures on natural disasters there until their companies paid their overdue taxes. The next day, Pustovoitenko ordered the tax authorities to seize the vehicles of the directors of non-paying companies. The list of automobiles slated for impoundment numbered 11,000. In addition, the tax police fined the company executives the equivalent of $1.8 million for their arrears. Once again, the move galvanized tax delinquent companies into taking some actions to pay part of their arrears, and the company directors again signed pledges of payment so they could go home. Despite Pustovoitenko's measures, revenue collection remained off target. In mid-September it was reported that the government had only collected 44 percent of the annual target at that point, making it doubtful that it would succeed in meeting its revenue projections for the year.

The economic problems were reflected in the continuing population decline. In December, the State Committee on Statistics reported that the country's population had fallen by an additional 205,000 over the year, leaving 50.09 million inhabitants. The decline was due to decreased birth rates accompanied by rising mortality rates since 1993, when the country's population peaked at just over 52 million.

CRIMEA

In October, the Crimean parliament approved yet another constitution for the autonomous republic. This was the fifth version of a constitution since 1992. Under Ukraine's national constitution adopted in 1996, the peninsula was to draw up its own basic law which could not contradict the Ukrainian constitution and which had to be approved by the Ukrainian parliament in Kyiv, as well as the local Crimean legislature. Previous versions of Crimea's constitution had been unacceptable to Kyiv over issues of citizenship, language (the Ukrainian constitution states that only Ukrainian has the status of state language, but allows for others to have official status), and the pro-Russian Crimean legislature's inclusion of a separate legal system for Crimea in its constitution. In the latest version, article 2 specifically stated that Ukrainian laws had precedence over Crimean laws, satisfying politicians in Kyiv. The regional constitution also provided for Sevastopol to remain separate from the Autonomous Republic of Crimea as an administrative-territorial unit. The Ukrainian parliament approved the latest version of the Crimean constitution on 23 December, and Kuchma signed it into law on the last day of 1998.

Although Kyiv approved the 1998 version of Crimea's constitution, it came under criticism from the Crimean Tatars. They claimed it did not guarantee the rights of Tatar returnees. (The entire population of Crimean Tatars had been deported in 1944, and legally allowed to return in 1956, although regaining their land and property proved problematic.) The Tatar congress in Crimea, the Kurultai, appealed to Kuchma to veto the constitution for failing to provide explicit guarantees for minorities. The Kurultai was particularly concerned that without a quota system for minority representation in the Crimean legislature, the 250,000 Tatars would be a permanent minority in the parliament, and might even be unrepresented altogether. This was a serious concern for the Tatars, since the majority of the Crimean population was ethnically Russian, and was often hostile to the Tatars over various issues. In the current Crimean legislature, there was not a single ethnic Tatar representative. Tatar leader Mustafa Dzhemilyev denounced Kuchma's decision to sign the Crimean constitution as a populist move to win Crimean votes in the upcoming presidential elections. The charges held some credibility since traditionally politicians in Kyiv had been supportive of the Tatars in Crimea and upheld the quota system in representation to counter Russian dominance on the peninsula. Crimean parliamentary speaker and head of the Crimean Communist Party, Leonid Hrach, dismissed the Tatar leadership as extremists. Dzhemilyev noted that Hrach was on record on a number of occasions for stating that the Crimean Tatars had been justly deported by Stalin in 1944.

SCANT PROGRESS IN ELECTION RUN-UP

The economic picture in Ukraine looked gloomy in 1998, and there was little reason to hope for any decisive reform programs to be implemented in the run-up to the October 1999 presidential elections. Most of the country's good news came from the international front, where Ukraine continued to be relatively successful owing to its generally cooperative attitude in international affairs. It was also fortunate that it is seen as a bulwark against Russian dominance in the region by other CIS states, its Central European neighbors, and Western countries. This has prompted all of these to be supportive towards Ukraine, and even lean on international financial institutions to help it out despite its own sorry record of economic reform. In the immediate future, however, the country's own leaders girded themselves for the upcoming election battle, and were more likely to resort to populism or currying support in the West or East in the upcoming presidential elections, rather than actually attempting to deal with the issues facing Ukraine.

Profile: SPEAKER OLEKSANDR TKACHENKO: A NEW OLD PLANET
by OLEG VARFOLOMEYEV

On 7 July 1998, the almost two-month-long marathon in the Ukrainian parliament for the post of speaker finished with the election of Oleksandr Tkachenko. The choice of this tongue-tied member of the Peasants' Party (SelPU), a former agricultural entrepreneur and, earlier, agricultural minister, was quite unexpected. Tkachenko, though he was deputy speaker in the previous parliament, had not been generally counted as a favorite of the election. In May, when the deputies started casting votes, it was expected that more radical leftists, the Socialist Party (SPU) leader and former speaker Oleksandr Moroz, or the Communist Petro Symonenko, would take the third post in the state hierarchy.

Tkachenko is a burly man of 60 with bushy eyebrows a la Leonid Brezhnev, whose language is the funny mixture of Ukrainian and Russian often spoken in countryside. He may produce an impression of just a simple mind from the village, despite the fact that he holds a candidate of science degree in economics. During his tenure of the speaker's post, he has been revealed as a clever and smart public politician with moderate "red" convictions. By the end of 1998 he was generally regarded as a potential strong candidate for the presidential elections of October 1999.

GLORIOUS PAST AND SKELETONS IN THE CLOSET

"I am no star, I am rather an undiscovered planet," Tkachenko told journalists who came to see the new speaker at his news conference soon after the July election. "Of course, I am not the first person in the state, but not the second either," he said, urging the amused representatives of the press to "study" him.

Tkachenko started out as a metalworker on a collective farm in Cherkasy Region. At the age of 24, after graduating from an agricultural institute, he worked as an agronomist. In 1966 he began moving up the career ladder in the Communist Party. Later on, Tkachenko graduated from the Higher Party School—the educational institution turning out top-level Communist Party functionaries. In 1985, Tkachenko returned to the land, as the first deputy chair of the Ukrainian Soviet Republic's government committee for agriculture.

The Soviet Ukraine's last year saw Tkachenko appointed the republic's agricultural minister. Later in 1991, Tkachenko ran in the first presidential elections of the independent Ukraine. Having no chance to win, he diverted a part of electors in the west of the country from the nationalist candidate Vyacheslav Chornovil in favor of the future president and his former Communist Party comrade, Leonid Kravchuk.

In December 1992, Tkachenko sets up the agro-industrial association People and Land. The following year, apparently thanks to Tkachenko's old ties in the Establishment, the state disbursed a $70 million loan from a U.S. credit line to People and Land for cultivation of corn, which the association would never return. In 1994, parliament set up an ad-hoc commission chaired by Professor Mykhaylo Chechetov to investigate into the alleged credit misappropriation. The commission apparently did not discover any wrongdoing, but its member, Les Tanyuk, in November 1994 called a press conference to express his disagreement with the commission's line. Along with misappropriation of state funds, Tanyuk accused People and Land of forgery of the loan agreements, alleging that the association was purposely misrepresented as a state organization to facilitate the loan approval. Tanyuk demanded an independent auditing of People and Land, but, later on, parliament shelved the issue. Tkachenko denied all the accusations, calling them intrigues of political lightweights.

Meanwhile, in May 1994 Tkachenko returned to politics. He was elected to the parliament, which gave him full immunity from prosecution. Later on, he became the first deputy speaker. On 4 July 1994, several factions disrupted the work of parliament, obliging Tkachenko to temporarily resign as deputy speaker. Three months later, Chechetov's commission officially rehabilitated him after some 15 checks into the business of People and Land. The official investigation by law-enforcement agencies was closed in July 1996.

Tkachenko's political opponents, however, did not forget the mysterious affair with the never-returned loan. The nationalist Rukh deputy Roman Zvarych sued Tkachenko in court, reportedly for the symbolic $70 million, after Tkachenko publicly called the recently immigrated from the United States Zvarych "a CIA agent." In 1996, Zvarych reported that a part of the U.S. $70 million loan had been used for buying cars, VCRs, and similar "agricultural" equipment. Last year, Zvarych continued his moral crusade against Tkachenko, accusing the prosecution and court of procrastination.

RELUCTANTLY IN OPPOSITION

The 1998 election of Tkachenko to the post of speaker by 232 votes out of 314 was a political compromise. The leftist factions and Hromada of former premier Pavlo Lazarenko adamantly rejected any reform-minded or President Kuchma–backed speaker. The right-of-center supporters of President Kuchma did not want the re-election of former speaker Oleksandr Moroz, a convinced antagonist of Kuchma, let alone the Communist Party leader Petro Symonenko.

Kuchma, reportedly manipulating the parliament vote through his loyalists in various factions, endorsed the replacement of Moroz, who was generally expected to be re-elected, with the seemingly more docile member of Moroz's Left Center faction, Tkachenko. The press continued to suggest that the administration may any time punish Tkachenko for "bad behavior" by taking the skeleton of the corn loan out of the closet and restarting a criminal investigation. Shortly before Tkachenko's election, the Kuchma-steered cabinet in an outward gesture of goodwill partially canceled People and Land's debts to state organizations.

For a few months, Kuchma and Tkachenko engaged in mutual assertions of loyalty and promises of long-time cooperation. Tkachenko took the president's side in defending Pustovoytenko's cabinet from leftist attacks in parliament. In October, he asked the deputies who had filed a motion demanding the dismissal of the cabinet for poor performance to withdraw their signatures from the document. Later in the same month, the votes of the Peasants' Party faction, of which Tkachenko remained the informal leader, were instrumental in saving the cabinet from no-confidence vote.

Those almost idyllic relations with the executive could not last for long. In Ukraine, all parliamentary speakers find themselves sandwiched between the reform-minded president, who has very wide constitutional powers, and the leftist-dominated, largely anti-system legislature, which strives to curtail the presidential power. Tkachenko, as a leftist, eventually began to talk about the need to amend the constitution concerning the power of the head of state, by transferring to the parliament the authority to appoint and dismiss the cabinet, prosecutor general, and head of the National Bank. The parliament voted down several economic decrees of the president, stymieing some badly needed reforms. Tkachenko rejected the idea of lifting Lazarenko's parliamentary immunity, which was suggested by Kuchma in an effort to bring the former premier, suspected of large-scale embezzlement, to court.

Kuchma, of course, did not like all this. The president and the media under his control began talking about a new confrontation of the parliament and the speaker with the executive. This confrontation got a boost when Tkachenko in winter supported the initiative of the "red" MPs to begin the process of abolishing the presidency.

UKRAINIAN LUKASHENKA

As the months passed after Tkachenko's election, it was gradually discovered that he is probably a no less vehement Slavic integrator and advocate of a return to the "glorious" Soviet past than his namesake, the Belarusian President Lukashenka. Along with Alyaksandr Lukashenka, the Ukrainian speaker also shares an agricultural background, an outward simple-mindedness, and a notorious inability to express himself clearly.

Tkachenko blasts reforms as foreign to the Ukrainian mentality. He promises that land will never be sold as long as he chairs the parliament. It may be surprising, though, to hear this from Tkachenko—a successful agricultural entrepreneur, who, managing the business of People and Land, had apparently succeeded in making some money. The independent weekly *Zerkalo Nedeli* on 11 July 1998 cited an anonymous poll in the Ukrainian parliament, which placed Tkachenko among the ten richest deputies.

Tkachenko brandishes the absence of private property on land in Ukraine as an "achievement" of the Ukrainian parliament and himself personally, as a veteran member of the mighty lobby of Soviet-era collective farm directors. Market reforms in agriculture have been hampered by the leftists in parliament ever since the independence of 1991.

In his address to the nation on Independence Day (24 August), Tkachenko contradicted himself, urging Ukrainians to "Remember with gratitude our prominent predecessors, who stood near the wellsprings of the Ukrainian state and were the heralds of freedom and independence," and in the following paragraph calling on compatriots not to be ashamed of the 70 years of the Soviet history.

During his December visit to Russia, he went as far as advocating a joint information sphere, single currency, customs union with Russia and Belarus, and joint Black Sea Fleet, provoking the indignation of the nationalists at home. The Rukh called for his dismissal for "anti-state statements" immediately after his return from Russia. Tkachenko remained unabashed, saying that he would sign under every word he said in Moscow.

A member of the anti-NATO inter-faction association in the parliament of 1994–1998, he called for a common defense doctrine with Russia in the wake of the December air strikes on Iraq to oppose "the impunity of the American and English."

Tkachenko may be somewhat less spectacular and generally more cautious in his statements than the nostalgic dictator in neighboring Belarus, but he shares with Lukashenka many convictions and ideals, including the glorification of the Soviet past and the desire to reunify with Russia.

TKACHENKO AND FOREIGN POLICY

When it comes to relations with "far abroad"—the post-Soviet expression invented to distinguish between the former USSR, or the "near abroad," from the rest of the world—Tkachenko often looks rather awkward.

During his meeting with Cuba's ambassador in December, he asked the Castro dictatorship to use its "influence in Latin America, especially in the Caribbean countries" to assist Ukraine in joining the World Trade Organization. Speaking to French President Jacques Chirac in September, Tkachenko announced that not only Ukraine and France, but also the two statesmen have "much in common historically." Tkachenko tells the French president that they were both agricultural ministers, created rural parties in their countries, and used to head local administrations—Chirac of Paris, and Tkachenko of Ternopil Region.

The negative attitude of Ukrainian leftists towards the West is widely known. Tkachenko hardly ever misses an opportunity to express his skepticism toward

Western credits. Several weeks after becoming speaker, in July he diplomatically explained to a visiting IMF representative Mohammed Shadman-Valavi that factions in parliament have "different views" on cooperation with this financial organization. "Most Ukrainians, even deputies, hardly understand such terms as the monetary system or the planned emission," he revealed to the IMF envoy.

Speaking in November on Ukraine's problems in dialogue with the European Union to Slovenian Premier Janez Drnovsek, Tkachenko was more open, saying, "We intend to actively search for other structures of integration." The speaker, a professed advocate of re-unification with the "elder sister" in the north, obviously meant Russia. "Our peoples will never forgive us if we do not reunify," Tkachenko once said, referring to Russia, Ukraine, and Belarus.

On receiving the news about Tkachenko's election in July, the speaker of the Russian Duma Gennadii Seleznev, an ardent proponent of a Slavic union, did not conceal his satisfaction. "I know Oleksandr Tkachenko well," he said. "He is in favor of integration." Besides the mutual respect and common views with Seleznev, Tkachenko is connected by friendly ties with Russian Federation Council Chairman Yegor Stroyev. The two men know each other since Soviet times, when Stroev was secretary for agriculture in the USSR's Communist Party Central Committee, and Tkachenko headed the agricultural ministry in the Soviet Ukraine.

The personal factor coupled with Tkachenko's pan-Slavic rhetoric undoubtedly helped the Ukrainian speaker during his 17–18 December 1998 visit to Moscow to persuade the Russian lawmakers to ratify the "big treaty" between Russia and Ukraine on 25 December. The Treaty on Friendship and Cooperation, signed by Kuchma and Yeltsin on 31 May 1997, was promptly ratified by the Ukrainian parliament. The Russian lawmakers, however, procrastinated with the ratification, dissatisfied with the Black Sea accords and reported violations of ethnic Russians' rights in Ukraine, and demanded that the Ukrainian parliament should first join the CIS Interparliamentary Assembly.

In 1998, Tkachenko several times publicly denied any intention to run for the Ukrainian presidency. However, come October 1999 Ukraine may be prepared to elect someone with a political program perfectly fitting Tkachenko's professed convictions. Polls conducted in 1996–1998 revealed that the share of those in the village who were against private ownership on land grew from 43 to 66 percent. Gallup polls in the summer of 1998 showed that 55 percent of the population would favor a presidential candidate who supports reunification with Russia and Belarus. The leftist electorate equals over 30 percent of the potential voters. As a moderate leftist, Tkachenko could attract many electors, who would otherwise be prone to vote for the significantly more "red" Socialists and Communists in protest against the economic hardships Ukraine is now living through.

DYNAMIC FOREIGN POLICY CONSTRAINED BY SLOW DOMESTIC REFORM

by OLEKSANDR PAVLIUK

1997 had been a year of major accomplishments in Ukraine's foreign affairs. In that year, Ukraine succeeded in signing a Charter on Distinctive Partnership with NATO, a major political treaty with Russia, border treaties with Romania and Belarus, and a historic Declaration on Accord and Reconciliation with Poland. That level of success was not sustained in 1998, although foreign policy continued to represent one of the country's very few positive achievements.

While maintaining its consistency, Ukrainian foreign policy became more dynamic, assertive (or even positively "aggressive"), and in many ways more coherent. Partly, this was explained by the growing confidence of Ukrainian diplomacy, building on its perceived accomplishments of the previous year. The new dynamics of Ukrainian foreign policy in 1998 had also much to do with the appointment at the beginning of April of Borys Tarasyuk, former ambassador to Brussels, as the new foreign minister. Starting with a re-structuring of the ministry itself, the new minister aimed at making Ukrainian foreign policy more targeted and proactive (rather than re-active). Particular importance was attached to Ukraine's involvement in the process of European and Euroatlantic integration.

Yet in the course of 1998 it became very clear that the making of Ukrainian foreign policy was increasingly constrained by the slow progress of Ukraine's transition. While Ukrainian diplomacy further intensified its international efforts, the efficiency of those efforts and the scope for foreign policy maneuvering were significantly limited by the country's growing domestic difficulties.

There were three main directions to Ukrainian foreign policy: European and Euroatlantic integration; regional cooperation within Central and Eastern Europe and the Black Sea areas; and relations with Russia.

EUROPEAN AND EUROATLANTIC INTEGRATION

As Minister Tarasyuk emphasized on several occasions, "Ukrainian foreign policy is neither pro-Western, nor pro-Eastern. It is pro-Ukrainian, as is defined by Ukraine's national interests." Yet, the Ukrainian foreign policy establishment believed that these national interests dictate the need for Ukraine's gradual "return to Europe." In 1998, the Western "vector" in Ukrainian foreign policy became even more pronounced. Foremost priority was given to Ukraine's relations with the European Union. Kyiv strongly reiterated that full membership in the EU remains the strategic goal for the long run, while getting EU associate status was its main foreign policy priority in the medium term. The year 1998 was an important stage in the development of Ukraine–EU cooperation. On 1 March, the Partnership and Co-operation Agreement (PCA) between Ukraine and the EU, which had been signed in June 1994, finally took effect after being ratified by all EU members. On 8–9 June, the first meeting of the Ukraine–EU Cooperation Council, set up in accordance with the PCA provisions, was held in Luxembourg.

At the meeting, the Ukrainian delegation headed by Prime Minister Valerii Pustovoitenko requested for Ukraine an associate member status with the EU. EU representatives rebuffed this application underscoring that it was premature to look beyond the PCA. On 16 October the second Ukraine-EU summit took place in Vienna, which emphasized "the unique and strategic partnership linking the European Union and Ukraine."

However, Ukraine–EU relations were marked by much mutual misunderstanding and often frustration. While the EU became increasingly disappointed with the slow pace of Ukraine's reforms, Ukrainian leaders blamed the EU for not having a clear, coherent, and inclusive strategy toward Ukraine and for being unwilling to even consider Ukraine as a prospect for full EU membership in the future.

In addition to cooperation with the European Commission, in 1998 Kyiv put more emphasis on bilateral relations with key EU member-states. Particular effort was made to improve relations with France, taking advantage of Jacques Chirac's early September visit to Kyiv—the first visit of the French president to Ukraine in seven years of Ukrainian independence.

In 1998, Ukraine continued to develop its on the whole successful relations with NATO. On 8 July NATO's Secretary-General Javier Solana visited Kyiv to mark the first anniversary of the Ukraine–NATO Charter on Distinctive Partnership. A State Inter-ministerial Commission on cooperation with NATO was set up in Kyiv, and on 4 November, President Leonid Kuchma approved a comprehensive State Program of Ukraine's Cooperation with NATO. The three-year program outlined practical steps Kyiv must take to implement the Ukraine–NATO Charter in various spheres: political, military, economic, scientific, and ecological. Ukraine became the first PfP (Partnership for Peace) country to elaborate such a program. Together with NATO, Ukraine actively participated in peacekeeping in the Balkans. On the whole, Ukraine's cooperation with NATO developed more successfully than with the EU, in part because the political support given by the United States to Ukraine through NATO ties was not replicated by any leading member-state of the EU.

Ukraine-U.S. relations were also struggling with difficulties, overshadowed by Ukraine's poor investment climate and economic performance. Both sides attempted to resolve those difficulties through negotiation and dialogue, particularly in the framework of the "Kuchma–Gore" commission whose regular meeting was held in Kyiv on 22–23 July. Despite the growing disillusionment with Ukraine's reform efforts, on 30 April Secretary of State Albright recommended to Congress a continuation of U.S. financial assistance to Ukraine in 1998. In turn and in response to the U.S. request, Kyiv agreed to abandon its participation in the Russian-Iranian nuclear power contract—a step which was financially, politically, and socially painful for Ukraine and for which, as believed by the Ukrainian government, Kyiv did not receive adequate U.S. compensation.

REGIONAL COOPERATION

Viewing itself as a country belonging simultaneously to both Central and Eastern Europe (CEE) and the Black Sea area, in 1998 Ukraine redoubled its efforts to enhance its regional role and strengthen ties with its neighborhood.

Kyiv has always viewed its relations with CEE states as crucial both for the ultimate success of Ukraine's internal transformation and for the strengthening of its regional identity. It was hoped that these relations as well as multilateral regional cooperation would anchor Ukraine more firmly in Central and Eastern Europe and help to avoid the emergence of a new dividing line on Ukraine's estern border—thus bringing the country closer to Western integrated institutions. Not surprisingly and symbolically enough, the newly appointed Foreign Minister Tarasyuk paid his first official visits to Budapest and Warsaw.

As in previous years, the most dynamic and promising cooperation was between Ukraine and Poland. The two presidents—Kuchma and Aleksander Kwasniewski—met six times during the course of the year (this was more meetings than Kuchma had with any other national leader in 1998). Among all other capitals, Warsaw demonstrated the most understanding of and international support for its eastern neighbor and actively advocated Kyiv's European accession aspirations. In turn, according to all polls of expert opinion in Ukraine, Poland was constantly ranked first among Ukraine's allies. Breaking with historical grievances, the emerging special partnership between Ukraine and Poland—the two largest countries in Central and Eastern Europe—has strong potential for development into a true pillar of regional stability. Informal trilateral cooperation between Ukraine, Poland, and Lithuanian, which had been launched in 1997, was continued in 1998. In May 1998, the Polish-Ukrainian economic forum took place in Rzeszow, Poland, attended by presidents Kuchma and Kwasniewski and joined by newly-elected Lithuanian President Valdas Adamkus.

While in 1997 most attention was given to the issue of NATO expansion, in 1998 Kyiv was preoccupied with the possible negative consequences of EU enlargement. Fears were growing in Ukraine that a new EU boundary could become a "dividing line," potentially more dangerous than the security implications related to NATO enlargement. The introduction of new border regulations and stricter visa policies instituted by neighboring CEE countries joining the EU in the first wave could, in Kyiv's opinion, seriously damage trade and human contacts between these countries and Ukraine, as well as the emerging forms of transborder and regional cooperation. To diminish the potential negative impact of EU enlargement, Ukrainian diplomats suggested starting expert consultations between Ukraine and the three CEE states joining the EU—Poland, Hungary, and the Czech Republic—and the European Commission (1+3+1 formula).

Another trilateral network which continued to develop during 1998 was cooperation between Ukraine, Romania, and Moldova. On 22 October, the second summit of presidents Kuchma, Emil Constantinescu, and Petru Lucinschi took place in Chisinau, Moldova. Earlier in the year on 14 August, one of the two Ukrainian-Moldovan-Romanian Euroregions—the Lower Danube—was finally created in accordance with the agreement achieved at the first trilateral summit in July 1997. At the Chisinau summit the three presidents noted their concern with the lack of progress in the final resolution of the problem of the breakaway enclave of Transdniester, and supported the complete withdrawal of all Russian troops from the territory of Moldova in line with the recommendations of the Organization for Security and Cooperation in Europe (OSCE). In 1998, Ukraine became much more active in seeking a solution to the Transdniester conflict. In March, a trilateral Ukrainian-Moldovan-Russian summit attended by presidents Kuchma and Lucinschi as well as Prime Minister Viktor Chernomyrdin and Transdniester leader Igor Smirnov, took place in Odesa. Kyiv also agreed in principle to send its observers to Transdniester if the mission is authorized by an OSCE or UN mandate.

On 4–5 June the Ukrainian city of Yalta hosted a summit of the Black Sea Economic Cooperation (BSEC), encompassing 11 Black Sea countries, at which it was decided to transform the loose grouping into a formal regional economic organization. Kyiv was a strenuous proponent of that decision. Later in June Ukraine also participated (as an observer) in the meeting of the Baltic Sea States Council, trying to develop and build upon its natural role as a link between the Baltic and the Black Sea areas.

Ukraine's strategic interest in the Black Sea region also stemmed from its vital need to gain access to oil from the Caspian basin in order to diversify its energy supply sources. In 1998, Ukraine intensified its diplomatic efforts aimed at being chosen as a transit country for export of the Azeri oil via Georgia to Europe. An agreement was reached with Warsaw to jointly investigate the economic feasibility of building an oil pipeline from Odesa through Brody to Gdansk. The year 1998 witnessed the steady, albeit slow, development of GUAM—a non-institutionalized regional cooperative initiative encompassing Georgia, Ukraine, Azerbaijan, and Moldova, created in October 1997. While Ukraine focused its hopes on economic and energy concerns, its GUAM partners, particularly Georgia and Azerbaijan, showed more interest in joint action against separatism, conflict resolution, and military cooperation.

RELATIONS WITH RUSSIA

In 1998, relations with Russia, which since independence had been the core preoccupation of Ukrainian foreign policy, remained uneven. The beginning of the year brought attempts of Ukrainian-Russian economic rapprochement. In February, a 10-year program of economic cooperation was signed between the two countries. The adoption of the program went in parallel to the growing interest of large Russian private businesses in privatization in Ukraine. Both events caused much debate inside Ukraine. While some hoped that this would help the country's economic growth, others were concerned with the potential negative impact of Russian economic penetration on Ukraine's sovereignty. However, both hopes and fears were subdued by the Russian financial crisis, which erupted on 17 August. The crisis had a direct negative impact on Ukraine and seriously damaged bilateral trade and economic cooperation. Mutual pledges were made to re-establish lost trade links and an agreement was reached to set-up a joint anti-crisis committee during Kuchma's visit to Moscow on 18–19 September. Yet immediate trade and economic interests of the two countries have remained varying and in some cases diverging, despite the still existing close economic interdependence.

In the political field, the most significant event was the ratification of the major political treaty on friendship and cooperation, signed by the two presidents in May 1997. After several postponements by the remaining opposition, the Russian State Duma finally ratified the treaty on 25 December. The long-awaited ratification of this basic document (although it was still to be approved by the upper chamber of the Russian parliament) was a major step forward in Ukrainian-Russian bilateral relations. Yet they still have a long way to go to become truly equal, neighborly, and cooperative; their ultimate future will primarily be shaped by domestic developments and the relative economic performance of the two countries.

Several problems remain unresolved, including trade relations, Ukraine's debts for energy deliveries; division of the former Soviet property; and demarcation and delimitation of the state border. Although the delimitation of the mutual border finally began in 1998, serious differences emerged, especially pertaining to the division of the continental shelf in the Azov Sea. Many in Russia still nurtured ideas of a "Slavic union" (or confederation), and Moscow remained suspicious of Ukraine's relations with the West, particularly with NATO, and often perceives Ukraine's attempts at European and Euroatlantic integration as a "zero-sum game" in which gains for Ukraine can only come at the expense of Russia's economic and security interests. Another noted change in Ukrainian-Russian relations was the declining role of the "Yeltsin factor," given the Russian president's poor health and his practical disengagement from active politics. The impact of this development is likely to be substantial, as in the past several years personal relations and agreements, as well as domestic political considerations, have played an important role in shaping the Russo-Ukrainian relationship. In this regard, the results of the October 1999 presidential elections in Ukraine will matter as well.

In 1998, most outside observers, as well as members of the Commonwealth of Independent States (CIS) themselves, recognized that the CIS had failed to develop into a stable and efficient regional organization and was in deep crisis. In its place several multi- and bilateral projects were gaining ground (GUAM, Central Asian Economic Community, and Union of Russia and Belarus), and most CIS countries were actively looking for stronger relationships with immediate neighbors beyond the former Soviet Union. Not surprisingly, the CIS summit in Moscow in April decided to set up a special intergovernmental expert forum to try to reform the CIS. Ukraine's attitude toward the CIS remained unchanged: Kyiv favored primarily the development of bilateral ties and economic cooperation, and suggested that its CIS partners concentrate on the creation of a free-trade zone.

DOMESTIC CONSTRAINTS

Events in 1998 demonstrated that Ukrainian foreign policy was increasingly complicated by the country's domestic difficulties. Ukraine's inability to effectively organize itself at home resulted in a growing imbalance between political declarations of the country's international intentions and ambitions on one hand, and the actual state of its economic and political transformation on the other. This imbalance particularly affected the Western vector of Ukrainian foreign policy, hampering Ukraine's prospects for European integration, and contributed to misunderstanding and mutual disappointment between Ukraine and the West—the EU in particular. Furthermore, the slow pace of economic reforms, weakness of major political institutions, and an overly complicated bureaucracy widened the distance between Ukraine and other more advanced CEE states. This has not only constrained Ukraine's efforts to play a more active role in the region, but threatened to bring about Ukraine's potential marginalization and regional self-isolation. In addition, Ukraine's internal weakness, together with its energy dependence on Russia, maintained its vulnerability to outside pressures and exerted a negative influence on Ukrainian-Russian relations.

The lack of progress on reforms also does not help to bridge the existing differences between various political forces, and hence prevented the formation of a stable national consensus on foreign policy issues. Such questions as Ukraine's cooperation with NATO (actively supported by its rightist and centrist political forces) or membership in the CIS Parliamentary Assembly (categorically demanded by its leftists, who threatened to block ratification of other international treaties if this was not implemented) remained politically divisive issues. Ukrainian political forces, both within and outside the parliament, demonstrated little potential for constructive cooperation regarding international issues. Even the country's political leadership was not unanimous on foreign policy priorities (while the president insisted that Ukraine's strategic goal was acquiring EU membership, the leftist chairman of the parliament repeatedly called for a "Slavic Union"), raising doubts as to the sustainability of Ukraine's European choice. Foreign policy was often used as a tool in the domestic political struggle—a tendency which is likely to increase in 1999, given the forthcoming presidential elections.

SOUTHEASTERN EUROPE

V

Slovenia
Croatia
Bosnia-Herzegovina
Federal Republic of Yugoslavia
Macedonia
Albania
Bulgaria
Romania
Moldova

Slovenia

Population:	1,990,000 (1995)
Capital:	Ljubljana (population 270,000)
Major cities:	Maribor (pop. 103,512), Celje (pop. 39,942), Kranj (pop. 36,808)
Area:	20,251 sq. km.
Major ethnic groups:	Slovenians 90%, small numbers of ethnic Serbs, Croats, Albanians, Hungarians, and Italians
Economy:	GDP growth: 3.2%
....	Inflation rate: 9.4%
....	Unemployment rate: 14.8%

SUCCESS STORY CONTINUES

by RUDOLF M. RIZMAN

To an outside and detached observer, Slovenian politics since 1991 exemplifies Francis Fukuyama's celebrated argument about the "end of history," identifying those countries that have successfully entered the arena of liberal democracy and in which sharp disagreements about the ends of political life have largely ceased. As most of the Slovenian population seems quite happy with such a status quo, a number of (conservative) Slovenian intellectuals worry that they have lost their very purpose: to stand as a vanguard of social change, and by implication, to enjoy a privileged and sacred position in society.

This does not mean that injustices do not occur and affect the lives of common people. The point is that people believe that the system is working and accept the "rules of the game." In the report of the ombudsman (an office for citizens' complaints) for 1998 we read that this institution received 3,300 complaints (15 percent more than the previous year) concerning inappropriate judicial and police procedures and administrative and social welfare problems.

Looking at major historical trends from the external point of view, the Slovenian political class takes very seriously the goal of attaining full membership both in the European Union (EU) and NATO, and seems to have among the best (if not the best) case among the EU aspirants.

The economy of course is crucial to success for both ordinary life and for EU entry. The Slovenian economy fared relatively well in 1998 in comparison to other post-communist economies and managed to avoid the negative consequences of both the Russian and Asian economic crises. Slovenia, with the highest per-capita GDP of the former socialist countries (close to $10,000), was the only transition economy that had never had to sign a "stand-by" agreement with the IMF in order to secure loans. This fact permitted her to take a more pragmatic economic course, avoiding the radical liberalization of capital markets that was a favorite demand of international financial institutions. Slovenia's more moderate approach helped to protect the exchange rate and the stock market from the above-mentioned international turbulences.

DIPLOMACY STRENGTHENS SOVEREIGNTY

Slovenia started the year as a new non-permanent member of the Security Council in the United Nations. (They will hold the seat for two years.) This fact may not be so important for larger states, but for a small country, which only came into existence as a sovereign state in 1991 and which had to struggle on a daily basis to be noticed and recognized in international politics, it meant much more, and also has multiple repercussions on its internal political life. By choosing

Slovenia, the international community sent a clear message to other states in the region—the former republics of what was Yugoslavia—that they should follow the Slovenian model of economic and political consolidation. Moreover, in August Slovenia's ambassador to the UN, Danilo Turk, took over as chair of the Security Council for the month of August, in the midst of the Iraq and Kosovo crises.

Slovenia also learned that its greater international exposure was a double-edged sword. First, it has to take stands on these complex international problems, where Slovenia had no recognizable interest or—due to being a newly-born state—no solid knowledge or experience, small diplomatic apparatus or expertise and the like. Also on occasion Slovenia found itself in the uncomfortable position of having to take sides in ongoing disputes between the European Union and the United States. A further example of the responsibilities which come with a more prominent international position was the episode where Slovenia initially supported an initiative in the UN to aim for a world free of nuclear weapons, and later withdrew its support when Washington tacitly expressed its discontent with this Slovenian foreign policy move.

A major breakthrough as far as the approaching the European Union is concerned was Slovenia's joining the formal process for EU entry that was opened in Brussels on 30 March. This followed Slovenia's ratification in June 1997 of the association agreement with the EU which had been signed in 1996 (but which had been held up pending amendment of the constitution to allow foreigners to buy real estate). The formal commencement of the EU entry process had a huge impact on political life. Thirty-one working groups were set up to harmonize Slovenian legislation with that of the EU, and in the course of the year parliament passed 170 laws adopting EU standards. The EU issued a progress report in November, which praised Slovenia as a democracy with a functioning market economy but urged further economic liberalization (including bank privatization). The report was sharply critical of the judicial and administrative bureaucracies, which they regarded as sluggish and under-staffed (noting an estimated backlog of 800,000 to 1 million civil cases).

This process triggered a debate both in the parliament and in civil society. The initial and unquestionable enthusiasm for EU entry was slowly evolving towards a more realistic view on integration, in recognition of one of the central truths of Western democracy: "there is no free lunch." Slovenian euroskeptics usually express worries concerning the fate of national sovereignty, given the danger that the small Slovenian state and culture (in particular language) will not be able to resist assimilationist pressures from larger European states; or more crudely that rich and cunning foreigners will buy Slovenian land. Although these concerns do not prevail in public opinion and among major power holders, they could reach a critical mass if the economy were to slide into recession.

Slovenian politicians worried when the new Social Democratic/Green government that took power in Germany in September demanded the lowering of German contributions to the EU budget, which would necessarily slow down the process of EU enlargement. In addition, Slovenian politicians were quite sensitive to recurrent suggestions from some Western politicians about the creation of "third Yugoslavia"—a new confederation of all the ex-Yugoslav states. Slovenia has been striving to establish itself as a Central-European rather than a Balkan country, and sees entry to the EU and NATO as a crucial step in putting its Balkan legacy behind it. So far Slovenia has been quite successful in convincing the international community of its political distinctiveness. It was rewarded in 1998 by a stream of distinguished international visitors (including the foreign ministers of UK, Russia, France, Italy, Austria, and U.S. Deputy Secretary of State Strobe Talbott). In November Prime Minister Janez Drnovsek made his first official visit to the United States. An important achievement was the first major military exercise of NATO outside its borders in Slovenia in November, under the title "Cooperation Adventure Exercise Exchange '98." Slovenian as well as foreign participants noticed that Slovenian military excelled in English language—something that is proving a problem for those armies (Polish, Czech, and Hungarian) which overtook Slovenia in being accepted for NATO membership. Small Slovenian units took part in peacekeeping operations in Bosnia (since November 1997) and Cyprus. In April it was agreed with Italy and Hungary to form a joint peacekeeping brigade, under Italian leadership.

Slovenia was less fortunate in solving open problems with her neighbors: in particular with Croatia, but also with Austria and Italy. It should be added that the relations with Hungary are exemplary. In dealing with Austria and Italy, Slovenia finds itself in an awkward position because the problems are relatively new and Slovenia no longer has the backing of the large and influential state that Yugoslavia once was. Austria demanded that Slovenia officially recognize and grant status to its "German minority" (which Slovenia estimates to be probably not more than 1,000 persons); while Italy pushed the rights of those Italians who fled the country after World War Two but now wanted to be able to buy the land that they left behind. Both countries support Slovenian entry to the EU, although the nationalistic right in those countries (Jorg Haider in Austria and Giancarlo Fini and Silvio Berlusconi in Italy) pressed their governments to make Slovenian entry conditional upon meeting those demands. Austria and Slovenia had to postpone the signing of a cultural agreement due to different treatments of "German minority" problem; but on 5 February it was announced that Italy would accept $62 million from Slovenia to compensate Italian citizens for property lost after they fled the country.

Problems with Croatia were of a more serious nature. Two in particular are worth mentioning: border disputes and arguments over the operation of the Krsko nuclear power plant in Slovenia, which was financed by the two republics in the former Yugoslavia and is jointly owned by them. Slovenia cut off electricity supplies to Croatia in July, citing non-payment for earlier deliveries. Also unresolved is where to draw the international sea border in the Piran gulf, which will determine whether Slovenia will have territorial exit to the international sea. The two states have repeatedly failed to find a mutually acceptable solution to these problems, and are likely to turn to some sort of international arbitration in the future. The two governments have asked former U.S. defense secretary William Perry to advise on the sea border dispute. There was still no resolution in sight of the long-standing dispute over the division of the former Yugoslavia's assets and liabilities. On 24 March Slovenia announced that it was withdrawing its permanent mission to the Brussels negotiations on this issue.

POLITICS AS USUAL

Slovenia has enjoyed a high level of political stability under Milan Kucan (president since April 1990 and re-elected in November 1997 for a second five-year term) and Janez Drnovsek (Liberal Democrat leader and prime minister since May 1992). On the domestic front, 1998 was certainly not a boring year. The governing coalition consisting of Liberal Democracy of Slovenia (LDS), Slovenian People's Party (SLS), and the small Democratic Party of Pensioners (DeSUS) was quite stable, although SLS leader Marjan Podobnik often shook it with arguments and political behavior more usually expected from an opposition leader. Podobnik tried to avoid the fate of previous conservative parties in the government (Janez Jansa's Social Democratic Party of Slovenia—SDS and Lojze Peterle's Slovenian Christian Democrats—SKD) who ended their period in office much weaker in terms of public support than when they were in the opposition. Podobnik and his party, who often adopt a political rhetoric of "honesty" and "morality," experienced serious setbacks when the weekly *Mladina* published documents revealing that they illegally financed their electoral campaigns in the past and were in debt to an Austrian bank. Podobnik sued *Mladina* and the matter had not been settled by year's end. Janez Drnovsek's LDS had a strong interest in keeping the coalition alive, and often yielded to the aggressive demands of Podobnik.

There were a number of other scandals in 1998 in Slovenian politics and they were becoming, it seemed, an indispensable part of its repertoire. Some critics explained their recurrence as the price that had to be paid for the relative absence of real social and economic problems in the country, while others blamed their frequency on the relative youth and inexperience of the political elite.

In April the opposition SDS accused Prime Minister Drnovsek of unconstitutional behavior, for allegedly signing a secret military agreement with Israel. Drnovsek, a popular figure, had little trouble shrugging off this accusation, particularly after Ivan Hvalica, a leading figure in the SDS, said that "we have constitutionally indicted you, and it is up to you to prove that the complaints are not true." In May the parliament decided the accusation was groundless. The opposition also launched accusations against two LDS ministers: Slavko Gaber (education) and Mirko Bandelj (interior). Defense Minister Tit Turnsek, from the SLS, had to resign in February after he accepted responsibility for a scandal involving a Slovenian military espionage vehicle which was confiscated by Croatian police after it crossed the Croatian border, either by mistake or on purpose (for a reward?). Turnsek's successor, Alojz Krapez, lasted only until October, when it was discovered that he assigned himself a large apartment under his ministry's control. The SDS also raised a charge against parliamentary speaker Janez Podobnik, from the SLS party (brother of Marjan Podobnik). The charge was later withdrawn, the purpose of the exercise being to warn the SLS that it should respect the interests of the conservative bloc to which it claims to belong.

The year also saw a more conflictual relationship between the state and the Catholic Church. The latter faces considerable difficulties in adapting to a democratic, secular political order. Church representatives frequently criticized the slow progress in the return of church property that had been nationalized after World War Two, and called for a more prominent role in the schools and media. The growing influence of the Catholic Church was reflected in support from a substantial proportion of conservative political bloc (in particular SDS, SKD, and to some extent SLS). Some commentators have tried to revise the historical record of events during the war in order to justify the Church's collaboration with the Nazi and Fascist occupier. Several times in the course of the year the Church challenged the legitimacy of the new constitutional order and the constitution itself: especially the right to abortion, the separation of state and church, and the secular nature of schools.

The past maintained a high visibility in these debates. Anton Drobnic, a state prosecutor and during the war himself a member of collaborationist armed units, issued a number of controversial statements which labeled the partisan resistance against Nazis and Fascist as merely serving as a tool of the communist seizure of power. Conservative politicians and some anti-communist intellectuals asked the parliament to pass lustration laws, which would ban and/or stigmatize the main officeholders of the previous regime. The parliament failed to agree either on lustration legislation or on a declaration of reconciliation, which had been proposed by the United List of Social Democrats (ZLSD, former communists). These episodes illustrate that the political spectrum in Slovenia—especially in the second half of 1998—was differentiated primarily through stands in the past rather than disagreements over contemporary policy choices.

On the level of local politics, politicians seemed to be more effective. In August 45 new communes were created, increasing the overall number to 191. The new communes were partly a response to a request from the Constitutional Court and partly a deliberate attempt by political parties to expand their spheres of interest. Other important decisions of the Constitutional Court, with far-reaching implications for political life, included the liberalization of conditions for political associations and the formation of political parties; a controversial decision on the implementation of a majoritarian electoral system; and last but not least the decision in principle on restitution of property to those who lost it half a century ago.

In the local elections for commune councils held in November the political parties tested their popularity and influence. The LDS won 23 percent of the vote, SDS 16 percent, SKD 12 percent, SLS and ZLSD 11 percent each, DeSUS 5 percent, SNS (Slovenian National Party) 2 percent, and independent candidates 12 percent. While the conservative bloc overwhelmingly controls the countryside, the left and liberal bloc controls the cities.

The responsibilities of government, both internal and international (especially in dealings with the EU), have apparently softened the previous "populist chauvinism" attitudes of the Slovene People's Party, thus (hopefully) leading to the emergence of a moderate conservative party as is seen in the established Western democracies. Although the Slovenian democracy continues to develop, it still lags behind its Western counterparts, which have seen a sharp decrease in party militancy over the past decade. In Slovenia in contrast the democratic path is still captive to the aggressive maneuvers of "parties of representation," appealing to voters not as free individuals but as members of an exclusive partisan group or self-centered community.

GLOSSARY

DeSUS Democratic Party of Pensioners of Slovenia
LDS   Liberal Democracy of Slovenia
SDS   Social Democratic Party of Slovenia
SKD   Slovenian Christian Democrats
SLS   Slovenian People's Party
SNS   Slovenian National Party
ZLSD   United List of Social Democrats

Croatia

Population:	4,800,000 (1991 census)
Capital:	Zagreb (pop. 994,000)
Major cities:	Split (pop. 207,000), Rijeka (pop. 206,000), Osijek (pop. 165,000)
Area:	56,538 sq. km.
Major ethnic groups:	90% Croatian, 3–4% Serbian
Economy:	GDP growth: 4%
	Inflation rate: 5.4%
	Unemployment rate: 18%

THE RISE OF THE OPPOSITION

by NEBOJSA BJELAKOVIC and SAVA TATIC

"Take a kilo of fresh spying and banking scandals, mix in half a kilo of intrigues and purges within [the ruling Croatian Democratic Union] HDZ, sprinkle with a bit of holy water—and you get 1998." This is how *Feral Tribune*'s Marinko Culic summed up the year in which President Franjo Tudjman's power machinery began to creak and the political opposition began to show significant electoral muscle. Not even a surprisingly Tudjman-friendly papal visit in early October managed to mitigate the political damage caused by a string of bank collapses featuring HDZ heavyweights and cronies, and revelations that state intelligence agencies had been spying on journalists and the arguably more liberal members of the ruling party.

While the Tudjman camp was busy infighting—for the first time since Croatia's independence—the leaders of the six key opposition parties agreed to create a joint electoral front in late August. Besides converting the newfound unity into electoral victories over HDZ in several early local elections, the opposition camp saw its nationwide popularity steadily rise over the second half of the year.

At the end of 1998, Tudjman himself trailed in popularity polls behind Social Democrats' leader Ivica Racan, which was an absolute novelty on Croatia's post-1991 political scene.

The media situation, however, remained immune to such substantial changes. The ruling party's monopoly over electronic media and its ill treatment of independent newspapers continued throughout 1998. Besides the judicial harassment, which independent media had been used to throughout the 1990s, evidence emerged in late summer that journalists were being spied on by state secret services. Even Interior Minister Ivan Penic implicitly acknowledged the existence of dossiers on the personal lives of select journalists.

Another novelty on the media scene was Forum 21, a lobby group established by state television employees to advocate privatization of the national broadcaster. Their independent-press colleagues were less than enthusiastic about joining ranks with Croatian Television (HTV) "dissidents," citing the years of loyal service that Forum 21 members have provided to the ruling elite. The semi-defection of hardened opportunists was a sign that power may have started to slip away from HDZ.

HDZ INFIGHTING

The emergence of open faction rivalry within the ruling HDZ was one of the main 1998 developments that could have a lasting effect on Croatian politics.

The intra-party friction became visible after the May death of Gojko Susak, Tudjman's minister of defense and the de facto second most powerful man in Croatia. (See accompanying document, "In Memoriam.")

Despite—or rather because of—his pre-war and wartime sins, Susak proved to be the only politician who was able to maintain the coexistence of two opposite factions within the ruling party. (Susak had been implicated in stirring up ethnic conflict in eastern Slavonia in 1991; ethnic cleansing of Serbs from reconquered Croatian territories in 1995; and backing Croat ethnic-cleansing campaigns in the 1993–1994 war against the Muslims in Bosnia-Herzegovina.) As the undisputed leader of the powerful, hard-line Herzegovinian lobby, the defense minister was able to keep the more extreme elements within the party at bay at times when the party's pragmatists held the day—that is, whenever Tudjman decided to yield to international pressure, be it over Bosnia or democratic standards within Croatia proper.

While battling lung cancer, Susak nurtured a fellow Herzegovina native Ivic Pasalic, a former physician and consummate HDZ apparatchik, as his political successor. As adept as he is in internal party politics, Pasalic definitely lacked the personal authority of his late political mentor and regularly figured as the least popular HDZ politician in opinion polls. The Herzegovinian lobby, however, continued to operate as efficiently as ever. When the new Defense Minister Andrija Hebrang, Tudjman's personal physician and former health minister, began interfering with the lobby's interests, he was fired within months.

Perhaps buoyed by widespread public speculation that he was Tudjman's most likely heir, Hebrang launched a daring investigation into the business practices of the army-run foreign-trade company RH-Alan. The move immediately gained him enemies among the members of the officer corps who had grown conspicuously rich during the 1990s. Hebrang reportedly wanted to sack the heads of military intelligence and procurement, Generals Markica Rebic and Vladimir Zagorac, but failed to secure Tudjman's support. The last straw that brought about the minister's demise was his proposal to transfer the administration of aid to Herzegovinian Croats from the Ministry of Defense to the Ministry of Finance. Hebrang resigned in October. General Pavao Miljavac, a man of establishment and continuity, was plucked out from active service to head the ministry.

By the end of the year, Pasalic had managed to successfully outmaneuver the most prominent HDZ pragmatists, such as presidential advisors and former prime ministers Hrvoje Sarinic and Franjo Greguric. Sarinic, who had earlier crossed swords with Pasalic over the Dubrovacka banka scandal, and Greguric were effectively sacked in the aftermath of a phone-tapping scandal featuring the involvement of several state intelligence agencies. The HDZ parliamentary majority dismissed all complaints about the illicit activity of the Croatian secret services despite the fact that the initiators of the November parliamentary hearing and targets of phone bugging were hitherto party heavyweights Sarinic and Greguric.

SPLINTERING AND UNITING

The rise in the fortunes of the anti-HDZ camp came largely thanks to the surge in popularity of the Social Democratic Party (SDP). The reformed communists had obviously benefited from the shift in public discourse from war rhetoric to ordinary worries, which fully vindicated SDP's consistent strategy of zeroing in on the social iniquities of Croatia's rampant crony capitalism.

The Social Democrats also profited from the split in the Croatian Social Liberal Party (HSLS), which only formalized the lingering rift between HSLS's two original leaders. Vlado Gotovac, the party's 1997 presidential candidate, and his faction broke off in January to form the Liberal Party (LS), thus further crowding the political center. Gotovac's decision came on the heels of his criticism of HSLS's other original leader, Drazen Budisa, for having flirted with HDZ after the 1997 local elections. According to several opinion polls, the split hurt both sides, as Liberal voters increasingly turned to the SDP, which consequently became the country's largest opposition party.

The antagonism between the Liberal leaders did not, however, prevent them from joining the leaders of SDP and three other major opposition parties—Croatian Peasants' Party (HSS), Croatian People's Party (HNS), and the Istrian Democratic Alliance (IDS)—at a 28 August meeting in Zagreb. The summit participants agreed on establishing a joint front vis-à-vis the ruling party, a platform that the opposition supporters had been calling for since 1991.

The new strategy bore its first fruits in the October early elections in Dubrovnik-Neretva County, where the opposition delivered a crushing defeat to HDZ, which was obviously still reeling from the Dubrovacka banka scandal.

In a further sign of unity, the opposition six boycotted the sessions of parliamentary committees during the November hearings related to the illicit activity of the Croatian secret services. On that occasion, opposition parties argued for the transparency of those institutions and for greater parliamentary oversight over their activities and budgeting.

Several opinion polls taken toward the end of the year indicated that the opposition six would soundly beat HDZ in the event of a general election, which should be held no later than January 2000. The path to an actual electoral victory, however, remains strewn with pitfalls. The issues of leaders' egos and inter- and intra-party friction, such as in the case of Gotovac's LS, were still likely to test the nerves of opposition supporters.

The particular onus of responsibility rests on the largest member of the loose alliance, the SDP. The good results the party obtained in the 1997 local elections and in the early elections in 1998 have boosted its self-confidence. Moreover, the electoral victories of SDP's counterparts in Italy, Great Britain, and Germany significantly improved its domestic image and international stature.

The favorable political winds and HDZ's sinking fortunes, may, however, tempt SDP leaders to try to go it alone against the ruling party. On one hand, such a strategy would rid them of the sometimes uncomfortable dealings with their political allies, such as IDS, with whom SDP has already had some ugly rows on the local level. On the other hand, it would mean ignoring the lesson that opposition parties in most of ex-Yugoslavia have been forced to learn time and again: for Balkan autocrats, being down does not necessarily mean being on the way out.

UNHAPPY MINORITIES, BULLIED BOSNIA

Minority issues and relations with ex-Yugoslav neighbors remained stuck between Zagreb's public pledges of benevolence and its reluctance to implement them.

While 1997 had witnessed an institutional and legal acknowledgment of the ethnic diversity within Croatia, expressed in new constitutional and education provisions, 1998 demonstrated that the ruling HDZ was not prepared to widely implement those provisions. Unsurprisingly, the questions of the return of refugees and Tudjman's attitude toward Bosnia-Herzegovina's unity continued to draw international criticism throughout the year.

The peaceful re-integration of the Serb-populated enclave of eastern Slavonia into full Croatian control featured triumphalist and revanchist statements and parades of Croatian militant right-wing parties. The events triggered a new exodus of Serbs from the region, especially in the first half of 1998.

In general, the return of the Serbs driven out of Croatia in 1995 was discouraged not only by the slow issuance of the necessary documents to those who were interested in returning but also by the state-tolerated violence against returnees, especially in the Krajina region. According to the Croatian Helsinki Committee (HHO), house burning, beatings, and killings of Serb returnees became almost a daily routine. The HHO also charged that Zagreb was intentionally slowing down internationally sponsored projects to clear land mines in areas previously populated by Serbs.

The latter, however, were not the only minority group to cry foul over the authorities' failure to comply with the Organization for Security and Cooperation in Europe standards for treatment of ethnic minorities. Italian and Hungarian minorities also complained about the lack of previously promised funds and textbooks for bilingual education. Moreover, state media often portrayed ethnic Italians and their political leaders as secessionists and disloyal citizens.

A similar tone was present in Zagreb's regional policy. Tudjman's speeches, such as the one at the Fourth HDZ Congress in February, continued to express territorial pretensions against Bosnia and unequivocal support for the Herzegovina hard-liners. Tudjman repeatedly indicated that there could be no deals with the Bosniac-Croat federation—including those on the federation's access to the port of Ploce—until Sarajevo signed the agreement about special relations with Zagreb, as stipulated in the 1994 Washington Agreement.

In response to Western pressure to soften his stand, Tudjman stepped up his anti-Western rhetoric and, in a pseudo-Tito move, set off to Russia to try to find at least some diplomatic understanding for his Balkan policies. No concrete results emerged from the mid-December visit. As there were no significant signs of its compliance with the Dayton provisions, Croatia remained outside European political, economic, and security integration processes.

A POTEMKIN VILLAGE IN BRETTON WOODS

From the mid-1990s onward, Croatia has acquired the reputation of a land of macroeconomic stability and microeconomic woe, as companies and individuals struggled with the side effects of a stern economic policy.

As in the previous years, inflation was kept under control (officially, at 5.4 percent) not least thanks to an increase in the central bank's base interest rate to 14 percent (up from 6 percent in 1997). Similarly, the official growth figure was solid at nearly 4 percent. The kuna's exchange rate remained stable for the fifth consecutive year.

Moreover, on the surface, Zagreb continued to make the right moves toward the reform of the economy. At the beginning of the year, the government introduced a 22 percent value added tax, drawing praise from the World Bank. The government also increased its privatizing effort by auctioning off a number of mainly smaller companies under a voucher-privatization scheme. But to take those figures as an accurate reflection of the health of Croatia's economy would be to ignore the substantial cloud behind a very thin silver lining.

The obvious down side of the government's economic policies was one of the highest costs of living in the post-communist world, despite the comparatively high average salaries as measured in dollar terms. According to official 1998 figures, one-third of Croatian citizens lived below the poverty line, while two-thirds of those who were employed made less than the average monthly salary (above $400).

The government's restrictive monetary policy has also not been conducive to investment, which in turn kept unemployment high. Official sources put the 1998 figure at 18 percent, while independent trade unions estimated the jobless rate at about 22 percent. The industrial sector was particularly hard hit. For example, by 1998, the workforces at each of the two communist-era export-oriented giants, Rade Koncar and Djuro Djakovic, had dwindled to about 4,000. In 1990, they had employed 23,000 and 18,000 workers respectively.

By 1998, the total number of employed had shrunk to roughly half of what it was in 1989. Because much of the workforce downsizing since 1990 was handled by means of early retirement packages, Croatia had less than two active workers per each retiree in 1998. As a consequence, the national pay-as-you-go pension scheme was reduced to disbursing pensions hovering around the existential minimum.

Beside the social costs, several negative macroeconomic trends were at play. The overvaluation of the kuna, which financial analysts estimate at between 30 percent and 50 percent, translated into rising imports and disincentives for exports or export-driven investment.

According to the Economist Intelligence Unit (EIU), Croatia's trade deficit was lower in 1998 than in the previous years due to an exceptionally good performance of the shipbuilding industry. Yet the gap between exports ($4.6 billion) and imports ($8.4 billion) was still wide enough to produce a serious current-account deficit ($1.5 billion), despite the solid earnings from tourism, transport, and remittances from abroad. In response, Zagreb turned to additional borrowing abroad, pushing its foreign debt to $7.6 billion, or beyond 30 percent of the gross domestic product ($20.3 billion, according to EIU). Although the absolute figure is not worrying by emerging-market standards, the same cannot be said of its dynamic: the foreign debt had almost tripled since 1994 ($2.8 billion).

Another systemically corrosive by-product of the stringent monetary policy was the liquidity squeeze in the real economy. That, coupled with the lack of financial discipline, led to high levels of bad debt, with both the government and businesses—even banks —commonly "rescheduling" or plainly defaulting on their liabilities. Official sources put the total bad debt for 1998 at 13 billion kuna (approximately $2 billion), while the Croatian Association of Employers operated with the sum of 67 billion kuna. The full gravity of the problem became evident when compared to Croatia's money supply, which has been oscillating around 12 billion kuna.

HDZ'S TRANSITION COMMISSARS

According to critics, the government's fiscal reforms had done little to undo the main features of a state-controlled economy. The tax reform, they charged, was initiated not to rid the economy of the heritage of state paternalism but to satiate the state's growing spending appetite. Since 1995, the state budget has grown by more than 15 percent annually. Nonetheless, the 1998 budget was roughly at a still manageable one third of the GDP.

While the fiscal reform has been conducted with reference to Western experiences—at least at the level of public relations—privatization was shaped by home-grown expertise. Much of Croatia's ownership-transformation history is littered with scandals, and its independent press has thoroughly documented the symbiosis between the ruling party and the country's *tajkuni* (a localized version of the word "tycoon"), essentially individuals who operate beyond the reach of the law as HDZ's "transition commissars."

Mechanisms have varied, but defaulting on liabilities remained the core element of the redistribution of the nation's wealth. That is why wholesale and retail chains were viewed as a prime possession for a *tajkun*. The scheme was simple: given the structure of the economy, large manufacturers had to rely on the traditional and well-established distribution channels; producers would deliver their wares for resale, and the *tajkun* would "forget" to pay for the goods, using instead the money generated from sales for acquiring new companies—often his own creditors.

Another popular scheme featured an even more direct involvement of the state. State enterprises were put up for auction, with prices often starting significantly below their market value, and the bidding somehow always went the way of privatization funds owned by HDZ loyalists, Tudjman's grandson included. The *tajkuni* then obtained soft loans from state-controlled banks to pay for the companies acquired at auctions. Following such successful acquisitions, *tajkuni* customarily dished out generous contributions to HDZ election campaigns.

Such schemes often assumed farcical proportions. Whenever the new owners ran out of working capital, state-controlled banks moved in as debt-collecting agencies, taking control over the bankrupt enterprise. The banks then either tried to sell it again to somebody else or continued to manage the company, but they never tried to collect the loans the *tajkun* originally took up in order to privatize the company.

The past year, however, brought signs that the machinery was not as well oiled as it used to be. The April collapse of Dubrovacka banka, a large regional bank with strong business ties to Herzegovina, was a result of the derailing of a secret takeover deal between the bank's top manager and regional HDZ bosses. Alleged ramifications led all the way up to Tudjman's political advisor Ivic Pasalic, by way of Croatia's most notorious *tajkun*, Miroslav Kutle.

Things worsened in the fall, when four smaller banks folded, combining for a loss of almost 2 billion German marks. The central bank intervened to stem the expansion of the crisis, but analysts predicted serious trouble for Croatia's banking sector in 1999.

GLOSSARY

HDZ	Croatian Democratic Union
HNS	Croatian People's Party
HSLS	Croatian Social Liberal Party
HSS	Croatian Peasants' Party
IDS	Istrian Democratic Alliance
LS	Liberal Party
SDP	Social Democratic Party

Document: *IN MEMORIAM*

Croatia's controversial Defense Minister Gojko Susak died on 3 May, after a long fight with cancer. The government declared 7 May a national day of mourning for the man credited with creating a modern Croatian army, through the help of arms-smuggling and covert advice from the United States. After fleeing Yugoslavia at the end of the 1960s, Susak emigrated to Canada and later ran several businesses, including a pizzeria. The "Pizzaman," as he was dubbed by Croatia's independent media, went on to raise millions of dollars among Croats in Canada

*and America, who bankrolled Franjo Tudjman's Croatian Democratic Union
(HDZ) party in 1990 elections.*

*Susak's roots were in the Herzegovinian town of Siroki Brijeg, where both his
father and an older brother were members of the fascist Ustashe movement during World War II. Susak, who returned to Croatia in 1990, exhibited anti-Serb
feelings even as a youth; while at university, he would karate-chop signs written
in Cyrillic, and he fled the country to avoid having to serve in the Yugoslav army,
which he perceived as Serb-dominated.*

*After joining President Tudjman's government, Susak became his henchman
in Bosnia and Herzegovina, where Croatian nationalists were attempting to link
their own para-state, Herceg-Bosna, with Croatia. Susak also bragged of firing
the first shot against the Serbs in 1991, when he and two other men started shooting shoulder-launched missiles at a Serbian village in eastern Croatia.*

*Susak's good friend, former U.S. Defense Secretary William Perry, delivered
the following remarks at the 7 May funeral:*

This is truly a sad occasion for me. I have come here not just as a representative
of the United States of America but as a friend of Gojko Susak.

Both Mrs. Perry and I express our deepest sympathy and the sympathy of our
countrymen to you, Djurdja, and to your children, and to Gojko's mother, brother,
and sister. Our thoughts and prayers are with you this day.

Gojko Susak's death is not only a great loss to his family and his friends. It is
a great loss for Croatia. What Shakespeare said about a great Roman I say about
a great Croatian: "Now there goes a man, we shall never see his like again."

Minister Susak's service to his country came at a crucial time. I think it is safe
to say that without him Croatia would have found the long and winding road to
independence and territorial integrity even more difficult and rocky than it was.

Gojko Susak was, as I found out on our very first meeting in 1994, a man with
certain, very important qualities. He was stubborn to be sure, but most of all he
was a patriot. He was a visionary in military matters, and his legacy will be that
one day the Croatian armed forces will be valued participants in Western security organizations. And perhaps most importantly, especially for forging the close
personal relationship we developed, he was a man of integrity. His word was his
bond. And to an American there is no higher praise.

The week after Croatia announced its independence Gojko left a comfortable
and prosperous job in Canada to return to Croatia and fight for his country's
freedom. In so doing, he saw his lifelong dream come true. He was living out his
view of freedom as expressed by the Croatian poet Ivan Gundulic:

"O beautiful, o dear, o sweet, freedom. A gift in which all bounty was given
by God to us. All the silver, all the gold, all the human lives, cannot be payment
for your pure beauty."

To Croatians he was crucial to the establishment of freedom here. To Americans he was crucial to the establishment of peace and stability in the region by

his support of the Dayton agreement. I often returned to him for help in removing the roadblocks that lay in our path of the Dayton agreement. But most of all, I always enjoyed working with Gojko. We saw each other many times. In Zagreb; in Washington; in Dayton; in Garmisch, Germany. It was always a pleasure to be in his company. I shall miss him very much.

In 1996 when I was secretary of defense, Gojko visited me in Washington. I gave a dinner in his honor. And at that dinner I closed my remarks with excerpts from a poem by one of our greatest presidents, Theodore Roosevelt. I believe that this captures the essence of Minister Susak:

"The credit belongs to the man who is actually in the arena, whose face is marred by dust and sweat and blood, who strives valiantly, who knows the great enthusiasms, the great devotions, who spends himself in a worthy cause. His place shall never be with those cold and timid souls who know neither victory nor defeat."

It was my honor to be here today to pay tribute to this remarkable Croatian patriot, to this remarkable man. God bless you, Gojko, and goodbye.

NOTE

Reprinted with kind permission from the Croatian Information Centre's *PRESS CUT*, in *Transitions* magazine, June 1998.

Bosnia-Herzegovina

Population:	3,200,000
Bosnian federation:	2,300,000
Republika Srpska:	900,000
Capital:	Sarajevo (pop. 350,000)
Major cities:	Banja Luka (240,000), Tuzla (pop. 240,000 including refugees), Zenica (pop. 160,000), Mostar (pop. 100,000)
Area:	51,233 sq. km.
Major ethnic groups:	Muslim 43.7%, Serbian 31.4%, Croatian 17.3%, other 7.6% (1991 census)
Economy:	(excluding Republika Srpska)
....	GDP growth: 25–35%
....	Inflation rate: 12.2%
....	Unemployment rate: 30–40%

A YEAR OF MIXED RESULTS

by GORDON BARDOS

The year 1998 marked Bosnia-Herzegovina's third full year of peace. Nevertheless, by year's end it was clear that the effort to create a viable state and a self-sustaining peace process was destined to be much more of a long-term effort than most observers had believed. Although widely publicized as the "Year of Returns," only a relatively small number of refugees and internally displaced persons in fact managed to return to their homes in 1998. The one territorial issue in Bosnia-Herzegovina unresolved at Dayton, the status of Brcko, remained such a point of contention that the international arbitration tribunal in charge of the town's fate had to postpone for the third time its ultimate decision. The city of Mostar was as divided as ever between the rival ethnic communities resident therein.

Bosnia-Herzegovina's second set of postwar statewide elections produced contradictory results. While the nationalist parties lost some of the support they had previously enjoyed, moderates backed by the international community such as Biljana Plavsic and Kresimir Zubak lost in their re-election bids against more nationalist opponents. On the other hand, Bosnia-Herzegovina did finally gain a common currency, common license plates, and a joint flag, and the international High Representative to Bosnia-Herzegovina, Carlos Westendorp, claimed that the 1998 elections showed that "steady, incremental progress towards a more moderate and pluralistic political environment" was being made.

The year 1998 also saw the international community take a much more forceful approach in the country. In December 1997, the Bonn Conference of the Peace Implementation Council gave the High Representative a mandate to break deadlocks in central institutions and to remove local officials. After Bosniacs, Croats, and Serbs in central institutions were unable to agree to such things as a common flag, currency, or passports, the international High Representative for Bosnia-Herzegovina unilaterally imposed his decisions on the bickering parties. When *elected* municipal leaderships in a number of small towns were considered to be obstructing the peace process, they were removed. Moreover, the international community also began to assume control over such things as media licensing, textbook and curriculum reform, and revamping the judiciary. The only similar attempts to reform entire states and societies on such a broad scale had come after the occupation of Nazi Germany and Imperial Japan.

DEVELOPMENTS IN REPUBLIKA SRPSKA

The international community's determination to play a more interventionist role was apparent early in the year. In January, opposition from moderate Serb parties and from Bosniac and Croat delegates in the Republika Srpska (RS) National

Assembly made it impossible for the more hard-line Serb nationalist parties (primarily the Srpska Demokratska Stranka, the SDS, and the even more nationalist Srpska Radikalna Stranka, SRS) to re-elect Gojko Klickovic as prime minister. After a particularly long session of the Assembly on January 16th, in the early morning hours of January 17th the hard-liners left in the mistaken belief that no decisions could be taken in their absence. International officials, however, managed to convince Serb moderates and Bosniac and Croat delegates to vote as a bloc, and succeeded in having the president of the Independent Social-Democrats, Milorad Dodik, elected as prime minister. Dodik thus became the first important publicly-elected postwar leader who had *not* played a role in the war.

Following RS President Biljana Plavsic's split with the Pale-based hardliners during the summer of 1997, the emergence of Dodik as RS prime minister gave the international community the more moderate Serb leadership that they had sought for years. But Plavsic and Dodik were limited in their ability to make drastic changes in the situation because their own hold on power was tenuous. After assuming office, Dodik quickly started to purge SDS-appointed factory managers in a number of important enterprises in January and February, and followed up this move in July when the general managers and editors of sixteen radio and TV stations in the RS were dismissed. Despite these moves, although Plavsic and Dodik enjoyed significant support in the western RS (primarily the area west of Bijeljina), the eastern RS (including the RS regions adjacent to Yugoslavia) remained firmly under the control of the SDS or the SRS. The Plavsic–Dodik government did manage to gain some measure of control over the eastern RS during the course of 1998, but the poor, predominantly rural municipalities in this region overwhelmingly supported SDS or SRS candidates in the 1998 elections. Nevertheless, the political center of gravity in the RS had by 1998 irrevocably shifted from Pale to Banja Luka.

The international agenda in Bosnia-Herzegovina suffered a setback in the September elections, when Plavsic was defeated by the SRS's Nikola Poplasen. (See accompanying interview.) Problems continued for the rest of the year after Poplasen refused to re-nominate Dodik as prime minister, and instead sought to create an all-Serb coalition government which would not rely on Bosniac and Croat votes in the assembly.

HERCEG-BOSNA

1998 also marked the first major postwar split among Bosnia-Herzegovina's Croats. Latent tensions had existed both during the war and into the post-Dayton period between Croats in western Herzegovina and their ethnic kin in central Bosnia, but they had nevertheless managed to maintain a significant degree of unity. This was in part due to the Croats' demographic position in B-H. Even before the war, the Croats had been the smallest of the three main ethnic groups (in numerical terms) in B-H. In the postwar period, however, their position had become even more precarious. Forced expulsions from the Posavina area and from Central Bosnia, together with a sizable voluntary out-migration, had cut the Croats' numbers in half—from over 800,000 in 1991 to less than an estimated 400,000 by 1998.

Because they were geographically located along the border with Croatia proper, many Croats in western Herzegovina (one of the most ethnically homogeneous areas in B-H even before the war) considered outright secession from B-H the logical move should the Dayton experiment fail. Geography, however, imposed a different set of considerations on their ethnic brethren in central Bosnia, given their location in small, isolated pockets of territory surrounded by far larger Bosniac populations. Consequently, Croats in Central Bosnia throughout the post-Dayton period had been much more eager to see the Dayton process succeed, and, as a result, exhibited a more cooperative approach toward the international community's efforts.

The differences between the interests of these two groups finally broke into the open in May, when a Herzegovinian hard-liner, Ante Jelavic, was chosen to replace the then-president of Hrvatska Demokratska Zajednica (Croat Democratic Community—B-H, or HDZ) Kresimir Zubak as HDZ—B-H president. Early in June, Zubak (also a member of the B-H presidency) announced the formation of his own political party, the Nova Hrvatska Incijativa (New Croatian Initiative, or NHI). Zubak acted with strong support from international officials in B-H, who believed they had finally found a "Croatian Plavsic" to weaken Croat nationalist resistance to the Dayton process. Their hopes quickly faded away, however, for Zubak's NHI fared poorly in the September elections, gaining less than 20 percent of the HDZ's votes, while Zubak himself came in far behind Jelavic in the race for the Croat seat in the B-H presidency.

Apart from these internal political squabbles, the Croats' Herceg-Bosna continued its existence as Bosnia-Herzegovina's unofficial third entity. It was also, in many respects, the most violent, with much of the violence occurring along Herceg-Bosna's strategic territory adjoining the border between Croatia and Bosnia-Herzegovina. A typical example of such violence occurred in April, when mobs protesting against the return of Serb refugees and displaced persons to the Drvar region went on a rampage, setting fire to the local International Police Task Force (IPTF) station, and killing an elderly Serb couple. In August, unknown assailants fired at Ukrainian Stabilization Force (SFOR) soldiers near Doljani, who were deployed to assist in the return of displaced Bosniacs. The most sustained effort to prevent the return of refugees, however, took place in Stolac municipality in southwestern Bosnia-Herzegovina, where throughout the year the homes of Bosniac returnees were bombed and burned on an almost weekly basis. On 10 December, a mob attacked IPTF members in the Stolac police station who were conducting an investigation into the harassment of Bosniac returnees. In the resulting melee, 24 monitors were forced to evacuate to Mostar. In all of these instances, international officials responded by removing local leaders from office, but this did little to improve the situation on the ground.

BOSNA

In contrast to the situation with the Croats and the Serbs, where there had been no significant alternatives to the ruling parties until the Zubak and Dodik affairs, a non-nationalist alternative had existed within the Bosniac body politic throughout the war and into the post-Dayton period. This alternative, personified by leaders such as Selim Beslagic, Zlatko Lagumdzija, and Sejfudin Tokic, was, however, rent by considerable infighting. Although all professed to be social-democrats, they were unable to bury their differences or unite enough to seriously challenge the rule of the Stranka Demokratske Akcije (the Party of Democratic Action, or SDA), led by Alija Izetbegovic. An effort by the OHR to forge an electoral alliance between these different factions that could challenge the SDA fell through in February. Izetbegovic himself refused to commit for another run as the Bosniac member of the joint presidency until late in the summer, but when it became clear that without him the SDA would split into moderate and hard-line factions, he relented. Consequently, the SDA-dominated "Coalition for a United and Democratic Bosnia-Herzegovina" was again able to win a significant victory in the September elections, and the SDA held on to power in every Bosniac-majority canton in the Federation.

THE FEDERATION

Although in theory the Bosniac-Croat Federation covers 51 percent of Bosnia-Herzegovina's territory, in reality it only covers less than one fifth of the territory, that making up the Federation's two ethnically-mixed cantons—Central Bosnia and Herzegovina-Neretva. In fact, after the emergence of the Plavsic-Dodik leadership in the RS, many international officials admitted that the main problem in implementing Dayton was the poor state of Bosniac-Croat relations.

Strongly divergent interests and goals separated Bosniacs and Croats on a wide range of issues in the post-Dayton period. On Brcko, for instance, Croats refused to attend the March arbitration proceedings as part of a united Federation delegation. American-backed efforts to integrate the Bosniac and Croat military forces (the Armija Bosne i Hercegovine, or ARBiH, and the Hrvatsko Vijece Obrane or HVO, respectively), gained little ground. In June, the United States halted its weapons supply program to the Federation Army because the two sides could not agree on common insignia and license plates for their vehicles. The long-awaited privatization program for the Federation, which was to have been enacted in 1998, had to be postponed until 1999 because of continuing disputes between Bosniacs, Croats, and the international community over how best to proceed. Similarly, little progress was made in dismantling "parallel institutions" such as the para-state structures of Herceg-Bosna, or of the wartime, Bosniac-dominated Republic of Bosnia-Herzegovina.

Croat dissatisfaction with the Dayton process also became increasingly evident during the summer of 1998, as high-ranking Croat officials started calling for a "re-cantonization" of the Federation. Essentially this meant splitting the existing multi-ethnic cantons into smaller, mono-ethnic Bosniac and Croat cantons. Others called for the formal recognition of Herceg-Bosna as the official third entity within B-H. Although international officials quickly announced that any revision of Dayton was out of the question, such remarks by leading Croat politicians showed that the HDZ had little faith in the Federation's long-term survival or viability.

It was on the ground, however, that the biggest problems in "bringing the Federation to life" were evident. Extremists on both sides repeatedly engaged in acts of violence and terror to prevent ethnic minorities from returning to areas from which they had been expelled. The most notable example was the above-mentioned case of Stolac, but such problems were evident in many other municipalities as well. A particular problem for Croat returnees were the hundreds of Mujaheddin fighters who stayed in B-H after the war, living in isolated villages in the hilly, heavily forested areas of Central Bosnia. In July, for instance, a Catholic church in Kakanj was bombed, and in the same month a Croat police officer was killed in Travnik. In Mostar, Croats "celebrating" Croatia's third place finish in the World Cup in July killed a young Bosniac woman and seriously wounded an elderly man when they fired shots into East Mostar. All told, the centerpiece of U.S. policy in B-H, the Bosniac-Croat federation, remained a complete failure.

REFUGEE ISSUES

Problems with the return of refugees were not limited to a few hotspots. In fact, very few individuals in the post-Dayton period have proven willing to return to their original homes if their native towns or villages are in territories controlled by other ethnic groups. Although the United Nations High Commissioner for Refugees had anticipated that there would be 50,000 such "minority returns" in 1998, by October less than 15,000 had taken place, and a good number of those went to the internationally-supervised area around the city of Brcko. The returns problem became all the more important as European governments, and especially Germany, began to repatriate (often involuntarily) refugees from Bosnia-Herzegovina who had made their way to Western Europe during the war.

What became increasingly evident by 1998 was that an absence of war was not enough for people to be willing to return. Local police forces and judicial systems had to be reformed to ensure returnees that their rights would be protected; property legislation had to be revised so as to provide the legal foundation with which individuals could reclaim their homes and apartments; education curricula had to be revamped so as not to offend minority groups; the economy had to provide jobs for current local residents as well as returnees; and so on. In the Republika Srpska, for instance, few Bosniacs and Croats returned to their homes despite the more moderate tone of the Plavsic–Dodik duo. This was at least in part due to the dire economic situation in the RS (at least in comparison to the economic situation in the Federation), which gave people little reason to go back to their homes.

Nor were refugee return problems confined to the RS. In July, the OHR advised international donor agencies to suspend funding projects in Sarajevo. The international community had previously decided to use Sarajevo as an example for the rest of Bosnia-Herzegovina, to show that it *was* possible to re-create a multi-ethnic society, but international officials became increasingly exasperated with the Izetbegovic government's obstruction of Croat and Serb returns to the capital.

THE QUESTION OF WAR CRIMES

The effort to apprehend individuals indicted for war crimes gained momentum in 1998. By year's end, over half of the publicly indicted individuals were either in custody or had died. After Dodik came to power in the RS in January, his government tried to persuade several Serbs on the list of indictees to surrender voluntarily. In this, they had some success: by April, five Bosnian Serbs had turned themselves in, either to SFOR troops or to RS police, of their own accord. Nevertheless, arresting those indicted for war crimes remained a very sensitive issue with considerable political risks. On 2 December, for instance, SFOR troops apprehended VRS General Radislav Krstic. Krstic was named in a so-called "sealed indictment" which had not been made public by prosecutors from the International Criminal Tribunal for former Yugoslavia (ICTY), and was arrested while on his way to an official meeting with SFOR officials. His arrest drew widespread condemnation from RS politicians across the political spectrum, and in Vlasenica two international officials were injured and a monitor's vehicle was destroyed in the protests following Krstic's arrest. SFOR also showed it was capable of making some very embarrassing missteps. In July, for instance, after weeks of surveillance and preparation, SFOR troops arrested two brothers in Prijedor and flew them to The Hague, whereupon ICTY prosecutors promptly announced that the two brothers were the victims of mistaken identity and released.

The two most well-known suspects on the ICTY's list were the Bosnian Serbs' wartime political and military leaders, Radovan Karadzic and Ratko Mladic. They remained at large throughout 1998. Mladic reportedly had moved to Belgrade where he was said to be working on his memoirs. Karadzic, on the other hand, spent most of his time in Bosnia-Herzegovina, moving between hideouts in the Kozara mountains west of Banja Luka, or in the hill country of eastern Herzegovina, with occasional trips to his native Montenegro. Western intelligence agencies had spent millions in the efforts to track and apprehend him, but by July news reports suggested that the operation had been abandoned.

INTER-ENTITY ISSUES

On the statewide level, inter-entity cooperation marked some modest improvements. After Dodik came to power in the Republika Srpska, agreements were quickly reached between the Federation and the RS on inter-entity rail cooperation and the adoption of common license plates. The latter move showed immediate results: between April and June alone, the number of vehicles crossing the Inter-Entity Boundary Line (IEBL) doubled (although, admittedly, the starting point was extremely low). In April, the transport and communications ministers of the Federation and the RS signed a memorandum of understanding intended to establish a joint postal service throughout Bosnia-Herzegovina. In June, the long-awaited common currency for B-H, the convertible mark, was finally issued. Bosniacs, Croats, and Serbs also managed to adopt some important legislation on their own. For instance, a Law on Customs Policy of B-H passed the B-H Parliamentary Assembly in September, and the ministers of trade and finance in the two entities agreed to commit themselves to removing obstacles to internal B-H trade. Although these agreements were promising, it remained to be seen whether they would be implemented in practice.

Bosnia-Herzegovina's central institutions also had some new blood injected into them in 1998. The September elections saw two of the original three members of the joint presidency, Momcilo Krajisnik and Kresimir Zubak, lose in their re-election bids. Zubak lost to a more hard-line Croat nationalist from Herzegovina, Ante Jelavic; while Krajisnik lost to the more moderate president of the Socijalisticka Partija–Republike Srpske (SP-RS), Zivko Radisic. (Due to the procedures in place for rotating the position of chairman of the joint presidency, Radisic replaced Izetbegovic as the first-among-equals in the B-H presidency.) In the B-H Council of Ministers, Svetozar Mihajlovic of Plavsic's Sloga coalition replaced the SDS-appointed Boro Bosic as the Serb co-chairman of that body. At year's end, however, it was still too early to tell if these personnel changes would aid in breaking the deadlock which had incapacitated central institutions for most of post-Dayton period.

In the legislatures of the two entities, the September 1998 elections resulted in the Party of Democratic Action (SDA) losing its absolute majority in the Federation House of Representatives, and for the first time in the postwar period the HDZ and NHI gained seats in the RS National Assembly. One practical and procedural issue of significant symbolic importance that was resolved was where central institutions would meet. For most of the post-Dayton period, sessions of the Joint Presidency and of the Council of Ministers had alternated between a location in central Sarajevo and one in the Sarajevo suburb of Lukavica on RS territory. In March, however, all three sides agreed that henceforth, all meetings of common institutions would be held in the Marijin Dvor complex in central Sarajevo.

TOWARDS A PROTECTORATE

The deadlock in the common institutions of Bosnia-Herzegovina led many observers to suggest that a "dependency syndrome" had set in, making B-H a de facto protectorate of the international community. What little progress was made in implementing the Dayton accords generally came only after a tremendous exertion of effort and time by international officials, as disagreements between

Bosniacs, Croats, and Serbs forced international officials to decide on the most pressing issues. In January, the international High Representative to Bosnia-Herzegovina, Carlos Westendorp, decided on the design of the new B-H currency. In February, he decided on the design of the new B-H flag. Westendorp also had to impose his decisions vis-à-vis the adoption of a law on the privatization of banks and enterprises and a law on telecommunications. In March, the international arbitration tribunal created to decide on the jurisdiction of Brcko, the one territorial issue in B-H left unresolved at Dayton, announced that it was delaying its award for another year—an implicit admission of the fact that large-scale instability was still possible in the country. In July, the UN Security Council voted to establish an international body to oversee reform of B-H's judicial system. The OHR and the OSCE also decided to set up a media monitoring commission charged with establishing a regulatory regime for broadcasting and other media to bring them up to European standards. During the course of the year, Westendorp also dismissed public officials (chosen in internationally monitored elections) in places such as Drvar, Stolac, and Vlasenica.

Given the precarious state of the overall peace process, on 8 December NATO foreign ministers decided that there was no room to change either the size or the force structure of the SFOR mission for the foreseeable future. In sum, three years after Dayton, the peace was still far from being "self-sustaining" and many international officials openly admitted that the international community would be in B-H for years, if not decades.

Interview: *DAYTON AND DEMOCRACY*

The biggest surprise of the September general elections in Bosnia was the victory of Nikola Poplasen, leader of the extreme nationalist Serbian Radical Party (SRS), in the Republika Srpska presidential elections. Poplasen beat President Biljana Plavsic, a moderate who had been championed by the international community. In his first public appearances after the election, Poplasen made an effort to tone down his rhetoric. Excerpts from a 28 September interview with Senad Pecanin, editor in chief of the Sarajevo magazine Dani, *follow.*

Dani: Are you aware of the international community's disappointment with your election?
Poplasen: . . . This obviously results from what has been attributed to the SRS and me personally, which has nothing to do with reality and my conduct and the SRS's [political] orientation thus far, and, especially, it has nothing to do with our intentions. . . . In other words, none of this talk about the SRS's isolationism,

the so-called ethnic cleansing, the so-called chauvinism, the so-called racism, is true. Those are nothing but lies. On the contrary, we are committed to openness, intensifying of all ties . . . and we will not only respect the Dayton agreement but insist upon its implementation.

Dani: "The Serbian Radical Party sees the future of Republika Srpska in its unity with Serbia and Montenegro, whereby the border with the [Bosniac-Croat] Federation of Bosnia and Herzegovina would become a state border, and the border with Yugoslavia would be erased." I believe you recognize these words of yours, and I am interested in whether your appointment to the office of the president of Republika Srpska changes anything in that frequently reiterated position.
Poplasen: Some political or historical goals may be achieved in five, ten, or 20 years. I have never given up on [our] general political goals, [that is] historic goals of the Serbian people and the SRS. . . . Within these [next] two years, the struggle for the Dayton agreement and for a Republika Srpska within the framework of the Dayton agreement is not in conflict with that citation you have read to me. The existence of the Serbian people in Republika Srpska and in other countries in the Balkans is possible and will be prosperous only on the condition that other peoples who live in the Balkans live in peace, and I would say, cooperating to a lesser or greater extent with the neighboring peoples, and there is nothing unusual about that. . . .

Dani: But in this case, you are against the preservation of the territorial integrity of Bosnia and Herzegovina.
Poplasen: I didn't say that we are going to reject—where does it say so?

Dani: Right here: ". . . whereby the border with the Federation of Bosnia and Herzegovina would become a state border, and the border with Yugoslavia would be erased."
Poplasen: Right, I'm talking about the long-term mandate. The Dayton peace agreement can be changed when the three peoples and the two entities agree to do so. . . .

Dani: Would you object to erasing entity borders?
Poplasen: Well, see, you're constantly stressing the entity borders as state borders. According to the Dayton agreement, they are only imaginary lines. . . .

Dani: Yes, but you know the cooperation between the entities is on the level of bad cooperation between two separate states.
Poplasen: We won't contest the joint functions of Bosnia and Herzegovina. . . . According to Dayton, the equality of entities and peoples is guaranteed. . . . The Dayton Bosnia and even the Dayton Republika Srpska are not in conflict with our long-term goals—we don't mind that. Why wouldn't we have good coopera-

tion with the people we were in conflict with until yesterday? . . . I cannot decide whether Republika Srpska will unite with Serbia, or whether Bosnia will become stronger, in ten years or so, but all the people who live here must make that decision in a legitimate and democratic way.

Dani: I saw your photograph in the foyer, probably from the battlefield. Did your combat experience help you gain a [chetnik] title [of vojvoda, or commander]? *Poplasen:* Yes.

Dani: Were you a good fighter?
Poplasen: That's for others to say. Probably, since I got the title, I was. I was both a fighter and a commander on several occasions.

Dani: Will you, from the office you hold, make possible the extradition of Radovan Karadzic to the tribunal in The Hague?
Poplasen: One of the primary duties of the president of the republic is to respect the constitution and laws of the republic. Something like that is not envisaged in our laws.

Dani: Will you support the request for the rebuilding of the Ferhadija mosque in Banja Luka?
Poplasen: Why would I support it? The president of the republic does not make decisions on that.

Dani: He doesn't, but [the president] is very important in any case. What is your personal opinion?
Poplasen: The institutions that have to decide will make a decision on it.

Dani: If you are asked to speak your mind, what will you say?
Poplasen: I will say that I am not in charge, because I am not.

Dani: But I am very interested in your personal stance on the issue.
Poplasen: I believe that many churches should come first, and the reconstruction of any mosque is the Bosniacs' business. . . . That is a religious right that we will not block either by laws or our conduct. I expect the same situation for other peoples in other areas.

Translated by Denisa Kostovi

NOTE
Reprinted with kind permission from *Transitions* magazine, November 1998.

Federal Republic of Yugoslavia___

Population:	11,100,000
Capital:	Belgrade (pop. 1,087,915)
Major cities:	Nis (pop. 247,898); Novi Sad (pop. 170,029); Pristina, Kosovo (pop. 108,020); Podgorica,
....	Montenegro (pop. 96,074)
Area:	102,350 sq. km.
Major ethnic groups:	Serbian 63%, Albanian 14%, Montenegrin 6%, Hungarian 4%, other 13%
Economy:	GDP growth: No reliable data
....	Inflation rate: No reliable data
....	Unemployment rate: 30%

HEADING FOR THE ABYSS

by GORDON BARDOS

In 1998, the already unstable situation in Yugoslavia took a significant turn for the worse. The perennial Albanian-Serb dispute in Kosovo became open warfare; Montenegro became increasingly estranged from what little was left of the Yugoslav federation; and international economic sanctions continued to prevent any resurrection of Yugoslavia's economy. Despite these problems, Yugoslav president Slobodan Milosevic was still in power at year's end. But there were some signs in the latter half of 1998 that opposition to his rule had spread to the highest levels of his regime, as both the secret police chief and the defense minister were purged.

THE MONTENEGRIN CHALLENGE

Perhaps the most serious challenge to Milosevic's rule since he rose to power in 1987 came after the Democratic Party of Socialists of Montenegro (Demokratska Partija Socijalista Crne Gore, or DPSCG) split into pro- and anti-Milosevic factions in 1997. In October of that year, the pro-Milosevic incumbent president, Momir Bulatovic, lost a hotly contested election to Milo Djukanovic, a former protégé who had broken ranks with Bulatovic's pro-Milosevic stance during the Serbian opposition demonstrations in the winter or 1996/97. On 14 January 1998, rioting erupted in the Montenegrin capital of Podgorica as Bulatovic's supporters staged a last-ditch attempt to prevent Milo Djukanovic from assuming office, attacking government buildings and police in the streets. Their efforts proved futile, however, and on the next day Djukanovic was sworn in as Montenegrin president after receiving a strong vote of confidence from the U.S. State Department. (Some observers attributed Bulatovic's failed coup attempt to the fact that the Army of Yugoslavia, the Vojska Jugoslavije, or VJ, refused to become involved.)

The struggle between Milosevic and Djukanovic continued throughout the year and was fought on a wide front. In May, Milosevic installed Bulatovic as Yugoslav federal prime minister after engineering the removal of another Montenegrin, Radoje Kontic. Kontic had drawn Milosevic's ire in January by refusing to support the use of VJ troops in Montenegro. Although the Djukanovic camp called Bulatovic's nomination unconstitutional, he remained in office. But Djukanovic's new policies in Montenegro continued to challenge Milosevic's hitherto unquestioned rule. (See accompanying interview with Montenegrin Prime Minister Filip Vujanovic.) For instance, Djukanovic frequently criticized Milosevic's approach to the Kosovo issue, and publicly announced Montenegro's willingness to cooperate with the International War Crimes Tribunal for the Former Yugoslavia (ICTY). Despite misgivings about Milosevic's Kosovo policies, however, the Montenegrins consistently refused to support Albanian calls for establishing Kosovo as the "third republic" of Yugoslavia, for fear that this would diminish Montenegro's importance. Soon after Djukanovic took office, the federal Yugoslav government suspended payments to pensioners in Montenegro, and in response the Montenegrins stopped payment of income and excise taxes to the federal government. By 1998, Montenegro was only paying its share of Yugoslavia's national defense budget. In September, the Montenegrin government refused to pay a "war tax" imposed by the federal government to fund the war in Kosovo, and Djukanovic even threatened to withdraw Montenegrin recruits from the VJ.

Montenegrin officials were also critical of the Milosevic regime's economic policies. For instance, they frequently threatened to introduce their own currency (or even to adopt the German mark) should the Milosevic government again begin to print money to cover deficits, as occurred in 1994–95 when Yugoslavia experienced severe hyper-inflation.

The new Montenegrin leadership also showed it was interested in pursuing a more independent foreign policy. This took several forms. For instance, the Djukanovic government began pursuing much more active relations with the other former Yugoslav republics, and members of the new Montenegrin government were frequently seen in Sarajevo, Banja Luka, and Skopje during the course of 1998. Djukanovic also strongly pushed for opening Montenegro's border with Croatia, which was of vital importance for resuscitating Montenegro's tourist industry. In December, Montenegro did in fact open its border with Croatia at Debeli Brijeg. Montenegro's independent foreign policy was not restricted to the Balkans. A Montenegrin office was opened at the European Union in Brussels, and plans were under way to open similar offices in London, Paris, New York, and Moscow.

WAR IN KOSOVO

The issue that dominated Yugoslav politics in 1998, however, was Kosovo. For the Serbs, Kosovo was considered the cradle of their civilization and identity as a nation, although by the 1990s 90 percent of the province's population was Albanian. In fact, the 2 million ethnic Albanians in Kosovo made them the largest ethnic irredenta population (as a percent of total population of the ethnic group) in the world when compared to neighboring Albania's population of 3.3 million. Adding to Kosovo's importance to Milosevic personally was the fact that he had risen to power based on his role as the champion of Serb rights in Kosovo. Thus, were he to admit that Kosovo was lost to the Serbs, it would be the final confirmation of his failure as the Serbian leader.

In late 1997, a heretofore little-known organization named the "Kosovo Liberation Army" (UCK) emerged onto the scene with a series of provocative attacks on Serbian police forces in the province. On 23 February 1998, the U.S. State Department's top Balkan envoy, Robert Gelbard, called the UCK "a terrorist organization." Western intelligence agencies acknowledged that the UCK was in part supported by radical Islamic groups with ties to Iran and experience in Bosnia.

Soon thereafter, the VJ launched a large-scale operation to destroy the organization. The most important action occurred in the village of Prekaz, the home of the Jashari clan in Kosovo's Drenica region, often described as the heart of the rebellion. During the Serb attack, over 50 people were killed, including women and children. Western powers subsequently threatened Milosevic with military force if he did not stop the crackdown. UN Security Council Resolution 1160 of 31 March 1998 condemned the "excessive use of force by Serbian police forces" and "acts of terrorism by the Kosovo Liberation Army." It also imposed an arms embargo on the Federal Republic of Yugoslavia (including Kosovo), and extended the mandate of the International Criminal Tribunal for the former Yugoslavia to cover potential war crimes in the province. Western mediation did succeed in reducing the level of violence temporarily, but with no viable political compromise in sight it was clear that the cease-fire would not last. Large-scale violence erupted again during the summer, and many analysts surmised that Milosevic had been given a tacit green light by Western powers to destroy the UCK, which lost much sympathy in the West because of its uncompromising positions and brutality.

Part of the difficulty in achieving a political solution to the Kosovo conflict lay in the fact that the Kosovars themselves were deeply divided. For most of the 1990s, Kosovar Albanian society had been led by the literature professor-turned-political leader Ibrahim Rugova, under whose guidance the Kosovo Albanians had built a shadow state in Kosovo, complete with its own government, school, health-care, and taxation systems. Milosevic tolerated this situation in part because he was preoccupied elsewhere, and in part because Rugova's passive resistance did not directly threaten Serb rule in Kosovo. Many Kosovars, however, became increasingly frustrated with Rugova's failure to provide tangible results from his policies. More militant factions within Kosovar Albanian society began to call for armed resistance to the Yugoslav state, and it was among these factions that the UCK was born. By 1998, tensions between Rugova's more moderate leadership and the UCK militants would make it extremely difficult for both the Serbs and the international community to find a competent interlocutor throughout the crisis.

To shore up his authority among Kosovars, Rugova held elections for his "government" in March 1998. Although Yugoslav authorities refused to recognize the validity of the elections, they did not prevent them from taking place. As expected, Rugova was elected "president" of the self-declared "Republic of Kosovo" with over 70 percent of the vote. Nevertheless, many members of the UCK refused to recognize Rugova's leadership, and tensions between the UCK and the moderates around Rugova persisted. The UCK, for its part, proved to be a disunited organization whose units were more a collection of armed clans than a disciplined, hierarchical fighting force. Throughout 1998, this would make it difficult to establish any sort of meaningful cease-fire.

An important part of the Kosovars' strategy had always been to "internationalize" the problem of Kosovo. The position of the Yugoslav authorities, however, had consistently been that Kosovo was an internal Serbian matter. In the face of increasing international pressure to allow foreign mediation in the Kosovo conflict, in April 1998 Milosevic held a referendum asking the Yugoslav population whether or not international mediation should be accepted. As was widely foreseen at the time, 95 percent of Serbs rejected the proposal.

Tensions continued to escalate, and in May the principal architect of the Dayton Accords, U.S. envoy Richard Holbrooke, turned his attention to Kosovo. Several days of intense negotiation resulted in Milosevic agreeing to meet with Rugova for talks aimed at re-establishing some form of self-government for the Albanian population in Kosovo. Talks between Albanians and Serbs began in the Kosovo capital of Pristina, but achieved little. In August, the VJ launched another major offensive against the rebel stronghold in the Drenica region. An important rebel-held town, Junik, fell on 16 August. Continued large-scale fighting led to approximately 250,000 people fleeing from their homes.

With the Balkan winter approaching, the prospect of hundreds of thousands of people freezing to death in the mountainous border region between Yugoslavia and Albania forced Western powers to act. In October, NATO leaders issued an activation order allowing military action against Yugoslavia. In yet another effort to prevent a showdown between NATO and Yugoslavia, Richard Holbrooke was dispatched to the area to try to wrest some concessions out of Milosevic. Some progress was made, and an agreement signed on 12 October, called for the insertion of 2,000 unarmed foreign monitors (the "Kosovo Verification Mission," or KVM) into the province and gave NATO aircraft the right to fly over Kosovo to monitor the situation. Yugoslav military and police forces were also to be reduced to their pre-February 1998 levels. Milosevic thereby was forced to reverse himself from his previously stated position that Yugoslavia would not agree to foreign mediation. On 24 October, UN Security Council Resolution 1203/98 paved the way for the verification mission, under the auspices of the Organization for Security and Cooperation in Europe (OSCE).

The weaknesses in the Milosevic–Holbrooke agreement quickly became apparent, however, as the cease-fire unraveled within weeks. Part of the problem was due to the fact that the UCK's obligations under the Milosevic–Holbrooke plan had been negotiated without the UCK's participation, so they did not feel obligated to live up to it. When VJ and Serbian police units pulled out of Kosovo, UCK forces moved in to the recently-evacuated areas. At the same time, the UCK had used the break in the fighting to raise money to rearm and reorganize after its summer defeats. By December, with the help of new weapons, UCK forces were even occasionally able to repel armored attacks by the VJ.

On the political front, U.S. diplomacy continued to try to find some compromise position between the factions, but to little avail. On 1 November, the first American interim autonomy plan for Kosovo was released, but was rejected by the Serbs as being too pro-Albanian. (In fact, this version barely mentioned Serbia at all.) A second American version came out on 2 December, but was then rejected by the Albanians as being too pro-Serb. At the same time, the United States's European allies, in what reminded many observers of the problems faced in ending the war in Bosnia, were becoming more and more disgruntled with the United States' unilateral diplomacy in Kosovo. Russia, for its part, since September under the leadership of Prime Minister Yevgenii Primakov, became much more vocal in its opposition to Western intervention in Kosovo.

By year's end, the cease-fire in Kosovo was hanging on by a thread, and there was little hope that any political compromise between the various factions involved could solve the problem. On 14 December, a column of 140 UCK members crossing the Yugoslav-Albanian border were ambushed by the VJ. Thirty-six UCK members were killed and several others taken prisoner. In the face of the renewed fighting and new calls for military action against Yugoslavia, Milosevic publicly warned that Yugoslavia would repel any NATO attacks. At the end of 1998, the death toll in the fighting was estimated at some 1,500 people killed and 250,000 forced to flee their homes to escape the fighting.

The international community, for its part, continued to insist that Kosovo remain a part of Yugoslavia, for fear that the UCK's professed goal, the secession of Kosovo and the creation of a "Greater Albania," would have severe repercussions throughout the region. Such a development would almost inevitably lead to the disintegration of Macedonia (itself facing a severe problem with the large Albanian population in western Macedonia, alongside Albania proper), and possibly lead to the long-dreaded wider Balkan war which could draw in Bulgaria, Greece, and Turkey. It would also have very negative consequences for the Dayton Accords in Bosnia-Herzegovina. Politically, negotiations were deadlocked by the Kosovar's insistence that an interim deal provide a clause allowing for a referendum on eventual independence, which Yugoslavia insisted was non-negotiable.

MILOSEVIC'S AUTUMN PURGE

Towards the end of 1998 there were increasing signs of serious opposition to Milosevic's policies even within his inner circle. In October, Milosevic sacked his longtime security chief, Jovica Stanisic, who had reportedly been opposed to Milosevic's crackdown in Kosovo, and to the heavy-handed way in which Milosevic had dealt with the opposition protests during the winter of 1996/97. Stanisic's removal was followed on 24 November by that of Momcilo Perisic, the Yugoslav defense minister. Perisic had grown increasingly critical of Milosevic's policies, indirectly accusing him of leaving Yugoslavia without allies, and had warned Milosevic against provoking a confrontation with NATO. After his dismissal, Perisic claimed that "Serbs have been fighting a war since 1991 and we still have no allies. Not even the Russian Federation has declared itself an ally. We have never been so isolated for so long and we have never [before] been without allies." In what was widely interpreted as a signal that he was willing to join with other anti-Milosevic forces, Perisic went on to say that he remained "at the disposal of the army, the people, and the state." Another key member of Milosevic's apparat to be dismissed at this time was Milorad Vucelic, the director of state-run television.

In each of these cases, individuals loyal to Milosevic's wife, Mira Markovic, were installed in place of the dismissed officials. In December, more purges in the military were carried out, most notably within the command structure of the Third Army, whose area-of-responsibility included Kosovo. (Notably, no changes were carried out in the Second Army, which was responsible for Montenegro). Apart from purging his inner circle, Milosevic also renewed his campaign against other important segments of society opposed to his rule. In October, a new law curtailing academic freedom was enacted. The new legislation removed the right to hire and fire faculty from faculty committees and transferred the right to deans who were political appointees. The deans were also given the right to change curricula to make them more acceptable to Milosevic's Socijalisticka Partija Srbije (Socialist Party of Serbia, or SPS). Some 130 professors at the University of Belgrade refused to sign a statement accepting the new powers given to the deans, and were all either suspended or terminated from their positions.

The Milosevic regime at the same time began to crack down on the independent media as well. On 24 October, the government imposed a $230,000 fine on the weekly *Evropljanin,* and on the night of 25–26 October police raided the offices of the popular *Dnevni Telegraf.*

Together with the changes in Montenegro, the international presence in Bosnia-Herzegovina, and the problems in Kosovo, Milosevic had increasingly less room to maneuver politically. Fortunately for him, however, the official Serbian opposition parties remained disunited, largely due to personal squabbling among the leaders of different opposition groups. Milosevic, moreover, continued to prove adept at co-opting members of the opposition when it proved advantageous for him. For instance, in March 1998 he had Vojislav Seselj, the extremist leader of the Serbian Radical Party (the Srpska Radikalna Stranka, or SRS), appointed a deputy prime minister of the Serbian government. Towards the end of the year, Milosevic began negotiating with one of his most vociferous opponents, Vuk Draskovic, the president of the Serbian Renewal Movement (Srpski Pokret Obnove, SPO), about bringing him into the government. (Draskovic did in fact become a deputy prime minister in the federal Yugoslav government in January 1999.)

RENEWED ISOLATION

Not surprisingly, Yugoslavia's diplomatic position improved little in 1998. Relations with Macedonia deteriorated after it agreed to the stationing of NATO troops on its territory. No significant progress was made in establishing diplomatic relations with Bosnia-Herzegovina either, because of Bosnia-Herzegovina's continued refusal to remove its suit against Yugoslavia for genocide before the World Court. Problems in Yugoslavia's relations with Croatia also persisted because of disagreements over the final status of Prevlaka, a strategic peninsula controlling access to the Bay of Kotor, home of the Yugoslav navy's only major port. This issue was a further strain for relations between Belgrade and Podgorica, with the latter intent on normalizing ties with Croatia as quickly as possible for trade reasons. Little progress was achieved on another important issue, the attempt to divide the former Yugoslavia's international debts among the former Yugoslav republics. The Federal Republic of Yugoslavia continued to insist on its rights as the sole legitimate successor state to the former Socialist Federal Republic of Yugoslavia, which would allow it to claim the latter's seat in the UN and its numerous diplomatic offices around the world.

The Kosovo situation, of course, also worsened Yugoslav relations with Albania. After Albania descended into large-scale anarchy in 1997, large parts of northern Albania effectively fell outside of the control of the Albanian government, and these regions provided the main supply routes for the UCK and home to its most important bases. Relations with Macedonia and Bulgaria also worsened after those two countries granted NATO the right to use their airspace for any possible military actions in Kosovo.

Yugoslavia's position vis-à-vis the West also deteriorated because of the Kosovo situation. International sanctions were re-imposed on Belgrade in March, and on 8 June, the EU banned new investment in Yugoslavia and instructed its member-states to freeze Yugoslav assets abroad. The United States, for its part, had gone through various twists in its approach to the Kosovo problem. Official Washington toned down its rhetoric about the UCK, and on 30 November, a State Department spokesman said that the United States saw Milosevic as the "root of the problem" in the former Yugoslavia, and that U.S. policy was aimed at supporting democratic opposition to his rule. Apart from a change in rhetoric, however, there was little evidence that the United States was seriously considering ousting Milosevic.

A WORSENING ECONOMY

Political crises and war in Kosovo were not the only problems facing the Yugoslav population in 1998. International economic sanctions continued into their sixth year, and refugees from Bosnia-Herzegovina and Croatia continued to burden the economy: by the late 1990s, the Federal Republic of Yugoslavia was home to the largest refugee population in Europe. The outbreak of war in Kosovo only exacerbated these problems. GDP in 1998 fell by 4 percent in relation to 1997 levels. Yugoslavia's economy also continued to suffer because of a U.S.-imposed "outer wall of sanctions" which prohibited Belgrade from obtaining loans from international monetary organizations such as the IMF or the World Bank.

Milosevic's regime itself, however, was in large part responsible for Yugoslavia's devastated economy because of its unwillingness to engage in any meaningful type of economic reform. A study completed by the Belgrade-based Center for Policy Studies in 1998 concluded that "The transition process, in the sense of the transition witnessed in the Eastern European countries, is yet to be seen here, while the developments we have seen in the last 10 years can only be described as a dead end." Independent economists in Belgrade called the economic program proposed by the Yugoslav government in 1998 the worst in 30 years. Among numerous objections, they cited a host of unrealistic assumptions in the plan, including an unfreezing of Yugoslav assets abroad, the restoration of ties with the IMF, the World Bank, and the Paris and London Clubs of international creditors, and the restoration of preferential trade status with the EU.

CONCLUSION

By any relevant measure, Yugoslavia's domestic and international situation was significantly worse at the end of 1998 than at the beginning of the year. Politically, Yugoslavia had disintegrated into three distinct and conflicting semi-autonomous entities (Montenegro, Kosovo, and Serbia proper), and the dynamics in the first two were following a course largely independent of anything that could be controlled from Belgrade. There was still no end in sight to the country's long-term economic decline, and on the diplomatic front there was little evidence that Yugoslavia could break out of its externally enforced international isolation. All told, the omens did not bode well for 1999.

Interview: *MILOSEVIC'S SHRINKING INFLUENCE IN MONTENEGRO*

Filip Vujanovic served as interior minister in the Milo Djukanovic government, acquiring the reputation of a moderate and pragmatic politician. When Djukanovic was elected president of Montenegro in October 1997, Vujanovic became the prime minister. He was interviewed for Transitions *in Podgorica by Milka Tadic, a journalist with* Monitor, *just after the May 1998 parliamentary elections.*

Transitions: Your coalition has said that the crisis in Montenegro is over. But what about the crisis in the Federal Republic of Yugoslavia?
Filip Vujanovic: The coalition victory means the end of the political conflicts that have shaken Montenegro. It also means that Montenegro has recognized its true interest in political reform, the democratization of political relations, and integration into the international community. [Slobodan] Milosevic's policy is

totally different: he stands for international isolation, backward economic policy, and autocratic rule. His policy no longer stands a chance in Montenegro—his candidate, Momir Bulatovic, was heavily defeated. I hope democratic forces in Serbia will find a way to defeat Milosevic through the model we promoted here and that democracy will triumph at the federal level as well. . . . We have good relations with all democratic parties in Serbia. Unfortunately, they are not strong enough to defeat Milosevic. Democracy, nevertheless, does have a future in Serbia.

Transitions: Some believe Milosevic will try to engineer unrest in Montenegro. What do you predict?

FV: I don't think he is going to change. . . . But our victory is a loss he cannot accept politically. That's why I think he will try to increase Bulatovic's influence in Montenegro. But Bulatovic won't be able to rule Montenegro from the federal level, although the federal government . . . can stop paying money into our pension and health funds, and it can deny us oil concessions. It can close the borders with Croatia and Albania, and it can make it more difficult for foreign tourists to come to Montenegro by maintaining visa requirements for travelers to Yugoslavia. Should any of this happen, Montenegro will establish mechanisms to protect itself.

Transitions: Your opponents maintain that your government has criminal connections. Is there any truth to these stories?

FV: Of course not. Under international sanctions it was well known that Montenegro depended on various channels for obtaining industrial materials, oil, and food. Those channels enabled Montenegro and its economy to survive. Even the international community tolerated them. A number of Montenegrins got rich quickly as a result. Of course, it is imperative that businesses are run in an appropriate fashion now. We are regulating conditions, and a number of people who got rich in that period will have to return some of that wealth to society through taxation.

Transitions: Montenegro's delegation in the Federal Yugoslav Chamber of Republics is dominated by Bulatovic's supporters. Will you change the delegation?

FV: Montenegro has to be represented in the Chamber of Republics by people ready to defend Montenegrin interests. Members of Bulatovic's party put their party's interests before those of Montenegro. Thanks to them, the federal government was fired and a new one, led by Bulatovic, was installed.

Transitions: Milosevic has to have the Chamber of Republics under his control, otherwise the federal parliament could vote him out. Aren't you afraid that he may not accept a new Montenegrin delegation?

FV: Of course he won't accept it, but the make-up of our delegation cannot depend on his good will. Montenegro can block any disadvantageous decisions. We can, for instance, block Milosevic's initiative to change the federal constitution and centralize state security services.

Transitions: The Montenegrin government no longer recognizes the federal government's authority. Milosevic doesn't recognize the Montenegrin government. Does FR Yugoslavia still exist?

FV: We don't recognize this federal government because we think it is illegitimate. We won't cooperate with such a government, although we still pay our dues to the federal budget. On the other hand, the federal government withholds federal budget funds.

The composition of the federal institution does not reflect the will of people of Montenegro. But I don't think Yugoslavia is in question. It's in our common interest to preserve Yugoslavia. But illegitimate federal institutions have to reflect the will of both Serbia and Montenegro. It is a difficult and complex job, but we will not give up.

Transitions: How does the present situation compare with the collapse of Yugoslavia?

FV: Milosevic is in a much more difficult situation today. He's lost his influence in Republika Srpska, where Milorad Dodik preserved his government—despite Milosevic's obstructionist attitude—and Biljana Plavsic remains president. Republika Srpska was very important to his overall position. By losing influence in Republika Srpska and here in Montenegro, Milosevic's influence in Serbia itself also shrank. I believe this new situation will serve as an incentive for democratic forces in Serbia to mobilize and bring down Milosevic's regime.

Transitions: Can Milosevic drag Montenegro into the Kosovo conflict?

FV: The Kosovo problem has to be solved by dialogue. The fact that it hasn't been is Milosevic's great failure. He neglected this problem, and it could have been resolved earlier. Now with all the fighting, it is difficult to achieve a solution. Talks between Albanians and Serbs cannot proceed without international mediation because of the great mistrust between these two peoples. The conflict could spread, but not to Montenegro.

Transitions: Albanians now talk of Kosovo as a third republic within Yugoslavia. What do you think?

FV: We are against giving Kosovo the status of a republic—it's one more step toward independence. Also, if Kosovo were a republic, the conception of the federal state would change. A broad autonomy would be the best solution. It would ensure Albanian rights in Kosovo itself and that Albanians take part in Serbia's and Yugoslavia's political life.

Transitions: What will be the priorities of the new Montenegrin government?

FV: Economic reforms are our priority. We will insist on privatization, now that we have clearly created a possibility for foreign investment. I hope that both the European Union and the United States have enough economic interest in the area to help reforms and transition in Montenegro. In the sphere of political relations, we will further affirm the principles of interethnic tolerance, respect for human rights, and the rule of law. In our foreign policy we will insist on establishing good relations with neighbors and former Yugoslav republics, and on connecting with the European Union, the United States, and Russia.

NOTE

Reprinted with kind permission from *Transitions* magazine, July 1998.

Macedonia

Population:	2,075,196 (1994 census)
Capital:	Skopje (pop. 450,000)
Major cities:	Bitola (pop. 80,000), Kumanovo (pop. 70,000), Prilep (pop. 70,000)
Area:	25,713 sq. km.
Major ethnic groups:	Macedonian 67%, Albanian 23%, Turkish 4%, Romani 2%, Serbian 2%, other 2%
Economy:	GDP growth: 5%
	Inflation rate: 2%
	Unemployment rate: 28%

DEFYING THE ODDS BY REMAINING STABLE

by STEFAN KRAUSE

After ruling the country for most of the time since it gained independence, the Social Democrats lost power in parliamentary elections in October and November 1998 and were replaced by ethnic Macedonian and Albanian parties widely regarded as "nationalistic" and "radical." However, the smooth transition of power and some easing of inter-ethnic tensions indicate that Macedonia remains relatively stable, for now.

The year 1998 in Macedonia started with nervous tension. The clashes between ethnic Albanians and security forces in the summer of 1997 had strained relations between the ethnic Macedonian majority and the sizable Albanian minority, and stiff prison sentences imposed on the mayors of Gostivar and Tetovo had poisoned the situation even more. There were fears that 1998 might bring about further deterioration of inter-ethnic relations and ultimately threaten the country's stability.

Those fears were underscored when in early January, and then in February, May, and July, a number of bombs went off in the capital city of Skopje and in other towns. The Kosovo Liberation Army (UCK) claimed responsibility for the January bombings, but as the year progressed, it remained unclear whether the UCK was really behind them or whether radical Albanians in Macedonia just tried to use that organization's name for their own goals. Shortly before the parliamentary elections in the fall, a number of ethnic Albanians were arrested for alleged involvement in the bomb attacks, but no hard proof implicating them was produced. As a matter of fact, many observers believed that the government in power at the time had them arrested during the election campaign period in order to prove its willingness to crack down on crime and to defend the interests of Macedonia.

In February 1998, the prison sentence of Gostivar Mayor Rufi Osmani, who had been sentenced to 13 years and eight months in prison following the violent clashes in Gostivar in 1997, was reduced to seven years. Still, this did little to ease tensions, especially after Osmani and his counterpart from Tetovo, Alajdin Demiri, were ordered to start serving their sentences in April. This decision was followed by large protest meetings of ethnic Albanians in Skopje and elsewhere. Inter-ethnic relations remained tense throughout the year and eased only with the advent of a new government. (See accompanying article, "Macedonia's Open Wound.")

PARLIAMENTARY ELECTIONS PRODUCE NEW MAJORITY

The main political event of 1998 was the third multi-party parliamentary elections since 1991, held on 16 October and 1 November. Those elections were held under a new electoral system, which had been adopted by wide consensus of the major political parties in July 1998. In previous elections, the 120 seats in the Sobranie (Assembly) had been filled in a two-round majoritarian system. Under the new system, 35 seats were to be allocated on a proportional basis among the parties passing a 5 percent threshold, while the rest would be contested in single-member constituencies (again in two rounds).

Throughout the year, the parties had tried to position themselves on the political scene, some forming coalitions in order to improve their chances in the vote, others deciding to go it alone. Those political maneuvers and the elections themselves resulted in a significant change of the party landscape.

The most important development in this field was the appearance of a new party on the political scene. On 21 March, the popular and charismatic Vasil Tupurkovski, who had been Macedonia's last representative in the collective Yugoslav presidency, announced the formation of the Democratic Alternative (DA). By self-description, the DA was a centrist party of civic (rather than national) orientation, although it did not go unnoticed that many of its top members had held high offices under Communist Yugoslavia.

After prolonged negotiations, the DA entered into a coalition with the Internal Macedonian Revolutionary Organization–Democratic Party for Macedonian National Unity (VMRO–DPMNE), headed by Ljubco Georgievski, a young poet who turned politician when democratic changes started in Macedonia. The VMRO–DPMNE, which had thus far been the main exponent of Macedonian nationalism, had toned down its rhetoric well ahead of the election campaign, focusing instead on economic issues and the fight against organized crime and corruption. The VMRO–DPMNE and DA formed the "Coalition for Changes" and agreed to field joint candidates in the single-mandate constituencies while running separate proportional lists.

This coalition agreement posed a problem for the Liberal Democratic Party (LDP), which had so far been the main centrist party and now risked being marginalized. The LDP only managed to form a coalition with the rather irrelevant Democratic Party of Macedonia, and would prove to be one of the big losers of the 1998 elections. As a result, the political career of LDP Chairman Petar Gosev, one of the more interesting political players of the past ten years, seems to have come to an end. In early 1999, Gosev announced his resignation as LDP chairman.

The main ruling party, the Social Democratic Union of Macedonia (SDSM) of Prime Minister Branko Crvenkovski, decided to contest the elections on its own, apart from a few strategic alliances in individual constituencies with its junior coalition partner, the Socialist Party of Macedonia (SPM). The SPM, for its part, in September formed a coalition with the Movement for Cultural Tolerance and Civic Cooperation, which comprised four small parties representing Roma, Turks, and Slav Muslims.

In another important pre-electoral development, the two main ethnic Albanian parties also decided to form an electoral alliance. The Party of Democratic Prosperity (PDP), which had been in the government for the past six years, and the more radical Democratic Party of Albanians (DPA) fielded joint candidates in single-member constituencies and a joint proportional list. Whereas the PDP enjoyed a numerical advantage with regards to the candidates in individual constituencies, the slots on the proportional list were split evenly between the two parties. The Albanian-party alliance was mainly tactical, as witnessed by the fact that it did not last beyond the elections.

The election campaign focused mainly on economic issues, the fight against corruption and organized crime, and closer integration into European and transatlantic structures. Nationalistic issues were conspicuously absent from most parties' campaigns. The Albanian parties hardly campaigned at all, knowing that in a country where ethnicity largely determines voting behavior they were assured most of the ethnic Albanian vote anyway.

The biggest election-campaign hit, though, was the DA's "Program for Reconstruction and Development," at the heart of which was the promise that Tupurkovski would raise $1 billion in foreign capital to improve the country's economy. Tupurkovski remained vague as to where the money would come from, and it was far from certain that even a fraction of this sum would ever materialize. The pledge helped, though, to raise Tupurkovski's popularity. If the failure to produce at least a substantial share of that sum does not backfire on him, he seemed to have positioned himself as the most serious contender for the 1999 presidential elections, provided he is backed by VMRO–DPMNE.

Unlike the 1994 parliamentary elections, in which the opposition boycotted the second round after claiming fraud, the 1998 elections were generally regarded as fair and democratic. Nonetheless, irregularities in individual constituencies forced a number of reruns. In one ethnic-Albanian constituency outside Skopje, irregularities were so serious that people in some polling stations had to vote well into January before the seat was finally filled.

There was also some concern about the role of the media during the election campaign since some of them (both public and private) openly side with one political camp or the other. Finally, there was widespread indignation about President Kiro Gligorov because of an interview he gave just one week before the first round of the elections. In this interview, he fiercely attacked Tupurkovski and insinuated that in 1992 Tupurkovski had been prepared to sacrifice Macedonian national interests in order to reach a settlement with Greece over the name issue. (Greece was refusing to recognize Macedonia's right to call itself by that name, arguing that this implied a territorial claim on northern Greece.) This interview was widely regarded as direct meddling in the election campaign by somebody whose official position requires neutrality in party-political affairs.

The elections themselves brought about a major shift in Macedonia's political balance. The outgoing government was soundly defeated, and the opposition took over. The "Coalition for Changes" won a remarkable outright majority of 62 seats in the new Assembly, with the VMRO–DPMNE winning 26.9 percent of the vote and 49 seats, and the DA 10.8 percent and 13 seats.

The SDSM, which at the end of the last assembly's term had 62 deputies, was reduced to 23.8 percent of the vote and 27 mandates. Its junior partner, the SPM, fared even worse, and only managed to elect its chairman into the new parliament. The SPM-led coalition failed to clear the 5 percent threshold, gaining only 4.1 percent. The LDP also fared worse than expected, and with 6.9 percent of the vote and four mandates might well be on its way to political irrelevance.

The Albanian parties managed to get a fair share of the votes and of the seats in the new parliament since their electoral alliance, which helped to concentrate the ethnic Albanian vote. Their proportional list received 19.6 percent of the popular vote. The PDP managed to get a total of 14 seats, while the DPA won 11 seats. The last seat in the parliament, finally, went to a representative of the Union of Roma.

"NATIONALISTS" AND "RADICALS" FORM NEW GOVERNMENT

After the elections, the "Coalition for Changes" opened preliminary coalition talks with the two Albanian parties and the LDP. Ultimately, the DPA was taken on board as the third partner in the new government. Such a development would have seemed highly unlikely before the elections, but the coalition talks went surprisingly smoothly. The idea of being in a government with an ethnic Albanian party—and the more radical one at that—might not have appealed to all VMRO–DPMNE followers, but it would almost certainly promote stability in Macedonia. In this regard, it is not that important whether the coalition was the result of subtle international pressure or whether Georgievski and other VMRO–DPMNE leaders really changed their minds on this issue.

Fulfilling one of the DPA's main demands, one of the first acts that the new government proposed and the parliament passed was an amnesty law with the basic aim of releasing Osmani, Demiri, and others convicted on similar charges. However, the amnesty also included drugs and arms dealers and was therefore highly controversial. President Gligorov vetoed it in January 1999, saying it violated the separation of powers.

The new Macedonian government was formally approved by the parliament on 30 November 1998. Led by Ljubco Georgievski, it included 27 ministers. Of those, 14 were VMRO–DPMNE members, eight came from the DA, and five from the DPA. The DA did surprisingly well in the coalition talks, given its numerical strength. Not only was the new chairman of the Sobranie a DA member, they also held a number of key ministerial positions, including Foreign Affairs, Internal Affairs, Economy, and Justice. The DPA, on the other hand, was put in charge of less important ministries, with the possible exception of Labor and Social Affairs. The positions of deputy ministers were divided among the three parties on a 8:8:5 quota for VMRO–DPMNE, DA, and DPA, respectively. Tupurkovski himself opted to stay out of the government and to become the head of the newly-created Agency for Reconstruction and Development, which will be in charge of bringing in foreign investment. DPA Chairman Arben Xhaferi also declined to join the government.

Not surprisingly, Georgievski named economic issues as the top priority of his government. Throughout his presentation to the parliament, though, he was rather vague when it came to concrete measures. The government pledged to present a comprehensive plan within three months. Apart from the economy, the fight against corruption and organized crime, integration into European and transatlantic structures, stable inter-ethnic relations, and improved ties with Macedonia's neighbors were at the heart of the new government's program.

One thing that became apparent at the very outset, though, was that the new government was not immune to Balkan political culture. The new coalition partners immediately started to divide the top posts in the public administration, the state agencies, and state-run enterprises among themselves, sacking top managers who had been appointed by the previous government. Those changes included the state media, which the government seemed to regard as an important tool for selling its actions to the public. The biggest publishing house, NIP "Nova Makedonija," in which the state held a 32-percent stake, was also affected by those changes.

ECONOMY STILL IN A PRECARIOUS STATE

It is obvious why economic issues were so high on the new government's agenda. On paper, the Macedonian economy looked quite good, with respectable GDP growth, a stable currency, and about the lowest inflation rate of all post-communist countries. Nonetheless, serious problems remained, many of them structural, and 1998 brought only some minor improvement to the general situation.

As in previous years, unemployment remained the biggest source of concern. According to official data, unemployment stood at 28 percent at the end of August 1998, but it is considerably higher in certain regions. Also, young people are particularly affected. The social welfare systems are on the brink of collapse. The old government raised pensions by 10 percent in the summer of 1998, obviously with the upcoming elections in mind, but the new government had to lower pensions to the previous level due to lack of funds.

Direct foreign investment also remained very low, but at least the trend was encouraging. In the first nine months of 1998, direct foreign investment amounted to about $160 million, a significant increase over a total of just $60 million for the years between 1993 and 1997. A few major privatization deals were also concluded in 1998.

Most encouraging was the significant growth in GDP, which was estimated at 5 percent for 1998 (compared to just 1.5 percent the previous year) and the drop in inflation from 3.6 to 3.0 percent. However, the trade balance remained negative, and the current account deficit rose from 8.3 percent of GDP in 1997 to an estimated 14 percent.

One of the biggest economic scandals of independent Macedonia, the collapse of the Bitola-based TAT savings house, was still not conclusively resolved. TAT, a pyramid scheme, collapsed in 1996, and some 23,000 people had lost a total of $65 million. On 1 July 1998, TAT owner Sonja Nikolovska was sentenced to eight years in prison, and others, including the former mayor of Bitola, received lighter sentences or were fined. However, the verdict was overturned in November 1998, and a new trial was scheduled for 1999. There was speculation that Nikolovska might get away with a lighter sentence if she can substantiate allegations implicating the former government in the scandal.

FOREIGN POLICY—SOME PROGRESS, SOME SETBACKS

Macedonia's foreign-policy situation was to a large extent determined by the Kosovo crisis. As fighting intensified in Kosovo, calls for the deployment of NATO troops on Macedonian territory increased. In May politicians demanded that NATO troops replace the UN Preventive Deployment Forces, whose mandate was nonetheless extended twice in 1998. NATO troops only arrived in December 1998 in the form of extraction forces which were to be used in the event that the international community needed to pull the OSCE monitors out of Kosovo.

The decision to allow the stationing of NATO troops on Macedonian territory was taken against warnings from Belgrade that this would be an unfriendly act and impair bilateral relations between Yugoslavia and Macedonia. Relations with Belgrade deteriorated at any rate, with the Macedonian government trying to keep a balanced regional policy, not upset inter-ethnic relations at home, and to improve its chances to draw closer to the European Union and NATO. In order to help the Kosovars without drawing Macedonia into the conflict, Gligorov in early 1998 proposed that a "corridor" for refugees be established in Macedonia in order to allow them to flee to Albania. This offer, however, was received coolly both at home and abroad and was not pursued any further.

Relations with Albania, meanwhile, strengthened. Then–prime minister of Albania Fatos Nano visited Macedonia several times during 1998, and several bilateral agreements were signed. With the apparent improvement of inter-ethnic relations in Macedonia, relations with Albania are largely unproblematic.

Macedonian-Bulgarian relations, on the other hand, still awaited a breakthrough. The contested issue of the existence or non-existence of a Macedonian nation and language continued to delay the signing of over 20 bilateral agreements, treaties, and conventions. Macedonia insisted that the official documents must be done in both state languages, while the Bulgarians continued to reject this demand. Sofia welcomed the election victory of the Macedonian opposition, which it regarded as more pro-Bulgarian that the old government, but despite some hints that Sofia might be willing to reach a compromise, there were no signs of a possible breakthrough by the end of 1998.

Until a few years ago, Macedonia's biggest problem was its southern neighbor, Greece. But ever since the signing of the interim agreement of 1995, relations between Skopje and Athens have improved. In 1998, Greece continued to be one of Macedonia's most important trading partners and the biggest foreign investor. Although no agreement on the contested issue of Macedonia's name was reached in 1998, relations seemed to gradually improve throughout the year. In a symbolic move, the head of the Greek liaison office was the first foreigner to congratulate the new speaker of parliament, Savo Klimovski, on his election. But at the end of the year most of this was forgotten, when on 22 December 1998, during a visit to Skopje, Greek Foreign Minister Theodoros Pangalos told the press that the issue of an ethnic Macedonian minority in northern Greece was non-existent. He referred to the local "Rainbow" organization, a group defending the rights of Greece's ethnic Slavs, as "a coalition of Stalinists, Slavo-Macedonians, and homosexuals," sparking fierce protests from the Macedonian side. It is likely that Pangalos was just testing the waters to see how willing the new government would be to compromise, but at any rate his statement did much damage and was a setback in the relationship.

GLOSSARY

DA	Democratic Alternative
DPA	Democratic Party of Albanians
LDP	Liberal Democratic Party
PDP	Party of Democratic Prosperity
SDSM	Social Democratic Union of Macedonia
VMRO–DPMNE	Internal Macedonian Revolutionary Organization–Democratic Party for Macedonian National Unity

Profile: *LJUBCO GEORGIEVSKI: POET TURNED PREMIER*

by STEFAN KRAUSE

Although only in his early thirties, Macedonia's new Prime Minister Ljubco Georgievski is not the youngest premier in the Balkans. His Albanian colleague Pandeli Majko is one year younger, and Branko Crvenkovski, from whom Georgievski took over, was only 29 when he became premier in September 1992.

On the other hand, Georgievski has played a leading role in Macedonian politics for almost a decade. Born in 1966 in the town of Stip, he studied comparative literature at the Faculty of Philology of Skopje University. In the late 1980s and early 1990s he published two books of poetry and a volume of short stories. With the disintegration of communist Yugoslavia approaching, Georgievski became a prominent figure in Macedonian intellectual and political circles, starting out as a student leader in the late 1980s. In 1990, he became the chairman of the newly established Macedonian Revolutionary Organization–Democratic Party for Macedonian National Unity (VMRO–DPMNE). Although he might have been picked because more experienced nationalist politicians regarded him as compromise figure, an inexperienced youth who could easily be manipulated and maybe later sacked by them, he has managed to hold on to that position ever since.

From the very outset, Georgievski was an ardent nationalist, unlike many other politicians who tried to reform federal Yugoslavia and keep Macedonia within that state. In the first Macedonian multiparty elections of 1990, VMRO–DPMNE became the single strongest party, and one of its leading figures, Nikola Kljusev, became head of an expert government supported by all major parties. Georgievski was elected to the ceremonial post of vice-president of Macedonia in 1991 but resigned from that position eight months later, dissatisfied with the slow pace of reforms and the fact that his party was increasingly being outmaneuvered by the more experienced Social Democrats, the main successor of the formerly ruling League of Communists of Macedonia.

In 1994, VMRO–DPMNE boycotted the second round of the parliamentary elections, claiming they were flawed and rigged to the advantage of the Social Democrats. The VMRO–DPMNE made a comeback of sorts in the 1996 local elections, winning a number of important municipalities. Before the 1998 elections, the party and its chairman decided to rid themselves of most of their nationalist rhetoric in favor of a pro-market approach and a focus on economic issues. This, along with widespread dissatisfaction with the Social Democrats, contributed to VMRO–DPMNE's victory in the 1998 elections and brought Georgievski into the premier's office.

Unless his government's performance is unusually bad (the precedent set by Bulgaria's Socialists in 1995–1997 should serve as a warning), Georgievski seems to have a long political career ahead of him. Following his election victory, he immediately sidelined some important figures from his party's leadership, saying they should not be burdened with party politics and rather should be allowed to concentrate on their government jobs. Interestingly enough, some party leaders who were also in the government retained their positions, and Deputy Foreign Minister Boris Trajkovski was newly appointed to the VMRO–DPMNE Executive Council, a clear sign that those people enjoyed Georgievski's trust. These maneuvers, which were expected to be confirmed by a party congress in 1999, indicate that Georgievski was clearly in control of his party, especially since there was no obvious candidate to replace him.

AN OPEN WOUND

by GORDANA ICEVSKA

As the October parliamentary elections neared, the fueling of ethnic tension became a campaign issue. Radicalism was growing in Macedonia, as is evidenced by not only the words of politicians but also the fights between Macedonians and ethnic Albanians, attacks on religious buildings, bomb explosions near government buildings, and the destruction of graveyards. Many Albanians in Macedonia idolize the Kosovo Liberation Army (UCK), and supporters of mutual coexistence were slowly being marginalized.

Discontent was sparked by the two main ethnic Albanian political parties in Macedonia, representing the interests of the country's Albanians (23 percent of the population according to official statistics, 33 percent according to their own). Only six months previously, Abdurahman Aliti, leader of the Party of Democratic Prosperity (PDP), and Arben Xhaferi, leader of the opposition Democratic Party of Albanians (DPA), were political enemies. Then they drew closer together and formed a coalition for the October parliamentary elections. Statements made by both warned of possible Albanian demands for autonomy, even secession.

The change in the PDP—which was part of the government—and the lack of criticism from the DPA were rooted in the Kosovo crisis. The first indication of the parties' new relationship came with their mutual declaration of support for the region. This was followed by protest meetings in support of Kosovo Albanians. Almost every ethnic Albanian in Macedonia is somehow connected to Kosovo; many have friends and relatives there. A few months previously people called out the names of party leaders at political meetings; by the time of the election campaign they were invoking the UCK. It was a catch-all term, implying support for Albanian brethren in Kosovo, calling for NATO to use military force in Kosovo, and cheering on the PDP and DPA.

Macedonian-Albanian tensions began to escalate back on 9 July 1997 when police followed a high-court ruling to remove the Albanian flag from local government buildings in Gostivar and Tetovo, both a few hundred kilometers west of Skopje. The flag in Gostivar was defended by several thousand Albanians who ended up first in police custody and then in the hospital. The beating of Gostivar Albanians—resulting in four dead and some 250 wounded—was not aimed at protecting Macedonian statehood. It was a show of strength designed to prove that the governing Social Democratic Union of Macedonia (SDSM) knows how to deal with the Siptari (a pejorative term for Albanians). The televised trials of the Tetovo and Gostivar mayors—both of whom were Albanian—resulted in sentences of two and a half and seven years, respectively, as a result of convictions for refusing to implement the high court's flag-removal order. The crackdown was also a way of diverting people's attention from economic problems: the day the flag was removed, the government devalued the national currency.

The events in Gostivar and Tetovo left deep scars. Ethnic Albanians felt even less loyalty to the country, while Macedonians had effectively been told that beatings are the best way to communicate with separatists. But, rather than feeling empowered, dozens of Macedonian families started selling their homes only days after the incident, moving to towns considered ethnically clean.

A CITY DIVIDED

The Macedonian capital Skopje is becoming ethnically divided. More and more Macedonian families are selling their homes on the left bank of the river Vardar and moving to the right. House prices have declined substantially on the left side, and buyers are mainly ethnic Albanians. At least one real estate agent in Skopje advises customers not to look for a flat or house where they don't belong. "Some of our clients say they don't let their flats to single people, pet owners, and Siptari," the agent explains.

Those who choose to live on the wrong side of the river face difficulties. "We bought land and started building a house," complains an ethnic Albanian doctor. "Three days after we started the work, local thugs broke in and ruined everything. They left a message with the neighbors that they don't want Siptari in their neighborhood."

A Macedonian mother has a different story: "We bought a flat on the left side of the Vardar because it was cheaper. We have lived here for five months, but we will probably leave. My son is ten years old and every time he goes out to play with the other children, he comes home crying. Albanian kids don't want to play with him."

Abdurahman Sejrani, a secondary-school teacher, recalls how Albanian pupils taken for their health check in a children's hospital in Skopje were met as they came out by Macedonian pupils shouting "Death to Siptari." They threw stones, and a fight developed. "Children are communicating only when they have school sports. They play football, but against each other, not in the same team," Sejrani says.

Not only children have resorted to fighting. Weapons are no longer taboo for ordinary people, and in police raids large quantities of arms are found more and more frequently. Border patrols are constantly uncovering arms being smuggled from or into Macedonia.

The number of incidents on the Macedonian-Albanian border has gone up, as well as on the Macedonian border with Yugoslavia.

Since December 1997, eight bombs exploded close to government buildings in several towns. The UCK claimed responsibility for planting three of the bombs, although some Albanian newspapers say all the bombs were planted by the UCK. The DPA's Xhaferi maintained that the UCK was not behind the explosions.

"The UCK has never planned any illegal terrorist activities, and the bombs don't have their signature," he said in an interview with the Skopje daily *Dnevnik*. "It's the work of those who want to destabilize Macedonia psychologically, so people will think that war is coming this way. This situation can benefit only those who want us to be prisoners of fear. . . . And it is normal that the effects of this fear are used by the ruling elite in Macedonia."

Macedonian political parties usually condemned Albanian political leaders for statements such as Xhaferi's, with the opposition PDSA getting more grief than Aliti's PDP. State and private media close to the Macedonian government even started to use the vocabulary of the Yugoslav state media, with talk of terrorists, separatists, and an endangered Serb population. They even suggested that Slobodan Milosevic was doing a good job with the Albanians in Kosovo.

NOTE

Reprinted with kind permission from *Transitions* magazine, October 1998.

Albania

Population:	3,249,136
Capital:	Tirana (pop. 270,000–300,000)
Major cities:	Durres (pop.130,000), Elbasan (pop. 100,000), Shkoder (pop. 81,000–100,000)
Area:	28,750 sq. km.
Major ethnic groups:	Albanian 95%, Greek 3%, other 2%
Economy:	GDP growth: 4%
	Inflation rate: 10%
	Unemployment rate: 16%

A KIND OF STABILITY

by FABIAN SCHMIDT

Albania in 1998 was continuing to suffer from its harsh political polarization. The opposition Democratic Party (PD) of former President Sali Berisha continued a parliamentary boycott, which it had started the previous year, demanding the resignation of the Socialist-dominated coalition government. Ignoring calls by the Organization for Security and Cooperation in Europe (OSCE) and the Council of Europe, the PD declined to participate in the parliamentary commission that was working on the draft constitution which parliament later passed in November.

The beginning of the year was marked by violent clashes in the northern city of Shkoder that started on 19 January, when a group of armed men attacked and seized a local police station. While the events caught much media attention, the episode was short-lived. For one day the group gained control over the city, but already the next morning special police forces entered the city and reestablished order. Even by the end of the year it was still unclear whether the attackers had political motives, since they have not been identified.

While the government was still struggling with the threat of crime, as the incident showed, it also was facing challenges from within. Following widespread allegations of government inefficiency and corruption, Socialist Prime Minister Fatos Nano conducted a government reshuffle in mid April, reducing the number of ministers.

Local by-elections on 21 and 28 June confirmed continuing popular support for Nano's coalition, which won in five municipalities and six smaller communities (while the opposition won in two municipalities and three communities). Nevertheless, the Socialist-led coalition remained fragile, and continued to face a strong challenge from the opposition Democratic Party. Former president and opposition leader Sali Berisha repeatedly made clear his intention to bring down the government, calling it "communist" and accusing Prime Minister Fatos Nano of political persecution of the Democrats.

SETTLING ACCOUNTS

The opposition challenge to the government was aggravated by the arrest on 23 August of six former high-ranking officials. Police arrested former Defense Minister Safet Zhulali, former Interior Minister Halit Shamata, the head of the anti-corruption agency Blerim Cela, and three other former high-ranking officials of Berisha's government. All of them were PD members. They were charged with committing crimes against humanity, in conjunction with their alleged roles in suppressing widespread unrest in spring 1997. The protests had then begun in southern Albania and led to the fall of Berisha's government.

General Prosecutor Arben Rakipi charged the six with ordering the use of chemical weapons, aircraft, and helicopters against civilians. Rakipi claimed he had documents signed by the defendants that prove they ordered such attacks against rebellious southern cities. Berisha, however, accused Nano of having trumped up the charges and of being behind the arrests. Nano, for his part, claimed he learned about the arrests only after they had taken place. The trial was not concluded by the end of the year.

That conflict shed light on the most problematic aspect of Albania's transformation into a state based on the rule of law, namely the politicization of state institutions, particularly the judiciary. Few Albanians trust the country's judicial system, which is considered corrupt and politically biased. A survey conducted by the World Bank in early 1998 indicated that many judges, prosecutors, and lawyers were more than willing to accept bribes.

The Socialists and their coalition allies had repeatedly accused Berisha of not respecting the independence of the judiciary when he was in office. Hence they made reform of the judiciary one of their priorities after winning the elections in July 1997. That reform also involved firing several appointees of Berisha's administration, including those whose professional credentials were questionable, having completed only crash courses organized by Berisha's government with the aim of quickly training post-communist judges and lawyers. Nonetheless, many employees of the current judiciary were still former communist-era officials, and the Democrats accused the Socialists of returning former communists to key positions.

The government found itself in a difficult decision in the wake of the arrests. It had to be cautious not to get the charges dropped, as this would have meant a sign of weakness towards the opposition and would also have undermined the independence of the judiciary, which the government has pledged to respect. Therefore, it had to provide proof that the cabinet was indeed willing and able to respect the work of the courts. But government inaction left the field open to Democratic charges that the prisoners had been detained for political reasons.

At the same time the conflict also showed that the Democrats continued to reject their role as an opposition party loyal to the principles of a democratic parliamentary system. Even though the Council of Europe and the OSCE urged the Democrats to take their parliamentary duties seriously, they did not halt their boycotts. Instead, they tried in vain to blackmail the government into accepting political compromises over various issues, using their presence at, or absence from, the legislature as a political lever.

Already in early 1998 in a bid to get the Democrats back to the parliament, OSCE representatives in Tirana began to mediate between the government and the opposition and started regularly observing parliamentary proceedings. Later the OSCE offered to monitor the trial of the six former officials in order to convince the Democrats that the proceedings would be fair and free from political interference.

VIOLENT OUTBREAK TRIGGERS NANO'S RESIGNATION

By the end of the year, however, the Democrats had not returned to the legislature. Rather, their strategy became one of confrontation. Berisha called on his supporters in August "to use all means" to overthrow the government.

Following several protest demonstrations at the end of August the Democrats increased their agitation following the killing of popular Democratic Party legislator Azem Hajdari on 12 September. Hajdari was shot by unidentified gunmen outside the party headquarters in Tirana. When unrest broke out at Hajdari's funeral in Tirana on 14 September, many observers feared that Albania was about to face a repetition of the violence and anarchy that took hold of the country in 1997 after the collapse of pyramid investment schemes. But two days later, both major political parties appeared willing to avoid violence.

As in March 1997, civilians seized tanks and roamed the streets, firing into the air with Kalashnikov automatic rifles and plundering shops. The opposition charged Prime Minister Fatos Nano with having organized the Hajdari killing, an allegation Nano vehemently denied. Within a few hours, opposition protesters managed to seize the prime minister's offices, the state radio and television building, and the parliament building. At least three people were killed in clashes with police by the end of the day.

But in contrast to 1997 special police forces were able to restore order quickly. Most protesters dispersed when police moved in, and only a small group of opposition supporters took shelter at the Democratic Party headq 'arters. They brought with them two tanks they had captured, and the next morning found them surrounded by police. Elsewhere, life in the city had returned to normal and shops opened again.

The riots, moreover, did not see the disorder spilling over to areas outside the capital. The only exception was the town of Kavaja—a Democratic Party stronghold near Tirana—where some opposition supporters built barricades on the country's main north-south road and captured the local police station the day after Hajdari's murder. Also, villagers from Lazarat, a small town overlooking the main road between Gjirokastra and the main Greek border crossing of Kakavija, blocked the road and robbed passengers. Lazarat, a Democratic Party stronghold, had long been notorious as a place where local villagers set up roadblocks and robbed travelers. In northern Albania, however, observers noticed that Shkoder, which many feared would be a likely theater for clashes between armed opposition supporters and police, remained calm.

The speed with which the government brought the revolt under control indicated that the government had managed to sufficiently rebuild its police forces to cope with major challenges. More important, the quick end to the revolt showed that there was no willingness in the population as a whole to support the violent means of small groups wanting to bring down a democratically-elected government.

Officials within the Democratic Party distanced themselves from the riots. Party leader Sali Berisha used state television after it was captured by his supporters to broadcast a call to all Albanians to refrain from using violence, a move that probably made it easier for police to restore order.

Subsequently Berisha strongly rejected accusations from Socialist Party and government officials that he had planned to stage a coup d'etat. Instead, he said, he remained committed to force the government to resign by means of peaceful protests. Despite a police ban and high tensions following the previous day's events, the Democrats began once more to stage peaceful protest demonstrations.

While the government showed that it was able to withstand the opposition challenge, internally the riots triggered considerable changes. Nano resigned on 28 September following the departure of Interior Minister Perikli Teta from the Democratic Alliance Party. Both resignations came after the five coalition parties failed to agree on government changes during intensive talks the same day. In a letter to President Rexhep Meidani, Nano said that he stepped down because squabbling within his own ranks had made it impossible to form a new cabinet. He added that "I am not receiving any credible signal of solidarity either from parts of the Socialist Party or from the coalition partners." Teta for his part told local journalists that "the Albanian political class is unable to bring the country out of the current grave political crisis," and described the country's leadership as "corrupt and incompetent."

A NEW BROOM

President Meidani on 29 September asked the 30-year-old Socialist Party General Secretary Pandeli Majko to form a new government. Earlier that day Majko won nomination from his party in competition with Foreign Ministry State Secretary for European Integration Ilir Meta and Deputy Prime Minister Kastriot Islami. Majko lacked ministerial experience but had been the leader of the Socialists' parliamentary group before and worked closely with Nano. He played a role in the 1990 student movement which brought about the collapse of communism and had mediated in the past between the Socialists and the opposition. But as Nano had done before, Majko ruled out new elections. Still, he offered dialog to Democratic Party leaders and stressed that "we must return the country to normality and not be guided by the psychology of revenge."

Western diplomats expressed the hope that Majko's nomination could put an end to Albania's highly polarized political climate. A diplomat in Tirana said that Majko was untainted by past association with the communist regime. He stressed that Majko "is very open, very well disposed towards the outside world," adding that "he doesn't have the baggage that people in their 50s and 60s have." Another diplomat there said "I'm sure he has enemies but it's not nearly as long a list of enemies as the average Albanian politician has." A diplomat in Brussels stressed that the government change was not "a victory for Berisha [but] a tactical move by the Socialists to keep their government intact. The government has not fallen and that is important."

The 30-year-old Socialist became Europe's youngest head of government on 2 October upon being sworn in by President Meidani. Parliament approved Majko's cabinet on 12 October. Among the key changes were the appointment of Minister for European Integration Ilir Meta as deputy prime minister and fellow Socialist Petro Koci as interior minister. Social Democrat Ingrid Shuli replaced fellow party member Gaqo Apostoli as minister for public works and transport, while Kadri Rapi succeeded fellow Socialist Anastas Angjeli as labor and social affairs minister. Angjeli replaced outgoing fellow party member Arben Malaj as finance minister. Majko told journalists on 2 October that he would seek a dialogue with the opposition Democratic Party and that his priorities were "a return to stability, drafting a new constitution and [solving] the Kosovo problem."

Berisha, meanwhile, repeated his call for new elections, but urged his supporters to show a "constructive spirit and sense of compromise in [a] dialogue which . . . should decide on an [interim] government with a broad base." He added that "the Democratic Party will not participate in this government [but] support its anti-crisis package [including] the restoration of public order [and] disarmament of the population." By the end of the year, however, the Democrats had not returned to take up their seats in parliament.

Nonetheless the coalition remained resolved to go ahead with drafting the country's new constitution and approving it by popular referendum on 22 November. The drafting of a new constitution had been a question of prestige to Albanian governments for several years. Berisha, while president in 1994, failed to get the two-thirds majority from within his coalition which he needed to pass his own draft constitution. When he then tried to pass the document by popular referendum the electorate defeated him in what many observers saw as a turning point in his political career.

But unlike Berisha, in November 1998 Majko received the backing of the electorate in the constitutional referendum, largely due to the coalition's efforts to bring the opposition on board. The parliamentary commission working on the draft not only included members of the governing coalition, but it was headed by the center-right opposition Republican Party legislator Sabri Godo. Godo repeatedly complained that the Democrats did not participate in the drafting process and stressed that their rejection was counterproductive.

Final results from the Central Election Commission showed that 93.5 percent of voters supported the law. Turnout, however, was a mere 50.57 percent. Representatives from the opposition Democratic Party, which boycotted the referendum and the parliamentary constitution drafting commission, claimed that the results were manipulated and declined to recognize the new constitution. They claimed that turnout was only 40 percent. International observers said the referendum was carried out correctly.

KOSOVO LOOMS

Berisha's strategy throughout 1998 seemed calculated to make the conflict in neighboring Kosovo work in his favor. With the eruption in February of open civil war in Kosovo between Serbian police and army and the ethnic Albanian separatist Kosovo Liberation Army (UCK), over 13,000 refugees fled into Albania. The UCK initially used bases in northern Albania to support its military operations in Kosovo, but by June Serbian forces had managed to bring the border area with Albania under control and to dry out the UCK's supply channels. Over 1,000 people were believed killed by the end of the year and 230,000 made homeless during the fighting inside Kosovo. The Albanian foreign ministry repeatedly charged Yugoslavia with border violations including shelling and sniping and with conducting massacres of Kosovo's civilian population. It also called for NATO military intervention there to stop the fighting.

Berisha had harshly attacked Nano over his moderate Kosovo policy in the past, especially following a meeting of the prime minister with Yugoslav President Slobodan Milosevic in December 1997. With the civil war starting in Kosovo, Berisha underlined the moderate nature of Nano's Kosovo policy, which did not openly advocate independence for the region. Berisha was fully aware that because of that policy, most Kosovars and many northern Albanians did not trust Nano's government.

The opposition tried to capitalize on the Kosovo conflict, demanding Kosovo's recognition as an independent state and Albanian assistance to the Kosovo Liberation Army. The new Majko government was forced to balance its position on the "national" agenda and used its fresh beginning to reach out to the Democrats by shifting their stance on Kosovo away from the approach favored by Nano. Majko, therefore, tried to promote national unity across the various parties in both Albania and Kosovo. He invited Kosovar leaders to Tirana, hoping to establish an all-Albanian round table that could agree on common strategies and principles the following year.

Majko's plan appeared ambitious considering the deep divisions among the Kosovars. The main gap Majko wanted to bridge was that between the Kosovo Liberation Army (UCK) on the one hand and shadow state President Ibrahim Rugova on the other. At the same time he intended to heal domestic political wounds between his party and the Democrats.

Besides the Kosovo conflict Albania suffered from the impact of the bombings of U.S. embassies in Kenya and Tanzania in August, in which over 200 people were killed. Following the bombings the U.S. embassy in Tirana began evacuating its non-essential personnel and a number of other U.S. citizens working in the country on 16 August. An Albanian Interior Ministry official said later that the U.S. Central Intelligence Agency (CIA) had gathered "serious evidence" that Islamic terrorists had been planning to blow up the American embassy there.

Earlier in the summer Albanian police had arrested four suspected Islamic terrorists in cooperation between the CIA and Albania's National Information Service. Some of them later admitted in court that they were agents of Osama Bin Laden, the fugitive Saudi national who was the key suspect in the embassy bombings. Media reports suggested that the African bombings may have been revenge-attacks after the Albanian arrests. Later that year police arrested another three suspects.

Meanwhile, Albania's relations with the Islamic world in 1998 were of an ambiguous character. While the previous government of President Sali Berisha had led the country into membership in the Organization of Islamic Conference (OIC) in 1993, Nano later denied that this membership was ever formally legalized. On 16 August 1998 he told *Zeri i Popullit* that "The OIC . . . never really included Albania, because the (membership) procedure started by Berisha was illegitimate." He added that "Albania has no other future but to be integrated in Europe." Nano stressed that Albania would continue to cooperate with other Islamic countries on a bilateral or multilateral level. Majko, however, changed that policy and officially acknowledged Albania's OIC membership in December following a call by Meidani to clarify Albania's position in the OIC.

ECONOMY STABILIZES

The economy was showing modest signs of recovery, following the collapse of pyramid investment schemes in 1997. GDP growth by the end of the year was estimated at 8 percent. Inflation dropped from 40 percent at the end of 1997 to 10 percent by the end of 1998. The official unemployment rate was 16 percent, though the real figure was estimated to be much higher. Albania's budget deficit amounted to a hefty 6.4 percent of GDP. The previous years' drastic devaluation of the Lek stopped, and it remained stable at between 150 and 154 to the dollar.

Finance Minister Anastas Angjeli presented the budget for 1999 to parliament on 29 December claiming that "We have been able to stop the economic decline of 1997 and restore the macro-economic stability in the country." The budget deficit expected by the government for 1999 was around 5.2 percent of GDP or $385 million, with revenues of $793 million and expenditures of $1.2 billion. Albania's foreign debts were $472 million. GDP growth was expected at 8 percent, with inflation at 7 percent. The government anticipated an increase of revenues by 19 percent as compared to 1998 and a rise of expenditures by 15 percent. The budget provided for a 10 percent increase of pensions and administration wages, as well as a 18 percent increase of student scholarships. Students had launched a hunger strike in December demanding better living conditions in dormitories and higher stipends. The government also planned to increase investments in public works by 32 percent. Angjeli pledged to increase tax revenues by 24 percent through tougher tax collecting. He also pledged to give the local government more financial autonomy.

Document: *"PARLIAMENT OF THIEVES"*

Political reconciliation in Albania took another turn for the worse on 7 July when the opposition Democratic Party made the decision to resume a boycott of parliament that it had ended four months earlier. Party chairman Sali Berisha said the Socialist-led government had initiated an aggressive campaign against the Democrats, including the creation of a parliamentary commission to investigate the civil unrest of 1997, which led to the deaths of about 2,000 people. The panel recommended an examination of Berisha's role in the unrest, saying that as then-president he was "legally responsible." In the speech excerpted below, which was made to supporters in Tirana, Berisha explained his reasons for the boycott. The text appeared 10 July in the Democratic Party's Rilindja Demokratike.

Brothers and sisters: The Democratic Party made a historic decision to boycott the parliament of thieves, the most corrupt parliament in Europe, on behalf of all those Albanians who hate illicit wealth and in the name of those Albanians who are ashamed of having in power the most corrupt government in the world. We boycotted parliament on behalf of all of you who have filled this square and who went away brokenhearted when we went to parliament because you knew all along that it was not the place for democrats to be. You knew that it was a parliament of the Albanian political mafia. You knew that it was a parliament of anti-national stands. . . .

We boycotted parliament to honor all the Albanians to whom faith in God and in the free vote is essential. We assure them that we are going to sacrifice everything in order to bring free and fair elections to Albania. We boycotted parliament in the name of 300,000 unemployed Albanians, who wake up every day with the fear of being unable to earn their daily bread. . . .

We boycotted parliament on behalf of those who are bombarded every day in Drenica, Decani, Rrahovec, and Smolice [in Kosovo] with bombs and grenades by the Serbs and whom [Yugoslav President Slobodan] Milosevic's ally in Tirana is dividing. . . . I appeal to the freedom fighters not to accept [Prime Minister] Fatos Nano's . . . Byzantine acts, because he can defend anything but the national cause. I appeal to the international community to give up the most corrupt man in Europe and the government that Albanians have abandoned. We demand free and fair elections because we deserve them.

NOTE
Reprinted with kind permission from *Transitions* magazine, August 1998.

Bulgaria

Population:	8,487,317 (1992 census)
Capital:	Sofia (pop. 1,190,126)
Major cities:	Plovdiv (pop. 377,637), Varna (pop. 297,090), Burgas (pop. 188,367)
Area:	110,994 sq. km.
Major ethnic groups:	Bulgarian 85.7%, Turkish 9.4%, Romani 3.7%
Economy:	GDP growth: 4.5%
....	Inflation rate: 10%
....	Unemployment rate: 11%

A YEAR OF CONSOLIDATION

by STEFAN KRAUSE

Compared to previous, turbulent years, 1998 was uneventful in Bulgaria. But it brought further stabilization and consolidation to a country that just a year to two earlier seemed on the brink of total collapse. The center-right government, surviving its first no-confidence vote, managed to work without major shakeups or scandals, although the pace of reform undoubtedly slowed down compared to 1997. The economy continued to recover and was further transformed, but privatization was slow.

As Bulgaria returned to a more normal state of things in this first election-free year since 1993, Bulgaria's political landscape changed as parties started positioning themselves for the 1999 local elections. In foreign relations, which were overshadowed by the Kosovo crisis, Bulgaria managed to stabilize its position. It was admitted to the Central European Free-Trade Area (CEFTA) and was chosen as the first host country of the new Balkan multinational force's headquarters. The dispute with Russia over energy issues was finally resolved. And a new media law was finally passed after years of wrangling and debates.

UNEVENTFUL "BIG POLITICS"

The political year started with a look back at the protests of January 1997 which had led to the downfall of the previous Socialist government. On 8 January Prime Minister Ivan Kostov released transcripts of a meeting of top Socialist politicians, in which former Prime Minister Zhan Videnov advocated the use of force against the demonstrators who blockaded and later stormed the parliament building. Two days later, government and opposition supporters rallied in Sofia to commemorate the first anniversary of the anti-Socialist protests. Although the demonstrations were peaceful, they highlighted the continued division in Bulgarian society and politics, with government supporters interpreting the events of winter 1997 as a victory of democracy while Socialist supporters saw them as some kind of coup d'etat.

On 15 January, the Bulgarian Socialist Party (BSP) announced it would file a no-confidence motion in the Kostov government over its health policies. The motion, which was formally brought forward on 22 January, was defeated on 29 January, with only 56 deputies voting for and 135 against. However, some non-Socialist deputies abstained or stayed away from the ballot.

In any event, the government managed to continue its work largely undisturbed by opposition challenges or internal strife. On the ministerial level, the government line-up remained unchanged, although some deputy ministers were sacked or resigned during the course of the year. But although Prime Minister

Kostov repeatedly stated that the government was on track as far as achieving its key reform objectives was concerned, he also admitted on 15 December that his party, the Union of Democratic Forces (SDS), had failed to establish a "proper dialogue with society." Already on 2 September, President Petar Stoyanov had urged the parliament to press on with reforms and warned legislators against complacency.

During the course of 1998, a number of significant pieces of legislation were passed by the parliament. They include the law on alternative military service and a lustration law which barred former high-ranking Communist officials and secret police agents from holding public office for five years. The lustration law was signed into force by President Petar Stoyanov, but in January 1999, the Constitutional Court declared that some of its key provisions violated the constitution.

On 5 October the government approved legislation to ratify the 1995 Framework Convention for the Protection of National Minorities. However, the convention was not ratified by the parliament in 1998, despite a previous intra-party agreement brokered by Stoyanov. Some legislators demanded that it should be accompanied by a declaration which would have watered down its provisions by effectively denying the existence of national minorities in Bulgaria. Inter-ethnic relations in general improved during 1998. For the first time in some 50 years, Bulgarian authorities in early September allowed circumcision ceremonies for Muslim boys, and both the prime minister and the president stressed the need to integrate the country's ethnic minorities.

But there were also problems in inter-ethnic relations. Racist attacks on Roma (Gypsies) continued in 1998. Roma also staged public protests against government neglect of their problems, and one Romany man set himself on fire on 2 June to protest the authorities' inertia. In early September 1998, ethnic Turks protested a decision by a district prosecutor to remove plaques commemorating ethnic Turks who in 1998 had been executed for alleged terrorist attacks. In late December, ethnic Turks complained about the desecration of a monument commemorating the forced assimilation of Bulgaria's ethnic Turks in the 1980s, although local authorities denied that the monument had been vandalized.

On 4 June the Constitutional Court ruled that the state must return the former royal family's property to ex-King Simeon II. A request by Prosecutor-General Ivan Tatarchev in December to have the Constitutional Court invalidate the 1946 referendum which abolished the monarchy failed, however, since the court decided that it is only competent to rule on issues pertaining to the current constitution.

On 6 August Bulgaria's long-time Communist dictator Todor Zhivkov died in a Sofia hospital, aged 86. Zhivkov had been at the helm of the Bulgarian Communist Party from 1954 to 1989. After his downfall, he was arrested and tried for abuse of power. His sentence was overturned in 1997, but he remained under house arrest for most of the rest of his life. His burial was attended by some 10,000 mostly elderly Bulgarians. Zhivkov's death sparked a controversy over his legacy. While President Petar Stoyanov called his rule "one of the darkest periods of recent Bulgarian history," the BSP said his name would be associated with "hard but creative work and a secure and easier life."

Another legacy of the socialist era was laid to rest in 1998. The Bulgarian authorities closed the case of Georgi Markov, a former dissident writer and journalist who was murdered with a poisoned umbrella in London in 1978, in an operation widely attributed to the Bulgarian and/or Soviet secret services. Investigations over preceding years had failed to produce any concrete evidence as to the perpetrators, and it is likely that the Markov murder will remain unsolved.

On 10 December the parliament amended the Penal Code, abolishing the death penalty and bringing Bulgarian legislation in line with that of the Council of Europe. Capital punishment was replaced with life in prison and it was recommended that those inmates waiting on death row since Bulgaria imposed a moratorium on capital punishment in 1990 should be granted clemency by the president.

PARTIES REALIGN IN ELECTION-FREE YEAR

Since the overthrow of the Communist regime, 1998 was only the second year (after 1993) during which no elections were held in Bulgaria. This gave the political parties time to concentrate on day-to-day politics, but it also offered them an opportunity to redefine their place in the party spectrum and conclude new alliances in preparation for the local elections scheduled for 1999.

As a result, the party system saw some significant changes in the center and on the center-left. The only party that remained largely unaffected by intra-party politics and realignments was the Union of Democratic Forces (SDS), the main force in the ruling coalition. The only significant development within the SDS was the 18 October announcement that it had transformed itself from a coalition of parties and groups into a single party, a development, however, that had started at least a year earlier and therefore came as no surprise.

In the center, four liberal parties formed a formal alliance on 10 July. This new grouping, named the Liberal Democratic Alliance, included the mainly ethnic Turkish Movement for Rights and Freedoms (DPS), the New Choice Liberal Alliance, the Liberal Democratic Alternative, and the Free Radical Democratic Party. Former Bulgarian President Zhelyu Zhelev was named honorary chairman of the new alliance. Given the relative strength of the DPS, which can rely on a large portion of the ethnic Turkish vote, the alliance is bound to do fairly well, although it remains to be seen how much of the non-minority, liberal vote it can take away from the SDS. Getting a fair share of that vote would be necessary for the Liberal Democratic Alliance to become a relevant political factor in the medium and long term.

Further to the left, a number of parties with a social democratic orientation also decided to join forces. They comprise the Bulgarian Social Democratic Party (BSDP) and the United Labor Bloc, which in December 1998 set up the Social Democratic Union. On 21 December, the Social Democratic Union in turn signed a cooperation agreement for the local elections with the Euroleft, which had been formed shortly before the 1997 parliamentary elections.

Meanwhile, the woes of the Bulgarian Socialist Party (BSP), the second-biggest political force, continued. During 1998, the BSP held talks with other leftist parties on coalitions and cooperation, but little came of them. The internal division within the BSP between reformers and traditionalists was not resolved, as witnessed by the fact that BSP Chairman Georgi Parvanov was reelected with only about 55 percent of the vote at the BSP party congress in early May. The BSP also continued to be plagued by declining membership numbers.

There were also some party-political developments in the non-Bulgarian political community. Already in 1997 some leading members had left the DPS to protest the decision of its chairman, Ahmed Dogan, not to form an alliance with the SDS. On 12 December 1998 the ethnic Turkish leaders within the United Democratic Forces (ODS, the alliance led by the SDS and forming the current government) announced that they would form the National Movement for Rights and Freedoms (NDPS). Most likely, this new group will remain allied to the SDS, since trying to go it alone would probably not secure them enough votes to survive politically.

ENERGY ISSUES HIGH ON THE AGENDA

Especially in the first half of 1998, a resolution of the dispute over Russian gas deliveries was high on the agenda. In 1997, Russia's energy giant Gazprom had signed an agreement with a newly-established company named Topenergy on the delivery of natural gas to Bulgaria. Topenergy was controlled by Gazprom itself, state-owned Bulgargaz, and Bulgaria's shady Multigroup business conglomerate. (See accompanying article, "Institutional Tug of War.") The Bulgarian government wanted to find an arrangement with Gazprom that would sideline Topenergy and Multigroup, and refused to let Topenergy act as an intermediary between itself and Gazprom. It also threatened to prevent transit of Russian gas through Bulgarian pipelines if no solution was found.

This dispute resulted in Russian gas deliveries for a number of Bulgarian towns being cut in early 1998. After both sides traded accusations back and forth for a while, talks on resolving the thorny issue were arranged. Those negotiations produced a preliminary agreement in March and a final one in April, according to which Gazprom would take over 100 percent of Topenergy's shares. Russian transit rights through Bulgaria were extended too. On the other hand, the agreement secured Bulgaria's supply with Russian gas, although the price was not disclosed. It was also agreed that Bulgaria could pay for part of Russia's gas deliveries in kind and in pipeline construction work. The new agreement is valid until 2010.

At the time of the Russian-Bulgarian talks, though, the government made it clear that it wants to be less dependent on Russian gas deliveries. An agreement with Royal Dutch Shell was announced in April, under which Bulgaria would be linked to a yet-to-be-built pipeline between Turkmenistan and Germany.

Bulgaria's controversial nuclear power plant at Kozloduy remained in operation in 1998, although malfunctions continued to be frequent. Still, the government rejected requests by the European Union and by neighboring states to close down the aging plant at the earliest possible date. On 14 September Ivan Shilyashki, the head of Bulgaria's State Energy Committee, said the four reactors at Kozloduy will be shut down between 2004 and 2012. In late November, a team of French, Swiss, and Russian experts said security of Kozloduy's two oldest reactors was "good." Considering Bulgaria's current dependence on energy from Kozloduy and its financial problems, this verdict will probably serve to keep the current reactors going.

ECONOMIC RECOVERY CONTINUES

Following the introduction of a currency board in 1997, tying the Bulgarian lev to the German mark, many economic indicators improved considerably in 1998. Inflation dropped below 10 percent (compared to some 600 percent in 1997), and the budget was in surplus. GDP grew by about 4.5 percent, although from a low base. Unemployment dropped from 13.7 to 11.0 percent. On the other hand, industrial production fell compared to 1997 as some of Bulgaria's key export markets experienced financial and economic trouble. As a result, the country also reported a trade deficit.

On 17 July, it was announced that Bulgaria would join the Central European Free Trade Agreement (CEFTA) on 1 January 1999. This move is expected to bring Bulgaria closer to the Central European countries that are on the fast track to entry into the European Union. On 30 July, the Bulgarian government and the IMF reached agreement on a three-year loan worth $840 million. The deal was backed by the BSP as well. The IMF formally approved the deal on 24 September.

Privatization was disappointing in 1998. Although the government aimed at launching a second wave of privatization, including most of the country's arms factories, results lagged far behind the government's plans which foresaw the privatization of 80 percent of the country's enterprises by the end of the year. However, the parliament on 4 December approved a government plan providing for the privatization of more than 1,000 state companies worth a total of $600 million for 1999. Already on 12 November, the parliament voted to reduce VAT from 22 to 20 percent in a move to encourage investment.

In December 1998, Bulgaria decided to peg its currency, the lev, to the Euro as of 1 January 1999. Since the introduction of the currency board, the lev had been pegged to the German mark at a rate of 1,000 leva to the mark. Already on 30 November, the government had decided to slash three zeroes from the lev as of 1 July 1999.

MEDIA—ALL IS NOT WELL

In the media sphere, attention in 1998 focused on the adoption of the electronic media law, which was finally passed on 23 September. Among other things, the new law provided for a revamped National Council for Radio and Television, which will license broadcasters and oversee their operations. Of the nine council members, four are appointed by the president, while five are elected by the parliament. Other provisions of the media law included a phasing out of state subsidies to public-service media and the introduction of a subscription fee and a ban on prime-time advertising on public electronic media.

President Petar Stoyanov on 28 September vetoed certain provisions of the new media law, the first time he used his veto since the advent of the Kostov government. Most importantly, he objected to a provision that broadcasts must be in the Bulgarian language, and to the prime-time advertising ban. On 20 November, the parliament overruled Stoyanov's veto on prime-time advertisement but heeded his other objections, thus opening the way for minority-language broadcasts. On 21 December, the parliamentary majority of the SDS elected five members to the National Council for Radio and Television. The vote was boycotted by the opposition which claimed that the SDS was using its majority in order to secure its domination of the council. Although the SDS claimed that only two of those five council members were also SDS members, it remains a flaw in the council's composition that it has no members who were nominated by the opposition.

Already before the adoption of the new media law, the previous National Council for Radio and Television on 17 January appointed new heads of the state-run media. Ivan Popyordanov became head of Bulgarian National Television, and Aleksandar Velev was appointed to the top position at Bulgarian National Radio. Both were professionals rather than party people, a deviation from previous practice. Popyordanov resigned from his position in November, saying the station needed new people to run it, but the real reason seems to have been that the council objected to his proposed programming scheme for Bulgarian National Television.

However, there were also problems in the media sphere, mainly stemming from the state prosecutor's habit of bringing journalists to court for alleged slander and libel of public officials. Despite appeals from Bulgarian journalists and international organizations, the Constitutional Court on 15 July ruled that relevant articles in the Criminal Code did not violate the Bulgarian constitution. Throughout 1998, there were also physical attacks on a number of critical journalists who were engaged in investigative journalism.

FOREIGN POLICY IN THE SHADOW OF KOSOVO

Foreign policy in 1998 was partly determined by the crisis in Kosovo and its regional repercussions. Bulgaria tried to contribute to a solution of the Kosovo conflict, putting forward a number of proposals. The government made it clear that it was opposed to independence for Kosovo and against a renewed embargo on Yugoslavia, which it fears would harm Bulgaria's economy. However, Bulgaria backed the international community's efforts, and on 23 October the parliament voted to allow NATO to use Bulgarian airspace for air strikes on Yugoslav military installations.

On 24 November the members of the newly-established multinational Balkan peacekeeping force decided that the first headquarters of that force will be located in the Bulgarian city of Plovdiv. The headquarters are to rotate among the participating states every four years.

Relations with Greece and Romania remained largely unchanged throughout 1998. Ties with Turkey, however, were improving as Ankara hailed Sofia's policy towards its ethnic Turkish minority. Both sides also announced that in the future there will be closer military cooperation, with Turkey pledging to help to modernize Bulgaria's army. Relations with Macedonia were strained throughout the Macedonian election campaign, with Macedonian officials accusing Sofia of supporting the then opposition and of meddling in Macedonia's internal affairs. Several Bulgarian journalists were denied entry into Macedonia over the election period. With the advent of a new government in Skopje, things improved, though. The issue of the existence of a distinct Macedonian language and nation, which Sofia still refused to recognize, remained unresolved throughout 1998, but first statements indicate that bilateral relations might improve with a more pro-Bulgarian government in office in Skopje.

INSTITUTIONAL TUG OF WAR

by BRIAN KENETY

On orders from Interior Minister Bogomil Bonev, police commandos and investigators from Bulgaria's organized crime fighting service on 26 August raided the Sofia headquarters of Multigroup, the country's largest private conglomerate.

Their mission was to search for documentation relating to four years of alleged illegal imports of $29 million in sugar by Bartex, a Multigroup subsidiary that has dominated the country's sugar sector. However, in less than an hour, with the search barely begun, an order came down from Prosecutor-General Ivan Tatarchev to call it off.

The aborted raid and the public accusations that followed underscored the chronic tendency of the country's crime-fighting institutions and their heads to work at cross purposes. "It seems that Multigroup is outside the law and is protected by a huge prosecutor's umbrella," said Bonev. "We were prevented from uncovering a crime, but we are not going to give up so easily." The minister accused Tatarchev of improper conduct and "illegal actions."

The prosecutor in turn threatened to launch a court action to depose Bonev for misusing his position. "If I find out that there was the slightest legal negligence [in carrying out the raid], Bonev will be held responsible according to the Criminal Code," he said. Tatarchev said he had not approved in the search warrant the presence of riot-gear commandos, who Bonev maintained had been necessary because "Multigroup is a notorious company, and we had reason to believe they would respond in a violent manner."

The center-right government of Prime Minister Ivan Kostov, which took office in May 1997, repeatedly stated its determination to limit the financial and political clout of what Kostov calls "parallel political powers" such as Multigroup, as his government seeks to recoup state losses from years of economic chaos and post-communist corruption. After the raid, Kostov himself said, "There is no such thing as a war with Multigroup. There is a war with those who do not abide by the law. If Multigroup observes the law, it will be treated as a normal company. If Multigroup has trampled on the law, the state will trample on Multigroup."

Kostov was pushing for amendments to the Judiciary Systems Act, which would overhaul the judiciary and more clearly define the roles of the investigative and prosecutorial branches. The draft bill put before parliament in September by Kostov's Union of Democratic Forces (SDS) also seeks to merge the prosecutor-general's office with the Supreme Judicial Council (which oversees the judicial branch). Critics of the bill said this would marginalize the prosecutor's office, which would answer to the justice minister, the council's ex officio chairman.

Georgi Karasimeonov of the Sofia-based Institute for Political and Legal Studies says the Bonev–Tatarchev conflict stems from the lack of clarity in institutional authority. "Clearly, the inter-institutional fighting is detrimental to Bulgaria and the fight against crime. There are similar problems with the whole judicial system, and here corruption very much plays a role at each step, from the choice of whom to arrest, to whether to pursue an investigation, to whether to prosecute, and the final decision of the judges."

Multigroup's roots go back to 1988, when champion wrestler Iliya Pavlov helped set up Multiart, Multigroup's precursor, under the tutelage of his father-in-law, then chief of the secret intelligence service. Ostensibly an exporter of Bulgarian artworks, Multiart allegedly ran a prostitution network before moving on to sanctions-busting after the onset of war in neighboring Yugoslavia.

Pavlov says his initial success—and capital—came from winning a contract to sell Soviet-era submarines for scrap metal. Ten years on, Multigroup remains a major force in the Bulgarian economy, with a declared 1997 turnover of $1.5 billion. Its 150 companies employ about 25,000 people. Exploiting a series of weak and corrupt governments in the first half of the decade, Multigroup secured a number of privatization deals and occupied key sectors of the economy. Today, there is scarcely an area in which it is not involved, from knitwear to banking, according to the respected weekly *Kapital*.

Multigroup was recently investigated for racketeering and tax evasion. Minister Bonev has publicly accused the holding of orchestrating murders and kidnappings and claimed that Prosecutor General Tatarchev was protecting Multigroup by thwarting probes. Pavlov denies the accusations, which he calls a smear campaign. He promised to cooperate fully with the continuing sugar probe and dismissed the head of Bartex, Spartak Zharov, who was fined $2.5 million for bypassing customs in importing 12,500 tons of sugar.

NOTE

Reprinted with kind permission from *Transitions* magazine, October 1998.

Romania

Population:	22,680,951 (November 1996)
Capital:	Bucharest (pop. 2,066,723)
Major cities:	Constanta (pop. 348,985), Iasi (pop. 337,643), Timisoara (pop. 325,359)
Area:	237,500 sq. km.
Major ethnic groups:	Romanian 89.4%, Hungarian 7.1%, Romani 1.8% (according to 1991 census—although Roma are generally estimated at 7% to 8% of the population)
Economy:	GDP growth: –4.8%
....	Inflation rate: 60%
....	Unemployment rate: 11%

THE PERILS OF COALITION POLITICS

by MATYAS SZABO

The high hopes with which Victor Ciorbea's government began its term in the fall of 1996 turned into a bitter disappointment during 1998. The mistakes and failures in implementing Romania's reform programs not only harmed the country's international image and economic credibility but also resulted in a deep coalition crisis that forced Ciorbea to resign. President Emil Constantinescu still believed at the time that "although the government lost a battle, the population would not lose the war," and hoped that the country would be able to recover from the "economic, social, political, moral, and communication-related" crises. However, the new prime minister, Radu Vasile, had to acknowledge soon after his nomination that his cabinet "argues more than any other government in Eastern Europe." The prevailing petty politicking and cabinet infighting affected all aspects of life in Romania, and by the end of the year most Romanians believed that life before 1989 was better than in 1998.

When Ciorbea was replaced by Vasile in April, Iliescu said that the "causes of the political and economic crisis will persist as long as the current coalition is in power, regardless of who is the prime minister." For his part, Vasile blamed the current opposition for stalling the privatization between 1990 and 1996. He said former communist countries that carried out economic reforms earlier were better off today than Romania. Most Romanians would probably agree with both of them, as a November public opinion poll revealed that 65 percent of the population believed their country was heading in the wrong direction.

POLITICAL CRISIS DEEPENS

The December 1997 cabinet reshuffle did not bring an end to the conflict between the governing National Christian Democratic Peasant Party (PNTCD) and its coalition partner, the Democratic Party (PD). On 7 January Prime Minister Victor Ciorbea rejected a call by the Standing Bureau of the PD to reinstate former Transportation Minister Traian Basescu, a PD minister who had been forced to resign after he refused to retract his criticism of the government's inability to reach decisions. Ciorbea said it would be "morally and politically wrong" to reinstate Basescu, and asked the Democrats to nominate another candidate for the portfolio.

The main differences between the two parties, however, went far beyond the "Basescu affair." PD politicians said the government had been distracted from its main task of reform by engaging in disputes over issues of minor importance, and warned that Romania might miss its chance to join NATO in a "second wave" if the reform program was not implemented. PD chairman Petre Roman reproached his allies for treating the Democrats as an "annex" of the other coalition parties, and warned on 8 January that the coalition "will either be one of equal partners or will not be at all." For his part, PNTCD chairman Ion Diaconescu stressed that the cabinet was "the best Romania can get," and said that the coalition must continue.

On 14 January the PD withdrew its support from Ciorbea, saying a new government should be formed by another prime minister. "The deadline for ending those negotiations is 31 of March, and the PD will quit the coalition if negotiations are not successfully concluded by then," read the statement from the PD's National Council. The reaction of the PNTCD was not surprising: Diaconescu said the Democrats' ultimatum amounted to "blackmail, demagogy, and hypocrisy."

Constantinescu played down the intensity of the conflict, saying on 17 January that "there is no genuine political crisis in Romania, but only a government crisis triggered by those with narrow party interests." As a temporary solution, he said the parliament would convene in an emergency session on 21 January in which the government's package of reform bills would be tied to a vote of no confidence. In a 21 January joint session the bicameral parliament voted by 225 to 170 to approve the request to tie the privatization law to a vote of confidence. Although the PD voted in favor of the law, parliamentary group leader Alexandru Sassu emphasized that "this should by no means be interpreted as a vote of confidence in the Ciorbea cabinet." For the first time since the coalition crisis emerged, PD ministers withdrew from the government bench during the debate. On 28 January the PD announced that it was withdrawing its ministers from the government, and although it still remained part of the ruling coalition it urged the replacement of Ciorbea as prime minister. Meanwhile, Ciorbea had outlined his government's 1998 economic program, and appointed the five ministers to replace PD cabinet members. Since Foreign Minister Andrei Plesu, an independent nominated by the Democrats, remained in the government, the PD's move created a unique situation in which a party both participated in the ruling coalition and adopted an opposition-like stance.

In the following couple of weeks Ciorbea had to fight a war that was waged against him on all fronts. PD representatives in the Senate's Commission on Local Administration on 17 February voted together with the opposition in rejecting a 1997 government regulation that allowed mayors and local councilors to be members of the government. Although the decision still had to be approved by the parliament, Roman warned Ciorbea that he had to resign as mayor of Bucharest, otherwise his premiership would "automatically cease" under the constitution. Constantinescu himself hinted on 2 March that Ciorbea might be sacrificed: after a meeting with the PNTCD leadership, he said that in order to resolve the ongoing political crisis, the PNTCD "must ignore party interests." The last blow for Ciorbea came when a group within his own party expressed "apprehension about the party's deteriorating image and isolation." The group, meeting on 25 March in Brasov, called for Ciorbea to be replaced by the party's

Secretary-General Radu Vasile. The same day, National Liberal Party Deputy Chairman and Justice Minister Valeriu Stoica said the crisis "must be resolved" even if the price was the sacrifice of the prime minister.

In a bitter speech broadcast live on national radio and television on 30 March, Ciorbea announced his resignation both as prime minister and as mayor of Bucharest. He said the "so-called victory" of his former political partners "will prove temporary and history will judge them harshly." The new cabinet will inherit the basis for a reform program that can be continued, Ciorbea noted, adding that he tried to be a "different type of premier, maybe ahead of history."

NEW PRIME MINISTER, BUT LITTLE CHANGE

Radu Vasile, an economic historian whom Constantinescu named prime minister-designate on 1 April, described himself as "a politician who does not yield to pressure." On 15 April, after the bicameral parliament endorsed his cabinet, Vasile said the coalition was committed to democratic and economic reforms and that no one should be surprised about "elements of continuity" between the new cabinet and its predecessor. Unfortunately, one of those elements of continuity was the constant cabinet infighting, which made Vasile declare towards the end of the year that "there is no other government in the region that would spend so much time criticizing steps taken by the government."

Despite an agreement signed on 6 April by members of the new coalition which significantly increased the power of the prime minister over his cabinet, Vasile failed to prevent the re-emergence of the coalition crisis. Throughout the second half of the year, virtually all parties within the ruling coalition tried to redefine the role they played in Romania's politics, and paid little attention to solving the country's burning problems.

First, National Liberal Party (PNL) deputy chairman Calin-Popescu Tariceanu said "the PNL must forge its identity and follow the example of the Democratic Party, whose popularity grew after the coalition crisis." Later he denied that he intended to signal the party's departure from the ruling Democratic Convention, saying on 1 June that he had only "a long-term process" in mind. It was also a reference to the future when Diaconescu said on 7 June that the PNTCD "must form the next government alone."

Second, Roman announced on 1 November that the PD had given an ultimatum to its coalition members, threatening to reconsider its participation in the coalition if reform steps were not implemented by spring 1999. The PNL, however, harshly criticized Roman and his party, saying that the Democrats "wish to reform provided that nothing is changed."

Third, the Romanian Alternative Party announced on 27 October that it was leaving the ruling coalition. Party Chairman Varujan Vosganian said the decision was prompted by the country's worsening economic situation, the delay in reforms, and the lack of respect for election campaign promises.

In order to speed up the reform process and to accommodate the demands of the coalition partners, Vasile on 23 September first dismissed Finance Minister Daniel Daianu, and then on 20 October accepted the resignation of Privatization Minister Sorin Dumitriu. Both ministers had been repeatedly attacked for failing to meet the planned pace of privatization and for being responsible for the heavy bureaucracy that hindered the reform process. The long awaited government restructuring, although announced by Vasile as early as mid-August, took place only in December. A "reshuffling psychosis," as PNL deputy chairman Valeriu Stoica put it, accompanied the "obsessive discussions" on the government's restructuring until 10 November, when leaders of the ruling coalition agreed on a plan to cut the number of ministries from 23 to 17. The restructuring, approved by the parliament on 16 December, abolished the privatization and reform ministries and, in a bid to speed up the reforms, transformed them into government departments under the prime minister's supervision.

ECONOMY CONTINUES TO DECLINE

The major factors that created the need for a government restructuring were not those "narrow party interests" that Constantinescu talked about in January, but differences of opinion among coalition partners as to how to speed up the privatization and reform process and stop the economy's decline. Daianu, an independent government member on a PNL slot who was credited by international financial organizations with having kept the budget deficit and foreign debt from spiraling out of control, had repeatedly warned against the danger of Romania's "Bulgarization." On 7 January he told journalists that the hardships caused by economic reform were not over, and Romanians would have to "tighten their belts" in 1998 even to achieve a "zero growth" of the economy. Daianu predicted that the 1998 budget deficit would not exceed 4.5 percent of the GDP and inflation would be around 30 percent, which, he noted, was in accordance with the recommendations of international financial institutions.

Negotiations with the International Monetary Fund, however, were stalled because of the looming coalition crisis. The IMF announced on 15 January that it was postponing a planned visit to Bucharest until the political situation there was clarified. After the IMF delegation's February negotiations with the government revealed that the two sides still disagreed on some details of the 1998 budget proposal, Daianu threatened to resign. He said the budget has to be changed every day to meet new demands, and refused to be an "accomplice in complicating even further the country's economic situation and negotiations with the IMF." As the positions of the IMF and the cabinet drew closer, Ciorbea said on 25 February that the budget would limit the deficit to 3.6 percent of GDP, but the IMF considered the government's projection of privatization revenues as overtly optimistic, and it suspended the release of a $86 million tranche from a $430 million standby loan because of the slow progress of economic reform.

After Ciorbea's resignation, Vasile pledged that his government would put Romania on the "road of no return" towards economic reforms. In line with his ambitions, on 22 April Vasile invited the IMF to re-negotiate the terms of the IMF standby agreement. Vasile argued that the government had restructured its budget and had a new program, which required new negotiations.

The draft budget, as adopted by the parliament on 26 May, allowed for 45 percent inflation and a budget deficit of 3.6 percent of GDP, and it foresaw an unemployment rate of 11.2 percent. Nevertheless, a press release that wrapped up an IMF delegation's visit at the end of June was non-committal about renewing loans to Romania and said an IMF mission might return in the fall to review the implementation of the government's reform program. The most dangerous adversary of that program, as Vasile noted on 30 June at a conference organized by the London *Economist* in Bucharest, was the "trade union–state managerial alliance." He said the state bureaucracy was the "mainspring of corruption," aided by ambiguous legislation passed by successive governments.

Yet another point of friction between Daianu and the coalition surfaced when the government approved on 2 July a $1.45 million loan for the purchase of 96 helicopters from the U.S. Bell Helicopter Textron company. According to the deal, after the purchase the U.S. manufacturer would buy 70 percent of the Gimbav aircraft company, which would then produce the helicopters. Daianu said he opposed the deal because Romania's military budget would have to be increased by 20 percent in the following nine years in order to cover the loan. On 21 July he even threatened to resign if the government upheld the controversial deal or if his earlier proposal to raise taxes in August was rejected by the cabinet.

In August Daianu came up with another proposal: he announced that he intended to cut the 1998 budget by some 8 trillion lei (almost $1 billion). He argued that the 1998 budget deficit might reach 5.5 percent of GDP. On 24 August he submitted the proposal to the government, and said he supported the State Privatization Fund's proposal to sell loss-making companies "for one dollar" to those willing to cover the companies' debts. In the second half of the year the economy continued to deteriorate. By year's end GDP would fall by 4.8 percent, while inflation ballooned to 60 percent.

Despite opposition from several ministries and trade unions, the government on 5 September approved Daianu's cuts. At the end of the month, however, the PNL withdrew its support from Daianu for failure to implement liberal policies in public finances. The same day Vasile dismissed Daianu, and replaced him with Traian Decebal Remes. The new finance minister's outline of the 1999 budget foresaw no deficit, providing that there were no payments for mass layoffs. The cabinet's plan to close 49 loss-making enterprises, that generated some 15 percent of total losses to the economy, was predicted to result in 70,000 people losing their jobs. The National Trade Union Bloc on 10 December protested against the plan, and numerous companies and trade unions launched strikes and staged protest actions against layoffs.

On 28 December the two main unions representing Romanian miners from the Jiu Valley set up a joint committee to prepare a general strike for early January. They demanded that two rail carriages be made available to transport miners to Bucharest. Citing the violence that followed miners' descents on Bucharest in 1990 and 1991, both the transport ministry and Bucharest's mayor rejected the demand.

HUNGARIANS THREATEN TO LEAVE THE COALITION

When Ciorbea announced his resignation, he thanked only his colleagues in the PNTCD and the ministers representing the Hungarian Democratic Federation of Romania (UDMR) for their cooperation. Indeed, the relationship between Ciorbea and the UDMR was the best possible, as Ciorbea's tenure was marked by a wish to grant ethnic Hungarians the basic rights that had been withheld from them. However, the new coalition headed by Vasile seemed to be hesitant about restoring minority rights demanded by Hungarians, making the UDMR repeatedly threaten to leave the coalition if the parliament failed to approve amendments to the education law and the establishment of a Hungarian-language university.

On 5 January Diaconescu promised that the coalition would respect agreements with the UDMR when the education law came up for debate in the Chamber of Deputies, while Plesu told Hungarian officials in Budapest that he saw no reason why a Hungarian university should not be set up in Romania. However, not all members of the ruling coalition were so committed to promises made to UDMR: George Pruteanu, the chairman of the parliament's education committee, told Max van der Stoel, the European Commissioner on National Minorities, that under international law Romania was not obliged to set up universities teaching in minority languages. Education Minister Andrei Marga and PD Chairman Petre Roman expressed similar positions, saying they supported separate sections for minorities within existing universities but not separate universities.

As the coalition crisis deepened, UDMR Chairman Bela Marko said Hungarians would not insist that their demands be implemented immediately, because the most important thing on the agenda was to ensure the passage of the budget. Constantinescu thanked the UDMR for its responsible behavior, saying the UDMR's contribution to the government coalition "goes far beyond that of an ethnic party."

With the new prime minister, supported by a group which earlier accused Ciorbea of neglecting the "national dimension" in the PNTCD's program, the fulfillment of promises made to the Hungarian minority were again postponed. The UDMR took a stronger position, announcing on 30 May that it would submit to the parliament a draft for setting up a separate Hungarian university in Cluj. The demand was received with hostility by virtually all coalition partners: Marga said universities "established on ethnic criteria" were likely to provoke ethnic tensions. A separate university in Transylvania, he added, could become the forerunner of "undesirable" movements.

On the same day when Hungary expressed its concern about the widespread anti-Hungarian campaign in the Romanian media, Vasile and Marga announced the establishment of a commission to examine the question of an independent Hungarian-language university. Diaconescu said on 22 June that a separate Hungarian university might become a "source of inter-ethnic conflict resembling that in the former Yugoslavia."

Hungarian Prime Minister Viktor Orban's visit to Romania on 25 July, and his support for the ethnic Hungarians' demand for a university, stirred up emotions. The main opposition Party of Social Democracy in Romania said Orban's statement that "if the university is not set up, there is nothing to talk about," amounted to "instituting joint sovereignty in Transylvania." Moreover, when Zsolt Nemeth, Hungarian Foreign Ministry State Secretary, said on 28 July that the Budapest cabinet is ready to finance a Hungarian university in Cluj, Marga said the issue "has been transformed into a state problem."

The dispute peaked in September, when the Chamber of Deputies' Education Commission rejected the amendment to the education law, proposed by Ciorbea's cabinet, which would have allowed the establishment of a Hungarian-language state university. A PNTCD parliamentary member argued that "the move emphasizes that Romania is a unitary state," and that a Hungarian university "would signify the first step toward federalism." The UDMR's Council of representatives decided on 5 September to leave the ruling coalition, unless an agreement was reached by 30 September. Leaders of the coalition failed to reach a compromise, and Marga's proposal to set up a "Danube University" for both the Hungarian minority in Romania and the Romanian minority in Hungary, was rejected even by Diaconescu, who pointed out that only several thousand Romanians live in Hungary.

Two hours before the expiration of the 30 September deadline, however, the government announced it would set up a Hungarian-German multicultural university, to be named "Petofi-Schiller" and to be supervised by the education ministry. Marga himself did not participate in the meeting that adopted the decision. His deputy, Mihai Korka, said it was absurd to limit teaching in the envisaged "Petofi-Schiller" university to minority languages, and his ministry would not agree to implement the government's decision unless tuition was concluded in Romanian as well. The other shortcoming of the "compromise" was that the German minority said their organization had not been consulted and that they did not need a separate university.

Nevertheless, the UDMR decided on 3 October to stay in the coalition. One and a half months later the Chamber of Deputies rejected the amendment to the education law, and adopted a version of the law which said multicultural universities must have Romanian sections. Moreover, the Bucharest Court of Appeals ruled on 10 December that the decision to set up the "Petofi-Schiller" university was unconstitutional as it introduced positive discrimination for a single national minority, preventing other minorities and the Romanian majority from receiving equal treatment. Despite Diaconescu's opposition, the government announced on 17 December that it would appeal the decision of the Bucharest court, but, as

Marko pointed out already in August, this was part of the coalition partners' "politicking" and "thinking more of the next elections than of the next generation."

OPPOSITION HAS LITTLE TO DO

The opposition to Ciorbea's and later Vasile's government from within the Romanian ruling coalition left little work for the country's opposition parties. The extreme nationalist pole of the opposition wanted early elections organized either by a "government of technocrats" or by one of "national unity" in which all parties were represented. The latter was initiated on 11 February when Corneliu Vadim Tudor, chairman of the Greater Romania Party (PRM) and Gheorghe Funar, leader of a dissenting wing of the Party of Romanian National Unity (PUNR), signed a protocol which they called the "first step on the road to set up the Great Alliance for the Resurrection of the Fatherland." The second step on that road was long postponed, as Funar could not reconcile with his expulsion from the PUNR in early 1997, and was busy with setting up a new political formation. On 25 April he announced in Cluj that he was launching the Alliance for the Unity of Romanians (AUR). PUNR leader Valeriu Tabara, however, contested in court Funar's right to use that name for the new party, as AUR was the name of the PUNR–Republican Party alliance in the 1990 elections. The Bucharest Municipal Tribunal accepted Tabara's appeal and rejected the registration of Funar's new party.

One month later Tudor proposed that Funar and his supporters join the PRM, offering Funar the position of PRM secretary general. Tudor repeated his invitation at the end of October, saying the offer "will be open till 31 December." Funar made up his mind and joined the PRM as secretary general on 16 November.

Former President Ion Iliescu's Party of Social Democracy in Romania (PDSR) has adopted a different strategy in making its voice heard in Romania's politics. Party deputy chairman Adrian Nastase said in January that, given the coalition PD's experience in ruling with the right, a future alliance between the two formations cannot be ruled out. Iliescu has also hinted at possible cooperation with the Democrats by saying the two parties "have much in common regarding doctrine." The tactics seemed to work. PD deputy chairman Traian Basescu and Nastase agreed in June to cooperate in the parliament on pending legislation. Nastase commented that the agreement could mark the beginning of a process of setting up a "social democratic pole in Romania," while Basescu stressed that cooperation between the two parties is a departure from past experiences. He added that in a democracy "today's opposition is tomorrow's government." The leadership of the PD, however, accused the PDSR of giving too much importance to their talks, and stressed that collaboration with the PDSR in local or general elections is not on the party's agenda.

The opposition's activity in 1998 ended with a parliamentary boycott and a failed no-confidence motion. On 20 November Iliescu announced that his party's senators and deputies would boycott the parliament's activities until the ruling coalition and the opposition agreed on a code of conduct. The PDSR, PUNR, and PRM ended the boycott only when Petre Roman proposed to them on 7 December to set up three mixed committees that would discuss the parliament's code and its legislative priorities. A few days after resuming their participation in the legislature, the three opposition parties moved a no-confidence motion in the cabinet, blaming it for economic failure and for the loss of international prestige. The motion was rejected on 21 December, bringing no end to the mutual accusations among coalition and opposition parties.

FOREIGN RELATIONS PUSHED INTO THE BACKGROUND
Overwhelmed with internal political and economic problems, Romania had little time in 1998 to deal with boosting its relations with foreign countries. After a very intensive year of diplomatic offensive ended with Romania's failure to be invited to join NATO in the first wave, in 1998 the country's foreign policy shifted more to regional cooperation.

President Constantinescu's continued efforts to persuade the West that his country was ready for a "second wave" of NATO expansion and European integration brought little satisfaction. A state visit to London on 12 March merely produced a non-committal statement on Romania's prospective NATO membership from British Defense Minister George Robertson, who said "the door of the Alliance remains open." NATO Deputy Secretary-General Klaus-Peter Kleiber on 15 June told Vasile that the decision on admitting Romania to NATO in a second wave of enlargement depended on the progress of the reform process in Romania. Vasile himself admitted on 27 June he said it was "unlikely" that Romania would be invited to join the military alliance in 1999. NATO membership remained a "major target" of Romania's foreign policy, but the hysteria that accompanied the country's bid for membership in 1997 must be avoided, he added.

Constantinescu remained optimistic and told the U.S. Congress in mid-July that Romania meets all the qualifications needed for NATO membership. But at the end of the year he accused the West of becoming "cynical and uninterested" in East-Central Europe. On 26 October he said in Oslo that the decision not to include Romania in the first wave of expansion "has been a serious mistake and mistakes must be paid for." Constantinescu argued that all threats to NATO security come from its southeastern tier and that Romania's membership would have been a solution to that problem.

Foreign Minister Andrei Plesu, meanwhile, was more concerned with southeastern European cooperation and improving Romania's ties with neighboring countries. Meeting with his Moldovan counterpart, Nicolae Tabacaru, Plesu said he preferred a "very good treaty" with Moldova to a "very quick one." The pending bilateral treaty must be "mutually acceptable" not only to the two countries' governments but also to "public opinion in Moldova and Romania," Plesu said in Chisinau on 20 February. According to Romanian media reports, Bucharest agreed not to mention the Molotov–Ribbentrop pact in the treaty, but insisted that the pact be called a "fraternal" one and be written in Romanian. One month later Plesu confirmed those reports saying that Bucharest was insisting on formulations emphasizing the "special ties" between the two countries, while Chisinau wants a "classic treaty of good neighborly relations."

Tensions also occurred in Romania's relationship with its northern neighbor, Ukraine. On 26 August Plesu told the U.S. Senate Foreign Relations Committee that the teaching of Romanian in minority schools in Ukraine was about to be replaced by the teaching of the "Moldovan language," and textbooks printed in Romanian were to be substituted by ones using the Cyrillic alphabet. The Ukrainian Foreign Ministry said those claims were "absolutely groundless" and part of a "political propaganda campaign" against Ukraine in the Romanian press. Later Plesu acknowledged the mistake, and called on journalists to display more "seriousness and responsibility" when reporting on the situation of the Romanian minority in Ukraine. That minority is "unfortunately divided into numerous rival factions" and it was one of those groups that proposed changing the official name of its language from "Romanian" to "Moldovan," he explained.

The success of Romania's foreign policy in 1998 was in its regional cooperation in the Black Sea zone and in the Balkans. On 26 February officials from Bulgaria, Georgia, Romania, Russia, Turkey, and Ukraine drafted guidelines for talks on confidence-building measures related to their naval forces in the Black Sea. As the conflict in Kosovo became more serious, Romania intensified its military cooperation with its neighbors. Meeting on the Greek island of Santorini on 11 April, the Bulgarian, Romanian, and Greek foreign ministers agreed to broaden cooperation and discussed the possibility of setting up a Balkan rapid deployment force. Only a few days later, the group, joined by Albania, Macedonia, and Turkey, agreed to set up the Multinational Peace Force in Southeastern Europe. The final agreement was signed in Skopje on 26 September and Italy was also among the signatories. U.S. Defense Secretary William Cohen said the establishment of the joint peacekeeping force was a step towards bringing security and stability in the region.

GLOSSARY

PD   Democratic Party
PDSR   Party of Democracy in Romania
PNL   National Liberal Party
PNTCD   National Christian Democratic Peasant Party
PRM   Greater Romania Party
PUNR   Party of Romanian National Unity
UDMR   Hungarian Democratic Federation of Romania

"A DISGRACE"

by BIANCA GURUITA

A rash of criminal libel convictions, including prison terms for three local journalists—one of whom was already behind bars—had freedom-of-press advocates in Romania reeling in 1998.

The first case, involving prison sentences handed down in July for two journalists in Iasi, set off a wave of front-page criticism in the media and by civic and media monitoring groups both at home and abroad. Another journalist is already in prison. Cornel Sabou, a journalist with the Trans-Press news agency in Baia Mare in northwest Romania, began serving a ten-month sentence on 22 August for his libel conviction.

In the Iasi case, Ovidiu Scultenicu and Dragos Stingu, working for the local newspaper *Monitorul*, were sued last year by police Lieutenant-Colonel Petru Susanu and his wife, Otilia, head criminal judge in the town. A 27 May 1997 article by the two journalists quoted a police source saying Susanu was to be fired from his position as chief of the criminal department, and that he was suspected of illegally obtaining funds. The source said Susanu intended to invest in a private bank; police are not permitted to involve themselves in business activities. Susanu was indeed fired, but on 23 July both journalists were convicted of libel and sentenced to one year in prison each.

The criminal code, in effect since 1968 and amended under the former government of Ion Iliescu in 1996, punishes libel with up to three years in prison, a fine, or both. Libel is defined as hurting someone's reputation by publicly stating falsehoods about him that could expose him to criminal prosecution or public contempt. Though Iliescu's government had stiffened the penalties, until 1998 no journalists had served time in prison since communism's fall.

Romanian newspapers called the Iasi trial "outrageous," "an abuse," and "a disgrace for Romanian justice." The accused journalists had requested the Supreme Court of Justice to move the trial to another town because Otilia Susanu was a judge in the Iasi court, as was her daughter, and her son-in-law was a prosecutor. The court rejected their request with no explanation. The journalists had no chance to get a lawyer, and their main witness, Iasi Police Chief Ioan Toarba, was not called to testify. The judge said the court could not find his home address to deliver a subpoena.

"Toarba was willing to come and prove in court that we did not write false information about Petru Susanu," said defendant Scultenicu. He and his colleague Stingu also were ordered to pay Susanu a total of 1.5 billion lei (about $170,000) in damages. And they were denied their civil rights, including parental rights—the type of punishment used in cases in which the defendant abuses his child and for people given longer sentences than the Iasi journalists. The court gave no explanation of why this was done, and legal experts said they had never heard of such a punishment for journalists before. The journalists were doing their jobs at *Monitorul* while waiting for their appeal, which was to be held in Iasi on 24 September.

Civic associations asked the Superior Council of Magistrates to charge the Iasi judge with abusing the law. The council is the only body in Romania that is allowed to analyze judges' activity, and in case of abuses it can dismiss or transfer them. Meanwhile, Otilia Susanu was promoted to the post of appeals court judge.

In the other case, journalist Sabou was sued by Mariana Iancu, head judge of the local court in Baia Mare, after he published some stories in *Ziua Nord-Vest*, a local daily affiliated with the national daily *Ziua*. Sabou based his articles on documents and quotes by sources—peasants who said the documents that Iancu obtained to help her mother obtain some farmland are false. The 12 peasants from the village of Ulmeni, in Baia Mare county, had (ultimately successfully) sued the judge's mother, accusing her of illegally obtaining land that was theirs. At the end of 1997, the Superior Council of Magistrates transferred Iancu to another court. The council did not say why the transfer was made.

The court in Bistrita, where Sabou was tried, said it had no choice but to give him a prison sentence on 25 May because he had been imprisoned for two previous convictions—robbery and desertion from the military. According to the court, that made him "a danger to society."

Sabou's appeal in the libel case was rejected, and the sentence became final on 3 April. Details on the previous convictions were not available. Monica Macovei, a Romanian human rights expert who agreed to take his case, said she did not yet have access to his criminal record. Legal experts were unable to explain the reason for Sabou's conviction. Macovei planned to help Sabou sue the Romanian state at the European Court of Human Rights in Strasbourg.

Meanwhile, Sabou's mother began a hunger strike on 26 August and asked President Emil Constantinescu to pardon her son. While Sabou was in jail, his wife, Camelia, gave birth to their third child. She told *Transitions* that Sabou is devastated and confused about his conviction, because he says he reported the truth.

Justice Minister Stoica was not eager to discuss problems inside the judicial system. He did say he will urge parliament to eliminate prison terms as punishment for libel, but his plans did not extend to removing libel from the criminal code, despite years of effort by journalists and human rights associations.

Many Romanian politicians are leery of decriminalizing libel and said journalists should be careful about how they criticize. "Politicians are scared to face a strong, free media," said Ion Iacos, vice president of Romania's Helsinki Committee. "Some are just not used to the idea, others simply cannot accept criticism." Senator Eugene Vasili said journalists and authorities were at war with each other, which damages a fledgling democracy. "The journalists try to undermine state institutions' authority, and institutions, to protect their authority, sometimes abuse the law." He believed freedom-of-information legislation would help. Eugene Vasiliu, chairman of the Senate's mass media committee, said he was working on such a law, under which he says journalists could protect their sources and not be blamed for what sources tell them. But he thought libel should remain a criminal offense.

NOTE

Reprinted with kind permission from *Transitions* magazine, October 1998.

THE SHADOW OF SECURITATE

by BIANCA GURUITA

Nine years after the end of Nicolae Ceausescu's brutal reign, the shadow of his notorious secret police, Securitate, still hangs over Romania. Securitate enabled the Communist dictator to keep a stranglehold on his people after he took power in 1965. Tactics ranged from the physical—real or imagined opponents of the regime were imprisoned, interrogated, tortured, killed—to the psychological: the pervasive feeling that Securitate was watching, as indeed it was. Thanks to its army of collaborators/informers, dubbed *securisti* in Romanian, Securitate knew what you had for breakfast, what you said to a friend. Your phone might have been bugged, your mail opened, your movements watched.

Securitate kept files on about 1 million people; it is unclear how many of Romania's 23 million citizens cooperated with the secret police; estimates range from 10 percent to 25 percent of the population. During the bloody mass revolt that ended Communist rule in December 1989, when about 1,200 people died, euphoric demonstrators shouted in the streets that they had conquered the fear of Ceausescu's iron arm—Securitate. Ceausescu and his wife, Elena, were executed by a military firing squad on Christmas Day after a quick trial.

It was to be the end of Securitate and its reign of terror. But Romania has been slow to address the issue of how to deal with Securitate's dark legacy. The government of former Communist Ion Iliescu, in office from 1990 to 1996, did not make much progress. The current government ran on a platform pledging to open the files. Then–Prime Minister Victor Ciorbea announced in fall of 1997 that within a few months, there would be a law on public access to Securitate archives. A year later, after protracted debates and delays, the proposal to let citizens see their own files and to reveal names of informers and Securitate officers had gotten only as far as the upper house of parliament. On 25 June the senate approved a version that the original proposal's architect criticized as weak and ineffective. The legislation now makes its way to the Chamber of Deputies and is not expected to see much movement there until 1999.

The driving force behind the legislation was Ticu Dumitrescu, a senator and president of the Former Political Detainees Association. Imprisoned under Ceausescu for ten years, three of them while still a student, Dumitrescu says he was tortured during interrogations, and even shown his files. "They left me for four hours to carefully read the reports Securitate had about me. I found in them details my friends and even some relatives of mine provided to Securitate."

But an upset Dumitrescu, after five years of working to get the law into parliament, walked out during the June vote. He accused senators of maiming the legislation, making it inefficient and pointless. "It is quite unbelievable we create through this law a council that is supposed to study the complete documents of Securitate archives without having free access to them. The political police files will remain in the hands of those officers who compiled them in the past. I feel betrayed. I know the Romanian people are continuously and shamelessly lied to."

Dumitrescu, a member of the main ruling party in the centrist coalition, the Christian Democrats (PNTCD), lost the support of his party for a year in August 1997 after accusing its leaders of dragging their feet on the law and being afraid to reveal Securitate's secrets. He admitted he is obsessed with the law, calling it "my only political stake: to disclose the dreadful Securitate once and for all because this is the only way to definitely split with the past." He said if access to the archives will be restricted, such a break will not be possible. "This makes us still Securitate prisoners."

The proposed law would allow citizens to see their own Securitate files. The files are said to include personal data and other details on Securitate surveillance subjects, including professional and social evaluations, and information on their relatives and friends. The law would also separate the structures within Securitate that acted as political police from departments that worked to protect the country's security on an intelligence and not a political basis. The public could find out whether public officials—including the president, the prime minister and his cabinet, parliamentarians, intelligence chiefs, military officials, religious leaders, judges, and public prosecutors—were Securitate collaborators or informers. The law would not entail prosecution of such public office-holders but would make their files public if they did not resign.

No political party openly expressed any opposition to the law, but all of them—both the ruling coalition and the opposition—proved by their senate vote in June that they wanted access to the files to be limited. Dumitrescu wanted the law to be applied by the National Council for Studying Former Securitate Archives, whose members would be nominated by the parties represented in parliament and be subject to parliamentary approval. A key point would be the council's access to the files. Dumitrescu wanted the council to have "the keys"—complete access to all the documents now in custody of the post-1989 intelligence services. But his senate colleagues said that could endanger national security. With a 109–7 vote, they changed the law to read that the intelligence agencies would remain the keepers of the files, and that the council would need their permission for any access. As senators did not specify what constitutes "national security," it would be up to intelligence agencies to decide whether to reveal a file.

The political police was created in 1948 with the assistance of the Soviet Union, which initially had a great deal of control over it. But Ceausescu set out on his own independent path, and from 1958 to 1959 an anti-KGB department was created within the agency. Securitate was reorganized several times, and in 1978, Ceausescu made it part of the internal affairs ministry and subordinated to him personally. This arrangement lasted until December 1989. Securitate's major departments included counter-intelligence for socialist countries, military counter-intelligence, economic counter-intelligence, the anti-terrorist department, and Department D—"disinformation and influence."

After Ceausescu's fall, Securitate was reorganized into several security agencies, the main ones being the Romanian Intelligence Service (SRI) and the Foreign Intelligence Service (SIE). Those two intelligence services, as well as the interior ministry and defense ministry, took over the Securitate archives. The archives are separated into three main categories: the criminal sector, which does not contain classified documents; the sector containing the files of those who were sent to forced labor camps; and the operative sector, which includes the files on informers and the individuals on whom they informed. The SRI got the largest share, including the last category, which would be what Dumitrescu's law covers.

About 22 percent of SRI employees had worked in the past with Securitate, but the government assures that they were not part of the political police under Ceausescu. The new intelligence agencies are forbidden to make arrests—their activity is limited to gathering data on security threats. In the past few years, their activity has focused on fighting organized crime. The current government says these agencies have made a great deal of progress and have changed to adapt to the new needs of an open society ruled by law.

Dumitrescu's proposed law defines Securitate as "those departments and those officers who maintained the discretionary power of the communist party by oppressing and restricting the fundamental rights of people." The law aims to expose the Securitate machinery by making public its structure and the names of political police officers.

Lack of a law on Securitate files has not stopped politicians from using leaked files to link their colleagues to the secret police. Parliament debates on the law were punctuated by periodic revelations in the media that ruling politicians had signed deals with Securitate. As fingers pointed and accusations were flung about, several officials resigned or were fired. In June, Health Minister Francisc Baranyi was forced to resign, and Democratic Party (PD) deputy Adrian Vilau lost his position as head of the parliamentary panel monitoring SIE, after their agreements with Securitate were made public.

Vilau said he had no regrets about his activity while he was a law student and said he did not harm anyone. His PD colleague Petre Roman, senator and party chairman, said the important issue was that Vilau hid his involvement from his party colleagues. Baranyi said he had been forced to sign at gunpoint in 1961 and did not consider himself an informer. Constantin Alexa, an SRI official, had leaked Baranyi's Securitate pledge to the media and was subsequently fired for it. He said in an interview on 10 August in the daily *Cotidianul* that Baranyi's SRI file shows the ethnic Hungarian acted against Romania's "national interest and security" after the overthrow of the Communists, and that he had links to Hungarian "separatists" and Hungarian intelligence. Baranyi's party, the Hungarian Democratic Federation of Romania (UDMR), represents Romania's 1.6 million ethnic Hungarians and was part of the ruling coalition.

These scandals are not new to Romanians; they are part of a series of sensational disclosures of politicians allegedly collaborating with Securitate. In the past nine years, several political careers were damaged and compromised by media printing excerpts of politicians' Securitate files. The files were leaked from SRI, which proved the agency has not managed to protect the materials against being used by various interests. The files became a blackmail tool in political debates, an unseen weapon impossible to counter.

Dumitrescu said only a probe of all Securitate documents would make it possible to really know whether a politician collaborated with Securitate and whether he caused any harm to anyone. "In any institution, the presence of an employee leaves traces: at the financial department, at the mailing department, inside the reports. There is not anyone whose activity cannot be discovered. That's why I fight for free and complete access," he says.

In the current cloak-and-dagger atmosphere, President Emil Constantinescu sought to head off media allegations that top ministers and intelligence chiefs, who make strategic decisions for the country, had ties to Securitate. In a televised statement, Constantinescu assured citizens a probe had shown that none of the members of the Supreme Defense Council—which includes the interior minister, the defense minister, the foreign ministers and the chiefs of Securitate successors SRI and SIE—had any connection with Securitate as "agents or collaborators." He said none is vulnerable to any form of blackmail, by internal or foreign sources, and promised that "the truth can never be hidden."

Meanwhile, Prime Minister Radu Vasile asked his ministers to write statements confirming or denying their involvement with Securitate. At an extraordinary meeting on 6 July, he opened the sealed envelopes in front of them and announced that all 23 cabinet members lacked any Securitate stigma.

Government records show that even if Securitate files were opened, the picture they would paint would be incomplete at best. Some people signed under duress but never cooperated; some say they gave information but never harmed anyone—the shades of gray are many. And thousands of files have been destroyed, including those of Communist collaborators. Mircea Gheordunescu, SRI deputy director, says Communist Party leaders in 1967 ordered Securitate to destroy the files of party members who were Securitate informers. An estimated 270,000 Securitate files were destroyed between 1971 and 1979, Gheordunescu said.

More disappeared after that. Dumitrescu accuses former Securitate officers of running a "Securitate-files black market." It started in December 1989, when some Securitate offices were vandalized and some Securitate files vanished. In June 1998, SRI revealed that in the first three months of 1990, 27,306 were destroyed by Securitate officers and another 1,876 files were stolen. Also in 1990, journalists working for *Romania Libera* newspaper reported that SRI tried to burn some Securitate files at a storehouse in Berevoiesti, near Bucharest. Virgil

Magureanu, Iliescu's SRI director, denied the agency tried to destroy the files. Nevertheless he promised "this kind of unfortunate incident will never happen again."

Justice Minister Valeriu Stoica, a backer of the law, said Romanian society needs not a purge but purification. "This can be done quite simply, if politicians assume the responsibility for their past, and do not try to bury it. If they do that and explain their past, I think first of all the public will understand them and only then maybe blame them. But they have to take responsibility." Senator Roman of the Democratic Party says he is pleased that the proposed law will at least ensure political control of the Securitate archives.

The law would attempt to separate people paid to provide anti-regime information on individuals from those forced to write various reports as part of their jobs, particularly those who had professional contact with foreigners. For example, Transportation Minister Traian Basescu says he did not sign any agreement with Securitate, but while he was a ship captain he wrote thousands of reports on his activity abroad. "You could fill a truck with my reports."

A 50-year-old journalist who worked for the international section of national radio says she had to write reports on every single interview with foreign personalities. "I had to hand those reports to the Securitate officer who had our section 'in custody.' The reports were in fact a summary of the interview. I always wrote— to make fun of that Securitate officer—that I never offered or received any presents. This was a job obligation. I never signed any agreement with Securitate, I never was asked to, and I knew very well that if I refused to write those reports I would have been jailed and my family destroyed. I just could not say no."

Ion Diaconescu, PNTCD president, who spent almost 20 years in Communist jails, says a distinction between different kinds of informers is absolutely necessary. He says informers were the lowest level in the Communist apparatus, and that "most of them were blackmailed to sign agreements with Securitate."

Calvinist pastor Laszlo Tokes, an ethnic Hungarian whose words of open opposition to the Communist regime sparked the 1989 revolt in Timisoara that led to Ceausescu's fall, was accused in the media in 1990 of making a Securitate pledge. He says he made many statements under duress, but that the statements solely concerned his pastoral work and his anti-Communist activity. Tokes was accused again in June, when extremist politician Corneliu Vadim Tudor said Tokes collaborated with Securitate under the code name Laszlo Ladislau. Tudor gave journalists a copy of an agreement Tokes allegedly signed with Securitate on 10 November 1982, which says Tokes agreed to provide Securitate with information on editing and distribution of the *Eilenpontale* religious magazine. Tokes denied this accusation, but his credit inside his party, the UDMR, has dropped. He is considered a radical within UDMR, and moderates may have used the document as a political tool in an effort to isolate him.

Tudor was the source of another disclosure. In 1995 he clashed with then-SRI director Magureanu and then-President Iliescu. In 1996 Tudor warned Magureanu that he had his Securitate officer file and threatened to go public with it unless Magureanu admitted his collaboration. Magureanu then provided the *Evenimentul Zilei* daily with some excerpts of his file. Magureanu said he "simply forgot" to reveal that he collaborated with the former secret police when he was sworn in as SRI director. This scandal seriously tarnished his image and boosted public mistrust in the SRI.

Only a few politicians have admitted on their own that they signed an agreement with Securitate. Senator Alexandru Paleologu, a refined intellectual, stated in 1990 that he signed such a document. "Even if you did not turn in anyone, you have to assume that you accepted a compromise. I needed to say that publicly to set me free of the obsession of guilt." Paleologu's courage gained him a great deal of respect, and his political career did not suffer at all.

Daniel Daianu, a respected economist, admitted in 1991 that he worked for Securitate as an analyst in the early 1970s. This did not prevent him serving as finance minister in Ciorbea's government, until his dismissal in September 1998. Ruling coalition politicians such as Diaconescu, the PTNCD party leader, have accused Iliescu's party of controlling the files. Diaconescu says Iliescu's Social Democratic Party of Romania (PDSR)—which ruled in 1990–1996—leaks files to undermine the government's credibility. Iliescu's party denied the charges.

Dumitrescu said Iliescu in fact was strongly supported by former Securitate officers to get into power. "It is quite clear that Iliescu would have been nobody today unless Securitate helped him to his political career," Dumitrescu said. Many believe this is the main reason that a law to open Securitate files was never considered during Iliescu's tenure, and that Iliescu's party ignored Dumitrescu's numerous attempts to get the legislation considered in parliament.

Though Iliescu never had Securitate on his agenda when in power, he says he now has changed his mind and favors a law to open the files. But observers note that he has nothing to lose by such a stance: any "no" vote by his opposition party would not be strong enough to make a difference. And though the PDSR consists of many former Communists, they probably would have nothing to worry about if a law was passed even if they were former securisti, because no files were kept on Communist collaborators with the secret police.

Some see Romania's Securitate archives as a potential Pandora's box. For others, it is a way to start coming to terms with the painful past. But no matter how the issue of access to the files is resolved, the legacy of Securitate is sure to linger for years to come.

NOTE

Reprinted with kind permission from *Transitions* magazine, September 1998.

Moldova

Population: 4,300,000
Capital: .... Chisinau (pop. 754,000)
Major cities: .... Tiraspol (capital of the self-proclaimed
"Dniester Republic," pop. 185,000), Balti
(pop. 158,000)
Area: .... 33,700 sq. km.
Major ethnic groups: .... Moldovan 65%, Ukrainian 14%, Russian
13%, Gagauz 3.5%
Economy: .... GDP growth: –8.6%
.... Inflation rate: 18.3%
.... Unemployment rate: 1.7% (1997)

FROM LEFT TO RIGHT, BUT NOT QUITE

by DAN IONESCU

Parliamentary elections, held on 22 March, were the main political event in 1998. They were won by the Communists' Party of the Republic of Moldova (PCRM), which garnered some 30 percent of the votes following an aggressive electoral campaign launched on 12 January by its leader, Vladimir Voronin (a former Moldovan interior minister in the final years of the Soviet era). The Communists skillfully capitalized on the older generation's nostalgia for the Soviet past, as well as on the omnipresent social hardships, including huge salary and pension arrears. Their political offer included a gradual restoration of "socialist relations" in the economy by strictly limiting the private sector, as well as full political, economic, and even military integration into the Commonwealth of Independent States (CIS). The price for years of continuously deteriorating living standards was mainly paid by the former ruling Agrarian Democratic Party (PDAM), whose popularity sank dramatically. By failing to pass the 5 percent parliamentary hurdle, the PDAM was de facto eliminated from the political game.

PCRM's victory was flawed, however, because it was unable to gain an absolute majority in parliament—they won only 40 out of 101 seats. The party was eventually forced into opposition by a loose center-right coalition set up on 21 April under the name of Alliance for Democracy and Reforms (ADR). This was made up of the Democratic Convention of Moldova (CDM), the pro-presidential Bloc for a Democratic and Prosperous Moldova (BMDP), and the Party of Democratic Forces (PFD), controlling 26, 24, and 11 parliamentary seats, respectively. Out of a total of 15 parties and blocs that had taken part in the election, those three center-right formations were—along with the Communists—the only ones to qualify for the new legislature.

On 23 April, BMDP leader Dumitru Diacov was elected parliament speaker—an influential position in Moldova's semi-presidential system. Though the composition of the new parliament was less complex than the previous one, parleys aimed at forming a coalition government without the Communists proved particularly laborious. Things were complicated by President Petru Lucinschi's insistence on having the last word in nominating the new prime minister. On 6 May, the president formally asked the parliament to appoint acting premier Ion Ciubuc rather than the young reformer Valentin Dolganiuc from the pro-Romanian Christian Democratic Popular Front (designated by the CDM) to head the next cabinet. Through his proxies in the BMDP, Lucinschi was able to help not only Ciubuc, but also Foreign Affairs Minister Nicolae Tabacaru, Defense Minister Valeriu Pasat, and Security Minister Tudor Botnaru retain their key posts in the new governmental team.

The rather hybrid cabinet was eventually approved by parliament on 21 May. Moldova thus found itself in a quite unusual political situation, with a government defining itself as center-right, although about one third of its members had already served in the previous left-wing, PDAM-dominated cabinet. This, of course, sharply contradicts the widespread perception of the right having returned to power in the Republic of Moldova after years of prevalence of the left.

Under the circumstances, ADR members had no choice but to content themselves with sharing the remaining portfolios, which they vowed to do according to the algorithm 2 (CDM) + 2 (BMDP) + 1 (PFD). The process, however, proved far from easy, with the Lucinschi-backed BMDP trying to get a bigger share of the pie to its partners' detriment. Bargaining over lesser ministerial positions, including deputy ministers and director-generals of departments, only ended in mid-June, when the CDM and the PFD accepted a compromise for the sake of keeping the fragile coalition alive. Growing dissent within the ADR continued to plague the activity of both the cabinet and the legislature. On 31 July, the BMDP joined forces with the Communist opposition in parliament in approving the transit of nuclear waste from Kozloduy, Bulgaria, to Russia—much to the dismay of its ADR partners.

Infighting within the ADR could only encourage the power-frustrated Communists in their attempts to shorten the government's life. In mid-September, they moved a no-confidence motion, attacking the cabinet's decision to cut social spending to reduce the budget deficit. This, however, was rejected by the parliament's Permanent Bureau, which voted against placing it on the legislative agenda. In late September the PCRM faction boycotted parliamentary debates in protest over "reformist" legislation, allegedly passed under pressure from international financial organizations. And on 6 November, the Communists moved another no-confidence motion, making the cabinet responsible for the ongoing economic crisis. Although this was supported by a majority of 38 deputies out of the 58 attending the 11 November session, it was short of the 50 + 1 majority mandatory in such cases.

Permanent political squabbling offered an opportunity to the president to renew his calls for a basic reform of the political system, aimed at turning the republic from a semi-presidential into a presidential one. In doing so, Lucinschi was resuming a drive launched by his predecessor and rival Mircea Snegur—an idea which Lucinschi used to oppose in his former role as parliament speaker (before being elected a president in late 1996). His latest appeal for more authority and powers, made on 10 December, was immediately seized by the Communists, who asked him to pass from words to deeds by dismissing the cabinet, proclaiming himself the premier of a "national salvation government" with Communist participation, and declaring a state of emergency because of the economic situation. Not surprisingly, Voronin's overtures were perceived by the democratic forces as an instigation to establishing a dictatorial regime.

ETHNIC MINORITIES AND LOCAL ADMINISTRATION

Constant malfunctioning within the central administration was matched by tension and dysfunction at local level. On 6 January, the Popular Assembly of the autonomous Gagauz-Yeri (a region inhabited by a Turkish minority professing the Christian faith) contested the validity of the Moldovan electoral law in the region. The mini-parliament later asked for a local plebiscite to be held on the same day with the parliamentary elections to decide on a new status for the region, as well as on its own constitution. Though the Central Electoral Commission gave the green light for the Gagauz referendum on 20 February, Moldova's Supreme Court nullified the decision on 17 March. On 14 May, the Gagauz Popular Assembly unanimously voted in favor of the region's basic law, despite government objections. Such maximalist policies, however, found no support in Turkey, the minority's protecting power. Visiting Turkish President Suleyman Demirel on 25 June thanked Moldova for the way it has solved the Gagauz issue, and promised financial aid for a series of regional projects, including a water supply project.

Toward the end of 1998, another minority based in the South, namely the Bulgarians from the Taraclia raion, came to public attention. The government announced plans to reform local administration by reducing the number of territorial units from 40 Soviet-style raions to only nine counties plus the Chisinau municipality. Ethnic Bulgarians, who form a majority in Taraclia, insisted that their region stay as a separate administrative unit, since inclusion into Cahul county would only open the way to loss of their cultural identity. In October the Bulgarian ambassador to Chisinau spoke out in favor of the minority, triggering an official protest on behalf of the Moldovan Foreign Affairs Ministry, which described his statements as interference in the country's internal affairs.

On 12 November, parliament passed the bill on reorganizing local government, but President Lucinschi returned it to the legislature asking, among other things, that the Taraclia district be preserved as a separate entity. On 23 December, the parliament rejected Lucinschi's appeal and adopted the law in its original form. The final voting provoked a new crisis within the ruling coalition, with vice-speaker Iurie Rosca (FPCD) calling for Diacov's dismissal if parliament yielded to Lucinschi's pressure. In response to the parliament's stance, local authorities in the Taraclia district decided to hold a referendum in January 1999 on whether the district's status should be changed or not.

NO BREAKTHROUGH ON TRANSDNIESTER

The tug-of-war over Taraclia's status renewed fears of separatism, which had been haunting the country since 1990–1992, when Transdniester chose to secede from Moldova. Relations with that breakaway region remained tense in 1998, especially since the leaders of the self-proclaimed "Dniester Moldovan Republic" continued to insist that their region should be recognized as fully independent.

Things were made worse by Russia's refusal to withdraw its troops from the region, situated hundreds of kilometers away from the its borders. Moscow continued to claim that its military presence on the Dniester was essentially a peacekeeping mission, and that a withdrawal of its forces could take place only after the conflict between Chisinau and Tiraspol (the Trasndniester capital) was fully settled. On 3 April, the Russian State Duma postponed again the ratification of an October 1994 Russian-Moldovan agreement on the troops' withdrawal. And in June, Duma deputy speaker Aleksandr Shokhin defended the Russian position at the Council of Europe Parliamentary Assembly session in Strasbourg in response to a withdrawal motion presented jointly by members of the Moldovan and Romanian delegations. The issue was discussed again at a meeting of the Organization for Security and Cooperation in Europe (OSCE) in Vienna on 9 July, at which the United States and the European Union once again urged Russia to honor its promise to withdraw all troops, military equipment, and ammunition from eastern Moldova.

For its part, in March the Transdniester leadership launched a drive collecting signatures in support of joining the Russia–Belarus union. The drive turned into a kind of non-binding referendum, according to which some 67 percent of the region's population supported the initiative. Such moves were encouraged by some extreme nationalist Russian politicians, including Vladimir Zhirinovsky. While visiting Tiraspol in late December, Zhirinovsky said that the Transdniester was "part of the Russian Federation" and appealed to President Boris Yeltsin to "undertake resolute action to recognize the Transdniester and establish direct economic ties with it."

Bilateral negotiations failed to bring any progress, the main stumbling block being Tiraspol's insistence on retaining all attributes of a distinct statehood, from its own flag and anthem to army and police. A meeting between Lucinschi and Transdniester leader Igor Smirnov in Tiraspol on 17 February raised some hopes of progress on economic questions. At a summit in Chisinau on 21 July, the two leaders again failed to agree on political issues, while reaching some limited understandings on electricity deliveries and re-commissioning a bridge over the Dniester at Dubasari, which had been severely damaged in the 1992 fighting. The advent of the center-right coalition in Chisinau in May was met with suspicion in Tiraspol, being used as a further pretext for blocking any attempt to find a solution to the conflict. In early June, for instance, Transdniester Supreme Soviet Chairman Grigorii Marakutsa accused the new cabinet in Chisinau of allegedly aiming at "Romanianizing the Moldovan Republic and unifying it with Romania."

The impact of international mediation endeavors also proved rather limited. A summit staged on 20 March in Odesa with the participation of Ukrainian President Leonid Kuchma and Russian Premier Viktor Chernomyrdin failed to resolve the main political questions. Ukraine was allowed to send peace-keeping observers to the buffer zone (in August, the Joint Control Commission, monitoring the truce in the security zone, fixed their number at ten only). By late September, it became evident that Tiraspol was not willing to reduce the numbers of its troops, while dragging its feet over further negotiations. This prompted the Moldovan side to announce on 6 October its decision to unilaterally reduce its forces. Despite Tiraspol's obstructive stand, the international mediators (Russia, Ukraine, and the OSCE) submitted in late November their own draft of an agreement, envisaging a special status for the breakaway region within a sovereign, independent, and territorially integral Moldova.

The relationship between Chisinau and Tiraspol was shadowed by a series of other issues as well. Tiraspol authorities banned Transdniester inhabitants from casting their votes in the Moldovan elections; threatened to impose an entry tax for non-residents, including Moldovan visitors; hampered Romanian-language education in the region, despite its financing by Chisinau; and, last but not least, refused to set free Ilie Ilascu and the members of the so-called "Ilascu group," jailed since 1992 on charges of terrorism.

ECONOMY AND SOCIETY

The Russian crisis had a serious impact on Moldova's economy, especially since Russia accounted for more than 60 percent of the country's exports. The collapse of the Russian market was mainly responsible for a 31 percent rise in the trade deficit, which reached $390 million in 1998. Foreign trade volume dropped by 19 percent, with exports diminishing by 27 percent as against 1997.

Despite earlier hopes of improving on the modest economic growth of 1997 (1.3 percent), in 1998 GDP dropped by 8.6 percent. Industrial production dropped by some 11 percent, while cereals production sank by 7 percent. Moldova's foreign debts reached some $1.3 billion by the end of the year, of which over $600 million was owed to the Russian gas company Gazprom. At the same time, the hard currency reserves of the National Bank halved from August to the end of the year (from $300 million to $150 million), mostly because of the bank's contribution to servicing the foreign debt (a total of $148 million was paid back in 1998), as well as to its sustained efforts to keep the national currency relatively stable. The Moldovan leu, however, fell in the same period from 4.7 to one dollar to 8.5, after reaching a record low of 10 to the dollar in early November. The annual inflation rate was 18.3 percent in 1998, as against 11.2 percent the previous year.

At the peak of the crisis, Lucinschi stated on 13 November that he might be forced to declare a nation-wide state of emergency. But the situation slightly stabilized in the following weeks, mainly thanks to the National Bank's ability to stabilize the currency. Despite the challenge posed by the Russian crisis, the new administration showed determination in revitalizing the reform process that had been practically frozen in the months preceding the March elections. Privatization made considerable progress, with nine key deals concluded with foreign investors, including the sale in October of a 52 percent stake in the Rezina cement mill to the French company LaFarge. The government and parliament also approved the privatization of the state telephone company Moldtelecom, which will take place in 1999.

The energy sector remained the economy's Achilles' heel in 1998, in view of the country's nearly total dependence on foreign sources of energy, including natural gas and electricity. On 26 February parliament approved the privatization of the Molodvagaz company, with 51 percent of its assets being taken over by Russia's giant natural gas concern Gazprom in part settlement for Moldova's debts. But in June, Gazprom threatened to cut gas deliveries by half unless Chisinau repaid its remaining debts. Also in June, Ukraine suspended electricity supplies after one of its reactors at Chornobyl was shut down. The Russian gas saga continued throughout the year, with Premier Ciubuc signing on 18 December in Moscow an agreement for 1999 providing for both an increase in the volume of deliveries and in the price paid by Moldova. In November, Ukraine again cut electricity deliveries by half, prompting Chisinau to seek emergency supplies in Romania. The move was hailed as a belated attempt to diversify energy sources and limit the dependence on the former Soviet space.

The critical economic situation was aggravated by the reluctance of international financial organizations to grant new credits to Moldova. The International Monetary Fund and the World Bank repeatedly delayed the release of new tranches from already agreed credits, mainly because of Chisinau's failure to streamline its budget, monetary, and fiscal policies. Moldova's 1998 budget, passed by parliament on 29 December 1997, was criticized as unrealistic and as making populist concessions to the electorate. On 16 July, the new legislature adopted a revised, more austere budget, which was described as "anti-social" by the Communists, who refused to take part in the vote. Towards the end of the year, both the IMF and World Bank expressed satisfaction over the line adopted by Moldova, including the draft for the 1999 budget, and signaled their willingness to resume lending in the immediate future.

Persisting economic woes were chiefly responsible for further deterioration of living standards in what was already one of the poorest countries in Europe. The minimum consumer basket amounted in December to some 600 lei ($75), while the average 1998 salary amounted to only 252 lei ($32). Over 80 percent of the population were believed to be living under the poverty threshold. The authorities proved unable to reduce the salary and pension arrears, which, by the end of the year, totaled over 1 billion lei ($120 million). The trade unions eventually decided to take action over this serious social plight. On 4 December, they staged a protest in front of the government headquarters, in which an estimated 20,000 to 40,000 people took part.

BETWEEN EAST AND WEST

Summing up his department's activity in 1998, Foreign Affairs Minister Tabacaru said on 29 December that, despite the impact of "political and economic cataclysms in neighboring countries," the year had been "full of achievements" for

Moldova's diplomacy. He quoted his country's striving to enhance its presence in international and pan-European organizations, such as the UN, the OSCE, and the Council of Europe.

Moldova, indeed, stepped up its efforts to re-orient its foreign policy toward the West. In January, Lucinschi visited NATO and EU headquarters in Brussels, where he held talks with NATO Secretary-General Javier Solana and European Commission Chairman Jacques Santer. Also in January, Defense Minister Pasat discussed in Washington with his U.S. counterpart William Cohen ways of strengthening military relations. Cohen seized the opportunity to praise Moldova's contribution to NATO's Partnership for Peace (PfP) program.

On June 10, Tabacaru addressed the UN General Assembly with an appeal to help find a lasting solution to the Transdniester conflict. During a further visit to Washington in August, Tabacaru signed agreements on establishing a joint Moldovan-U.S. committee for improving military cooperation, and on a program for the training of Moldovan soldiers by the U.S. military. Besides, Tabacaru was informed on 19 August that the United States decided to include Moldova in its Action Plan for Southeast Europe—a move that aroused optimism in Chisinau about the prospects of bilateral relations.

Also in August, a ten-day PfP exercise took place at an airfield in Chisinau, in which U.S. and Moldovan military medical corps simulated an airlift of civilians affected by a natural disaster. On 28 September, Solana paid a short visit to Chisinau, where he discussed with Lucinschi and other Moldovan leaders the country's participation in the PfP, as well as the Transdniester conflict. While reaffirming Moldova's interest in closer cooperation with NATO, Lucinschi nevertheless stressed his county's neutral status. This caution appeared to be a response to repeated accusations of "flirting with NATO" leveled by the Left.

OSCE continued to play an important role as a mediator in the peace process on the Dniester. On 2 June, the organization marked five years of activity in Moldova; and in early July, OSCE Secretary-General Giancarlo Aragona discussed in Chisinau with Lucinschi the ways to settle the conflict. Aragona's successor, Polish Foreign Minister Bronislaw Geremek, also pledged to intensify mediation efforts. Moreover, Polish President Aleksander Kwasniewski told Lucinschi in Warsaw in late October that his country was willing to join the Transdniester mediators. At a meeting in Oslo on 3 December, OSCE foreign ministers called for reinvigorating talks between Chisinau and Tiraspol.

According to Tabacaru, 1998 marked a turning point in Moldova's relations with the European Union. On 15 July, the Coordinating Committee adopted in Brussels a cooperation program for 1998–1999. However, the EU dismissed as "premature" a request by Moldova to join the European Conference, a forum that brings together 15 candidates to EU membership. Among the EU states, France offered Moldova moral support during the initial phase of the turmoil provoked by the Russian crisis. On 4 September 4, French President Jacques Chirac paid a one-day visit to Chisinau—the first ever by a leader of a major Western nation. France already ranked first among foreign investors in Moldova. These Westward diplomatic steps should not disguise the true situation with respect to Moldova's foreign policy priorities. The Russian Federation remained Moldova's main strategic partner, and relations with the countries belonging to the CIS retained their special significance, despite the crisis. The ritual pilgrimage of senior Moldovan officials to Moscow continued throughout 1998, the best example being offered by the new-old premier. Ciubuc discussed in Moscow prospects for long-term economic cooperation with his Russian counterpart Viktor Chernomyrdin on 17 March; the same issue was tackled again there with the new Russian premier Yevgenii Primakov in late October; finally, on 17 December, Ciubuc had to fly again to Moscow to coax the Gazprom management not to cut off gas supplies.

However, relations with Russia were not free of tension. They were shadowed not only by the August financial crisis, but also by long-standing issues, such as the State Duma's refusal to ratify the basic bilateral treaty signed in 1990 with the former Soviet state, or the 1994 agreement on troops withdrawal from Transdniester. Though the Moldovan side tended increasingly to believe that a new treaty should be drafted to replace the "historically outdated" 1990 one, it could hardly agree with the perception prevailing in the Russian Duma— dominated by leftists and nationalists—that Transdniester had to be seen as a separate entity. In a message addressed to Lucinschi in late June, President Yeltsin confirmed Kremlin's official position, thus indirectly playing down the Duma's stance on the issue.

A further source of tension lay in Russia's aspiration to preserve its supremacy in the Commonwealth of Independent States. The 29 April CIS summit in Moscow highlighted the friction within the organization. While visiting Chisinau on 7 May, CIS Executive Secretary Boris Berezovskii had to admit that the CIS must rid itself of the still prevailing "Big Brother mentality." Thus it was not surprising that some countries continued to look for alternative cooperation alignments, such as GUAM (Georgia-Ukraine-Azerbaijan-Moldova), set up in the fall of 1997. Significantly, senior officials from the GUAM countries, including Moldovan Premier Ciubuc, chose Washington as the venue to issue on 6 October a joint declaration urging closer cooperation in order to overcome the world economic crisis. Moldova also showed interest in plans to set up a multiple transportation network between Central Asia and Europe via the Transcaucasus. In September, Lucinschi joined the presidents of seven other countries at the TRACECA conference in Baku. Earlier, Lucinschi took part in the Yalta summit of the Black Sea Economic Cooperation organization on 4 June.

Despite cooperation within the CIS and GUAM, relations with neighboring Ukraine were complicated by disputes over border delimitation and the treatment of ethnic minorities. On 10 March, Premier Ciubuc protested Kyiv's decision to push the border 100 meters into Moldovan territory to prevent the building of an oil terminal at Giurgiulesti. Bickering over the terminal went on for several months, with Ukraine putting forward ecological arguments against a project that could pollute the Danube delta. Ukrainian Foreign Minister Borys Tarasiuk discussed the issue in Chisinau on 17 July; and on 4 August Premier Ciubuc reached in Kyiv an agreement on a territorial swap that resolved the dispute. On 15 November Ciubuc laid the foundation stone for the terminal. As for the Moldovan minority in Ukraine's Odesa province, a cultural organization in Chisinau on 9 September issued a protest against pressure by local authorities on minority teachers to define the language they used as "Moldovan" rather than Romanian. As mentioned above, Ukraine in 1998 intensified its participation in mediating the Transdniester conflict. In October, President Leonid Kuchma proposed that a new summit be held in Kyiv on 27–29 November, but the plan failed to materialize.

Relations with Moldova's other neighbor, Romania, remained rather complex. The two states were unable to finalize a bilateral basic treaty, with Bucharest insisting that the treaty be called a "fraternal" one, and Chisinau showing preference for a classic treaty with no special connotation. However, an earlier request that the document included a reference to the 1939 Molotov-Ribbentrop secret pact that led to Romania losing Bessarabia to the Soviet Union was apparently abandoned even before Romanian Foreign Minister Andrei Plesu visited Chisinau on 19 February.

One of the most sensitive issues in relations with Romania was that of dual citizenship, which was reportedly solicited by an increasing number of Moldovans. On 26 August the Moldovan Supreme Security Council described the trend as "abnormal" and asked for legal steps to prevent it. Russian-language media in Chisinau even spoke of a "tacit assimilation of Moldova by Romania." Fears of pressure for union with Romania led the new center-right government to continue the policy of its predecessor in denying the legal registration of the Bessarabian Metropolitan Church, re-established in 1992 under the subordination of the Bucharest Patriarchate. The only officially recognized church remained the Moldovan Orthodox Church, subordinated to the Moscow Patriarchate.

Apprehensions aside, the two states continued the by now traditional policy of small steps. On 21 January, a Moldovan-Romanian trade center was inaugurated in Chisinau. Lucinschi met his Romanian counterpart Emil Constantinescu on 21 February in Galati and on 10 October in Bucharest. Among the priorities discussed on those occasions was the question of breathing life into the Euroregions of the Lower Danube and Upper Prut, whose creation was agreed the previous year by Romania, Moldova, and Ukraine. Trilateral cooperation was discussed on 22 October in Chisinau by the presidents of the three countries, who also signed a document urging Moscow to withdraw its troops from the Transdniester region.

GLOSSARY

ADR   Alliance for Democracy and Reforms
BMDP Bloc for a Democratic and Prosperous Moldova
CDM   Democratic Convention of Moldova
PFD   Party of Democratic Forces
PCRM Communists' Party of the Republic of Moldova
PDAM Agrarian Democratic Party

CULTURAL AWARENESS

by IULIAN ROBU

The decision by two Moldovan radio stations to devote much of their air time to rebroadcasting programming from Russia prompted emotional accusations that the stations have sold out Moldovan national interests in favor of quick cash. But the issue also points to a growing trend. To be successful in Moldova—where Romanian is the official language, but Russian-speakers make up over 30 percent of the population—many stations feel they can't afford to ignore the country's minorities.

In mid-1997, Eldoradio, a Moldovan station, initiated a radical facelift by signing a rebroadcasting deal with Evropa Plius, an independent, Moscow-based commercial station. Soon, Eldoradio slashed its Romanian programming and now does little more than rebroadcast Evropa Plius's music, news, and talk shows. In spring 1998, Polidisc, another Moldovan station, made a similar move when it started to broadcast the programs of Russkoe Radio, another private Russian station, 15 hours a day. Some of the Russian programming is superior to that of Moldovan stations, especially news. Russkoe Radio also places a heavy emphasis on the Russian pop music adored by a considerable segment of Chisinau listeners.

These advantages enabled Polidisc and Eldoradio to quickly attract a considerable amount of advertising. Valerii Galupa, Polidisc's executive director, says income from selling local ads already covers the fee the station pays to Russkoe Radio and still leaves the station with a profit. He added that it made more financial sense for his station to rebroadcast Russkoe Radio than to develop original programming—even if it would have been of the same quality. This last point particularly distresses people who have worked to create indigenous shows. "When we introduced Russian-language programming, we were able to sell more advertising, until the two [Moscow-based] radio stations came in," says Corneliu Durnescu, executive director of Radio d'Or.

When it debuted in October 1996, Radio d'Or had pledged to broadcast exclusively in Romanian. A year later, the station had to respond to market realities and by 1998 was broadcasting four hours a day of Russian programming, produced in-house.

More competition may be on the way, because two powerful stations from Romania are also entering the fray. The Radio Contact company has 22 local stations scattered throughout Romania with a combined market share of around 30 percent—first among commercial networks. In June, the Moldovan branch office received a license. Although part of a larger network, each Radio Contact station adjusts its music and current-affairs content to the local market, according to Viorel Balan, Radio Contact Chisinau's programming director; the station has already introduced two news bulletins in Russian. Balan says Radio Contact plans to expand into a nationwide network and will also take into account the needs of other local markets—such as in the south, home to much of the Gagauz minority. Pro FM, another powerful Romanian station, was slated to enter the Moldovan market in the near future.

According to Catalin Giosan, the station's Chisinau director, Pro FM is planning to address exclusively the Romanian-speaking population, but if market research shows the need, Russian-language programming might be added.

The "invasion from the East," as the boom in Russian programming was dubbed locally, raised complaints that young Romanian-speaking broadcasters might soon find themselves with limited chances to develop their skills. But the tone of the debate suggests something deeper: the mixed feelings some Romanian-speakers have about all things Russian, given the forced Russification of the language and culture during the almost-50 years of Soviet rule. "Russian was planted here; it didn't grow by itself," says Valeriu Saharneanu, chairman of the Journalists' Union. When the Soviet Union absorbed Moldova after World War II, users of Romanian were forced to write their language, which uses a Latin alphabet, in Cyrillic; this form of Romanian was given the official name of Moldovan. Mere mention that the Romanian language or Romanian culture was native to Moldova could lead to severe persecution.

Critics have also based their reservations on more concrete grounds. They say that the stations have violated one of the key conditions stipulated in their licenses—that at least 30 percent of programming must be in Romanian. The validity of this claim is generally recognized, although Polidisc has a more ambiguous case (the station has another frequency that continues to run Romanian-language programming). Legally, nothing can be done: the quota rule, introduced in 1995, is not in the Law on Audio-Visual Media. As a result, courts do not have a sufficiently strong legal reason to sanction a station that violates the quota, says Anton Coval, head of the Law and Licensing Department of the Coordinating Council for Audio-Visual Media, the licensing body. In 1997 the council warned Eldoradio to stop broadcasting only Evropa Plius, but the threat went no further. "We can't make order [on the air waves] because of the imperfect laws," Coval laments.

The council is considering a revamped media law, which would cure its legal impotence by specifically mentioning quotas. Some council members are thinking of going a step further by raising the Romanian-language quota to 60 percent for commercial stations and 70 percent for public stations. Another idea is to provide economic incentives to stations that have a high percentage of Romanian-language programming—a change favored by many Romanian speakers.

NOTE

Reprinted with kind permission from *Transitions* magazine, September 1998.

RUSSIAN
FEDERATION

VI

Domestic Politics
Foreign and Military Policies
Economic and Social Policy

Domestic Politics

Population:	147,700,000
Capital:	Moscow (1994 pop. 8,793,000)
Major cities:	St. Petersburg, (pop. 4,883,000, Nizhnii
	Novgorod (pop. 1,425,000, Novosibirsk
	(pop. 1,418,000)
Area:	17,075,400 sq. km.
Major ethnic groups:	Russian 81.5%, Tatar 3.8%, Ukrainian 3%
	Chuvash 1.2%, Bashkir 0.9%, Belarussian
	0.8%, other 8.8%
Economy:	GDP growth: –4.6%
	Inflation rate: 84%
	Unemployment rate: 11.8%

ECONOMIC CRISIS YIELDS MASSIVE POLITICAL FALLOUT
by LAURA BELIN

The central event of 1998, the economic crisis that engulfed Russia in August, had profound consequences for both elected officials and those who wielded political influence behind the scenes. No one's fortunes changed more than President Boris Yeltsin's, whose political standing eroded as dramatically as did the value of the ruble. Although the constitution providing immense presidential powers remained unchanged, by the end of the year Yeltsin's position was weaker than at any other time in his presidency.

YELTSIN FADES PHYSICALLY AND POLITICALLY
Yeltsin displayed a familiar leadership style during the first three months of the year. First, he maintained a balancing act between opposing factions in the government. During the second half of 1997, controversies over economic policies, especially privatization, had highlighted discord between Prime Minister Viktor Chernomyrdin and First Deputy Prime Ministers Anatolii Chubais and Boris Nemtsov. In January, Yeltsin signed off on a redistribution of duties that favored the prime minister at the expense of the so-called "young reformers." Chernomyrdin gained the authority to oversee the finance ministry, budgetary and monetary policy (formerly Chubais's domain), and the fuel and energy ministry (for which Nemtsov had been responsible). Three weeks later, Yeltsin promised—albeit in ambiguous language—that Chubais and Nemtsov would stay in the government until 2000.

Equally important, the president sought to distance himself from the government's policy failures. He pledged to call the government to account for its poor performance in 1997, when economic growth registered a meager 0.4 percent. Yeltsin's rhetoric was tough. But his health remained a question mark. Following a two-week spell in the hospital in December 1997 for what officials termed a respiratory infection, Yeltsin took two weeks of vacation in January 1998 and postponed scheduled trips to India and Chechnya. In March, he urged journalists to stop speculating about his health, only to be forced three days later to return to the hospital with another acute respiratory infection. The illnesses raised questions about whether the president was suffering from a degenerative ailment or serious complications stemming from his past heart disease.

Meanwhile, Chernomyrdin was gaining stature and looking increasingly presidential. When the cabinet held an expanded session on 26 February, a session at which heads were expected to roll, the president left early, leaving Chernomyrdin to grill ministers. Yeltsin sacked four cabinet officials in early March, but none held senior posts; the core of the Chernomyrdin government was left intact. Moreover, the prime minister, who had rarely sought the limelight, began to raise his public profile. In March he was to begin regular weekly appearances on a nationwide television show.

Chernomyrdin's television career was abruptly cut short when Yeltsin sacked the government on 23 March. During his five years as prime minister, Chernomyrdin had survived many rumors concerning his imminent demise. When the ax finally fell, virtually no one had seen it coming. The prime minister learned of his fate when he arrived at the Kremlin for what he thought would be a routine Monday morning meeting with the president.

Yeltsin gave only a vague explanation for his decision. He said the government lacked "fresh approaches" and should focus on solving social and economic problems, putting political infighting aside. In keeping with the law on the government, which required the entire cabinet to step down if the prime minister left office, Yeltsin fired the whole government. But he issued separate decrees firing Chernomyrdin, Chubais, and Interior Minister Anatolii Kulikov, making clear that some ministers were "more fired" than others and would not be returning to the cabinet.

As recently as January, Yeltsin had promised to leave Chernomyrdin's government in place through 1999. What changed his mind? Some argued that Yeltsin came to view Chernomyrdin as a threat to his personal power. He sacked the government just a few days after leaving hospital, perhaps to emphasize that he was still the central figure in Russian politics.

Whatever the reason for firing Chernomyrdin, the choice of his successor seems to have been impulsive. The Kremlin initially announced on 23 March that Yeltsin would serve as acting prime minister indefinitely. That arrangement was legally untenable, since the constitution named the prime minister as the acting head of state should the president's health fail (hardly an improbable scenario). Apparently Kremlin officials quickly realized the potential for a constitutional crisis, because within a few hours, Yeltsin named 35-year-old Sergei

Kirienko as acting prime minister.

To call Kirienko a dark horse for the job would be an understatement. He had only four months' experience as fuel and energy minister and was the deputy head of that ministry for just eight months before that. Before the spring of 1997, he was a banker and oil company chief who had never worked in the capital. Like several others from Nizhnii Novgorod, he found work in Moscow on the coattails of Nemtsov, who was governor of that region before becoming first deputy prime minister in March 1997.

At first, many commentators and politicians believed that Yeltsin would eventually abandon Kirienko in favor of a more experienced candidate, perhaps Moscow Mayor Yurii Luzhkov or a prominent regional leader. But after the State Duma rejected Kirienko's candidacy on 10 April, Yeltsin renominated him within the hour. The constitution was the Kremlin's trump card. It stipulated that if the Duma voted down the president's nominee for prime minister three times, the president was obliged to dissolve the lower house of the parliament and call for new Duma elections within four months.

Communist Party leader Gennadii Zyuganov vowed that his party's members would never support Kirienko, but cracks in the Communists' resolve appeared early in the game. Duma Speaker Gennadii Seleznev, a senior member of the Communist faction, repeatedly expressed concern about allowing Yeltsin to dissolve the Duma and rule by decree.

Yeltsin also held out a carrot for wavering Duma deputies. A few days before the second vote on Kirienko, the president instructed influential Kremlin official Pavel Borodin to take care of the deputies' needs if they showed a "constructive approach" toward Kirienko. (Borodin's duties included allocating cars and apartments.) Meanwhile, Kirienko and Yeltsin aide Sergei Shakhrai played "good cop, bad cop" with the Duma. Kirienko promised to work with the parliament if confirmed. Shakhrai outlined a grim scenario for the Duma should the deputies reject Kirienko three times. Not only would Yeltsin dissolve the lower chamber, Shakhrai warned, he would issue a decree changing the electoral law to eliminate proportional representation, currently used to select half the Duma deputies.

The opposition in the Duma withstood the pressure a second time, voting down Kirienko in a show of hands by a wider margin than in the first vote. Nonetheless, Yeltsin immediately renominated Kirienko, and his brinksmanship paid off. Despite pledges by Communist leaders to stand firm, a sizable minority of Communist deputies and their allies opted to protect their parliamentary mandates despite misgivings about Kirienko's inexperience. They were emboldened by the fact that the final vote was held by secret ballot. In the end, Kirienko was confirmed with 25 votes to spare. Only Grigorii Yavlinskii's Yabloko faction remained unanimously opposed to his candidacy.

Notwithstanding his victory over the Duma in April, that same month Yeltsin suffered a rare defeat at the hands of the Constitutional Court. The judges ordered the president to sign the so-called "trophy art" law, which prohibited transporting abroad any artifacts acquired by the USSR during the Second World War. (In 1997, Yeltsin had vetoed that law a second time, after both houses of parliament overrode his first veto. The proposed law was causing problems in Russia's relations with Germany.) The ruling removed one of Yeltsin's key tools to block parliamentary initiatives at a time when the upper house of the parliament, the Federation Council, was increasingly willing to override his vetoes. Following the trophy art ruling, Yeltsin was forced to sign several laws that he would have preferred to veto a second time. One that gained widespread attention in Russia and the international financial community was a law setting limits on foreign ownership of shares in Russia's electricity monopoly, Unified Energy Systems.

The appointment of the Kirienko government generated ill will among Communist Duma deputies. In 1997, the Communist leadership had advocated roundtable talks with the government and presidential administration. But in May 1998, Zyuganov announced that his party no longer favored "dialogue" with the authorities. The Communists soon collected enough signatures in the Duma to launch impeachment proceedings, and in June the Duma formed a commission to consider impeachment charges. Though there was little chance of removing Yeltsin from office, the commission served as an insurance policy. The constitution forbids the president from dissolving the Duma once two-thirds of deputies have passed an impeachment motion, and the commission could rapidly draft such a motion.

Soon after the Kirienko government took office, the economic situation in Russia worsened, with low commodity prices and tax receipts contributing to fiscal problems and a collapse in the stock and bond markets (see "Russian Economy: Farewell to Orthodox Market Transition"). The government drew up an "anti-crisis program," but many of its parts required parliamentary approval. As during the battle over Kirienko's confirmation, Yeltsin was not disposed toward negotiating with legislators. Government and Kremlin officials warned the Duma and Federation Council that any delay in passing the anti-crisis program would harm the Russian economy. In July, after the Duma rejected key parts of the plan, the authorities sought to implement several policies through presidential decrees and government directives, though some of those decrees were of dubious legality.

In any event, the anti-crisis plan failed to live up to its name. The August ruble devaluation and default on government securities severely tarnished Yeltsin's authority and credibility. He had staked much political capital on the Kirienko government and had promised as late as 14 August that there would be no devaluation. Less than a week later, the ruble was released from its peg and lost two thirds of its value. Yeltsin dismissed Kirienko and named Chernomyrdin as acting prime minister. But this time it was not so easy for Yeltsin to blame the government for the economic failures. For years, some of Yeltsin's opponents had demanded his resignation. In August, such calls for the first time appeared to be more than political rhetoric. Some journalists began to predict the president's imminent departure—perhaps immediately, perhaps in the autumn. The rumors persisted even after Yeltsin declared on nationwide television in late August that "I am not going anywhere."

For two weeks after nominating Chernomyrdin, Yeltsin attempted to use the same strategy that had secured Kirienko's confirmation. He and Chernomyrdin met with key members of parliament and he vowed to support Chernomyrdin to the end. Kremlin officials again hinted that if new parliamentary elections became necessary, they might be held under a different electoral system. The conventional wisdom held that the Duma would confirm Chernomyrdin. After all, the same deputies had confirmed him two years earlier, following Yeltsin's re-election. Moreover, Chernomyrdin had developed a fairly good rapport with opposition members of parliament, who viewed him as the lesser evil compared to Chubais and Nemtsov.

Duma leaders demanded a wide-ranging political agreement in exchange for a confirmation vote. They wanted more power for the legislature, including the right to confirm senior cabinet officials and the right to hold no-confidence votes on individual ministers. In exchange, the Duma would freeze the impeachment hearings, refrain from holding no-confidence votes for at least three months, and move swiftly on key legislation. Those demands proved too much for Yeltsin, who insisted on maintaining the balance of power outlined in the constitution. The Kremlin favored an agreement under which the president would agree not to dissolve the Duma and the deputies would act quickly on legislation and refrain from no-confidence votes.

Sensing that the economic crisis had profoundly weakened Yeltsin, and perhaps fearing retribution from voters if they confirmed a prime minister who had already run the government for five years, the Communists walked away from a deal they would no doubt have accepted a year earlier. The Duma voted down Chernomyrdin's candidacy by a wide margin on 31 August.

At first, the Kremlin's game plan remained unchanged. Yeltsin immediately renominated Chernomyrdin, who made policy pronouncements and otherwise behaved as if confirmation was a foregone conclusion. But when the Duma rejected him again convincingly on 7 September, Yeltsin paused before naming another prime ministerial candidate. Intense negotiations took place. Some politicians lobbied for the appointment of Moscow Mayor Yurii Luzhkov, but Luzhkov was reportedly demanding that Yeltsin step down before the end of his term. Yabloko leader Yavlinskii was among those who proposed Foreign Minister Yevgenii Primakov as a compromise figure.

In the end, Yeltsin blinked. Primakov was a surprising choice, given Yeltsin's famous reluctance to act in response to external pressure. Moreover, the president's most vocal critics in the Duma were the ones most pleased by the Primakov's candidacy. In the wake of the economic crisis, Yeltsin in effect acceded to a Communist request he had rejected many times before: to appoint a government that a majority of Duma deputies could support.

Primakov's confirmation went smoothly, but this shored up Yeltsin's position only temporarily. During a brief trip to Central Asia in October, the president appeared more feeble than ever. Television footage showed him nearly fall over during a ceremony and later take nearly 30 seconds to sign his own name to a document. The same month, the Constitutional Court finally ruled on a year-old appeal concerning whether the president could run for re-election in 2000. Although the president had repeatedly denied having plans to seek a third term, Kremlin lawyers argued that he should be entitled to run again, since he was first elected president in 1991 under a different constitution. However, the court ruled that Yeltsin was currently in his second term and therefore ineligible to seek re-election.

In November, the Constitutional Court took away another presidential lever against the Duma. The judges ruled that the electing half the Duma deputies by proportional representation was consistent with the constitution. Yeltsin himself imposed that electoral system in a 1993 decree, but presidential advisers came to believe that proportional representation worked to the advantage of opposition groups, since it was the Communists who had the most extensive party organization in the country and thus scored high on the party list vote. The Kremlin had hoped that the court would strike down the system and give the Duma more reason to fear dissolution.

By the end of the year, Yeltsin appeared weak and politically isolated. In November, he was hospitalized with pneumonia, and two weeks later he briefly visited the Kremlin in order to sack his chief of staff, Valentin Yumashev, and three deputy heads of the presidential administration. Yumashev had worked closely with the president for years, and had been the ghost-writer of Yeltsin's memoirs. His replacement, Nikolai Bordyuzha, had a reputation for loyalty but was relatively new to high office, having served as Federal Border Guards chief from December 1997 to September 1998 and Security Council secretary thereafter. For the third December in a row, Yeltsin spent part of the month convalescing. The center of power drifted toward Primakov, who took the president's place on an official visit to India, the same trip that had been postponed from January 1998 because of Yeltsin's ill health.

LESSON FOR OLIGARCHS: BE CAREFUL WHAT YOU WISH FOR . . .

One of the most important political developments of 1997 was the outbreak of clan warfare among the business elites who had helped bankroll Yeltsin's 1996 re-election campaign. The struggle continued along similar lines for the first half of 1998, but the economic crisis ruined some of the "oligarchs" and dramatically reduced the wealth and political influence of others.

Russia's political intrigues in early 1998 conformed to the pattern set during controversies over privatization the previous summer. Opposing sides battled it out in the media, since most leading newspapers and television networks were financially dependent on "sponsors" in the business community. Media financed by Vladimir Potanin's Oneksimbank supported the government's "young reformers," as did fully state-owned Russian Television, the Channel 2 network. Media linked to Boris Berezovskii's LogoVAZ empire (in particular the 51 percent state-owned Russian Public Television and the newspaper *Nezavisimaya gazeta*), Vladimir Gusinskii's Media-Most empire (especially NTV and the newspaper *Segodnya*), and the gas monopoly Gazprom tended to support Prime Minister Chernomyrdin. For their part, Chubais and Nemtsov warned against "crony capitalism" and letting "oligarchs" determine Russia's economic policies.

If Yeltsin expected the March government reshuffle to put an end to political infighting, he was far too optimistic. Unconfirmed media reports saw the hand of Berezovskii behind the sacking of Chernomyrdin; the businessman was said to be displeased with the government's plan to privatize the oil company Rosneft, and the decision to allow Oneksimbank to handle State Customs Committee funds. Whether or not he favored Chernomyrdin's departure, Berezovskii certainly did not approve of the Kirienko appointment. Newspapers under his financial control *(Nezavisimaya gazeta* and *Novye izvestiya)* published several articles attacking Kirienko' s record. Behind the scenes, Berezovskii lobbied to keep Nemtsov out of the new cabinet and urged Yeltsin to choose former Security Council Secretary Ivan Rybkin as prime minister.

Yeltsin warned Berezovskii in April that he would "drive him out of the country" if he did not stop trying to influence the composition of the new government. After Kirienko's confirmation, the president defied vigorous opposition from some business elites and kept Nemtsov on as a deputy prime minister (the new cabinet had no first deputy prime ministers). The virtually unknown Viktor Khristenko became deputy prime minister in charge of financial issues. He had served as deputy governor and later presidential representative in Chelyabinsk Oblast before becoming deputy finance minister in spring 1997, when Chubais was in charge of the finance ministry. As deputy prime minister in charge of social issues, Yeltsin appointed Oleg Sysuev, who had joined the government in 1997 at the same time as Nemtsov and quickly became identified with the "young reformers."

In another rebuke to Berezovskii, within a week of Kirienko's confirmation Yeltsin gave his blessing to the appointment of Chubais as chief executive of Unified Energy Systems. *Nezavisimaya gazeta* and Russian Public Television had argued strongly against giving Chubais that job. On 30 April Yeltsin agreed with other CIS presidents to appoint Berezovskii as CIS executive secretary. But there was no disguising the fact that the Kirienko cabinet was a victory for the "young reformers."

Throughout the short tenure of Kirienko's government, the "information war" that began in 1997 continued unabated. The same media that had attacked Chubais and Nemtsov now found fault with the "political lightweights" in Kirienko's cabinet. (At age 45, Sysuev was the oldest of the four highest-ranking ministers.) During widespread railroad blockades by striking coal miners in May, Russian Public Television and NTV, among others, put the blame squarely on the government's incompetence. In contrast, state-run Russian Television and newspapers funded by Oneksimbank characterized the protests as misguided, costly, and counterproductive, since corrupt coal industry executives (not the government) were responsible for wage delays.

Following steep declines in the stock and bond markets, Yeltsin tried to forge a consensus among top businessmen in support of the government's economic program. In early June, he met with leading bankers and heads of major companies in the energy industry. The meeting involved businessmen on opposing sides in the ongoing political dispute; Berezovskii and Gusinskii were there alongside Chubais and Potanin. In mid-June, Kirienko held two meetings with the same group of "oligarchs" within a three-day period. Kremlin officials even floated the idea of forming a special council of business elites to advise the government—a strange proposal, given the government's purported opposition to "crony capitalism."

In the end, no such council was formed. Instead, Kirienko embarked on a risky showdown with Gazprom in a desperate attempt to show the government was serious about collecting taxes. The gas monopoly contributed roughly a quarter of all federal tax revenues, but it had amassed sizable tax arrears. On 2 July, Kirienko announced that if Gazprom did not pay its taxes in full, the government would seize some company property and cancel a "trust agreement" under which chief executive Rem Vyakhirev managed a 35 percent state-owned stake in the gas monopoly. Boris Fedorov, whom Yeltsin had appointed as head of the State Tax Service in May, refused to honor an agreement to reduce Gazprom's tax bill, which the company's management had obtained while Chernomyrdin was in office.

Vyakhirev denounced the "provocation" against his company, as did a host of media outlets that were already unfavorably inclined toward the Kirienko government. The propaganda war raged for several days, with some media hailing the government's resolve to collect taxes. Outlets sympathetic to the gas monopoly (in some cases part-owned by Gazprom) decried the government's "Bolshevik" methods and drew attention to the huge debts owed to Gazprom by non-paying consumers, among them many government-funded organizations.

During the Gazprom controversy, some media raised the volume in their criticism of Yeltsin as well. On 10 July, the editor-in-chief of *Nezavisimaya gazeta* called for the creation of a "Provisional State Council" to take power and preside over early presidential and parliamentary elections. Yeltsin quickly ruled out any prospect of a "coup" or early election, but the newspaper continued to lobby for a change of political leadership.

Gazprom and government officials quietly reached an agreement on a tax payment schedule in late July. But the 17 August ruble devaluation and default on government securities sealed the fate of the Kirienko government. Yeltsin's decision to bring back Chernomyrdin was widely viewed as a victory for the "oligarchs"; Nemtsov resigned the day after Kirienko was fired. But once Yeltsin sacrificed Chernomyrdin and picked Primakov, the influence of the top bankers immediately began to wane.

Primakov was the first Russian prime minister to have broad-based support in both houses of parliament. He was consequently less reliant on the "oligarchs" for political backing. Although his government agreed to provide financial assistance to a few "socially important" banks, Primakov's policies were expected to benefit Russian industrialists more than the bankers and the oil and gas lobby, which had done well during Chernomyrdin's tenure. Some business elites were dissatisfied with the new premier within weeks of his appointment. But by that time Yeltsin's own position was too weak for him to sack Primakov, even if the "oligarchs" could have persuaded him to do so.

Furthermore, top businessmen were licking their wounds after the financial crisis. The banks that had invested heavily in government securities suffered huge losses, and some oil companies faced possible asset seizures by foreign creditors. By the end of the year, the business empires of Aleksandr Smolenskii (founder of SBS-Agro) and Vladimir Vinogradov (founder of Inkombank) were in tatters. The economic downturn harmed Gusinskii's Media-Most empire as well, since advertising revenues dropped sharply.

During the battle over Kirienko's confirmation, *Nezavisimaya gazeta* had warned that the president would win a Pyrrhic victory if installing the Kirienko government provoked the "oligarchs" to oppose Yeltsin himself. Similarly, the fall of the Kirienko government and the "young reformers" can be considered a Pyrrhic victory for the "oligarchs." After August, Russia's richest men found both their net worth and their future prospects for political influence significantly reduced.

PRESIDENTIAL CANDIDATES PREPARE FOR 2000

Throughout the year, leading candidates to replace Yeltsin prepared for the next presidential election. Moscow Mayor Yurii Luzhkov appeared to be the rising star in the pack. He continued to forge economic agreements with various regional leaders, and the Moscow city government expanded the number of newspapers under its financial control. Most important, Luzhkov founded a new political movement, Fatherland. At the time of its founding congress in December, Fatherland claimed the support of some 20 governors and many mayors. By the end of the year those endorsing Luzhkov for president included Sergei Shakhrai, a longtime Yeltsin ally who had held various government and Kremlin posts until Yeltsin sacked him in June; and former Federal Border Guards head Andrei Nikolaev, who won a by-election to the Duma with Luzhkov's help in April 1998. Longtime Yeltsin spokesman Sergei Yastrzhembskii went to work for Luzhkov soon after the president fired him in September (Yastrzhembskii had reportedly urged Yeltsin to appoint Luzhkov prime minister). Luzhkov strongly supported the Russian-Belarusian Union, to which he wished to add Yugoslavia, and spoke out on behalf of ethnic Russians in former Soviet republics. For instance, in March he accused the Latvian authorities of pursuing a "policy of genocide and discrimination against our former compatriots." The 1998 economic downturn could win Luzhkov some support, since he had long called for more steps to promote domestic industry and had criticized "monetarist" economic policies and the International Monetary Fund. On the other hand, the economic crisis dealt a blow to businesses in the capital, threatening to impair Luzhkov's fund-raising abilities and tarnish his image as the man who brought prosperity to Moscow.

Aleksandr Lebed, who placed third in the first round of the 1996 presidential election, kept his hopes alive for 2000 by winning election as governor in resource-rich Krasnoyarsk Krai. He won easily despite the fact that Luzhkov and several celebrities personally campaigned on behalf of the incumbent. Lebed had some celebrity backing as well from French film star Alain Delon, but his own charisma and hefty financial support from Boris Berezovskii, among others, contributed more to his victory. Berezovskii claimed not to support Lebed for president but explained that he wanted to preserve Lebed's political viability with the hope of drawing "patriotic" votes away from Luzhkov in the next presidential race.

Opinion polls consistently showed Communist leader Zyuganov commanding about 20 percent support in a hypothetical presidential race, giving him an excellent chance of making a runoff election. But disunity within Communist ranks was apparent throughout 1998. In the spring, there was an abortive attempt by radicals to establish a "Leninist-Stalinist platform" within the party. On the other end of the spectrum within the party, Duma Speaker Gennadii Seleznev in October announced his intention to run for president. Although Seleznev would have virtually no chance of victory, any rival Communist candidate would harm Zyuganov's prospects for reaching the second round. Luzhkov might attract votes from "patriots" who were not strong Communists but had supported Zyuganov in previous elections. Zyuganov and Luzhkov flirted with an alliance in September, but both the Communists and the mayor backed off, presumably to avoid alienating their core constituencies.

Yabloko leader Yavlinskii, the fourth-place finisher in the last presidential election, did not gain much ground in opinion polls in 1998, but he held on to his base and looked poised for a possible role as kingmaker. He also won the support of the popular private network NTV, although Luzhkov received generally favorable treatment on that network as well. The economic collapse confirmed that Yavlinskii acted wisely in refusing invitations to join the government on several occasions since 1996.

Liberal Democratic Party of Russia leader Vladimir Zhirinovsky, who came in fifth in 1996, continued to make headlines with occasionally outrageous rhetoric and scuffles with political opponents. However, as in previous years, in key Duma votes he usually supported the government. Probably inspired by Lebed's example, Zhirinovsky announced plans to run for governor of Leningrad Oblast in 1999. When that election date was postponed, Zhirinovsky said he would run for governor of Sverdlovsk Oblast instead.

Two prominent politicians saw their hopes of gaining the presidency fade in

1998. The big loser of the year was undoubtedly Viktor Chernomyrdin. When he was prime minister, he had consistently denied harboring presidential ambitions. Within a week of his dismissal in March, he announced that he would run for president after all. The move appeared to be a desperate attempt to forestall defections from his Our Home Is Russia movement, whose claim to be the "party of power" now looked decidedly shaky. Several regional leaders left Our Home Is Russia, and Luzhkov appeared most likely to win their support. Even as prime minister, Chernomyrdin had lacked charisma and his prospects in a future presidential election were questionable. Having been rejected by the president in March and by the Duma in September, Chernomyrdin's chances seemed close to zero.

As for Boris Nemtsov, he remained politically active after leaving the government, founding the Young Russia movement and forming a center-right coalition with Anatolii Chubais, Yegor Gaidar, and Boris Fedorov. But the economic crisis probably closed the door on a presidential bid by the rising star of 1997 who was once, fleetingly, regarded as Yeltsin's chosen successor.

Sidebar: *THE COMMUNISTS AND THE JEWISH QUESTION*

by LAURA BELIN

Following the 1996 presidential election, the conventional wisdom in Russia held that the Communists had missed their last chance to gain power and that, consequently, anti-Communist rhetoric would gradually fade as a political weapon. But surprisingly, anti-communism experienced a revival in late 1998. For the first time in five years, some prominent politicians called for banning the Communist Party. In addition, the relationship between the party and the mainstream media, never a friendly one, became more acrimonious than at any time since the 1996 presidential campaign.

The catalyst for these developments was the appointment of the Yevgenii Primakov government in September. Although a wide range of political groups, including Grigorii Yavlinskii's Yabloko movement, welcomed Primakov, others in Russia's "democratic" camp were less comfortable with the new premier. They had been despondent when President Yeltsin replaced the liberal Foreign Minister Andrei Kozyrev with Primakov in January 1996, a move widely viewed as a sop to the Communists and Vladimir Zhirinovsky's Liberal Democratic Party of Russia after their strong showing in the December 1995 parliamentary elections.

The return of Viktor Gerashchenko as Central Bank chairman under Primakov and the appointment of Communist Party member Yevgenii Maslyukov as first deputy prime minister in charge of economic policy aroused more concern about the government's "drift to the left." Former government officials like Russia's Democratic Choice leader Yegor Gaidar and Forward, Russia! leader Boris Fedorov blamed Gerashchenko's lax monetary policy for the rampant inflation in the early 1990s. Although Maslyukov was a moderate voice in the Communist Party (he had defied his colleagues to join Sergei Kirienko's government as trade and industry minister), he nonetheless advocated monetary emissions and trade policies that disturbed those who supported the economic strategy of previous Russian governments.

Many Moscow journalists were also wary of the new government. Some complained that cabinet officials became less accessible to journalists following Primakov's appointment. In September and October, numerous media reports played up fears concerning the government's economic plans. For instance, *Kommersant-Daily* published an alleged draft plan that involved banning the use of U.S. dollars.

Meanwhile, Communist leader Gennadii Zyuganov renewed his push for "supervisory boards" at Russia's nationwide television networks. He had intermittently advocated establishing such boards for years, since coverage on major television networks was with rare exceptions slanted against the Communists. Journalists condemned efforts to increase outside supervision of their activities.

In this charged atmosphere, Communist firebrand Albert Makashov (who had participated in the October 1993 assault on the Ostankino television tower) handed the media a stick with which to beat his party. At an anti-government rally in October, he called for quotas on Jews in high office and for "shipping off to another world" various unnamed "kikes, shylocks and bloodsuckers." The comments provoked an uproar, but Makashov refused to retract his statements and made more anti-Semitic remarks in subsequent interviews.

The scandal escalated in November, when the Duma rejected a proposed motion to censure Makashov. Duma Speaker Gennadii Seleznev was the only member of the Communist faction to vote for censure. President Boris Yeltsin issued a statement condemning "any attempt to insult ethnic groups." Prominent businessman Boris Berezovskii, who is Jewish, advocated banning the Communist Party on the grounds that they were inciting ethnic hatred. Gaidar and former First Deputy Prime Minister Anatolii Chubais also endorsed a ban. Not all shared their view: Primakov worried that banning the party with the largest representation in parliament "may destabilize the situation." Duma Foreign Affairs Committee Chairman Vladimir Lukin of Yabloko warned against turning Communists into martyrs, while Moscow Mayor Yurii Luzhkov said Makashov's "disgraceful" and "savage" remarks did not justify banning an entire party.

But the controversy kept the Communists in the unflattering media spotlight for some time. In fact, Communist leaders portrayed the scandal as an attempt by the media and the architects of failed economic policies to deflect public attention from their miserable living standards. Not long after the Duma declined to censure him, Makashov accused an NTV journalist of "acting worse than the worst of the yids." Meanwhile, Zyuganov issued a statement concerning "provocative attacks on our party," which alleged that "the haters of Russia are trying hard to force the so-called Jewish question on us." The statement charged that "the servants of criminal capital" were "the main organizers and instigators of a new wave of anti-Semitism in Russia."

The media certainly made the most of the scandal—some journalists even suggested Communists might have planned the November assassination of Duma deputy Galina Starovoitova, a vocal critic of Makashov. But Communist leaders also helped keep the controversy alive. In mid-December, Duma Security Committee Chairman Viktor Ilyukhin, a more high-ranking party member than Makashov, asserted during a meeting of the Duma's impeachment commission that "large-scale genocide [against the Russian people] would have been less serious if the president's entourage and the government included representatives of other ethnic groups and did not consist exclusively of Jews." The Duma voted down a motion to condemn Ilyukhin's remarks, and some members of the Communist faction called for revoking the accreditation of television networks in response to their coverage of Ilyukhin.

However, the controversy appeared unlikely to have far-reaching political consequences. In December, the Procurator-General's Office announced it was considering criminal charges against Makashov, but prospects for a trial were slim, as the Duma would no doubt block any motion to lift his immunity from criminal prosecution. Despite the president's 12 November call for "urgent radical measures" to stop "manifestations of ethnic and political extremism," a serious effort to ban the Communist Party seemed highly improbable. Yeltsin had tried that route once, in the wake of the August 1991 coup, only to have his decree overturned by the Constitutional Court. Besides, banning the country's largest political party ahead of parliamentary and presidential elections scheduled for 1999 and 2000 would fatally undermine the fairness of the balloting. But the events of late 1998 demonstrated that at least some Russian politicians continued to believe in anti-communism as a powerful rallying cry.

GOVERNORS EMERGE STRONGER

by NATAN SHKLYAR

Russia ended 1997 in the midst of a power struggle between the federal authorities and the regions. The driving force behind the battle was the 1996 institutional change mandating that regional executives be elected by their constituents rather than appointed by the president. The August 1998 economic crisis abruptly upset the precarious balance of power that was evolving from the tug-of-war between center and periphery, and by the end of the year regional leaders emerged strengthened while the federal center was largely inactive. At the same time, no serious threats to the integrity of the federation materialized, separatism being an unsustainable policy for most regions, which still depended heavily on subsidies from the federal center.

ELECTIONS SECURE REPUBLIC PRESIDENTS, OUST REGIONAL GOVERNORS

Although President Boris Yeltsin and his associates debated the possibility of returning to the post-1991 practice of appointing governors, regional elections continued across the country. Incumbent leaders of ethnic republics who stood for re-election in 1998 were, with few exceptions, overwhelmingly re-elected. Ingushetiya's President Ruslan Aushev and Chuvashiya's Nikolai Fedorov won with strong majorities. Mordoviya's President Nikolai Merkushkin and Bashkortostan's President Murtaza Rakhimov won by banning key opponents from their races. In Bashkortostan, a ruling by the Russian Supreme Court reinstating opposition candidates was simply ignored. Dagestan's leader Magomedali Magomedov changed an ethnically-balanced constitution to win a second term, removing opposition candidates along the way. One key exception was in North Osetiya, where Aleksandr Dzasokhov defeated incumbent republican President Akhsarbek Galazov. And in Kareliya, Communist Prime Minister Viktor Stepanov lost to Petrozavodsk Mayor Sergei Katanandov.

Governors of the ethnically Russian regions, oblasts, and krais had more difficulty at the polls, often falling to the mayors of regional capitals. On the same day that Kareliya's Stepanov lost, Smolensk Mayor Aleksandr Prokhorov, backed by both local Communists and the presidential administration, unseated Governor Anatolii Glushenkov. Incumbents also fell in Lipetsk and Penza.

Perhaps the most watched gubernatorial race of the year took place in Krasnoyarsk Krai, where former general Aleksandr Lebed defied the polls and surged from behind on 17 May to defeat incumbent Governor Valerii Zubov. Lebed focused his campaign on the rural areas of the krai and enjoyed the support of magnate Boris Berezovskii and Anatolii Bykov, a Rossiiskii Kredit Bank vice president who chaired the Krasnoyarsk Aluminum Plant (KrAZ) Board of Directors and allegedly had ties to the criminal underworld. Lebed's victory set him on the path for presidential elections scheduled for June 2000.

Supporters of the incumbent governor won key legislative elections in regions like Orel, Volgograd, Nizhnii Novgorod, Rostov, and Krasnodar, and in the republics of Chuvashiya and Kalmykiya. The Communist Party and other opposition groups did particularly well in the 1998 legislative elections, often changing the regional status quo. For example, Communists did well in Smolensk, Krasnoyarsk, Orel, Orenburg, Omsk, and Volgograd, but lost many seats in the Kemerovo and Chuvashiya legislatures, where they had once been strong.

Governor Eduard Rossel saw his support drop in the Sverdlovsk legislature, but he managed to maintain a slim majority despite gains by the Communists and the supporters of Yekaterinburg Mayor Arkadii Chernetskii, a Rossel rival. St. Petersburg's December elections resulted in a highly fractured city parliament that was strongly divided on its future relations with Oblast Governor Vladimir Yakovlev.

REGIONAL ECONOMIES WEATHER THE CRISIS

Economically, the year can be divided into two periods, before and after the crisis that began on 17 August. While the economy appeared relatively stable at the beginning of the year, there were already clear signs of trouble. Most regions began 1998 with mounting wage and pension arrears, and blamed the center for not transferring the money required to make the payments. The vast majority of Russia's 89 regions remained heavily dependent on federal transfers, with only a handful actually contributing to the federal budget. Industrial giants, long overdue for restructuring, remained dormant across Russia, their employees not paid for months and with few hopes for orders in the near future. Primorskii Krai, in the Russian Far East, suffered from chronic energy shortages, mostly because federal and regional agencies failed to pay their utility bills to the local power producer, Dalenergo. Slumping oil prices on world markets severely undercut federal tax revenues and hurt regions such as Tatarstan, home to some major oil refineries.

The harsh economic conditions inspired people across the country to take to the streets, demanding payment of long-overdue salaries and pensions. Teachers, medical workers, nuclear scientists, and pensioners blocked traffic in regions as diverse as Chelyabinsk, Perm, Irkutsk, and Nizhnii Novgorod. Coal miners from Sakhalin and Primorskii Krai to Kemerovo and Komi were especially active in May, blockading railways and causing millions of rubles in losses from delayed cargo and passenger trains, until the government appeased them with short-term federal handouts and promises of future payments. Protests were supposed to culminate in a nationwide trade union and Communist-sponsored rally on 7 October, but the actual turnout was poor and the action's impact meager.

When the crisis hit in full force on 17 August, the regions were less affected by it than Moscow, mainly because regional banks had very limited exposure to the GKO (treasury bond) market. Governors had mixed reactions to the crisis, with some imposing price and export controls on essential goods while others stuck with market mechanisms. Prices for consumer goods began to rise drastically despite attempts to avoid that scenario. Administrative measures were generally ineffective and led to shortages of many goods, since suppliers chose not to sell them for artificially low prices. Price controls and export quotas were difficult to enforce, and many governors quietly abandoned them within a few weeks. Although a number of businesses closed, waiting for the situation to stabilize, some local producers and exporters benefited from a weaker ruble and the disappearance of imported goods from the domestic market.

The adverse effects of the crisis were compounded by the drought that plagued much of central Russia and resulted in one of the worst harvests since the end of World War II. Fortunately, Russia still had about 20 million tons of crops stored from the phenomenally successful harvest of 1997. The residents of the Far North faced the winter with shortages of heating fuel and mounting wage arrears. Following the example of the center, many of the regions defaulted on their foreign and domestic debts, although the cities of Moscow and St. Petersburg remained solvent. Direct foreign investors, like ICN-Pharmaceuticals, generally cut back their operations while in principle reaffirming their commitment to the Russian market. Authorized by federal legislation, some regions introduced a new sales tax, thus raising hopes of higher revenue in 1999.

FEDERAL AUTHORITY WANES

Yeltsin's chronic poor health, a weak presidential administration, frequent government reshuffles, and the economic crisis made it difficult for the Kremlin to define and enforce a coherent policy toward the regions. With hopes of bringing regional separatism to heel, the Kremlin started the year with the presidential administration threatening to scrutinize all regional laws to determine whether they complied with federal legislation. The justice ministry estimated that between one-third and one-half of all regional laws were unconstitutional. Meanwhile, the center continued signing legally questionable power-sharing agreements with regions, bringing the total number of agreements to 46 of the 89 regions (the last was a treaty with the city of Moscow signed 16 June). The ethnic republics generally favored the use of such bilateral treaties because they gained significant concessions from Moscow, but several leaders of the ethnically Russian oblasts objected to them, calling for a consistent federal policy toward all regions.

The presidential administration, which had once monopolized regional policy, yielded control over this issue to the government. After Yeltsin appointed Viktoriya Mitina in November 1997 to be his regional policy aide, the Kremlin's grip on the regions weakened. Mitina was not able to keep assertive regions in line, and the election of a former convict as Nizhnii Novgorod mayor, as well as Lebed's victory in Krasnoyarsk, were the last straws triggering her dismissal in May. A former KGB officer, Vladimir Putin, replaced Mitina and took a much more hard-line approach toward delinquent regions. His staff collected meticulous information on how governors spent federal subsidies. However, Yeltsin transferred Putin to head the Federal Security Service in July, and Yeltsin again appointed a weak aide, Oleg Sysuev, to run regional policy. A former mayor of Samara and deputy prime minister in the Chernomyrdin and Kirienko governments, Sysuev openly admitted in October that the presidency had transferred responsibility for regions to the government. Although there was some talk in Moscow about reducing the number of regions from 89 to as few as eight to make the federation more manageable, this idea never came close to implementation.

Fiscal federalism remained the focal point of center–periphery relations, as Moscow and the regions battled over tax revenue allocation. It became common for regions to complain that the center never transferred promised subsidies for wage and pension payments, and for Moscow to counter that the money had been sent long ago. Moscow tried to keep tight control over how governors spent federal subsidies, for instance preventing Sverdlovsk from creating its own regional bank with federal money. Due to the poor transparency of fiscal transfers, however, many governors managed to use funds for purposes other than those outlined in the federal conditions attached to grants. To address this problem, the Kirienko government began signing special treaties with regions requiring them to comply with federal standards in revenue allocation, tax collection, and debt restructuring in exchange for access to further federal subsidies. Chelyabinsk and Khakasiya signed such agreements, making their relations with the center more transparent, whereas St. Petersburg, Perm, and Krasnoyarsk refused to comply. The effort apparently was abandoned after Kirienko's removal.

In an attempt to keep unruly leaders in line, Moscow flexed its law enforcement muscle by cracking down on corruption among regional officials. In Tula, Vologda, Kemerovo, and Vladimir oblasts former governors were prosecuted on various charges of bribery, embezzlement, or abuse of power. Federal agents also arrested current deputy governors in Tver, Voronezh, and Kursk oblasts on charges ranging from bribery to embezzlement to improper conduct. Regional auditors also found that public funds had been used improperly in Nizhnii Novgorod and Leningrad oblasts. Finally, a special team of federal agents conducted a thorough investigation of corruption and crime in the highest echelons of Dagestan after armed groups temporarily took control of the republican administration building on 21 May.

GOVERNORS GROW STRONGER, BUT FACE CHALLENGES

With Moscow's strength waning, the governors gained considerable leverage. For instance, Kemerovo's Aman Tuleev used miners' strikes to force more subsidies and autonomy out of Moscow while Sakha (Yakutiya) sought to secure its gold reserves independent of Moscow. Ethnic republics relied on nationalist and separatist threats to assert their authority, as in the case of Tatarstan's citizenship law passed on 16 April. This legislation permitted residents to be citizens of Tatarstan without being citizens of Russia. Except for Chechnya's on-going independence campaign, the only outright separatist threat came from Kirsan Ilyumzhinov, the eccentric president of Kalmykiya, who announced in November that he would declare his republic an associate member of the Russian Federation if the center did not fulfill its financial obligations. Ilyumzhinov retracted his threat, however, as soon as Moscow reprimanded him. Nizhnii Novgorod defied the Constitutional Court's authority in February by directing local companies to pay salaries before paying taxes, directly contradicting an earlier ruling. Also, Moscow Mayor Yurii Luzhkov ignored the court's decision to outlaw residential registration requirements. Finally, the economic crisis challenged the loyalties of local military commanders, who found their ill-fed and poorly clad troops increasingly dependent on regional authorities for supplies and infrastructure.

Chechnya remained a unique case. Separatists held Yeltsin's envoy to the region, Valentin Vlasov, hostage for six months before releasing him. Vlasov's predicament only highlighted Chechen President Aslan Maskhadov's waning influence in the region as several field commanders, backed by thousands of armed troops, opposed him for not taking a hard enough line against Moscow. Although Maskhadov backed Chechen independence, Moscow considered him a more reliable negotiating partner than most other Chechen leaders. As the republic's problems only grew worse, Moscow seemed even more inclined to accept Chechnya's de facto withdrawal from the Russian Federation and to build up a tighter security ring around Chechnya's borders. Federal promises to rebuild the Chechen economy were not realized. Perhaps the most remarkable feature of Chechnya's political limbo was that oil from Azerbaijan, which in November 1997 had started to flow across the province to the Russian port of Novorossiisk, continued to cross the territory with only occasional interruptions in the course of the year.

One of the most significant methods of power consolidation for regional governors was acquisition of partial regional ownership in various enterprises. In some cases, like Sverdlovsk and St. Petersburg, the governor offered banks tax breaks as well as licenses to operate with the regional budget funds in exchange for a controlling stake in the bank's stock. (The success of such plans has yet to be demonstrated.) Rostov Oblast gained control of Rostselmash, a giant producer of agricultural machinery, while Bashkortostan created a state-run monopoly in the revenue-generating energy sector. Samara's governor, in contrast, persuaded the federal center to transfer ownership of several large enterprises to the oblast in exchange for forgiving federal debt to the region. Nizhnii Novogorod did the same, taking advantage of the chaos surrounding the financial crisis. Perhaps the biggest coup for regional leaders was Yeltsin's decision to transfer 33 percent of the ownership of Unified Energy System, the electric power grid monopoly, to regional governments. This move greatly inhibited the company's ability to collect debts for power usage from delinquent regional governments and enterprises as well as its capacity to institute higher electricity rates. The August financial crisis and resulting governing paralysis in the center presented regional leaders with vast opportunities to strengthen their positions. Indeed, the so-called "oligarchs" were badly battered by the collapse of their financial empires, which were heavily tied to the government's GKO pyramid scheme. Similarly, oil and gas barons were weakened by the slumping prices on international markets. On the other hand, regional governors have secured greater federal concessions and pocketed many regional banks and industrial enterprises.

Successive new prime ministers in Moscow clearly recognized the growing importance of the regional leaders, but most governors rejected federal overtures to join the cabinet. In Primakov's government only Vadim Gustov, governor of Leningrad Oblast, gave up his elected seat to become first deputy prime minister in charge of regions, CIS, and youth affairs. Primakov also invited leaders of the eight regional associations into the presidium, or inner circle, of the cabinet of ministers, theoretically allowing them to participate in the highest level of policy making. In practice the inclusion of the governors in the presidium gave them little additional power, however.

Although regional leaders signed a number of bilateral treaties with other regions, the governors have failed to act as a united front in their dealings with Moscow. Consequently, they did not capitalize on their growing power potential as an elite group. Federation Council meetings showed that governors see themselves first as lobbyists for their particular region, and only then as senators with a national agenda. Tomsk Oblast Governor Viktor Kress, who heads the Siberian Accord regional association of 19 republics, krais, and oblasts, said that the association's member regions cannot focus solely on economics because their interests are too divergent.

AN EYE TOWARDS THE PRESIDENTIAL ELECTION

With Yeltsin's authority waning and presidential elections approaching in 2000, Luzhkov and Lebed led the charge among governors in the race to win the presidency. Although the crisis considerably battered the Moscow economy, Luzhkov was still planning to ride on his reputation as a successful administrator who presided over the economic rebirth of the city. Of course, his major disadvantage was the traditional resentment felt in the provinces against the capital. To promote his candidacy in the regions, Luzhkov founded the Otechestvo (Fatherland) political movement on 19 December and spent a good part of the latter half of 1998 establishing a presence in almost every region.

As Luzhkov's campaigning intensified and his influence spread throughout Russia, many mid-level regional officials began to view Fatherland as the new "party of power." This perception brought many regional leaders into Luzhkov's orbit. A large number of governors attended the party's 19 November preliminary organizational conference. Governor Ivan Sklyarov of Nizhnii Novgorod openly backed Luzhkov's candidacy, and in Irkutsk a vice governor chaired the local Fatherland branch. In Samara, Voronezh, and Tver local politicians, businessmen, and journalists were competing for power positions within the new party, which they hoped will promote their political ambitions should Luzhkov win the presidency.

Lebed has had greater difficulty turning his governorship into a presidential launch pad. By the end of the year his popularity in Krasnoyarsk was rapidly declining. Most local residents grew resentful of Lebed's frequent absences and his reliance on Muscovites to run the krai's affairs. Most importantly, Lebed had a falling out with his powerful supporter Bykov, who openly said that backing the general was a mistake because he was simply using the region as a stepping stone for his presidential ambitions. Lebed's Honor and Motherland movement and the Popular-Republican Party have failed to develop effective regional networks, and Lebed himself was not successful in gathering the support of other regional leaders, even in Siberia.

SEEKING FOREIGN TIES

Foreign policy and international trade were areas of both contention and compromise for the Kremlin and the regions in 1998. Governors were very bold in making foreign policy pronouncements. When rumors began circulating that Yeltsin might transfer the southern Kuril Islands to Japan in order to normalize relations between the two countries, the governors of Sakhalin Oblast and Primorskii Krai vocally defended the islands as traditionally Russian territory. Saratov's Governor Ayatskov said he would unilaterally close the oblast's border with Kazakhstan to halt the illegal flow of alcohol, arms, and narcotics. Ayatskov also visited Ukraine in July and November to sign trade agreements and develop an economic basis for increasing Russian influence in Ukraine.

Sometimes the foreign activities of Russian regions touched on sensitive international issues and went directly against Moscow's policy line. For example, some regions developed trade ties to Georgia's rebellious province of Abkhazia and some sent representatives to a conference that recognized the Turkish policy on Cyprus. Dagestani residents clashed with their neighbors across the Azerbaijani border.

Driven by the desire to keep regional foreign activities limited to economics, the Russian Ministry of Foreign Affairs created a special department to coordinate the regions' foreign policies. Moscow and Irkutsk, however, clashed over how to share power and profits from potentially lucrative energy export deals to China. Unfortunately, foreign direct investment in the regions dropped from about $4 billion in 1997 to only $2 billion in 1998.

Foreign leaders sometimes sought to avoid Moscow by appealing directly to the regions. Belarus President Alyaksandr Lukashenka worked hard to develop bilateral relations with Russian regions where the governors opposed Yeltsin. He visited Primorskii Krai and Murmansk Oblast, and the governors of Orenburg, Krasnodar, Tula, Yaroslavl, Stavropol, Kostroma, and Vladimir visited him in

Minsk. Although the Kremlin does not like Lukashenka's active networking in the regions, Belarus has signed agreements with 55 regions.

Overall the governors gained increasing authority in their newly elected positions during 1998. Throughout the year, it became evident that in addition to its enormous economic problems, Russia had yet to establish an effective federal structure. Yet the weakness of individual regions and Moscow's capacity to redistribute revenue among them suggest that the overall integrity of the Russian Federation is not in danger. At the same time, debates about the number of regions in the federation, whether regional executives should be elected or appointed, and whether bilateral treaties are acceptable suggest that the very structure of federal relations will continue to change.

Sidebar: *MURDER SILENCES STAROVOITOVA AND ROKHLIN*

by LAURA BELIN

Two high-profile murders in 1998 stunned the Russian elite and even cynical observers of the Russian political scene. In July, a single shot to the head claimed the life of Duma deputy and retired Lieutenant-General Lev Rokhlin, 51. Four months later, two assailants gunned down Duma deputy and legendary democratic activist Galina Starovoitova at the age of 52.

Rokhlin and Starovoitova were far from the first prominent Russians to be murdered, nor even the first Duma deputies killed. But their deaths were the most shocking since the still-unsolved murder of television journalist Vladislav Listev in March 1995.

Rokhlin and Starovoitova came from vastly different backgrounds and entered high politics under different circumstances. But both held firm beliefs that ultimately drove them into opposition to President Boris Yeltsin, whom they had supported early in their political careers. Neither hesitated to criticize what they viewed as disastrous policy failures, and while the Russian media frequently broadcast their opinions, neither's advice was heeded by the authorities.

THE LONGSTANDING POLITICAL ACTIVIST

Galina Starovoitova got an early start in expressing her political views. As a 22-year-old student in Leningrad in 1968, she signed a letter opposing the Soviet-led invasion of Czechoslovakia and was subsequently questioned by the KGB. For most of the next 20 years, she lived in Leningrad and devoted herself to scholarly work in the fields of ethnography and sociology. In 1987 she moved to Moscow as a senior associate of the USSR Academy of Sciences' Center for the Study of Inter-Ethnic Relations. From that time onward, she spoke out in favor of the right of Nagorno-Karabakh, populated mainly by ethnic Armenians, to secede from Azerbaijan. This stance earned her immediate and lasting popularity in Armenia. In May 1989, she won a seat in the USSR Congress of People's Deputies from a district in Yerevan with more than 75 percent of the vote in the first round, even though she had never lived in Armenia.

Starovoitova became active in the Inter-Regional Group in the Congress of People's Deputies and was an ally of renowned dissident Andrei Sakharov. In June 1990, voters in Leningrad elected her to a seat in the RSFSR's Congress of People's Deputies, where she became a member of the Democratic Russia group. A supporter of Boris Yeltsin, then chairman of the RFSFR Supreme Soviet, Starovoitova joined his Supreme Consultative Council and became his adviser on nationalities questions following the August 1991 coup attempt. She held that post until November 1992.

In the first few months after the collapse of the USSR, Starovoitova was considered an influential member of Yeltsin's circle—some Russian media even mentioned her as a possible candidate for the post of defense minister. Although some Democratic Russia activists disagreed with Yeltsin's economic policies, Starovoitova supported those policies and acting Prime Minister Yegor Gaidar. After becoming a co-chairman of the Democratic Russia movement in 1993, she supported Yeltsin throughout that year in his battles with the parliamentary opposition in the Supreme Soviet, even as some of the president's erstwhile allies condemned his use of force to disband the parliament.

Starovoitova finally broke with Yeltsin over the war in Chechnya, which she viewed as a "crude use" of "notorious tools of imperial policy." During the campaign before the 1995 parliamentary elections, Democratic Russia threw its support behind Grigorii Yavlinskii's Yabloko movement (which, of all the movements in the "democratic" camp, had the best election prospects). Meanwhile, Starovoitova campaigned successfully as an independent for a Duma seat in St. Petersburg. She did not join the Yabloko faction in the Duma.

After a brief attempt to run for president in 1996, which ended when the Central Electoral Commission refused to register her as a candidate, Starovoitova worked to secure Yeltsin's re-election. She later said she had sought to run for president with a view toward eventually calling on her supporters to vote for Yeltsin.

But Starovoitova no longer had the president's ear. She spoke out on many topics, particularly those relating to human rights and ethnic relations, but she remained a marginal figure on the political scene. In April 1998, she even parted ways with Lev Ponomarev and Gleb Yakunin, with whom she had long shared the chairmanship of the Democratic Russia party.

THE ACCIDENTAL POLITICIAN

Whereas Starovoitova was a political veteran by the time she won a Duma seat, career soldier Lev Rokhlin was an accidental politician. He was awarded a medal for his service in Afghanistan in the early 1980s but did not gain nationwide fame until he commanded the force that led the ground assault on Grozny, the capital of the breakaway republic of Chechnya, in January 1995. He retained a good reputation despite that war's unpopularity, thanks to his refusal of a medal offered for his service in Chechnya.

Rokhlin became politically active only in September 1995, when he agreed to become the number three candidate on the party list of Prime Minister Viktor Chernomyrdin's Our Home Is Russia movement, three months before the elections to the State Duma. He did not actively seek the spot, nor was he the movement's first choice—he was approached after better-known figures, including retired Colonel General Boris Gromov, had defected from the prime minister's bloc. Like many political groups that year, Our Home Is Russia wanted a general on its election list. Rokhlin agreed to run, he said at the time, because he thought increased access to government officials would help him in lobby on behalf of the chronically under-funded military.

After the parliamentary election, Rokhlin announced plans to return to military service. His declared intention prompted some commentators to accuse Our Home Is Russia of defrauding the electorate, since the bloc's top two candidates, Chernomyrdin and film-maker Nikita Mikhalkov, had already declined to take up their seats in the Duma. Rokhlin changed his mind under pressure and was eventually appointed chairman of the Duma's Defense Committee.

For a while, Rokhlin remained loyal to the government, and he supported Yeltsin's re-election in 1996. He spoke out frequently on military issues. Immediately after the presidential election, he made public accusations of corruption at high levels in the military. At the same time, together with Aleksandr Lebed, he successfully promoted the candidacy of Igor Rodionov for the post of defense minister.

During the second half of 1996, Rokhlin became more critical of some official policies. After Russian troops were withdrawn from Chechnya, he cautioned that the federal government was far from finding a long-term solution to the problems there. In one interview, he warned that in the future the breakaway republic would become a hub for terrorism in the Caucasus region. In February 1997, he embarrassed the governments of Russia and Armenia when he revealed during a speech to the Duma that Russian officials had illegally transferred a large quantity of weapons to Armenia from 1994 to 1996.

But it was not until the summer of 1997 that Rokhlin made a final break from the Yeltsin regime. Increasingly frustrated at funding shortfalls for the Russian armed forces, and angered by the May 1997 dismissal of Defense Minister Igor Rodionov, Rokhlin waited until the Duma adjourned for summer recess, then issued an appeal blaming Yeltsin for dire conditions in the armed forces and for the war in Chechnya.

Yeltsin was outraged, as were leaders of Our Home Is Russia, but it was impossible to dislodge Rokhlin from the chairmanship of the Defense Committee while the Duma was not in session. He continued to criticize the president over the summer and set about creating a new movement to support the armed forces and defense industry. Undeterred by Yeltsin's vow to "sweep aside the Rokhlins with their counterproductive actions," he held public meetings in several cities to drum up support.

In Moscow, his most prominent supporters were Communist Party leaders. By the time his Movement to Support the Army held its founding congress in September, Rokhlin was calling for public protests to force Yeltsin to resign. His increasingly radical rhetoric estranged him further from his former allies. At one press conference, he even claimed that the presidential administration was planning to discredit him politically and perhaps "physically eliminate" him. But the Communists and their allies held enough Duma seats to block the removal of Rokhlin from the chairmanship of the Defense Committee. Responding to charges that he betrayed Our Home Is Russia by denouncing the president and government and by forming an opposition movement, Rokhlin replied, "I didn't betray them—they betrayed me."

In subsequent months, Rokhlin faced a criminal investigation for allegedly vowing to oust Yeltsin's "hated regime" (he denied calling for unconstitutional means of political struggle and claimed some opponents and media misinterpreted his remarks). By the end of 1997 he was demanding Yeltsin's impeachment. Yet Rokhlin was dissatisfied with his new political allies also, accusing the Communists of complicity in a "plot" to remove him from the Defense Committee. Communist Party leader Gennadii Zyuganov denied the existence of such a plot, but the Communists did agree to a redistribution of the committee chairmanships that forced Rokhlin out in May 1998.

During the last months of his life, Rokhlin announced that his Movement to Support the Army would sue the defense ministry for failing to meet its financial obligations toward military personnel. He also vowed to sue Defense Minister Igor Sergeev for alleged "crimes" committed against the armed forces while carrying out military reform. In less than three years one of the army's most prominent generals had become one of the loudest critics of Russia's commander in chief and military leadership.

SKEPTICISM GREETS MURDER INVESTIGATIONS

News of Rokhlin's death spread the morning of 3 July 1998. He had been shot in the head while lying in bed at his dacha. Suicide was ruled out, but investigators quickly seized on another simple explanation: family violence. Within hours, an interior ministry spokesman announced that Rokhlin's wife, Tamara, had confessed to killing her husband with his own gun, on which her fingerprints were found.

However, Rokhlin's daughter and son-in-law claimed Tamara Rokhlina was innocent. They denied Rokhlin had been drunk the night of his murder or had argued with his wife. They alleged that she had confessed only because her family's lives had been threatened. They further alleged that a second bullet was found embedded in a wall of another room at the dacha, and speculated that hired killers murdered Rokhlin and forced his widow to fire a shot into a wall. Rokhlin's allies charged his death was politically motivated. Several newspapers echoed their skepticism about the official version of events and suggested military officials or the special services might have been involved in the murder. Nevertheless, investigators charged Tamara Rokhlina with murder a week after her husband's death and arrested no other suspects in the case.

The investigation into Starovoitova's death inspired even less confidence among leading politicians and journalists. There was no mistaking the murder for anything other than a contract killing. On 20 November 1998, two assailants approached Starovoitova and her aide, Rulsan Linkov, in the stairwell of her St. Petersburg apartment building and shot her in the head. The murder weapon was a very rare type of gun, used most often in covert military operations.

Who put out a contract on her life, and why, provoked intense speculation. Some political allies, notably Linkov and Yegor Gaidar, called it a political killing and pointed the finger at "red-brown" forces. After all, she was one of the staunchest critics of the Communists. In 1992 and 1993, she advocated legislation that would have barred former workers in the apparatus of the KGB or Communist Party of the Soviet Union from serving in the government—with the exception of those who "clearly abandoned totalitarianism in August 1991." Shortly before her death, she sharply condemned anti-Semitic statements made by Communist members of the parliament. The very day of her murder, she had advocated a Kremlin meeting to discuss political extremism in Russia.

But Starovoitova was just one of many opponents of the Communists, and not even a particularly influential one. Many commentators instead linked her death to local politics in St. Petersburg. She was killed shortly before local elections, in which she was backing candidates opposed to St. Petersburg's powerful governor, Vladimir Yakovlev. The St. Petersburg election campaign was a bruising battle—alleged criminals were running for office in many districts, and there were widespread reports of bribing voters and various dirty tricks against candidates who were opponents of Yakovlev. The governor himself added fuel to the fire when he failed to turn up at Starovoitova's funeral, which was attended by many members of Russia's political elite. One newspaper claimed that Starovoitova had been in possession of a tape recording of a conversation linking Yakovlev to organized crime figures.

Although investigators did not rule out a political motive for the killing, leaks from law enforcement authorities repeatedly tried to suggest that money lay behind Starovoitova's murder. Anonymous sources in the security services charged that on the day of her death she had been carrying some $900,000 in cash—purportedly to finance campaign activities. (Starovoitova's aide Linkov vehemently denied such reports.) One newspaper alleged that she was a co-founder of three dozen companies that took money abroad and erroneously claimed Linkov was not injured in the shooting. Journalist Brian Whitmore of the *St. Petersburg Times* argued that the St. Petersburg branch of the Federal Security Service "has been doing everything possible to create this 'commercial' version [of the murder], which doesn't exist." In addition, several St. Petersburg journalists claimed that investigators interrogated them seeking incriminating information about Starovoitova and her political allies.

At year's end the authorities had charged no one in connection with Starovoitova's murder, and the case seemed destined to join the ranks of other high-profile political killings that would remain unsolved for years, perhaps permanently.

The murders of Rokhlin and Starovoitova underscored that even the politically prominent are not immune from lawlessness in Russia. Yet the killings did not appear to leave a lasting mark on the country's political landscape. Rokhlin's death did not alter the government's approach to military reform policy. Viktor Ilyukhin, the Communist chairman of the Duma Security Committee, took over the leadership of the Movement to Support the Army, making it increasingly likely that the movement will fade into the background as an appendage to the Communist Party.

After Starovoitova's death, a few commentators expressed the hope that the murder would at last unite the disparate groups in Russia's "democratic" camp, but nothing of the kind happened. Going into the 1999 parliamentary elections, at least three or four political parties and movements appeared set to compete for votes among those who once supported Democratic Russia in the early 1990s.

Foreign and Military Policies _____

A REAR-GUARD ACTION: FOREIGN AND MILITARY POLICIES IN 1998

_by_ SCOTT PARRISH

At a January 1999 news conference summarizing the accomplishments of Russian foreign policy over the past twelve months, Russian Foreign Minister Igor Ivanov tried to put the best face on a difficult and disappointing year. "Russia has not only retained its status as a key player on the international arena in the past year. It has objectively strengthened it," Ivanov claimed. Attempting to underline Russia's claim to great power status, Ivanov insisted that "an overwhelming majority of nations recognizes that the solution of crucial contemporary problems is inconceivable without Russia's direct involvement, [and] consideration of its interests." Few observers were fooled, however. One Russian newspaper described Ivanov's remarks as "a tedious collection of trite phrases," and offered a harshly contrasting assessment: "Russian diplomacy has never before had such a bad year."

Ivanov, a career diplomat who became foreign minister when his predecessor Yevgenii Primakov was appointed prime minister in September 1998, had to face harsh realities. The August 1998 financial collapse and continued military weakness further undermined Russia's already eroding international standing. Russia found itself marginalized on many significant international issues during 1998. While it has been clear since 1992 that Russia could not sustain the global role of the Soviet Union, in 1998, even Russia's reduced role as a major regional power came into question. Russian leaders often found themselves with few means to effectively defend Russian interests. NATO enlargement proceeded apace, and the NATO-Russia Founding Charter signed in 1997 failed to deliver the consultation and cooperation that Russia had hoped for. In the Balkans, Russian views about how to resolve the Kosovo conflict had little impact on Western policy. Relations with the United States declined as the Clinton administration showed little deference to Russian preferences. Moscow also watched as its economic weakness prompted the Commonwealth of Independent States (CIS) to fall into even deeper disarray in 1998. As in previous years, relatively good news for Moscow came from the East, where ties with China and India remained warm, and relations with Japan continued to slowly improve.

For the Russian military, 1998 was another disastrous year. While Defense Minister Igor Sergeev began to take some serious steps toward creating a smaller and more efficient military, continued budgetary shortfalls hampered his efforts. It seemed unlikely that Sergeev would receive the economic resources and political support he needed to carry out his reform program anytime soon. While some new funds may be spent on maintaining Russia's nuclear forces, most of the military seemed set to continue its long-standing decline, at least as long as President Boris Yeltsin remains in office.

CHILLY RELATIONS WITH THE UNITED STATES

Relations with the United States continued to deteriorate during 1998. The August 1998 financial collapse and the subsequent removal of Sergei Kirienko's government of "young reformers" convinced many in Washington that the attempts to promote a transition in Russia to democratic market capitalism had failed. The appointment of former Foreign Minister Yevgenii Primakov, who was widely (if somewhat unfairly) viewed in Washington as anti-Western, did little to improve the situation. In this generally bleak climate, no substantive progress was made on outstanding bilateral issues. While the U.S.-Russian relationship remained a mix of cooperation and competition, as the year ended discordant notes seemed to dominate. Talk of a "strategic partnership," common a few years ago, was jettisoned.

Many of the disputes that divided Russia and the United States reflected their markedly differing preferences about the "rules of the game" that order the post–Cold War international system. These preferences are strongly shaped by each country's relative power position. As the most powerful country in the world, the United States often prefers unilateral solutions to international issues. By contrast, a weak Russia prefers multilateral solutions, where it can use international institutions and norms to bolster its position and constrain the United States. When the United States and Great Britain bombed Iraq in December 1998 in response to Iraq's failure to implement UN disarmament resolutions, the harsh condemnation that followed from Moscow was not just the result of Russian interest in future trade and debt repayments from Iraq. It also reflected widespread concern that if the United States could unilaterally bomb Iraq, it might act unilaterally against Russia itself at some point in the future.

The deterioration of U.S.-Russian ties can also be traced to the domestic political weakness of both presidents, Yeltsin and Clinton. Yeltsin's increasingly frail health undermined his leadership, and Clinton, facing the threat of impeachment, could not pick up the slack in the bilateral relationship. The two presidents met in Moscow in September, but the lack of concrete results from this meeting—it produced only two modest arms control agreements—highlighted the stagnation of U.S.-Russian ties. Yeltsin unintentionally underlined this point with an excruciating performance at the closing news conference of the summit, where he seemed unable to grasp his surroundings, sat mute for over a minute after one reporter's question, and then responded with unintelligible comments.

With such debilitated leadership, and guided by divergent approaches to international politics, the United States and Russia failed to resolve almost all of the myriad issues dividing them during 1998. Aside from Iraq, the United States continued to accuse Russia of failing to control the leakage of missile and nuclear technology to Teheran, and some Western analysts believe that the Shahab-3 medium-range missile, which Iran tested in July 1998, utilizes Russian technology. That same month, the United States sanctioned several Russian organizations for allegedly shipping missile and nuclear technology to Iran, a charge Russia denied. Strategic arms control likewise remained frozen, as the Russian State Duma, which had come close to holding a long-delayed vote on the ratification of START II in December 1998, again postponed the issue following the U.S. and British bombing of Iraq. Russian officials also continued to criticize U.S. ballistic missile defense programs, saying they threatened to undermine the 1972 ABM Treaty. In the second half of the year, a trade dispute over alleged dumping of Russian steel on the U.S. market added an additional sour note.

There were still a few bright spots of bilateral collaboration. U.S. nuclear security assistance to Russia, granted under the Cooperative Threat Reduction program (also known as the Nunn-Lugar program), continued to make real strides toward securing Russian nuclear, chemical, and biological weapons. Joint teams of Russian and U.S. experts were upgrading security at over 50 sites in Russia where nuclear materials are stored, for example. U.S. financing made possible the accelerated dismantling of Russian ballistic missile submarines (SSBNs), intercontinental ballistic missiles, and heavy bombers under START I.

STAGNATION IN EUROPE

Russia continued to have difficulty finding its place in the new Europe during 1998. The Russia-NATO Founding Act signed in 1997, while avoiding a crisis, had not yet led to a new level of cooperation between Russia and the alliance. Despite the agreement, Russian elites remained suspicious that an assertive NATO will exclude them from playing a significant role in European security affairs. At the December 1998 meeting of the NATO-Russia Permanent Joint Council, Russian Foreign Minister Ivanov praised the "positive atmosphere," but emphasized Russian objections to the possible unilateral use of NATO forces to enforce a peace settlement in Kosovo, where civil conflict festered for much of 1998. In addition, Russia feared that the revised NATO strategic doctrine scheduled to be announced at the alliance's 50th anniversary in April 1999 would codify a new role for the alliance as an international policeman, operating without UN Security Council approval. Russian diplomats expressed concern that the new NATO doctrine would retain the option of first use of nuclear weapons. Although the new German Social Democratic/Green coalition government floated the idea of NATO adopting a no first-use policy in November 1998, this trial balloon was promptly deflated by Washington. Talks on the revision of the 1990 Conventional Forces in Europe treaty, which Russia wants revised to take account of NATO enlargement, failed to produce any results during 1998.

Russian relations with the European Union countries remained warmer than with the United States. But the impact of the August 1998 financial crisis and the advent of the Primakov government has also led the EU to somewhat distance itself from Russia. At the Russia–EU summit in October, for example, only a few minor agreements were signed. The EU leaders, while offering humanitarian food aid to Russia, urged Prime Minister Primakov to issue a sensible economic program and conclude negotiations on assistance with the IMF, and did not promise to intervene with the fund or offer any independent financial aid package.

The electoral defeat of German Chancellor Helmut Kohl in September 1998 removed one of the staunchest European advocates of close collaboration with Russia. Newly-elected Chancellor Gerhard Schroeder, mindful of significant German investment in and loans to Russia, pledged not to change the strategic approach of German foreign policy, but added during his December 1998 visit to Moscow that "Germany's financial capabilities are more or less exhausted," and Russia will have to rely on the IMF and World Bank for economic assistance in the future. A number of Russian commentators opined that the election of Schroeder opened a new and more difficult phase in Russian-German relations.

Russia also made little progress during the year in Eastern Europe and the Baltics. The issue of NATO enlargement remained an irritant in relations with virtually every country in the region. Ties with the Baltic States have been particularly strained by this issue. At year's end Russia had still not signed a border treaty with either Latvia or Estonia. Tensions over the issue of the Russian minority in these two countries did ease somewhat during 1998, however, as Moscow praised the adoption of revised citizenship laws that will make it easier for many Russians resident there to acquire citizenship.

MORE TROUBLE IN THE CIS

Russian relations with the CIS states remained mixed, at best, during 1998. The economic crisis in August undermined Russian claims to regional leadership, and complicated bilateral ties. Overall, Russia made some strides forward in ties with Ukraine, Belarus, and Armenia, but relations with the Central Asian states, Moldova, Azerbaijan, and Georgia stagnated or deteriorated. Furthermore, the CIS itself remained completely moribund, and signs appeared that some of its members, such as Azerbaijan and Uzbekistan, were actively considering withdrawal from a number of CIS agreements, including the 1992 Tashkent collective security treaty.

Ties with Belarus remained good, with the authoritarian Belarusian President Alyaksandr Lukashenka continuing his push for economic and political union. Belarus has been a reliable ally for Russia in such international institutions as the United Nations and the CIS. The defeat of the "young reformers" in Moscow, who had previously undermined attempts at union with Belarus for economic reasons, appeared to increase the likelihood that the latest Russian-Belarusian integration agreement, signed by Lukashenka and Yeltsin in December 1998, might be implemented. Previous such declarations, however, have been largely ignored in practice. Relations with Ukraine were more unsteady, as the Russian parliament refused to ratify the Russian-Ukrainian friendship treaty signed in 1997 for most of the year. Even after the Duma approved the treaty on 25 December 1998, the Federation Council refused to quickly follow suit, and opponents of the treaty, led by Moscow Mayor Yurii Luzhkov, vowed to fight on against its approval. Disputes over Russian natural gas shipments to Ukraine, unpaid debts for such shipments, and transit fees for Russian gas exported westward through Ukraine remained chronic irritants to bilateral ties. On the other hand, significant progress was made toward demarcating the Russian-Ukrainian land border during 1998, and the overall tenor of political relations between the two countries remained good.

In the Caucasus, Russia improved its links with Armenia, but relations with Georgia and Azerbaijan remained rocky. Little progress was made during 1998 toward resolving the Nagorno-Karabakh or Abkhaz conflicts. Politicians in both Georgia and Azerbaijan view Russia as deliberately manipulating these conflicts to undermine their independence and sovereignty, a charge Russia denies. Nevertheless, ties with Baku, already unstable because of the ongoing dispute over how to manage the oil resources of the Caspian basin, further deteriorated in late 1998, as Russia stepped up its military ties with Armenia, dispatching MiG-29 fighters and S-300 air defense missiles to a Russian military base there.

RELATIVE SUCCESS IN THE FAR EAST

As has usually been the case in recent years, while Russian foreign policy suffered defeats in the West, it made at least some modest gains in the East. Relations with China remained warm, and ties with India also continued to improve, putting Russia at the apex of an Asian "triangle." In December 1998, premier Primakov even proposed the formation of a Russian-Chinese-Indian "strategic partnership" to counterbalance the United States. The seemingly insoluble problem of the southern Kuril Islands, however, continued to hamper ties with Japan.

In 1998, China proved to be a reliable supporter of Russian views on many important international issues, while also remaining the largest market for Russian exports of military hardware. China joined Russia in criticizing U.S. policy in Iraq and the Balkans, and also supports Russian opposition to U.S. plans to develop ballistic missile defenses. These common points were publicly highlighted at several meetings between top Russian and Chinese officials, including an informal summit between Chinese President Jiang Zemin and Yeltsin in December. Although this meeting was held in a hospital room owing to one of Yeltsin's periodic illnesses, it did result in the signing of a border demarcation agreement and a joint statement reflecting the warm political ties between Beijing and Moscow.

Brisk sales of Russian military hardware to China also continued. As of October, Russian officials estimated that Chinese orders accounted for about $2.5 billion of the $8 billion in outstanding arms export contracts. Beijing took delivery of a second advanced Kilo-class (project 636) diesel-electric submarine from Russia in December 1998. China is the only country to which Russia has sold this advanced submarine, and Beijing has ordered two Sovremennyi-class missile destroyers, as well as S-300 and Tor-M1 air defense missile systems. Russia is also providing assistance to the Chinese nuclear submarine program. The first of the Russian SU-27 fighters to be produced under license in China in accordance with a 1997 contract rolled off the assembly line in late 1998, and China has expressed interest in purchasing SU-30 fighter bombers as well as licensing the technology for their production.

Some Russian and Western analysts questioned whether Russian-Chinese cooperation was as substantial as it appeared on the surface. While U.S. global dominance currently gives the two countries a powerful incentive to cooperate, should that incentive weaken, Russian-Chinese cooperation might flounder as well. Skeptics also point to the continued weakness of Russian-Chinese trade, which has not come close to the $20 billion/year target set by the two governments, but has instead shrunk. According to Chinese figures, after a 10 percent drop in 1997, bilateral trade turnover in 1998 dropped by another 10 percent, falling to $5.5 billion. There also remains a deep suspicion toward China among much of the Russian elite, especially in the Siberian regions that border China. And for both China and Russia, U.S. power is threatening, but Western markets and technology remain attractive, so that neither really regards the other as an alternative to the West.

The atmospherics of the Russian relationship with Japan improved in 1998, but the linked issues of concluding a peace treaty formally ending World War II between the two countries and resolving their territorial dispute over the southern Kuril Islands continued to pose an seemingly intractable obstacle to the full normalization of Russian-Japanese relations. Yeltsin and then Japanese Prime Minster Ryutaro Hashimoto agreed in November 1997 to push for a peace treaty by 2000, but little progress has been made toward that goal since. A summit meeting between Yeltsin and Prime Minister Keizo Obuchi in November 1998 produced a joint declaration that called for the formation of two new bilateral commissions to intensify discussions of the peace treaty and Kuril issue. One commission will address "border demarcation," while the other discusses "joint economic activity" on the disputed islands. Russia advocates expanding economic ties before resolving the territorial issue, while Japan has insisted that the Kuril issue must be resolved before relations can be fully normalized.

Russia continued to cement ties with India during 1998, as symbolized by Prime Minister Primakov's December visit to New Delhi. This trend continued despite India's nuclear weapons tests in May. Russia joined the other declared nuclear powers in condemning the Indian tests, but refused to punish India for its defiance of global nonproliferation norms. Instead, just weeks after the Indian tests, in June Atomic Energy Minister Yevgenii Adamov signed a renewed deal with India for the construction of two VVER-1000 power reactors at a site near Kudankulam. Like China, India remains a major purchaser of Russian arms. Russia reported during 1998 that it was providing assistance to the Indian nuclear submarine program, and India expressed interest in purchasing T-90 tanks and S-300 air defense missiles, and possibly the aircraft carrier Admiral Gorshkov.

Russia also continued to build links with the rest of Asia. In July 1998, Russia was accepted as a member of the Asia-Pacific Economic Cooperation forum (APEC), a goal that Moscow had long sought. Ties with South Korea continued to improve. Although trade was hurt by the Russian economic crisis, Seoul agreed to reschedule much of the Soviet-era debt and continue accepting raw materials and military equipment as payment. Relations with North Korea remained rocky, as talks in December on a new friendship and cooperation treaty to replace the 1961 pact that expired in 1996 made little progress. Moscow also expressed some annoyance with the August test-launch of a Taepodong-1 intermediate-range missile by North Korea, which passed near Russian territory without advance warning.

COLLAPSING MILITARY CONTINUES TENTATIVE REFORM

Seven years after the collapse of the USSR, Russia must still transform the bloated military it inherited from the Soviet Union into a smaller, cheaper force better suited to coping with the potential threats of the twenty-first century. Neglect of the military has been one of the hallmarks of post-Soviet Russia. Not until 1997 did President Yeltsin begin to address the military reform issue with more than empty rhetoric. During 1998, under the leadership of Defense Minister Igor Sergeev, the Russian military continued to take tentative steps toward reform. Completing this task will require both sustained attention from the national political leadership and sufficient economic resources, neither of which is likely under current circumstances.

Sergeev aimed to consolidate and downsize the Russian military. During 1998, overall armed forces personnel were reduced by more than 400,000. The Air Defense Forces and Air Force were also merged into a single service branch, creating a new four-branch structure. Sergeev intended to reduce the number of services to three—air/space, ground, and navy—by about 2005. This reorganization will also reduce the number of military districts from 8 to 6, with the new districts to be transformed into operational commands to create a more streamlined command structure.

Sergeev also took steps to improve readiness. Undermanned and ineffective units in the ground forces were combined into more combat-ready units. One reason for the failure of the Russian military in Chechnya was that virtually all forces dispatched there were "composite" units hastily patched together from undermanned units that had not previously trained together. According to the Russian General Staff, by the end of 1998, seven new combined units designed to have "permanent readiness" had been formed, each staffed at 80 percent of wartime levels and having 100 percent of wartime equipment. The Air Force took similar measures, and its new commander, Colonel-General Anatolii Kornukov, appointed in January 1998, claimed to have raised the level of airworthiness of aircraft from 40 to 80 percent.

While these steps certainly represent progress, extremely serious obstacles to the revival of the Russian military persist. The most obvious is the inability of the financially strapped Russian government to fund the military. According to Sergeev, the military "got barely one-third of the allocations stipulated in the [1998] budget." The military newspaper *Krasnaya zvezda* reported in January 1999 that while the original 1998 military budget was 81 billion rubles, that was subsequently cut to 60 billion ($2.5 billion at the post-August exchange rate), and ultimately "less than half this [reduced] amount was allocated to the army and navy." Repeated government promises to repay military wage arrears remain unfulfilled. At the end of 1998, the debt of the military to its troops, suppliers, and other creditors totaled 70 billion rubles. The draft military budget for 1999 envisioned defense spending of 91 billion rubles, but actual allocations will certainly be lower.

At this level of funding, Russia cannot sustain even 1.2 million troops. Funds for combat training are lacking. Even the Russian General Staff admits that "the standards of personnel training remain low." Owing to fuel and parts shortages, Russian Air Force jet pilots now average only 5–8 hours of flight training annually. NATO considers 150 hours a year the minimum for flying proficiency. Other more serious personnel problems persist. (See accompanying article, "Discharge of the Light Brigade.") The conscription system continues to fail. Its regulations exempt 80 percent of the draft pool, routinely leading to the induction of medically unfit, mentally unstable, or criminal recruits. Shortages of qualified noncommissioned officers and junior officers have become critical. Even by official statistics, 13 percent of all "initial officer posts" remain vacant, and in the first 10 months of 1998, 18,000 officers under age 30 left the armed forces. Without well-trained leadership, morale remains low, and unit cohesion is virtually nonexistent. Desertion, violent crime, corruption, and suicide are also rampant. Some 500 servicemen were killed on active duty during 1998, while another 800 died while off duty. Some of these deaths were accidental, but at least a few hundred of them were probably suicides or the result of violent crime. Housing, health care, and food supplies are also less than adequate. For many Russian young men, military service has become a horror to be avoided by all possible means.

Russian military equipment is also rapidly becoming obsolete, as funds are unavailable to buy new hardware or conduct adequate maintenance. Only Russian nuclear forces are receiving substantial new hardware, with the deployment of the first regiment of 10 SS-27 Topol-M ICBMs in December 1998. Even the nuclear forces face funding shortages, and weaknesses have emerged in the Russian early warning system of radars and satellites, for example. These have reportedly left Russia potentially vulnerable to a surprise missile attack and may raise the risk of accidental nuclear war. Nevertheless, the new Russian leadership, according to a November 1998 speech by First Deputy Prime Minister Yurii Maslyukov, has singled out nuclear forces as an area that must be funded to maintain Russian great power status. While supporting START II, Maslyukov called for the annual production of 35–40 SS-27s, and urged the commissioning of "several" new Borei-class ballistic missile submarines by 2010. Otherwise, argued Maslyukov, obsolescence will reduce Russian strategic nuclear forces from their current levels of about 6,600 warheads to at most 930 by 2007. The availability of resources to carry out this policy is questionable, however, as is its strategic logic. As even the Russian national security concept approved in 1997 acknowledged, the most likely threat to Russian national security is not nuclear aggression but rather internal or regional conflicts, perhaps spilling over into Russia from the Caucasus or Afghanistan and Central Asia. Nuclear weapons are unlikely to have much utility in such conflicts, and if Russia is not able to revive its conventional forces, it may find itself unprepared for them. Despite this, 1998 ended with the military leadership embroiled in debate over whether Russia should create a unified strategic nuclear command.

As in 1997, these horrific conditions spawned much speculation that the military might rebel. Nevertheless, the probability of a military coup or revolt still seems low. Both the officer corps and soldiers are too demoralized. During early 1998, some viewed the "Movement to Support the Armed Forces, Defense Industry, and Military Research," headed by then chairman of the Duma defense committee, Lev Rokhlin, as an organization that could catalyze such a development, but the movement seemed to die along with Rokhlin, who was mysteriously murdered in July 1998. Threats by Krasnoyarsk governor Aleksandr Lebed in July 1998 that he would take "responsibility" for a strategic nuclear missile base in his region unless Moscow paid the back wages of its troops highlighted a more probable, although still unlikely scenario: the disintegration of central authority over the military and the emergence of some form of regional warlordism.

DISCHARGE OF THE LIGHT BRIGADE

by VICTOR KALASHNIKOV

The Russian army, reeling from the war in Chechnya and facing brutality within its ranks, has found a new enemy: itself. On the eve of widespread demonstrations across Russia in October—which brought angry citizens into the streets demanding payment of back wages and the resignation of President Boris Yeltsin—Viktor Anpilov, leader of the radical Working Russia movement, commented with a sense of malicious joy at the prospect of his striking workers being met by troops of the Russian army. "What a chance!" he exclaimed to Russian television. "The authorities have ordered troops into the major cities to hold protesters in check. We'll bring them over to our side!"

At the last minute, Prime Minister Yevgenii Primakov declared partial payment of the soldiers' back wages, thus subverting Anpilov's mock recruitment drive. But Anpilov's jest provokes the question: how reliable a force is today's Russian army? Several factors have converted the once undefeatable and legendary symbol of Russian might, whose last great manifestation was the Red Army, into a potential source of domestic tension and a receptive ground for radicalism of any color.

First, there is a desperate lack of funding. The Moscow-based Soldiers' Mothers Committee, an organization of about 2,000 women whose sons have been drafted, appealed to Yeltsin to cancel the draft in autumn 1998 in reaction to reports that just twice-daily meals are about to be introduced in some units. In St. Petersburg, an organization of army officers formed a Homeless Union of their own to pressure Moscow to demand their rights to decent shelter as guaranteed by the Russian constitution.

Secondly, military service in Russia has lost much of its meaning and objective over the past several years, as the empire dwindles and its arch-enemies have disappeared. The new foes, in the view of many servicemen, are sitting in the Kremlin itself. The Chechen war had a particularly harsh effect on morale; the experience of fighting fellow Russians, say psychologists brought in by the army to deal with the discord, destroyed the friend–foe dynamic essential to maintaining military discipline and ended whatever esprit de corps remained after the breakup of the Soviet Union. Many in the army feel they are living in a hostile environment in their own country—that the military is engaged in a continuous battle within itself.

SOLDIER VS. SOLDIER

Violence within the army has increased dramatically; according to official figures, 50 soldiers were killed by their fellow servicemen in 1997, and thousands were injured in beatings. Army studies have concluded that most of these incidents bear no relationship to ethnic or regional tensions among soldiers (those from Moscow vs. those from the provinces for example); rather, the roots are in the abysmal and abusive living and work conditions. One-third of these attacks were committed by officers—70 percent of whom served in Chechnya—against subordinate soldiers. The most technically sophisticated units hold the lead in the decline of discipline and rising violence. For example, the Strategic Rocket Forces showed the highest—around 25 percent—increase of violations of service regulations in 1998, followed by the navy with 20 percent.

Dozens of officers have been prosecuted for abusing their troops over the past year. The abuses are not only physical; numerous officers force their troops to toil as a slave-like workforce at their private country homes or "rent" them to private firms.

There has also been an alarming rise in suicides within the military ranks. Between January and August, the Russian Army reported 276 suicides, among both soldiers and officers. In October, two top officers—a major and a lieutenant colonel—committed suicide in Moscow; an investigation revealed that their families were starving. An average of two to three legal proceedings related to killings and suicides in the Russian Army are initiated daily by the military prosecutor.

Those who are sickened by the violence and the abusive conditions are simply abandoning their posts. More than 12,000 delinquencies were registered in the first 10 months of 1998—notably higher than in 1997. Some 40,000 men are on the run from the army across Russia, according to the Soldiers' Mothers Committee, which has helped found a network of military service centers across the country where soldiers who leave their unit for short periods of time can request counseling and, in conjunction with the Military Prosecutor's Office, an investigation into charges of abuse. A recruit who has not unequivocally refused to return to the service is not treated as a deserter; the service centers offer the prospect of either reintegration into the unit—without the severe disciplining arising from desertions—or even discharge, if their charges of abuse or medical problems prove true. Valentina Melnikova, head of the Soldiers' Mothers Committee, says the centers serve more than 2,000 runaway draftees each year, many of whom come with complaints of aggressive bullying, theft, hunger, and illness. Nearly a third of those who have reported to the centers have obtained discharges on medical grounds, indicating serious health damage sustained during their period of compulsory service.

THE PEOPLE'S ARMY

As it heads toward the all-volunteer force that Yeltsin declared to be his aim by 2000, and with about 10 percent of its intended conscripts dodging the draft in 1997, the Russian army continues to shrink. Today, the Russian army is a 2.3 million-strong force; by the year 2000, that will be reduced to 1.8 million, and by 2005, the army has stated its ranks will be reduced to 1.5 million. The number of draftees has declined accordingly: from 530,000 in 1996 to 300,000 in 1998, and an estimated 200,000 in 1999.

In the run-up to 2000, every Russian man between the ages of 18 and 27 is still subject to two years of compulsory military service (three years in the navy)—with a few exemptions related to family or educational status. As the semiannual autumn conscription began in October, new draftees were entering a force that has undergone profound demographic changes. Those who have the means to evade service are doing so in ever-increasing numbers: according to Melnikova, a payment of $3,000 to $7,000 placed in the correct pocket can ensure one's exclusion from the draft. Other means are also coming to light, including "temporary" enrollment in elite officer-training academies, intended to provide a high level of education to those planning a military career (thus exempting students from conscription as low-level recruits). Many leave the institutions after just two or three years, fulfilling their compulsory service by getting an education, then fleeing into private business or civilian colleges. (That loophole was just closed, however: the newly adopted Military Service Law provides a disincentive for such maneuvers by equating one year of compulsory service with two years in a military school.)

The caliber of those conscripted is declining precipitously, according to three-star General Vladislav Putilin, the deputy head of the army general staff, responsible for recruitment and mobilization. The number of drug- and alcohol-addicted conscripts has soared ten times over the past four years. The percentage of those who have dropped out of school after only four years of education before being drafted has increased a hundred-fold since 1985. Thirty-seven percent of young men were neither employed nor studying at the time of their spring conscription in 1998; an ever greater proportion of conscripts are coming from lower social strata and from the impoverished countryside. "We're in the process of becoming a genuine workers' and peasants' army," Putilin has joked, bitterly. "The army will increasingly have to perform social rehabilitation rather than military training."

NOTE
Reprinted with kind permission from *Transitions* magazine, November 1998.

Economic and Social Policy

FAREWELL TO ORTHODOX MARKET TRANSITION

by RADOSLAV K. PETKOV

Nineteen ninety-eight was the year which clearly showed that the Russian economy could not transform itself along the path established by Poland, Hungary, and the Czech Republic. In contrast to those successful post-socialist transitions, Russia did not and could not generate the internal consensus for market reforms that would put the country on a convergence path to the developed capitalist economies. Russia's size and geopolitical position posed a different civilizational choice.

The country had to find a way to reform a distorted Soviet economy while at the same time preserving its territorial integrity and providing for the subsistence of 150 million people. The orthodox market approach was not up to the task. It was unable to address the chronic deficit of effective political and economic institutions in post-Soviet Russia, which undermined any, including market-oriented, reforms. Price liberalization, privatization, and macroeconomic stabilization did not—and could not by themselves—establish the incentives for microeconomic reforms and forge a public consensus for fundamental change in the way the economy was run. The financial crisis in the summer of 1998 pulled aside the veil of price stability and a strong ruble, revealing the bare-bones of an unreformed economy made up mostly of inefficient enterprises and loss-making farms.

THE ECONOMY GRINDS TO A HALT

After Russia registered a small positive growth in 1997 of 0.8 percent, the government expected gross domestic product (GDP) to increase by 2 to 4 percent in 1998. The decline of world commodity prices and the Asian financial crisis which began in October 1997, however, had a devastating effect on Russia's exports and undermined the financial stability which was the precondition for recovery in the real economy. In the first half of the year, Russia's GDP declined 0.5 percent. The downturn continued in the third quarter with a 7.6 percent drop in output. For the year, Russia's GDP fell 4.6 percent to 2.68 trillion rubles ($280 billion at the average exchange rate).

Industrial production continued its downward trend and fell 5.2 percent for the year. The sharpest decline was recorded by light industry and car manufacturing (-12 percent), metallurgy (-8 percent), mechanical engineering and metal processing (-7 percent), and chemical and petrochemical industries (-7 percent). Due to the replacement of sharply-reduced imports with locally produced goods, output grew on average 3.1 percent in October–December 1998, mostly in the engineering and food industries. This growth was from a very low level, however, and did not conceal the lack of corporate sector reform in Russia. Only 29 out of 89 federation subjects recorded stable or increased production volumes in the period January–November 1998. Eighteen regions recorded a fall in industrial output in excess of 10 percent.

The demonetization of the economy meant that the share of barter in inter-enterprise transactions continued at around 50 percent. Total arrears (including payables to suppliers, budget, and wage arrears) increased to 40 percent of the total amount due in 1998. Debts to energy providers alone exceeded 130 billion rubles. Domestic customers alone owed the natural gas monopoly Gazprom more than $14 billion at the end of 1998, a sum equal to 3 percent of Russia's 1997 GDP ($452 billion).The punitive tax system and lack of clear regulations pushed at least 20 percent of the economy underground. The share of the "unofficial" economy in the trade sector was estimated at 60 percent. For example, about 14,000 Russian companies registered in Cyprus to arrange for inter-enterprise payments offshore.

The situation in the agricultural sector was even more distressing. Delay in land reforms, lack of financing for agricultural equipment and fertilizers, and depressed producer prices (often manipulated by corrupt rings of middlemen) caused a 12 percent drop in agricultural production in 1998. According to Agriculture and Food Minister Viktor Semenov, the utilized arable land in the country had declined by a quarter since the early 1990s, the number of cattle halved, mineral fertilizer use dropped to 15 percent of its former level, and the fleet of agricultural machinery decreased between 45 and 55 percent. Compounding these problems, a severe drought in 1998 led to a grain harvest of 48.5 million tons, down from 89 million tons in 1997 and the worst since 1953.

The decline in production and agricultural activity naturally translated into falling employment and depressed living standards. The unemployment rate rose from 9.3 percent in May to 11.8 percent in December. Nearly a third of the unemployed came from the agricultural sector. The average monthly salary during the first half of 1998 ($173) fell as a result of the summer financial crisis and ensuing ruble devaluation to $60 in December. Real incomes declined by 12 percent according to the World Bank, while Goskomstat figures show that the crisis pushed 30 percent of the Russian population (about 43 million people) below the poverty line (measured by a monthly subsistence wage of 522 rubles). The decline in living standards was especially drastic in the regions which depended heavily on imported food, medicine, and supplies. Shortages of essential foods and medicines appeared in Sakhalin, Kamchatka, Dagestan, and the Russian Far North.

THE SUMMER FINANCIAL CRISIS

The financial situation in Russia at the beginning of 1998 was precarious. The chronic federal government deficits made the country increasingly dependent on external borrowing (mostly from the IMF and the World Bank) and short-term government securities (GKOs). In June 1998, the total value of outstanding GKOs reached 436 billion rubles ($70 billion). Foreigners, who in 1996 were admitted to the GKO market partly under the insistence of the IMF, held 30 percent of the outstanding short-term government debt. The financial crisis in South East Asia, however, made foreign investors increasingly nervous of Russia's ability to pay its debts and maintain a stable ruble that would protect the value of their GKO holdings. Falling world energy prices added to their fears. Russia, which depended on energy exports for 70 percent of its foreign exchange earnings, saw its foreign exchange reserves falling to $13.6 billion in early July from a high of $24 billion in April 1997.

To continue to fund Russia's budget deficits, foreign investors in GKOs required higher interest rates, which in turn added to the government debt service and, consequently, the need to issue additional treasury bills. This vicious circle received a fresh bout of intensity in late spring, when the Russian government and the IMF failed to reach an agreement on a 1998 austerity plan and the Fund delayed the next $670 million disbursement of a three-year $9 billion IMF loan. Worried at the prospect of ruble devaluation and the possibility of defaulting on the short-term government debt, investors sparked a massive sell-off on Russia's stock and GKOs markets in late May and early June. By the end of July, foreign holdings of GKOs were reduced from about $20 billion to $13 billion. This put heavy pressure on the ruble as investors converted their ruble earnings into dollars. With limited foreign reserves to defend the ruble, the Central Bank raised the interest rate to commercial banks to 150 percent. The Ministry of Finance offered yields on government securities of 110 to 120 percent, but did not find buyers even at these sky-high rates. The government, facing a severe payments crunch, turned to the international financial institutions for help. Anatolii Chubais was appointed special negotiator and sent to Washington for talks with the U.S. Treasury Department and the IMF. After round-the-clock negotiations, the two sides announced on 13 July that Russia would receive $14.8 billion in loans from the IMF, the World Bank, and Japan in 1998. The IMF would loan Russia $12.5 billion for the year, of which $11.2 billion was in the form of a new stabilization loan approved under the condition that Russian government adopt a tough anti-crisis program, including significant changes in the tax system. The new stabilization package also included a combined $7.8 billion in loans for 1999. Thus, Russia was set to receive $22.6 billion of international financial support before the end of 1999.

On 20 July, the IMF board of executive directors approved the rescue package and authorized the first disbursement of $4.8 billion—$600 million less than originally planned, as retribution for the failure of the Russian parliament to pass all of the tax measures required by the IMF. One million dollars of the IMF funds were immediately used to pay off short-term government debt. The remaining funds went to boost the Central Bank's foreign exchange reserves. A second IMF tranche of $4.3 billion was to come in September, and a third one of $2.1 billion in November. The IMF program assumed, however, that restored investor confidence would bring down interest rates and induce foreign investors to roll over their GKO holdings, thus alleviating immediate pressure on the federal budget. Foreigners were expected to roll over $3.5 billion of the $4.8 billion they held in GKOs maturing by the end of 1998. Russian banks were expected to roll over an additional $7.7 billion. In a deal managed by the investment bank Goldman Sachs, foreign and local investors agreed to exchange $6.4 billion of GKOs for seven- and twenty-year Eurobonds, priced 9.2 percent over the benchmark U.S. treasury bills. After the swap, $10.7 billion of GKOs remained to be redeemed by the end of September 1998. The Russian finance ministry, at the same time, estimated that taxes collected in the second half of the year would be 106 billion rubles ($17 billion at the time), markedly less than the 146 billion rubles ($23 billion) in total debt service.

The announced finance gap intensified speculations of imminent ruble devaluation and sparked a massive sell-off in the stock market in early August. During the week of 10 August, the Russian stock market plunged 25 percent. The ruble was pushed out of the Central Bank–set corridor of 6.2 to 6.5 per dollar, while GKO yields soared to 125–140 percent. At those prices, the finance ministry canceled three consecutive GKO auctions, dashing hopes that it could roll over its debts. On 13 August, George Soros wrote a widely-publicized letter to the *Financial Times*, claiming that the meltdown in Russia's financial markets had reached its "terminal phase" and urging a 15–25 percent ruble devaluation and the introduction of a currency board. President Boris Yeltsin and the Russian government were quick to dismiss the idea of devaluation, claiming that the exchange policies already in place could return stability to the financial market. They changed their minds over the weekend of 15–16 August, when it became clear that another G-7 bailout was not going to materialize. In a joint statement on 17 August the government and the Central Bank announced a new anti-crisis package including:

- Introduction of a crawling peg for the ruble that would allow it to float within currency corridor limits of 6 to 9.5 rubles per dollar (allowing the ruble to effectively fall by up to 30 percent).
- Restructuring of ruble-denominated government securities maturing before the end of 1999 into new, longer-term securities (effectively defaulting on GKOs).
- A 90-day moratorium on the repayment of credits received from nonresidents, insurance payments on credits backed by securities (margin calls), and payments under currency futures contracts. The moratorium applied to private borrowers with Russian resident status, i.e., commercial banks and companies that had taken loans from foreign financial institutions.
- A ban on nonresidents investing in ruble assets with maturities of one year or less.

The decisions of 17 August were meant to provide debt service relief, stop the drain of foreign exchange reserves on defending the ruble, and protect local banks, which had amassed huge obligations to foreign creditors (these were in addition to the direct purchases of GKOs by foreigners). The immediate result, however, was financial panic and selling on the stock and foreign exchange markets. On 18 August the ruble fell 12 percent against the dollar. Banks lost their most liquid assets, GKOs, and froze payments of wages, pensions, and business transactions. Prices of imported and some domestic consumer goods rose sharply. In the last week of August only, wholesale prices increased by 30 percent, with a knock-on effect feeding through at retail level. In the period 17 August–9 September, prices of imported foodstuffs increased by 100–500 percent, while prices of Russian products went up by 50–100 percent, before falling toward the end of the month. In Khabarovsk, in the Russian Far East, basic goods such as butter, salt, and sugar increased four times in price in the first week of September, yet remained scarce even at those levels. In an effort to protect local consumers, some governors like Aleksandr Lebed in Krasnoyarsk and Aman Tuleev in Kemerovo imposed price controls and prohibited export of certain goods outside their regions.

FISCAL POLICY

The proximate cause of the August financial crisis was a chronic fiscal deficit, which in turn was the result of an unreformed economy that produced few taxable profits. On the revenue side of the federal budget stood an inefficient and narrowly based tax regime, which placed a heavy burden on the top 100 corporate taxpayers (Gazprom alone contributed about 20 percent of Russia's tax income) while leaving many individuals untouched. As a result, the federal government collected taxes equivalent to 10 percent of GDP in 1998, one of the lowest tax collection levels in the world. On the expenditure side, 42 percent of revenues in 1998 went to service interest payments on domestic and foreign debt. The federal budget deficit for 1998 was 3.2 percent of GDP, down from 7 percent in 1997, but still above the IMF requirement of 2.8 percent. Government revenues amounted to 302 billion rubles, while expenditures were 389 billion rubles. Taxes provided 81 percent of all budget revenues in the period January–November 1998. The VAT (value-added-tax) brought in 36 percent of budget revenues, excise duties 18 percent, profit tax 12 percent, and foreign trade tax 12 percent. With realized revenues only 82 percent of the target set in the 1998 budget, the government had to cut expenditures. Actual spending in 1998 came to 78 percent of the budgeted amount. Servicing the government debt in January–November accounted for 30 percent of spending, national defense 14.6 percent, the social sphere and culture 14.5 percent, and law enforcement and state security 7.7 percent. The federal government remitted 29 billion rubles, or 9.2 percent of the total spending, to Russian regions by way of financial aid. Wage arrears to public sector employees grew steadily from the beginning of 1998, reaching 12.4 billion rubles in June.

To address the worsening fiscal situation and to meet the IMF's requirements for the July package of financial assistance, the government drafted a new anti-crisis program. The program planned to bring in an additional $17.4 billion in revenues by expanding the tax base and to cut $12 billion of budgeted spending in 1998, including on government administration. On 15 July the lower house of the Russian parliament, the Duma, gave preliminary approval to cutting the profit tax from 35 percent to 30 percent, imposing a uniform tax on small businesses, and extending state regulation of alcohol production. The Duma rejected, however, the proposed universal 5 percent sales tax and approved a revised version of that law, which would allow regional authorities to introduce a sales tax only on luxury items (such as furs and travel agencies) and not on essentials such as bread, meat, milk products, and children's goods. The Duma passed a law revising the income tax scale, but in a substantially different version from the government's draft. Whereas the government sought a 20 percent tax rate for incomes between 20,000 and 100,000 rubles, the Duma approved a 15 percent rate on annual incomes from 20,000 to 40,000 rubles and a 20 percent rate on incomes between 40,000 rubles and 100,000 rubles. The Duma also refused to levy income tax on interest earned from bank deposits that were less than 10 times the minimum monthly wage.

Altogether and in contrast to most commentaries, the Duma was fairly cooperative, agreeing to 12 of the government-proposed bills and rejecting only two. Yeltsin enforced by decree the elements of the government anti-crisis program that the Duma failed to approve. He also vetoed the reductions in profit and excise taxes because the Duma failed to approve the laws that would have made up for the lost tax revenues. Yeltsin decreed a standard 20 percent VAT and mandated that VAT be paid immediately upon delivery of goods and not after their sale. The implementation of tax reforms, however, was derailed by the August financial crisis.

MONETARY POLICY

Russia's monetary policy was tight in the first half of the year and was moderately loosened in the second half, partly to accommodate the needs of a severely demonetized economy and partly to absorb the shock of the 17 August ruble devaluation. Money supply for the year, measured in accordance with IMF standards to include cash, deposits in national currency, and foreign currency deposits in the banking system, grew from 452 to 631 billion rubles, or by 40 percent—but this meant a contraction in real terms, taking into account the rate of inflation (84 percent for the year as a whole). The average monthly rate of money supply growth was 2.8 percent. In January–August 1998, money supply actually fell by 4 percent, and in September–December grew by 45 percent. Between October and December alone, 23.5 billion rubles were printed. According to

Finance Minister Mikhail Zadornov, 16.5 billion of them were channeled into circulation, and the remaining amount went to the Finance Ministry for the repayment of short-term state debt. The sharp devaluation of the ruble in the second half of 1998 resulted in an increase in the estimated foreign currency component of the money supply from 18 percent as of 1 January to 29 percent at year's end.

Average inflation in the first seven months of 1998 was 7 percent. Following the August crisis, inflation soared to 38 percent in September, 4.5 percent in October, 5.7 percent in November, and 11.6 percent in December. Inflation for the year was 84.4 percent. In retrospect, the combination of tight monetary policy (designed to hold down inflation); heavy dependence on short-term foreign financial inflows (to plug the fiscal gap); and a pegged exchange rate proved explosive for Russia's balance of payments and precipitated the August financial crisis.

THE BANKING SYSTEM

The Russian banking system in 1998 continued to fail to effectively mediate between the real economy and the available financial resources. Instead of lending to the productive sector, Russian banks channeled available resources to the short-term debt market and engaged in security speculation. The GKO portfolio of the sector amounted to $27 billion at the end of June 1998, with the state-owned Sberbank holding 50 percent and the rest of the banking system 10 percent of its assets in GKO. Russian banks borrowed around $10 billion from foreign financial institutions in order to finance these operations, and built very risky portfolios totaling $6 billion in forward contracts. After the GKO market collapsed and the value of the ruble fell, Russian banks lost 50 percent of their total assets and more than half of their liquid assets. The volume of foreign exchange credits fell 12 percent, while ruble-denominated credits fell 16.5 percent. Worried depositors fled from the banking system. Between August and October 1998, household deposits in hard currency halved to $3 billion. Ruble-denominated deposits fell to $6 billion (their lowest level in four years), bestowing on Russia one of the lowest per capita savings rates in the world.

To restore the payments system, the Central Bank lent 55 billion rubles to commercial banks in the aftermath of the crisis. On 17 August the government announced plans to support the 12 largest Russian banks—Sberbank, Vneshtorgbank, Vneshekonombank, Oneksimbank, National Reserve Bank, Menatep, Most Bank, Inkombank, Bank of Moscow, Alfa Bank, SBS-Agro, and Rossiiskii Kredit—by helping them form a pool of resources to sustain each other. The idea did not materialize. Two of the banks in which Gazprom was a major shareholder—the National Reserve Bank and Inkombank—merged on 25 August. Three other major banks—Oneksimbank, Most Bank, and Menatep—followed suit, setting up a bank holding company to which each of the banks was to contribute 51 percent of its shares. A widely anticipated bank consolidation, however, did not take place: after August, only 68 banks were shut down out of a pre-crisis total of 2,552.

In December 1998, the Central Bank announced a program of restructuring the banking sector. The program divided the banking system into four groups. The first group of 862 banks with sufficient capital and no liquidity problems did not need support. The second group of 398 banks considered fundamentally sound, but experiencing some liquidity problems, would receive Central Bank support. The third group of the 18 largest and considered most socially important banks would also receive help. The fourth group of 275 insolvent banks with no chance of survival would be bankrupted. In early December, the government and the Central Bank created the Agency for Restructuring Credit Organizations. Its duties would be to bankrupt insolvent banks, help salvageable banks by injecting liquidity and restructuring their debts, and attract new investments into the sector. The Agency's share capital of 10 billion rubles, however, was considered by many as inadequate for any real impact. The Central Bank itself estimates the overall cost of recapitalizing the banking system at 140 billion rubles.

PRIVATIZATION AND FOREIGN INVESTMENT

Revenue from privatization sales in 1998 came to 15.2 billion rubles, exceeding the original target of 8.1 billion rubles. The result, however, was mostly due to the ruble devaluation: in pre-devaluation rubles, the privatization revenues would have only amounted to 4.3 billion rubles. About 85 percent of privatization receipts came from the December sale of a 2.5 percent stake in Gazprom to the German Ruhrgas for $660 million. The other major privatization sales planned for 1998 were canceled. The auction of a 75 percent stake in the major oil company Rosneft failed after the two expected bidders—Royal Dutch Shell Group and British Petroleum—failed to submit bids by the deadline of 26 May at the initial asking price of $2.1 billion. The privatization of an additional 25 percent in the telecommunications company Svyazinvest (a 25 percent stake had been sold in 1997 to a consortium led by George Soros) was also canceled due to unfavorable market conditions.

In the first nine months of 1998, Russia received $18.6 billion in foreign capital, compared with $35.2 billion in the same period of 1997. Direct investment was a paltry $1.5 billion (compared with $4 billion in 1997), portfolio investment came to $7.3 billion (or 39 percent of the total), and other types of investment totaled $9.9 billion (53 percent), including foreign official credits. Net foreign investment in government securities plunged to $500 million, from $10.7 billion in the same period of 1997. After the August financial crisis, a significant number of foreign direct investors and businesses decided to scale back or terminate their operations. Those companies that closed at least some of their operations include IBM, Philips Electronics, White Nights (an oil joint venture), Subway Sandwich Shops, Tetra Travel, and US West.

FOREIGN TRADE

In 1997 Russia ran a trade surplus of $17.5 billion. In 1998, the country's export performance weakened significantly, mostly because of falling world commodity prices. Russia exported $4.21 billion worth of oil, a decrease from 1997 of $2.9 billion, or 41 percent. Imports also declined, especially after the ruble devaluation in the second half of the year. Dollar-denominated imports fell by 50 percent in the period September–November 1998, compared with the same period in 1997. For the year, imports fell by 25 percent to $58 billion and exports declined by 17 percent to $75 billion. The trade surplus was $17 billion. Exports to countries outside the CIS totaled $59 million and to the CIS $16 billion, down from $70 billion and $19 billion respectively in 1997. Imports from the CIS amounted to $15 billion and from the rest of the world $43 billion, down from $19 billion and $53 billion in 1997.

With exports of energy resources and other primary commodities accounting for 80 percent of the country's merchandise exports, Russia, in retrospect, was slow to devalue the ruble. Other commodity exporting countries such as Canada and Australia engineered a gentle devaluation of their currencies in 1997–1998 and prevented a current account calamity of the Russian magnitude. The Russian government and the IMF, however, held to a strong ruble as an anchor of low inflation for too long.

TOWARD A NEW ECONOMIC POLICY?

Following the August crisis and the confirmation of Yevgenii Primakov as prime minister, the Russian government and the Central Bank, headed by its former governor Viktor Gerashchenko, began to draft a new anti-crisis economic program. After several drafts were leaked as trial balloons in the press, the final version of the economic program was published on 15 November. The program articulated the main principles of the Primakov government's economic policy and described plans to strengthen the state's role in "shaping and developing the market and its social orientation." The overarching goal of the program was "transition of the market economy to socially-oriented economic growth." Earlier drafts of the economic program were widely criticized for proposals for capital and price controls, national industrial policies, and lax monetary and fiscal regimes.

The final program heeded elements of that criticism, and laid out general principles capable of attracting guarded support from Western observers. One such pledge was "holding inflation in 1999 to a level of not more than 30 percent" by "rigorous control of prices for the output of natural monopolies, refusal to allow abrupt movements in the floating ruble rate, and increasing the supply of goods to cover the demand of those able to pay." The other main sections of the program addressed normalizing the population's living conditions, restoration and development of the real sector, and executive power as a means of enhancing economic initiative. Measures to improve the availability of essential foodstuffs and medicines included reduced import duties and price controls, debt relief for domestic producers of such items, and compensation to poor citizens for price increases. The section on the real economy emphasized the need for tax reform aimed at broadening the tax base, lowering the tax burden on producers, and decreasing the general level of indebtedness (the latter being a major propellant of the barter economy).

The government also announced plans to lower VAT rates from 20 percent to 15 percent in 1999 (with 1 percent going to finance agriculture and the coal industry), reduce the profit tax from 35 percent to 30 percent, and decrease employers' social security contributions from 39.5 percent to 32 percent of the payroll. The program also envisioned increasing the efficiency of federal and state budget expenditures and transferring "operational and executive powers from federal executive bodies to those of constituent parts of the Russian Federation." The program was full of good general intentions, but lacked specific measures to achieve the desired results. The task of stabilizing the economy and restoring growth would thus remain the major challenge for Russia in 1999.

NOTE

The macroeconomic data cited in this article is compiled from the Russian State Committee for Statistics, the Central Bank, the United Nations 1998 Economic Surveys of Europe, Bank of Finland, Standard & Poor's, and the Economist Intelligence Unit.

SOCIAL FALL-OUT FROM AUGUST CRASH

by PENNY MORVANT

After the relative stability of 1997, living standards fell sharply in Russia in 1998 in the aftermath of the August financial crisis. Average per capita income was down by more than 16 percent in real terms by the end of the year, while unemployment, wage arrears, and the number of people living below the poverty line had risen. The economic crises and accompanying political turmoil also pushed social welfare reforms off the agenda.

The financial crash was preceded by a series of high-profile protests by miners, who blockaded the Trans-Siberian railway, but the total number of work days lost as a result of strike action over the year was lower than in 1997. As in previous years, the long-expected "social explosion" failed to materialize and most Russians appeared to adopt individual rather than collective strategies to cope with the stresses of post-Soviet life. Russia's overall crime rate climbed by almost 8 percent in 1998 after a period of relative stability mid-decade, while corruption at all levels became ever more evident and openly acknowledged.

President Boris Yeltsin may have declared 1998 the "year of human rights," but the country's actual record was uneven at best. Authority over Russia's penal system was finally transferred to the justice ministry in keeping with a commitment Russia made to the Council of Europe, but prison conditions remained harsh. Arbitrary arrests and detentions continued, and the judiciary was still dogged by delays. Implementation began of a controversial law on religion enacted in 1997, with the legislation thus far causing fewer problems than many had foreseen. At the local level, however, restrictions on religious freedom as well as on other civil liberties grew as the capacity of regional governors to act independently of the center increased.

LIVING STANDARDS FALL

The impact of the economic crisis on Russians' living standards was becoming apparent by year's end. Real after-tax income fell by 16.3 percent in 1998, with a particularly sharp decline in the later months. According to Goskomstat figures cited in *Russian Economic Trends*, for example, average wages were 14 percent lower for 1998 as a whole but the December figure was 40 percent down in comparison with the same month the previous year. The percentage of people living in households with average per capita income below the poverty line as defined by the labor ministry was about 24 percent, 3 points higher than in 1997 and roughly equivalent to the figure back in 1994.

Consumer expenditure fell sharply in real terms but held up better than income data would suggest, implying that actual income exceeded reported levels, and perhaps that households were running down what savings they had left after bank failures and resurgent inflation had taken their toll. Consumer expenditure in December 1998 was 16 percent down on December 1997, with most of the fall attributable to lower spending on non-food items (down 26 percent) and services (down 10 percent); expenditure on food dropped by 9 percent.

The unemployment rate (measured according to International Labor Organization methodology) rose only marginally in 1998, increasing by half a point to 11.8 percent by the end of December. The percentage of unemployed registered with the Federal Employment Service fell in comparison with 1997, but that was probably due primarily to long delays in the payment of benefits and to other disincentives to register.

Statistics on Russian living standards in general are notoriously unreliable. Individuals and companies under-report income to evade taxes, while official data tend to understate poverty because the official poverty line is artificially low and delays in wage and benefit payments are not always taken into account. Goskomstat's shortcomings hit the headlines in May, when the organization's head, Yurii Yurkov, was arrested following allegations that he and other officials had systematically distorted data to help major Russian companies cheat on taxes. Nevertheless, the gloomy picture painted by government statistics was borne out by sociological survey data. A December poll by the Public Opinion Fund showed that four out of five Russians believed their lives had become more difficult during the year, while a survey conducted by the Institute of Parliamentary Sociology found that seven out of ten respondents did not expect matters to improve in 1999. Survey data also lent credence to the unemployment trend identified in the official statistics, if not the numbers themselves: the All-Russian Center for the Study of Public Opinion put the jobless figure at 18.4 percent in December, up from 18 percent in November 1997.

The deepening economic crisis and political upheaval also squeezed out social sector reform. A 12–point program setting out the main social and economic tasks to be fulfilled by the Russian government in 1998 included beginning pension reform and targeting social protection to the most needy. The government adopted a pension reform program in May envisaging three types of benefit: a minimum "social pension" for which all with a minimum work record would be eligible; earnings-related pensions; and additional personal pensions financed through voluntary contributions to government-monitored private pension funds. Deputy Economics Minister Andrei Sharonov said in November, however, that implementation of the reform had been put off "indefinitely" as a result of the August crisis. The government also continued to float the idea of raising the retirement age and eliminating pensions to those who were still working, but encountered stiff resistance from the State Duma and trade unions. Another of the goals outlined in the 12–point program was enacting a new Labor Code by 1

January 1999 to replace the one adopted in 1971, but the government did not approve a new code in principle until late December, let alone submit it to the parliament for consideration.

WAGE ARREARS PILE UP, BUT PROTESTS ARE MUTED

Paying off arrears in both pensions and wages was at least in rhetoric a major priority for the governments of Viktor Chernomyrdin, Sergei Kirienko, and Yevgenii Primakov. Nevertheless, the state sector wage backlog climbed from 4.9 billion rubles at the end of 1997 to 13.7 billion ($550 million) a year later. Total enterprise wage arrears increased from 40 billion to 56 billion over the same period. Two pension increases in late 1997 and a new formula for calculating pensions introduced in February 1998 put additional strain on the Pension Fund. The government sought in the summer to increase mandatory individual pension insurance payments from 1 to 3 percent of the wage to make up the shortfall but was unable to push the measure through. Despite the prominence given to social stabilization measures by the new Primakov government, in early January 1999 Deputy Prime Minister Valentina Matvienko acknowledged that overdue pensions still amounted to 29 billion rubles and that future pension increases would not keep pace with inflation.

Wage arrears continued to be the main cause of strikes and other forms of labor protests, which were most prevalent in the education sector. The "rails wars" in the spring and summer, in which miners blockaded the Trans-Siberian railway and staged a three-month picket of the Russian government building in Moscow, were the most visible and radical form of protest. But two days of protest action organized by the main official trade union group on 9 April and 7 October attracted a relatively low turnout and the number of working days lost due to labor disputes in 1998 was down to 5.24 million from 6 million in 1997. The number of people seeking to claim back wages through the court system rose, but was still small.

As in previous years, Russians proved more concerned with individual survival strategies than with collective action, possibly because of a reluctance to lose what little they had; a belief that protest would yield few results; and the absence of individuals or movements capable of harnessing discontent. A survey carried out in September–October suggested that almost three out of every four now grew some of their own food in an attempt to make ends meet. Simon Clarke, a specialist on Russia's labor force, argues, however, that the dacha makes little net contribution to the food budget of urban Russians once the costs of transport, rent, and so on are taken into account. He contends that the dacha, like secondary employment, provides another mechanism for those who are already relatively comfortably off to increase their security by diversifying their sources of income.

CRIME AND CORRUPTION FLOURISH

The crime rate climbed by 7.7 percent over the year, with a 10 percent increase in serious crimes, which accounted for almost 60 percent of all offenses. Without a doubt, the crime that most shocked the nation was the November killing in St. Petersburg of democratic deputy Galina Starovoitova (see essay by Laura Belin), which was reminiscent of the 1994 assassination of *Moskovskii komsomolets* journalist Dmitrii Kholodov and the slaying a year later of TV star Vladislav Listev. Her murder, like Kholodov's, is thought to have been linked to a corruption investigation. Score-settling among criminal groups was another important motive behind such "contract killings." The northern Caucasus, notably areas in and around Chechnya, were the most lawless, with a particularly high rate of abductions.

Heavy bureaucracy, complex and contradictory regulations, a tradition of cronyism and informal links as well as a general lack of respect for the law meant that corruption continued to flourish. A study by the Economist Intelligence Unit gave Russia the highest score on its corruption scale, while another international survey gave Russia a score of 2 on a scale of 0—most corrupt—to 10—least corrupt. Around 18,000 officials at various levels of seniority were arrested on corruption charges during the year. Interior Minister Sergei Stepashin said that in twelve of Russia's 89 official regions such offenses had been committed by officials at the level of "deputy governor or higher."

There were renewed allegations about the involvement of police and security services personnel in racketeering and other crimes. A senior Federal Security Service (FSB) officer claimed in November that FSB officers had been involved in a plot to kill financier and former CIS Executive Secretary Boris Berezovskii. He said his motivation for speaking out was to draw the attention of the current FSB head to the need to purge officers who were using the agency for "private and mercantile" rather than constitutional goals. Vadim Radaev of the Institute of Economics in Moscow argued that state agencies were being commercialized, acquiring a form of "customary rights" to exercise violence in the marketplace.

Senior politicians accused their colleagues of corruption and were, in turn, the object of such allegations, as *kompromat* continued to be an important instrument of political intrigue. Three members of the liberal Yabloko faction in the Duma sent Primakov a letter in early November posing 16 questions about allegedly suspicious activities of members of his government, including First Deputy Prime Minister Yurii Maslyukov, First Deputy Prime Minister Vladimir Gustov, and Deputy Prime Minister Gennadii Kulik. Gustov suggested that the anti-corruption campaign was "an attempt to make up for lost time in the presidential race."

UNEVEN RECORD IN HUMAN RIGHTS

It was another mixed year for human rights. On 1 September, after many delays, responsibility for overseeing most of the penal system was transferred from the interior ministry to the justice ministry in line with a commitment Russia gave when it joined the Council of Europe in 1996, reaffirmed in an October 1997 presidential decree. The change meant that criminal investigation and internment were no longer the prerogative of a single government agency, but it is unlikely to have much practical impact for several years. Chronic overcrowding, decaying infrastructure, and violence against detainees by correctional staff continued to render prison conditions harsh and even life threatening. The number of prisoners infected with the HIV virus rose again—up around 500 percent between September 1997 and October 1998—and tuberculosis rates soared. In August doctors said that a new multi-drug-resistant form of the disease had taken hold, leading a number of international NGOs to write to Yeltsin warning that Russia's penal institutions had become the "incubator of a new illness."

Several hundred prisoners continued to sit on death row, waiting for their cases to be reviewed by a presidential commission on clemency. The government renewed its pledge in August to abolish the death penalty by the following April, but later in the year a number of senior officials were quoted as saying that violent criminals should be put to death. Early in 1999 the head of the Kremlin clemency commission said that all death sentences passed since the institution of an unofficial moratorium on executions in August 1996 should be replaced by life or 25-year prison sentences by the summer and that a Constitutional Court ruling stipulated that no new death sentences could be handed down until all defendants potentially facing execution could exercise the right to a jury trial. Jury trials were currently available in only nine regions.

The judicial system in general still suffered from poor financing, leading to a huge backlog of cases and leaving judges more susceptible to corruption, intimidation, and manipulation by political officials and criminals, particularly at the local level. There was a partial victory for Aleksandr Nikitin, the defendant in what is arguably the late 1990s' most famous case, viewed as a test of human rights commitments and the independence of the judiciary. A retired naval captain, Nikitin was arrested in February 1996 on charges of espionage for his part in a report by a Norwegian environmental movement on radioactive contamination by Russia's North Sea Fleet. When his case finally went to trial in St. Petersburg in October, the judge concluded that the evidence presented by the prosecution did not support the indictment and returned it for further investigation. Nikitin, however, remained under house arrest and could still face a 20-year prison term.

The Russian parliament ratified the European Convention on Human Rights and the European Convention for the Prevention of Torture and Inhuman or Degrading Treatment, but NGOs and the media continued to report numerous cases of abuse by law enforcement as well as correctional staff. In two landmark trials in the Urals republic of Mordoviya in February six police officers were convicted on charges of torture. In April, for the first time in recent years, OMON special police detachments used force against demonstrators, dispersing students protesting against education reforms in Yekaterinburg. The practice of hazing new recruits in the armed forces continued: according to the Military Prosecutor's Office, 57 servicemen died and 2,735 were injured as a result of bullying in the first 11 months of the year. The number of non-combat deaths declined but the military suicide rate was up, as were the number of appeals for help to groups such as the Moscow-based Soldiers' Mothers Committee.

In May the post of human rights commissioner (or ombudsman) was finally filled. The law establishing the position had gone into force over a year earlier but State Duma deputies were unable to agree on a candidate. After months of political haggling, Oleg Mironov was approved as part of a larger political deal involving a number of Duma committee posts. Mironov, a communist not known for his interest or expertise in human rights, appeared unlikely to be as outspoken an advocate of human rights as Sergei Kovalev, the holder of a similar post in the early 1990s who was fired for opposing the Chechen war. In the regions, progress on establishing bodies analogous to the federal Human Rights Commission suffered setbacks. Reflecting the shift in the balance of power in Russia in favor of the regions, at least eight governors violated federal law by abolishing such commissions.

The process of issuing regulations governing the implementation of a controversial law on religion passed in 1997 was completed by October. The law, aimed ostensibly at combating dangerous religious cults but regarded by many as an attempt to discriminate against members of foreign religions in favor of the Orthodox Church, distinguishes between "religious organizations" and "religious groups," which enjoy fewer privileges, and requires both to re-register with the authorities. The re-registration process was not scheduled to be completed until the end of 1999. An NGO challenged the constitutionality of certain provisions of the law, and the case was accepted for review by the Constitutional Court in November. Several international religions had re-registered successfully at year's end but others, such as the Jehovah's Witnesses, reported difficulties in some localities. Some regional governments were said to be citing the new law as justification for obstructing the activities of minority groups, such as the Khakasiya Lutheran Church. The increased decentralization of power, it appeared, had boosted the capacity of local elites to act in an arbitrary and discriminatory manner with regard to religious freedom as well as other civil liberties.

BRINGING THE MONEY IN

by SVETLANA MIKHAILOVA and ROZA TSVETKOVA

As the Moscow branch of the State Tax Inspectorate raided one of Moscow's flea markets, until the last moment none of the 40 participating tax inspectors knew where they were going. The goal of the operation was to check whether the vendors used cash registers, with which all indoor trading premises must be equipped. The operation, code-named Shuttle, started at midday, when the inspectors were taken by bus from their offices to the Dynamo flea market.

Having split into groups of three (two inspectors and a tax police officer in each), they entered the market building. Inspector Vladimir Smirnov requested to see the papers of one of the traders. "Again?" grumbled Elena P., giving him a folder that contained her trading license. The license was OK, but she did not have a cash register.

"You'll have to come to your local tax office," said the inspector. "As it is your first offense, you are liable to a 4,000 ruble [$640] fine." Elena was baffled. "Not a single vendor in this market has a cash register. Why do I have to suffer?" "Bad luck," shrugged the inspector and proceeded to his next victim.

Nikolai R., a footwear trader, had neither a cash register nor a license. He thought that the fee he had paid for holding his stall was enough. He, too, had to sign the protocol. But unlike Elena, he didn't look upset: trading without a license involves a much smaller fine than trading with a license and not having a cash register. The conclusion is simple: it is better to trade illegally than to have proper papers but no cash register.

Mikhail K., the next vendor, was trading in women's underwear and cheap jewelry. He didn't have a cash register either. At the sight of the tax inspectors near his stall, he got agitated, although not in the least frightened. "Tell me what exactly the law says," he demanded. When the law was quoted to him, he burst out laughing. "Can you repeat your joke?" he asked.

At 1:30 P.M., an order to terminate the operation came by radio from Gennadii Yermolaev, the chief inspector of the Moscow Tax Office. The inspectors were invited to the market office. The vendors screamed at them from all sides. "What cash machines? They don't even have electricity here! It is the market administration that must be fined!"

The law on the obligatory use of cash registers, which came into force in 1993, is ignored by all 200 Moscow flea markets. Feliks Oganov, deputy director of the Dynamo market, feigned ignorance. When he was shown a pamphlet with rules, according to which the market administration has no right to allocate a stall to a vendor without a cash register, he claimed he had never seen it before. "Markets will never have these machines," Oganov said. "Fire regulations do not allow us to have electricity. If we make the vendors buy their own portable cash registers, they will have to raise prices for their goods, and the whole idea of flea markets will become irrelevant."

The results of the operation Shuttle were as follows: there was not a single cash register at the market, but only 39 vendors—the ones the inspectors had time to catch—were fined for the absence of cash registers, and 21 for trading without licenses. Around 160,000 rubles will go to state coffers after the raid.

Bringing in money is a top priority for the tax inspectors. The recently developed system of checking real estate property owners, introduced by Boris Fedorov, the newly-appointed chief of the State Tax Inspectorate, was capable of bringing a lot of cash to the state budget. That was proven by the inspection of a prestigious residential high-rise building in Kudrinskaya Square. According to the Moscow Tax Inspectorate, the average rent for a flat in such a building should be between 12,500 and 94,000 rubles. The majority of Moscow landlords, however, are guilty of tax evasion as well as of renting their flats out without proper contracts, which makes it impossible for tax inspectors to prove anything. As it happens, the federal budget loses about 200,000 rubles in unpaid taxes from this building alone—a sum that would be sufficient to pay one month's pensions to 854 retirees or one month's salaries to more than 280 doctors or teachers.

On 11 June, the officers of Moscow Tax Inspectorate No. 3 visited every flat in one high-rise. The tenants of 216 flats were either absent or refused to open their doors, and the inspectors, who have no right to intrude on private dwellings, had to leave them alone. The 28 (all foreigners) who let the tax inspectors in let their landlords down, because it turned out than none of the flat owners was paying tax for renting to foreign citizens.

Dmitrii Chernik, chief of the Moscow State Tax Inspectorate, is determined to improve the tax legislation. He is convinced the law has to state clearly that any undeclared income, received from a rented-out property, is qualified as deliberately hidden. Therefore, the fine for such evasion has to be increased. Also, he stands for the obligatory registration of tenancy contracts with notaries and the police, who should be obliged to pass this information on to tax authorities. "Anyone who rents his flat and receives income from it must pay taxes," Chernik said, adding that only half of Moscow landlords are currently registered with the Tax Inspectorate. "At the moment, the law does not allow us to enforce taxes on them when they are not properly registered."

Chernik said that tax dodgers would be made liable for the whole period of tax evasion and would have to pay 10 percent of the owed sum in fines on top of it. "It is not so hard to find out for how long a flat has been rented by asking either the owner himself or his neighbors," he said. It is unlikely that the landlords will succeed in persuading all their neighbors not to spill the truth. The next step would be to establish cooperation with foreign companies that provide rented accommodation in Moscow for their employees and to track down tax dodgers with their help."

NOTE

Reprinted with kind permission from *Transitions* magazine, August 1998.

TRANSCAUCASUS & CENTRAL ASIA

VII

Georgia
Azerbaijan
Armenia
Kazakhstan
Uzbekistan
Tajikistan
Kyrgyzstan
Turkmenistan

Georgia

Population:	5,000,000
Capital:	Tbilisi (pop. 1,066,000)
Major cities:	Kutaisi (pop. 194,000), Rustavi (pop. 29,000), Batumi (pop. 123,000)
Area:	70,000 sq. km.
Major ethnic groups:	Georgian, Armenian, Russian, Azerbaijani, Ossetian, Greek, Abkhaz (percentage breakdown unavailable)
Economy:	GDP growth: 3%
	Inflation rate: 11%
	Unemployment rate: 2.6%

A DIFFICULT YEAR

by STEPHEN F. JONES

1998 was a difficult year for Georgia—generously one might describe it as two steps forward and one step back. President Eduard Shevardnadze, who turned 70 in 1998, described the year as a "test of strength for Georgian statehood." It was a year when corruption, the control of law enforcement bodies, and the problem of human rights abuses, particularly in the penitentiary system, were supposed to be aggressively tackled. In some spheres like foreign policy and to a lesser degree in democracy-building, the Georgian state made important gains. In other areas, such as the economy, human rights, or control over national territory, progress was less impressive.

Georgia remained a weak state: popular legitimacy was still fragile, it still lacked the means to ensure effective national security, and it remained vulnerable to outside interference. For the West, Georgia remained the star of the Caucasus. Under Shevardnadze's leadership, the country has adopted major democratic and market reforms, oriented itself toward Western economic and security structures, and promoted regional security with its neighbors. But in 1998, there were serious signs of popular disillusion with the Western model of development (in particular with the policies urged on Tbilisi by the IMF). Catastrophic corruption, the ineffectiveness of the ruling pro-Western party—the Citizens' Union— and economic stagnation opened up avenues for populist nationalist parties with easy cures. The gains of the Labor and Socialist parties (whose names do not reflect their ideological namesakes in the West) in the November local elections reflected growing resentment with Shevardnadze's reform program. The tension with Aslan Abashidze, the local Georgian "Pasha" in Achara (Ajaria) (an autonomous republic in Georgia) significantly increased in 1998. Abashidze attempted to extend his influence beyond the borders of his own autonomous republic, and became a more serious opponent for Shevardnadze.

ASSASSINATIONS AND COUPS

The year began badly, with a spectacular assassination attempt on Shevardnadze. On 9 February, 20 assailants armed with rocket-propelled grenades attacked his motorcade as it was returning from the State Chancellery to his governmental residence in Krtsanisi. Two bodyguards and one of the assailants—an ethnic Chechen—were killed. Shevardnadze escaped unhurt thanks to his armor-plated Mercedes (a gift from the German government) and the skill of his driver. The assassination attempt raised a number of issues: first, the political system's overdependence on one man. In an extraordinary parliamentary session following the assassination attempt, politicians expressed their fears that political chaos would have inevitably followed the removal of Shevardnadze. Second, there was a frenzy of speculation as to who was behind the attack. Was it organized crime resisting Shevardnadze's anti-corruption campaign; ex-president Zviad Gamsakhurdia's followers seeking revenge; or (the most likely in Shevardnadze's own mind) was it Russian circles attempting to destabilize Georgia, to bring it back into the Russian sphere, and end the prospects for the export of Azerbaijani oil across Georgia? Third, questions were raised once again about the effectiveness of the security ministry, which had been directly culpable in the 1995 attempt on Shevardnadze's life.

Following the February assassination attempt, the assailants fled to Samegrelo, the regional base of the Zviadist movement (followers of ex-president Gamsakhurdia) in Western Georgia. There they seized four UNOMIG (United Nations Observer Mission in Georgia) hostages, among others, in the hope of exchanging them for their captured comrades. The hostages were released unharmed after six days, and Gocha Esebua, the leader of the attack on Shevardnadze, escaped. He was later killed. According to Georgian government officials, the evidence suggests that local Zviadists led the assassination attempt, and were financed and trained by anti-Georgian elements in Russia. Russia was implicated in a second threat to Shevardnadze's life on 26 April, when two military aircraft, due to escort Shevardnadze's plane returning from Turkey, were sabotaged on a Russian-manned military airport in Georgia. As a result, Defense Minister Vardiko Nadabaidze, known for his pro-Russian orientation, was dismissed. The interior and security ministries followed suit with a wave of senior dismissals.

In October, there was an attempted coup in Western Georgia led by a former Gamsakhurdia supporter, Lieutenant-Colonel Akaki Eliava, the commander of the Senaki military base. The attempted coup, which lasted only one day and involved only a few hundred soldiers, was poorly organized but demonstrated the continued unpopularity of Shevardnadze in Samegrelo, the failure of Shevardnadze's policies of reconciliation, the fragility of the state, and the inefficiency of the government's security structures. Shevardnadze blamed certain interests (i.e., the Russians) opposed to the construction of the Baku-Supsa oil pipeline, and who aimed to undermine foreign investment in Georgia. Eliava evaded capture and at the end of 1998 was still at large in the forests of Samegrelo.

POLITICAL CHALLENGES

Shevardnadze's popularity, and that of his party—the Citizens' Union—declined in 1998, battered by economic stagnation, the late payment of salaries, perceived defeat in Abkhazia, and passivity against corruption. The parliamentary ad hoc anti-corruption commission remained ineffective, and Shevardnadze's call for a special anti-corruption agency consisting of young highly-paid incorruptibles— "an alien body within the state structure," as he described it—was still not in place by the end of the year. Shevardnadze faced local elections in November, and came under pressure from angry reformists in his party, such as parliament chairman Zurab Zhvania, who argued that dishonest ministers discredited his policies. Zhvania argued that the non-implementation of laws had brought the whole reform program to a halt and Georgia to the "edge of the abyss."

In response to this pressure, Shevardnadze dismissed almost his entire government in July, leaving in place the three power ministers (Interior, Defense, and Security) for reasons of "security." The new administration was headed by the former ambassador to Moscow Vazha Lortkipanidze. Shevardnadze proposed a new governmental structure—a cabinet of ministers headed by a "prime minister" to replace the ineffective coordination of ministries in the State Chancellery, but it required a constitutional amendment. A number of the most corrupt ministers were forced out such as Pridon Injia (communications minister) and Niko Lekishvili (state, or first, minister). Others with an equally corrupt reputation, such as Kakha Targamadze (interior minister), were left in place although a number of reformers gained ministerial rank such as Lado Chanturia at the Justice Ministry. There were further dismissals throughout the year—Jemal Gakhokidze, security minister, after the attempted coup in October, customs chief Tamaz Maglakelidze, and a slew of generals after the appointment of the reformist defense minister, Davit Tevzadze, in April. The youngest cabinet minister, 28-year-old Finance Minister Mikhail Chkuaseli, resigned in November in light of the deteriorating economic situation, to be replaced by Davit Onoprishvili. But these cabinet reshuffles made little difference in a system where, on Shevardnadze's own admission, half the economic activity was hidden and untaxed.

Shevardnadze, through the Citizens' Union, maintained control of the legislative agenda. But from May onwards, after a serious defeat in Abkhazia (see the accompanying article by Jonathan Cohen) and what looked like a rigged June by-election in Lagodekhi that overturned a socialist victory, the parliamentary opposition attacked the government aggressively, calling for Shevardnadze's resignation. An alliance of three parties—Labor, Socialists, and the Union for Democratic Revival from Achara—emerged, sponsored by Aslan Abashidze, Shevardnadze's potential rival for the presidency. The local elections in November vindicated the accusations of Zhvania and other reformers within the Citizens' Union that the authority of the government had eroded due to a corrupt executive structure. Thirteen parties and blocs took part. Barely a third of the voters participated, and while the Citizens' Union secured the largest number of seats in most councils (*sakrebuloebi*) at the local level, it failed to gain a majority on many city and regional councils. The Labor and Socialist parties, which had campaigned on anti-market issues and promised wage, pension, and health improvements, captured the Tbilisi and Rustavi city councils. The Labor Party did well because in part the United Communist Party, which had a similar platform, was not permitted to participate after late registration (brought about by the Central Election Commission objections to its lack of a required regional organization). Abashidze's Union for Democratic Revival won all 30 seats on the Batumi City Council.

Local government has little power in Georgia (regional and district governors are still appointed by Shevardnadze), but opposition-controlled councils proved troublesome. For example, the Tbilisi council resisted municipal privatization plans. The councils will be important platforms for the opposition in the run-up for national elections in October 1999.

HUMAN RIGHTS

The extra-parliamentary opposition, though a thorn in Shevardnadze's side, was small and disorganized. The ex-president's widow, Manana Arvchadze-Gamsakhurdia, continued to stage demonstrations, as did a small number of refugees (officially, internally displaced persons or IDPs) under the leadership of Boris Kakubava, the leader of the Coordinating Committee of Political Parties and Public Organizations from Abkhazia and South Ossetia. Rather brutal suppression of their demonstrations and a refusal to permit a congress of refugees in Tbilisi (subsequently reversed) led to accusations of civil rights abuse. There were similar questions raised when a local journalist reporting on homosexuality in an army unit in Akhaltsikhe was suddenly drafted despite his claims for exemption based on a 1997 law offering alternative service. In the wake of a series of police beatings, the international organization Human Rights Watch has pointed out that the police force lacks proper training and an understanding of civil rights. Georgian journalists and NGO representatives, in a protest letter in September, called for the resignation of the commander of the Special Police and the chief of the Tbilisi police, and a thorough reform of the police and the interior ministry. The penitentiary system, where there is a high incidence of tuberculosis and continued practice of torture, remained unreformed in 1998 despite a call from the Council of Europe and the Third International Conference of Human Rights (which took place in Warsaw in October) to punish all those who used torture in Georgia. A judicial reform, introduced to purge corrupt and incompetent judges through the introduction of tough qualifying examinations, came to a temporary halt in 1998 after a judge, based on a clause in the constitution, persuaded the Constitutional Court to permit him and others to serve out their 10-year terms (until 2001). Parliamentary deputies announced their intention to introduce amendments to the law to reverse the decision of the Constitutional Court. The continuing problems in the operation of the judicial system were revealed by the flawed trial of Jaba Ioseliani, the former leader of a powerful militia called Mkhedrioni, and 14 other defendants. Convicted of high treason and terrorism (they were accused of organizing an 1995 assassination attempt against Shevardnadze), they were jailed for terms of three to 15 years.

THE ECONOMY

The Georgian economy showed a decline in GDP growth rates in 1998, down to 3 percent compared to 11.3 percent in 1997, while inflation was held to 11 percent. Real growth was undoubtedly higher due to the large size of the illegal economy but GDP had nevertheless shrunk to about one third of its size in the mid-1980s. Imports continued to rise and exports fall, producing a widening trade deficit. Although Georgia was not in arrears with its foreign debt, it stood at $1.75 billion, with repayments a crushing burden for Georgia's small economy (with total GDP of about $5 billion). Around 74 percent of households officially received less than 300 lari ($150) per month, which put them on the poverty line. Wages were often paid months in arrears due to the lack of government revenue. Government pensions, at a monthly average of 14 lari ($7), were 40 million lari in arrears. The social safety net was minimal, with a newly-privatized health service and medicines that most people cannot afford.

The fundamental problem remained the inability of the state to gather sufficient tax revenues. Tax receipts for the first three quarters of 1998 were 5.3 percent of GDP, even lower than in 1997. This can be explained by corruption, a complicated and punitive tax system, a large illegal sector, and a lack of a sense in society of tax-paying as a citizen's obligation. There was little incentive for small businesses to join the legal economy, and foreign investors were discouraged by complex regulations that were manipulated to extract bribes. Georgia's financial policy—relatively tight control over the money supply, low inflation, and a stable exchange rate—was barely sustainable in Georgian economic conditions.

The Russian crisis in August tipped the Georgian economy into recession. As Georgia was flooded with cheap Russian imports and export demand in Russia declined dramatically, pressure on the lari, or the demand for dollars, increased significantly. The lari had been relatively stable for two years, but slipped dramatically from 1.3 to the dollar to over 2.00 by the end of the year. So ended one of Shevardnadze's proud economic achievements. The depreciation of the lari led to a major budgetary crisis, major asset losses by banks (approximately 24 million lari), and a surge in consumer prices of between 30 and 80 percent.

More positively, international oil companies such as Chevron, which uses Georgia as transit for its oil from Kazakhstan, promised greater investments and priority for the Eurasian trade corridor that crosses the Caucasus. Foreign experts predicted, based on oilfields in Kakheti, that Georgia could be self-sufficient in fuel by 2002, and oil was expected to begin flowing through the Baku-Supsa pipeline in early 1999.

The IMF, while continuing to urge for a tight money policy, provided funds to bolster Georgian reserves which had been lost in trying to support the lari. The European TACIS program (Technical Aid for the CIS) continued to invest significantly in Georgian ports and transport infrastructure.

MINORITIES AND THEIR TERRITORIES

In 1998, tensions increased with many of Georgia's ethnic minorities. The Abkhazia issue was the most serious problem. There were more frequent meetings and negotiations, both bilateral and multilateral, between both sides in 1998 than in previous years, and the Geneva process provided an important forum for talks on practical problems of cooperation until the two major issues—the return of refugees and Abkhazia's political status—could be resolved. But in 1998 there were no significant results from either the Geneva process or from the discussions under the auspices of the Commonwealth of Independent States (CIS). The latter, on Georgia's initiative, recommended an expansion of the role of the CIS Peace-Keeping Force (PKF) in Abkhazia beyond the small security zone at the Georgian-Abkhazian border.

Meanwhile, illegitimate Abkhazian local elections in March and the activity of the Georgian partisans in the Abkhazian region of Gali increased tensions. In May, these tensions exploded after Georgian partisans ambushed and killed 17 Abkhazian policemen. The Abkhazian response, with the PKF looking on, was a military sweep through Gali leading to the expulsion of 30,000 Georgian inhabitants who had trickled back to the region. It led to a major domestic crisis in Georgia and reduced the possibilities for compromise. The passive role of the PKF led to demands from the Georgian opposition for the withdrawal of the Russian military from Georgia entirely. The withdrawal of the PKF from Abkhazia would have led to a renewed war. Demonstrations of refugees in Georgia and Georgian military exercises in a region adjacent to Abkhazia did not prevent some progress in talks in Athens in October, when for the first time representatives of the Georgian Abkhazian government in exile were present. However the impasse on repatriation of Georgian refugees remained unresolved in 1998 and a meeting between Shevardnadze and Vladislav Ardzinba, the Abkhazian leader, planned for the fall, never took place.

The situation in South Ossetia, by contrast, continued to improve in 1998. Shevardnadze met with Ludvig Chibirov, the leader of the South Ossetians, in Georgia in June. Both declared their willingness to accept the principle of asymmetrical federalism (that is, recognizing that South Ossetia's status differed from other regions within Georgia) and anointed 1998 the "year of repatriation." However, despite relatively free travel between Georgia and South Ossetia, a reduction in the number of military posts (from 60 to 12), and a United Nations High Commissioner of Refugees program to rebuild houses, very few of the refugees from either side returned.

Two other regions presented problems for the center in 1998. Meskhet-Javakheti is a region occupied by a large Armenian population adjacent to the Republic of Armenia. One of the poorest regions in Georgia, it is better integrated into the neighboring Armenian economy than with Georgia. In 1998, Javakh, a local Armenian society that claims to represent most Armenians in the region, continued to demand autonomy and greater social and economic investment from the center. It even drew up its own constitution. Tense relations with Tbilisi worsened when Georgian soldiers entered the region on 13 August anticipating a joint exercise with Russian troops from the local garrison in Akhalkalaki (located inside Meskhet-Javakheti). They were met by armed Armenians and were forced to turn back. Many Georgians suspected a provocation from the Russian garrison, which is a major employer in the region and a supporter of Armenian claims for autonomy. The situation is complicated by the claims of Meskhetian Turks, who were expelled from the region in 1944 and now demand resettlement. The Georgian government drew up a bill for their gradual return but the pace was too slow for a group of Meskhetian exiles who demonstrated in Tbilisi in September. They were promptly picked up by the police and transported across the border to Russia.

More alarming for the authorities and for Shevardnadze in particular, was the growing assertiveness of Aslan Abashidze, Chairman of the Acharan Supreme Council. The Acharan autonomous republic, which is predominantly ethnically Georgian but approximately 50 percent Muslim, has been out of Tbilisi's control for some time. In March 1998, Abashidze, taking advantage of the Georgian constitution which postponed the definition of relations between the center and Georgia's autonomous units until the country was territorially united, passed legislation to enhance Achara's autonomy. He created his own National Security Council and established direct elections for the Chair of the Acharan Supreme Council. He strongly resisted the transfer of border protection from Russian to Georgian troops despite a Russo-Georgian agreement and accused Tbilisi of assassination plots and a desire to remove Achara's autonomy. In June at his party's congress delegates called for an end to the autocracy of Tbilisi, the impeachment of Shevardnadze, and the withdrawal of the Acharan party—the Union for Democratic Revival—from the Georgian parliament. In the November elections, Abashidze attempted to broaden his appeal outside Achara and allied with the parliamentary opposition to Shevardnadze.

FOREIGN POLICY

1998 was a successful year in Georgian foreign policy. Georgia's priorities were continuing integration with Western economic and security structures; the promotion of the Eurasian transportation corridor; the reestablishment of Georgian border control; the development of its alliance with Ukraine, Moldova, and Azerbaijan; and better-defined relations with the CIS.

Georgia asserted greater independence from Russia over the course of the year. In March, during a visit by William Cohen, U.S. secretary of defense, Georgia signed an agreement on military and security cooperation with the United States, which included finance for equipping the Georgian army and extending participation in NATO's Partnership for Peace program, (PfP). The United States began work on a new system of air traffic control for Georgia, Congress allocated $18 million for Georgia's frontier defense, and the Pentagon promised 14 transport helicopters. In June, U.S. Deputy Secretary of State Strobe Talbott visited Georgia and in September, NATO Secretary General Javier Solana followed. Georgia signed a series of military and energy agreements with Turkey, a NATO member and partner in the Eurasian transport corridor. In March, Turkish Prime Minister Mesut Yilmaz visited Georgia. Turkey awarded the Georgian defense ministry $5.5 million for military programs and offered to train 50 Georgian cadets in its military academies. Joint meetings were held with Turkey and Azerbaijan to support the proposed Baku-Tbilisi-Ceyhan pipeline in April and again in October. Visits by the Bulgarian and Romanian prime ministers suggested their interest in economic partnership with Georgia, including the transport of Central Asian oil to Europe through Georgia and the Balkans.

Relations with Armenia dramatically improved in 1998 with half-a-dozen high level visits, including Armenian President Robert Kocharyan's visit in November. Major agreements were signed on transport (a significant reduction in transit tariffs for Armenia) and Armenian integration into the Eurasian corridor project. Russia continued to be Georgia's least cooperative partner. There was a prolonged dispute between the two sides on the number of military objects Russia should return to Georgia. Russia continued to refuse the extradition of Igor Georgadze, Georgia's former security minister who was involved in the 1995 assassination attempt against Shevardnadze. The removal of Russian frontier guards from Georgia's land and sea borders with Turkey caused considerable ill will in Moscow. Georgia's informal alliance with the GUAM states (GUAM stands for Georgia, Ukraine, Azerbaijan, and Moldova); its increasingly close relations with the European Union and NATO; and its lack of commitment to CIS agreements (Georgia refused to sign 11 CIS agreements at the Moscow CIS summit in November) were clear signs that Russia was losing influence in Georgia.

Thus 1998 was a year of mixed success for Georgia: increasing independence from Russia, but increasing dependence on Western aid. Its weak statehood, underlined by an extremely fragile economy, made Georgia vulnerable to outside interference. At the same time, there was continuing progress toward democracy, although popular disillusion and corruption remained serious obstacles to its consolidation.

ABKHAZIA: PEACE POSTPONED

by JONATHAN COHEN

After four years of unstable cease-fire, the frozen conflict between Georgia and the disputed territory of Abkhazia came very close to war in spring of 1998. Hostilities on the border between Abkhazia and Georgia had an intensity not witnessed since the autumn of 1993, when 13 months of fighting ended with Abkhazians in control of the region and most of the Georgian population of Abkhazia displaced.

Precise information about the events is difficult to come by, because both sides put their own slant on the numbers killed. Nevertheless, the United Nations military observers in Georgia (UNOMIG), established in August 1993, suggested a death toll of several hundred and the displacement of some 30,000 people. Although a cease-fire was renegotiated on 25 May, the hostilities were a reminder of how fragile the situation is and how impervious to resolution the conflict seems to be. The recent conflagration will undoubtedly have consequences for the prospects of a peaceful settlement, as well as the stability of Georgia and oil transit routes through the Caucasus as a whole.

A cease-fire had been in place since May 1994, maintained and monitored by UNOMIG and peacekeepers from the Commonwealth of Independent States (CIS), first deployed in July 1994. But despite negotiations mediated by the Russian Federation and the UN, problems continued. Abkhazia remains unrecognized by the international community. There is little common ground for a resolution of the basic dispute on the political status of Abkhazia. Abkhazians demand sovereignty; Georgia is prepared to grant autonomy within an asymmetric federation. To Abkhazians, autonomy, reeking of Soviet federalism, is yesterday's debate. They demand an equal rather than a subordinate relationship between the respective authorities in their main city of Sukhumi (called Sukhum by the Abkhazians) and Tbilisi, and talk of confederation. There is a further contradiction: Georgia requires a safe return of the people displaced by the war (internally displaced persons, or IDPs) before the issue of Abkhazia's status can be defined. Meanwhile, the Abkhazians, fearing they will again be a minority in their own homeland, demand a determination of the political and legal status of Abkhazia before the issue of IDPs can be resolved.

The mutual antagonism and distrust that have littered the past five years have meant that reconciliation and accommodation, even before the latest outbreak of fighting, was not an immediate prospect. At best, Georgia and Abkhazia enjoyed a volatile stability.

Nevertheless, events over the past year, while not foreshadowing an imminent solution, suggested that progress could be made.

TWO STEPS FORWARD . . .

One heartening sign was the meeting of Georgian President Eduard Shevardnadze and Abkhazian President Vladislav Ardzinba, in Tbilisi on 14 August 1997. The meeting—which took place on the fifth anniversary of the Georgian attack on Abkhazia—might have encouraged reconciliation, but it was also an attempt by its convener, Russian then-Foreign Minister Yevgenii Primakov, to reassert Russia's waning influence over the peace process. The meeting led to criticism of both Shevardnadze and Ardzinba—from both their respective parliaments and the public, who are generally less receptive to a negotiated settlement and more fearful of the possibility of concessions. Nevertheless, in November 1997 negotiating teams met in Geneva, which led to the establishment of the Coordinating Council, with three working groups on security, IDPs, and socio-economic development. In addition to the formal agreement to intensify negotiations, other bilateral contacts between Georgian and Abkhazian officials presaged a more positive dynamic.

In early 1998 a small but symbolic agreement eased telephone restrictions between Sukhumi and Tbilisi. International communications were also improved, although this meant Abkhazian calls had to be routed through Tbilisi. Another step toward stabilization was the dispatch of a UN needs assessment mission to Abkhazia in February under the auspices of the Coordinating Council. This signaled that rehabilitation and development needs in Abkhazia could be important in a wider political dialogue.

Grounds for optimism remained shaky, however. In practical terms, the new working groups on security and IDPs made no progress, the latter unable even to meet because of disagreements over composition and agendas. The negotiations continued to leave Abkhazians feeling pressure from both Georgia and the international community. The economic blockade, in effect since December 1994, and the activity of irregular, armed Georgian formations (terrorists in Abkhazian terms, partisans in Georgian) penetrating into Abkhazia, contributed to Abkhazians' discontent and diminished their faith in the impartiality of any mediation.

It is easy to overestimate the extent of the blockade. Despite restrictions, produce can be illegally imported into Abkhazia across the Psou River, by boat from Turkey, or across the Inguri River border with Georgia. Although the blockade has a significant economic impact, trade restrictions are secondary as a barrier to trade exchanges and economic recovery—the principal constraint is one of resource deficiency. Nevertheless, the key impact is psychological. The Georgian strategy of trying to strangle Abkhazia in the hope of weakening the regime or forcing it toward compromise only entrenches anti-Georgian feeling and creates a siege mentality among Abkhazians. They have survived the hardship so far and see no reason why they cannot continue to do so—although 20–25 percent of the estimated 250,000 population of Abkhazia receives aid from agencies such as the International Committee of the Red Cross. The blockade also gives the

Abkhazians an excuse to blame someone else for their economic plight. Furthermore, it has an impact on their negotiating strategy: their self-sufficiency makes political accommodation to remove the blockade an unacceptable concession.

. . . THREE STEPS BACK

The Gali district (called Gal by the Abkhazians) is on the Abkhazian side of the border with Georgia. Largely inhabited by Georgians, it has long been a sensitive area. The pre-war population was 90,000, of which 95 percent were Georgian—overwhelmingly Mingrelian—with their own distinct language and identity. In the aftermath of the war a spontaneous process of return has seen as many as 50,000 of these come and go across the border, outside the official, failed repatriation scheme, negotiated in 1994. Old people, women, children, and some men crossed the border to tend their crops and then returned to Zugdidi (a regional city on the Georgian side of the border with Abkhazia) either to sell them, to benefit from the distribution of humanitarian aid, or to escape rising tensions. A bridge over the Inguri between Zugdidi and Gali provided the only legitimate crossing point, but a couple of other bridges and 22 fords enabled people to cross informally. The overwhelming majority of returning IDPs did not officially register in Abkhazia, which created another source of tension, with Abkhazian militia often detaining people for lack of appropriate documentation. One side's legitimate detention, however, is the other's harassment and a source of extortion.

In this atmosphere, lawlessness has flourished. Guerrilla activity, an issue since the end of the war, took on a new intensity. Between June 1997 and April 1998 more than 60 serious, organized incidents occurred, including placement of land mines or bombs, hostage-taking, and killings. Georgian guerrillas have targeted Abkhazian militia and CIS peacekeeping forces. In turn, Abkhazians have attempted to root out guerrillas. Inevitably, civilians have been victims. Some of the activity was also aimed at reclaiming the bodies of victims of the fighting: hostages have been taken or people killed to provide a currency to negotiate the release of a corpse or a hostage.

Guerrilla activity has not been uniform. The White Legion was the largest and reputedly the best-organized group. Others included the Forest Brothers, the Liberation Army, and Cobra. Their activities can be characterized in terms of four levels of professionalism and support. At one level, a local in the Georgian villages in the Gali district, who has a grudge, or has maybe had too much to drink, might take his hunting rifle to kill an Abkhazian. At a second level, locals might stage minor operations, typically disorganized and relatively independent, possibly as a response to Abkhazian militia patrols. A third level involved recruits from among IDPs in Georgia, possibly former soldiers, acting in groups of ten to 20 and armed with Kalashnikov assault rifles and anti-personnel and tank mines. These were becoming increasingly professional; there was conjecture they were linked to the Tbilisi-based Abkhazian government-in-exile (consisting of Georgian deputies elected to the Abkhazian parliament in 1991). The Georgian government knew of their existence but did not seek to control them, and was vocal in distancing itself from their activities. A fourth level of guerrilla activity, which sometimes operated beyond the Gali district, was highly professional and well-trained, with sophisticated weapons. As IDPs operating alone could hardly achieve their level of professionalism, they were likely to be controlled in part by the Ministry of State Security.

In the first months of 1998 the military significance of guerrilla activity was limited. Continuous attacks were reminders of the problem, not decisive steps to re-ignite conflict. But the psychological impact fueled a cycle of retaliation. By May the guerrillas thought they were winning the struggle for lower Gali (the southern part of the Gali district). Abkhazian militia entered this region at their peril. The returnees in the region were increasingly in control of their own affairs, depending on one another for security needs, although ironically still receiving and paying for electricity from Abkhazian authorities. They were open to accusations from Abkhazians that they were either harboring or supporting guerrillas. Tensions were expected to increase: either guerrillas would try to reach beyond the Gali district in a more consolidated way (and there had already been attempts to place bombs in the neighboring district of Ochamchira and in Sukhumi), or Abkhazians would strike back, fearing that they might lose the Gali district entirely.

This could not be countenanced: the loss would have begun the dismemberment of Abkhazia and created a launch pad for guerrilla attacks deeper into Abkhazia. The fertile land and the critically important Inguri hydroelectric power station (providing 30 percent of its energy to Abkhazia and 70 percent to Georgia) are too significant to cede to Georgia without a fight.

THE NOOSE TIGHTENS

The political stalemate created periodic increases in tension—especially around CIS summits, when the peacekeeping forces' mandate was renewed, and at times of negotiations. Tensions had certainly been increasing since February, when a blockade over the Inguri bridge was imposed by disgruntled IDPs in advance of discussions about the renewal of the peacekeepers' mandate. The CIS summit on 29 April endorsed a resolution reiterating a 1997 proposal to extend the security zone throughout the Gali district, linking the restoration of Abkhazia's economy to the repatriation of IDPs and the creation of joint Georgian-Abkhazian local administrative bodies with representation from the UN and Organization for Security and Cooperation in Europe (OSCE) representation. Abkhazians had previously rejected all these measures and did so again, protesting that the peacekeepers' mandate could not be amended without their consent.

Following the summit declaration, a public meeting of Abkhazians in Ochamchira on 7 May called for an end to the terrorist attacks, withdrawal from the negotiations, and a mobilization to clean up the Gali district, implying that all Georgians should be kicked out. Two days later, Bezhan Gunava, a Georgian parliamentary deputy, accompanied by Germane Patsatsia, leader of the Abkhazia parliamentary group in Tbilisi, crossed the Inguri into Abkhazia under the protection of the Forest Brothers guerrilla group to distribute humanitarian assistance. The visit, the first of a Georgian official to Abkhazia without the formal permission of Abkhazian authorities, was seen as a provocation.

On 14 May, the Abkhazian parliament adopted a resolution condemning the summit declaration, calling on Ardzinba to revoke the CIS peacekeeping mandate and to reject further Russian mediation. Whether or not Abkhazians felt they could survive without the presence of the CIS forces, the parliament was clearly prepared to push a more radical agenda than Ardzinba.

The reason for the new conflagration was unclear. A premeditated Abkhazian operation, one guerrilla attack too many, and a Georgian attempt to retake the Gali district by Independence Day on 26 May have all been mooted. On 18 May, a guerrilla attack was reported by the Georgian media to have left 20 Abkhazian militia dead. Abkhazian sources put the figure at six. The attack sparked a strong Abkhazian response: on 20 May some 1,500 Abkhazian militia entered the Gali district. Although guerrillas formed the main contingent of Georgians fighting Abkhazians, interior ministry troops also participated. By the time a cease-fire was established (localized fighting continued for several days), almost all Georgians in the Gali district had crossed the Inguri. From the east bank of the river they were able to see the smoke as Abkhazians burned their villages—diminishing the chances of a further repatriation once the situation stabilizes.

The Abkhazian response was predictable: they either had to accept the loss of the Gali district or retaliate. As a result, a large contingent of people has again been displaced. The process of return to the Gali district, not to mention the rest of Abkhazia, has been put off indefinitely. The IDPs, who have been waiting to return for almost five years, still have their expectations raised by Georgian politicians. Meanwhile, Abkhazians hope the IDPs will assimilate into Georgian society and not want to return—another unlikely prospect. The uncertain status of IDPs could fuel the cycle that led to the resumption of hostilities, providing fertile ground for future guerrilla activity. They now feel betrayed by their own government, the Russians, and the international community.

A large, alienated constituency once again resides in western Georgia. Zugdidi's population has swollen to almost double as a result of displacements from Abkhazia. Those marginalized by displacement join those marginalized by the split in Georgia's political life. Western Georgia was the stronghold of the ousted Georgian leader Zviad Gamsakhurdia and the word "Zviadist," a term of abuse in Tbilisi, retains a positive resonance for many in Zugdidi and Mingrelia. Shevardnadze is far from popular there: people live with the consequences of war in a way that those in Tbilisi do not. In Tbilisi, Abkhazia is one of a number of important issues, but not the only one. The intense criticism that Shevardnadze faced as a result of the May hostilities has undermined his authority. As one opposition politician commented, "You can't wave a red rag at a bull without a dagger in your other hand." Yet while the illusion was created that the Gali district could be retaken, the reality is more humiliation for Georgia. Opponents claim Georgia might be better able to resolve the Abkhazian conflict without Shevardnadze, who was leader when the war commenced, but others suggest that if the main factor that has guaranteed Georgian stability is removed, the situation will deteriorate.

THE RUSSIAN FACTOR

The mantra of Russian culpability is heard on both sides. Georgians damn the Russians for mounting an ineffective peacekeeping operation, which reputedly allowed Abkhazians to move heavy weapons into the security zone. Abkhazians condemn the peacekeepers for having allowed Georgian guerrillas to penetrate the security zone. Clearly, the peacekeepers failed to separate the opposing sides. Expressions of concern about their efficacy are not new, but the rationale to maintain them has diminished, especially from the Georgian perspective. They have not created conditions for IDP return. The Russians have increasingly demanded a curb on guerrilla activity, trying to save their own credibility. The UNOMIG has not been immune from criticism either, since it too was unable to protect the IDPs. The idea of deploying a protection force of 300 in Abkhazia to secure the role of UNOMIG has been mooted in the UN Security Council since March, but this will not secure the process of return to the Gali district. Georgians might be waiting for NATO, or a broader internationalization of peacekeeping with possibly Ukrainian and Turkish contingents. But at a time when events in Kosovo had led to the displacement of far fewer people but received far greater international attention, it was unlikely that the international community would sanction the deployment of a significant body of troops in Georgia. In any event, even if a peacekeeping operation could effectively separate the parties, the questions of status and IDP return will not go away. Furthermore, the debate in Georgian society about the nature of future relations with Abkhazia is lackluster.

Discussion at the political level is not mirrored in society, and while Georgian and Abkhazian leaders may haltingly engage in dialogue with one another, there is little attempt to do so with their populations. Many in Tbilisi see machinations concerning the struggle for oil pipeline routes as the stimulus for the latest bout of conflict. With a decision on the major pipeline to export Caspian oil due in the autumn, an argument commonly heard in Tbilisi was that Russia destabilized Georgia to prevent a Georgian-Turkish pipeline, in favor of a northern route through Russia. Russia's track record in the Caucasus is such that Moscow is rarely blameless and is certainly an unreliable ally. This should, however, give both Georgia and Abkhazia pause for thought. Both sides know the danger of relying on Russia to sort out their problems. Development on these grounds seems hardly likely to remove the identity, security, and democratic deficiency matrix that has made the conflicts in the Caucasus so intractable.

NOTE
Reprinted with kind permission from *Transitions* magazine, July 1998.

Azerbaijan

Population:	7,529,000
Capital:	Baku (pop. 1,550,000)
Major cities:	Genje (pop. 232,000), Sumgait (pop. 190,000)
Area:	86,600 sq. km.
Major ethnic groups:	Azeri 90%, Russian 5%
Economy:	GDP growth: 10%
	Inflation rate: 1.1%
	Unemployment rate: 10–15%

A TIME FOR PATIENCE

by FARIZ ISMAILZADE and JASON PELLMAR

Azeris and foreigners alike looked upon 1998 as the year in which the main sources of contention in Azerbaijan would be resolved: that is, the conflict in Nagorno-Karabakh and the route of the main oil export pipeline. Unfortunately, no progress was made in resolving either problem. No one was more distraught at this impasse than the 900,000 refugees and internally displaced persons who seven years after fleeing their homes were still unable to return to their homeland, the Armenian occupied Nagorno-Karabakh and six adjacent districts, and as a result were living in tent camps, dug-outs, and railway cars. October did see fresh presidential elections which left Heydar Aliev in power—accompanied, perhaps, by a false sense of security.

PRESIDENTIAL ELECTIONS

In October current President Heydar Aliev, the chairman of the ruling New Azerbaijan Party, ran for election to his second term in office. His election campaign was predominantly based on achievements in domestic and international affairs, such as the stabilization of the republic's internal situation, the May 1994 cease-fire with neighboring Armenia in the Karabakh conflict, an increase in foreign investment in the oil and gas sector, and a somewhat more impressive macroeconomic development than in the other Newly Independent States.

International organizations such as Freedom House, the Organization for Security and Cooperation in Europe (OSCE), and the Institute for Democracy, as well as the domestic opposition, exerted pressure on the authorities of the Republic of Azerbaijan to considerably improve the electoral process. The government moved to fulfill its commitments to the OSCE by formally abolishing censorship in August and by approving a new Citizenship Law in September granting full citizenship to the 260,000 refugees who had arrived on the territory of Azerbaijan from January 1988 till January 1992. The authorities generally responded positively to concerns raised by the international community and indicated their willingness to meet international standards in the conduct of the election. The new Law on the Election of the President of the Republic, as amended on 10 July 1998, showed significant improvement over the previously existing law. In response to the opposition's demands, Aliev proposed two changes in the electoral law, including reducing the minimum turnout for a valid election from 50 to only 25 percent and allowing individuals to sign the nominating positions for more than one presidential candidate. Both these changes were adopted by the parliament, the Milli Majlis. The opposition stood to benefit from the alteration making it easier to collect a sufficient number of signatures for presidential nominees. The print media was allowed to express a wide variety of views and each candidate was given an equal amount of airtime in accordance with the new election law.

However, not all aspects of the election ran smoothly. From the outset, the leaders of six major opposition parties, including the Popular Front of Azerbaijan, the Azerbaijan Democratic Party, the Liberal Democratic Party, and the Social-Democratic Party boycotted the elections claiming that the basic conditions for holding democratic elections were not met. They denounced the presidential election law as "undemocratic," demanded that the political censorship in the country be lifted, and urged an end to human rights violations. A particular point of contention was the role of the Central Electoral Commission. The law enabled the Milli Majlis and the president to appoint 12 members each to the commission. Although the law stated that the members must be politically unaffiliated, it was still easy for those in power to pack the commission with their supporters, especially given the preponderance of Aliev supporters in the Milli Majlis. (The opposition only has eight seats in the 125 strong Milli Majlis, which is dominated by the pro-Aliev New Azerbaijan Party.) President Aliev offered four seats in the Central Election Commission to the disgruntled opposition on 4 August, in addition to a fifth seat from the parliament quota. The opposition was unwilling to compromise unless full parity was achieved. Prior to the elections, a series of demonstrations organized by several opposition parties took place in Baku. On 16 August, some 5,000 people took part in an opposition rally to protest the "anti-democratic elections for the Azerbaijani president" slated for 11 October. Interior Minister Ramil Usubov used an estimated 500 plain-clothes police "to stave off provocation from the opposition." Police detained 106 people in Baku overnight, but the majority of the dissenters were soon released.

The Central Election Commission had six contenders registered: incumbent president Heydar Aliev, elected in 1993 and nominated by the New Azerbaijan Party; Etibar Mamedov, nominated by the Azerbaijan National Independence Party; Firudin Hassanov, appointed by one of the three registered Communist Parties; Khanhusein Kazimili, Chairman of the Social Prosperity Party; Ashraf Mehtiyev, Chairman of the Association of Victims of Illegal Political Repression; and Nizami Sulimanov, Chairman of the Independent Azerbaijan Party.

The official results reported a turnout of 3,289,221 voters (around 77 percent of the registered electorate). Aliev led with 2,556,059 votes or 78 percent of votes cast, followed by Mamedov with 389,662 votes (12 percent), Sulimanov 270,709 votes (8 percent), Hassanov 29,244 votes, Mehtiyev 28,809, and Kazimili 8,254.

Following the announcement of the election results, Mamedov, who came in second, declared the elections fraudulent and accused Heydar Aliev of tampering with the election results. A Soviet-era dissident and prominent opposition member, Mamedov had appeared to be highly popular among Azeris, not least because of his reputation as a clean politician—one who had never held any government office. Mamedov supporters held a series of public demonstrations in Baku, as well as other major cities. Government authorities used police force in order to control the situation.

The presidential elections of 1998 were also criticized by leading international human rights groups and the OSCE Election Observation Mission. The OSCE report found "clear evidence of ballot stuffing" and concluded that "the overall legal and administrative framework governing the election process fell short of meeting the international standards for a genuine election competition." Thus, the presidential elections failed to portray Azerbaijan as a country moving toward democratization and liberalization. Cynics speculated that Aliev supporters, anxious to assuage the president's vanity, went overboard in pushing his vote tally to landslide proportions. A more modest victory—which, independent polls suggested, Aliev could probably have achieved without fraud—would have attracted less internal and external criticism.

RIGHTS AND WRONGS

On 26 March President Aliev signed a decree declaring that an attempted genocide of the Azeris had taken place in 1918. This was an attempt to counter Armenian claims of their 1915 genocide at the hands of the Turks, by officially noting the killings of Azeris that took place in Baku and other major cities in 1918 at the hands of the Armenian Dashnaktsusun Army, under the leadership of Red Army Commissar Stepan Shaumyan. The decree was widely publicized in secondary schools and universities and acted as a catalyst in spurring the desire to further study Azerbaijani history.

In January criminal charges were brought against the former speaker of the Milli Mejlis, Rasul Guliyev, for embezzlement and misappropriation of $25 million through deals with foreign importers of Azerbaijani crude oil. In 1992–93 Guliyev had worked as the deputy president of the State Oil Company of Azerbaijan (SOCAR). Chief Prosecutor Eldar Hasanov expressed his desire to have Guliyev extradited from the United States, where he had resided as a political refugee since September 1996. Guliyev published in the United States two books—"Oil and Politics" and "The Road to Democracy"—criticizing the policies of the Azerbaijani leadership. In April the Milli Mejlis stripped Guliyev of his immunity from prosecution as a parliamentary deputy. In June Guliyev fought back from exile: in an interview with a Moscow paper he accused Aliev of embezzling $900 million, and of complicity in the loss of territory to Armenia in 1993 as part of the plot to undermine then-President Elchibey and secure his own return to power. In December new embezzlement charges were filed. In December, in the wake of Aliev's triumphal reelection, new charges accusing Guliyev of insulting the president were filed. While their leader stayed at a safe distance, moving between Turkey and the United States, six deputies of the parliament who supported Guliyev broke away from the ruling New Azerbaijan Party to form the Democratic Party.

Later in the year there was another scandal, this time around former president Abulfaz Elchibey. In November Elchibey, an old political rival of Aliev, accused the current president of involvement with the Kurdish Workers' Party (PKK), which threatens Turkey with separatism. President Aliev could not tolerate such an accusation and charges were filed against Elchibey for insulting the president, an offense punishable by up to six years in prison.

NO PROGRESS OVER NAGORNO-KARABAKH

The year of 1998 brought no improvement, let alone solution, to the crisis in Nagorno-Karabakh. While the OSCE Minsk group co-chairs France, Russia, and the United States searched for proposals that would bring about a peaceful resolution of the conflict, neither Armenia nor Azerbaijan was willing to make concessions. Negotiations broke down when the Minsk group co-chairs came up with the "Common State" proposal. This new proposal suggested that Azerbaijan and Nagorno-Karabakh form a Common State on the basis of a horizontal, rather than a vertical relationship. While this proposal was welcomed in Yerevan and Hankendi (Stepanakert), Baku categorically refused it, claiming that the proposal did not guarantee the territorial integrity of Azerbaijan and was biased towards the Armenian side. Azeri ruling officials generally believed that the "Common State" proposal came out of the Russian foreign ministry and did not conform to the 1996 OSCE Lisbon summit's conditions of autonomy for Karabakh. The "Common State" proposal would effectively recognize the sovereignty of Karabakh, which could potentially serve as the basis for an independence movement.

Unfortunately, the OSCE's gradual distancing from the Lisbon summit's principles created even greater stagnation in the search for a solution to the conflict. Some 900,000 refugees and internally displaced persons of Azerbaijan struggled to survive in tent camps for the seventh consecutive year and there were still no viable solutions in the making.

The year of 1998 also saw the further militarization of Armenia by Russian supplies of S-300 surface to air missiles and MiG-29 fighter jets. Armenia has gradually been transformed into the only ally of Russia in the Caucasus, since Azerbaijan and Georgia have chosen to align themselves with the Western powers. Russia's militarization of Armenia was of deep concern to Azeri authorities, who claimed that the balance of power in the Caucasus has been upset. As a result, they redoubled their efforts to create an alliance with Turkey and NATO.

Skipping ahead, it is worth noting that in January of 1999, while President Aliev was in Turkey for medical treatment, the chief advisor to the president Vafa Guluzade openly suggested moving an American military base from Incirlik in Turkey to Azerbaijan. This suggestion highly angered Russia and Iran. Azeri authorities justified their stance declaring the necessity to counteract the Armenian militarization.

INDECISION OVER OIL

In 1998 the key question of how to secure the future export of Azerbaijan's oil wealth to world markets remained unresolved. Speaking in December, U.S. Commerce Department advisor Jan Kalicki described 1998 as "the year in which the euphoric rush to the Caspian was tempered by rational expectations."

In late 1997 the Azerbaijan International Oil Consortium (AIOC) and the Azerbaijani government had witnessed the first fruits of the 1994 "Contract of the Century," the deal signed in 1994 for the development of Azerbaijan's offshore resources. The first ("early") oil from the Chirag field was pumped in November 1997 through the northern pipeline, across Chechnya to the Russian Black Sea port of Novorossiisk. Excitement over the success of the AIOC raised hopes that agreement over the route for the Main Export Pipeline, which will carry the larger volumes of oil (up to 100 million tons per year) expected in the future, would be concluded in 1998. The Main Export Pipeline is expected to run from Baku to the Georgian Black Sea port of Supsa, with an extension down across Turkey to the Mediterranean port of Ceyhan. Although it is economically less favored than a pipeline across Iran, the Baku-Ceyhan pipeline was considered by the United States to be the most politically beneficial, since it would served to bind NATO member Turkey with the Caucasian and Central Asian countries, while bypassing fickle Russia and the hostile state of Iran.

The initial informal agreement of Azeri, Turkish, and American governments had been made in favor of the Baku-Ceyhan route. Hence in the words of President Aliev: "The decision of the Azerbaijani government and of the Azerbaijani president is known. There are many ways to transport the main oil to the international market. But for Azerbaijan—the one and only—the most beneficial and the most reliable is via Baku-Georgia-Turkey to Ceyhan." Aliev spoke these words on the occasion of his 75th birthday (10 May 1998), where 19 state delegations including Eduard Shevardnadze of Georgia and Suleyman Demirel of Turkey gathered in Baku for a private commemoration.

However, the collapse of oil prices in the world markets in the wake of the 1997 Asian crisis created hesitation among the oil companies in the making of a final decision. The Clinton administration persistently tried to influence the oil companies with various bonuses and persistent negotiations by Richard Morningstar, the energy advisor to the U.S. president in regards to the Caspian region. In October 1998 the presidents of Azerbaijan, Georgia, Kazakhstan, Turkey, Uzbekistan, and U.S. Energy Secretary Federico Peña signed "The Ankara Declaration" endorsing the Baku-Ceyhan pipeline as the main route for transportation of Caspian oil to the world markets. However, the decision to actually sign a contract to commence construction was postponed indefinitely.

Meanwhile, the AIOC continued the re-construction of a small Western pipeline, passing via Georgia to the Black Sea port of Supsa. This $500 million pipeline will be the second outlet for "early oil" and will decrease the dependence of Azerbaijan on the northern (Russian) route, which is quite unstable due to the political turmoil in Chechnya and rapidly changing Russian policies. Actual oil production in Azerbaijan remains modest, since progress in developing off-shore fields has been held back by lack of drilling equipment and other delays. Azerbaijan extracted 9 million tons of oil, up from 5 million the previous year.

ECONOMIC REVIVAL

In 1998, the real GDP compared to 1997 increased by some 10 percent. This was one of the highest results among the former Soviet Republics and the countries of Eastern Europe. Industrial production rose by 1.1 percent and capital investment by 62 percent. Fourteen production sharing agreements (PSAs) were signed with foreign oil companies resulting in $1.6 billion in foreign investments and contract bonuses. Macroeconomic stability resulted in an inflation rate of 1.1 percent, one of the lowest in the post-Soviet world. U.S. trade turnover with Azerbaijan nearly doubled in 1998 to $127 million, frcm $68 million in 1997. Close cooperation with the IMF and the World Bank and implementation of European Union's TACIS programs (various technical assistance projects) created a good foundation for further economic development. Despite these positive developments, the unemployment rate has remained high, with an official estimate of 10–15 percent. Trade with the foreign countries also experienced a deficit of $167 million.

In September Azerbaijan hosted the "Silk Road Summit" of 32 countries under the auspices of the European Union. The "Baku Declaration" on the development of the transport corridor of Europe-Caucasus-Asia (TRACECA) was signed. If implemented, the "Silk Road" project will encourage much greater investment in the region, as well as promote stability and long-term economic development. The significance of the conference was further illustrated by the attendance of the Armenian Prime Minister Armen Darbinian.

FOREIGN AFFAIRS

In 1998 President Heydar Aliev visited Great Britain and Japan. Both of the visits turned out to be successful in terms of increasing bilateral cooperation and attracting investments to the Azerbaijani economy. During his visit to the UK, President Aliev discussed cooperation with NATO under the Partnership for Peace program and signed three Exploration, Development and Production Sharing Agreements (EDPSA) for oil projects with SOCAR (State Oil Company of Azerbaijan Republic). The fourth contract concerned major hotel construction in Baku and was signed with Morrison Construction.

On his first official trip to Japan, President Aliev created a joint economic commission to attract more Japanese investments into the Azerbaijani economy. Japan committed itself to the further development of the Silk Road Corridor, considering itself historically linked to Azerbaijan via the Silk Road, which extends from Europe through the Caucasus, Central Asia, India, China, and finally, to Japan. The Azeri State Oil Company SOCAR signed a preliminary agreement with Japanese Mitsui that would give it a 15 percent share in the development of the Kurdashi oil field in the Caspian Sea. In order to modernize a key power plant near Baku and a petrochemical facility, loans were promised by Japan's Economic Cooperation Fund and the Nichimen Company, respectively. Finally, Japan pledged $1.2 million to humanitarian aid projects, implemented by the United Nations High Commissioner for Refugees (UNHCR), to better the conditions of the refugee and displaced person population. Prime Minister Hashimoto also promised to support Azerbaijan in its bid for membership in the World Trade Organization (WTO) and the Asian Development Bank.

The year of 1998 brought some major disappointments in Azeri-American relations. After the visit of Azeri President Aliev to the United States in 1997 and his meetings with President Clinton, Azerbaijan hoped for a radical change in the U.S. Congress's discriminatory policy towards Azerbaijan. Section 907 of the Freedom Support Act, passed in 1992 under pressure from the Armenian diaspora, prohibits any assistance from the U.S. government to Azerbaijan, in response to Baku's alleged blockade of Armenia. However, a congressional resolution that would have lifted Section 907, allowing direct governmental aid to Azerbaijan and removing the stigma of being a pariah state, was narrowly defeated. The resignation of U.S. Congress Speaker-Designate Bob Livingston, a long-time supporter of oil interests, even further crushed the expectations of Azerbaijan. Thus, despite pressure from Secretary of State Madeleine Albright and President Clinton, the U.S. Congress remained loyal to the Armenian electorate and refused to get rid of the obstacle in the U.S.-Azeri developments and promotion of democracy in the region.

Azerbaijan's relationship with Russia hit rock bottom in 1998. Russia's constant supply of weapons to Armenia provoked irate reactions from Azeri officials. Furthermore, the Russian government failed to properly investigate the illegal arms transfer to Armenia, which they admitted took place in 1993–96. Their silence seemed to legitimize the deliveries, which were arguably illegal under the Conventional Forces in Europe treaty limiting conventional weapons. Failing to find support from Russia in regards to the Karabakh crisis, Azerbaijan was pushed towards NATO. In a bid to bring Azerbaijan back into its orbit of influence Russia extradicted former Prime Minister Suret Huseinov to Azeri authorities. Huseinov was accused of organizing the anti-government coup in 1995 in Ganja. After the failure of the coup he sought refuge in Russia as a political refugee. The trial of Huseinov opened in Baku on 14 July. He was charged with a variety of offenses ranging from treason to drug-dealing. He pled guilty only to illegal weapons possession and living in Russia under a false identity.

Similar trends were experienced in relations with Iran. Iran's support of Armenia, its inequitable policies in the northwestern province of Iran, home to 20 million ethnic Azeris, and its advocacy for the division of the Caspian Sea into equal sectors were the major reasons for the bilateral tensions. The Azerbaijani government, fearing the spread of Islamic fundamentalism from the south, forbade the functioning of numerous pro-Islamic groups and parties. In its turn, Iran, concerned with the possible prosperity of Azerbaijan Republic and the potential willingness of the Iranian Azeri province to secede, sought to further strength the ties between Iran and Armenia. Finally, unwilling to accept Western, especially American, influence in the Caspian region, Iran called for a reevaluation of the status of the Caspian Sea, thus refusing to recognize the current oil contracts. However, Iran did buy $180 million worth of Azebaijani oil, making it Baku's biggest single customer.

The visit of NATO Secretary-General Javier Solana to Baku in late September opened a new phase in NATO-Azerbaijan relations. Azeri President Aliev discussed in his meeting with Javier Solana the issues of mutual cooperation, Azeri-Armenian conflict, participation of Azeri soldiers in the CentrasBat-98 exercise in Macedonia, and the Russian supply of weapons to Armenia. The Secretary-General emphasized the importance of peaceful means in the resolution of the Nagorno-Karabakh conflict and urged a negotiated solution on the basis of the 1996 Lisbon documents. He also focused on the expansion of Azerbaijan's role in the Partnership for Peace program of NATO.

1998 witnessed a significant shift in Azeri-Israeli relations. Following the initiation of Turkish-Israeli defense cooperation in 1996, Azeri authorities also drew closer to cooperation with Israel. A short visit of Israeli Prime Minister Benjamin Netanyahu to Baku in September 1997 and his talks with President Aliev encouraged more active support of Jewish lobby groups of Azeri positions. In June, eight major Jewish lobby groups in the United States decided to take on the influential Armenian Assembly of America to clear Azerbaijan's name in Congress and end the sanctions imposed by Congress in 1992 at the urging of Armenian-Americans. At the same time, a group of Azeris launched a radio service for the Iranian Azeri population using an Israel-based transmitter. This caused much displeasure from the Iranian authorities, who accused Azerbaijan of "inviting the Zionist regime into the region."

Altogether, the year of 1998 can be considered a successful year in Azerbaijan's foreign policy. The replacement of Foreign Minister Hasan Hasanov by new young diplomat Tofik Zulfugarov brought fresh ideas and enthusiasm into the work of the foreign ministry. Hasanov was dismissed for misappropriating a $10 million loan from Turkey, which was intended for the construction of a diplomatic center in Baku. In the course of the year numerous additional countries opened embassies in Azerbaijan and cooperation with the European Union and other international organization intensified.

However, despite energetic efforts to become a member of the Council of Europe, Azerbaijan was refused membership in this organization (as was Armenia), due to the inability to solve the Karabakh conflict and the failure to hold municipal elections. In order to meet the Council of Europe's membership criteria, President Aliev signed a law abolishing capital punishment and called for minor reforms in the police and prison system.

A NATION'S DIGNITY

by ARIF ALIEV

The Baku city court has been keeping close watch over the dignity of the citizens of Azerbaijan. After a bizarre trial that ended 7 July, Judge Zahid Agayev ruled that an article by journalist Elmar Husseynov had "insulted" the Azeri nation and ordered him to publish a refutation and pay a fine of 16,000,000 manat (about $4,100) to a refugee fund. The prosecutor had only asked for half that sum.

The case began on 27 February, when policemen raided newsstands throughout the city and confiscated the issues remaining from the February press run (3,000–5,000 copies) of the independent magazine *Monitor*. Funded by its staff and edited by Husseynov, the glossy, 72-page monthly runs political and economic analysis, usually critical of the authorities.

The action stunned local journalists, who scrambled to find a reason for such an extraordinary undertaking by the police (the last time a paper was confiscated was in 1993, when the anti-government newspaper *Azadlig* ran a cartoon that apparently offended President Heydar Aliev). What had made the authorities so angry this time? What particular article had pushed them into committing such an obviously illegal act? Some thought it might have been an article on Rasul Guliyev, the former speaker of the Azerbaijani parliament, now in the camp of the radical opposition. Or it could have been several articles exploring the clannish character of the ruling elite and its monopoly on the sale of strategic raw materials. Or was it the exposé on widespread torture in Azerbaijan's jails? Neither the presidential administration nor the Ministry of Information and Press provided any hint, telling the press only that they were not familiar with the confiscation.

Several journalists' organizations and a number of independent publications then launched a joint protest action, which included appeals to the president and the general prosecutor. Their efforts eventually coaxed an explanation out of the Baku police, who claimed to have confiscated *Monitor* for rather noble aims: to protect the moral health of their fellow citizens and stop attempts to incite conflict among the country's various regions. The statement from the police chief of Baku also alleged that several articles had tended toward "misinformation and complicity in the enemy's propaganda."

The police failed to specify exactly which article or articles had been so threatening. Unexpectedly, Eldar Namazov, the head of the president's secretariat, provided an answer. In an article published by the daily newspaper *Panorama*, he wrote that the main danger to "the moral health and the unity of the nation" stemmed from a February piece by Husseynov, entitled "Azerbaijanis Are the Nation of the 21st Century." Exploring questions of national identity, Husseynov had concluded that Azerbaijanis lacked any distinctive "high quality" or "clear-cut national idea." But, he wrote, this could be used to the country's advantage: "We represent a society that is quite amorphous and free of any national prejudices. We can make cosmopolitanism and supranational identity the trump card of the Azerbaijanis. . . . We can combine the most valuable qualities that are of crucial importance for the future information era. . . . We have all the necessary preconditions to become a real nation. Not an industrial nation, but rather a nation of a new format."

But Namazov claimed that Husseynov had insulted the nation and complained that the authors of such articles are punished in civilized countries, while in Azerbaijan people try to defend them. He then appealed to the country's leaders to defend the country's dignity.

The president's aide proved to be right in his psychological calculations. He touched on the fragile national identities of those living in a fledgling country, and his call for support was soon accepted. The state media launched tales of alleged intrigue organized by "the agents of foreign states" and "the hostile forces to Azerbaijan" represented by Husseynov and his magazine. The culmination of the campaign was a lawsuit filed by three professors from Baku State University—Yagub Makhmudov, Seidaga Onunlakhi, and Gurban Mamedov—who accused Husseynov of libeling the nation and sought damages equal to *Monitor*'s yearly revenues.

By even agreeing to hear the case, the Baku city court violated the country's mass media law, which stipulates that those who consider themselves insulted can sue only after the editorial staff of the offending publication has refused to publish a refutation or apology. *Monitor*'s editors say they never received any such request. It is also still unclear who authorized the three professors to represent the interests of the entire nation. The trial itself resembled an academic dispute, with the plaintiffs citing not facts but abstracts from old manuscripts and academic literature.

Monitor cannot afford to pay such an enormous amount in damages—though other media have said they would try to help out—and has appealed the decision. In addition, another libel lawsuit may be in the offing: the Interior Ministry has threatened to sue Husseynov over the prison torture article, which the editor insists was based on earlier reports by human rights organizations.

The case's final outcome is yet to come, but one thing is clear: everybody is talking about the court's verdict, and nobody remembers the illegal confiscation of *Monitor*.

NOTE

Reprinted with kind permission from *Transitions* magazine, August 1998.

UNCERTAINTY HANGS OVER FUTURE OF NAGORNO-KARABAKH

by EMIL DANIELYAN

The long-running Nagorno-Karabakh conflict continued to bedevil the political life of the Caucasus region in 1998. In Armenia, it caused a change of government. In Azerbaijan, it clouded plans to implement multi-billion-dollar oil contracts signed with the world's leading companies. Armenian President Levon Ter-Petrossian failed to convince the public, and more importantly his entourage, that more concessions to Azerbaijan is the only way to prosperity. Ter-Petrossian's conciliatory remarks, openly expressed in September 1997, were rejected by his "power" ministers and the leadership of the self-proclaimed Nagorno-Karabakh Republic (NKR).

But the ouster of Ter-Petrossian and the hard-line takeover in Yerevan did not lead to a shift in the international climate against Armenia, as many had feared. By the end of 1998 it was the Armenian side that accepted a new peace plan put forward by the Organization for Security and Cooperation in Europe (OSCE), while Azerbaijan turned it down.

The year began with the first serious clash between the two dissenting groups in the Armenian side, which left Ter-Petrossian with no chances of success. At a two-day meeting of Armenian and Karabakh leaders, those who had real power levers, refused to go along with Ter-Petrossian's conciliatory approach. Prime Minster Robert Kocharian, Defense Minister Vazgen Sarkisian, and Interior and National Security Minister Serge Sarkisian found the existing OSCE plan unacceptable. The plan, accepted by Azerbaijan, called for a phased solution to the conflict whereby Karabakh's status would be determined during the last stage of the peace process. Ter-Petrossian argued that it was a chance to break the deadlock. His opponents countered that Karabakh should have an internationally guaranteed status before returning occupied Azerbaijani territories.

Yet at the heart of the debate apparently was a deeper issue. The plan would reportedly grant the region a high degree of autonomy within Azerbaijan. This seems to be what Ter-Petrossian implied in his Karabakh discourse. He argued that the time was working against the Armenians as oil-rich Azerbaijan will able to build up its military power and reverse the status quo after several years. These ideas were welcomed in Baku, where they raised hopes for an imminent settlement.

Ter-Petrossian's opponents, supported by the opposition, refused to accept anything less than "horizontal ties" between Karabakh and Azerbaijan. The NKR leadership grew particularly outspoken in its condemnation of Ter-Petrossian's stance. It was obvious that a showdown was just a matter of time. And it came on

3 February. "Only time will tell who wants to sell Karabakh and who really cares about its people," Ter-Petrossian said in his resignation speech. It was not clear what proportion of Armenia's population endorsed his vision. There was certainly no mass enthusiasm about it, not least because the ex-president never stated explicitly what Armenians should give up in Karabakh.

The change of government in Armenia received a negative reaction, and not only from Baku. Although there was no international criticism, Western analysts and the press saw gloomier prospects for a breakthrough. Russian President Boris Yeltsin noted only that "tough people" came to power in Yerevan.

The hardening of Armenia's position later in the year was thus no surprise. In early May, Armenia officially demanded that the OSCE Minsk Group present a new "package" plan. Later in the month, the group's Russian, U.S., and French co-chairs toured the region to study the new situation. No new peace proposals were unveiled in Baku, Yerevan, and Stepanakert. Throughout the summer Armenian and Karabakh officials claimed that the mediators were ready to advance new proposals but faced strong resistance from Azerbaijan, which stuck to the existing plan. In late June, Armenian Foreign Minister Vartan Oskanian warned that if Azerbaijan refused to compromise and embarked on a military build-up in the coming years, Armenia would consider unification with Karabakh or recognition of its independence. The statement was immediately condemned by Azerbaijan and the mediators. By compromise, Yerevan understood an "unconventional" status for Karabakh. Andorra was cited as an example. A tiny principality sandwiched between France and Spain, it is nominally headed by the French president and a Spanish bishop.

Mediation activities were put off until after the Azerbaijani presidential election in October. In the meantime, a government crisis erupted in Karabakh where Prime Minister Leonard Petrosian resigned in June after falling out with the NKR's powerful Defense Minister Samvel Babayan. The Karabakh parliament, controlled by Babayan's supporters, refused to allow President Arkadi Ghukasian to assume the duties of prime minister. The crisis was settled with the appointment of a compromise figure. In late September, local elections were held in Karabakh. As usual, they were denounced as illegitimate by Azerbaijan. But there was no reaction from the international community this time.

Karabakh was also a major issue during the October presidential election in Azerbaijan. The incumbent President Heydar Aliev was criticized by opposition candidates for being too soft on the Armenians. Some of them called for a military solution to the conflict. Aliev's anticipated victory gave a green light to the resumption of the Minsk Group's shuttle diplomacy. On 9 November the mediators brought a new "package" plan to Baku and then to Yerevan and Stepanakert. It proposed that Azerbaijan and Karabakh form a "common state." What that meant in practice was unclear as details of the proposals were kept secret. Top Azerbaijani officials rejected them immediately after talks with the mediators. Vafa Guluzade, Aliev's foreign policy adviser, said the plan contained no reference to Azerbaijan's territorial integrity, calling it "ambiguous." A French OSCE negotiator explained that the co-chairs tried to avoid using terms like "autonomy" and "territorial integrity" that had caused controversy between the conflicting parties.

There was a different reaction to the plan in Armenia and Karabakh. Oskanian found it a major improvement over the previous OSCE document. His Karabakh counterpart, Naira Melkumian, said it constituted "serious progress" in the Minsk Group's initiatives and "may allow us to get out of the deadlock." Not surprisingly, on 26 November Yerevan and Stepanakert announced official acceptance of the plan, albeit with unspecified "reservations."

The absence of relevant information made it difficult to judge how different the new OSCE plan was from the previous one. According to Kocharian, it was "substantially different." Its rejection by Azerbaijan may substantiate this assertion. On the other hand, representatives of the former Armenian government maintained that the two documents were virtually identical except their format. The previous plan would reportedly have given Karabakh de facto independence while technically keeping it part of Azerbaijan. It was unknown if the new one envisaged a "common state" between two equal parties as the Armenians wanted. Information was also scarce on other sticking points such as Karabakh's army and its overland connection with Armenia.

But it may be argued that with its approval of the OSCE proposals the Armenian side had significantly improved its international standing. Ter-Petrossian therefore proved wrong in 1997 in predicting that the West and Russia would force the Armenians into accepting the then current proposals. Even if OSCE concessions were minor, the mediators did scrap those proposals, returning to the package strategy. And even if this meant little progress in the peace process, the Armenians will not be the only party to blame for that, something which was prevalent in the West after Ter-Petrossian's ouster by the "hard-liners." Whether a protracted status quo is more beneficial to the Armenians or Azerbaijanis is a different question.

In addition, Azerbaijan turned down an invitation by the Council of Europe to attend hearings on Karabakh held in Paris in mid-December. Invitations were also extended to Armenia and the unrecognized NKR. Baku insisted that the Azerbaijani community of Karabakh, displaced by the war, also participate as a separate party. It did not back down even after the Council of Europe proposed to include representatives of the Karabakh Azerbaijanis in Azerbaijan's delegation.

Also in 1998, pressure from the Clinton administration and oil multinationals was again insufficient to get the U.S. Congress to repeal serious restrictions on American aid to Azerbaijan. Known as Section 907 of the 1992 Freedom Support Act, they were imposed due to efforts by the Armenian-American lobbying groups.

By and large, the year did not bring certainty in the future of the decade-long Nagorno-Karabakh conflict. Growing Western interest in the Caucasus (primarily motivated by the oil riches of the Caspian Sea) did not result in the kind of involvement seen in Bosnia or Kosovo. Mediation efforts were led by diplomats only. Western politicians did not go any farther than calling for a "peaceful settlement." Perhaps this was because they have a powerful rival there, Russia, whose positions in the Transcaucasus are much stronger than in the Balkans.

In any event, the chances of major progress will remain slim without more assertive international mediation. The Armenians are unlikely to agree to anything less than what they were offered by the OSCE in 1998. It remains to be seen what Azerbaijan's final position will be.

Armenia

Population:	3,754,300
Capital:	Yerevan (pop. 1,200,000)
Major cities:	Gyumri (207,000) (pre-earthquake figures), Vanadzor (146,000) (pre-earthquake)
Area:	29,800 sq. km.
Major ethnic groups:	Armenians 93.3 percent, Kurds 1.7%, Russians 1.5%, other 3.5%
Economy:	GDP growth: 7.2%
	Inflation: −1.3%
	Unemployment 12%

CHANGE OF LEADERSHIP WITHOUT POLITICAL REFORM

by EMIL DANIELYAN

A change of leadership did not bring democratization to Armenia in 1998. The ouster of President Levon Ter-Petrossian by his former close associates, a development which would had been inconceivable just a few months before, had no decisive impact on the oligarchic nature of Armenia's political system. Public opinion remained the least important of the factors shaping political developments. The pre-term presidential election in March failed to break a state vote-rigging machine that had come into existence under Ter-Petrossian. Ensuing events left little hope that future elections will be free and fair.

As observers predicted, differences developing within the Armenian government since 1997 on how to end the Nagorno-Karabakh conflict reached breaking point and one of the dissenting sides had to go. Ter-Petrossian and his Armenian Pan-National Movement (HHSh) had been advocating a policy of concessions to Azerbaijan. By the beginning of 1998 they had lost most of their power levers. On the other side of the government barricade were Prime Minister Robert Kocharian, his key ministers, and the leadership of the self-proclaimed Nagorno-Karabakh Republic (NKR).

The two sides reportedly clashed at a meeting of Armenia's security council in early January. It then became obvious that a showdown was inevitable, and it was sparked later in the month with what initially seemed to be assassination attempts against figures close to the HHSh. On 20 January, Ter-Petrossian's chief bodyguard said his car had come under fire as he drove 50 kilometers west of Yerevan. General Romain Ghazarian survived unscathed although his Toyota jeep was shown riddled with bullets. The next day, the commander of the Armenian interior troops was hospitalized after gunmen wounded him in the legs. On 22 January, in a bid to take the initiative, the HHSh demanded from Ter-Petrossian "resolute steps to counter the outbreak of terrorism" in the face of a "paralyzed" government. An HHSh leader, Ara Sahakian, said Armenia was in "diarchy" and the president should "bring clarity into the executive."

Yet the balance of forces finally swung to the Kocharian camp when the hard-line Defense Minister Vazgen Sarkisian on 23 January threw his weight behind it. Sarkisian expressed his open defiance to Ter-Petrossian, accusing the HHSh of stage-managing the assaults. What followed then was a series of behind-the-scenes actions that saw remaining presidential loyalists driven out of government. The first of them, former interior minister Vano Siradeghian, stepped down as mayor of Yerevan on 30 January. That Ter-Petrossian too had to go became clear the same day, after the Yerkrapah Union of Karabakh war veterans (Sarkisian's well-organized force) demanded his resignation.

The Armenian president was left with no other choice on 3 February as his loyal HHSh lost its majority in parliament. The HHSh faction shrank from 96 to 56 deputies overnight, with dozens of them defecting to the Yerkrapah group, which quadrupled its membership to become the biggest in parliament. Later in the day, Ter-Petrossian went on state television to tell the nation that he was resigning to prevent "instability" in Armenia. He said he had taken the decision after a "demand by bodies known to you." The resignation signaled a temporary "defeat of the party of honorable peace in Armenia," Ter-Petrossian said.

Ter-Petrossian's resignation marked the end of an epoch in the history of contemporary Armenia. Elected president by a huge margin in 1991, Ter-Petrossian effectively destroyed his reformist image in September 1996 when his re-election is widely believed to have been secured by fraudulent means. Ironically, those who helped him falsify the vote were the ones who eventually ousted him. Ter-Petrossian could counter brutal pressure from the Kocharian camp only with a solid base of popular legitimacy, something which he no longer had after 1996.

Kocharian assumed duty as Armenia's acting president the next day, promising that the fresh election will be free and fair. His repeated statements that the 16 March poll should "consolidate" rather than "polarize" the nation raised hopes for a long-awaited political reform in Armenia. Vazgen Manukian, chairman of the opposition National Democratic Union (AZhM), who many believe had won the 1996 election, announced that Ter-Petrossian's resignation ushered Armenia into a "new epoch of democracy."

Indeed, Kocharian's first actions were encouraging. On 9 February, he legalized the Armenian Revolutionary Federation (HHD or Dashnak party) bringing to an end its long stand-off with the authorities. A few days later he released HHD activists, sentenced to various prison terms during the allegedly political trials of 1995–97. By legalizing the Dashnaks, Kocharian obtained a new influential ally with dominant positions in the diaspora. Only three days after his release from jail, Dashnak leader Vahan Hovannisian announced the HHD's support for Kocharian's candidacy because he "symbolizes the unity of the nation."

But as the date of the voting approached, the new regime increasingly relied on its predecessors' tactics of using government levers to cling to power at any cost. Largely left intact, the old-new "power class" (top bureaucrats, local bosses, businessmen with government connections) received a clear signal as to whom to "work for." Ter-Petrossian was gone but his vicious machine remained in place.

On 27 February, Manukian alleged that "police, former KGB, and local government officials have united" and "intimidated people" to vote for Kocharian. But it was not only the heavy presence of law-enforcement officials in the Kocharian campaign that shattered Manukian's initially upbeat calculations.

Karen Demirchian, Armenia's long-time Soviet-era leader, emerged from political oblivion in mid-February to join the presidential race, rapidly gaining ground against the two front-runners. It was widely believed that Demirchian was pressured by the regime into running for president and hence stealing the protest vote that would otherwise go to the AZhM. Demirchian was the Communist Party first secretary from 1974 to 1988 and was campaigning on a "social democratic" platform. Many Armenians, impoverished by the collapse of the command economy, wanted him back in the hope that he would re-establish the living standards of ten years earlier.

Apart from the state apparatus, Kocharian's bid was backed by a group of former opposition parties that had rallied behind Manukian in 1996. The pro-Kocharian forces formed on 4 March a loose electoral alliance called Justice and Unity. Expecting sweeping policy changes from the new Armenian leader, they enabled him to claim broad support. It later proved to be insufficient for ensuring a clean election.

DEJA VU DURING AND AFTER ELECTIONS

Hours after voting got under way on 16 March, reports started coming in of armed men entering polling stations, beating opposition observers and stuffing hundreds of ballots (marked for Kocharian) into boxes. Right after the polls closed in the evening, six opposition candidates, including Demirchian and Manukian, issued a joint statement saying that the "elections cannot be considered free and fair regardless of their results." It said the voting had proceeded in the "atmosphere of widespread breaches of law, intimidation and falsification."

The charges were denied by the Central Election Commission and Kocharian, who only acknowledged "minor irregularities" and "omissions." Official figures said Kocharian won the first round with 39 percent of the vote, followed by Demirchian (31 percent), Manukian (12 percent), and Communist leader Sergei Badalian (11 percent.) None of the major opposition parties endorsed Demirchian for the run-off voting. The latter lacked credible organizational structures to prevent vote manipulation on 30 March. Not surprisingly, Kocharian was declared the winner with 59 percent of the vote to Demirchian's 41 percent.

The former Communist boss refused to accept his defeat saying that the "people were not allowed to express their will." However, he declined to launch a campaign of mass protests, as demanded by his activists. Demirchian wanted "no splits in the society."

In its preliminary statement, the Organization for Security and Cooperation in Europe (OSCE) said that despite irregularities the election was a "step forward . . . toward a functioning democracy." Its final report was more strongly-worded, noting that the ballot had not met its "standards."

The aftermath of the election went smoothly for the authorities. There was no united opposition to deal with, as had been the case in 1996. In fact, most of the former opposition parties enthusiastically rallied behind Kocharian. Those remaining in opposition refused to accept the new president's legitimacy, but did not join Demirchian's cause, since they deeply mistrusted him.

The radical reshuffle of the opposition camp brought about a new picture. On its right were Manukian's AZhM and several liberal parties that had split from the HHSh at various times. As time went on, they increasingly cooperated with the former ruling party (hitherto an arch-enemy) in attacking the government in parliament. The Armenian Communists (less hostile to the ruling regime) continued to firmly hold the far left position in the political spectrum. Closer to the center was the People's Party of Armenia (HZhK), established by Demirchian in May. It rapidly expanded throughout the country and claimed 15,000 members by end-1998.

OLD POLITICAL SYSTEM LARGELY UNTOUCHED

Few of the new pro-government parties were rewarded with major posts. The Dashnaks, the most influential amongst them, were given the ministries of education and culture and a gubernatorial post. The force which had most of the levers was Sarkisian's Yerkrapah Union. It controlled parliament, several ministries, and most provincial administrations in Armenia. Yerkrapah brought under its tutelage the "power class" formerly loyal to Ter-Petrossian. This fact meant growing disaffection with Kocharian within the ex-opposition. They had expected him to bring to justice allegedly corrupt officials who had built fortunes during the independence years. A large-scale corruption crackdown was even less likely after the murder of Prosecutor-General Henrik Khachatrian in August. (According to the official version, he was shot dead by one of his subordinates.)

It also turned out that Kocharian's pledge to curtail his sweeping powers amounted to proposing nothing more than cosmetic changes in the constitution. The issue that caused the greatest controversy was how to elect Armenia's next parliament. Yerkrapah found itself alone in advocating a law that would allocate most parliament seats under the majoritarian, single-seat system. The other major parties insisted that parliamentary elections based on the proportional system would be more difficult to falsify. In November, Yerkrapah, which was formally transforming itself into a political party, pushed through in the first reading of its draft law on elections. The move was condemned by the opposition, who threatened to boycott the elections scheduled for 1999.

The 1999 elections will determine the correlation of Armenia's political forces for several years to come. Ending the year, Defense Minister Sarkisian told his loyalists that they were the main support base of Kocharian. This suggested that Yerkrapah will make every effort to keep its majority in parliament. The problem is that it is not the only group supporting the president. This led some observers to predict a tough competition among pro-government groups as well. The clash of interests may thus be stronger than it was during the 1998 election. Strangely, this prospect leaves the door open for a democratic change in Armenia.

THE ECONOMY: NICE FIGURES, SLOW CHANGE

In purely macroeconomic terms, 1998 saw a major improvement over the preceding year. But the faster economic growth and low inflation did not mean a substantial rise in living standards in Armenia, which still suffered from huge unemployment.

Nonetheless, the government claimed an "economic breakthrough" as GDP growth hit 7.2 percent alongside a 1.3 percent fall in consumer price level, the first ever deflation in Armenia. In 1997, the growth had been just 3 percent and inflation 22 percent. As of late September 1998, exports were up 12 percent and imports almost unchanged compared with the same period in 1997. Exports fell considerably in the fourth quarter as a number of large Armenian enterprises lost their markets in Russia in the wake of the August financial crisis. The government also attributed the price deflation to the Russian crisis, as the much cheaper Russian imports reduced the overall consumer price index.

The government said it had managed to prevent a massive spillover of the crisis on Armenia, pointing to a mere 4 percent depreciation of national currency against the U.S. dollar during 1998. The government's good tax collection record was a strong back-up to its tight fiscal and monetary policies. Second, state treasury bills covered only a fraction of Armenia's budget deficit. Over 95 percent of the deficit in 1999 was to be financed through the much cheaper external borrowing. And perhaps more importantly, most Armenians have long ceased to rely on the state for their survival, which meant the latter can get away with paying meager salaries and pensions. However, money transfers from thousands of Armenians working in Russia were one of the ways to get by. Estimated at $50 million per annum, those transfers were reduced to a trickle by the crisis.

The government's privatization policy faced serious difficulties, with only one third of the remaining 480 medium-sized and large state enterprises sold off at auctions in 1998. Most of them were under heavy debt burden and therefore not competitive. The famous Yerevan Brandy Factory was one of the few exceptions. It was bought by France's Pernod Ricard group for $30 million. By the end of 1998 over 75 percent of Armenia's GDP was generated by the private sector.

Direct foreign investments reached $210 million by the end of the year. This figure is modest by international standards, but still higher than the total amount of investments in the Armenian economy during the previous five years.

Armenia's economic performance was praised by the International Monetary Fund and World Bank, with new loans being approved in late December. The IMF approved the last $59 million tranche of its $154 million Enhanced Structural Adjustment Facility, agreed in 1996. The concessional ESAF loans are designed for low-income countries to strengthen their balance of payments. The World Bank, for its part, announced a $65 million loan package to finance Armenia's budget deficit. The two institutions also endorsed the government's economic program and budget for the next year. With a planned 18 percent rise in its volume, it projected roughly the same deficit level of 5.3 percent of GDP.

Vahram Nercissiantz, the World Bank's former representative to Armenia who became President Kocharian's adviser in August, had said that Armenia would need a steady growth rate of 10–12 percent per year if its people were to see considerable improvement of life soon. Analysts agree that such a growth can only be export-oriented. The country still imported 3.6 times more than it exported. The huge current account deficit only slightly decreased to 21.5 percent of GDP in 1998.

Officials admitted that an underdeveloped infrastructure, weak banking system, and undeveloped capital market are a serious obstacle to the influx of foreign investment. The Kocharian government maintained that the unresolved Nagorno-Karabakh conflict was not the main factor hindering economic development, contrary to the view prevailing in the West.

The year saw some improvement in the country's communications with the outside world. In June, Georgia lowered by 26 percent tariffs for cargoes transported to and from Armenia across its territory, enabling the latter to save $8 million in annual transit fees. In December, Yerevan unveiled an agreement with Georgia and Bulgaria on a regular ferry link across the Black Sea, which it said would help Armenia restore rail communication with the outside world. Transport officials said it could boost external cargo turnover by 20–30 percent in 1999.

Many experts cited another factor stifling economic activity in Armenia. It is widely believed that problems with the rule of law discourage many entrepreneurs from doing business there. There seemed to be little progress in ensuring equal conditions for businessmen after the change of government in February. The political class which supports Kocharian is not enthusiastic about a truly free market. Political connections with leading officials remained vital.

It appears that in a country like Armenia, fair economic competition is impossible without fair political competition. This first of all means democratic elections, which Armenia stopped having from 1995 onwards.

PROCEEDING WITH A "COMPLEMENTARY" FOREIGN POLICY

The international isolation which Levon Ter-Petrossian had warned might befall Armenia over its stance on Nagorno-Karabakh did not materialize in 1998. The relations of the new government in Yerevan with the rest of the world underwent no major changes. Armenia's foreign policy was based on what the authorities described as the "complementary" principle. An example of this was both "having Russian military bases and close ties with NATO," as Foreign Minister Vartan Oskanian put it. Military cooperation with Moscow was accompanied by efforts to intensify contacts with the West and Europe in particular.

A policy shift occurred only with regard to neighboring Turkey, Armenia's traditional foe. Shortly after Kocharian became president, Yerevan announced that it would pursue international recognition of the 1915 genocide of over one million Armenians in the Ottoman Empire. Moreover, it said the issue should be included on the "agenda of the Armenian-Turkish dialogue." Ankara has consistently denied that the mass killings constituted a genocide. The previous Armenian government did not raise the genocide issue in its dealings with Turkey. Many in Armenia concluded that the softer line did not bring any reciprocity from Turkey, which had given its unconditional backing to Azerbaijan in the Karabakh conflict and kept its border with Armenia closed. The 1915 genocide, which for decades traumatized the nation, was also seen as a point of potential political leverage over Turkey. On 29 May the lower house of the French parliament infuriated Turkey by formally recognizing the genocide. In June, Armenia threatened to veto the choice of Istanbul as the venue for the next OSCE summit, but backed down later in the year. In a sign of defusing bilateral tensions, Oskanian said in December that the two countries were engaged in a behind-the-scenes "dialogue," but did not elaborate. It may well be that U.S. calls for Ankara and Yerevan to "build a stronger relationship" played a role in that statement.

One result of the serious Turkish-Armenian differences is the continued presence of Russian troops in Armenia. This military cooperation received a new impetus in July with a visit to Armenia of Russian Defense Minister Igor Sergeev. It produced an agreement to "upgrade" the weaponry of the Russian bases. In late 1998 Moscow began deployment of modern MiG-29 fighter jets in Armenia, ostensibly to replace older planes. It was understood that the Russians would start deploying their long-range S-300 anti-aircraft missiles in Armenia in 1999.

Political ties with Moscow were mostly outside the framework of the Commonwealth of Independent States (CIS). It remained an ineffectual organization despite attempts by its new executive secretary Boris Berezovskii to reform it. Kocharian agreed with Berezovskii in that use of economic incentives was the best way to try to revive the CIS.

At the same, "integration in European structures" was considered another top priority by the authorities. "Armenia is part of the European family," Kocharian said in June. The European Union's presence in the region was manifested through its TRACECA project (Transport Corridor Europe Central Asia and Caucasus), which aims to revive ancient commercial routes linking Europe and Central Asia through the Caucasus. With Kocharian praising the idea for contributing to "peace and stability in the region," Armenia sent for the first time an official delegation to Baku in early September to attend a big international conference on TRACECA. It was led by Prime Minister Armen Darpinian. In December, an EU-Armenia commission held its annual meeting in Yerevan. Foreign Minister Oskanian predicted the start of a "political dialogue" with the EU after their Agreement on Partnership and Cooperation, signed in 1996, takes effect in mid-1999.

Likewise, the U.S.-Armenian relationship did not seem to suffer from Ter-Petrossian's resignation. Unlike Ter-Petrossian in 1996, Kocharian was congratulated by Bill Clinton upon being elected president. The existence of a large and influential Armenian-American community was still a major reason for Washington's fairly friendly attitude towards Yerevan. The volume of American aid to Armenia was expected to remain unchanged at roughly $135 million in 1999.

Kazakhstan

Population:	17,300,000
Capital:	Almaty (pop. 1,200,000). The capital moved to Akmola in December 1997.
Major cities:	Karaganda (pop. 613,000), Shymkent (401,000), Akmola (pop. 280,000)
Area:	2,717,300 sq. km.
Major ethnic groups:	Kazakh 43%, Russian 36%, Ukrainian 5.2%, German 3%, Uzbek 2%, Tatar 2%
Economy:	GDP growth: –2%
....	Inflation rate: 8%
....	Unemployment rate: 4%

NAZARBAEV GEARS UP FOR LIFE PRESIDENCY

by BHAVNA DAVE

Politics in Kazakhstan in 1998 were overshadowed by preparations for the presidential election which took place on 10 January 1999. The election was held two years ahead of schedule and not precipitated by any apparent political crisis, indicating that in personalized regimes of the sort in place in Kazakhstan the need for self-legitimation is more important than obtaining a popular mandate when it comes to calling elections. Although Nazarbaev obtained an 80 percent mandate to stay in office until the year 2006, he may have tarnished his image as a leader committed to democratic reforms. The Organization for Security and Cooperation in Europe (OSCE) and most international organizations refused to send election observers, accusing the regime of giving insufficient time to the opposition to prepare, barring candidates on grounds of "minor administrative convictions," and widespread intimidation of voters in order to maximize the vote for the incumbent.

The Nazarbaev regime made it clear that its perspective for rule extends beyond the current term in office. Sergei Tereshchenko, an ex-premier who was recalled from political oblivion and appointed Nazarbaev's electoral campaign head, maintained that another 15–20 years will be needed to transform Kazakhstan into a "civilized and democratic state," a transformation to be presided over by Nazarbaev personally. He also declared that the election campaign team was being expanded into a political party called Otan (Fatherland), which will field its candidates in the local and parliamentary elections, and support Nazarbaev as their candidate in the 2006 elections.

ELECTORAL POLITICS IN THE "OASIS OF STABILITY"

Although a sense of apathy and cynicism pervaded a large stratum of the population, particularly its younger members, who increasingly felt alienated from "palace" politics, there was also a grudging recognition that no alternative to the present regime exists—a belief that personalized leaderships typically seek to cultivate. With no rival to himself within the government, and an opposition almost totally disempowered by a sustained use of the state law and order machinery to prevent any public activity, Nazarbaev in all likelihood would have won the elections even without an elaborate campaign or a crackdown on his opponents. By all overt indicators, Kazakhstan was quite successful in 1998 in reinforcing its carefully-cultivated image as an "oasis of stability," continuing to preach interethnic friendship, religious tolerance, and social harmony, and sidelining those viewed as undermining this image. Indeed by mid-1998 the economy appeared to have attained a degree of macroeconomic stability, a new pension reform had been successfully launched, and wages and foreign investment were among the highest in the Commonwealth of Independent States (CIS). The latter half of 1998, however, exposed the vulnerability of Kazakhstan's economy in the face of the Asian and Russian crises and the continuing fall in prices of oil and metals—its two principal exports. These crises eroded the vision of development and prosperity articulated in Nazarbaev's *Strategy 2030* (a blueprint for development through the year 2030, issued in October 1997)—a vision that had already rested on an exaggerated expectation of returns from the country's oil and mineral wealth. Seeking to insulate itself from the unfolding economic crisis, the leadership responded by tightening its hold on politics and attending first to the routine business of elections, rather than responding to pressing economic matters.

The first indicator of early presidential elections came on 30 September when Nazarbaev proposed an amendment to the constitutional provision requiring a 50 percent minimum voter turnout, punctuating it with a proposal to limit the power of the presidency and create a stronger parliament. In a pattern reminiscent of the Soviet-era top-down mobilization of popular will, parliamentary deputies soon urged that presidential elections be held earlier in order to avoid an overlap with the Russian presidential elections in December 2000. They also proposed amendments extending the presidential term from five to seven years, and removing the clauses that had limited the president to two terms in office and had set 65 as the maximum age limit for a presidential candidate.

Within a week the parliament approved these amendments and scheduled presidential elections for January 1999. The opposition was caught unprepared for what were to be the first multi-candidate presidential election (the previous two presidential mandates in 1991 and 1995 were derived through referenda), and was therefore inclined to boycott them. However former premier Akezhan Kazhegeldin, who lost his job in October 1997, allegedly by resigning on health grounds, emerged as a challenger to Nazarbaev. As he returned to Kazakhstan in spring 1998 after nearly six months' absence, purportedly for convalescence, Kazhegeldin was soon elected as head of Kazakhstan's Union of Industrialists and Entrepreneurs. Nazarbaev had honored his role in "promoting market reforms" by presenting him with the National Medal of Honor—an award generally reserved for members of the government—and expressed hope that Kazhegeldin would soon return to active politics.

In the meantime, various opposition parties and their leaders organized a Movement for Free Elections, holding public rallies and demonstrations, only to be arrested, briefly imprisoned, fined, and ultimately disqualified from contesting elections for these peccadilloes. An amendment to the law on elections passed in May disqualified any person with a standing court conviction from running for any public office. Murat Auezov and Galym Abilseitov, the two leaders of the opposition Azamat and potential candidates, were thus disqualified for having attended these rallies, while the third leader Petr Svoik had already been convicted earlier for "inciting ethnic hatred" in an article he wrote in the newspaper *Karavan*.

As the parliament was gearing up in early October to pass amendments to the constitution to pave the way for early presidential elections, and as Kazhegeldin's candidacy appeared likely, a conflict flared up between the ex-premier and the government. Kazhegeldin reported an assassination attempt against himself, and alleged that his aide Mikhail Vasilienko had been unlawfully detained while delivering proposals for constitutional amendments drafted by the Businessmen's Association. The authorities dismissed these allegations as publicity seeking devices.

Although the opposition viewed Kazhegeldin as an ally—he also participated in the demonstrations for free elections—his desire to contest elections received lukewarm support. The government used familiar bureaucratic means to stall his candidacy. Kazhegeldin was barred from contesting the elections for defying an order by a local judge to appear in court for having attended the unsanctioned anti-election rally. As the deadline for registration approached, Nazarbaev "regretted" his being barred from contesting elections, and urged the Supreme Court to overturn the ruling against Kazhegeldin. Kazhegeldin's immense financial resources, international connections, and support from U.S. lawyers and human rights organizations failed to reverse the court decision. Having worked for long years in Moscow, Kazhegeldin lacked an independent clientele or a regional base within Kazakhstan to offer an effective challenge from within the power circles. Despite his favorable image in Western media for his stance in favor of foreign investment, he lacked credibility before the people or the opposition, who saw him as an enriched state functionary rather than a forceful voice for economic reforms.

Serikbolsin Abdildin, leader of the Communist Party and a former speaker of parliament, was the only non-governmental leader to contest the elections. The other two contestants, Gani Kasimov (head of the Kazakh Customs Committee) and Engels Gabbasov (a parliamentary deputy), were seen as inside figures posing as an "independent" candidates. Among others to declare candidacy were Baltash Tursynbaev, who resigned his post as ambassador to Turkey. He was immediately appointed as a deputy premier, presumably a "reward" to pull him out of the contest.

In the less than five weeks available to them, the candidates were required to collect 170,000 signatures—roughly 2 percent of the registered voting population—and pay an election registration fee of nearly 2.5 million tenge (about $30,000). Large, elaborate billboards praising the president and his achievements appeared all over the country as Nazarbaev unleashed a high-profile electioneering campaign visiting various provinces. Identifying Nazarbaev with all state symbols, the state-controlled media slid into eulogies, flashing messages such as "Nursultan Abisheevich—We know him," which made his rivals look all the more marginal and irrelevant.

THE SUBORDINATION OF MEDIA

The past year hit the independent newspapers fairly hard as the authorities took sustained actions against *21-iy vek* (21st Century) and *Karavan* for publishing criticism of the government. A bomb allegedly planted by state security officials damaged the offices of *21-iy vek*—a newspaper financed by Kazhegeldin—in September. The publication of articles by Petr Svoik and extracts from Kazhegeldin's new book in *Karavan* triggered an aggressive reaction from the authorities, who also accused the newspaper of publishing pornographic material and illegal advertisement. Svoik was accused of "inciting ethnic hatred" and seeking to "destroy the state" in an article published in March titled "Kazakhstan and Russia: A New Union?" Kazhegeldin came under attack for suggesting that Nazarbaev personally was to blame for promoting "weak authoritarian tendencies," which were undermining the creation of an open, reform-oriented economy. While newspapers could still criticize the government and other officials, personal criticism of Nazarbaev was deemed unacceptable. *Karavan* lost much of its financial clout as a result of the criminal proceedings and heavy fines and was effectively brought to heel by the authorities.

THE BLOSSOMING OF THE NEW CAPITAL?

In 1997 Nazarbaev had decided to move the nation's capital from Almaty to the northern city of Akmola. In 1998 the new capital was given another positive boost by gaining a new name—Astana, or simply, "the Capital." Nazarbaev accused foreign journalists of habitually presenting the distorted translation of Akmola—"White grave," instead of what he regarded as the correct translation, "Holy shrine." To do away with the bleak and distorted image of the new capital, official documents subsequently defined "White blossoming" as a more accurate translation. A flurry of construction activities continued with the financing by foreign firms, notably from Turkey, Switzerland, China, and Japan. Altogether, a total of $188 million was spent on government buildings and $250 million on other construction. The Japanese Agency for Economic Cooperation allocated $170 million for the development of a new international airport. Lured by special pay and other incentives, some 3,500 officials were relocated to Astana from Almaty. No foreign diplomatic missions had moved to the new capital by year's end, however. Any public discussion on the financial drain caused by the development of Astana and its long-term viability as the capital remained implicitly proscribed.

MORE PERSONNEL SHUFFLING

Nazarbaev issued periodic warnings to the Balgimbaev government to speed up economic reforms. The past year saw a further consolidation of the structure of two parallel, but highly unequal, structures of governments—the prime minister and his cabinet on the one hand and the president and his ever-growing apparatus consisting of various extra-constitutional agencies and committees towering over the prime minister and his cabinet on the other. Among some notable changes were the dismissals of Asygat Zhabagin, the energy minister, and Baltabek Kuandikov, the head of the state oil company Kazakhoil, allegedly for their involvement in private business and for failure to limit domestic increases in oil and electricity prices despite a worldwide fall in energy prices. They were replaced by young technocrats Mukhtar Ablyazov and Nurlan Kapparov respectively.

There were signs of discontent among regional officials over the prerogative of the center in the collection and redistribution of revenues to the regions: a policy that appeared to punish poorer regions without rewarding those generating greater revenues. The abolition of four oblasts (provinces) in 1997 was justified on the grounds of their being financially unsustainable. There was also some fear that the western oil-producing regions, as well as the more developed northern regions, may become more assertive vis-à-vis the center. Almaty's Mayor Viktor Khrapunov urged special taxation privileges for the former capital. Nazarbaev continued to rule out regional autonomy, rejecting demands to make the *akims* (regional governors) directly accountable to people by subjecting them to popular election. The office of the *akim* remained one of the least transformed positions within the administration since Soviet times.

POPULATION CONTINUES TO DECLINE

Kazakhstan prepared for its first post-independent census—slated for spring 1999. The government needed to cross a psychological barrier by establishing a clear majority of Kazakhs (estimates ranged between 42–52 percent of the total). It was also hard-pressed to demonstrate progress toward the unrealistic target of a total population of 25 million by the year 2030. Kazakhstan's population was estimated at 15.6 million in 1998, down from 16.8 in 1991. Kazakhstan's leaders look over their shoulder at neighboring Uzbekistan, whose population is 24 million and growing fast. Since 1991, over 2.17 million people have left Kazakhstan, a primarily Germans, Russians, and other Slavs. Although emigration of Russian-speakers slowed down in the latter half of 1998 due to Russia's economic troubles, it may accelerate if Kazakhstan's economy declines.

As a result of economic difficulties and growth in urbanization, the birth rate among Kazakhs had slumped to 1.5 percent—the lowest for several decades. Decrying the presence of a significant number of single Kazakh women, some deputies introduced a motion to legalize polygamy as a means of raising birth rates among Kazakhs, arguing it to be an integral aspect of nomadic culture. The bill was rejected as the majority emphasized that Kazakhstan was "not just an Asian state," but also aspired to become a "civilized, European-type" state.

While the government continued to intensify repatriation of the Kazakh diaspora, it failed to counteract a notable increase in the brain-drain of Kazakhs to Russia and the West. Concerns also mounted over a growing presence of "guest-workers," traders-cum-settlers, and refugees. Expansion of trade and relaxation of border control with China also reinforced the fears of an influx of Chinese settlers. While only 2,000 Chinese were officially registered, some estimates put the number as high as 100,000, revealing exaggerated fears of gradual assimilation by their huge eastern neighbor. The Chinese embassy protested the mistreatment of Chinese settlers by Kazakh officials as well as the widespread stereotyping and prejudices. Incidentally, China also donated $100,000 to Kazakhstan to conduct its census.

A LOOMING ECONOMIC CRISIS

In January 1998, Kazakhstan became the first CIS state to adopt a new pension scheme, modeled on Chile, shifting the responsibility for pension from the state to the individual. It stipulated a mandatory 25.5 percent of the total income contribution of each employee toward his or her total income into a pension fund— 15.5 percent to the State Pension fund and 10 percent to private funds. The World Bank offered a loan of $300 million aimed to address social protection and the creation of a regulatory framework.

Wages continued to rise in the past year with the monthly per capita income of $120 being one of the highest in the CIS. However, glaring economic inequalities between the newly-rich and the common people made these figures irrelevant. A study by the International Federation of the Red Cross revealed that 73 percent were living below the government-defined poverty line of $50 per person per month. The official sources put unemployment at 4 percent whereas the Independent Federation of Trade Unions put it as high as 25–28 percent.

Kazakhstan's GDP is estimated to have fallen by 2 percent last year, due to the Asian economic crisis, which triggered a slump in demand for oil and metals. The IMF forecasted a zero growth scenario in 1999. Although Kazakhstan managed to control inflation—down to 8 percent from 15 percent the previous year—its currency, the tenge, weakened slightly in the last quarter of 1998. Its foreign currency reserves went down from $2 billion to $1.3 billion as the government drew on them to support the tenge in the aftermath of the Russian crisis. Kazakhstan denied that Russian financial meltdown has had any serious impact on its economy, claiming that a high degree of autonomy had been attained. However, there was a 50 percent drop in its trade with Russia in the months following the August crisis.

Kazakhstan gains 30 percent of its export revenues from oil—exporting almost half of its oil production. Despite an increase in oil extraction, labor problems and antiquated equipment resulted in a contraction in oil refining as Kazakhstan's three major refineries were operating at less than half their capacity. Kazakhstan was estimated to have lost about $1–1.5 billion last year due to the slump in oil prices, which was partly responsible for the decision to halt oil privatization.

The past year proved to be one of the worst for grain harvest in the last 40 years. Compared to 12.3 millions tons in the previous year, only 7.3 million tons could be gathered due to adverse weather conditions.

RELATIONS WITH NEIGHBORS

After protracted talks, Kazakhstan finally signed an agreement on the division of the northern sector of the Caspian Sea bed with Russia. However, the sea's legal status remains unresolved as yet, since Iran continues to regard the Caspian as an internal sea which should be subject to joint exploitation by the littoral states. Kazakhstan indicated that it will renew its participation in the CIS Collective Security Treaty later this year.

Relations with the neighboring Central Asian states remained cordial, with Kazakhstan signing a treaty of "eternal friendship" with Uzbekistan. The marriage of Nazarbaev's youngest daughter to Kyrgyz President Askar Akayev's oldest son was likely to deepen kin ties between the two states.

Kazakhstan continued to forge close economic ties with China, signing a 15 year cooperation plan in the oil, gas, and telecommunication sectors. Trade between the two countries totaled $100 million in the first quarter of 1998, up some 20 percent. China offered a $100 million loan to small business. Kazakhstan began its first shipment of oil to China (by rail) and may supply up to 1 million tons to China in 1999. Construction began on the first segment of a 3,000 kilometer long pipeline, estimated to cost upwards of $3 billion, for transporting oil from western Kazakhstan to China. The first stage will link the country's western oil fields to the eastern cities of Kazakhstan—which are currently dependent on oil imports from Russia. An agreement resolving disputes over the 1,700 km border between Kazakhstan and China was signed by the two countries. Kazakhstan has shown its willingness to fully cooperate with China in curbing the activities of Moslem Uighur separatist groups, who were active in support of their fellow ethnics across the border in the Chinese province of Sinkiang. This policy stance by Kazakhstan's government has caused resentment among its own Uighur communities.

FUTURE UNCERTAIN

The economy is likely to offer the biggest challenge to the current regime and belie hopes of a smooth sailing due to oil and natural resources. Kazakhstan approaches the end of the millennium amidst predictions of zero growth, impending austerity measures, and continuing uncertainties about its ability to turn oil into a cash resource. In this climate, the strategy of holding rather frequent and unwarranted elections, the extensive use of state resources and media in sidelining the opposition, delegitimating any criticism of the regime, and propagating the view that no viable alternative no Nazarbaev exists, may well prove to be counterproductive in the long term. The fact that the government took the whole electoral exercise very seriously—and is now contemplating early parliamentary elections—suggested how insecure and narrow was the social base of the leadership despite its almost complete control over the political system.

Uzbekistan

Population:	22,200,000
Capital:	Tashkent (pop. 2,200,000)
Major cities:	Samarkand (pop. 388,000), Namangan (pop. 291,000), Andijan (pop. 288,000)
Area:	447,000 sq. km.
Major ethnic groups:	Uzbek 74.5%, Russian 6.5%, Tajik 4.8%, Kazakh 4.1%
Economy:	GDP growth: 1%
....	Inflation rate: 30–40%
....	Unemployment rate: 0.3%

CRACKS IN THE MONOLITH

by CASSANDRA CAVANAUGH

Uzbekistan's authoritarian government moved into crisis mode in 1998, as the economy grew much more slowly than estimates predicted, import earnings dropped precipitously, and the currency sank further from convertibility. President Islam Karimov reacted with vigor—by sacking high government officials and continuing to wage war against independent Muslims. The virulence of both reactions, however, spoke more to latent instability than to a president secure in his rule. To an outside observer it looked as if at least some of the crises were of Karimov's own making.

BATTLING DISORDER

The implications of corruption for domestic politics stood at the center of President Karimov's agenda for 1998. In an address to parliament at the end of the year the president remarked that "The larger the number of state officials, the more justice is violated." Acting on this belief, or perhaps on a desire to clear out all sources of potential opposition before parliamentary elections in 1999 and a presidential vote in 2000, he spent much of the year dismissing senior officials. The first deputy prime minister, the head of the State Tax Service, the finance minister, the long-serving minister of public health, and First Deputy Prime Minister Ismail Jurabekov, as well as the governors of Samarkand and Navoi viloyats (provinces), were all dismissed during the year, as official announcements discreetly stated, "in connection with [their] transfer to another post." Karimov had manipulated power in the past by constantly rotating regional governors; his fear of Jurabekov, his longest-serving deputy prime minister and a scion of the powerful Jizzakh-Samarkand clan, seems rooted in fact. But 1998's wave of sackings took on a new aspect. For the first time, a senior government official, Murudullo Kurolov, the head of the State Tax Committee, was not only fired, but arrested and charged with corruption. The unlucky man's assistant committed suicide by jumping from a fifth floor window the day of the arrest.

Shortly after the arrest, Karimov issued a decree banning "lavish celebrations," intended to prevent the kinds of showy displays of wealth at traditional large gatherings such as weddings. "False ostentation has a negative effect on the upbringing of our youth," the decree read; but, the negative effect Karimov probably had in mind was on the increasingly impoverished population, who looked on resentfully as the governmental elite grew fabulously rich. Karimov's attempt to incite this populist anger and mobilize it in his favor was fully on view during his 9 November address in Samarkand, in which he explained the dismissals of the region's top bureaucrats (the governor or hakim, Alisher Mardiev, had been appointed only three years earlier), and lashed out at nepotism, which he labeled "tribalism." For the first time, the government acknowledged the common practice of new regional governors clearing out their entire state apparatuses and packing them with family members and supporters. Karimov specifically accused Mardiev not only of filling such profitable state posts as the heads of local trade departments, bazaars, and traffic police with close relatives, but also of using state funds to organize astronomically expensive wedding celebrations. Moreover, the president cited a 25 percent increase in serious crime in the region under Mardiev's watch, including violent crime and especially economic crime and bribery.

Having called for a "new political force" to emerge to cleanse the republic of such offenses, President Karimov continued the technique of manufacturing pluralism, and even intensified efforts in preparation for parliamentary elections in December 1999. Two new political parties held their founding conferences in 1998: both the Social Democratic party led by a former opposition figure and the Fidorkorlar ("those who are self-sacrificing") espoused nothing which could be construed as diverging from the president's own policies. Karimov himself repeatedly stated his commitment to building a democratic state, but observed that of the "four or five parties and movements in Uzbekistan, none of them really meet the standards of a real party." As for the national opposition parties hounded out of existence in 1993, Erk ("freedom") and Birlik ("unity"), their leaders remaining in the country began to suggest that they would try to field candidates for the parliamentary elections. However, over the summer the regime rejected feelers sent out by foreign diplomats and Erk members on the possible return of their exiled leader, poet Mohammad Solih.

Despite official denials of censorship or state control, the domestic media in Uzbekistan remained completely unfree, while alternative sources became less and less accessible. As with political parties, the Uzbek government created "independent" media outlets, such as the Yoshlar television channel which began broadcasting in September, which lacked any political or even critical social content. Or, as in the case of the new "non-state" news agency, a member of the presidential apparatus was appointed as chief. In December, the state-run radio issued a blistering criticism of Radio Liberty and BBC Uzbek service broadcasts, while shortly thereafter Uzbek-language BBC broadcasts were removed from medium-wave, possibly in retaliation for series of programs on human rights). Few Uzbek journalists were likely to take up Karimov's repeated calls to become more critical after the August sentencing of Samarkand satirist Shodi Mardiev to 11 years imprisonment for his jibes against corrupt local officials, or the outrageous October verdict condemning Kyrgyz journalist Rustam Usmonov to 14 years in a strict-regime camp for writing about corruption in Andijan. Journalists from the Russian Federation were also subject to harassment: in August two were beaten on the street in the capital in full daylight after returning from investigating persecution of Muslims in the Fergana Valley.

"SUCH PEOPLE SHOULD BE SHOT IN THE HEAD!"

Islam Karimov's Islamophobia reached a new and murderous peak in 1998, as evinced by his statement, cited above, before parliament in May assessing what should be done about those he accused of Islamic fundamentalism. What began as a wave of arrests of thousands of Muslims suspected of associating with independent imams yielded a series of sensational show trials, a law intended to place all religious organizations under complete state control, and a continued avalanche of state propaganda against so-called "Wahabis."

At the end of 1997 several police officers in the sensitive Fergana Valley region were brutally murdered. These events, which most observers understood as part of an ongoing struggle among local criminal groupings, set off the arrest of thousands, resulting in at least one death, presumably from beatings, in pre-trial custody. Many of those arrested had small quantities of drugs or ammunition planted on them during their arrest. Witnesses confirmed that police used this technique openly; one man swept up in May recounted that he was advised to confess—if he did not, larger quantities of drugs could always be "found" in his home. The initial roundups culminated in the trial of eight young men before the Supreme Court in July; the accused murderer, Tolib Mamajanov, stated during the trial that the murders, to which he confessed, were an instrument of Islamic justice. Mamajanov was sentenced to death, and his accused associates to lengthy prison terms. However, all the men exhibited signs of physical mistreatment; several stated in court that police had abused them to force their confessions. As in the trials which followed, prosecutors and judges spent most of the time outlining the depredations and the risk to national security of so-called "Wahabis," including several leading imams who were forced into hiding (such as Obidkhon Nazarov) or "disappeared" by the state, and paid little if any attention to the supposed crimes at issue in the proceedings.

Who were these "Wahabis" that President Karimov believed should be shot? The branch of Sunni Islam which predominates in Saudi Arabia originated in the eighteenth century as a type of Islamic Protestantism. In Soviet parlance, "Wahabism" was used as a slur against those attempting to maintain religious traditions, or to revive adherence to basic Islamic precepts; Karimov seems simply to have carried over this practice. The victims of Uzbekistan's 1998 crackdown shared several characteristics, but only a few overlapped with the type of fundamentalism implied in the label "Wahabi," such as emphasizing Koranic rituals like the five daily prayers, or pilgrimages to local shrines traditional in the region's own Islamic heritage. They may wear beards, and their female relatives may wear a hijab (veil). Though Uzbek assertions that homegrown fundamentalists were being trained in Afghan and Pakistani military camps date back several years, no concrete evidence has ever emerged.

The state's efforts to submit all aspects of religious life and all religious believers to its surveillance and control entered a new phase in May with the passage of the new, ironically named Law on Freedom of Conscience. Though the law has created some obstacles for non-Muslim faiths, barriers to the registration and operation of Christian and Jewish congregations have largely been lifted, in response to international pressure. Not so for restrictions on "unofficial" Islamic practice, confirming the impression that the law was intended to limit opportunity for Islamic communities to develop into centers of social activism. Not only did the statute mandate re-registration of religious communities, but it set the minimum number of congregants at 100, rather than at 10 as previously mandated. Proselytism, private religious teaching, and wearing of "ritual" dress in public places were all forbidden. This final provision was used to expel nearly 60 young men and women from institutions of higher learning for wearing beards or hijab. Many unregistered mosques were confiscated from their congregants and turned into public buildings, while a decree forbid giving the call to prayer over a loudspeaker. Finally, the chairmen of neighborhood or village associations, who for several years had been appointed and paid by the state (not elected by their communities) were instructed in 1998 to investigate local residents who wore religious dress and regularly attended services, and to supply to state officials information on where, about what, and with whom they pray.

Already the repression has had the opposite effect to that intended, provoking the kind of social activism it was presumably intended to prevent. In January a group of female family members of those arrested held a protest demonstration in front of government buildings. Later in the spring an even larger group of supporters of the imam Obidkhon Nazarov gathered in front of his family's apartment; the demonstration effectively blocked attempts to evict the Nazarovs. Groups of expelled students repeatedly took their case to the courts, but have found no relief.

Sooner or later, many observers believe, Karimov's bete noire of an Islam-fueled outbreak of social unrest is likely to come true, as believers lose all hope in the possibility of justice or the rule of law, and turn to other means to redress their grievances. Islamic parties in neighboring Tajikistan and Afghanistan, now more secure in power than ever, would no doubt be happy to assist them in this task.

RELATIONS WITH TAJIKSTAN REACH NEW LOW

Uzbekistan's relations with its neighbors entered a severe crisis in November, when a rebel Tajik commander based in Uzbekistan attempted an armed insurrection in Tajikistan's northern Leninabad province. While Uzbekistan issued vehement denials, captured rebels confessed they were trained and housed by Uzbek military and security specialists. Evidence shows that the rebels had launched earlier raids on Tajikistan, such as the August assassination of a local mayor, from Uzbek territory. It seemed clear that Colonel Mahmud Khudaiberdiev, himself half-Uzbek, and supported by the province's former leader, another ethnic Uzbek, acted with the government of Uzbekistan's knowledge, if not its covert support. The coup attempt, quickly put down by Tajik government forces together with fighters from the United Tajik Opposition (UTO), dealt a severe blow to Uzbekistan's likely aim of destabilizing the current cooperation between

Tajikistan's sitting government and the Islamist UTO, and in fact strengthened their union in the face of a common outside foe.

Karimov's sensitivity to the fact that members of an Islamic opposition had entered the government of his southern neighbor was no doubt increased by the success of the Taliban in maintaining control over most of the territory of Afghanistan in 1998, including the capture of Mazar-i-Sharif in August. He expressed fears of Taliban expansion in several international fora, calling on the United Nations to intervene in the conflict, and making a defensive alliance the centerpiece of relations with Kazakhstan, Uzbekistan's neighbor to the north. Though Uzbek-Iranian antagonism is longstanding, Foreign Minister Abduaziz Komilov traveled to Teheran in November to provide impetus to the peace process; he continued on to Pakistan, a country whose support for the Taliban has alienated Uzbekistan in the past. In an unprecedented step, it was reported that while in Pakistan Komilov met with a senior Taliban leader. Finally, fear of a Taliban invasion was a factor (among others) in prompting a warming in Uzbek-Russian relations. Not only did Uzbekistan and Russia sign a defense pact during President Boris Yeltsin's October visit to Tashkent, but they pledged together with Tajikistan to halt the spread of "Islamic fundamentalism." Relations with neighboring states in the Commonwealth of Independent States remained close, with visits exchanged with President Nursultan Nazarbaev of Kazakhstan, and successful negotiation with President Askar Akayev of Kyrgyzstan for continued Uzbek natural gas supplies. The thorny problem of regional water cooperation also moved closer to a solution, with the signing of preliminary agreements between those three countries on use of water and hydroelectric power in the Syr-Daria and Naryn river basins.

Improved Uzbek-Russian ties were counterbalanced by a cooling between Uzbekistan and the United States. Though the U.S. government continued to provide significant foreign aid in the form of technical assistance ($32 million in 1998), American frustration with the slow pace of economic reform grew evident as the year progressed. With regard to political and social reforms, treatment of religious minorities in particular sparked American interest, though concrete expressions of displeasure were few. Accordingly, the United States continued to fund some of the most needed projects to promote Uzbekistan's energy producing industries, providing $215 million through the Export-Import Bank to develop natural gas infrastructure. As Uzbekistan, which reportedly saw an 11 percent increase in drugs trafficking in 1998, continued to cooperate with the United States on drug interdiction, one of the U.S.'s major strategic concerns in the region, relations are unlikely to deteriorate conclusively.

Less concerned with the lack of political reform than the Americans, the European Parliament moved to ratify the Partnership and Cooperation Agreement signed with Uzbekistan in 1996. Though ratification had been initially suspended for two years, due to Uzbekistan's total non-compliance with the human rights provisions of the agreement, intense lobbying in 1998 by a Uzbek government thirsting for international recognition seems likely to push the agreement towards ratification in early 1999.

ECONOMIC BELT-TIGHTENING

In the wake of the financial crisis in Russia, its largest trading partner, Uzbekistan was forced to shift its economic estimates for 1999 sharply downward. The real impact of the crisis is difficult to state, given the government's refusal to release accurate economic data; while government figures claim a 4.4 percent rate of growth for 1998, the Economist Intelligence Unit (EIU) estimated actual growth of only 1 percent. Export earnings were further hit by the continuing drop in world prices for cotton and gold—the two largest export commodities. The poor cotton harvest struck another blow to state finances, coming in 12 percent lower than in 1997 in absolute tonnage, with a yield 14 percent lower in tons per hectare. The overall volume of foreign trade fell by 28 percent and exports by 23 percent. The government compensated with cost-cutting measures, vowing in July to reduce the number of state officials by a quarter. Yet wage hikes of nearly 50 percent for state workers passed in the same month seemed sure to offset whatever savings would be achieved.

Despite these problems, the government remained intransigent in its opposition to fundamental economic reforms. Karimov viewed the type of IMF-driven economic reform carried out in Russia as a threat to his rule, founded on the maintenance of a stable (if gradually declining) standard of living for his people. Privatization limped along, with the government unwilling to relinquish control of major enterprises. One major stumbling block to both international financial support (the IMF halted loan disbursements in December, 1996) and foreign direct investment was the status of the Uzbek currency, the som. The som remained unconvertible, while the state controlled access to hard currency through a system of permits. Exchange rates were set by the state for different types of transactions. Potential foreign investors lacked guarantees on expatriation of profits, and so had little incentive to enter Uzbek markets. Meanwhile, the state controlled export commodities, and restricted the amount and kind of goods which could be imported. With legal access to hard currency difficult or impossible to obtain, ordinary citizens, who preferred to hold their savings in dollars to protect them from 30–40 percent annual inflation, were forced onto the black market, where rates at the end of 1998 were nearly four times higher than the official bank exchange rate. The advertising campaign launched at the end of 1998 to persuade them to deposit their dollars in the National Bank (complete with television spots showing women in traditional dress drawing dollars from their dowry chests) seems to have had little effect. President Karimov insisted that the stringent economic policies and currency devaluation demanded by the IMF would cause social unrest, but in 1999 he may have no choice but to yield, since hard currency reserves were thought to have hit ruinously low levels.

Tajikistan

Population:	6,000,000
Capital:	Dushanbe (pop. 600,000)
Major cities:	Khojent (Leninabad) (pop. 180,000), Kulyab (pop. 70,000), Kurgan-Tyube (pop. 45,000)
Area:	143,100 sq. km.
Major ethnic groups:	Tajik 64.9%, Uzbek 25%, Russian 3%, other 7.1%
Economy:	GDP growth: 5.3%
....	Inflation rate: 2.7%
....	Unemployment rate: not available

PEACE DOES NOT BRING AN END TO THE FIGHTING

by BRUCE PANNIER

As 1998 ushered itself in, Tajikistan had officially been at peace for six months after five years of civil war. There had been incidents which temporarily put peace at risk, but the Tajik government of mainly former Communists and the United Tajik Opposition (UTO) with Islamic groups at its core did not allow sporadic outbreaks of violence to ruin their agreement on reconciliation. There were even signs of active cooperation between the former enemies. But 1998 proved that it is one thing to lay down arms and another to be friends and cooperate in rebuilding so much that was destroyed.

On the domestic front, the process of healing the country's grave wounds began. The peace accord had been signed back in June 1997 by President Imomali Rakhmonov, representing the Tajik government, and Said Abdullo Nuri, leader of the UTO, but as the new year began there was little progress in implementing the terms of the agreement.

In line with the peace accord a National Reconciliation Commission was formed and met for the first time in Tajik capital, Dushanbe, in mid-September 1997. The 26-member commission, with Nuri as its chairman, had equal representation from both sides. The commission was charged with forwarding proposals for amendments to the country's constitution so that free and fair elections to parliament could be held 12–18 months after the commission's first meeting. Complaints by the UTO leadership in early January that the government was slow in fulfilling certain terms of the accord led the UTO to walkout of the commission. UTO representatives went back to the Reconciliation Commission one week later when it was clear the government would begin handing over top posts in the government to UTO members, another term of the accord and the UTO's primary complaint. The UTO left the commission again in May due to a decision by Russia, Uzbekistan, and Tajikistan to form a "troika" aimed at combating religious extremists and subsequent legislation passed by the Tajik parliament banning the activities of religious political parties. The UTO left the commission again briefly in late September when one of its leaders, Otakhon Latifi from the democratic wing of the UTO, was murdered in Dushanbe. The UTO demanded, and received, better security arrangements before they returned to the commission.

Amid these events, members of the commission, particularly Nuri, were often torn from their duties to mediate armed disputes which plagued Tajikistan during 1998. By the end of 1998, not one proposal on amendments to the constitution had been forwarded by the commission to the parliament for approval.

Giving over seats in the government to UTO representatives was visibly more successful. The temporary departure of the UTO from the National Reconciliation Commission in January prompted the government to start naming new officials. UTO members became the ministers of economics and foreign trade, water resources, labor and employment, and chairman of the country's customs committee. Another complaint which sparked the walkout from the commission was the slowness in giving official amnesties to UTO members and releasing from jail those who had been arrested for their part in the civil war. Having received his amnesty the number two man in the UTO, Hoja Akbar Turajonzoda, returned to Tajikistan from Iran in February. He became first deputy prime minister.

Though the UTO received more places in the government during the year, their nominee for defense minister was rejected by the government side on several occasions. That nominee, Mirzo Ziyayev, was among the most capable UTO field commanders during the civil war. Popular among his men and very influential among the UTO in general, Ziyayev had fewer friends on the government side which fought against him. He had enough influence in the UTO that its leadership refused to withdraw his candidacy. But Ziyayev complicated his own situation when he incautiously remarked to journalists during the summer that Samarkand and Bukhara, the second and third largest cities of present-day Uzbekistan, are historically Tajik cities. He remained the UTO nominee for defense minister at the end of 1998.

Although the UTO received its share of high-profile posts during 1998, it will also need officials at regional and local levels if it is to stand a chance in the planned elections. In post-Soviet Central Asia controlling candidates' access to local meetings, factories, schools, and other gathering places has been key to electoral victory. That, and the power to select local election committee representatives, were in the hands of the village akims (leaders), the mayors, and the governors. The UTO did not receive many of these positions and if Tajikistan does go ahead and hold parliamentary elections in 1999, as planned, this may become an issue of contention.

GUNS STILL AT THE READY

Although the work of the National Reconciliation Commission and the reality of the two sides sharing power was a signal achievement, steps towards reconciliation were constantly sidelined by fighting, usually close to, if not in, the capital of Dushanbe.

After five years of fighting both sides were spent. Government and UTO armed forces together were probably between 25,000 and 30,000 men. Battles in central Tajikistan from February 1996 to the spring of 1997, alone, left thousands of these dead. With no military victory for either side, there was only a paper signed thousands of kilometers away pledging the two sides would work together. On the ground in Tajikistan trust came hard. Neither side was disarmed. There were those on both sides who had gained much during the war, reputation or wealth or both. Perceptions of cheating by one side were inevitable, as were further clashes. In January the first incident occurred on the outskirts of the capital. UTO members set up a road block and government troops arrived. Fighting began and the UTO fighters ranks swelled to 500 led by field commander Rahmon "Hitler" Sanginov, who would make news again in 1998. Somehow, the UTO fighters took Dushanbe's deputy mayor and other officials from the city administration hostage and successfully bargained for the release of comrades languishing in government jails.

It was a sign of things to come. In February UTO fighters hijacked two food trucks 100 kilometers east of Dushanbe. The government soldiers guarding the trucks were beaten and their weapons taken. On 9 March the police station in Rogun, 75 kilometers east of Dushanbe, was attacked, one policeman wounded, others beaten and their weapons seized. One week later, "unidentified gunmen" killed five policemen and one civilian at a roadside checkpoint in Karabulok, 70 kilometers east of Dushanbe. A week later six policemen were killed in Kofarnikhon, 25 kilometers east of Dushanbe. That turned into a week long battle between government forces and "unreconciled" elements of the UTO which left 20 people dead. Over 100 government troops were taken captive during the fighting, but were released later, after UTO and government representatives came to mediate.

Fighting broke out again on the outskirts of Dushanbe in late April and stray mortar shells even landed near the presidential palace in downtown Dushanbe. There was rarely one entire month without some clash. But these were not always between the former antagonists. Just days before the end of the year fighting broke out between the forces of two UTO field commanders, Rahmon Sanginov and Khojali Pirmuhammadov, immediately following a meeting between the two men in the National Reconciliation Commission's building.

All these and other such occurrences paled beside the two worst examples of violence in Tajikistan in 1998. The first was an international incident. In late July three United Nations officials, Japanese political science professor Yutaka Akino and two army officers from Poland and Uruguay, together with an interpreter, entered UTO-controlled territory in central Tajikistan. They were on their way to verify UTO troop positions. On a remote section of road in this mountainous region they were stopped and executed. When that news became public there was a mass exodus of foreign aid workers, including the UN mission to Tajikistan. With the help of the UTO leadership, three men were quickly caught and charged with the crime. However, the UN demanded that a full investigation be made and not only the perpetrators but those who ordered the execution and their motives be made clear. Despite the capture of suspects who admitted their crime, by year's end, the UN still had not received satisfactory information which would allow it to return all its staff to Tajikistan.

The bloodiest violence came when a former colonel from the Tajik army made a sudden return to an unexpected part of Tajikistan. Colonel Mahmud Khudaberdiyev was a decorated veteran of the Soviet occupation of Afghanistan. When the civil war started in Tajikistan he led a unit of the Popular Front, a para-military group which helped government forces during the war. They were particularly antagonistic towards members of Islamic groups. Khudaberdiyev was made the commander of the Tajik army's First Brigade, the best unit in the Tajik army. His unit was based in Kurgan-Tyube (Kurgan-Teppe) in south-central Tajikistan not far from the border with Uzbekistan. Khudaberdiyev, like many of the leaders from the Popular Front, became something of a warlord. He controlled the area around his unit's base and fought or declined to fight for the government as he wished. Competition for control of the local economy had earlier led to fighting between Khudaberdiyev's unit and another unit of the Tajik Army, with Khudaberdiyev coming out as the winner. In early 1996, he marched on Dushanbe to force the removal of some government officials. In early 1997, without orders, he marched on, and captured, the western Tajik city of Tursunzade, which was ruled by bandits but officially under government control. President Rakhmonov ordered him to withdraw immediately; Khudaberdiyev ignored him and was "punished" by being named commander of the rapid reaction force of the presidential guard.

He did not agree with the terms of the peace accord and less than three months after its signing declared that no Islamist would be permitted in his section of Tajikistan. He moved to section off the entire Khatlon Oblast from Dushanbe's control. The government reacted in force and drove this once valuable ally from the country. More than one year later, in early November, Khudaberdiyev returned leading an armed force. Instead of reappearing near his former base area in Kurgan-Tyube, Khudaberdiyev's attack targeted Khujand in the northern Leninabad region, Tajikistan's second largest. Khudaberdiyev's forces, with surprise on their side, enjoyed some successes in the first two days of fighting. The government, allied with the UTO, gradually poured in enough troops and weaponry to turn the tide. Hundreds were killed during the five days of fighting and significant damage was done to the area, but Khudaberdiyev escaped, again. There was the mystery of why Khudaberdiyev chose Khujand instead of Kurgan-Tyube, an area he was more familiar with and where he undoubtedly still had supporters. This puzzle was seemingly solved when Khudaberdiyev made a statement that he was allied to former Tajik Prime Minister Abdumalik Abdullajonov. Abdullajonov was from the Leninabad Region and remained popular there, though he now headed an opposition party from his home in exile. Nothing was heard from Abdullajonov until after the attack crushed. Then Abdullajonov issued a statement denying that he was party to the violence in northern Tajikistan.

TESTY NEIGHBORS

As it turned out, Khudaberdiyev's attempted coup in the north caused more damage to Tajikistan's relations with neighboring Uzbekistan than it did to Tajikistan's infrastructure or cooperation between the government and the UTO.

Tajikistan's foreign relations seemed ready for a change to the better at the beginning of 1998. Rakhmonov met with Uzbek President Islam Karimov and Russian Prime Minister Viktor Chernomyrdin in January. Those two countries had done the most to prop up Rakhmonov's government during the dark days of the civil war. President Rakhmonov visited Uzbekistan right after the New Year. Karimov had greatly helped, and by some accounts greatly influenced, Rakhmonov during the civil war. Rakhmonov was known to call Karimov "Father" on occasions as a sign of respect. Karimov was among those who were not satisfied with the Tajik peace accord and brought the question up when he saw Rakhmonov. But all accounts show the two got along well and within days of Rakhmonov's arrival to Uzbekistan, he and Karimov were in Ashgabat, Turkmenistan, meeting with the presidents of Kazakhstan, Kyrgyzstan, and Turkmenistan. The summit yielded little of regional importance but was the beginning of Tajikistan's return to the community of its neighbors. During the civil war even those neighboring states helping Dushanbe did so as much to keep the "disease" in Tajikistan as to help President Rakhmonov.

Not long after the summit reports began to circulate that Tajikistan would join Kazakhstan, Kyrgyzstan, and Uzbekistan in the Central Asia Union. That did happen in late March. Rakhmonov's mid-January meeting with Chernomyrdin was also a success. Chernomyrdin said Russian troops guarding the Tajik-Afghan border would remain while necessary and promised Moscow would make additional loans to Tajikistan.

But both these countries dragged Rakhmonov into a mess in May. The Uzbek president made an official visit to Moscow at that time and following his meeting with President Boris Yeltsin, it was announced Russia, Uzbekistan, and Tajikistan were forming a "troika" to combat the spread of religious extremists. During the Tajik civil war the UTO were the "religious extremists" and the announcement in Moscow was ill-received by many in Tajikistan.

Continued violence in Tajikistan, especially the killing of the UN officials, prevented Tajikistan from energetically developing its foreign relations. However, during 1998 Rakhmonov became more independent from both Uzbekistan and Russia. Regarded as a stooge of Moscow or Tashkent in the war years, Rakhmonov's new alliance with the UTO gave the Tajik president the opportunity to speak his mind on regional matters. With the exception of Uzbekistan, the other countries in the region and Russia, who had all signed on as guarantors of the peace, were very supportive of efforts by the two Tajik groups to mend fences.

Khudaberdiyev's raid on Leninabad in November unwittingly forced a change in Rakhmonov's relations with Uzbekistan. Even as Khudaberdiyev's forces were being beaten back by government and UTO forces, questions were being raised in Dushanbe as to how and from where these rebels entered Tajikistan. It was not difficult to figure out that they surely crossed over from Uzbekistan. To use the Uzbek president's own words, the Leninabad Region "sticks out like a tongue into Uzbek territory." During a special session of parliament, Rakhmonov named

Uzbekistan as involved in Khudaberdiyev's attempted coup. Other Tajik officials said Khudaberdiyev had trained, under Uzbek army officers, in northern Afghanistan, then in Uzbekistan's Jizzak region before finally striking at northern Tajikistan.

Tashkent's reaction was swift. Uzbekistan pulled its battalion out of the CIS peacekeeping force guarding the Tajik-Afghan border two weeks after Rakhmonov accused Uzbekistan of playing a part in the Leninabad rebellion. Tashkent claimed those troops were no longer needed in Tajikistan as they were originally stationed there to guard against UTO forces in Afghanistan. Few believed this reasoning and when Uzbekistan closed the border with Tajikistan and shut off natural gas supplies to its neighbor it was obvious that relations between the two countries would never be the same.

These actions pushed Tajikistan towards Moscow. In some ways the choice was inevitable. Russia continued to provide security along Tajikistan's border with Afghanistan. The UTO were back in Tajikistan, legally, but another, arguably worse Islamic threat in Afghanistan had finally made its way to the border. Fighters of Afghanistan's Taliban movement overran the last major bastion of resistance, the northern city of Mazar-i-Sharif, in early August. Not long after, Russian border guards sighted groups of armed men near the Tajik border, presumed to be Taliban fighters, though in Afghanistan a man with a gun is not an uncommon occurrence. Still, Uzbekistan's one battalion did not compare to the 25,000 soldiers in Tajikistan under Russian command. And despite the economic problems which began in Russia in August, Moscow remains more likely to help Tajikistan financially than Tashkent may ever be able to do.

But, at year's end Tajikistan could count on none of its immediate neighbors for help. Relations with Kyrgyzstan were amiable but not significant. In any case it is hard to imagine what Kyrgyzstan could do for Tajikistan. Relations with China have rarely been a factor for the Tajik people, and the huge neighbor to the east has historically been a potential threat to the area now called Tajikistan. Tajikistan supported their kinsman, ousted Afghan President Burhanuddin Rabbani, in the conflict there and continued to provide an airbase in the city of Kulyob for use by Rabbani's defense minister, Ahmed Shah Masoud. At the end of 1998 Masoud's forces were the only major obstacle to the Taliban, so friendly relations between Dushanbe the new masters of Kabul was out of the question. Tajikistan's best friends at the end of the year were, and were likely to remain for some time, Russia and Iran.

Economically, Tajikistan began to crawl out from the ruins in 1998. In 1997, Tajikistan recorded the first growth in GDP since it became an independent country in 1991, at around 5.3 percent. There were signs of improvement in agriculture and industry but this reflected more the relative absence of fighting rather than resulting from reforms.

Fields were farmed again and industrial output in the first five months of the year increased over 1997 figures by 8.5 percent. But further progress was hindered by the inability to pay wages (or pensions) and the country continued to thrive on black market activity.

Tajikistan was promised loans in May by the International Monetary Fund, $120 million over the next three years, and the World Bank, $60 million. Along with two organizations, donors pledged an additional $150 million over the next three years, all for reforms in the banking system and country's infrastructure. However, these loans were dependent on Tajikistan demonstrating that progress towards peace and stability, and 1998 showed that will not be easy.

Tajikistan has rich potential wealth in metals, precious metals, and agricultural products, but its transport access to world markets is limited. The Karakorum Highway, running from China through eastern Kyrgyzstan and Tajikistan then into Pakistan and on to India, may help now that the full length of it is open. But Tajik roads between the lowland west and mountainous east are often closed during the colder months, closing the Karakorum Highway to most of Tajikistan.

Kyrgyzstan

Population:	4,698,108
Capital:	Bishkek (pop. 650,000)
Major cities:	Osh (pop. 220,000), Jalalabad (pop. 75,000)
Area:	198,000 sq. km.
Major ethnic groups:	Kyrgyz 52.4%, Russian 21.5%, Uzbek 12.9%, German 2.4%, other 8.3%
Economy:	GDP growth: 1.8%
	Inflation rate: 18.4%
	Unemployment rate: 3.1%

WAITING FOR THE GOLD RUSH

by BRUCE PANNIER

Kyrgyzstan began 1998 headed in the right direction. The previous year the country made great economic progress. Driven by the first full year of production at the Kumtor Gold Mining Operation, in 1997 Kyrgyzstan had managed to cut its trade deficit by more than 60 percent. Its industrial output increased by almost 50 percent compared to 1996 and its currency was the most stable of all the countries in the Commonwealth of Independent States (CIS). There was no reason to believe 1998 would not be the same.

Economic news, good and bad, was once again in the center spotlight in 1998. The economic performance in 1997 kindled hopes in Kyrgyzstan that 1998 would revive the earlier optimism and turn the country into an example of a state successfully emerging into a market economy. Neighboring CIS Central Asian states were still waiting for the oil, natural gas, and metals in their soil to be extracted and exported. But Kyrgyzstan's major development project, the Kumtor gold mine, was already up and running and preparing to increase production. Other gold mining projects were expected to begin operations in 1998.

Even the value of water flowing from Kyrgyzstan's mountains had increased after talks with neighboring Kazakhstan and Uzbekistan opened the door to cash payments to maintain water supplies. Previously Kyrgyzstan had used its own funds to maintain, or try to maintain, the many reservoirs and dams along numerous rivers. Several of those rivers meet and form the Syr-Daria, one of Central Asia's largest rivers, bringing water to Uzbekistan and Kazakhstan. Agreement was reached to give money to Kyrgyzstan to maintain the reservoirs and dams or to compensate the country with coal and natural gas. Unfortunately, little of this assistance had actually materialized by the end of 1998.

There were many public posters in Kyrgyzstan, particularly in the north, proclaiming "Kumtor-Golden Cooperation." The joint venture between Kyrgyzstan's state gold company—Kyrgyzaltyn—and Canada's Cameco Corporation had extracted 17 tons of gold in 1997 out of an estimated 514 metric tons at the site. The site was mined on a small scale during Soviet times but had not been fully developed due to its distant location—4,000 meters high in the mountains not far from the Chinese border. But even with an increase in production, Kumtor could not contribute to the Kyrgyz economy as it had in 1997, due to falling gold prices on the world market.

In addition, something of a disaster happened near the site in May. One of four trucks traveling to the Kumtor operation on 20 May overturned into the Barskoon River, spilling 1.7 tons of cyanide (which is used to leach gold from the ore). The Barskoon River flows into Issyk-Kul, the country's biggest lake and major tourist attraction. When news of the spill got out, hotels on the north shore of the lake lost between 50 and 80 percent of their summer business. Local merchants also suffered. But none suffered as much as the inhabitants of the village of Barskoon near the south shore of Issyk-Kul.

The spill itself was bad enough, but the response to it caused an even broader scandal. Reports in some media and testimony from people near the scene indicate the drivers of the trucks intended to do nothing except pull the truck out of the river. It was the chance passing of a Russian border guard who understood the seriousness of the accident that finally prompted someone to call down river and tell people there not to drink or bathe. The village was sealed off so tightly that even some aid could not get in. At first government officials told journalists there was no problem because the area's water system had been shut off. Barskoon, however, does not have water in pipes or from the tap, people take it from the river. Officials both from the government and from the company played down the incident, saying it was not serious. They were certainly wrong about the effects as the entire village and its surrounding area were evacuated to the other side of Issyk-Kul for a short time, four people died, and hundreds were admitted to hospitals.

The bad publicity hampered operations at the mining site during the summer months when the site was most accessible to the giant vehicles making the trip. The accident also posed a problem for the government. Obviously some compensation should come for the victims of the spill. But the Kyrgyz government is a partner in the mining operation. Good economic news in 1997 did not mean the Kyrgyz government was in financial shape to pay out millions of dollars for compensation. Finally, months after the accident a figure of $8.4 million restitution was given by the Kyrgyz special commission assessing the area.

TENSION WITH NEIGHBORS

Regionally, Kyrgyzstan looked to profit from a new understanding of the cost of water. Kazakhstan and Uzbekistan had agreed in 1997 that they should help in the cost of maintaining reservoirs along rivers originating in Kyrgyzstan but flowing into the two countries. Arable land is rare in much of Central Asia, giving water value it has in few places. Given the massive scale of the dam projects built in Soviet times, regulating the flow of water was a problem involving more than one country. But despite talk payment for upkeep or possibly bartering for water with supplies for power stations in Kyrgyzstan, little of anything was sent to Kyrgyzstan. The chances of money from Uzbekistan were diminished by an accident involving a reservoir overflow, causing a flood which killed several dozen people in Uzbekistan. The Uzbek government complained about the lack of advance warning, which could have saved lives. Kyrgyzstan claimed lack of funds had left the country unable to send planes to check on melt from glaciers or rapidly rising water levels in high mountain reservoirs.

As to supplies of natural gas, Uzbekistan shut that off on the eve of winter, citing debt for supplies already received. It was only when Kyrgyzstan began negotiating with Russia's Gazprom that Uzbekistan agreed to renew supplies. Kazakhstan was unable to provide heating and energy for its own population in part because supplies had been redirected to ensure that the new, and rapidly growing, capital in the northern city of Astana would not be without power.

FALLOUT FROM RUSSIAN CRISIS

Though more rapid growth was evident in the Kyrgyz economy for the majority of 1998, the Russian economic crisis which began in mid-August eventually hit Kyrgyzstan also. Halfway through 1998 industrial output was up 28 percent over the figure for the same period in 1997. This was by far the most impressive growth figure of all the CIS economies, as had also been the case in 1997. The national currency, the som, had been introduced in May 1993 at an exchange rate of 4 som to one U.S. dollar. By mid-summer 1998, its exchange rate was around 17 to one dollar.

When the Russian financial crisis began at that time, the Kyrgyz government, like all the other CIS governments, forecast minimal repercussions. But, like many of the CIS countries, Russia was Kyrgyzstan's leading trade partner and the effects didn't take long to reach the Central Asian state. Kyrgyzstan's National Bank had set aside $200 million to defend the som. At an early September session of the Kyrgyz parliament, then Prime Minister Kubanychbek Jumaliev admitted the Russian crisis was having an impact but that the situation in Kyrgyzstan was stable. Jumaliev noted the GDP had risen by 4.5 percent in the first eight months of the year compared to figures from 1997.

But one month later Marat Sultanov, the chairman of the National Bank, said "In Kyrgyzstan we were prepared for the Russian crisis and even predicted it, but not on such a scale." Sultanov continued that the som had lost 17–18 percent of its value in the months since the August crisis. That was optimistic as the official trading rate at currency exchange points in Bishkek was 22–22.5 som to one dollar, which was more than a 30 percent devaluation. By year's end it was trading at over 30 som to one dollar and that was an improvement from mid-November when it briefly traded at 35–37 som to one dollar. In November Sultanov said about half the foreign currency reserves spent were used to buy government securities from investors who were pulling off their business deals.

Despite what Prime Minister Jumaliev said in September, Kyrgyz GDP recorded growth of just 2 percent by year's end. Kumtor saved Kyrgyzstan again by providing 37 percent of the country's industrial output, but the falling price of gold on world markets kept Kumtor from doing more. Also during those first nine months Kyrgyz exports brought in $345 million but imports cost the country $521 million. Trade with Russia had fallen by 150 percent, and worse, after cutting the trade deficit by two thirds in 1997, Kyrgyzstan was suddenly right back where it ended 1996.

HEADS ROLL

Though much of Kyrgyzstan's hard luck was probably unavoidable, somebody's head had to roll for this bad chain of events. Kyrgyzstan's Accounts Chamber had already reported to the president, the prime minister, and other leading government officials that the country had lost about $20 million due to economic crimes. The same report said the figure for 1998 was up by 150 percent in the first nine months. President Askar Akayev decided in December it was time to use these pieces of information, and launched an anti-corruption campaign. One of the first victims was Prime Minister Kubanychbek Jumaliev. Jumaliev had been appointed prime minister in April just after Russia named Sergei Kirienko to the same position. The reasoning was the same: a new face and a fresh approach to problems which baffled old Soviet bureaucrats. Jumaliev, a former student of Akayev in his university days, replaced Apas Jumagulov, who was a veteran politician and a notable survivor in the minefield of Kyrgyz politics.

Jumaliev was to suffer the same fate as Kirienko, who was ousted in August. At a session of the country's Security Council in December Akayev told Jumaliev that he had not accomplished a single one of the tasks Akayev had set for him. Akayev told the session that Jumaliev and his government had totally failed to stave off the effects of Russia's economic problems. So, just before the end of 1998, Jumabek Ibraimov, a man in poor physical health, became the third prime minister Kyrgyzstan had in eight months.

Amid these problems there was one positive event in October. Late that month Kyrgyzstan received the news that it had been admitted to the World Trade Organization, the only country from the CIS to be a member. While this promised to be of great help to Kyrgyzstan in the future its immediate impact was to stir resentment among other CIS countries. This was especially true among Kyrgyzstan's partners in the CIS Customs Union, Russia, Kazakhstan, and Belarus. Since being formed by those three countries in 1994 the union had not met many of its goals, such as regulating tariff rates between member states. But that did not stop complaining from Moscow, Minsk, and Astana that Kyrgyzstan would not be able to comply both with CIS Customs Union regulations and its new obligations as a member of the WTO. Other CIS countries may also have been envious, since Uzbekistan's decision to cut off supplies of natural gas to Kyrgyzstan (see above) came shortly after the announcement of WTO membership was made.

In domestic politics, two other significant events took place during the year. In July, the Constitutional Court ruled that Akayev had only been elected once as president. According to Kyrgyzstan's constitution a person can be elected to that office only twice. The court decided that Akayev's selection as president of the Soviet Socialist Republic of Kirghiziya by the Supreme Soviet in 1990 did not count. Neither did his direct election as president in 1991, as the constitution had changed in the interim. Thus Akayev's election in 1995 was deemed to be his "first" election to the presidency. Complaints that this ruling was a distortion of the constitution limiting a president to two terms fell on stony ground. The Constitutional Court decision practically assures that Akayev will once again run, and win, in the presidential elections scheduled for December 2000. He did tell a Russian journalist in October he would not run if the country failed to show signs of improving, but at the time he said that, the full effects of Kyrgyzstan's economic problems were not yet visible.

On 18 October, the country held another referendum on amendments to the constitution and conducted on the initiative of Akayev, not the parliament. A similar referendum had been held in February 1996, not long after Akayev was elected president. The February 1996 referendum was a series of changes, some unrelated to one another, but the only vote possible was "yes" or "no" to the entire package. It was approved by the country fairly easily and vastly increased the powers of the presidency.

The October 1998 referendum was nearly the same. It included a question on the possibility of private land ownership in land, and one on changing the structure of the country's parliament. Seats in the People's Assembly were to be reduced from 70 to 38. The People's Assembly usually meets twice a year to pass legislation approved by the Legislative Assembly, which had its seats increased by the referendum from 35 to 67. This shift should weaken the Legislative Assembly. Another factor weakening the latter was the fact that the referendum removed some of the immunities the deputies had previously enjoyed. There had already been proof of corruption in the ranks of the parliament as deputies were caught up in scandals in the past. New exposure to the laws could be used to quiet criticism from parliamentary deputies in the future.

These developments did not go unnoticed. Opposition groups attempted to hold a demonstration against the proposed changes in the structure of the government during the last weekend of September. But militia and security ministry troops arrived in sufficient force to ban the meeting and arrested several of the organizers. There were also serious doubts about private land ownership. Few people in Kyrgyzstan had the money necessary to buy the land they were farming. No program had been set up to offer loans to farmers to buy the land on which they lived. Fear spread through some areas that many could become a kind of neo-serf, bound to their plot of land and forced to work for a wealthy landowner while receiving paltry wages. Announcement began just before the day of the vote that there would be a five-year moratorium on the purchase of land, but during that time the registration process for ownership could begin.

As a last note, an event not seen in Central Asia for more than a century took place in Kyrgyzstan in July, a royal wedding of sorts. Askar Akayev's son, Aidar, married the daughter of Kazakhstan's President Nursultan Nazarbaev, Aliya. They held their reception at Akayev's house on the shore of Issyk-Kul (no word that anyone went swimming), attended by heads of state and Russian pop stars. Akayev later said in an interview, he gave his son some gifts and $150. The Kyrgyz president didn't have any of the local currency with him at the reception. The way 1998 ended suggests that Akayev's son was better off with the dollars, for now.

Turkmenistan

Population:	4,460,000
Capital:	Ashgabat (pop. 400,000)
Major cities:	Chardzhou (pop. 164,000), Tashauz (pop. 114,000)
Area:	490,100 sq. km.
Major ethnic groups:	Turkmen 77%, Uzbek 9.2%, Russian 6.7%, Kazak 2%, other 6.1%
Economy:	GDP growth: 4.7%
....	Inflation rate: 19.3%
....	Unemployment rate: not available

THE FALTERING OIL STATE

by ALEXANDER COOLEY

Oil wealth is a mixed blessing for developing countries. While it floods a state's budgetary coffers with revenues, it also promotes the formation of state-dominated institutions that are antithetical to both economic and political liberalization. These patrimonial and distributive policies are difficult to change, even when a decline in oil income creates intense fiscal pressures for economic diversification and institutional reform.

Turkmenistan's post-Soviet oil-led economic strategy has been a variant of this general pattern of petro-state development. From 1991 to 1993, a steady stream of revenues allowed the state to preserve its Soviet-era social spending, thereby avoiding the painful economic transitions undergone by other countries in the Commonwealth of Independent States (CIS). Indeed, the Turkmen strategy was to avoid "transitioning" altogether, as authorities planned to use oil and gas export revenue to preserve the state-dominated political and economic hierarchies of the Soviet era. In 1993, however, external factors—Russia's denial of access to European natural gas customers and CIS customer payment problems—severely curtailed the amount of gas Turkmenistan could sell, and the state's gas production and economy have since collapsed.

Despite early optimistic forecasts, gas production in 1998 slumped to an independence-era low and the economic free-fall continued. Yet, Turkmen authorities continued to implement policies akin to other oil states, showing no signs of initiating substantive reforms in either the political or economic spheres. Specifically, developments in 1998 can be grouped into three broad areas.

First, the political system remained what can be best termed "authoritarian-patrimonialism," as efforts at democratization were cosmetic in nature. President Saparmurat Niyazov maintained his absolute dictatorial power, regularly purged bureaucracies and ministries for not fulfilling their duties, and cemented local and regional loyalties to the center by disbursing patronage in the form of state subsidies.

Second, the state did not initiate any substantive liberalizing economic reforms or construct the institutions necessary for market-oriented economic activity. Major industries and enterprises continue to be operated (exclusively or in foreign partnership).

Third, 1998 underscored Turkmenistan's foreign policy of "pragmatic neutrality." The Central Asian state continued to distance itself from Russia and the CIS, preferring, instead, to forge ties with external partners that could potentially assist with the construction of the pipelines necessary for the resumption of

capacity-level gas exports. On this front, new diplomatic initiatives were under-
taken, most notably a visit by President Niyazov to the United States.

POLITICS AS USUAL

President Niyazov rules by decree as head of the Democratic Party of Turkmenistan, the sole legal party. Under the title of "Turkmenbashi" (Chief of all
Turkmen), he remains the center of a personality cult and his images adorn
Ashgabat's streets, public monuments, and cultural festivals. Despite proclamations in February 1998 that Niyazov would cede many of his powers to the parliament and introduce new parties, his rule continued unchecked. Elections for
parliament and local administrations that were held in April offered only pro-
government candidates and the reported voter turn-out of 99 percent suggested
that they were less than fair.

Once again, international human rights and political monitoring organiza-
tions rated Turkmenistan among the most repressive dictatorships in the world.
All oppositional political activity was forbidden, external media (including Rus-
sian newspapers) were banned and the government controlled the domestic press.
In 1998, the U.S.-based Human Rights Watch group referred to Turkmenistan as
"one of the most repressive and abusive governments in the world." Freedom
House's annual rating of political freedoms around the world once again placed
Turkmenistan in its lowest tier of 13 countries described as "not free."

Prior to his April visit to the United States, Niyazov confirmed this interna-
tional reputation by arresting his former foreign minister and political dissident
Abdy Kuliev. Kuliev was detained after his arrival from a six-year exile in Russia on charges that he was a criminal and, like all dissidents, a "drug dealer." He
was later released after heavy U.S. pressure, along with five other dissidents.
Government officials were purged throughout the year. On May 20, Oil and Gas
Industry and Mineral Resources Minister Batyr Sarjayev was dismissed, and in
September Niyazov fired Defense Minister Danatar Kopekov, the chief of the
general staff, and the deputy defense minister after an embarrassing incident
involving military desertions and hostage-taking in the western part of the country. As usual, Niyazov also selectively removed local administrators and agricultural officials and threatened others with jail if they did not improve their
performance. Despite these upheavals and persistent rumors of the president's
ill-health, no obvious potential successor emerged on the political scene. One
concrete positive step in the area of human rights was taken at a conference of
the Organization for Security and Cooperation in Europe (OSCE) in Oslo where
Turkmen Foreign Minister Boris Shikhmuradov announced a moratorium on the
death penalty. The minister further stated that the president would soon reduce
the number of laws providing for capital punishment. The measure was made in
order to bring Turkmenistan in step with OSCE "humanistic values."

THE ECONOMY

Consistent with its expectations of future hydrocarbon-based wealth, Turkmenistan implemented few real reforms in 1998, as the economic situation remained grim. After a disastrous 26 percent GDP decline in 1997, official statistics announced that GDP in 1998 grew for the first time since independence—by about 5 percent. Like all official economic data, however, this figure must be treated with caution and is disputed by Western economic information-gathering organizations. GDP at the end of 1998 was still less than 60 percent of its 1991 level. Agriculture increased output by 24 percent relative to 1997 while the construction sector was up by 13 percent. Industrial output continued its decline (down 4 percent) and accounted for just 29 percent of the country's GDP.

The main cause for the decrease was the near halt in natural gas production and export. In 1998, the gas industry accounted for just 1 percent of GDP compared with 8 percent in 1997 and 65 percent in 1993. Inflation showed signs of stabilizing at around 20 percent, but artificial currency controls continue to make the unofficial exchange rate for the manat about 100–150 percent higher than its official 1998 closing of 5,200 per U.S. dollar. The banking and finance sector remained a shambles, even after a new plan to avoid a financial meltdown was enacted by merging several banks according to their sectoral specialization. For the second year in succession, the current account balance was negative, with estimates ranging from $450 million to $650 million.

While the government claimed that most of the country's 16,000 businesses were privately owned, the large hydrocarbon, power, and textile industries with export potential remained firmly under state control. Rumors that Turkmenistan would finally enact an IMF-backed structural adjustment plan were again proven false. While authorities indicated that such a program might be implemented in 1999, they disagreed with the IMF over fundamental issues and Turkmenistan remained the only former Soviet state that had not yet adopted an IMF-approved program.

Turkmenistan's fiscal problems remained acute. The government continued to heavily subsidize the economy, especially food production, agriculture, and utilities. Tax collection was particularly problematic, as the tax code was full of contradictions and disincentives and was practically unenforceable. In 1998, income taxes constituted only about 8 percent of total government revenues. As a result, the state had difficulties in meeting public sector wage payments and continued to turn to short-term external financing for its domestic investment projects.

In turn, this aggressive borrowing created repayment problems that threatened to destroy Turkmenistan's already low credit rating. As of the end of 1998, the government was in default on about $100 million in foreign debt (after a fall restructuring plan) and was due to pay $200 million to external creditors in 1999. The external debt of $1.5 billion gave the country one of the highest debt-to-GDP ratios of the former Soviet states, about 75 percent. For 1999, the parliament approved a budget spending total of 20.5 trillion manat ($4 billion) and projected a deficit of 1.3 percent of GDP, a seemingly ambitious goal. While showing some improvement over 1997, agriculture also remained a problem sector. State subsidies to the agro-industrial complex totaled more than $1 billion, but the sector continued to remain unprofitable, as cotton production only reached about half of the target level over the past five years. The 1998 cotton harvest was estimated at 690,000 tons, an improvement of 60,000 tons on 1997's disastrous yield, but well below the official 1998 plan of 1.5 million tons. Still, the export-value of the crop was estimated at $900 million, which would make it the state's largest foreign currency earner. Niyazov announced that agricultural officials will be held criminally liable if they fail to meet next year's target of 1.3 million tons.

Despite state proclamations that reforms were yielding measurable results, inefficient methods, an aging capital stock, artificially low state-procurement prices, and widespread corruption and embezzlement continued to choke the farm sector. Farmers still did not have the right to own land and instead had to operate on lease arrangements with the state. While peasants officially had a right to long-term leases (10–15 years), local administrators and governors regularly intervened and set their own short-term leases. Consequently, farmers in many areas stopped the normal crop rotation meant to ensure soil fertility and cotton yields per hectare plummeted. Reports for 1998 indicated that average cotton yields fell to between 800 and 900 kilograms per hectare, the worst on record. The only good news on the agricultural front was the announcement that 1.24 million tons of grain (the best to date) had been harvested.

Even though Turkmenistan's revenue base continued to diminish, there was no let-up in the state-sponsored construction of factories and grand-developmental projects. "White elephants" have been a hallmark of Turkmenistan's domestic investment, as many projects were approved for political-symbolic reasons rather than their economic merits. Construction now accounts for about a quarter of GDP, making it a larger sector than either agriculture or industry. The major state-commissioned projects for 1998 included: a textile complex near Ashgabat ($17 million), a pharmaceutical plant ($5 million), a fiber-optic communications line ($22 million), an international medical center ($26 million), a second runway for Ashgabat's airport ($85 million), four flour mills ($71 million), and a grain mill complex ($20 million). All of these projects were completed with at least partial external funding, with Turkey leading the way, and all will operate under state control.

OIL AND GAS SECTOR DEVELOPMENTS

The gas sector, once the fiscal bedrock of Turkmenistan, has continued its slide. Through the first eleven months of 1998, production totaled a paltry 11.5 billion cubic meters (bcm), a 28 percent decline on the previous year. Gas production had slumped to a fraction of its 1989 peak level (89 bcm) or even 1993 level

(65 bcm). External factors were primarily responsible for this decrease. In 1993, Turkmenistan was excluded by Russia from sharing in revenues from gas exported to hard-currency paying East European customers (about 11 bcm), and was forced to export to only CIS customers. The loss of these revenues was further exacerbated by the inability of cash-strapped CIS countries such as Ukraine, Georgia, and Armenia to pay for their gas. These countries owed upwards of $1 billion to Turkmenistan and often repaid arrears with barter goods as opposed to currency, further adding to Turkmenistan's fiscal problems. Ukraine's summer 1998 repayment of $259 million of its $713 million debt opened the way to another agreement to deliver 20 bcm of gas in 1999, but Ukraine's previously demonstrated inability to pay and Russia's Gazprom's desire for a share of the market may ultimately scuttle the deal.

A top priority of Turkmenistan's foreign policy has been to reach agreements for the construction of new gas pipelines to service non-CIS customers. The beginning of 1998 was marked with the inauguration of the Turkmenistan-Iran natural gas pipeline (Korpedze-Kord). Publicly hailed as one of the most important events in Turkmenistan's brief independent history, the pipeline's completion was more a symbolic victory than an economic one. The pipeline's capacity is only 3–3.5 bcm a year, and Turkmenistan will not receive actual revenues for a couple of years in order to cover Iran's construction costs. Nevertheless, Korpedze-Kord was the first new pipeline, independent of Russian control, to transport gas to a non-CIS country.

In late June, a group of U.S. companies headed by Amoco announced plans to construct a 750-mile pipeline to transport gas from western Turkmenistan to Turkey and the European market. With a projected capacity of 35 bcm of gas a year, the $2.4 billion project will originate in Turkmenbashi, extend across the Caspian Sea to Baku, traverse Georgia, and link up with the main Turkish gas transportation grid in Erzurum. Work on the Turkish leg of the project began in 1998 and was scheduled for completion by the end of 1999.

While these new pipeline plans were being pursued, others were officially dropped. In November, U.S.-based UNOCAL officially withdrew from the Central Asia Gas Pipeline Consortium. UNOCAL owned a controlling 54 percent stake in the consortium, which had been planning an ambitious Turkmenistan-Afghanistan-Pakistan pipeline. UNOCAL officials cited the political uncertainties in Afghanistan and lower prices for oil as the reasons for its decision. The $2 billion project, in partnership with Gazprom (Russia), Delta Oil Company (Saudi Arabia), and Rosgaz (Turkmenistan), had been in doubt for some time since the Taliban seized control of most of Afghanistan.

Another heavily publicized project was shelved when the British-Dutch company Shell announced in late December that its projected Turkmenistan-Iran-Turkey natural gas pipeline would be postponed indefinitely. Shell officials disclosed that two pipelines to Turkey were unfeasible and that the trans-Caspian route was more attractive to both parties than a trans-Iranian route that was vigorously opposed by Washington.

On 22 April the U.S. Export-Import Bank for the first time approved the financing of a hydrocarbon-related project in Turkmenistan. A $96 million long-term loan was announced for the sale of compression equipment needed for a gas pipeline upgrade. However, little additional progress was made towards securing Western financing for the more ambitious projects that the Turkmen government covets.

The collapse of the gas sector prompted the Turkmen government in 1998 to aggressively pursue the expansion of the oil sector. Oil production during the first eleven months increased to 5.8 million tons or 126,000 barrels/day, the highest output since independence, though plummeting world oil prices in 1998 reduced revenue increases. In June, Niyazov announced the signing of a resolution on the licensing, production, and exploration of hydrocarbons in the Garashsyzlyk territory, which in effect created the country's first national oil company. The new company was comprised of four departments of the Turkmenneft state concern and will be exclusively responsible for concluding production-sharing agreements for developing Garashsyzlyk, the source of 80 percent of Turkmenistan's oil.

A number of agreements with foreign oil companies were signed in 1998. The most prominent of these was the deal with Mobil to develop the Kyapaz field in the Caspian Sea, however the accord was shelved pending the resolution of the status of the disputed field with Azerbaijan. In October, the French company Total was awarded a feasibility study for constructing the Turkmen stretch of a Kazakhstan-Turkmenistan-Iran pipeline designed to provide Iranian refineries with 75 million tons of crude oil on a swap basis. Another agreement was reached with British Monument Oil and Gas and Malaysia's Petronas to transport oil from western Turkmenistan along the Caspian to Iran, also on a swap basis. In late November, Petronas reported that it had struck the first gusher at the Liyanov Vostochnyi field on Turkmenistan's Caspian shelf. In December, Niyazov invited Russia's Lukoil for the first time to explore the Caspian area for cooperative agreements.

Turkmenistan also signed agreements to upgrade refining capacity with the Turkish Gamma Company ($140 million) and the French-Iranian consortium of Technip and NIOC ($196 million). A deal to produce basic refined oil products was closed with Germany's Mannesman and Japan's Itochu, while Nishio-Ivai and JGX initialed a $200 million accord to produce 90,000 tons of polypropylene a year. The total worth of these oil-related projects exceeds $1 billion and will be supervised and financed by Israel's Merhav through long-term loans.

CASPIAN SEA STATUS

Nineteen ninety-eight also saw measurable shifts in Turkmenistan's policy on the Caspian Sea. Historically, Turkmenistan's position on the division of the sea has fluctuated. Initially, Turkmenistan supported the position advanced by Kazakhstan and Azerbaijan, that a new international legal regime should be constructed to divide the sea into national sectors. In late 1996, Turkmenistan reversed this position in accordance with the Iranian and Russian view that all of the Caspian be held in common among the littoral states. In early 1997, this position was again abrogated as Niyazov publicly laid claim to the Azeri-claimed Chirag oil fields, questioning Azerbaijan's right to exploit Kyapaz (referred to as Serdar by Turkmenistan).

In February 1998, Turkmenistan and Azerbaijan announced an agreement to divide the Caspian into respective national sectors along the median line, although Turkmenistan maintained its claims over the Azeri part of the Chirag field. Throughout the year, relations were again strained as the joint Azeri-Turkmen committee made no progress in resolving the dispute. Indeed, Mobil announced shortly after winning the tender for Kyapaz from Turkmenistan that it would not take any further steps until its legal status had been permanently resolved. Kyapaz occupies 400 square kilometers in area and is estimated to contain between 150 million and 200 million tons of oil. Turkmenistan had awarded the tender, in part, to protest Azerbaijan's 1997 signing of a production-sharing agreement to develop the field with the Russian companies Lukoil and Rosneft. The companies withdrew from the agreement shortly after Turkmenistan voiced its "uncompromising" objections.

Optimism for reaching a general solution to the Caspian issue was bolstered in 1998 as Russia eased its position. Russian officials were now ready to accept the basic principle that the seabed and property rights to mineral deposits be divided into national sectors, although they continued to advocate that the actual waters of the Caspian be regarded as common and managed by an international regime. The Iranian position remained solidly in favor of a joint basis for resource management, since their portion of the Caspian coastline is fairly small, and has few potential oil fields located within it. A November summit in Moscow among the littoral states produced no agreement.

FOREIGN POLICY DEVELOPMENTS

In other foreign policy developments, Turkmenistan attempted to broaden its external ties in the hope of obtaining political and economic support for its pipeline needs. The major foreign policy event of 1998 was Niyazov's trip to Washington and his first official visit with U.S. President Bill Clinton, however, the Turkmen president failed to achieve either of his major trip objectives. First, U.S. officials dispelled the notion that an exception to the U.S. sanctions on Iran would be granted to any pipeline projects involving Turkmenistan. Second, the Turkmen president failed to secure U.S. financing for a Caspian pipeline project. Indeed, in a statement released on the day prior to Niyazov's arrival, U.S. officials downplayed the potential significance of Caspian oil. In a May visit to a Turkmenistan, U.S. Eximbank chairman James Harmon reiterated that the United States would only finance trans-Caspian infrastructure projects on their commercial merits.

Nor did Niyazov manage to improve his country's public image on the human rights front. Even before the visit, international organizations were highly critical of the Clinton administration's decision to receive the Turkmen president. At an appearance at Johns Hopkins University, the president maintained that "no one has been arrested in Turkmenistan for political reasons," a statement that was plainly contradicted by the recent jailing of former Foreign Minister Abdy Kuliev. In interviews with major U.S. newspapers, Niyazov stated that democratic institutions and political opposition parties would be introduced gradually and in a manner that was consistent with the traditions and social norms of the Central Asian state.

Niyazov's other major 1998 diplomatic initiatives included official visits to China and Turkey, both potential gas customers. Turkmenistan reaffirmed its skepticism of the CIS and other regional attempts at cooperation, and broke ranks with other Central Asian countries (particularly Uzbekistan) by taking an official stance of neutrality towards Afghanistan's Taliban government. Along with Pakistan, Turkmenistan was playing an active role in mediating the conflict between the Afghan government and warring factions in the north.

Finally, Turkmenistan made a concerted effort in 1998 to expand its ties with major (non-CIS) international organizations. In early November, Turkmenistan acquired full membership of the Asian Development Bank (ADB), thereby guaranteeing preferential access to the bank's financial resources and related technical assistance to support economic reforms. In September, the Permanent Council of the OSCE opened its first office in Ashgabat. The European Bank for Reconstruction and Development also announced the initiation of a $35 million loan to support small businesses in the wake of its $50 and $30 million loans for the construction of an Ashgabat-Mary highway and the modernization of the Turkmenbashi seaport.

PROSPECTS

Turkmenistan continued to falter as a result of its stubborn adherence to its policy of gas-led development. While President Niyazov's claim in 1992 that his country would soon become the "Kuwait of the Caspian" seems somewhat farcical, the Turkmen president seems unrelenting in his attempts to emulate the developmental patterns of the wealthy Gulf states. Developments in 1998 brought an almost perverse new twist to this goal: Turkmenistan's policies were consistent with those of oil-states even though it was currently receiving very little income from its hydrocarbon exports.

As always, officials remained optimistic about the future and anticipated that 1999 will bring real growth and an increase in living standards for the state's relatively small population. Certainly, Turkmenistan's gas export problems are external and political in nature, and the country does have the potential to be a significant producer. But such promises have been made every year since independence and have always proven to be hollow. Grand export pipelines are expensive and will take years to build even under the most favorable of political and commercial circumstances. Barring some unexpected political upheaval, the short-term prospects for development under current policy are bleak. As many of its neighbors turn the economic corner, Turkmenistan will continue to wait for the arrival of its "black gold."

Interview: *BUILDING DEMOCRACY THE EASTERN WAY*

After being hospitalized and undergoing heart surgery in fall of 1997, Saparmurat Niyazov, leader of Turkmenistan since the country's independence in 1991, has granted few interviews. So it was quite a coup when Olga Solomonova, a reporter for Trud, *a Russian daily newspaper, convinced the president to participate in a wide-ranging discussion that touched on the Turkmen opposition and Niyazov's definition of democracy. Excerpts of the interview, which was published on 13 January, are below.*

Trud: Saparmurat Atayevich, there is the concept of "Western democracy." But does an "Eastern" exist?
Saparmurat Niyazov: I contend there is not a Western and Eastern democracy. There is democracy. And it develops in various countries, you will agree, in various forms, inasmuch as every country has its own peculiarities. In Turkmenistan we have a traditional Eastern society with our own customs, traditions, and mentality. Are you asking how to combine traditionalism with reformism? From the start we refused to copy any model. We tried to find our own path, taking into account world experience and our own national specifics. I am certain that an artificial, rushed introduction of new democratic institutions in a traditional society cannot be fruitful. I don't want to accuse anyone, but what happened in Tajikistan when they tried to impose democracy from above? It broke up the society and the people. We adopted a constitution in which it is written that we are building a legal, democratic, and secular government that guarantees all rights and freedoms of a person. But we are heading toward this gradually, trying not to allow a decline in the people's lives, confrontations of various social groups, and not disturbing society.

Trud: Apparently, the opposition you have is unusual in that nothing is heard about it. Or is it that there simply is no opposition?

SN: If by opposition you mean an organized political force with clear tasks, goals, and platforms, then we don't have any such thing. Of course, there are certain people, uncoordinated groups of Turkmen, for example in Moscow and abroad, who are not satisfied with the present course. But one can hardly consider them normal opposition. Our society is not politicized. Therefore, apparently, there has been no success in forming a second party: they couldn't collect enough votes. Yes, and our only party—the Democratic—can and does exist because I myself head it.

Trud: That your authority in Turkmenistan is very great is obvious at first glance: portraits of the president, monuments, busts at every step. How do you regard this?

SN: Do you want to ask whether this is a display of a "personality cult?" Well, again I would remind you that this a traditional Eastern society, where there has always been an infatuation with the leader, possibly at times even excessive. But a personality cult is nonetheless a communist phenomenon. Incidentally, if you consider that pensions and wages paid out without any delays, free education and health care, absence of interethnic conflicts and a peaceful, safe environment in cities and villages constitutes a "cult," then call it that. But for me as head of the government the main thing is to peacefully get through the complicated transition period without excesses and conflicts and arrive at genuine democracy.

Translated by Bruce Pannier

NOTE
Reprinted with kind permission from *Transitions* magazine, March 1998.

Contributors

Andrea Adams is a student of political science at Creighton University. She spent the summer of 1998 working as a research assistant at the Russian Center of Public Opinion and Market Research (VTsIOM) in Moscow.

Arif Aliev is the chairman of Yeni Nesil, the association of journalists of Azerbaijan.

Gordon Bardos is program officer at the Harriman Institute, Columbia University. He is currently working on a full-length study of the post-Dayton period in Bosnia-Herzegovina.

Laura Belin is studying for a Ph.D. at Oxford University. From 1995 to 1997 she worked as a research analyst on Russian domestic politics at the Open Media Research Institute (OMRI) in Prague. From 1997 to 1998 she covered Russian affairs for Radio Free Europe/Radio Liberty's Newsline.

Nebojsa Bjelakovic is a doctoral candidate at the political science department of Carleton University, Ottawa, Canada. He received a B.A. from Belgrade University and an M.A. from the Institute of Central/East European and Russian-Area Studies at Carleton. He specializes in Russian foreign policy and Balkan issues.

Cassandra Cavanaugh is a Ph.D. candidate in Russian and Soviet History at Columbia University. She is a research associate for Central Asia in the Europe and Central Asia (Helsinki) division of Human Rights Watch.

Terry D. Clark is an associate professor of political science at Creighton University in Omaha, Nebraska. A graduate of West Point with a Ph.D. from the University of Illinois at Urbana-Champaign, Clark has published extensively on political institutions and public opinion in Russia and Lithuania.

Jonathan Cohen is programs associate with the London-based non-governmental organization Conciliation Resources.

Alexander Cooley is a visiting assistant professor of political science at Johns Hopkins University. He is also a Ph.D. candidate in political science at Columbia University and Harriman Institute Mosley-Backer Fellow, 1998–1999.

Andrew Cottey is a lecturer in the Department of Peace Studies at Bradford University. He has worked for the EastWest Institute, Saferworld, and the British American Security Information Council and has been a NATO Research Fellow. He is author of *East-Central Europe After the Cold War* (Macmillan/St. Martin's Press, 1995) and editor of *Subregional Cooperation in the New Europe* (Macmillan/ St. Martin's Press, 1999).

Emil Danielyan works for Radio Free Europe/Radio Liberty's Armenian service in Yerevan. From 1996 to 1997 he was an analyst intern at the Open Media Research Institute in Prague.

Bhavna Dave is a lecturer in Central Asian politics in the Political Studies department of the School of Oriental and African Studies, University of London. She previously worked as a research analyst at the Open Media Research Institute in Prague. Her major areas of research are ethnic relations, politics of language, religion, and clan networks in Central Asia.

Jeremy Druker is director and editor-in-chief of *Transitions Online* magazine, based in Prague.

Sharon Fisher is a Ph.D. candidate at the School of Slavonic and East European Studies (SSEES) at the University of London, writing on national identity and state-building in Slovakia and Croatia. She previously worked as the Slovak analyst at OMRI and the Radio Free Europe/Radio Liberty Research Institute.

Bianca Guruita is a reporter at *Nine O'Clock*, a Bucharest English-language daily.

Gordana Icevska is a journalist at the Skopje daily *Dnevnik*.

Dan Ionescu is a broadcaster with Radio Free Europe/Radio Liberty, Prague, where he edits a daily program for the Republic of Moldova. He was formerly a research analyst with the RFE/RL Research Institute (1984–94), Munich, and a senior research analyst at OMRI, Prague (1995–97).

Fariz Ismailzade is a political science student in Baku. In summer 1999 he was an intern at the Center for Strategic and International Studies in Washington.

Steven C. Johnson is editor in chief of *The Baltic Times*, an English-language weekly in Riga.

Stephen F. Jones is an associate professor of Russian and Eurasian Studies at Mount Holyoke College in Massachusetts, and is the author of over 50 articles and chapters. He is currently completing a book entitled *Georgian Social Democracy: In Opposition and Power.*

Victor Kalashnikov is a Moscow-based writer and was a contributing editor to *Transitions.*

Brian Kenety is a Sofia-based correspondent for the Inter Press Service.

Stefan Krause works in Skopje as a political analyst for the International Crisis Group, an international analysis and advocacy organization. Previously, he was a research analyst at the Open Media Research Institute in Prague, specializing in Bulgaria, Macedonia, and Greece.

Joan Lofgren is a Ph.D. candidate at Columbia University in political science, writing a dissertation on nationalism and privatization in Estonia. She is currently a researcher at the University of Tampere, Finland, in a project on research and innovation in Russia.

Alexander Lukashuk, former editor in chief of Belarus Publishers in Minsk, was a member of the Belarus Parliamentary Committee on Political Repression from 1990 to 1995. He works for the Belarusian Service of Radio Free Europe/Radio Liberty in Prague.

Ustina Markus is a specialist on the former Soviet Union with the Department of Defense. Before joining the DoD she worked for OMRI and its predecessor, the RFE/RL Research Institute, as a specialist on Ukraine and Belarus. She has a Ph.D. from the London School of Economics.

Jan Maksymiuk is a regional specialist (Belarus, Ukraine, Poland) for Radio Free Europe/Radio Liberty's Communications Division.

Svetlana Mikhailova is a journalist with the Moscow weekly *Vremya.*

Penny Morvant works for the BBC in London. From 1995 to 1997 she worked as a research analyst specializing in social issues in Russia at OMRI in Prague.

Bruce Pannier covers Central Asia for Radio Free Europe/Radio Liberty's News and Current Affairs division. From 1995 to 1997 he was an analyst at OMRI.

Scott Parrish currently works as a senior research associate at the Center for Nonproliferation Studies (CNS) of the Monterey Institute of International Studies in Monterey, California. Formerly he covered Russian security and foreign policy at OMRI in Prague. He has a Ph.D. in political science from Columbia University and has taught at the University of Texas at Austin.

Oleksandr Pavliuk is director of the Kyiv Center of the EastWest Institute. He graduated in International Relations at Kyiv State University, and has a doctoral degree in history from the Ukrainian Institute of International Relations. He is author of *Ukraine's Struggle for Independence and U.S. Policy* and has published articles in *Foreign Affairs* and *Security Dialogue*.

Jason Pellmar is majoring in anthropology at Wesleyan University. In 1999 he conducted fieldwork in refugee camps in Azerbaijan for Relief International.

Radoslav K. Petkov is deputy director of the Economic and Regional Development Program of the EastWest Institute. He is one of the authors of the Institute's *Russian Financial Crisis Assessments* and *Rebuilding Russia* Discussion Papers. He has a B.A. in Economics and Politics from Eugene Lang College in New York and an M.A. in Economics from the New School for Social Research.

Andrejs Plakans is a professor of history at Iowa State University. He is the author of *The Latvians: A Short History* (Stanford, CA: Hoover Institution, 1995).

Rudolph M. Rizman is a professor of sociology at the University of Ljubliana.

Iulian Robu is a journalist and translator based in Chisinau.

Andrzej Rudka is president of PECAT (Policy Education Center on Assistance to Transition) Foundation in Warsaw and a consultant on economic restructuring issues.

Peter Rutland is a professor of government at Wesleyan University and an associate of the Davis Center for Russian Studies at Harvard. From 1995 to 1997 he was assistant director for research at OMRI in Prague. He has written *The Myth of the Plan* (Hutchinson, 1985) and *The Politics of Economic Stagnation in the Soviet Union* (Cambridge University Press, 1993).

Fabian Schmidt is working as the Tirana Project Director of the Institute for Journalism in Transition and was a media regulation advisor with the OSCE during the 1997 elections. He worked as a research analyst focusing on the southwestern Balkans at OMRI from 1995 to 1997. Schmidt is currently working on a Ph.D. thesis on democratic institution building in Albania.

Natan Shklyar is a research associate at the EastWest Institute in New York and the managing editor of the EWI *Russian Regional Report*. He holds a B.A. in Diplomacy and Foreign Affairs from Miami University of Ohio.

Ben Slay is a senior economist at PlanEcon, Inc., in Washington, D.C., a position he formerly held at OMRI in Prague. He is the author of *The Polish Economy: Crisis, Reform, and Transformation* (Princeton University Press, 1994) and the editor of *De-Monopolization and Competition Policy in Post-Communist Economies* (Westview Press, 1996).

Tim Snyder, an academy scholar at Harvard University, is working on a book on Poland's eastern policy. His book *Nationalism, Marxism, and Modern Central Europe* was published by Harvard University Press in 1998.

Jonathan Stein is a Research Associate at the EastWest Institute Prague Center, where he has recently completed an edited volume on ethnic minority parties in post-communist Europe. He also writes quarterly reports and forecasts on Eastern Europe for the Economist Intelligence Unit.

Matyas Szabo is academic coordinator of the Southeast European Studies program at the Central European University in Budapest. He has an M.A. in sociology, and worked as research fellow at the Center for Study of Nationalism in Prague. In 1995–96 he was an analyst intern at OMRI.

Sava Tatic is the managing director at the Media Development Loan Fund in Prague. He was formerly electronic publications editor at the Institute for Journalism in Transition in Prague. He holds a graduate degree in European studies from the Central European University (CEU) and a graduate diploma in international relations from the School of Advanced International Studies (SAIS) at Johns Hopkins University.

James Toole is a Ph. D candidate at Brandeis University in Newton, Massachusetts.

Roza Tsvetkova is a journalist with the Moscow weekly *Vremya*.

Milada Anna Vachudova has a B.A. from Stanford and a Ph.D. in political science from Oxford University. She is a fellow of the Center for European Studies at Harvard University and of the EU Center of New York University. She is the author of *Revolution, Democracy and Integration, East Central Europe Since 1989*, forthcoming from Oxford University Press.

Oleg Varfolomeyev works for the BBC in Kyiv and writes on Ukraine for the Jamestown Foundation *Monitor*. In 1996–97 he was an analyst intern at OMRI.

Claire Wallace is a professor of sociology at the Institute of Advanced Studies in Vienna. She formerly taught at the Central European University and Lancaster

University. She is the author (with Sijka Kovatcheva) of *Youth in Society: The Construction and Deconstruction of Youth in East and West Europe* (St. Martin's Press, 1998).

Rory Watson is European correspondent for the *Glasgow Herald* and former deputy editor of the *European Voice* in Brussels.

Index

Sanginov, Rahmon, 409
Santer, Jacques, 48, 49, 286
Sarinic, Hrvoje 197
Sarjayev, Batyr, 422
Sarkisian, Serge, 379
Sarkisian, Vazgen, 379, 384, 387
Sassu, Alexandru, 261
Schiffer, Claudia, 86
Schroeder, Gerhard, 109, 323
Schuster, Rudolf, 88
Scultenicu, Ovidiu, 270
Securitate, in Romania, 273–278
  collaborations with, 275–278
  history of, 274–275
  legislation to open files of, 273–274
Seleznev, Gennadii, 179, 296, 303, 305
Semenov, Viktor, 333
Sergeev, Igor, 317, 320, 326, 390
Seselj, Voijslav, 156, 222
Shadman-Valavi, Mohammed, 179
Shakhrai, Sergei, 296, 302
Shamata, Halit, arrest of, 241
Sharetsky, Syamyon, 157
Sharonov, Andrei, 343
Shaumyan, Stepan, 371
Sheremet, Pavel, 154
Shevardnadze, Eduard, 354–356,
  358–359, 362, 366
  assassination attempt on, 353–354, 373
Shikhmuradov, Boris, 422
Shilyashki, Ivan, 253
Shokhin, Aleksandr, 283
Shuli, Ingrid, 245
Shushkevich, Stanislau, 7, 158
Shydlouski, Alyaksei, 157
Siimann, Mart, 143–144
Siradeghian, Vano, 384
Skele, Andris, 133–134
Sklyarov, Ivan, 312
Skubiszewski, Krzysztof, 112, 113–114
Slomka, Adam, 102
Slovak Democratic Coalition (SDK),
  84–85, 87–88
Slovak National Party (SNS), 87–88
Slovakia, 83–99
  and Austria, 89
  banking in, 89
  and Czech Republic, 89
  democracy in, 4
  economy of, 88–89
  and elections in, 86–88

Slovakia *(continued)*
  and European Union accession, 3, 50,
    90
  and Great Britain, 89
  and Hungary, 89
  media in, 85–86
  and NATO, 3
  political parties in, 85–86
  politics in, 84–86
  presidency in, 88
  privatization in, 89
  religion in, 88
  and Roma, 89
Slovenia, 188–204
  and Austria, 191
  border disputes, 191–192
  and Catholic Church, 193
  and Croatia, 191–192
  economy of, 189
  elections in, 193–194
  and European Union accession,
    189–191
  and Germany, 190
  and Italy, 191
  lustration laws in, 193
  and NATO, 189, 191
  political parties in, 192
  politics in, 192–194
  and United Nations, 189–190
  and United States, 190
Slovenian Christian Democrats (SKD),
  192–194
Slovenian People's Party (SLS), 192–194
Slovenian National Party (SNS),
  192–194
Smerek, Jan, 87
Smirnov, Igor, 183, 283
Smirnov, Vladimir, 348
Smolenskii, Aleksandr, 302
Snegur, Mircea, 281
Snyder, Timothy, 110
Social Alliance (PS), in Poland, 102,
Social Democratic Party (SDP), in
  Croatia, 196, 198
Social Democratic Party (SDRP), in
  Poland, 119
Social Democratic Party of Slovenia,
  192–194
Social Democrats (CSSD), in Czech
  Republic, 73, 76–81
  government of, 79–81